Projects in Speech Communication

Perfection Learning®

Editorial Director	**Carol Francis**
Executive Editor	**Jim Strickler**
Senior Editor	**Gay Russell-Dempsey**
Permissions Editors	**Karyn Morrison**
	Kate Winzenburg
Design Director	**Randy Messer**
Design Team	**Tobi Cunningham, Robin Elwick, Emily Greazel, Deb Bell, Mike Aspengren, Jane Wonderlin**
Picture Research	**Anjanette Houghtaling**

Contributors

Pupil Edition

Lisa Dillman	Education Writer, former teacher, playwright
Lisa L. Owens	Curriculum Writer, former competitor and tournament judge in Iowa high school speech and debate
Karen Peterfreund	Education Writer, former English teacher

Teacher's Wraparound Edition

Sheryl A. Reda	Communication Consultant

Acknowledgments

Text Credits

Excerpt from *Fish Lips.* Copyright © 1987 by Amy Tan. First appeared in Seventeen Magazine. Reprinted by permission of the author and the Sandra Dijkstra Literary Agency.

"The Truth About Caffeine." Reprinted courtesy of www.best-speech-topics.com

Reprinted by arrangement with The Heirs to the Estate of Martin Luther King Jr., c/o Writers House as agent for the proprietor New York, NY. Copyright 1963 Dr. Martin Luther King Jr; copyright renewed 1991 Coretta Scott King.

Excerpt from Nobel Prize Presentation Speech by Professor Ole Danbolt Mjøs. Copyright © 2007. Reprinted by permission of the Nobel Foundation.

Excerpt from column by Mary Schmich. Printed in the *Chicago Tribune,* June 1, 1997.

Excerpt from *Humor in the Court,* 1977, and *More Humor in the Court*, 1994, by Mary Louise Gilman.

Excerpt from *The Portable Plato,* translated by Benjamin Jowett. NY: Viking Press, 1968.

(Acknowledgments continued on page 634)

Printed in the United States of America

1000 North Second Avenue
P.O. Box 500
Logan, Iowa 51546-0500
Tel: 1-800-831-4190 • Fax: 1-800-543-2745
perfectionlearning.com

3 4 5 6 7 RRD 13 12 11
[hardback] ISBN-13: 978-0-7569-9059-6
[hardback] ISBN-10: 0-7569-9059-9

Projects in Speech Communication

Perfection Learning®

Review Board

Review Board for *Projects in Speech Communication*

Projects in Speech Communication has been developed with the guidance of an outstanding panel of expert teachers.

Senior Consultant

Diana B. Carlin, Ph.D.
Department of Communication Studies
University of Kansas

Professor Diana Carlin teaches a variety of courses on political debates, speechwriting, and women in politics. She is the author of secondary textbooks on debate and public speaking and is a former high school teacher and forensics coach.

Teacher Reviewers

Linda L. Alderson, Director of Forensics and UIL Academic Coordinator
Boling High School (retired)
Boling, Texas

Russell Kirkscey
Speech Teacher
Blanco High School
Blanco, Texas

Anna J. Small Roseboro, NBCT
Communication Arts and Sciences Department
Calvin College
Grand Rapids, Michigan

Mary Schick
Speech and Debate Teacher/Coach
Miami-Dade County Public Schools
Miami, Florida

Stephen Douglas Williford
Speech Teacher
Harding Academy
Memphis, Tennessee

Cynthia Woodhouse
Language Arts/Debate Teacher
West Senior High School
Iowa City Community Schools
Iowa City, Iowa

Standards Compliance of *Projects in Speech Communication*

Projects in Speech Communication supports state standards as well as the K–12 Standards of Communication developed by the National Communication Association.

Projects in Speech Communication Overview

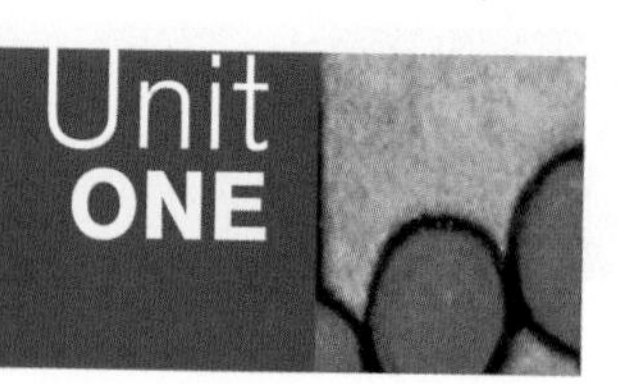

Communication Basics

Interpersonal Communication

Group Communication

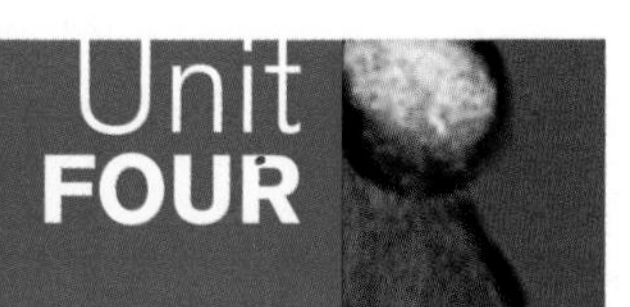

Public Speaking

Types of Presentations

Mass Communications

Communication
SOURCEBOOK

Speeches, Commentary, and Humor

Projects in Speech Communication
Special Features

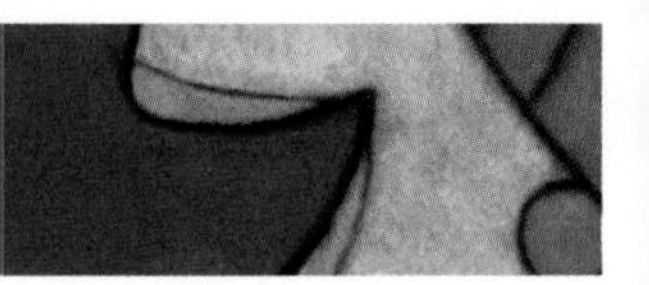

Chapter Projects

Engaging "Learn-by-Doing" Activities

Project	Page	Concept	Participants
1. Instant Replay	4	communication elements	group
2. "Who's on First?"	24	avoiding misunderstandings	partner
3. Silence, Please!	46	nonverbal communication	partner
4. Listen Here	64	listening for main ideas	group
5. What Do *You* See?	86	perceptions	individual
6. Different People, Different Talk	112	language choices	partner
7. Lend Me Your Ear	136	types of listening	partner
8. Work It Out	152	problem-solving	partner
9. "So Tell Me About Yourself . . ."	174	interviews	partner
10. Power to the Group!	198	nature of groups	group
11. The Group Roles On	214	member roles	group
12. Got a Problem? Here's the Solution.	230	problem-solving	whole class/group
13. You're Out of Order!	254	parliamentary procedure	whole class/group
14. Get to the Point!	276	thesis statement	partner
15. Says Who?	296	reliable sources	group
16. Map It!	320	graphic organizing	partner
17. Worth a Thousand Words	350	visual and audio aids	group
18. The One That Got Away	372	effective language	individual
19. Check It Out	394	rubric creation	group
20. Here's How	422	process presentation	partner
21. The Triple Play	450	logic, emotion, and ethics	group
22. And the Winner Is . . .	478	award/acceptance speeches	whole class
23. Bring It to Life	508	speech competition events	whole class/partner
24. Media Crystal Ball	542	role of media in modern life	group
25. Technology Tales	562	technology pros and cons	partner

Diversity

Communication in a Diverse World
explores similarities and differences across cultures and gender.

Gender Journey relies on first-hand research to draw conclusions about gender differences.

(See pages 109, 197, 275, 419, 539, and 591.)

Traditions and Change

Communication Past and Present
explores historical developments of communication styles and traditions, from scribes to computer chips, and from Cicero to Dave Barry, to name just a few.

(See pages 20, 42, 60, 82, 104, 132, 148, 168, 190, 210, 226, 250, 268, 292, 316, 346, 368, 390, 414, 446, 504, 534, 558, and 586.)

Careers and Jobs

Is This Job for Me? explores careers that use the communication skills discussed in the chapter.

Workplace Workout presents an on-the-job scenario related to unit themes to analyze what went wrong and suggest strategies to make it right.

(See pages 108, 196, 274, 418, 538, and 590.)

Media

Two full chapters, 24 and 25, explore media and technology and their impact on communication. In addition, **Director's Cut** and **Media Master** offer opportunities to create media projects.

(See pages 109, 197, 275, 419, 539, 576–577, and 591.)

Unit One

Communication Basics

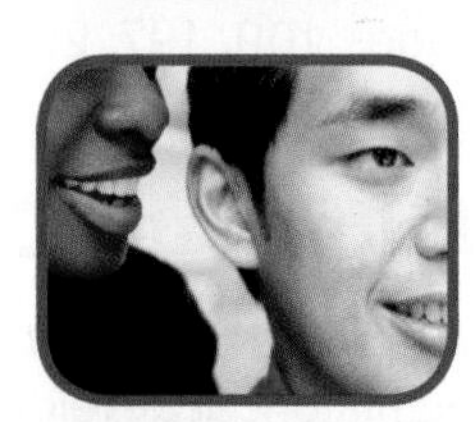

There is only one rule to become a good speaker: learn how to listen.
– Anonymous

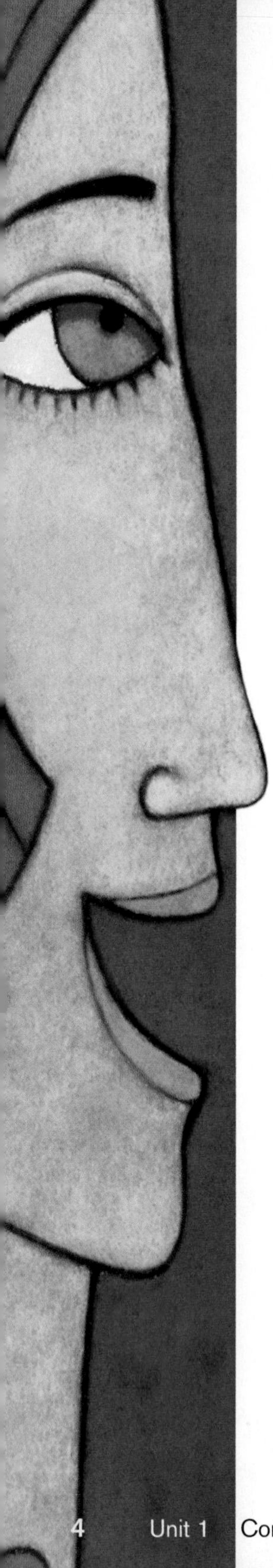

The Fundamentals of Communication

ESSENTIAL QUESTION

What is communication?

Chapter Project: Instant Replay

You communicate so naturally that you may not even think about the process. This project will help you become aware of elements you use in the communication process.

With a small group, you will create a short, attention-grabbing scene that demonstrates the communication process. One group member will be the "announcer." You will present your scene once straight through. Then you will repeat the presentation, freezing when the announcer says "freeze" at agreed-upon spots. Like a sports analyst looking at an instant replay, he or she will identify and explain each element in the communication process. The presentation should take no more than two to three minutes. Refer to the CAPS guidelines below as you work.

The rubric on page 19 shows the traits on which your presentation will be evaluated.

CONCEPT	the communication process has many elements
AUDIENCE	classmates and teacher
PURPOSE	identify the components in the communication process
SITUATION	creative classroom demonstration

KEY VOCABULARY

- communication
- metacommunication
- message
- receiver
- sender
- encoding
- decoding
- feedback
- context
- channel
- interference
- intrapersonal communication
- interpersonal communication
- person-to-group communication
- mass media

Suggest three topics you think these students might be discussing. What evidence did you use to make your suggestions?

Speak Up!

What comes to mind when you hear the word *communication*? Write a brief definition. In turn with your classmates, share your definition as your teacher writes it on the board. Which definition appears most often? Which did you find most inventive? Which was the most surprising? Keep these definitions in mind as you read this chapter.

Pages 6–16 will provide the information you'll need to complete this project.

The Importance of Communication in Daily Life

Communication is a process for exchanging ideas and creating meaning. To appreciate how important communication is, try to imagine life without it. How would you interact with your friends and family or learn anything at school? How would citizens take part in their communities and governments? Would you be able to work at a job?

KEY POINT

Communication has vital social, academic, civic, and professional importance.

Social Importance

Communication is how you connect with others. It's how you meet people, work in groups, make friends, and fall in love. Most people feel that these personal connections are the key to happiness. In fact, in some societies, the worst punishment a person can receive is being shunned, or prevented from communicating with others.

Academic Importance

Virtually every aspect of school life depends on communication. Good communication skills help students and teachers express themselves clearly and understand others as they clarify meaning and ask questions.

Civic Importance

A thriving society relies on good communication. That's why the First Amendment to the United States Constitution guarantees freedom of speech. Freedom and democracy depend on the open exchange of ideas. Through such exchanges, citizens establish the laws of the land. Through communication, people also set up the rules and practices of such organized groups as the Girl Scouts and after-school clubs.

Choices

Good communicators naturally attract many friends and acquaintances. These connections often open up new opportunities socially, at school, during after-school activities, and on the job. Think about your own life. How might strong communication skills expand your choices?

Communication in a DIVERSE WORLD

A World Without Language

She was strapped to a chair all day and confined in a crib of wire mesh every night. From 20 months until age 13, not a soul held her, soothed her, or spoke to her. "Genie," as she has come to be known, lived in severe deprivation at a critical stage of her infancy and girlhood. Her life and the lives of other unfortunate children like her throughout the world have helped scientists understand more about human language and how vital it is to human development.

When Genie was found in California in 1970, the only sound she made was a whimper. She became the subject of intense instruction and study by linguists, psychologists, neurologists, and others. Within a year she could recognize many new words, but she remained silent for the most part. When she did begin to speak, Genie spoke much like a two-year-old, a word here and a word there. Later, she began using two words together ("little marble," "two hand") and then three words. However, Genie's speech did not continue to develop as hoped. She was never able to construct a question, despite hours of instruction. She understood little grammar. Four years after she began to put words together, her progress had stalled–her speech sounded like a "garbled telegram."

Universal Grammar Linguist Noam Chomsky developed the theory that all human brains come equipped at birth with a "Universal Grammar" from which all human language in all its diversity has developed. According to Chomsky, Universal Grammar allows a child to understand his or her native language simply by being exposed to it. The human brain appears to be hard-wired with a "language acquisition device" (LAD). When the LAD is short circuited early on for a long time, the child's ability to fully communicate can be damaged for life, as in Genie's case. When a child is nurtured and surrounded by language, the LAD allows the healthy learning of language. Despite the diversity of world languages, the human ability to develop language is universal.

A nurtured child easily picks up language because of the "language acquisition device" built into the human brain.

Standards for Communication Decisions

Your earliest communication choices were simple. For example, you learned to say "please" and "thank you." As you grew older, the choices became more complex. Each time you communicate you make four kinds of choices, those related to 1) yourself, 2) your listener, 3) the occasion, and 4) the task.

Taking yourself, your listener, the occasion, and the task into account will help you establish a standard for making appropriate communication decisions.

Self

Effective communicators consider themselves first. They ask, *What am I trying to say? How do I feel about what I am saying? How can I say it most appropriately?* Answers to those questions explain why you choose to thank your aunt for a gift, call a friend with a sympathetic word when she's unhappy, or hold your frightened little brother's hand.

What might the speaker do to receive a better response from the listeners?

Listener

Effective communicators also consider their listeners. They ask, *How is the listener responding to what I am saying? How can I adjust what I am saying to get a better response?* You might, for example, feel like telling your chemistry teacher, "This test grade is unfair." But if you stand in your teacher's shoes you might see that your best approach is to offer solid reasons why you deserve more points. By thinking about your listener, you are likely to get your message across in as clear and forceful a way as possible.

PROJECT PREP

With your **project group**, act out two different versions of a scene. In the first, explain to a friend why you turned in a paper late. In the second, explain to your teacher why the paper was late.

Occasion

Often the best guide for knowing how and what to communicate is the where and the when—the occasion, or the situation. When you consider the occasion as you make communication decisions ask, *How would I describe the occasion? What is my role in the occasion? What is the role of my listener?*

Task

You make communication decisions based, in part, on the task you are trying to accomplish. When you consider the task as you make communication decisions ask, *Do I care somewhat or a great deal about this task? How can the task be accomplished? What is the role of my listener in this task?*

A Model of the Communication Process

When texting a friend, do you ever type "jk" for "just kidding" after saying something you don't mean? If you do, you are commenting on your communication—standing back from it and explaining the communication itself to your friend. You are using **metacommunication**, or communication about communication. Metacommunication allows you to think about and discuss communication strategies as you communicate. Creating a model, or representation, of the communication process is one way to use metacommunication to understand all the elements of the process.

Message, Sender, and Receiver

What happens when you really need to communicate something and do it well? When your **message** really matters—such as when you're explaining why you missed class or signaling a left turn on your bike or asking someone to help you with an important project—you need your audience, or the **receiver** of that message, to understand. As the **sender** of that message, you must be sure your meaning is clear to the receiver.

Key Elements in the Communication Process	
Message	the idea the sender is trying to communicate to the receiver
Sender	the one who initiates the message
Receiver	the target of the message
Feedback	the response the receiver gives to the sender
Context	the time or place where communication occurs
Channel	the means used to transmit the message from sender to receiver
Interference	anything that blocks or hinders the message or feedback from being properly received

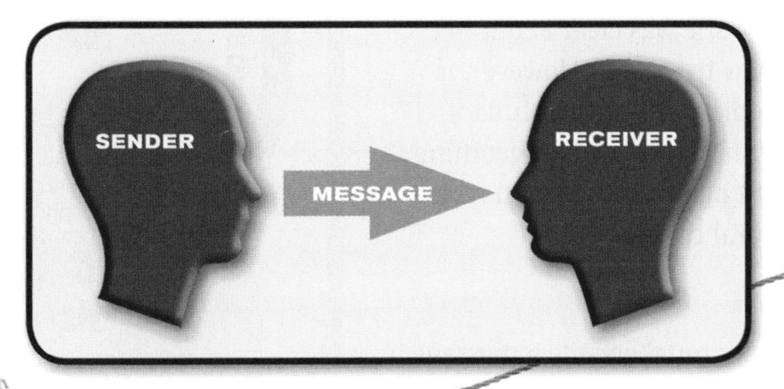

Communication involves making your meaning clear to the receiver.

Lily is going over the details of the junior class float with Minh. How would you assess his response?

Notice the communication elements in this scene: During a homecoming planning meeting in the school art room, Lily (the sender) tells Minh (the receiver) that she wants him to design the junior class float for the parade (the message). She tells Minh what the job entails and assures him his artistic skills make him the right person for the job.

Encoding

Before sending her message, Lily had to "translate" her ideas into words and gestures that Minh would understand. The process of turning ideas into messages is called **encoding**. In this case, Lily didn't need to give much thought to encoding her message. It happened on the spot because she was clear about her message and how to send it. However, if Lily were to speak to the entire student body about volunteering for homecoming tasks, she might plan, practice, and revise her speech several times.

Decoding

Just as the sender must encode a message, the receiver must "translate" the words and gestures into meaning. This process is called **decoding**. Minh hears Lily's words and sees her body language and interprets those signals to draw meaning from the message. In this fairly simple exchange, Minh would very likely be able to decode on the spot. In a different communication setting, as you will see on page 11, Minh might wonder, "What did she mean by that?" and need more thought to decode the message.

Feedback

Communication is a two-way process that relies on **feedback**, the receiver's response to the sender. Feedback turns the receiver into a sender and the original sender into a receiver. Even if the feedback is wordless (a shrug, a high-five, or a raised eyebrow), it helps complete the communication cycle and perhaps open up a new one. Whether he agrees to design the float or not, Minh's feedback will tell Lily that her message was successfully received.

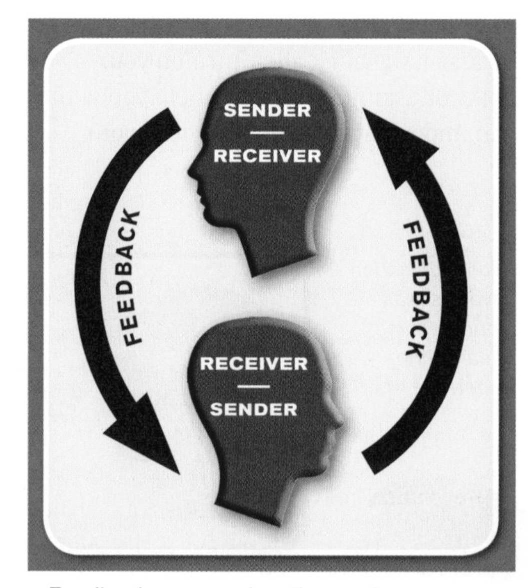

Feedback occurs when the receiver transmits a message back to the sender.

Context

All communication occurs in a specific situation, or **context**. The context of a communication is shaped in part by the time and place in which it occurs. The social setting—who is participating—and the psychological setting—the state of mind of the participants—also help define the context.

Out of context, Minh may have no idea Lily is referring to this kind of float when she calls to him.

Imagine a different context for Lily's communication to Minh. Suppose on a Saturday she sees Minh on a city bus with his friend from another school. This shift in context makes a difference in how Lily's message is sent and received. Lily waves and calls out to Minh, "I'd like to use you for the float." Minh's mind could easily be on everything *but* school and homecoming as he rides the bus with a friend. He may be surprised to run into his schoolmate in this setting. He may not realize or remember that Lily knows anything about his artistic skills. If he and Lily aren't good friends and don't typically run into each other, he might not even recognize her outside of school. In this context, when Lily mentions the float, Minh may have no idea what float she means. He might be distracted by thoughts about whether to introduce Lily to his friend.

Compare Contexts

	Context 1	Context 2
Time	Thursday after school during a homecoming committee meeting	The Saturday before the committee meeting
Place	Art room	City bus
Social setting	Friendly, business-oriented get-together	Chance meeting between Lily and Minh, who is with a friend
Psychological setting	Minh's mind is on homecoming; he knows what Lily is talking about when she speaks to him	Minh is caught off guard seeing Lily outside of school; he does not understand Lily's meaning; he may be confused and embarrassed

Channel

The means used to transmit a message from sender to receiver is called the communication **channel**. Messages are transmitted through many different channels, big and small. Those messages can be both verbal and nonverbal. Examples include:

- television programs broadcast on available channels
- daily newspapers delivered to subscribers' homes
- advertisements posted on billboards
- online updates posted to members of a networking site
- daily announcements over the school's PA system
- dinnertime conversation with the family
- gestures such as pointing a finger when giving directions.

In the interaction at school and on the bus, Lily communicated orally (channel) to Minh. She could have communicated through a different channel instead, such as in writing by posting a list of students' assigned tasks on the bulletin board or sending an e-mail.

Interference

Even in its simplest form, communication is rarely perfect. Anything that blocks or distorts communication is called **interference**. Interference can come from different sources, including the context, the sender, the receiver, and the channel.

As you've seen, the *context* of a Saturday bus ride could be a source of interference for Minh, since his mind might be on other matters entirely. Lily as the *sender* could be another source of interference if she expresses her message in language that is too vague for Minh to decode accurately.

Which of these communication channels do you use most often?

What if Minh, the *receiver*, doesn't recognize Lily at all out of the context of school? His confusion could be another source of interference. Or maybe he had an argument with her last year, so when he sees her now he puts up his defenses, blocking clear reception.

Maybe Lily is sitting too far away from Minh for him to hear what she says. Or what if she simply waves to Minh on the bus and then later sends him an e-mail about the float—but he doesn't get it because she used an old address. In these examples, the *channel* becomes the source of interference.

PROJECT PREP

With your **project group**, work up a mock cell phone conversation. Include at least three forms of interference.

Expanding the Communication Model

So far, the communication model represents relatively simple exchanges, communication between two people. The model can also be expanded to represent two other common communication situations: group communication and public speaking.

Group Communication

Think back to the homecoming meeting in the art room (page 10). Now add two more people, Chuck and Alicia, into the discussion. Although adding them complicates exchanges, it does not change the terms of the communication process.

For example, the *context* for communication is the same. Lily is communicating the same *message*. Now, however, everything she says in the meeting—whether it's directed at a specific individual or the whole group—has three *receivers*, each of whom provides feedback to Lily and each other.

What happens if Chuck and Alicia say nothing as Lily tells Minh she'd like him to design the float? Suppose Chuck smirks and Alicia slams her notebook shut. Whatever their feelings, their reactions create meaning for Lily and Minh. Lily may interpret both actions as negative. She may think Chuck and Alicia are unhappy about Minh's assignment. Minh, on the other hand, may interpret the *feedback* differently. He may think that Chuck seems relieved that he didn't get such a big task and that Alicia seems angry at Chuck's reaction.

Public Speaking

The basic communication model applies to public speaking situations as well. The *sender* is the speaker, and the *receiver* is the audience. *Feedback* can include applause, no applause, gasps, laughter, and questions. *Interference* can be noise, a bad microphone, or audience prejudice. *Context* can include the type of venue, the audience size, what the audience already knows, and the audience's attitude about the subject or the speaker.

Clapping is a way to send a speaker positive feedback.

Is This Job for Me?

Search: Motivational Speaker

In a hushed auditorium, the spotlight follows a young man as he moves easily across the school stage telling his chilling story. He was a high school dropout. He headed into a downward spiral and found himself living on the street, addicted and hungry. Only with the helping hands of a youth agency was he eventually, and after a long, painful struggle, able to pull himself back up to life. He is at the assembly to inspire students to stay in school and to avoid the nightmare he found himself in. In fact, he tours the country, speaking at one high school after another, to spread his message of caution and hope. He is a *motivational speaker*, a public speaker who provides engaging, educational, and uplifting speaking services based on personal expertise acquired through education or life experience.

Does a job as a motivational speaker interest you? Measure yourself with this personality inventory to find out if you have the traits of a motivational speaker. Are you:

- ✓ Articulate?
- ✓ Keenly aware of listeners' responses?
- ✓ Enthusiastic?
- ✓ Flexible?
- ✓ Personable?
- ✓ Dramatic?
- ✓ Quick on your feet?
- ✓ Comfortable in front of an audience?

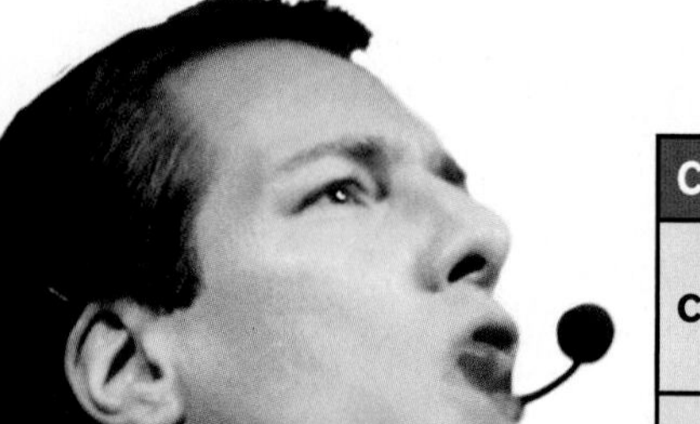

Clients	What You Would Do
Corporations	Motivate the sales force or inspire workers to achieve their personal best in their jobs
Professional associations	Inspire members to achieve greater results with dedication and the use of "best practices"—techniques known to work
Training film productions	Provide an inspirational face and/or voice to help people learn job or other skills through video training
Community organizations	Motivate fundraisers and volunteers
Religious institutions	Urge members to give generously so the organization can fulfill its purpose

Refining the Definition of Communication

You began this chapter by thinking about the question, "What is communication?" You probably have a good general idea of what communication is. Now that you know more about the interplay of elements within the process, you can refine your definition.

Communications experts have come up with this definition: "Communication is the negotiation of a shared meaning." *Negotiation* means "give and take." Every time you communicate you give and you take. You share your understanding. You also try to understand others, ask questions, and solve problems. You negotiate to reach an agreement or a shared meaning.

TechConnect The messages you exchange with others every day—handwritten notes, e-mails, shrugs, winks, text messages, voicemail messages—are all considered communication. When such communication fails (missed calls, misunderstood words or signals), shared meaning is the missing puzzle piece. Metacommunication and feedback can improve the chances of negotiating shared meanings between senders and receivers.

Characteristics of Communication

In addition to defining what communication is, experts have identified what communication *does* as a way to understand it better. They have observed that communication:

- **never stops.** Even when you stop talking, you continue communicating with your silence. You can sit in class and say nothing, but you are still communicating. You're creating meaning as someone interprets your silence as boredom or someone else thinks you're acting snobbish. Everywhere you turn, meaning is created within you, and you create meaning in others.
- **always changes.** In the simplest of conversations you naturally move dynamically from one thought or topic to another.
- **varies.** Changing any one of the elements, or variables, in the communication process changes the communication act itself. Even a seemingly simple act of communication involves many variables, making communication a complex process.

TechConnect *The reply to their e-mail is the feedback this family needed to know they were understood.*

Communication is ongoing, dynamic, variable, and complex.

Levels of Communication

Another way to understand communication is to identify the levels on which it occurs. Communication occurs on four different levels depending on the number of people involved in the communication process.

- **Intrapersonal communication** is communication within ourselves. Our inner thoughts include words and images. Before communicating with others, we use those thoughts to create the meaning we want to transfer with our message. Intrapersonal communication takes place when we think about the messages others send us. Without intrapersonal communication, no communication would be possible.
- **Interpersonal communication** occurs in contexts where two or more people actively participate in exchanging messages. Conversations, small-group discussions, and interviews are examples. The largest group that allows effective interpersonal communication is about ten to fourteen people.
- **Person-to-group communication** is the level of communication usually called public speaking. Examples include lectures, project reports, and speeches. The speaker addresses the audience as one receiver.
- **Mass media** is a level of communication that uses technology to bring the same message to large groups of people. Print media such as books and newspapers allow large numbers of people to read the same message. Electronic media such as radio and TV send audio and visual messages to millions of people at the same time. The Internet allows a vast audience to not only see a given message, but also to interact through online forums, Web logs, and videoconferencing.

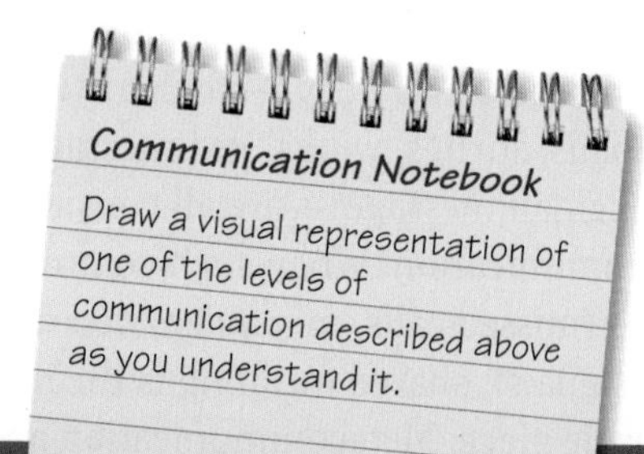

Intrapersonal communication

Interpersonal communication

Person-to-group communication

Mass media communication

PREPARING THE PROJECT

Begin your project by looking back at the **Project Prep** activities in this chapter and using the directions below.

Make Connections

Discuss with your group how your definition of communication may have changed as you read pages 6–16. Share your personal understanding of the role communication plays in your life. Discuss and summarize these important points:

- the role communication plays in your social, civic, academic, and personal life
- the ways in which you consider yourself, your listener, the occasion, and the task when making communication decisions
- the parts played by the message, the sender, the receiver, the feedback, the context, the channel, and possible interference in the communication process
- the four levels of communication.

Focus

Briefly review the group project you are working on: the "instant replay" presentation demonstrating and analyzing the communication process.

Plan

Brainstorm ideas for the scene you will use to demonstrate the communication process. Come up with three or four good ideas and then choose one among them that the group likes best. Talk through the scene to make sure the following will be possible:

This group is brainstorming a script for a communication scene.

- The sender's message will be concise and meaningful.
- The receiver's response must clearly show that the message was understood.
- The feedback between receiver and sender should be evident.
- Some form of interference should occur to obstruct communication.
- All members of the group are involved in the presentation.

Surefire Brainstorming

To get the best results from brainstorming:

- work cooperatively toward a goal
- let ideas flow rapidly
- don't judge ideas—just let them flow
- try looking at things in a fresh way
- build on the ideas of others and try unlikely combinations.

Develop

With your group, develop a script for your presentation. "Cast" the parts, being sure to include each group member. Decide where you want the announcer to call "freeze" to identify the communication elements. You might want to add some visual effects, even choreography. If your group does add a communication channel in addition to speech (such as gestures or diagrams) be sure the announcer names all the channels you have used.

Practice

Practice your presentation as often as needed until you all feel that you will have no trouble. Ask someone to time you to be sure that you do not go over three minutes. If your demonstration is running long, decide what needs to be cut and practice again without that part.

PRESENTING THE PROJECT

Use the strategies that follow to help make your presentation as good as it can be.

Your group should now be ready to share the project: demonstrating the communication process and analyzing it in an instant replay. Go over the CAPS guidelines on page 4 and the rubric on the next page to be sure that your project meets requirements.

Managing Nerves

If you are like many other people, you may feel anxious about making a presentation in front of a group of people. To feel as confident and ready to present as you can, take the time to prepare fully. Try to know the presentation, and your part in it, backward and forward. Make it your own by knowing it so well that nothing can trip you up.

When you work with others, everyone needs to be "on board" with the presentation. You and the members of your group should rehearse together and time your presentation as often as necessary to feel secure in what you are doing.

In addition to being fully prepared, you may also want to feel that you look your best. Then you won't be distracted by worries of what others may be thinking of your appearance. You might also want to use relaxation methods, such as deep breathing and muscle-relaxing meditation to calm your nerves. Consciously imagine each of your muscles relaxing as you inhale and exhale slowly.

If you prepare carefully, look your best, and use relaxation techniques, when your turn comes, you will walk to the front of the class and begin your presentation with confidence and energy.

Meditating helps relax the body and quiet the mind.

EVALUATING THE PROJECT

Evaluate the presentations using the following rubric.

Score the demonstration on each point, with 4 being "outstanding" and 1 being "needs much improvement."

Come up with an overall score and write a brief paragraph that explains your score.

Understanding of the Communication Process	Demonstration of the Communication Process	Creativity and Originality	Preparation and Use of Time
4 Presenters showed insight into the communication process.	**4** Presenters' demonstration helped illuminate the communication process.	**4** The presentation was attention-grabbing and unique, interesting, and fun.	**4** The presentation flowed smoothly and was neither too short nor too long.
3 Presenters understood the communication process.	**3** Presenters' demonstration was helpful in understanding the communication process.	**3** The presentation was attention-grabbing, interesting, and fun but not very original.	**3** The presentation progressed fairly smoothly and was neither too short nor too long.
2 Presenters did not seem to understand some elements of the communication process.	**2** Presenters' demonstration was minimally helpful in understanding the communication process.	**2** The presentation was fairly interesting and fun but not original or attention-grabbing.	**2** The presentation had a few awkward moments and went a bit over or considerably under the time limit.
1 Presenters misunderstood much of the communication process.	**1** Presenters' demonstration did not help in understanding the communication process.	**1** The presentation was not original or attention-grabbing and only moderately fun and interesting.	**1** The presentation was not smoothly executed and went well over or under the time limit.

Communication *Past* and Present

Mass Communications

From Gutenberg . . .

In about 1450, a humble German printer named Johannes Gutenberg created a simple device that soon had enormous impact.

The device: the printing press

The impact: a world of communication spinning so fast and so wide that it is still slightly dizzying

While Asians had long used block printing successfully, Gutenberg was the first to use moveable type to mass-produce books, creating about 180 copies of his famous Bible in 1455. This book, now called the Gutenberg Bible, led to a new way to communicate.

Printing was costly at first—the average clerk would have to work for three years to buy a Gutenberg Bible—but it was not nearly as costly as the only alternative: handwritten books. Books scribed by hand took well over a year to copy and only the extremely wealthy, often clergymen, could afford them. Gutenberg's press was able to produce six pages at a time. Once the technology was working at peak efficiency, books and newspapers flew off the presses. Books became affordable even for working people.

By 1500, the new presses were being used throughout Europe. Classic Latin and Greek texts, the source of inspiration for Renaissance scholars, were translated for the middle class, and the intellectual and artistic influence of Renaissance thinkers spread. Scientific publications became a major catalyst for a new scientific movement. As the demand for books grew, other trades also flourished, such as papermaking and binding. As economies grew and publishing thrived, more people learned to read, and with a more literate population, societies grew stronger.

For the first time in history, writers were sharing ideas with people they would never meet and who might not even live in the same country or speak the same language. Books printed with moveable type created a worldwide net before anyone ever heard of the electronic age. You can e-visit the British Library's copies of Gutenberg's Bible at http://www.bl.uk/treasures/gutenberg/homepage.html.

. . . to the Internet

It took an army of people to make the Internet what it is today, but one of the most impressive inventors was Paul Baran. In 1962 he was trying to design a communications network that could continue to operate after a nuclear attack. Applying digital technology and the concept of "redundancy," or use of additional components in case original components fail, he rejected the centralized switching operations then in use. He devised instead a network of nodes that would route information from one node to the next in a system called "distributed communication."

In an interview with *Wired* magazine, Baran recalls predicting in 1966 that people were going to do their shopping "via a television set and a virtual department store. If you want to buy a drill, you click on Hardware and that shows Tools and you click on that and go deeper."

Baran's predictions were right. Since then, the network he designed, later named the Internet, has expanded exponentially. Worldwide and accessible to anyone with a computer and a modem, the Internet is now made up of millions of smaller networks that connect governments, businesses, schools, and individuals.

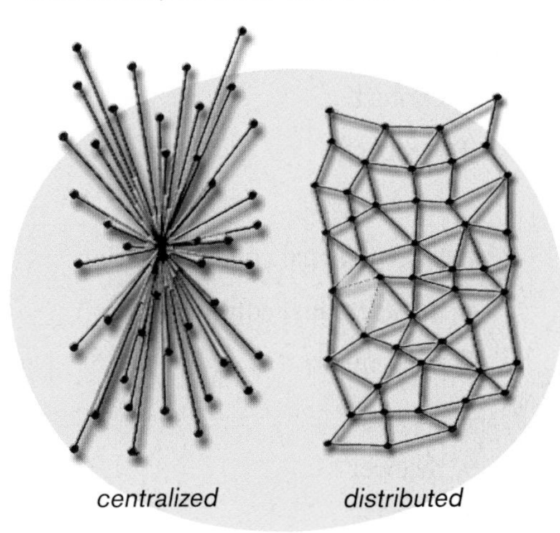

In 2008, about 1.25 billion people were using the Internet. At any time, night or day, people can communicate in some way. They can send and receive e-mail, conduct business, visit sites where they can learn or play, stream videos or music, exchange ideas in chat rooms, and transfer files.

Gutenberg could never have imagined this global interconnectedness. He might be happy to know, however, that he inspired a popular Web site. Project Gutenberg, which offers a collection of 6,267 free e-books, is made possible by thousands of volunteers. Visit them at http://www.gutenberg.org/catalog.

Chapter 1 Review

Using Vocabulary Words

For each of the following terms, answer two questions:

- What is it?
- What is an example?

1. channel
2. context
3. feedback
4. interference
5. interpersonal communication
6. intrapersonal communication
7. mass media
8. message
9. receiver
10. sender

Reviewing Key Ideas

1. Explain the importance of communication.
2. List the four things to keep in mind when making communication decisions. Provide an example of how each can affect communication.
3. Identify the seven key elements in the communication process.
4. Draw a simple communication model using the elements of sender, receiver, message, feedback, and context. Briefly explain your positioning of context in the diagram.

Reflecting on Your Project

With your small group, discuss which parts of your project went especially well and which gave you the most trouble. Come up with two or three strategies for dealing with trouble spots in future projects.

Responding to the Essential Question

Use the headings in this chapter to help you write a brief chapter summary that answers the question, "What is communication?" Compare your summary with a partner's to see if you both covered the main points.

Extending Your Understanding

Everyday Life

1. With a partner, observe other pairs or groups communicating at lunchtime. Discuss examples of interference that you see.
2. Think about two communications you wish to initiate. For each one, use a channel you would not usually be likely to use. Discuss how changing the channel may affect how the receiver interprets your message.
3. Focus on an object in your room at home. Engage in some intrapersonal communication about any personal meaning you find in it. You can talk out loud or write yourself notes. Does the meaning you find surprise you?

In the Media

4. Listen to a radio advertisement and identify the main message the sender wants the audience to receive. Compare conclusions with another listener to see if you identified the same intended message. Discuss any differences.
5. Watch an interview on a television news program. List at least two examples of interference in the communication between the interviewer and the subject. Discuss whether the interference affected the end result of the communication and ways the interference might have been avoided.
6. Read an advice column in your local newspaper in which an expert answers a reader's question. Describe how the element of feedback is represented in this communication.

Research

7. Research famous speechwriters in history. Choose one who interests you and prepare a three-minute profile of him or her using at least two sources (books, articles, or Web sites). Present your profile to the class along with photos and a passage from one of your subject's best-known speeches.
8. Research the definition of communication using a variety of sources (dictionaries, encyclopedias, books, articles, or Web sites). Apply the CAPS model to your research and illustrate as needed. Present your research to the class.

Interpreting Graphics

Copy the model diagram on a separate sheet of paper. Then label the elements in the communication process that are represented in the diagram.

Additional Projects

1. **Group Project:** In a small group, select a common group activity at your school. Examples include band practice, class discussions, and assemblies. For the class, act out both successful and unsuccessful communication using your chosen activity. After your presentation, ask your classmates what went right and what went wrong.
2. **Individual Project:** Illustrate or build a communication model that's specific to one situation. Sample ideas include a coach talking to a team, a three-way conversation, a competition debate, and a dog-training session. Brainstorm your own list of ideas and then choose one you'd like to work on. Consider how your model differs from the one presented in this chapter. Display your finished model in class.

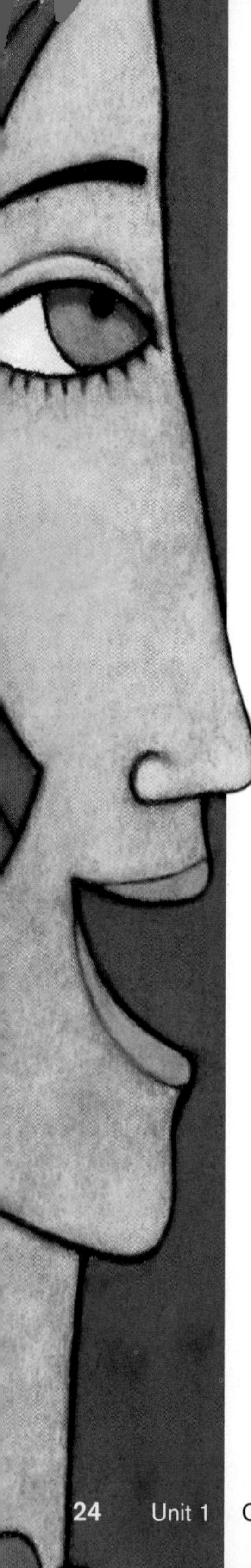

Oral Language

ESSENTIAL QUESTION

How can people use language to achieve effective oral communication?

Chapter Project: "Who's on First?"

If you are misunderstood, how do you feel? You might feel as frustrated as Abbott and Costello in their famous comedy sketch, "Who's on First?"(See page 28.) This project will help you send and receive clear messages to avoid misunderstandings.

With a partner, you will develop a two- to three-minute scene that features a face-to-face conversation between two characters who continually misunderstand each other (either consciously or unconsciously) because of different language choices each makes. Be creative and have fun with it—the exchange can be funny, serious, or somewhere in between. Refer to the following CAPS guidelines as you work on your scene.

The rubric on page 41 shows the traits on which your presentation will be evaluated.

CONCEPT	language choices can affect both the literal meaning of what you say and what a listener thinks you are saying
AUDIENCE	partner, classmates, and teacher
PURPOSE	practice effective oral communication
SITUATION	creative classroom scene

KEY VOCABULARY

denotation	economy
connotation	grace
usage	abstract
colloquialisms	concrete
syntax	dialect
substance	idiom
style	jargon
clarity	

Speak Up!

Many words have so many synonyms that some just can't be substituted in every context. An easy example is the adjective *good*. Depending on how it is used, it can mean beneficial, enjoyable, valid, honorable, nice, or well-behaved. Take a moment to substitute each of those synonyms for *good* in this sentence:

That was a *good* movie!

Which ones make sense in this context? Which ones don't make sense? Which ones make sense but change the sentence's meaning?

Come up with your own quick list of varied synonyms for the adjective *bad*. Use your imagination. Then try out the different words in the sentence below.

That was a *bad* movie!

What indicates that these students are communicating effectively?

BACKGROUND FOR THE PROJECT

Pages 26–38 will provide the information you'll need to complete this project.

Identifying Characteristics of Oral Language

Oral communication is the use of spoken language to convey ideas. Think about how much a speaker conveys in the following simple sentence.

> Language is the most important tool in our communication toolbox.

Chances are you have no problem understanding that sentence. The question is, why?

Starting from the first word, the speaker focuses attention on the topic of language. Based on personal knowledge and experience, you start predicting where the sentence might go from the word *language* alone. The speaker then guides you with all the words that follow to his or her intended meaning. The sentence goes on to point out a relationship among all communication elements and asserts that language is the most important element. The metaphor of language as a tool in a toolbox adds another layer of meaning to the sentence. Not bad for just ten simple words.

Every day you manipulate *thousands* of words in your communication. No wonder, then, that you are likely to find yourself caught up in the problems and opportunities of language.

These teachers are both giving lessons on the same basic topic–language skills–to two different audiences. What different language choices might they make to communicate with their classes?

Features of Language

Language *is* the single most important component of oral communication. Every language, whether spoken or written, has similar features. The words and sounds differ from language to language, but the characteristics of language are the same.

Use of Symbols

All languages use symbols to represent things and ideas. If you want to communicate a thought about a dog, you don't need to have an actual dog handy to point to. Instead, you use the word *dog* and let that stand as a symbol for the animal.

What feature of language explains why all of these words can mean dog*?*

Social Understanding

There is no real reason why the idea of a dog should be represented by the word *dog.* In fact, speakers of other languages do not use the word *dog*—they have their own symbolic words for it. However, speakers of the same language agree on the meanings of these symbols and understand one another. English speakers simply agree that *dog* means a furry four-legged animal that barks. Social acceptance of the meanings of words is a characteristic of language.

Use of Grammar

Languages also all organize into a system the symbols they use to stand for ideas. The grammar of a language provides a system by which words—and the ideas they represent—can be put into relation to one another. Grammar allows speakers to say something *about* a dog, not just name it.

Flexibility and Change

The system of language is so flexible that a speaker can create a sentence that was never before created. Further, language is always changing. Words, meanings, and even grammar "rules" have changed over the centuries and continue to change today. New words always come into the language, sometimes arriving with never-before-known technological changes (*gigabyte* and *Internet,* for example). Words also change meanings. In the 1960s, the word *radical* brought to mind protesters with extreme views. In the 1980s, it was often used to mean "hip" or "cool."

Oral language is characterized by symbols, social acceptance of meaning, grammar, flexibility, and change.

Denotation and Connotation

One way to understand differences in meaning is to examine a word's various shades of meaning. Shades of meaning are the subtle differences in ideas that a word can convey. If you hear the word *pencil,* for example, you might think of a yellow, wooden object with sharpened lead at one end and an eraser at the other end. However, some people might think of a mechanical pencil or an artist's pencil or a flat carpenter's pencil. Fortunately, the meaning of *pencil* can be cleared up quickly. Imagine the difficulty, however, in clearing up any misunderstandings that might arise from far more abstract words such as *honor, freedom, friendship,* or *love*.

Words convey meaning through their denotations and connotations. A word's **denotation** is its explicit, literal meaning, its "dictionary definition." Language requires that people share the same basic denotation for most words. English speakers agree on the denotation of *dog* and don't picture a giraffe when they hear that word.

A word's **connotation,** however, conveys subtle shades of meaning. Connotation is a word's implied or suggested meaning. Connotations can involve emotions, images, or memories—the associations a listener makes with a word. Connotations are generally positive or negative. If you are a letter carrier who has to dodge territorial dogs all day, you are likely to have a negative association with the word *dog*. If you grew up with a cheerful, slobbering sheepdog, the word *dog* is likely to have a positive connotation.

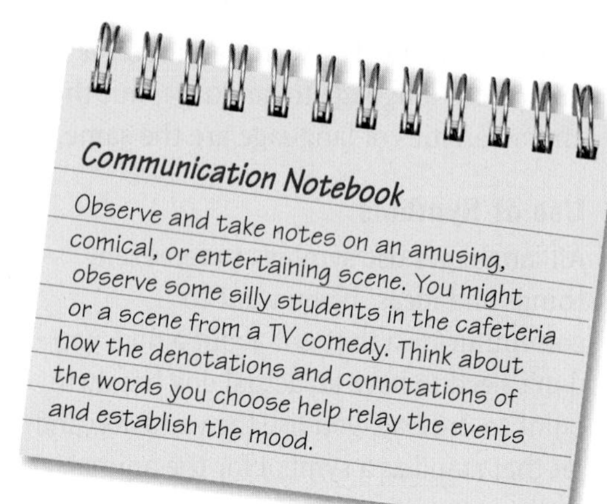

The following words are synonyms for the word "funny." Note the differences in connotation.

funny	He told a funny story.
amusing	He told an amusing story.
comical	He told a comical story.

"Funny" suggests laughter. "Amusing" suggests something less than "funny," perhaps something slight or inconsequential."Comical" suggests something more involved and far more humorous than merely "funny."

PROJECT PREP

With your **project partner** or as your teacher directs, watch a video, DVD, or Web presentation of Bud Abbott and Lou Costello's classic six-minute comedy routine, "Who's on First?" Watch it once all the way through. Then replay it, jotting down any ideas it sparks for your own project.

Search **Lawyer**

Do you know what the word *use* means? The nine judges of the Supreme Court struggled with defining that simple word when a case came before them in 1995. According to a federal law, for some crimes, the "use" of a gun imposes an automatic 5-year prison sentence. But what exactly does it mean to "use" a gun? If a defendant has an unloaded gun locked up in a drawer, is that gun in "use"? In a landmark decision, the judges unanimously ruled "no" even though prosecutors were trying to argue "yes."

Every day, in countless courtrooms across the country, *lawyers*–professionals trained in legal principles and case law–argue over the meanings of words. At times a person's life and liberty may depend on how key words are defined.

Does a job as a lawyer interest you? Measure yourself with this personality inventory to find out if you have the traits that make a successful lawyer. Do you:

- ✓ Enjoy theory and abstract ideas?
- ✓ Seek the truth through analysis?
- ✓ Work well alone?
- ✓ Trust your own beliefs and understandings?
- ✓ Dislike ordinary detail?
- ✓ Look to the future?

If you become a lawyer, you might have the following job opportunities.

Clients	What You Would Do
Corporations	Write contracts that spell out the exact terms of business relationships
Government	Prosecute or defend criminals; protect the rights of children; do research for a judge
Individuals	Defend people accused of crimes; argue a case for civil wrongdoing
Nonprofit organizations	Argue a case on behalf of people whose interests are served by the organization

Analyzing Standards for Using Oral Language

Speakers who get their messages across clearly choose and organize their words and adapt their messages as needed for specific listeners.

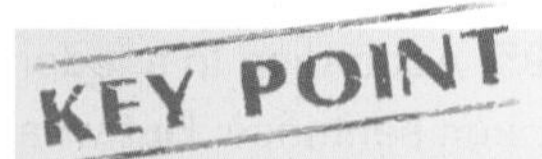

Making solid language choices requires adapting to the situation you're in, your purpose in communicating a message, and your audience, or listeners.

For example, imagine that your older brother's best friend has been hired as a teacher at your school. His name is Thomas Johnson. You've known him all your life as Tommy, and you often call him by the nickname "TJ." What should you call him?

Think about the *situation.* School is a public place with an established set of behaviors, including how students address teachers. Calling your brother's friend Mr. Johnson when other students are present is probably a good decision. Your *goal* is to have him and other *listeners* understand from your word choice that you recognize and respect Mr. Johnson's role.

How might you modify your choices if you run into him after school, when the hallways are empty? Or what if you see Mr. Johnson in the parking lot? Your choices will vary with different circumstances.

Levels of Usage

Language **usage** is the relationship of language to the specific situation, purpose, and audience. Effective communicators match the level of language to the situation and audience. The chart below shows the two main levels of spoken English usage: Standard and Nonstandard.

Standard Spoken English	Nonstandard Spoken English
Language at this level can be: • formal and technical • informal or general • conversational. People use this in both formal and informal situations. You would use it for an oral presentation in class or maybe when you're trying to make a good impression on someone. General rules of grammar and usage apply.	Language at this level can include elements of Standard Spoken English and also be: • slang • familiar mainly to a certain region or culture • invented or coined. Many people use this in everyday communication and in any truly comfortable or informal exchange. It can be appropriate in some formal situations, too, when the audience shares an understanding of any nonstandard terms or connotations.

Distinguishing Oral Language from Written Language

In most of speech—public and private, formal and informal—you strive for usage that allows your listeners to feel comfortable with what you say and how you say it. In that process you use **colloquialisms**, words and phrases that are generally characteristic of spoken language and not of standard written language.

Oral language is less formal than written language because it contains more contractions, more colloquialisms, and sentence fragments. Also, it is usually composed "on the spot," and listeners allow for "looser" language usage. In addition, speakers modify spoken language through tone of voice, volume, and facial expression or gesture.

However, listeners do not have an "anything goes" attitude. Listeners still expect certain conventions of vocabulary, **syntax** or word order, proper usage, and other characteristics of language use. These expectations will vary according to audience and situation, but the expectations are definitely there.

PROJECT PREP

Think about the language you used in your last written paper. Then think about how you might talk about the topic of that paper in an informal conversation. What are some of the differences in language? Talk about them with your **project partner.**

Can you identify possible differences in situation, purpose, and audience that would explain the language choices in the following chart?

Standard Written English	Standard Spoken English	Nonstandard Spoken English

I will express my attitudes about the use of pre-taped interviews on television by analyzing the differences between spontaneous live interviews and those conducted on film and edited to fit a given program.	I'll talk about my reactions to the kinds of interviews you see on TV, noting the differences I found between pre-taped interviews and live, face-to-face interviews.	To me, those pre-taped TV interviews look totally staged and bogus. You don't really see people talking that way in real life. Come on.

Effective communicators adjust their language according to the purpose, situation, and audience.

Making Communication Choices

While all oral language shares certain characteristics, each speaker uses oral language in a different way. Effective speakers make communication choices based on what works best for their own style, their listeners, and the situation.

Appropriateness for Speaker

As a speaker, you want to choose language that makes you feel comfortable, allows you to express your personality, and helps you communicate your intended message to listeners. How you make those choices defines your language style.

Language and Style

Style is *how* something is said or done. Style is different from content—*what* is said or done. In basketball, for example, many players dunk the ball. Yet, Michael Jordan had a style of dunking that set him apart from others. He dunked (*what* he did) with a degree of acrobatic grace (*how* he did it). In fashion, anyone can wear a hat. However, some people make wearing a hat an act of style by wearing it off to the side or inside out. These choices show personal style.

Michael Jordan's dunking style was all his own.

In addition to an athletic and fashion style, people also have a language style. Everyone uses language in a unique way. You may know someone whose conversation is always spiked with humor. Another person might use words sparingly. Still another might have an anecdotal style, peppering her speech with sayings and stories.

Every message has both substance and style. **Substance** is the content—the message communicated through the denotations of words. This part of the message can be summarized, explained, and paraphrased. The speaker's **style** is the way the message is expressed. It is determined by word choice, connotation, syntax, and organization. Style can be described, but it cannot be summarized or paraphrased.

Read through the following short passages. Imagine that the speakers are addressing the student council. Note that the passages contain the same substance but different styles.

Speaker A

We have an issue on today's agenda that needs our immediate attention. The principal discussed it directly with Jamal, so I've asked Jamal to address the group.

Speaker B

Hey, guys, you probably noticed the red flag item from Principal Martinez on our meeting list. Since Jamal heard it straight from the principal herself, I'll let him go ahead and fill you in.

Clarity, Economy, and Grace

A speaking style most likely to convey a clear message is characterized by clarity, economy, and grace. Read this chart to learn about these aspects of style.

Components of Style			
	Clarity	**Economy**	**Grace**
Definitions	**Clarity** or clearness of style means selecting understandable, precise words and placing them in a clear order. Style enhances the message. Above all, your message must be accessible to your audience. Any stylistic choice you make should further the clarity of your message.	**Economy** in style means that the speech expresses an idea briefly and pointedly.	**Grace** is the expression of your ideas in an appealing and skillful manner. A graceful style is pleasant to hear and memorable—even eloquent.
Examples	The Book Drive Campaign is an important part of our school's support of community literacy.	The goal of our Book Drive Campaign is 100% participation from all students and school employees.	The Book Drive Campaign shows our commitment, our caring, and our capacity to give.
What to avoid	• words that are unfamiliar to your audience • poorly constructed sentences • poor organization • a lack of transitional words and phrases	• wordy explanations of simple ideas • unnecessary repetitiveness	• phrases and sentences that sound awkward • lack of parallel structure
Negative examples	The Book Drive Campaign, which we certainly endorse and which is important, is a part of our community service work. We support community literacy, and of course, service, the point of this being that we are committed.	We have many goals this year, but one of our goals involves the total participation of all students and employees of the school to the tune of 100% as givers to the community literacy work to which we are so committed.	The Book Drive campaign shows how committed we are, that we care, and the capacity to give.

Appropriate Choices for the Listener

Another consideration in making communication choices is to think about what is best for the audience or the listener. Choose language that allows the listener to focus on and understand your message.

Shared Meanings

People generally share the denotations of most words. But sometimes your listeners will not share the connotations you use. These tips can help you avoid problems.

- Think about your audience before you speak. What words will likely be unfamiliar? Make substitutions whenever possible.
- If you must use an unfamiliar word, be sure to supply a clear definition for it as you speak.
- If you and the audience are likely to share the denotative meaning of a word but not the connotative meaning, try to replace that word with another that has a shared connotation. If you can't make a suitable replacement, explain your use of the term to help the audience understand the connotation you're using.

Imagine, for example, that you're reading a picture book to your five-year-old cousin. Afterward, you say, "Wow, that thief was such a snake!" Your young cousin is confused and says, "Snake? I didn't see a snake anywhere!"

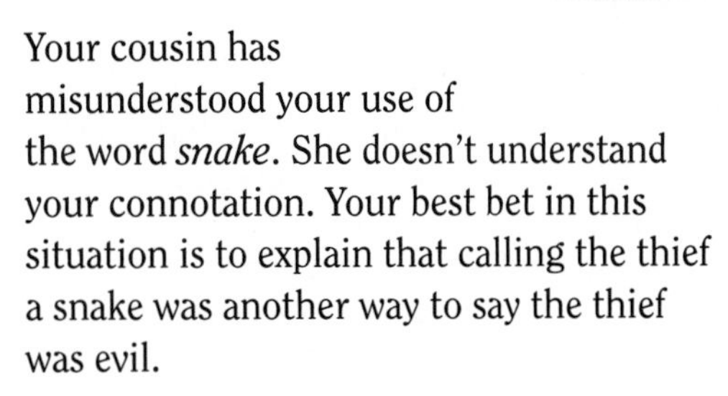

Your cousin has misunderstood your use of the word *snake*. She doesn't understand your connotation. Your best bet in this situation is to explain that calling the thief a snake was another way to say the thief was evil.

If you suspect that your communication has gone off track because you do not share a word's denotation or connotation, put yourself in your audience's place. What do you think the person or group *thinks* you mean by the word? Can you substitute something else or define the word in the context of your message? You may want to just directly ask someone to share his or her understanding of a word. (No doubt you've asked, "What do you mean by that?" many times.) It might be the only way to clear up confusion and give you clues to shape the rest of your communication.

Abstract and Concrete

Abstract words refer to general concepts or ideas. **Concrete** words refer to specific items or processes you can see or instantly identify. Abstract language has its place, but choosing concrete words will help your audience understand your message. One way to improve the effectiveness of your oral communication is to choose concrete language over abstract language when possible. If you must use abstract words, offer concrete examples to illustrate your meaning.

Abstract Language	Concrete Language
"I want my freedom."	"I'm ready for summer vacation."
Shondra had a problem with her sister.	Shondra thought her sister was wrong to bully the neighbor kids.
Marcus hoped to be successful one day.	Marcus wanted to finish medical school and provide free care to elderly patients without health insurance.

PROJECT PREP

Sketch two different scenes, each with the caption "Nicole makes a contribution." Share them with your **project partner** and discuss the differences in meaning.

Dialect

Another variety of language that may cause problems for an audience is dialect. A **dialect** is a language pattern—often regional—that is different from the dominant or typical language pattern. Dialect can differ from the dominant language in vocabulary, pronunciation, or syntax. In most cases, dialect does not hinder communication. In fact, many audiences find dialect charming or interesting if it is understandable. People who speak a dialect of English are at no disadvantage when speaking with an audience who speaks the same dialect. When a speaker addresses another audience, however, dialect becomes a factor. For example, in some regions of the country, people might commonly say, "He is sure enough going to be there." In other parts of the country, this expression is unusual. You must decide—as a communicator—which elements of dialect belong in conversation and in a speech and which do not.

The terms below illustrate some dialectical differences between English spoken in the United States and English spoken in the United Kingdom. If someone told you it was parky outside, would you know to wear a coat?

American English	British English
• good-bye	• cheers
• bathrobe	• dressing gown
• steal	• nick
• Popsicle	• ice lolly
• car muffler	• silencer
• telephone booth	• call box
• police officer	• bobby
• chilly	• parky
• apartment	• flat

Idiom

An **idiom** is an expression that means something other than the literal meaning of its words. An example is the expression "spill the beans." You know that means to tell a secret or spoil a surprise. If you say you "feel like a million bucks" or are "on top of the world," you are saying you feel good, not that you actually feel like money or are sitting atop the world. Keep your audience in mind when communicating with idioms. Try not to use expressions your listeners won't understand. Most idioms are commonly known, but some are regional, making them part of a dialect.

Jargon

The technical vocabulary of a hobby, occupation, or other specialized activity is called **jargon**. Avoid jargon unless you are speaking to people who typically use the same jargon. Jargon may confuse audiences outside the specialized group. For example, many people you might encounter would have no idea what you're talking about if you uttered this jargon-filled sentence:

I *downloaded* my friend's *podcast* on my *cell* and then *uploaded* it to my audio library *software* before *syncing* that with my *MP3 player*, creating a *backup* on my *external hard drive*, and then *ripping* a *disc* so my dad could listen to the show in his car.

Understanding your audience will help you adjust your choice of words so listeners receive your message and don't feel ignorant or out of touch—or worse, that your intention was to show off or put them down.

Looking in a horse's mouth is one way to tell how old and healthy it is. Questioning the quality of a gift you have received is impolite, so "Don't look a gift horse in the mouth" has come to mean, "Be grateful for the gift."

Appropriateness for the Situation

Another consideration in making appropriate communication choices is to think about what is best for the situation or occasion. Are you speaking in a private conversation, to a group of classmates, or to a potential employer? You won't use the same level of language to speak to a friend about a homework assignment that you will use to persuade a potential employer to hire you as a clerk in a music store. Choose language that shows that you understand the formality or informality of the situation or occasion.

Appropriateness for the Purpose

One final consideration in making appropriate language choices is to think about what is best for your purpose or task. Are you speaking to instruct, to persuade, or to describe? If you are speaking to instruct, you will use language that is direct and active. If you are speaking to persuade, you will use language that appeals to logic or emotion. If you are speaking to describe, you will use language that appeals to the five senses. Choose language that effectively accomplishes your purpose for speaking.

Imagine that you're in charge of educating other students about the upcoming school charity drive. (You have a fixed audience of your peers in this case.) How might your purpose differ with each of the following situations? Think about the different language choices you might make in each situation.

Topic	Possible Situations	Purpose
School charity drive	• assembly	• introduce the topic to all students
	• volunteer work groups	• provide in-depth details and assign tasks
	• one-on-one conversations	• offer guidance and advice to individuals

What is the speaker's purpose in each situation? What language is appropriate for each situation?

Comparing Two Styles of Language

Is how you say something (style) as important as what you say (substance or content)? Here are two speeches about the same topic. Each speech has a decidedly different style.

- How would you evaluate each speech in terms of clarity, economy, and grace?
- Is one speech more effective than the other? If so, which one, and why?

Audience: The student body

Situation: Two students are running for president of the student council

Purpose: To persuade voters to cast their votes in favor of a candidate

Speech A

Thank you for attending this assembly to consider our choices for class president. I appreciate your time and your attention. When you go to the polls on election day, I want you to know why you are casting your votes for me. First, I am a leader. My peers look to me for guidance and encouragement. I am captain of a successful debate team, and I led the school marching band to victory at our last competition. Second, I am a listener. I consider varying points of view before making decisions. Recently, the band purchased new uniforms. There were many opinions regarding which uniform to select. I listened to the different points of view and suggested a compromise that made everyone happy. Finally, I am committed. I will not take my duties lightly. You will see evidence of my presidency through new school programs and community service projects. A vote for me is a vote for leadership, diversity, and commitment.

Speech B

Hey everyone. Thanks for showing up here so we can lay it all out for you to help you see who you want leading the way. I know that you all have tons of other stuff to do, so I won't take much of your time. I'll make it simple—I want to be your leader! I am a leader, you know that. I got the whole school behind that car wash fundraiser last year. You know I listen to you guys, too. You can always grab me in the hall or give me a shout on my cell and I'll be there to listen. Another thing—I'm like a bulldog when it comes to sticking with things. There'll be some real changes if I win, so just do it—vote for me!

PREPARING THE PROJECT

Begin your project by looking back at the **Project Prep** activities in this chapter and using the directions below.

Make Connections

Discuss with your partner what you learned about oral language in this chapter. Summarize:

- the characteristics of oral language
- the role of denotation and connotation in conveying meaning
- the differences in level of usage
- the ways in which you consider your listener, the occasion, and your purpose when making communication decisions about language standards.

In their comedy skits, Bud Abbott (left) usually portrayed a character whose serious tone helped Lou Costello (right) draw laughs.

Focus

Briefly review the project you are working on: the "Who's on First?" comedy (or drama) of language errors and misunderstandings.

Plan

Brainstorm at least five ideas for the scene you will enact. Talk them over and decide on one to develop into your presentation. Double-check that your idea demonstrates the effect of language choices on how well—and how poorly—a message gets across. Then, to get a feel for your project, improvise a few exchanges using the idea you settled on.

Develop

With your partner, create a draft of your conversation. Be sure you have included plenty of clear examples of language choices that have multiple shades of meaning. Go over the CAPS directives on page 24 to be sure that your scene is on target.

Practice

Practice a number of times. Try practicing in front of a live audience—your family or your friends. If they have useful comments to improve your presentation, consider reworking parts of your conversation. Also be sure to time your presentation so that it fills out the time limit.

PRESENTING THE PROJECT

Use the strategies that follow to help make your presentation as good as it can be.

If you can grab the attention and interest of your audience right way, you will have a good chance of keeping their interest through your presentation.

Surefire Warm-Ups

To get your energy level high for a strong start to your presentation, warm up ahead of time with activities that get your body moving. Stretch your muscles gently, as an athlete would before a workout, or try something more vigorous like imaginary jump rope.

Engaging Your Audience

Here are some specific ways to get your audience interested right from the start.

- Raise the curiosity of your listeners about what is unfolding before them.
- Try something unexpected and fresh.
- Warm up before your turn comes so you are alert and ready. Keep your energy level high.

EVALUATING THE PROJECT

Evaluate the presentations using the following rubric.

Score the demonstration on each point, with 4 being "outstanding" and 1 being "needs much improvement."

Come up with an overall score and write a brief paragraph explaining that score.

Understanding of Language Choice and Multiple Meanings	Demonstration of Mis-communication	Creativity and Originality	Preparation and Teamwork
4 Presenters showed insight into language choice and multiple meanings.	**4** Presenters' demonstration helped illuminate miscommunication.	**4** The presentation was attention-grabbing, unique, interesting, and fun.	**4** The presentation flowed smoothly and the partners played off each other well.
3 Presenters understood language choice and multiple meanings.	**3** Presenters' demonstration was helpful in understanding miscommunication.	**3** The presentation was attention-grabbing, interesting, and fun, but not very original.	**3** The presentation progressed fairly smoothly and the partners worked together well.
2 Presenters did not seem to understand some aspects of language choice and multiple meanings.	**2** Presenters' demonstration was minimally helpful in understanding miscommunication.	**2** The presentation was fairly interesting and fun but not original or attention-grabbing.	**2** The presentation had a few awkward moments and the partners stumbled over each other at times.
1 Presenters misunderstood much about language choice and multiple meanings.	**1** Presenters' demonstration did not help in understanding miscommunication.	**1** The presentation was not original or attention-grabbing and only moderately fun and interesting.	**1** The presentation was not smoothly executed and the partners did not work together well.

Communication *Past* and Present

Neanderthal Speech and Musical Sounds

From Neanderthals . . .

What image comes to mind when you see the word *Neanderthal*? Hairy creatures cavorting and chattering excitedly like monkeys?

Or do you picture the early humans in the film *Quest for Fire,* who communicated in word-like sounds? Evidence suggests that Neanderthals, the closest known relatives of modern humans who may have lived 230,000 years ago in Europe, might indeed have used language much as we do today. Three main pieces of evidence for this view are 1) the tools they fashioned, 2) various structures in their skulls, and 3) DNA extracted from Neanderthal fossils.

The complex and job-specific tools Neanderthals created show that they were probably able to think symbolically. Many scientists believe that making and using tools goes hand-in-hand with larger brain capacity, which in turn makes language creation possible. As intriguing as this theory is, the use of tools alone falls short of proving that Neanderthals had language.

More evidence does seem to exist, however, in the tongue, larynx, neck bone, and ear of the Neanderthal skeleton. In 1983, scientists in Israel found a small Neanderthal neck bone that supports the tongue. They hypothesized that this bone enabled the Neanderthal tongue and larynx to produce speech. More evidence was found in the hypoglossal canal, which carries a nerve that allows tongue muscles to move. Some scientists feel that the Neanderthal tongue may have been even more agile than ours. Additionally, a discovery in the middle ear of these early humans seems to show that they could differentiate distinct sounds. So it would seem that Neanderthal anatomy had the potential for hearing and producing speech. But was their speech actual language?

Geneticists contend that for Neanderthals to have made the leap from primitive one- and two-word sentences to a language rich in vocabulary, grammar, and word order would have required a shift in their genetic makeup. A piece of evidence discovered in Spain seems to support that possibility. A gene which is connected to language acquisition in humans was extracted from a Neanderthal fossil. This gene is one of several existing in humans today that play a recognized role in how humans learn language.

. . . to Modern Humans

One researcher has theorized that Neanderthal language was more musical than ours. Neanderthals may not have separated language and music into two distinct areas of the brain as modern humans do. However, studies show that modern human speech vocalizations actually correspond remarkably with the 12-tone scale of music.

Researchers Dale Purves, Deborah Ross, and Jonathan Choi at Duke University recorded speakers of English and speakers of Mandarin Chinese as they vocalized vowel sounds. The scientists then used a machine called a *spectrum analyzer* to compare the underlying sounds in those vocalizations to the sounds in the 12-tone scale. The human ear can't hear sounds at that level, but the spectrum analyzer picked up surprising similarities.

All vocalizations come from the same source in the body, the vocal cords in the larynx, powered by the lungs' air stream. The sounds are then shaped and modified by the soft palate, tongue, and lips. Each of these body parts is unique in each human, just as each person's eyes or fingertips are unique. The researchers found, however, that despite all that variety, 70% of human vocalizations recorded in the study matched up with ratios that musical intervals have. These hidden similarities between human speech and the musical scale may help explain why the use of a scale divided into 12 tones sounds so right to humans. Perhaps it would also have felt right to Neanderthals, though that will never be known for sure.

Chapter 2 Review

Using Vocabulary Words

Explain the relationship between the words in each of the following pairs.

1. denotation, connotation
2. usage, colloquialisms
3. substance, style
4. abstract, concrete
5. dialect, idiom

Reviewing Key Ideas

1. Identify and briefly describe the different levels of usage in oral language.
2. Discuss the importance of considering situation, purpose, and audience as you make appropriate oral language choices.
3. Define *jargon* and list two or three examples.
4. Describe how clarity, economy, and grace serve as benchmarks for good oral communication.

Reflecting on Your Project

With your partner, discuss the ways you worked well together. Also discuss changes you might make in work styles and how you would divide the tasks if you were to work on a similar project in the future.

Responding to the Essential Question

Prepare a one-minute oral summary of the main chapter concepts to answer the question, "How can people use language to achieve effective oral communication?"

Extending Your Understanding

Everyday Life

1. Pay attention to conversations going on around you in class, during softball practice, at the mall, or at home. Make a list of interesting examples of dialect, idiom, or jargon you hear. Try to work some of them into your own conversations tomorrow. Don't forget to consider situation, purpose, and audience as you speak.
2. Seek out students at your school who speak English as a second language. Interview them about any problems they encounter understanding oral communication from native English speakers.
3. If you take a foreign language class, ask your teacher about denotations and connotations in the language you are studying. Identify a pair of words with similar denotations but greatly different connotations.

In the Media

4. Work with a partner to memorize Abbott and Costello's "Who's on First?" routine. Transcripts are widely available online, as are videos of their performance. As you learn the material, discuss how each speaker in the routine does or does not modify

his language as the conversation unfolds. What advice would you give two people who have that much difficulty understanding each other? When you're ready, perform the routine for another classroom.

5. Watch a commercial. Record a number of the key words used in the ad. Analyze the connotations of those words and offer an explanation of why they might have been chosen.
6. Watch a talk show on a cable channel and another on a public broadcasting station. Compare the level of usage of the participants. Give specific examples.

Research

7. Research the professions of TV journalist and print journalist to discover the significance and specific applications of oral language in those jobs. Conduct online, video, and print research and also interview people working in those fields, if possible. Share your research with the class.
8. Research famous American speeches and select one that you think serves as a model for effective oral communication. Share it with your class, along with any background information you find to place the speech in context. Be sure to back up your opinion with several reasons why the speech addresses its situation, purpose, and audience.

Interpreting Graphics

Are pictures worth a thousand words?

Look closely at this photograph, and then try to put into words what you see. Write a paragraph describing the scene as accurately as you can. Then discuss what oral language can communicate that pictures cannot, and vice versa.

Additional Projects

1. **Group Project:** In a small group, discuss this phrase from the Constitution of the United States: "All men are created equal." Explain what each word in that sentence means, with examples. For abstract words, give concrete examples. Present your ideas to the class in a creative way.
2. **Individual Project:** Create a glossary of terms used in the hobby or sport or other endeavor you know best. Identify terms that would be jargon for people who are not familiar with your endeavor, and write definitions in plain English that everyone could understand.

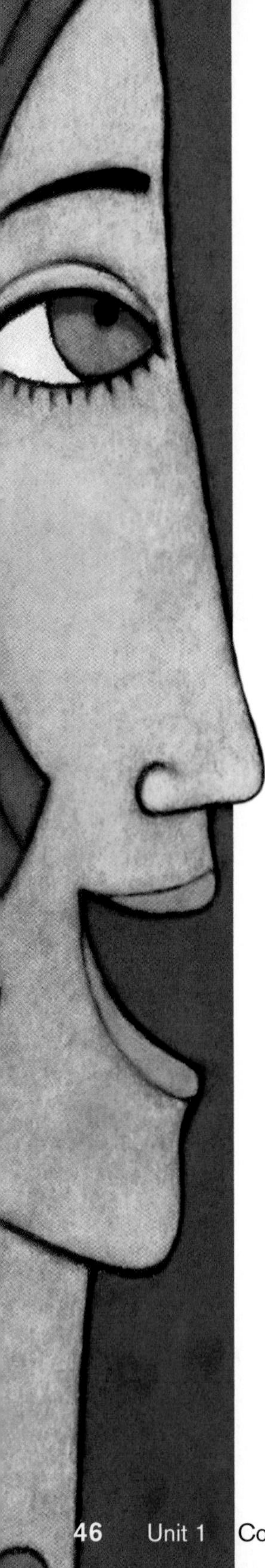

Nonverbal Communication

ESSENTIAL QUESTION

How and what do people communicate without words?

Chapter Project: Silence, Please!

Have you ever been more pleased—or more hurt—by the look on someone's face than by any words spoken? This project will help you understand how expressive wordless communication can be.

With a partner, you will present a two-minute conversation in which two people communicate without using words. Your exchange can be friendly or hostile, funny or tragic. Use your imagination. Classmates will take note of your body language, facial expression, gestures, and movements to evaluate how well you complete this activity. Refer to the following CAPS guidelines as you work to meet this challenge.

The rubric on page 59 shows the traits on which your presentation will be evaluated.

CONCEPT	nonverbal communication can be as effective as the spoken word
AUDIENCE	partner, classmates, and teacher
PURPOSE	to practice effective nonverbal communication
SITUATION	a two-minute wordless "conversation"

KEY VOCABULARY

- nonverbal communication
- body language
- multi-channeled
- emphatic gestures
- descriptive gestures
- posture
- stance
- proxemics
- communication imperative
- mannerism
- credibility

Sign language is a highly developed form of nonverbal communication. List some of the gestures you use to express information without words.

Speak Up!

Your voice can say one thing while your body says something completely different. Say the sentences at the left while your body indicates the thoughts at the right.

Your Voice Says	While Your Body Says
Yes, Mother, I'd love to clean my room.	Cleaning my room is the last thing I want to do.
I don't care which movie we see.	Nobody ever does what I want.
Yeah. I'll go rock climbing with you.	Man! Rock climbing terrifies me.

BACKGROUND FOR THE PROJECT

Pages 48–56 will provide the information you'll need to complete this project.

Types of Nonverbal Communication

The letters on a keyboard can be used to make all the possible words in our language. Why, then, do people who communicate casually with friends by e-mail or instant message use smileys so much? The answer is that even though there are thousands of words to choose from, people communicate with much more than words. Anything people communicate beyond the literal meaning of words is called **nonverbal communication**. For example, in face-to-face exchanges, you often signal your feelings about what you are saying through your **body language**—gestures, eye contact, posture, facial expression, and even how close you stand to another person. Just like those smileys, your body language conveys a message without the use of words. (See page 56 for body language customs in other cultures.)

These people are communicating with words but they are also sending messages through their bodies. What is each person communicating nonverbally to the others? How can you tell?

Communicating with Body Language

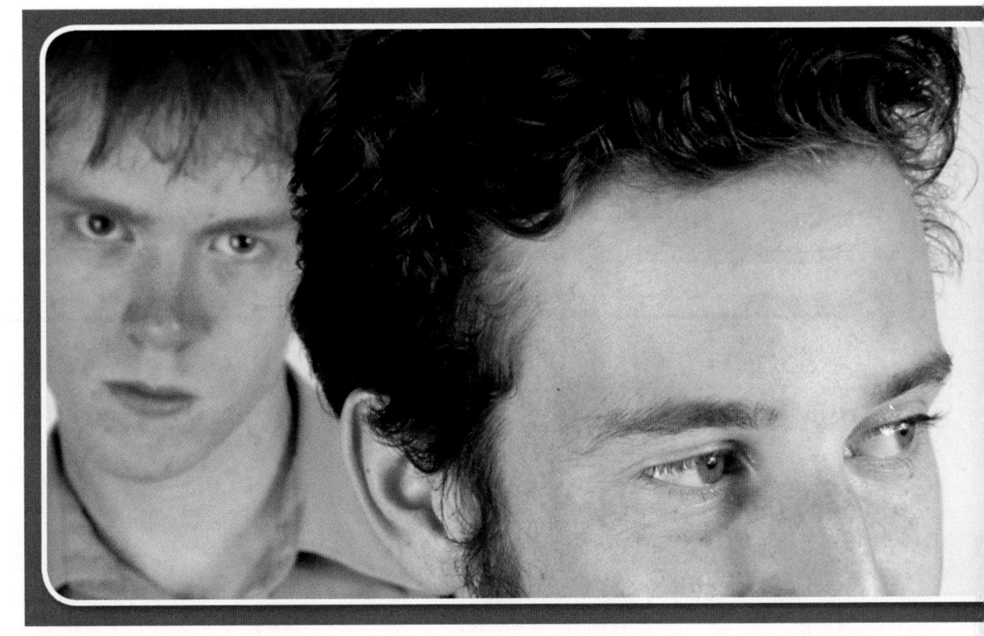

What do their facial expressions tell you about what these people are thinking?

You can often tell what people are thinking by their body language. Sighing or looking out the window might signal boredom or distraction. Folding the arms or moving away can show resistance. A shake of the head or a frown usually shows disagreement. Nonverbal communication may not be effective when expressing complicated, deep ideas, but it is a powerful means of communicating attitudes and subtle shades of meaning. You may not know *why* the person is bored, resistant, or unhappy, but you can learn to read the signals.

In Chapter 1, you read that the means used to transmit a message is called the *channel* and that not all channels use words. Nonverbal channels transmit messages via facial expression, gestures, movement, and even silence. Most of our communication is **multi-channeled,** conducted through both the verbal and nonverbal channels.

To express exactly what you mean, become aware of the ways you communicate nonverbally and the effect your nonverbal communication has on your overall message. Understanding the different types of nonverbal communication can help you clarify your messages and interpret the messages of others.

Facial Expressions

If you watched TV with the sound turned off, you would still be able to understand a lot just by looking at facial expressions. Often you can tell how someone feels by noting a raised eyebrow, a wrinkled brow, or a tight-lipped smile. Facial expressions add very clear meanings to verbal communication and can turn a plain message into a sparkling one.

The smile is a facial expression understood around the world to mean the same thing: good feeling. Smiling may not be appropriate in all situations, but it does put people at ease, and it also shows your pleasure in communicating with them.

Because facial expressions are such a natural and spontaneous part of your communication, you may not always be aware of the ones you are using. In fact, the naturalness of facial expressions is one reason they convey messages so powerfully. Listeners can tell if a speaker is overdoing facial expressions and will likely regard that speaker with less trust than a speaker whose expressions appear natural. Too much facial expression is sometimes called "mugging."

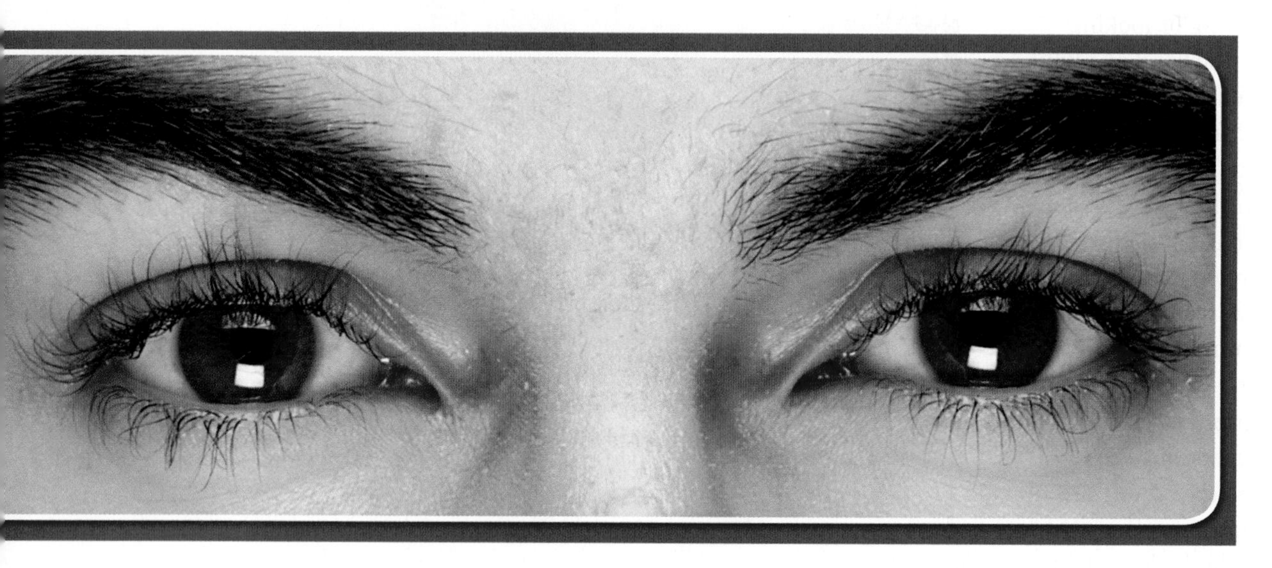

Eye Contact

Have you ever heard one person say to another, "Look at me while I'm talking to you!" The speaker is asking for eye contact so that he or she can confirm that the person is really listening. Most people in the United States view eye contact as a way to acknowledge someone's importance.

Both speakers and listeners should make eye contact. People trust someone who can "look them in the eye." In addition to honesty, eye contact conveys earnestness, sincerity, confidence, and expertise. Speakers who rely too heavily on notes, looking up at their audience infrequently, are seen as insincere, incapable, or weak. In a small group, speakers should make eye contact with all the listeners, moving from one person to another. Speakers in front of a large audience should make eye contact with all the sections of the audience.

Eye contact does more than validate the importance of your listeners. It is also a key part of interpreting feedback. A communicator who really looks at listeners can see through their nonverbal messages if they are having trouble understanding, or if they agree, disagree, or appear to be losing interest. A good speaker will pick up on these cues and adjust his or her comments to the needs of the listeners. Without eye contact, those cues would go unnoticed.

Gestures

Gestures are the movements of the limbs, body, or head. Gestures typically come in two types:

- **Emphatic gestures** allow a speaker to emphasize spoken words. Such gestures include shrugging, nodding, enumerating, and pointing.
- **Descriptive gestures** allow a speaker to help listeners visualize spoken words. For example, a speaker describing something flat or smooth might use a flat hand in a palm-down position to help listeners picture it.

What does this gesture convey?

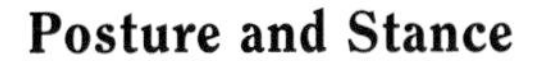

Posture and Stance

How you hold your body is your **posture**. How you distribute the weight of your body on your feet is your **stance**. Posture and stance are important to both speakers and listeners.

In speakers, an upright posture (standing or sitting) can improve breathing and sharpen alertness. It also conveys interest in and respect for the subject being discussed.

In listeners, posture and stance communicate a general attitude. For example, if listeners slouch in a chair or at a desk (even if it's because they're tired), others will likely read their posture as communicating a lack of interest or boredom. On the other hand, sitting or standing with good posture creates a favorable impression—listeners appear to be more a part of the communication.

In which photo do these girls look friendlier? Why?

Movement

Movement of the entire body from spot to spot is another type of body language. Moving often makes communicators feel more at ease. It also is a key part of controlling distance. The distance between two people can communicate the level of familiarity and other important messages. (See page 53.) Too much movement, however, can distract from a message and make a communicator look scattered, disorganized, or inattentive.

KEY POINT

Our bodies send positive and negative messages through facial expressions, eye contact, gestures, posture, movement, and appearance.

Which student is dressed more appropriately for a speech in history class on the Electoral College? Why?

PROJECT PREP

Go over the six types of body language with your **project partner**. Together, work up a short exchange in which one of you says a sentence and the other responds with a gesture, a facial expression, or a movement.

Appearance

A message is almost impossible to separate from the communicator. The way a communicator looks will usually help or hurt the message. Different communication situations call for different levels of formality in speech and presentation as well as in appearance.

Dress is one of the most important factors in appearance. Communicating effectively means dressing in a way that will put others at ease and fit the occasion. For a speech at school, for example, boys would probably wear tucked in shirts. For a speech at City Council, girls might wear skirts or slacks rather than jeans.

Cleanliness and grooming are also part of appearance. Most people respond positively to good grooming. A hairstyle that does not fall in the eyes allows for better eye contact. Also, while makeup may be appropriate in certain communication situations, it should draw attention to your face in only a positive way.

Communicating with Space

Have you ever felt uncomfortable because someone you did not know well stood too close to you during a conversation? Everyone has a zone of personal space that he or she expects others to respect. You would probably feel comfortable only if certain trusted people entered that space.

The control of space is another nonverbal behavior that affects communication. The use of space, called **proxemics**, differs from culture to culture, so no rule covers every place and situation. Below is a chart of the distances between a sender and receiver (or receivers) that carry meaning in the United States.

PROXEMICS IN THE UNITED STATES

3 inches to 18 inches
intimate: 2 people sharing

1.5 feet to 4 feet
personal: small groups talking

4 feet to 12 feet
social: party conversation

12 feet to 20 feet
public: public speaking

Proxemics, how close we want to be to others, can be influenced by our culture, our gender, or by work or social contexts.

Think about a large group discussion you've participated in. Sometimes pairs get closer to each other to share private information. What effect on the rest of the group might such proxemics cause?

The Crowded Elevator

What happens in a situation in which we can't keep our bubble of personal space around us? Think of the last time you were in an elevator with a group of people you did not know. People in an elevator are forced to move into personal space in a social context. Some people look at the elevator floor indicator or down at their shoes. They are avoiding the embarrassment of looking at strangers within their personal space.

Space in Public and Work Settings

Think about the space arrangements chosen or enforced by people in a communication situation. If a public speaker is elevated on a stage and kept distant from the audience, how intimate can a message be? If an interviewer is behind a desk, does the person being interviewed feel at ease? Would it be better if the interviewer were seated facing the interviewee with no desk between them?

PROJECT PREP

With your **project partner**, arrange yourselves in a way that reflects one of the proxemics discussed on this and the previous page. You might want to ask classmates to identify the social situation your arrangement suggests.

Gender Differences

Males and females often have different levels of comfort in personal space. For example, studies have shown repeatedly that males feel more comfortable when people they do not know well sit across the table rather than next to them. For females, studies indicate the opposite. Females seem to feel more comfortable when people sit next to them.

The Effects of Nonverbal Communication

People attach meaning to all kinds of nonverbal behavior. Looking someone in the eye conveys meaning, just as *not* looking someone in the eye conveys meaning. Everything you do, or don't do, communicates *something*. The idea that you are never *not* communicating, whether you are aware of it or not, is called the **communication imperative.** The communication imperative is a key concept when studying nonverbal behavior and analyzing your own. Those aspects of your nonverbal communication that you can thoughtfully control should be consistent with the message you want to convey. Nonverbal communication can actually contradict the message you mean to send.

Analyzing Mannerisms

A **mannerism** is a distinctive behavior. If a person repeats a mannerism often, others tend to identify that distinctive behavior with the person. You need only think of the comedians who make you laugh by mimicking the behaviors of public figures to understand how closely you associate people with their mannerisms.

Some mannerisms are harmless, but others can distract from the intended verbal and nonverbal messages. Try to eliminate from your speech any of the following mannerisms:

- playing with jewelry
- flipping or twirling your hair, or repeatedly moving it from your face
- holding a hand in front of your mouth while speaking
- "rolling" your eyes
- slouching
- using the same hand gesture repeatedly, such as stabbing with a finger.

Analyzing Credibility

Listeners look for physical cues that your message is believable. For example, if you tell someone, "I'm really interested in what you have to say," that person expects direct eye contact from you and perhaps a nod of the head and an interested smile. Conversely, if you yawn and check your watch while professing your interest, the other person will probably feel your words are not ringing true.

Nonverbal behavior has an impact on trust and **credibility.** Credibility means believability, or worthiness of belief. Because people have less control over their nonverbal behavior than over their verbal communication, nonverbal messages are more convincing than verbal ones if the messages contradict. If you say "yes" but at the same time shake your head, "no" will be the stronger message. If you want to be trusted, match your nonverbal communication to what you say.

Communication in a DIVERSE WORLD

The Message in the Movement

Some body language seems to be universally understood throughout the world. Smiling, laughing, and shaking the head in disagreement share the same meaning in all cultures. Other kinds of nonverbal communication, however, mean different things to different people. If you visit another country, try to learn something about that culture's nonverbal communication customs so you can avoid misunderstandings.

Cultural Differences in Body Language

One of the most important cultural disagreements about the meaning of body language concerns eye contact. Most western cultures, such as those in Europe, regard eye contact as Americans do—as part of a positive, respectful exchange. In Japan and many cultures in Africa, Latin America, and the Caribbean, however, people who make eye contact in certain situations are considered rude and disrespectful. In many Arabic cultures, eye contact that is more prolonged than most Americans would feel comfortable with is the norm. In these cultures it communicates sincerity and truthfulness.

The bow shows not only respect in Japan but also status. Visitors are wise to learn the customs for showing rank.

Cultural Differences in Proxemics

While people in the United States tend to reserve two feet of space for very personal interaction, other cultures view the same distance as more appropriate for social interactions. For example, North Americans tend to require a larger bubble of personal space around them to feel comfortable than do Europeans, especially those from Spain and Italy. People in Arabic cultures tend to stand very close while talking. While you cannot know the spatial variations for all cultures, you can be tolerant and understanding of those whose proxemics differ from yours, just as you would expect members of other cultures to be for you.

PREPARING THE PROJECT

Begin your project by looking back at the **Project Prep** activities in this chapter and using the directions below.

Make Connections

Discuss with your partner all the important elements of nonverbal communication as you remember them. Share any personal examples of events in your life in which nonverbal communication made an impact. Finally, think about the following:

- how body language impacts verbal communication
- the six types of body language
- the concept of personal space
- how mannerisms and culture influence our perceptions of nonverbal communication.

Focus

Briefly review the project you and your partner are working on: the two-minute conversation without words. Be sure you both understand what you will be doing.

Plan

Brainstorm ideas for your nonverbal conversation. Come up with three or four good ones and then choose the one you both like best. Talk through the scene and decide the following:

- Will the scene be funny or dramatic?
- How will you begin your presentation?
- What facial expressions, gestures, and movements will you use? Try to use as many as you can.
- What will happen in the middle of the scene?
- How will you end the scene? Try to make your ending as dramatic or funny as possible.

Develop

With your partner, develop a "script" for your nonverbal scene. Talk about the characters you are playing and what motivates them in this scene. Work on your movement, gestures, and facial expressions as you discuss the script.

Surefire Impact

Use these techniques to make a strong nonverbal impact.

- Be sure your gestures, facial expressions, posture, and movement support your intent.
- Adapt your appearance to reflect the situation and the listener's expectations.
- In public speaking, use appropriate lighting, space, and media to accomplish your task.

Practice

Practice your presentation as often as needed until you both feel that you will have no trouble. Ask someone to time you. If your scene is running long, cut and practice again without that part. If it is short, add to it and practice it again.

Use the strategies that follow to help make your presentation as good as it can be.

You and your partner are almost ready to present your nonverbal conversation. Before you do, go over the CAPS guidelines on page 46 and the rubric on page 59 to be sure your project is on the right track. Also try the suggestions below for grabbing your audience right away.

Getting Off to a Good Start

Plan ahead for how you can make an instant impact on your audience. You are inviting them into the world of nonverbal communication—how will you extend that invitation? Will you, like the mute performers in *Blue Man Group,* come out wearing blue makeup on your face? Be prepared with whatever device, if any, you decide to use to capture attention right from the start.

From the opening moments of the show, the audience members know they are in for something special from Blue Man Group.

EVALUATING THE PROJECT

Evaluate the presentations using the following rubric.

Score the demonstration on each point, with 4 being "outstanding" and 1 being "needs much improvement." Come up with an overall score and write a brief paragraph that explains your score.

Understanding of the Elements of Nonverbal Communication	Demonstration of a Nonverbal Conversation	Creativity and Originality	Preparation and Use of Time
4 Presenters showed an understanding of nonverbal communication.	**4** Presenters' nonverbal conversation was instructive and very enjoyable.	**4** The presentation was unique, well-performed, and interesting.	**4** The presentation flowed smoothly and was neither too long nor too short.
3 Presenters understood most aspects of nonverbal communication.	**3** Presenters' nonverbal conversation was enjoyable but not very instructive.	**3** The presentation was unique, well-performed, and somewhat interesting.	**3** The presentation progressed fairly smoothly and was neither too long nor too short.
2 Presenters did not seem to understand many elements of nonverbal communication.	**2** Presenters' nonverbal conversation was somewhat enjoyable but not instructive.	**2** The presentation was fairly interesting and well-performed but not unique.	**2** The presentation had a few awkward moments and went a bit over or under the time limit.
1 Presenters misunderstood most elements of nonverbal communication.	**1** Presenters' nonverbal conversation was neither enjoyable nor instructive.	**1** The presentation was neither unique, well-performed, nor interesting.	**1** The presentation was not smoothly executed and went well over or under the time limit.

Communication *Past* and Present

Shake on It

From the "Right Hand of Friendship"...

Some nonverbal expressions have a long history. The handshake is a good example. This quick, powerful interaction has been around for centuries. There are many

theories about how the handshake originated. One looks to Biblical times and the Book of Galatians, in which Paul indicates that in Jerusalem he met with James and John, both of whom extended the "right hand of friendship." Some anthropologists believe, however, that the handshake originated in medieval Europe. Certain knights at that time were known to pull their concealed swords on unsuspecting strangers. To convey that they had no such intentions, peaceful knights took to offering an open hand to show that they had no hidden weapons. Soon, all manner of men adopted this greeting. Even today, males are more likely to shake hands when they meet than are females.

English Quakers in the 1600s adopted the handshake, replacing the more formal, upper-class bow. Thomas Jefferson is given credit for further popularizing the handshake during his presidency, perhaps believing it to be a more democratic form of greeting than the bow.

. . . to the "High Five"

In contemporary America, the "soul brother handshake" became popular in the 1960s in African American communities. It is an extended handshake, with a gripping of thumbs and a hook clasp of the fingers following the traditional handshake. The hand slaps of the "gimme five" or "high five" variety followed and are still popular.

The classic handshake, however, remains an expected part of social interactions, regardless of gender, class, or occasion. The handshake communicates friendliness and observance of social convention. It helps put others at ease. It is as much a part of communication in the business world as the phone call or the e-mail.

A good handshake has these qualities:

- The whole hand is involved, not just the tips of the fingers.
- The palm is vertical, thumb on top.
- The grip is firm, but polite. A limp or loose grip (the wet fish grip) is almost universally seen as a sign of weakness. Too tight a squeeze will be resented as aggressive or intimidating.
- The up-and-down "pump" is not exaggerated. A few pumps (1–3) are enough. Unless you are very close friends, hanging on to another person's hand longer than 1–3 pumps is usually perceived as too intimate.

Chapter 3 Review

Using Vocabulary Words

For each of the following terms, answer two questions:

- What is it?
- What is an example?

1. body language
2. communication imperative
3. credibility
4. mannerism
5. multi-channeled
6. nonverbal communication
7. posture
8. proxemics
9. stance

Reviewing Key Ideas

1. Give two reasons why nonverbal communication is important to the creation of meaning.
2. Explain why audiences might place more faith in nonverbal communication than in verbal communication.
3. List the six types of nonverbal communication and provide an example of how each can alter or improve an audience's understanding of a speaker's message.
4. Identify the four principal spatial distances and the types of communication common to each.

Reflecting on Your Project

With your partner, discuss which parts of the project went especially well and which gave you the most trouble. Come up with two or three strategies for making the hard parts easier on a future project.

Responding to the Essential Question

Use the headings in this chapter to help you write a brief chapter summary that answers the question, "How and what do people communicate without words?" Compare your summary with your partner's to see if you both covered the main points.

Extending Your Understanding

Everyday Life

1. Observe interactions of others in a social setting—perhaps at a school sporting event or on a field trip. Discuss the nonverbal behaviors you see, including use of space.
2. Seek out people your age from other cultures. Use the six types of nonverbal communication as a guide to ask about differences in nonverbal communication between their native culture and the culture they are now in.

3. Keep track of the ways you may be using gestures, facial expressions, and silence to communicate with others. How do people respond to your nonverbal messages?

In the Media

4. Rent an old silent movie such as *The General* with Buster Keaton or *The Gold Rush* with Charlie Chaplin. Take note as you watch the actors perform. How do they go about silently conveying emotion? What gestures, movements, and facial expressions do they use?
5. Watch an interview on a television news program. Try to find examples of instances in which the person being interviewed displayed mannerisms.
6. Read articles by famous mimes about how to express feelings and concepts without the use of words.
7. Look through magazines and newspapers and study the body language of the people in the photographs. What kinds of nonverbal messages are they sending?
8. Find a Web site that shows images illustrating the use of sign language. Learn as many signs as you can and share them with your classmates and family.

Interpreting Graphics

Look at the graphic above. On a separate sheet of paper, draw a representation of the people who would fit into each group.

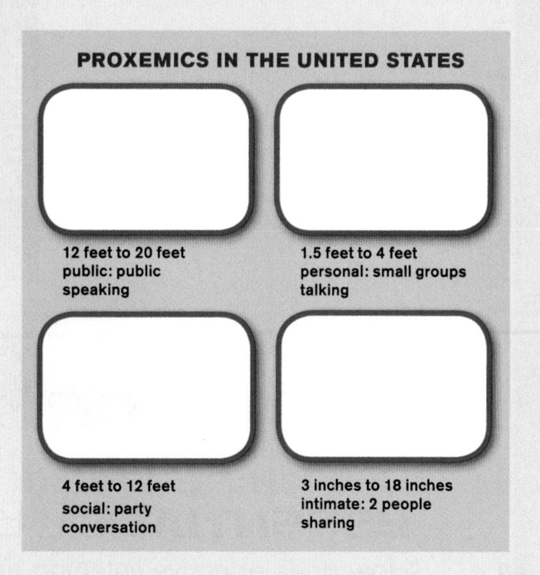

Additional Projects

1. **Group Project:** In a small group, research some aspect of being an interior designer or architect, two careers that deal with public spaces. Look for information on how the use of space is important in each. Do your research separately and then come together to share your findings. Write a report based on this information. Bring pictures, drawings, blueprints, or other examples to show the class.
2. **Individual Project:** Research the "dress for success" concept in at least two sources, from books, articles, or Web sites. List the suggestions you find about clothing and makeup. Apply the CAPS model to your research and present your research to the class. If your teacher permits, consider the use of costumes to help you make your points.

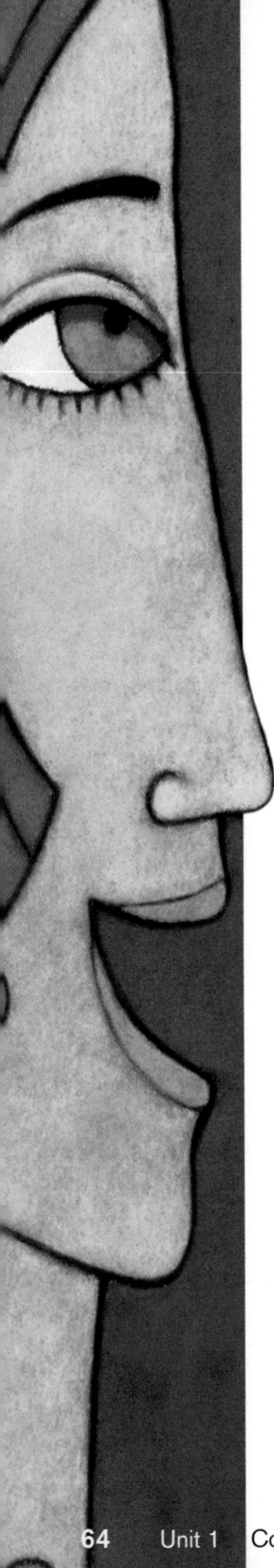

Listening

ESSENTIAL QUESTION

How does effective listening help people communicate meaningfully?

Chapter Project: Listen Here

Few things feel as satisfying as knowing you have been *heard*. Many people are so involved in expressing their own ideas, however, that they sometimes forget to listen carefully. This chapter will help you sharpen your listening skills.

In a group of four, you will plan a brief presentation that offers listeners four points of information. Choose any subject you like, but be sure to include four main points, facts, or events that you want your listeners to remember. When you finish your presentation, you will call on listeners to tell you the main points. Be ready to offer ways to help improve listening skills to anyone who has trouble remembering the main points. The whole presentation should be no longer than three minutes. Refer to the following CAPS guidelines as you work.

The rubric on page 81 shows the traits on which your presentation will be evaluated.

CONCEPT	good listening skills are essential to good communication
AUDIENCE	classmates and teacher
PURPOSE	sharpen listening skills
SITUATION	two-minute group presentation followed by one-minute listener response

KEY VOCABULARY

hearing	empathic listening
listening	listening barriers
active listening	selective listening
critical listening	paraphrase
precision listening	summarize

The gap between what one person says and another person hears can make the game of "telephone" hilarious–and demonstrate the importance of careful listening.

Speak Up!

Play a quick game of "telephone" with your classmates. Your teacher will quietly speak or whisper a message to a student in the front of the room. That student will repeat what he or she hears to the next person, taking care to not let others hear. The message is then passed from student to student to the back of the classroom. The last person should share the message received with the rest of the class. Is it the same message your teacher communicated?

BACKGROUND FOR THE PROJECT

Pages 66–79 will provide the information you'll need to complete this project.

The Listening Process and Its Components

Listening is an act you do on purpose, and it requires specific skills and ways of thinking. Understanding the listening process will help you become a better communicator.

Listening vs. Hearing

What's the difference between listening and **hearing**? You hear things all the time. You hear classmates rustling papers during a test. You hear your friend's TV while talking on the phone. Hearing is passive—you hear even when you don't want to. Hearing requires only that you receive sound waves and implies no intention.

Listening, however, is an intentional act and an active process. **Active listening** requires that you concentrate on what you are hearing, attach meaning to it, and react to it. Without active listening, you can't understand the message and you can't give feedback. Think about the part listening plays in the following scene:

Ruby has agreed to babysit for Ms. Micelli's son James. Ms. Micelli tells Ruby that James should be in bed in one hour and that Ruby can read to him before bed. She gives Ruby her cell phone number and points out other important numbers on the refrigerator. Then she says, "Once James is in bed, you can help yourself to a snack—anything but the cupcakes on the counter. Any questions?"

Ruby replies, "No, I think I got everything. I'll read James a story and see that he gets to bed on time. I'll probably grab a soda later (and I won't let those cupcakes tempt me). I know what to do if I have any questions or problems before you get home."

Ruby has given Ms. Micelli the feedback required. She let Ms. Micelli know that her message was received and understood. Communication was successful because Ruby was truly listening instead of just "hearing."

PROJECT PREP

Before meeting with your **project group** for the first time, think about your personal listening skills. Write down a few skills you can use to help your group's communications go smoothly.

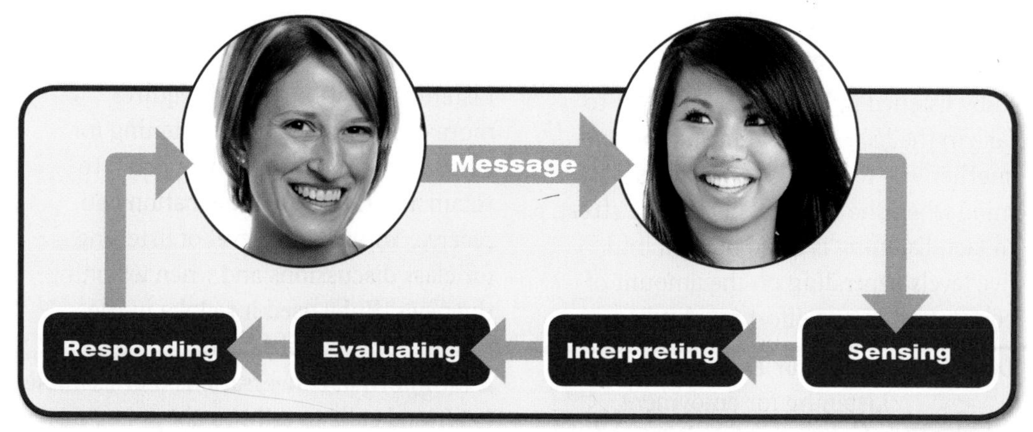

The stages of the listening process progress from simply hearing to thinking through the response.

Stages of the Listening Process

Ruby went through all four stages of the listening process:

Stage 1—*Sensing,* or simply hearing the words. Before you can listen, the speaker must have your attention. When the speaker has your attention, you are able to hear and receive the intended message.

Stage 2—*Interpreting,* or deriving meaning from the words. At this stage you make sense out of the words for your own understanding.

Stage 3—*Evaluating,* or judging what the message is about in context. How you evaluate the message determines in large part how you will respond to it.

Stage 4—*Responding,* or turning listening into a two-way process. This step allows you to offer feedback, advice, or a similar reaction. You and the speaker must listen to each other and respond for successful communication.

Imagine that Ms. Micelli sees Ruby on the street the following day. Ms. Micelli tells Ruby that she would like to talk to her about something. Ruby is curious and responds, "Sure, what is it?" Ms. Micelli says, "I think we should sit down. Let's duck into the soda shop." Ruby is somewhat worried by this suggestion and says, "Is everything okay, Ms. M?" Ms. Micelli assures Ruby that everything is fine, that she just needs to get off her feet, and they can talk more easily indoors. "Okay, Ms. M," says Ruby. "And the sodas are on me."

Once again Ruby has gone through all four stages of the listening process. Ruby has sensed (or heard) Ms. Micelli and given her the attention she requires. Ruby has also interpreted and evaluated Ms. Micelli's request, asking, "Is everything okay?" Continually listening and giving feedback, Ruby finally determines how best to respond to Ms. Micelli's request. She agrees to Ms. Micelli's suggestion and offers one of her own.

There are four stages of listening: sensing, interpreting, evaluating, and responding.

Levels of Listening

Ruby listened to Ms. Micelli one way to take in the babysitting information and another way to gauge Ms. Micelli's state of mind when she ran into her on the street. In fact, listening is often divided into five levels depending on the amount of concentration and effort involved.

Level 1 Listening for Enjoyment

Listening for enjoyment, or appreciative listening, requires very little active involvement or concentration. Examples include watching television or listening to a favorite CD or radio station. The stakes are low. If you miss a joke or a song, the only thing you lose is a moment of amusement.

You can also listen for enjoyment in certain social situations. You can listen to your parents talk about a shared memory. You can listen to your friend play the guitar. The listening is polite and communicates to others that you consider them to be important. Any social situation, however, can require a move from listening for enjoyment to a higher level of listening. If you don't pay close attention, you may miss cues that tell you that your parents' conversation is now more serious or that your friend would like a thoughtful critique of his or her guitar playing.

Level 2 Listening for Information

Listening for information requires more concentration than listening for enjoyment. At this level, you listen to retain and recall the information you receive. You use this level of listening for class discussions and when watching the news. Ruby used it to take in the instructions for babysitting. You also use it for informal conversations. For example, if a friend calls to tell you about her car trouble, you listen closely for information and use it to help you track the thread of your conversation and participate in it fully. You may be able to respond with a similar experience or help your friend solve her problem. If you let your friend talk *without* listening for information, you may make off-topic or even inappropriate responses. You'll run the risk of confusing or insulting your friend.

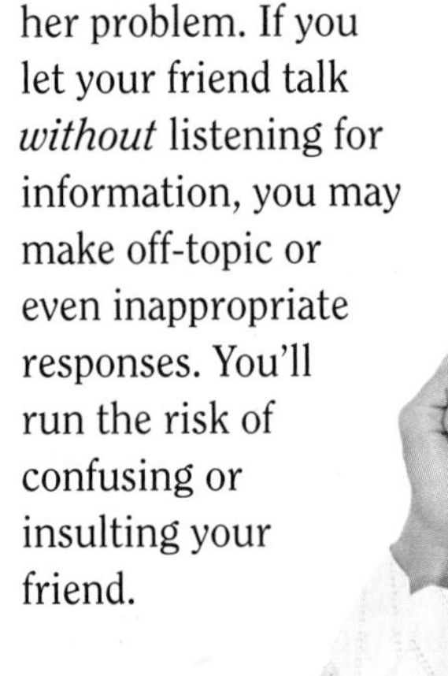

Level 3 Critical Listening
This next level is an even more active process. **Critical listening** involves analyzing and evaluating the information you take in so you can use it to further your communication. Your goal is to retain information, but at this level you are also questioning the information and testing what you hear against other information.

A critical listener gives thoughtful and perceptive feedback to the speaker. For example, Ruby took in Ms. Micelli's instructions and very effectively communicated her understanding of that information by mentioning the most important points.

Critical listening does not mean "being critical." Harshly judging someone or what that person says—being critical—is simply being unkind. When you listen critically you listen to evaluate what you hear—and then you carry out the process of testing what you hear against other information. That requires a high level of involvement and concentration. (For more on critical listening, see pages 138–140.)

Level 4 Precision Listening
When you pay attention to details that give you clues to the speaker's emotion or state of mind, you are practicing **precision listening**. Precision listeners hear more than just the facts. They also pick up on the subtle changes in a speaker's voice. Remember Ms. Micelli's response when Ruby asked, "Is everything okay?" She used precision listening to quickly evaluate Ruby's words and tone of voice (worried) just as Ruby tried to pinpoint Ms. Micelli's feelings. Ms. Micelli's response showed that she understood Ruby's state of mind.

To practice precision listening, tune in to both the substance and the style of a message. A subtle rise in volume or an extended pause, for example, can change how any message is interpreted. If your older brother says, "I've been accepted at U of W," you might detect enthusiasm or disappointment in his voice. At face value, his words don't tell you the whole story. But factoring in his delivery will give you clues about his state of mind. If he emphasizes the "I," he might be expressing pride or even confusion about being accepted. On the other hand, if his tone is flat throughout, he might not be happy about the news. As a precision listener, you can hear the subtleties of the message and understand its full context. And your feedback will help your brother shape the rest of what he says, just as other precision listeners can help you shape the things you say.

Level 5 Empathic Listening
This level is the most difficult to master. Along with concentration, retention, and judgment, **empathic listening** requires that you use *empathy*, the ability to share and understand the speaker's feelings. Empathic listening requires qualities that don't always come easily. Here's an example: You share wonderful news with a friend—something you are really excited about—and your friend just says, "That's nice" with no emotion. Your friend lacks empathic listening skills—no sharing of your feelings occurred. Mindy, in the scene that follows, however, listens empathically to her friend George's good news.

George runs up to Mindy and says, "Guess what! I just bought a car with the money I earned as a lifeguard last summer!"

Mindy, jumping up and down, yells, "Oh, Georgie, that's great! How did you save all that money? What kind of car did you buy? Where is it? Can I have a ride?"

Mindy knows how to respond with real empathy and enthusiasm. Her feedback tells George that his news is a big deal and that she is excited for him and shares in his happiness. (For more on empathic listening, see pages 142–143 in Chapter 7.)

From easiest to most difficult, the five levels of listening are listening for enjoyment, listening for information, critical listening, precision listening, and empathic listening.

Mindy and George share an empathic moment.

PROJECT PREP

Each member of your **project group** should make a cartoon illustrating one of the five levels of listening. Refer to the chart below for help. Share your cartoons with the rest of the class.

Five Levels of Listening

	Listening for Enjoyment	Listening for Information	Critical Listening	Precision Listening	Empathic Listening
Motive	Entertainment	Gathering facts, opinions, and other information	Listening with the intent to judge or evaluate	Understanding substance and style for clues about meaning	Listening to help others
Definition	Listening passively for one's own pleasure	Listening to acquire information for recall	Listening to evaluate the speaker's information	Listening for clues about the speaker's feelings or state of mind	Listening to understand why a speaker feels as s/he does
Skills Required	None	Concentration May require note-taking skills Retention	Concentration May require note-taking skills Retention Analysis Reflection	Concentration May require note-taking skills Retention Analysis Reflection Recall of details Willingness to evaluate how something is said as well as what is said	Concentration Retention Reflection Empathy Suspension of judgment
Application Example	Listening to a TV comedy	Listening to a class lecture Listening to a coach's game plan	Interviewing a potential student council candidate	Listening to gauge people's opinions on a new school policy	Listening to people on different sides of a conflict express themselves

Overcoming Barriers to Effective Listening

You'll recall from Chapter 1 that *interference* is anything that blocks communication. Interference can create barriers to effective listening. Knowing about **listening barriers** can help you shape your messages in a way that will help your listeners overcome barriers.

Imagine that a student is unhappy because he is not allowed to wear his favorite t-shirt on school grounds. The principal, who understands the reason why such shirts are prohibited, may not want to argue its merits with the student. These two may have put up listening barriers before they even meet. With effort, however, they can break down their listening barriers. The student might begin by politely expressing his dissatisfaction with the policy. The principal might be tempted to interrupt, but she too is polite and is also impressed by the student's respectful tone. Hearing the other person out is usually the best approach. In this case, the student is heard and the principal gets insight into her student—and the two have a friendly and productive conversation. Each understands the other's point of view.

Listening barriers can result from physical interference, such as background noise or a mumbling speaker. They can also result from mental interference, such as a closed mind. Barriers can also go up because of cultural interference, such as an unfamiliar language or traditions. These are all conditions that reduce the likelihood of a message being understood. Actively working to reduce listening barriers helps understanding, and both speakers and listeners share in the responsibility.

Physical Barriers to Listening: Impaired Hearing

The most common physical barrier to listening is the inability to hear. For the many people with deafness or other hearing impairments, understanding messages is not associated with *listening*. Sign language, lip-reading, or some combination of both techniques facilitates communication. In the United States and Canada, American Sign Language (ASL), which calls for seeing rather than listening, is a common communication method.

Mary Apondo teaches sign language to colleagues at Othoro School, Kenya.

RESUME **Is This Job for Me?** FIND JOB MONEY | POST RESUME | EDUCATION | CAREER ADVICE |

Search: Sign Language Interpreter

Every time there is an assembly at school, Jamie is there using her talented hands and exceptional listening skills to translate for the students. Jamie has been a *sign language interpreter*, an interpreter for the deaf, for more than 10 years. One of her students is Joey, who was born unable to hear. Jamie has been signing to him since kindergarten. Now a sixth grader, Joey watches as Jamie signs all the words that the speaker is saying, just as she signs all the words that pass back and forth in Joey's classroom.

Interpreters like Jamie serve as professional communicators wherever people come together–in schools, hospitals, senior citizen facilities, public meetings. Many universities in the United States and Canada offer interpreter training programs. Most offer an associate degree as well as certification. You can find many of them on the Internet.

Do you think you would enjoy learning sign language and translating for a deaf or hearing-impaired person? Measure your potential with this personality inventory to find out if you have the traits of a sign language interpreter. Are you:

- ✓ Good at listening?
- ✓ Able to stay focused for long periods?
- ✓ Sensitive to others' needs?
- ✓ Good with languages?
- ✓ Outgoing and friendly?
- ✓ Able to ignore distractions?

If you become a sign language interpreter, you might have job opportunities in the following organizations.

Clients	What You Would Do
Schools	Interpret and translate for hearing-impaired or deaf students as well as teach hearing students how to communicate by signing
Courtroom	Translate testimony for hearing-impaired jurors, witnesses, or defendants
Television/ Theatre	Provide translations and descriptions of sounds for hearing-impaired or deaf viewers
Religious institutions	Translate sermons or other community service announcements for hearing-impaired or deaf members; interpret and translate thoughts and ideas of deaf members for the congregation

You can use many of the strategies and skills in this chapter when communicating with people who have hearing impairments. As in any communication, people who sign or lip-read expect your attention, concentration, and understanding. Try to make your messages understandable for everyone. Use these strategies to help make sure your message comes through.

- Be sure that you have the person's attention before speaking. This might mean waiting for him or her to finish a task and look up at you.
- Speak slowly and clearly. Raise your voice slightly, but don't shout.
- Maintain eye contact. Be sure the person can see you clearly. Face the person when speaking, checking often for understanding. You might need to wait a little longer for a response.
- Meaningful facial expressions and gestures can help convey your message.
- Be prepared to repeat your message when necessary. Repeat an entire sentence rather than just a word or phrase.
- Be aware of whether members of a larger audience have hearing impairments. Enlist someone to offer ASL for public communication.
- **TechConnect** Use visual aids (videos, slide presentations, posters) and written material to supplement your message.
- Don't cover your mouth, eat, drink, or chew gum while speaking.

TechConnect *Supplementing messages with a video or PowerPoint presentation can help overcome listening barriers.*

What mental barrier to listening might this young man be experiencing?

Mental Barriers to Listening

The most common mental barrier to listening is a lack of concentration. Everyone's mind wanders sometimes, even when a real effort is made to listen. The brain processes words at the rate of more than 500 per minute. Yet most speakers communicate at 125–250 words per minute. In other words, you think faster than a speaker talks. Actively listening for information, listening critically and with precision and empathy, will help you stay focused on the speaker. The more you focus, the better you will become at filling that extra listening time with judgment, analysis, and understanding.

Your state of mind can be another mental barrier to listening. Your attitudes about yourself, other people, ideas, and events influence how well you listen. If an audience is hostile toward or not interested in a speaker's topic, they are not likely to listen well. Sometimes an audience comes prepared to listen for enjoyment, as at a rock concert, but the performer may want them to also listen for information, to learn about a personal charity, for example. In such cases, the speaker will need to change the audience's attitude in order to fulfill his or her communication goal.

Language can be a listening barrier when you travel to a foreign country.

The tendency to actively plan what you want to say while someone else is speaking is another common barrier to listening. The only way to overcome this practice is to concentrate. Periodically remind yourself to listen and not speak unnecessarily. Help your listeners in turn by allowing enough time for them to process your comments.

Another common mental barrier goes up when you engage in **selective listening**. This occurs when you block out anything you don't want to hear, paying attention only to information that coincides with your own interests or beliefs. An example might be when adults share their views about what's wrong with today's music. You may appear to be listening, but when you begin hearing the same old comments you quickly tune out. You may, however, tune in again when a positive remark is made.

Cultural Barriers to Listening

Cultural barriers to listening can include language, vocabulary, accents, and customs. When people from different cultures try to communicate, both parties need to pay special attention. A Canadian and a Bulgarian might need to overcome language barriers to communicate with each other. And while Australians and Americans both speak English, they may face barriers because they use different vocabulary.

Most of us find cultural accents intriguing and fun to hear. Sometimes, though, accents can make listening difficult. In increasingly multicultural societies, listeners in all settings (academic, business, and social) need to concentrate and make the effort to understand speakers with a variety of accents.

Actively taking responsibility for receiving the intended message—so that both speaker and listener are working toward effective communication—will help you overcome cultural barriers. One strategy to find common ground is to listen for overall content and key words.

Solving Common Listening Problems

Barrier	Explanation/Example	Applying What You Know
Competing noises	Noise (locker doors slamming, clashing cafeteria trays)	• Speakers should choose a suitable location for communication. • Speakers can speak up to overcome competing noises.
Blocked view	Seating arrangement makes viewing the speaker difficult	• Speakers should try to place themselves so others can see them. • Listeners can adjust their positions to see better.
Poor speaking volume	Speaker does not "speak up"	• Speakers should adjust volume as required by the situation. • Speakers can use a microphone. • Listeners should let a speaker know when they can't hear.
Listener's physical condition	Being tired or ill presents physical barriers	• Speakers should communicate when audiences are physically able to listen and should reschedule for a better time, if necessary. • When possible, listeners should be well-rested and prepared to listen.
Listener's attitude	Listening selectively or being mentally unprepared to listen (being bored, prejudiced, or hostile)	• Speakers should try to capture and keep their listeners' attention. • Listeners should try to overcome any negative attitudes. • Speakers should work on using a pleasant, engaging voice. • Speakers should try to anticipate listener needs and modify messages as necessary.
Vocabulary or language	Speaker's language may be problematic (vocabulary and accent differs from your own)	• Listeners should be open to working around differences in vocabulary or language.

Communication Notebook

You've heard the riddle, "If a tree falls in a forest and nobody hears it, does it still make a sound?" Think about this variation on that riddle: "If a person says something and you don't really listen, does communication take place?" Draw a diagram to help you with the riddle. Then answer the question in a brief paragraph.

Academic Listening

One of a successful student's most important skills is effective academic listening. In Stephen R. Covey's book *The Seven Habits of Highly Effective People,* one important concept is "seek first to understand, then to be understood." You must listen in order to understand, and understanding is the basic key to academic success.

Using good listening skills will help you communicate effectively with everyone at school—classmates, teachers, coaches, other school staff. You can talk with others easily, experience fewer misunderstandings, and have greater success with your schoolwork if you are a good listener. Use the following strategies in any situation at school that requires precision listening.

Concentrate

Stay focused so you can avoid letting your mind wander. Look at the speaker and put yourself in his or her place. Do not think about something else while trying to listen. To really hear, you must stay tuned. For all levels of listening higher than enjoyment, do your best to concentrate on one thing only.

Practice

Try a few listening exercises, such as listening to something while purposely tuning out background sounds. Simply being aware of background sounds can help you find ways to ignore them and keep your focus on what you are listening to.

Listening while ignoring distractions takes practice.

Prepare

Take time to prepare yourself for listening. Position yourself so that you can hear properly. When appropriate, consider doing research ahead of time if you're going to listen to someone speak on a new topic. Research might include reading an assignment in a textbook, a handout, an e-mail, or a Web site. Take notes if that helps you.

Note Key Words

Listen for key words. Often, a speaker will clue you in when he or she is about to say something important. The word "however," for example, usually means the person is about to make an exception to what was just said. The phrase "for example" signals that a particular case that makes the speaker's message clearer is about to follow (and might be worth jotting down).

Write It Down

Even the best listeners can benefit from taking notes when they want to retain information. You take notes for class, and you scramble to find a pen and paper when someone gives you their phone number. Studies show that just the act of writing down important points helps people remember information, even when they never refer to the notes again.

Paraphrase or Summarize

Good listeners often find that they can retain a speaker's information when they **paraphrase**, or restate, the speaker's words or **summarize** the content in a word or two. Doing so can show the speaker you understand, as well as reinforce the message in your own mind. On page 66, Ruby summarizes Ms. Micelli's babysitting instructions. To paraphrase Ms. Micelli's message, Ruby could instead say, "I understand the bedtime routine and know where I can reach you." Either way, she shows Ms. Micelli that she has received and understood her instructions.

If you want to understand and remember what your teacher is saying, listen carefully and write down the important points.

Improve your academic listening by concentrating, practicing, preparing, listening for key words, taking notes, and summarizing.

Begin your project by looking back at the **Project Prep** activities in this chapter and using the directions below.

Surefire Vocal Impact

Practice speaking loud enough so that the people in the back of the room can hear you.

Make Connections

Share an instance of the role listening has played in your life. Then discuss:

- the difference between listening and hearing
- the stages of the listening process
- the five levels of listening
- the physical, mental, and cultural barriers to listening.

Focus

Briefly review the group project you are working on: a three-minute presentation that offers listeners four pieces of information and suggestions for listening effectively.

Plan

Brainstorm ideas for your project. What will your four pieces of information be? How will you incorporate the ideas and how will you each present them?

Develop

Outline your presentation. Decide the overall focus of your presentation and the four main points you will include. Come up with four strategies to improve listening.

Practice

Practice your presentation as often as needed until you all feel comfortable.

PRESENTING THE PROJECT

Use the strategy that follows to present your project.

Your group should now be ready to share the project. Go over the CAPS guidelines on page 64 and the rubric on page 81 to be sure that your project meets requirements.

Listening to Group Members

In a group of four, one of you is probably the driving force, two of you are contributors, and one of you may feel left out. This pattern is normal in a group, but it doesn't mean the quiet person *should* be left out. Just be sure to listen carefully so that everyone's ideas are heard.

EVALUATING THE PROJECT

Evaluate the presentations using the following rubric.

Score the project on each point, with 4 being "outstanding" and 1 being "needs much improvement."

Come up with an overall score and write a brief paragraph that explains your score.

Understanding of the Listening Process	Information and Strategies Offered for Listening	Creativity and Originality	Preparation and Use of Time
4 Presenters showed insight into the listening process.	**4** Presenters' information and strategies were very helpful.	**4** The presentation was inventive, unique, interesting, and fun.	**4** The presentation flowed smoothly and was neither too long nor too short.
3 Presenters understood the listening process.	**3** Presenters' information and strategies were somewhat helpful.	**3** The presentation was inventive, interesting, and fun but not very original.	**3** The presentation progressed fairly smoothly and was neither too long nor too short.
2 Presenters did not seem to understand some elements of the process.	**2** Presenters' information and strategies were only slightly helpful.	**2** The presentation was fairly interesting and fun but not inventive or unique.	**2** The presentation had a few awkward moments and went a bit over or under the time limit.
1 Presenters misunderstood much of the listening process.	**1** Presenters' information and strategies were not helpful.	**1** The presentation was not inventive, unique, interesting, or fun.	**1** The presentation was not smoothly executed and went well over or under the time limit.

Communication *Past* and Present

The Gift of Listening

From Trumpets . . .

Inventors have always sought ways to help the hearing-impaired. The overview that follows highlights some types of hearing aids people have used for the last 200 years.

The small end of this ear trumpet was placed in the ear. The speaker spoke into the flared end.

1800 The earliest firm known to manufacture hearing aids commercially is established in London. Their products include ear trumpets and acoustic urns.

The acoustic urn was placed on a table. The person with hearing impairment held the end of the tube to the ear to help hear the other people seated at the table.

1836 The first known British patent for a hearing aid is issued for a curved earpiece worn behind the ear.

1879 The Rhodes Audiophone, a device that picks up sound waves and transmits them through the bones of the skull, is introduced.

The upper edge of the audiophone was held against the teeth. Tension allowed adjustment for sound pickup.

. . . to Implants

1902 The carbon hearing aid, based on Bell's telephone and using a 3-volt battery, appears in limited quantities. Its sound amplification was not very strong, however.

With the carbon hearing aid, the receiver was attached to the woman's clothing; the battery resided in her handbag, and the earpiece was carried in the hand.

1920 The power vacuum tube hearing aid helped those with severe hearing loss from the 1920s through the 1940s.

1952 Transistor hearing aids replaced vacuum tubes. Transistors needed only one battery, which lead to practical, streamlined units.

A practical way to wear a hearing aid–eyeglasses.

Today With the advent of digital circuitry, hearing aids can now be as invisible or colorful as the wearer requires. Utilizing DSP (digital signal process) chips, they are flexible and powerful.

A new development for the profoundly deaf is the cochlear implant, consisting of two parts. One part is placed behind the ear and contains a microphone, speech processor, and transmitter. The other part is implanted surgically under the skin and stimulates the auditory nerves of the inner ear with electronic impulses. These give wearers a representation of sounds that can help them understand speech.

Chapter 4 Review

Using Vocabulary Words

From the list below, choose three sets of two terms that you think are connected. Write a sentence for each set explaining the connection between the terms. Example: ***Critical listening*** *focuses on hearing the facts, while* ***precision listening*** *also requires attention to a speaker's feelings.*

active listening

critical listening

empathic listening

hearing

listening

listening barriers

paraphrase

precision listening

selective listening

summarize

Reviewing Key Ideas

1. Explain the difference between *listening* and *hearing*.
2. List and briefly define the four stages of the listening process.
3. Explain why empathic listening is the most difficult level of listening to achieve.
4. Identify three common types of barriers to effective listening.

Reflecting on Your Project

With your group, discuss how well you listened to other group members. Then identify one or two listening strategies that might help you work together in the future.

Responding to the Essential Question

Use what you learned in this chapter to write a one-page personal experience essay in response to the question, "How does effective listening help people communicate meaningfully?" Write about a specific time when your good listening skills helped you understand a speaker. Compare your essay with a partner's to see if you both described the good listening skills highlighted in the chapter.

Extending Your Understanding

Everyday Life

1. With a partner, practice the art of listening for enjoyment. As you listen to music or a radio talk show, pay attention to any clues your partner gives that signal the need for you to switch to the listening-for-information level. Jot down those clues on a sheet of paper for your reference.
2. During your next conversation with a family member, listen for main ideas and the key words that indicate that something important is coming. See if you can guess what the speaker will say next.
3. Identify possible cultural barriers to listening that may be affecting your communications with a friend or acquaintance. Discuss them together and work out ways the two of you can help each other listen and be listened to when you talk.

In the Media

4. Take notes while watching the evening news on television. Concentrate on one news story, and really listen to the details. Afterward, summarize the story for a friend without referring to your notes. Then invite your friend to paraphrase the story for you. Discuss whether the note-taking helped you retain information and how well you feel your friend "heard" your summary.
5. Watch a television talk show such as *Oprah*. Discuss the host's use of empathic listening with guests. Did the host seem to understand what the guests were feeling? Did he or she frequently interrupt the guests or listen while they completed their statements?

Research

6. Research the use of lip-reading and ASL as methods of "hearing" in at least two sources: articles, books, or Web sites. Apply the CAPS model to your research and present your findings to your class. During your presentation, be sure to demonstrate examples of each communication method.
7. Research the career of psychologist, a job that requires the use of superior listening skills. Find information about necessary training and the key reasons that active listening is so important to a psychologist's success with patients. Present case studies from books or Web sites to the class.
8. Research the ways classroom teaching techniques have evolved over the years from the straight lecture approach to a more interactive approach. Look for information about how listening skills played into the changes in teaching philosophy and present it to your class in an interesting way.

Interpreting Graphics

Copy the graphic organizer below onto a sheet of paper. Use the organizer to write a sentence describing when you would use each of the levels of listening.

When I Use	
Listening for enjoyment	
Listening for information	
Critical listening	
Precision listening	
Empathic listening	

Additional Projects

1. **Partnered Project:** Select a process to explain to a partner. Your partner will play the role of student, and you will play the role of teacher. When you've detailed the process, have the student summarize what he or she recalls. Discuss possible reasons why some elements of the process were included in the summary and others were not.
2. **Individual Project:** Visit a different classroom and lead students in a round of "telephone." Discuss how much each message changed from beginning to end. Then offer the group strategies they might use to improve their chances that the end message matches the initial statement.

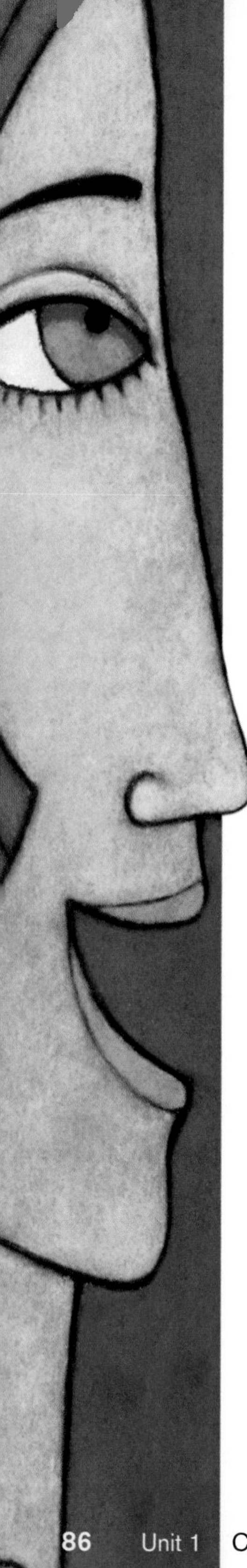

Influences on Communication

ESSENTIAL QUESTION

What influences your ability to communicate effectively?

Chapter Project: What Do *You* See?

Nobody else sees the world and communicates ideas in exactly the same way you do. This project will help you understand why.

Plan and present a two-minute discussion of a work of abstract art. You will present the art in class and give a brief summary of your interpretation. You will also analyze what factors led you to this interpretation. Refer to the following CAPS guidelines as you work to meet this challenge.

The rubric on page 103 shows the traits on which your presentation will be evaluated.

CONCEPT	how people see themselves and others helps shape communication
AUDIENCE	classmates and teacher
PURPOSE	demonstrate how perceptions influence communication
SITUATION	two-minute discussion and analysis of artwork interpretations

KEY VOCABULARY

- perception
- interpret
- self-concept
- misperception
- stereotype
- snap judgment
- attitude

Explain why you think talking with this girl would be easy or difficult.

Speak Up!

Turn to a partner and share three words that describe your unique personality. Don't think too hard about it—just do it!

creative FUNNY
LOUD nervous
fierce CHAOTIC

BACKGROUND FOR THE PROJECT

Pages 88–101 will provide the information you'll need to complete this project.

Perception of Self and Others

Perception is the process of using your senses to gather and process information about your environment. It is how you become aware and make sense of everything you encounter in your world. For example, you arrive home, open the door, and smell fresh-baked bread. Your brother is setting the table, and you hear the oven timer going off. Your dad greets you and says, "Five minutes." Evaluating all you smell, see, and hear, you understand that it's almost dinnertime.

You use perception to enhance your understanding of messages and their senders. Perception allows you to assign meaning to all the information you take in. The more accurate your perception, the better you can understand. This chapter explores several major influences on perception and how they affect the communication process.

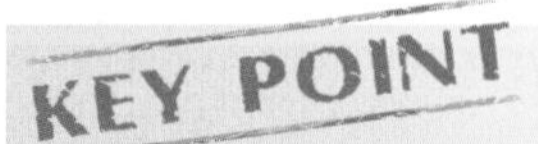

Perception identifies, organizes, and makes sense of information.

The Stages of Perception

Perception requires that you process the information around you in three stages: take it in, organize it, and interpret it.

Stage 1: Taking in the Information Every minute, you are taking in sensory information. You encounter millions of information pieces every day. You listen to a classmate's history report. You feel the breeze against your cheek in the park. You taste your orange juice at breakfast. You see hundreds of advertisements all around you. In most situations, you focus on just one or two sensory details at a time instead of the full range of things you are capable of perceiving. If you run into a friend, you focus on him or her—the face, the voice, the message. You filter out all the other sounds and smells and movements around you.

If you are visiting Times Square in New York for the first time, you might focus on only the sights, filtering out the sounds.

Stage 2: Organizing the Information Once you take in sensory information, your brain sorts it so you can properly interpret it (see Stage 3). The organization happens automatically, helping you avoid overload from too much complex data flying around. Objects and ideas are sorted by such characteristics as number, size, color, function, and social category. These characteristics are already stored in your memory from past experiences. Consider these examples.

- You immediately determine that someone is short or tall or the situation is good or bad.
- You decide that a group is made up of students or construction workers.
- You quickly see that there are four empty seats in the movie theater.

Chloe's friends have commented that her style is "unique." If you were Chloe, how would you interpret the word unique*? How might you interpret it if you were her mom? Her little brother?*

Stage 3: Interpreting the Information During this stage, you **interpret** the information—your brain assigns meaning to it. Meaning comes from your memory, which taps into the whole of your life experience. That experience includes your culture, environment, relationships, individual experiences, education, beliefs, attitudes, and emotions. No two people take in and organize the same information in exactly the same way.

These variables in experience produce varying interpretations and perceptions that affect communication. Whether you are a sender or a receiver, your perceptions will guide your communication choices.

For example, you might listen with interest to someone who knocks on your door trying to raise money for a cause. Your dad, in contrast, already contributes to many causes and charities, and he may also be in the middle of making dinner. So before the fundraiser even begins to talk, he might cut the conversation short with a polite, "No thanks. We're busy now." Perception differences have influenced communication.

Why Perceptions Differ

Perceptions differ because people differ. You are different from the student who sits behind you in Spanish class. He is different from the girl who lives next door, and she is different from her best friend. Each human being is unique and will arrive at his or her perceptions through a variety of filters. As your brain works through the three stages of perception, it does so on the basis of your personal physical functions, background, mood, and reasons for perceiving.

Physical Functions

The physical functions that affect your perceptions include how you are "hardwired," or how your brain works. They also include such characteristics as your health, age, sharpness of senses, gender, and size. Superior hearing or poor eyesight might affect you. You might be older than the person with whom you're talking. You might feel tired or hungry or sick. If you're recovering from a bad case of the flu, for example, you might decline when a friend offers a bite of a chili dog. Your friend perceives the chili dog as appetizing; you do not.

Background

Different backgrounds result in different perceptions. Kylie, a talented cellist, invites Christina to a Friday-night concert. Christina envisions a rock concert and says yes immediately. Kylie has grown up enjoying classical music and is thrilled that Christina will join her at a symphony concert. Christina's perceptions—based on her background of going to pop music concerts—have not prepared her for the symphony. Each girl perceived "Friday-night concert" differently.

SEATED WOMAN (MARIE-THERESE), Pablo Picasso, 1938

PROJECT PREP

For 20 seconds only, look at Picasso's portrait of Marie-Therese pictured on the left. With the painting out of sight, write down everything you recall about it. Compare your list with that of a classmate. This warm-up will help with your **project.**

Mood

Everyone has good days, bad days, and in-between days. Because of your mood, you might react very differently to the same set of circumstances at different times. If you're apprehensive about a big test you're studying for, you might snap at your little sister when she asks you to play Candyland with her. If she asks you the same thing the next day, and you're feeling relieved and proud because you aced the test, you are more likely to give her a much friendlier response.

Focus

Your reasons for perceiving also affect what you perceive. Your mind focuses on different things at different times. That focus will vary depending on what you're thinking about. If you are studying Spanish, hearing a couple speaking "en español" may catch your attention in a way it never did before. Or maybe you are hoping to buy your first cell phone. You find yourself suddenly perceiving different models and their styles, colors, and features.

Self-Concept

How would you describe yourself *to* yourself? Whether you come up with a few descriptions or dozens of them, your list reveals your **self-concept**, or how you see yourself. Your self-concept affects your behavior, your communication style, and even how others perceive you. Do any of the words below apply to you?

How Self-Concept Is Formed

You began to form a unique self-concept at a *very* young age—as soon as you started interacting with the world. Your self-concept may remain relatively fixed for long periods of time, but there are countless opportunities for it to change and evolve. As you interpret your experiences and observations—either positively or negatively—you continually shape and reshape your self-concept. How you interpret others' reactions to you affects your self-concept also. Your self-concept is shaped by your:

- **experiences.** May regularly wins the half-mile race at local track meets. This experience contributes to her perception that she's a good athlete.
- **observations.** Victor looks in the mirror today and is not pleased. This observation causes him to feel unattractive. He decides not to ask May for a date.
- **interactions.** A writing contest judge tells Franco that she loves the short story he submitted. This reinforces Franco's perception that he's a good writer.

Misperceptions and Mistakes

You are bound to form a **misperception**, or flawed conclusion, about yourself from time to time. When you do, your self-concept will be less than accurate. You might be mistaken about something simple, like the exact shade of your hair. You might perceive yourself to be much more adept at Sudoku than you really are. Or you might have a major misperception about your appearance, personality, or talent. People with negative self-concepts often concentrate on a single failure and unnecessarily apply that negative perception to other aspects of themselves.

Zach struggled with piano lessons as a youngster. He couldn't keep up with the practice schedule or learn new music, so he quit. As a high school senior, he perceived that he had no musical talent. Recently, however, Zach took a dare and tried out for the school musical. The play's director cast Zach as the male lead.

Emily's situation is the reverse of Zach's. Playing the piano and learning new songs came easily to her. Based on these talents, she perceived herself to be musically talented in all ways. When she auditioned for the school musical, though, her voice was less than stellar. She did not understand why the director did not cast her. Zach's and Emily's misperceptions had an impact on both self-concept and behavior.

Correcting Mistakes

You can't entirely avoid misperceptions about yourself, but you can work to identify and correct them. Periodically check in with yourself to reflect on the perceptions that make up your self-concept.
Ask yourself:

- How do I see myself right now?
- How would I like to see myself?
- How do others see me right now?
- How would I like others to see me?

Jake may see himself as Wonder Boy, but do his friends?

Next, consider discussing your self-perceptions with someone who knows you well. You might talk with your best friend, a sibling, or a trusted adult. Tell that person, "I see myself as __________ and __________." Or, "I think Genevieve believes I am __________ and that you think I am __________."

Listen to your confidante's feedback about your perceptions. Note where his or her perceptions differ from yours and discuss possible reasons. For example, you might perceive that everyone enjoys the witty comments you make during movies. But your confidante may suggest that the friends you see movies with regard your jokes as constant interruptions. You can use that knowledge to update your own self-concept and the behavior you exhibit.

Making changes to your self-concept can take time and work. But when you make a positive change in your behavior—such as not talking during movies—you will receive positive feedback. Others will notice, and their perceptions of you will change. Those changes should affect your self-concept in a positive way.

PROJECT PREP

Follow the directions above for reflecting on your self-concept. Answer each question honestly. Then share your perceptions with someone and ask them to give you honest feedback. This insight should help you with your upcoming **project**.

Self-Concept and Communication

Your self-concept affects the way you both "talk" to yourself and interact with others. It acts as a filter for all of your experiences.

Intrapersonal communication is your inner dialogue. It is the thinking you do as you process information to make decisions, solve problems, or just talk yourself through a situation. Consider the following examples.

Kevin wonders what his physics teacher meant when she said his perspective on an experiment was "unusual." Kevin thinks it over. The teacher seems to like him, and he's currently earning an A in class. His positive self-concept leads him to believe that "unusual" is a good thing. Because he has had positive experiences in class, he is more likely to send himself a positive message.

Use clues from the photo to evaluate this person's self-concept.

If the teacher were to say the same thing to Alicia, however, the situation might be different. Alicia sees herself as one step behind the other students. She is earning a C despite studying hard. Alicia's negative self-concept might cause her to perceive that "unusual" means "dumb." Because Alicia has had negative experiences in physics class, she is more likely to send herself negative messages. And where Kevin's self-concept might inspire him to work harder, Alicia might decide that it's not worth her trouble.

Interpersonal communication refers to your communications with others. Most people present different versions of "self" at different times. If you had plans for three different dinners—one with a good friend, one with your principal, and one with a complete stranger—you would present a different self each time. You'd feel completely comfortable with a friend and conversation would flow easily. You might be on your best behavior for your principal and would choose your words carefully. With a stranger, you might feel awkward and have little to say or you would ask questions to find something in common. Your self-concept will probably vary in the company of each person, causing you to change your behavior from one situation to another.

The feedback you receive from others affects your behavior. For example, if you are loudly criticizing the football team from the stands, a few disapproving looks from other fans might cause you to tone down your comments. Likewise, others might join in as you cheer on the team. Such positive feedback might encourage you to increase your enthusiastic support.

What perceptions of these people do you form based solely on their appearance?

Perception of Others

Your perception of others plays a big role in your communication choices. Forming accurate perceptions of others will go a long way toward achieving successful communication. Not surprisingly, people with accurate self-concepts are more likely to accurately perceive others. Ashley knows that she excels in language arts subjects because she has a strong affinity for them. To do well, she doesn't put in extra study time beyond completing assignments. Ashley also knows that her friend Darius does not share her natural instincts for language arts. She understands that Darius does well because he spends many hours studying the material. Ashley's perceptions of Darius are accurate.

Forming Perceptions of Others

You start forming your perception of others the second you meet someone. You probably notice physical characteristics first. Examples include facial features, body type, and skin color. Next you notice social characteristics such as a person's personality, attitude, and speech patterns. You also notice the person's hairstyle and clothing choices. You also may identify aspects of your own personality when trying to perceive others' traits. As always, your judgments will affect your perception.

Misperceptions about Others

Because each person's thought processes are unique and influenced by many competing forces, misperceptions of others do happen. The following examples illustrate common reasons for misperceptions.

- **Physical characteristics:** You notice a boy your age with red hair and freckles just like yours. You think you should meet him. One possible misperception might be that this person also thinks that sharing red hair and freckles is a good reason to strike up a conversation when, in fact, he may not. Another is that he will be like you because you share a similar appearance. Assuming a connection based on physical characteristics can be a mistake.

What misperceptions might the people in this cartoon be experiencing?

- **Social characteristics:** If the classmate at the beach doesn't acknowledge you when you wave and say "hi," you might decide that she is antisocial. A possible misperception might be that you thought she saw or heard you when she didn't.
- **Stereotyping:** A **stereotype** is an oversimplified image or idea about a person or a group. At a party, you meet Lisa and learn that she lives in a very wealthy neighborhood. You assume she is stuck up. Lots of misperceptions are applicable here. Where Lisa lives doesn't necessarily mean she is rich, and being rich doesn't necessarily mean she is stuck up (or shallow, or spoiled, or any of a dozen other stereotypes).
- **Snap judgments:** You introduce yourself to Darrell. He doesn't greet you with a smile, so you make a **snap judgment**, an opinion based on one quick bit of information. You assume that Darrell is unfriendly or bad-tempered. But perhaps Darrell just got braces and is uncomfortable showing them, or maybe he just doesn't show emotion in the same way you do.
- **Feelings:** If you meet fun-loving Hans when you're in a bad mood, you might find him annoying. You might misperceive him as phony, when he is a genuinely friendly and sincere person.

Misperceptions about others include assuming qualities based on their physical makeup and social status, applying stereotypes and making snap judgments, and allowing personal feelings to get in the way.

Correcting Misperceptions

Just as you check for misperceptions of yourself, check for misperceptions about others and work on correcting them. Ask yourself, "Do I have enough information about this person to form opinions? If not, what information might be helpful?" A good place to start is to verbally check your perceptions with the other person, as in the examples below.

Remember that people naturally change. A friend who was grumpy yesterday may not be grumpy today, and someone who gave an awkward report in class may speak with authority in a Sunday School class.

Perception of Others and Communication Your perceptions affect your communication in both positive and negative ways. If you feel good when you meet someone, you will communicate that positive attitude, and your exchange will probably be positive. If you make snap judgments and assign negative stereotypes of "rich snob" to Lisa and "unfriendly grouch" to Darrell, your interactions with them will be based on misperceptions. Your ability to communicate with them will be weakened. Continually reassessing your perceptions of others will help you see each individual's point of view. Others will also be reforming their perceptions of you. The more you work on understanding others, the more they will try to understand you, and the more effective your communications will be.

Other Influences on Communication

Perception of self and others is not the only influence on communication, though it is a powerful one. Other forces that influence your communication are your knowledge, attitudes, needs and priorities, and culture.

Knowledge

You may not be able to recall every bit of the knowledge you've ever learned. But you *have* collected vast amounts of knowledge in your lifetime. Your knowledge of how the world works affects the following communication choices:

- **those with whom you communicate.** Should you talk to your school guidance counselor about a problem you're having in class? Should you tell your lab partner that someone is spreading gossip about him? Your knowledge and experience will guide you to the right choice.
- **what you are able to communicate.** What can you tell someone about how an MP3 player works? What can you communicate about your musical tastes? If you don't have knowledge of a subject, there is little you can communicate about it.
- **when you are able to communicate.** Should you call your friend at 3 A.M.? When is the best time to ask your boss for a raise? Social knowledge will help you conform to expectations.
- **what means you should use to communicate.** Should you use e-mail to ask someone to the dance? Should you break up with your steady over the phone? Your knowledge of norms will be your guide.
- **special ways of communicating.** Can you use American Sign Language to communicate? Are you able to speak Mandarin Chinese?

Attitudes

An **attitude** is an opinion or general feeling. Your attitude about communication can be influenced by your self-concept. For example, someone who sees herself as a shy, clumsy speaker may not enjoy interacting with others as much as someone who thinks of himself as outgoing and quick-witted. That attitude will affect the success of the communication.

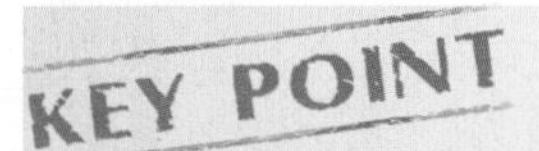

Your knowledge, attitudes, needs and priorities, and culture can all influence how well you communicate.

Needs and Priorities

Your personal needs and priorities also affect your communication decisions. As you mature, learn, forge new relationships, and enter the workforce, your interpersonal needs will continue to evolve. Listed below are a few common communication needs. The accompanying images illustrate these needs in action.

Communication Needs

love	acceptance
Telling your mom that you love her	Knowing your friends like you "as is"
pleasure	**friendship**
Calling your grandpa just to say hi when you should be studying	Sharing a problem with the student whose locker is next to yours
attention	**relaxation**
Feeling that what you say matters to others	Spending Saturday morning in an online chat room

Culture

Your culture and the cultures of the people you encounter can also influence communication in many ways. Cultural differences include language, customs, and nonverbal behaviors. Different social roles or expectations based on gender or race within a culture can also affect communication between individuals or groups.

Compare the individuals in the settings below. How might their cultural differences influence the way they communicate?

- The popular kid vs. "the loner"
- A man in a family vs. a woman in the family
- The only child vs. one of seven children
- A single-parent home vs. a two-parent home
- A student in the 21st century vs. a student in the 18th century
- Growing up Japanese in the U.S. vs. growing up Japanese in Japan
- A Republican rally vs. a Democratic rally

PROJECT PREP

Select one of the cultural duos presented above. With a partner, discuss ways the two might communicate given their differences. Then act out a short encounter.

Social and Ethical Responsibilities of Communicators

Communication is powerful. It can have the power to help you make friends, but it can also give you the power to create enemies. It can improve your social, family, and academic life, but it also has the potential to harm someone else's. You can use communication to improve society, but you can also use it to hurt society. Communication can be misused to restrict an individual's choices instead of to increase them.

Because communication can be so powerful, it carries social and ethical responsibilities. These responsibilities include sorting through your perceptions, misperceptions, and interpretations. They also include adapting your message to fit the situation, purpose, and audience. As a communicator, you are also responsible for avoiding stereotypes, snap judgments, and other misperceptions.

The chart below shows the principles of ethical communication. These principles might seem simple, yet they are anything but. For example, what do you do if the socially and ethically responsible message, or the truth, hurts others' feelings? Making the "right" communication choice is often complicated, requiring serious thought and much practice.

Making the ethical communication choice is not always easy.

Characteristics of communication	Implications for communicators
Socially and ethically responsible communication is . . .	Socially and ethically responsible communicators . . .
honest	tell the truth
polite	respect others' feelings
mutual	listen to and acknowledge others' communication
helpful	consider the effect of their communication on others
potentially life-changing	enable others to be better, personally and academically

Is This Job for Me?

Search: Mediator

With the 2005 World Cup qualifying games just a few weeks away, the union of the U.S. Soccer team was holding out for higher pay. Their employers, the U.S. Soccer Federation, felt the union's demands were too high and threatened to use minor league replacements. Neither side wanted that result. So on a cold day in a hotel near Chicago's O'Hare airport, officials from the union and the federation met to hash out their differences. One person at the meeting, however, was on neither side. That was the *mediator,* a neutral party who helps guide the opposing sides through hard-to-break-down differences. By the next day, the two sides had come to an agreement. The players agreed not to strike, the Federation agreed to pay more money, and the regular players took to the fields.

Does a job as a mediator sound interesting to you? Measure yourself with this personality inventory to find out if you think you have the traits to become a mediator. Do you:

- ✓ Listen attentively?
- ✓ Have insight into interpersonal relationships?
- ✓ Have a knack for "reading" others?
- ✓ Quickly synthesize information?
- ✓ Know how to resolve conflicts?
- ✓ Communicate clearly and decisively?
- ✓ Have a strong sense of fairness and objectivity?
- ✓ Handle pressure well?
- ✓ Know how to keep information confidential?

If you become a mediator, you might find job opportunities in the following organizations.

Employers	What You Would Do
Law Firms	Mediate disputes between opposing sides in legal cases
Government Agencies	Mediate disputes between countries or other governmental agencies
Corporations	Mediate employee disputes or disputes between corporations
Independent Consulting Firms	Mediate legal, social, corporate, governmental, school, or personal disputes

PREPARING THE PROJECT

Begin your project by looking back at the **Project Prep** activities in this chapter and using the directions below.

Make Connections

Use a notebook to summarize this chapter, including:

- perception of self
- perception of others
- the three stages of perception
- why perceptions differ
- social and ethical aspects of communication.

Write one or two sentences explaining how perception affects communication.

Focus

Reread the description on page 86 of the two-minute interpretations of a piece of abstract art. Think of three specific ideas that you learned that you can apply.

Plan

Find a copy of an interesting work of abstract art. Freewrite to capture your impressions: how does it make you feel? What does it bring to mind? What does it represent to you?

Surefire Freewriting

Keep your pen or pencil moving to let your ideas flow freely.

Develop

Write a draft of your presentation. Try it out by reading it out loud. Have you included plenty of clear examples of how perceptions can affect the interpretation of this piece of art? Look over the evaluation rubric on page 103 and be sure you have addressed each point.

Practice

Do several practice runs of your presentation in front of an audience of friends or family, if possible. Be sure that you don't go longer than two minutes.

PRESENTING THE PROJECT

Use the strategy that follows to help make your presentation as good as it can be.

Involving the Audience

A discussion of art is a great way to gain audience participation. As you present your project, be sure to include questions that your audience can answer, at least in their minds. Draw on universal feelings and concepts that will have a strong impact.

EVALUATING THE PROJECT

Evaluate the presentations using the following rubric.

Score the interpretation on each point, with 4 being "outstanding" and 1 being "needs much improvement."

Come up with an overall score and write a brief paragraph explaining your score.

Demonstrating How Perceptions Affect Interpretation of Art	Creativity and Originality	Preparation	Time Limit
4 Presenter used many clear examples of how perceptions can affect the interpretation of a piece of art.	**4** Presenter found a creative and unique way to complete the project.	**4** Presenter was very well prepared.	**4** Presenter used all of the time well, with no empty spaces, and did not go over or under the time limit.
3 Presenter used a few clear examples of how perceptions can affect the interpretation of a piece of art.	**3** Presenter showed creativity and originality in presenting most parts of the project.	**3** Presenter was well prepared.	**3** Presenter used the time well, with only one or two awkward spots, and did not go over or under the time limit.
2 Presenter used very few clear examples of how perceptions can affect the interpretation of a piece of art.	**2** Presenter showed creativity and originality in some parts of the project but not others.	**2** Presenter was mostly prepared.	**2** Presenter used the time well, with only one or two awkward spots, but went slightly over or noticeably under the time limit.
1 Presenter used no clear examples of how perceptions can affect the interpretation of a piece of art.	**1** Presenter did not demonstrate creativity or originality.	**1** Presenter seemed unprepared.	**1** Presenter did not use the time well and went considerably over or under the time limit.

Communication Past and Present

Stereotypes Through History

Stereotypes are based on perceptions about what people in a certain group are like. They can be positive or negative, expressed by a word, a phrase, or an image. One recent study suggested that Americans are stereotyped as open-minded, friendly, and generous—and also as self-centered, arrogant, and impatient. The Japanese have been stereotyped as smart and organized, but reserved and exacting. Stereotypes can be problematic because they often appear to contain a grain of truth. Of course not all Americans are open-minded and not all Asians are smart, but it often seems that a good many of them are. But there are also many stingy Americans and a good number of outgoing Japanese. Each person is an individual.

From Historical Times . . .

For as long as humans have been interacting and forming perceptions, they have also been creating stereotypes. Stereotypes are often related to race, ethnicity, gender, and socio-economic status. Following are just a few examples from earlier periods in American history.

Gender Stereotyping: Women from Colonial Times to the 1920s From the American Revolution until the 1920s, American women were second-class citizens, unable to own property or to vote. If single, they paid taxes but had no political power at all. If married, they were entirely dependent upon the will of their husbands. They were stereotyped as being too emotional and weak to understand social and political issues. They finally won the right to vote in 1920.

Woman Devotes Her Time to Gossip and Clothes Because She Has Nothing Else to Talk About. Give Her Broader Interests and She Will Cease to Be Vain and Frivolous.

What messages about women do you think this cartoon conveys?

Ethnic Stereotype: The Irish in the 19th Century Irish immigrants coming to America in great numbers were stereotyped as heavy drinkers who hated to work and loved to fight. Later, they were characterized as the typical policeman on the beat. When John F. Kennedy became president of the United States, the Irish stereotype took yet another turn.

Occupational Stereotyping: Scientists in the 19h Century The "mad scientist" stereotype was popular in the 19th century.

It portrayed scientists as eccentric men with rumpled clothing and wild hair who were obsessed with their work. The "absentminded professor" was a very common stereotype also. People of high intellect in general were often looked upon with distrust and even disdain.

. . . to Today

Stereotyping continues into modern times. Following are just a few examples from today's world.

Gender Stereotyping: Men in the 21st Century Today, a common stereotype of men is that they all love football and wouldn't think of being ballet dancers. Men who pursue dreams that are not condoned by male culture often struggle within themselves as well as with those who oppose them.

Billy Elliot did a grand jeté around gender stereotypes when the title character in the movie gave his all to ballet.

Political Stereotyping: The Modern Era When the French government decided not to support U.S. involvement in Iraq, many Americans, particularly those in the government, were furious. In protest, House Republicans renamed French fries "American fries." Characterized as weak, disloyal, and irresponsible, the French became the brunt of nighttime comedians. For their part, the French responded with political cartoons such as the one below.

In 1886 France gave the Statue of Liberty to the United States. What point do you think this cartoon is expressing?

Occupational Stereotyping: Hollywood Actors in the 21st Century You've heard the stories and seen the news clips. A young Hollywood starlet drives her car into a pole, runs over the toes of a photographer, and spends millions of dollars on a birthday party. Young actors who reside in the Los Angeles area are often stereotyped as having little talent and even fewer brains. In fact, young actors in Hollywood are not very different from young people everywhere: some of them are foolish and conceited, and some of them are bright and caring.

Chapter 5 Review

Using Vocabulary Words

For each term listed below, make a box and divide it into four sections. In the top left section, write the word. In the top right section, draw an illustration of the word. In the bottom left section, give an example of what the word means to you. In the bottom right section, write the opposite of that word.

Word	Illustration
Example	Opposite

1. attitude
2. interpret
3. misperception
4. perception
5. self-concept
6. snap judgment
7. stereotype

Reviewing Key Ideas

1. Define *perception*.
2. List and briefly define the three stages of perception.
3. Explain why perceptions differ.
4. Discuss how your self-concept is formed.

Reflecting on Your Project

Write some thoughts in your notebook about how your presentation went. Note at least two aspects of your presentation you thought could have gone better. Check your perceptions with a classmate to see if he or she agrees with you. Discuss strategies for improving those areas for the next time you work on such a project.

Responding to the Essential Question

Use what you learned in this chapter to write a one-page, non-rhyming poem in response to the question, "What influences your ability to communicate effectively?" Share your poems in small groups.

Extending Your Understanding

Everyday Life

1. The next time you go to the movie theater, practice using all of your senses to gather information about your environment. Arrive early enough before your movie starts so you can spend a few minutes in the lobby selecting sensory data to process. If you go with a friend, share and compare your lists of noticeable things in the lobby.
2. During your next family meal, close your eyes as the food is brought to the table. See if you can guess what's cooking by using senses other than sight.

3. At a school sporting event, scan the crowd for someone you've never seen before. Check yourself for any stereotypes or other misperceptions you automatically assign by sight alone.
4. The next time you snap at someone at home, take a step back to think about ways your mood may have affected your perceptions of the other person. Did your mood cause you to misperceive the other person's message or intention?

In the Media

5. Watch back-to-back episodes of your favorite classic sitcom with a group of friends and try to identify all the stereotypes portrayed.
6. Watch an interview on a TV news show. Pay close attention to how the interviewee's self-concept affects his or her answers to the reporter's questions. What conclusions can you draw about how the person's self-concept affected that communication?

Research

7. Research examples of stereotyping in advertising. Create a stereotype-free poster that advertises a product of your choice. Present your ad to the class, along with several examples of magazine or Web ads that rely on stereotypes to sell products.
8. Research the career of private detective, a job that relies on accurate perceptions. Find information about necessary training, and the key reasons that perception skills are so important to a detective's success solving cases and working with people. Present examples from books or Web sites to the class.

Interpreting Graphics

Write a few sentences identifying possible stereotypes in the picture below.

Additional Projects

1. **Partnered Project:** Write a two-minute scene depicting a conversation in which one character's skewed perception of the other character creates significant communication problems. Brainstorm ideas and write the scene together. Then perform it for another classroom. Afterward, ask your audience, "What just happened?" Prepare your own explanation to share with them.
2. **Individual Project:** Read Edgar Allan Poe's "The Tell-Tale Heart." Write a one-page essay that explores the main character's self-concept. Share your essay in class and answer any questions about your reasoning.

Unit One

Culminating Activities

In this unit you have explored communication basics: the elements of communication, oral language, nonverbal communication, listening, and factors that influence communication. The activities on these pages will help you apply your understandings to situations in everyday life.

Workplace Workout

Ryan had been working at the electronics store for just a week. A co-worker named Gwen was showing him how to handle returned merchandise. Gwen reminded Ryan of his bossy older sister. When Gwen was explaining the return process, Ryan was thinking about his sister and felt Gwen too was being bossy.

Gwen also used a few terms that Ryan didn't know, such as *manufacturer incentive* and *rebate*. Ryan didn't want to look stupid so he just nodded and said, somewhat impatiently, that he understood.

Ryan got his first return on a busy Saturday afternoon, and he couldn't remember the procedure. He was embarrassed to ask Gwen, so he kept trying different things on the cash register as the checkout line got longer and longer. Finally the cash register froze—and he had to turn to Gwen for help after all. Ryan was humiliated and when he got home later that afternoon told his parents he didn't want to go back to that job.

What Went Wrong? With a partner, use the terms from the communication model to analyze the interaction between Ryan and Gwen. Identify the purpose, audience, and occasion for the exchange. Then draw a model with the elements labeled and show where in the process successful communication broke down.

Make it Right Then with your partner, re-enact the scene between Gwen and Ryan to show a successful communication experience. Your characters can use asides (times when they step out of character and speak directly to the audience) to explain the improved communication. Present your reenactment to the class.

GenderJourney

With a small group, obtain a copy of a recent yearbook. Choose a class (eighth graders or sophomores, for example) and count the number of individual photos for that class. Assign each group member a page or more of photos to tally the number of males who are smiling in the photos and the number of females who are smiling. Record the results on a two-column chart. When all the results are in, compile them into one master chart. Then, in discussion with your group, explain what the results might mean, referring to information in Unit 1 to help you. Write a paragraph to share your explanation.

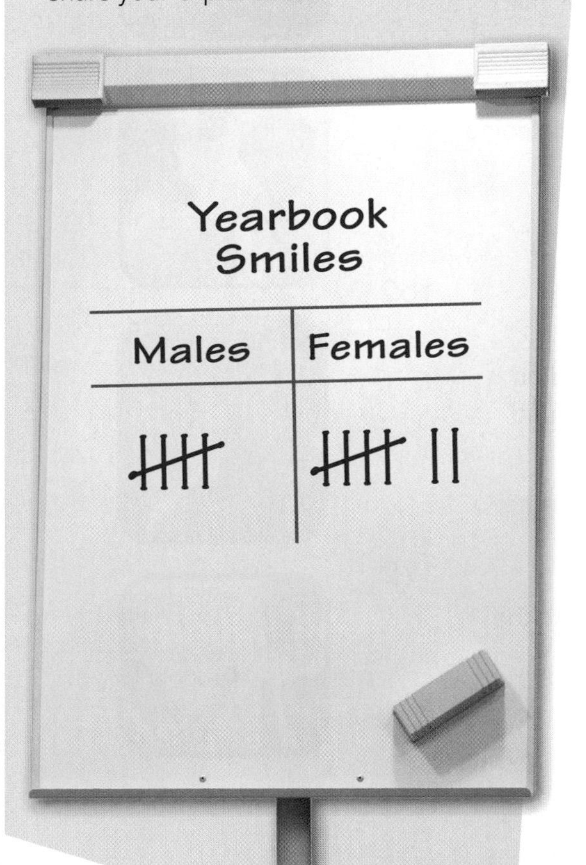

Media Master

With a partner, create a script for a 30-second anti-drug radio advertisement aimed at middle school students that would be played on a rock music station. Use information from Unit 1 to make sure you shape the message to the audience in all possible ways.

OWN IT!

Unit 1 began with an anonymous quote: "There is only one rule to become a good speaker: learn how to listen." (See page 3.) Think back over what you learned in Unit 1. Think about the projects you worked on and the other activities you completed. Think about your own real-world communication. Does what you learned in Unit 1 support the idea expressed in that quote? If not, what "one rule" would you come up with to become a good speaker? Write a paragraph or create a visual to express your response.

Unit Two

Interpersonal Communication

Each person's life is lived as a series
of conversations.
– Deborah Tannen

Effective Interpersonal Communication Strategies

ESSENTIAL QUESTION

What strategies enhance interpersonal communication?

Chapter Project: Different People, Different Talk

You talk one way with your teenage friends and another with adults or younger children. This project will help you become aware of communication strategies that work in a variety of situations.

With a partner, you will role-play two one-minute conversations on the same topic. Each of you will play yourself one time. The second time, you will play the part of a different person—another teenager, a grandmother, child, teacher, coach. Classmates will try to guess who the different person is in each conversation based only on your language choices and communication decisions. Refer to the following CAPS guidelines as you work to meet this challenge.

The rubric on page 131 shows the traits on which your presentation will be evaluated.

Concept	different social contexts affect the way people communicate
Audience	"mystery" conversation partner
Purpose	practice effective interpersonal communication strategies
Situation	creative classroom demonstration

KEY VOCABULARY

duration	relevant
intimacy	sincere
protocol	paralanguage
assertive	volume
courteous	rate
tact	inflection
specific	

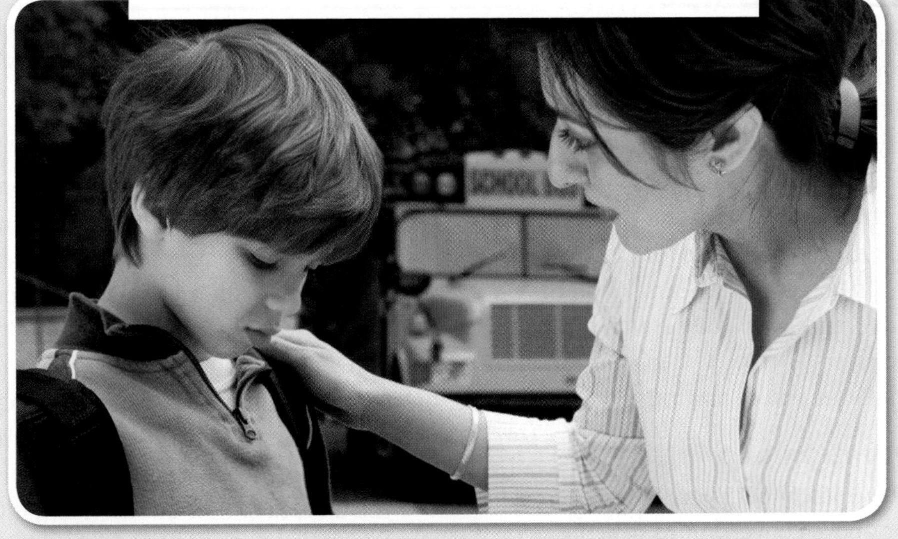

Describe, in two or three sentences, a likely context for the communication in this photograph.

Speak Up!

What do you say when someone says, "Hi! How are you?" Your answer may depend on who's asking. Explore how you tailor what you say to the social context. List the different people you're likely to meet on an average day. Think about how you would respond to each one's greeting.

Person Who Asks "How are you?"	Your Response
An adult neighbor	"Fine, thanks. How are you?"
The school bus driver	"I'm OK."
A good friend	[You roll your eyes.] "Don't even ask!"

Pages 114–128 will provide the information you'll need to complete this project.

Interpersonal Relationships

Imagine that you're walking down the hall after school to a play rehearsal. You exchange greetings with friends along the way. You make a study date with a student in your history class. A friend walks part of the way with you, and the two of you talk about your plans for the weekend. When you get to rehearsal, you have a conference with your drama teacher about your part and your interpretation of the character you're playing.

Duration and Intimacy

How you conduct yourself in each of the above conversations depends on your relationship with the other person. Two major factors define relationships. One is **duration**—the length of time you've known the person. The second is **intimacy**—how close you feel and how much trust you have in sharing personal information.

Duration and intimacy help define interpersonal relationships and shape communication decisions.

Often, the longer you've known someone the more intimate your relationship, but not always. For example, you may have known the cashier in a neighborhood store all your life, but you wouldn't tell him your personal secrets. On the other hand, you might share intimate facts about yourself with a doctor or nurse you've just met. The chart below gives you an idea of how duration and intimacy work together in daily social relationships.

Variations on a Theme: Interpersonal Relationships

	High Intimacy	Low Intimacy
Long Duration	• Family members • Lifelong friends • Neighbors *Characterized by high trust, high self-disclosure, development of personal meanings, physical closeness*	• Letter carrier • Bagger at the corner store • School bus driver *Characterized by little personal self-disclosure, restricted topics, less physical closeness*
Short Duration	• Social Worker • School counselor • Physician *Characterized by high levels of self-disclosure, limited topics, high urgency*	• Casual acquaintance • Person behind you in line • Someone you talk with at a football game *Characterized by small talk, reduced importance, little or no personal information*

Situation in Interpersonal Communication

Just as the duration and intimacy of your relationship affect what you say and how you say it, so does the situation in which you are speaking. Imagine that you are getting an award from your school. The award ceremony will be in the auditorium, and parents and faculty will be present. You are expected to give an acceptance speech. What will you say in your speech? "Thanks! This is so cool"? Probably not. An award ceremony in front of adults is a formal event, and what you say in your speech must reflect the formal nature of the event.

Formal situations, such as the award ceremony, call for more formal dress, behavior, speech, and topics of conversation than do informal situations, such as running into a friend at the mall. For most adults, formal situations arise because of work or social events. For students, formal situations arise in school and through other academic pursuits as well as some family events.

The interpersonal relationships in the military are governed by formal and strict expectations.

Expectations in Interpersonal Social Situations

	Personal/Private	Professional/Academic
Formal	**Funeral** • Association of people is personal. • Appropriate dress, behavior, and language are expected. • Conversation topics are restricted.	**Formal business meeting, classroom discussion, interview** • Association is based on shared goals or interests. • Appropriate dress, behavior, and language are expected. • Mode of communication is well-defined and topics are predetermined.
Informal	**Conversation with a close friend** • Association is by personal choice. • Language and behavior are intimate and informal. • Expectations are based on previous experiences as friends.	**On-the-job break time, hallway conversation** • Association is based on mutual goals or interests. • Behavior is less formal, but topics and language are still influenced by relationship. • Communication may have impact on future meetings.

Entertaining friends with clever comments is one interpersonal communication purpose.

Purpose in Interpersonal Communication

Remembering your purpose is another key to making good communication choices. For example, if you make a campaign speech during a school election, your purpose is to persuade fellow students to vote for the candidate you support. When you tell your parents about an upcoming class trip, your purpose is to convince them the trip is a good idea so they will give you permission to go.

PROJECT PREP

With your **project partner**, create two versions of a 15-second scene showing how situation and purpose affect communication choices. Think of a situation to use for both scenes, but change the purpose in the second version. Write or act out your scenes.

Even in casual conversation you have a communication purpose behind everything you say. Suppose you are telling a friend about an article you read on bicycling. Depending on the focus of the article, your communication purpose could be to entertain your friend, inform her, educate her about cycling, warn about some danger, or maybe just impress her with how much you know. Your purpose would affect the way you talk about the article you'd read. For example, if it was a humorous article and your purpose was to entertain your friend, you'd use a lighthearted tone. If it was a sobering warning about the injury rate for cyclists who don't wear helmets, you'd use serious language.

Strategies for Effective Communication Decisions

Consider how the *type of relationship*, the *situation*, and the *purpose* affect the following communication between Kayla, editor of the school newspaper, and Victor, a reporter. Victor wrote an article on the school's new dress code, and Kayla has some problems with it. She invites Victor to her office and offers him a seat. "If we wanted an article about how *students* feel about the dress code, this would be it. You really nailed that," she says, complimenting him. "But that's not what we want this article to do. We're trying to get the administration to rethink their decision." Kayla sees that Victor looks puzzled. "What we have to do, Vic, is make a case for getting rid of the code based on logic and reason, not on how the students feel about it." Victor understands. He promises to turn in a revised article by 3:00 the next day. Kayla thanks him, saying, "You're the best!"

In the meeting between Kayla and Victor, both participants are aware of the nature of their relationship, the situation, and the purpose. They understand that their relationship and situation are governed by **protocol**—specific conventions of behavior— and that their communication has an important purpose. In this case, Kayla follows protocol in inviting Victor to her office, offering him a seat, and, as his superior on the paper, leading their discussion. She informs him up front about the purpose of their meeting—to discuss his article for the paper. She accomplishes her purpose by using the following strategies for making good communication decisions.

Be Assertive

When you are **assertive**, you express yourself directly and forcefully. Kayla is assertive in her conversation with Victor. She quickly gets to the heart of the problem and doesn't mince words. She lets Victor know how his article differed from the goal and what the article needs.

Assertiveness is just as important when you are reacting instead of initiating. When you disagree with someone, you have the choice of expressing your disagreement or not. You may have good reasons to say nothing. For example, the issue may not be all that important to you, or you may prefer to wait for a more appropriate time. But if you remain silent just because you are afraid to express your views, try to become more assertive. Assertive communicators are not reluctant to say what they believe needs to be said.

Be Courteous

When you are polite and respectful of others you are being **courteous**. Courtesy is the use of good manners and adherence to accepted rules of behavior. You learn the rules early in life: "Say *please* and *thank you*. Don't interrupt when someone else is talking." If you follow them you can't go wrong. Kayla is courteous when she asks Victor to sit down and when she thanks Victor at the end of the conversation. She politely expresses her appreciation of Victor's cooperation as well as her confidence in him as a reporter, both of which show kindness and courtesy.

Victor knows how to revise his article because Kayla was very clear about her communication purpose.

Kayla's courtesy, tact, and sincerity have earned her the respect of the whole newspaper staff.

Use Tact

Successful communicators also use **tact**, the quality that allows people to speak without giving offense. In discussing Victor's article with him, Kayla is assertive, but she is also tactful. She uses tact to tell Victor that his writing is strong, and she says, *"What we have to do, Vic, is make a case for getting rid of the code based on logic and reason."* By using the word *we,* Kayla tactfully includes herself in the effort to solve the problem.

Be Specific

The more **specific**, or detailed and particular, communication is, the less chance there is for misunderstanding. What would have happened if Kayla had told Victor in general terms that his story wasn't what she was looking for? Would he have been able to rewrite his article in the way she wanted? Probably not. By clearly defining the purpose of the article and explaining specifically how the article could be rewritten, Kayla is able to communicate her message effectively.

Make It Relevant

Effective interpersonal communication is **relevant**—connected to the issue at hand. Kayla and Victor are both discussing the same topic: Victor's article for the school paper. Neither talks about anything else. If Victor had tried to change the subject, Kayla would probably have thought him uncooperative and even silly. If Kayla had wandered off the subject, Victor would probably have been confused about what Kayla wanted him to do and perhaps have questioned her dedication to the paper.

Good communication is relevant to the context and to the communication that has already taken place. You can change the subject or introduce new information or ideas only if the new subject relates to the situation, the audience, and the overall purpose, and if the listener understands its relevance.

Mean It

Listeners judge a message by how **sincere** it is. A sincere message is honest, natural, and believable. It is heard as representing the speaker's true feelings. Interpersonal relationships depend on sincerity. If two people are talking and one feels the other is not sincere, trust breaks down. If the listener cannot trust that the speaker really believes what he or she is saying, what point is there in continuing the conversation?

Effective interpersonal communication is assertive, courteous, specific, relevant, and sincere.

Choose the Appropriate Level of Usage

As you read in Chapter 2, situation, purpose, and audience help you choose your words. For example, if you are being interviewed for a job, the situation calls for you to use Standard English, not slang or informal English. If you were trying to help someone understand how to use a computer, the purpose would steer you away from technical jargon. If you were talking to a child, knowledge of your audience would prevent you from using big words and formal language. You use the level of usage that allows listeners to feel comfortable with what you say and how you say it.

Monitor Body Language

When Kayla talked to Victor she was assertive, courteous, specific, relevant, and sincere. But what if, as she was talking, she sighed, looked at her watch, and had an expression on her face that showed annoyance? How would that have changed the effectiveness of her communication? Or imagine that Victor slouched in his chair and looked at his feet, refusing to make eye contact with Kayla. What message would that send?

You can do all the right things—be assertive, courteous, specific, relevant, sincere, and use appropriate language—but if you're not careful, your body language can undermine your message. Body language can send messages that can support or contradict what your words are saying. Facial expressions, gestures, posture, lack of eye contact, movements, even the way you dress all communicate meaning.

What kind of language do you think this woman is using with her grandson?

Match your body language and paralanguage to the intended meaning of your communication.

Communicate with Paralanguage

Paralanguage is the use of vocal effects to express meaning. Paralanguage is *how* something is said. Paralinguistic cues tell the listener when the speaker is nervous, upset, bored, or just kidding. They also help the listener understand the specific shade of meaning a speaker is conveying. The three paralinguistic cues that are most important in shaping the meaning of words are **volume**, **rate**, and **inflection**.

- **Volume** Raising your voice or giving special emphasis to words helps listeners interpret what you're saying. Consider a simple sentence such as "This is my art project." How does the meaning of the sentence change when different words are said with greater stress? See for yourself. Say the sentence below three times, each time saying the word in italics louder than the other words and with greater stress.

  This is my art project.

  This is *my* art project.

  This *is* my art project.

  Which way would you say this sentence if you were responding to this question: "That's an interesting lump of clay, but where's your art project?"
- **Rate** The rate at which you speak also adds meaning to what you say. By speeding up or slowing down, you can communicate eagerness, excitement, reluctance, care, and other attitudes.
- **Inflection** The third paralinguistic cue is inflection. Inflection is a change in the pitch of your voice. Your voice can rise, getting higher, or fall, getting lower. The most familiar example of inflection is the way your voice rises at the end of the question: *What do you want me to do?* When your voice falls at the end of a question, it can suggest impatience or disgust. Listen to the effect when you let your voice fall at the end of the question: *What do you want me to do?* In American English, rising inflection at the end of a sentence can turn a statement into a question: *That's your cat?*

Rising inflection at the end of a statement can also suggest uncertainty, apology, or a hint of embarrassment. Suppose someone asked, "How are you getting to the prom?" Try saying the answer by letting your voice fall a bit at the end: "My dad's driving us." Then say it again, this time letting your voice rise at the end. Which way makes it clear that you are perfectly comfortable with the transportation arrangements?

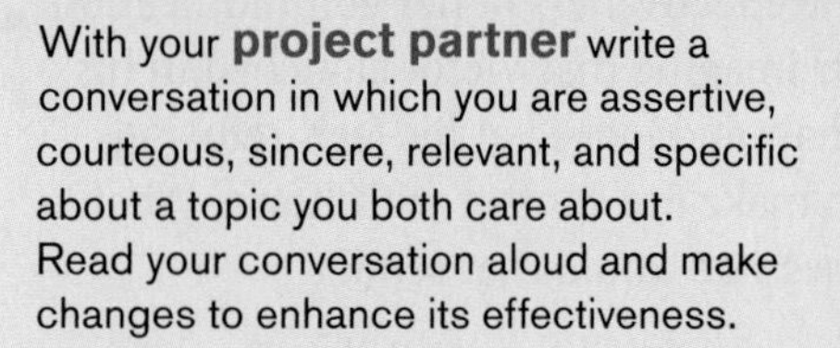

PROJECT PREP

With your **project partner** write a conversation in which you are assertive, courteous, sincere, relevant, and specific about a topic you both care about. Read your conversation aloud and make changes to enhance its effectiveness.

Communication in a DIVERSE WORLD

He Says, She Says: Gender and Body Language

Researchers have studied the body language of Americans and have observed distinct differences in the body language of women and men.

Men take up more space when they are sitting or standing. They extend their arms and legs away from their body, and the effect is that they look larger.

Women take up less space when they are sitting or standing. They keep their arms and legs close to their bodies, and appear smaller as a result.

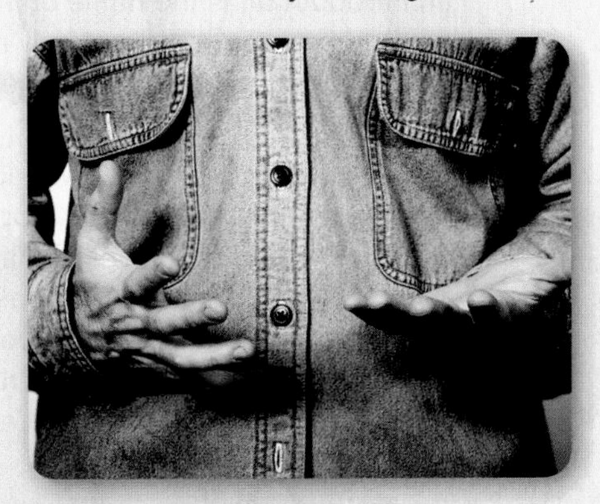

Men tend to gesture away from their bodies.

Women tend to gesture toward their bodies.

Researchers have interpreted these differences in body language as subtle signals that women have less power than men and are inclined to be nurturing, while men are self-confident and in control. However, there are always exceptions. Also, this research was done with people of your parents' generation and older. Observe your classmates. Are the males and females of your generation still sending the same gender-specific messages with their body language?

Introduce the younger person first when introducing an adult and youth.

Applying Decision-Making Strategies in Everyday Communication

Your everyday interactions put you in the same kinds of situations again and again. You meet new people. You introduce people to one another. You make apologies, give directions, and take part in conversations. Even in these familiar situations, you can improve your communication with good decision-making.

Making Introductions

Making introductions is not only a courteous thing to do, it is also important for effective communication. When people don't know each other's names or their relationship to other people in the conversation group, they can't communicate well together.

Introducing Others

If you are introducing two people who don't know each other, provide the following information.

- **Names** The most important part of an introduction is the name of the person. Say each name clearly so each person can hear and remember the other's name.
- **Relationship** Mention how each person is connected to you. For instance, "Grandma, this is Tina Slocum. She goes to my school." If you are introducing someone your own age to an adult, always introduce the younger person first: "Dr. Larman, this is my friend Nat Rose."
- **Relevance** In some situations, you may need to explain why people are present. For example, if you head up a committee of students and faculty planning a fundraising event, you might indicate the knowledge or expertise members bring to the committee as you introduce them.

Introducing Yourself

Sometimes you will need to introduce yourself. Follow the same guidelines that apply to introducing others. Say "hello" and give your name. If necessary, explain your role in the situation. For example, "Hi, Mrs. Patel. I'm Wendy Makar, Logan's friend from school. Logan asked me to come and rehearse our lines for the school play."

If someone else is introducing, remember these suggestions.

1. **Listen carefully.** Pay attention to the person's name and any other information offered.
2. **Make a "name note."** Try to connect the name with something that will help you recall it later.
3. **Make eye contact** with the person you are being introduced to. Eye contact is courteous and helps to begin the process of developing a relationship.
4. **Shake hands.** You may not want to shake hands when you are being introduced to someone your own age, but when you are being introduced to an adult, offer your hand. Then shake the person's hand in a firm and friendly manner.
5. **Smile.** In most situations, a smile will convey goodwill.
6. **Speak.** Typically, courtesy calls for saying something like, "I'm happy to meet you." In some situations, "Hello" is enough. Some people like to use the person's name as a way to help them remember it. If you want to initiate a conversation, you may want to provide an opening for a response from the person. For example, "It's an honor to meet you, Ms. Creech. I love your books. I've read every one of them."

Introducing yourself with a friendly smile and handshake can help relax you even in a formal situation.

Making Apologies

Everyone makes mistakes. If your mistakes hurt other people, apologize. To understand what makes an apology an effective communication, think about apologies people have made to you. What is the most important thing you expect in an apology? It's probably sincerity. Most people are very forgiving if they believe that the person apologizing recognizes his or her mistake and is truly sorry for it. In addition to being sincere, here are some more suggestions for making and accepting apologies.

1. **Name it and claim it.** Being specific is important when apologizing. Don't just say, "I'm sorry." Acknowledge the wrong you did (name it) and accept responsibility for it (claim it).
2. **Offer an explanation.** Briefly tell why you made the mistake. People you have wronged or disappointed often appreciate knowing what brought your mistake about.
3. **Offer to make things right.** If an error is correctable, offer to correct it. If it is not, tell what you will do in the future to be sure it won't happen again.
4. **Keep it brief.** People often ramble on when they are nervous, but curb that impulse. Respect the other person's time, and get to the point.
5. **Be sincere.** The important thing about an apology is that you really mean it.

Here's an example of an effective apology.

Victor, it was wrong of me to read your journal when I found it on the table. I should have just returned it to you. I know you're upset that I read it, and I'm so sorry that I didn't respect your privacy. Please accept my apology. I'll never do such a thing again.

When someone apologizes to you, try to be brief and gracious. You may not always be ready to forgive and forget, but you can at least acknowledge the apology.

I was very upset by what you did, but I appreciate your apology.

Sincere apologies have great healing power.

Giving Directions

Think of how many times during a typical day you have the opportunity to give directions. A visitor wants to know how to get to the principal's office. A fellow student needs help accessing an Internet resource. A friend wants to learn a new dance move. Each of those situations involves giving directions. When you give directions, you try to transfer knowledge and skills to others so they can accomplish a goal.

Ben Turpin, actor in American silent films, illustrates how not to give directions.

Imagine that someone asked you how to get from the school to a familiar shop. You would probably think about the following things:

- how to keep your directions simple
- how to state the directions clearly
- getting feedback so you'll know your directions are understood.

Simplicity, clarity, and understandability will help ensure that you successfully transfer your knowledge. Here are some other tips for giving directions.

1. **Begin by communicating the goal.** If you are giving directions to a store, you might say, "I'm going to give you the easiest route even though it is actually a little farther." If you are helping someone find a book in the library, clarify the correct title of the book so you can give accurate directions.
2. **Know where you are starting.** If the person asking for directions is new to your city, you can't rely on familiar places or landmarks. If the person looking for a book is uncertain about the title, you may have to start with the author and go from there.
3. **Break the directions into steps**, offering small quantities of information, bite-sized steps that people can digest and remember.
4. **Check for understanding.** Look at the person to see if he or she is following what you are saying. Ask if your directions are making sense. If they aren't, go back and explain a step again.
5. **Don't talk down to your listener.** You're probably helping someone do something that you can do with ease, but never lose patience. Treat every listener with respect.

Making Requests

Everyone needs help once in a while. When making a request, remember to think about the purpose, the situation, and the audience. Here's how.

Giving homework directions to a young child requires great clarity.

1. **Figure out who is able to help you.**
2. **Decide how assertive you should be.** A request can take the form of a question (Will you help me?), a statement (I need your help), or a command (Help me!). In emergencies you may need to give commands, but most people respond better to requests that take the form of questions or statements.
3. **Be specific.** "Could I see your notes from Tuesday's history class? I was home sick and didn't get the timeline Ms. Kirk handed out." If you don't provide the extra information, you might have to make another request and impose on the person's time again.
4. **Determine the best situation.** Choose a time and place most comfortable and convenient for the person to whom you are making the request.
5. **Communicate a time frame.** "There's a test this Friday, so I'll need to have your notes from Tuesday by Thursday afternoon, if possible."

Participating in Conversations

Conversation is the spontaneous, informal spoken exchange of messages. Many people believe it is an art—and that some people are simply better conversational artists than others. But conversation also involves skills that you can learn to develop your art. Think about the following characteristics of conversation.

1. **Conversation is oral.** That is, conversation takes place out loud with two or more people participating.
2. **Conversation is spontaneous.** Because it is oral, it is immediate and spontaneous. Although you monitor what you say, you don't plan it in advance. No one "scripts" a conversation.
3. **Conversation is informal.** Some conversations are more formal than others, but usually conversation follows few rules other than the rules of basic courtesy.
4. **Conversation involves taking turns.** Some speakers don't give their listeners a chance to speak. Some listeners want to speak before their turn, and others remain silent when it's their turn to speak. Taking turns keeps conversations flowing.

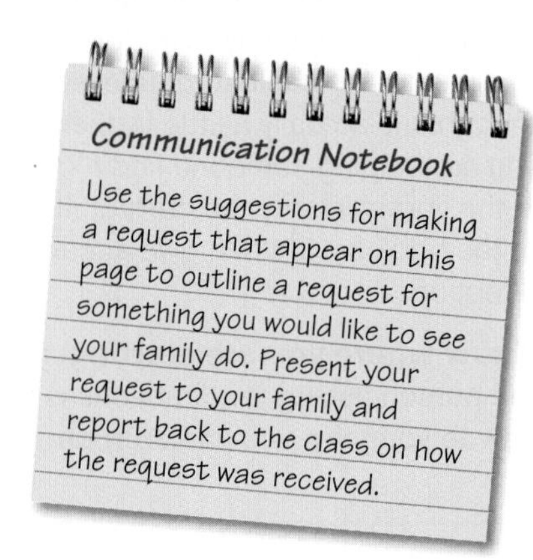

Conversation also requires good listening skills. If you listen well, you will be able to effectively apply the strategies you read about on pages 116–120 that are fundamental to all interpersonal communication.

1. **Relevance** Effective conversation maintains a relevance or logic of its own. A thread runs through it, tying together the ideas shared by the participants. Listening helps a good conversationalist move gracefully from one topic to another.

2. **Tact** Conversations are sometimes about difficult and demanding topics. Good conversationalists try to make others feel comfortable about speaking and sharing their ideas. A good conversationalist tries to minimize embarrassment.

3. **Courtesy** Good conversationalists are courteous. They don't interrupt. They're patient when a topic becomes less interesting to them. They make eye contact with listeners and other speakers. They use language that others will understand, and they refrain from using words or expressions that embarrass or offend.

4. **Sincerity** Good conversationalists are genuinely interested in listening and speaking to others. They listen in a way that makes the speaker feel important. They speak in a way that makes the message seem important. They show their involvement in the conversation with appropriate nonverbal behavior, such as leaning forward, making eye contact, and nodding in agreement as they listen.

What nonverbal message is this listener conveying?

KEY POINT

Use decision-making strategies and good listening skills to participate appropriately in conversations for a variety of purposes, including making introductions, apologies, and requests and giving directions.

TechConnect *Technology creates some communication problems while solving others.*

Telephone Conversations

TechConnect Like all other communication, phone conversations are affected by your relationship with the other person, the situation, and the purpose of the call. But phone calls have special challenges. Since you can't see the person on the other end, you can't interpret body language. Given the potential distractions, you are also likely to give the call less than your full attention. Call-waiting and the ability to put people on hold can also add to the disruption. You can, however, follow a few basic guidelines to get past these challenges.

- **Speak clearly.** When leaving a voice message, slowly and clearly state your name, reason for calling, and number. Your outgoing voicemail message should also be clear and brief.
- **Reduce interference.** Turn off the radio, CD or DVD player, or TV. If you are talking to someone else when you get the call, ask the new caller if you can call back (and do so as quickly as you can). If you are waiting for an important call while talking to someone face-to-face, forewarn the person about the call.
- **Get the message.** When taking a call for someone else, say, "I'm sorry, he (or she) is not available. May I take a message?" Write down the caller's name (ask for a spelling if you have any doubts), repeat the phone number, and ask for the best time to call back.
- **Respect the caller's time.** Unless your call is urgent, don't make calls before 9:00 A.M. or after 10:00 P.M. If you use call-waiting and put people on hold, don't keep them hanging on for longer than a few seconds.

Talking on a cell phone presents special communication challenges. For more on cell phones, see Chapter 25.

PROJECT PREP

With your **project partner**, act out two different versions of a phone call. In the first, demonstrate poorly handled phone use. In the second, set things right by demonstrating good phone use.

PREPARING THE PROJECT

Begin your project by looking back at the **Project Prep** activities in this chapter and using the directions below.

Make Connections

Discuss with your partner how your ideas about communication changed as you read pages 114–128. Share what you learned about your own communication decisions and any patterns that you were not aware of before. Discuss and summarize these important points:

- how the type of relationship between speakers affects communication
- how situation and purpose affect communication
- strategies for effective communication.

Focus

Briefly review the task: to role-play two different one-minute conversations showing different communication choices for different people. You each play yourself once and someone else once.

Plan

Settle on a topic you might discuss. Then choose two different conversation partners that you and your partner will role-play. Make sure you select people who will allow you to show differences in:

- communication purposes
- levels of usage
- body language
- assertiveness.

Develop

Both of your conversations will be on the same topic. Think about how the relationship with the other person and your purpose affect what you say and how you say it. Keep your "mystery" conversation partner a mystery by not using words that would give the identity away. For example, if your mystery person is your coach, don't say, "Well, coach, that was some game!" Your communication choices should be the only clues.

If possible, capture your practice on video so you can watch and learn from it.

Practice

Practice your presentation as often as needed until you both feel that you will have no trouble. Ask someone to time you to be sure that you do not go over one minute for each conversation. Test your presentation out on listeners to make sure you are giving enough clues in language choices for the mystery identity to be revealed.

Surefire Rehearsing

To get the best results from rehearsing:

- keep in mind who you and the other person are supposed to be
- speak up when something doesn't sound real for that person
- share your ideas about what the other person would say and about how it would be said.

PRESENTING THE PROJECT

Use the strategies that follow to help make your presentation as good as it can be.

People who give performances impersonating such figures as Mark Twain and Ben Franklin stay in character by learning as much as possible about the person and historical era.

You and your partner should now be ready to share the project with your classmates demonstrating how communication changes depending on who your partner is in a conversation. Go over the CAPS guidelines on page 112 and the rubric on page 131 to be sure that your role-played conversations meet the requirements.

Staying in Character

For the person playing herself or himself, staying in character isn't a problem. The problem is remembering who the other person is supposed to be and talking to that person as if she or he were someone else. For this reason, the person who is playing the part of someone different needs to get in character and stay in character. Here are some tips that can help.

- Before you begin the conversation, take a few seconds to think about the person you are portraying. Try to imagine yourself inside that person's skin.
- As you listen, use your body language to reflect the person you are representing. Ask yourself how the person you are portraying would sit or stand. When would he or she smile or raise an eyebrow?
- React–both in body language and in actual comments–the way your character would. Does what you're hearing please you or distress you? Express what your character would feel.

Practice facial expressions and body language your character might use.

EVALUATING THE PROJECT

Evaluate the presentations using the following rubric.

Score the demonstration on each point, with 4 being "outstanding" and 1 being "needs much improvement."

Come up with an overall score and write a brief paragraph that explains your score.

Relationships and Conversations	Levels of Usage	Creativity and Originality	Preparation and Use of Time
4 Presenters skillfully reflected the different nature of the interpersonal relationships in their conversations.	**4** Presenters' level of usage was different in each conversation and appropriate to the listener.	**4** Presenters found a creative and unique way to complete the project.	**4** The presentation flowed smoothly and stayed within the time limit.
3 Presenters' conversations reflected a fair amount of difference depending on the interpersonal relationship.	**3** Presenters' level of usage varied somewhat from conversation to conversation.	**3** Presenters showed creativity in the project.	**3** The presentation progressed fairly smoothly and stayed within the time limit.
2 Presenters' conversations reflected some difference depending on the interpersonal relationship.	**2** Presenters' level of usage varied a little from conversation to conversation.	**2** Presenters showed creativity in some parts of the project but others were less inspired.	**2** The presentation had a few awkward moments and went a bit over or noticeably under the time limit.
1 Presenters' conversations reflected very little difference.	**1** Presenters' level of usage did not vary at all.	**1** Presenters did not demonstrate creativity or originality.	**1** The presentation was awkward and went well over or under the time limit.

Communication *Past* and Present

Say Hey!

From Greetings Past . . .

Hey and *hi* have a lot in common. Both seem to have started out as expressions of surprise or attention-getting rather than greetings. Greetings relied more on gestures than words. According to a French etiquette book published in 1838, a gentleman of good breeding may greet people in the street in one of the following ways: with "an inclination of the head, a gesture with the hand, [or] the touching or doffing of the hat." The book further cautions that a gentleman should not speak to a lady until she indicates that she has noticed him by an inclination of her head. Stopping in the street to talk with friends is definitely frowned upon. "If you have anything to say to anyone in the street, especially a lady, however intimate you may be, do not stop the person, but turn round and walk in company; you can take leave at the end of the street."

Hi used as a greeting is chiefly a North American development, according to the *Oxford English Dictionary.* It first appeared in print in 1862 in a book called *Went to Kansas,* by Miriam D. Colt. It took a bit longer for *hey* to transition from attention-getter to greeting. Its transition began in the southern United States. A survey done in the 1960s by the *Dictionary of American Regional English* found that *hey* was used as a greeting primarily in Arkansas, Louisiana, Mississippi, Florida, Georgia, and the Carolinas. Since then, people throughout the country have taken to using *hey* as a friendly greeting.

. . . to Greetings Present

The idea of using *hey* as a greeting may have started in the 1950s with baseball great Willie Mays, who was nicknamed the "Say Hey Kid." According to one story, when Mays, who was from Alabama, joined the New York Giants in 1951, he didn't know the other players' names right away, so he greeted his fellow players by saying, "Hey, man. Say hey, man."

According to another account, the nickname was inspired by Mays' reluctance in his rookie year to talk to the press. When approached by a reporter, he would say, "Say what? Say who? Say where? Say hey!"

Two New York sportswriters both claimed credit for giving Mays the name of "Say Hey Kid." The nickname stuck and may have reinforced a new meaning to *hey*.

Hey in casual conversation is also often used now for effect or emphasis. You hear it especially in the expression *but hey*: "Michael ate all the pizza, but hey, I wasn't hungry anyway."

Chapter 6 Review

Using Vocabulary Words

With a partner, look at the list of vocabulary words at the beginning of the chapter. Use the words to play "Connect Two." Choose two words that you think belong together. Tell how you think the two words are connected.

State your reason this way: "I would connect _____ and _____ because ______."

EXAMPLE: *I would connect tact and courteous because they both have to do with being polite and treating someone with kindness.*

When you've "connected two," it's your partner's turn. Think about what you learned in this chapter and try to be creative about the words you connect and why you think they belong together. There are no wrong answers as long as you can come up with a good reason why two words belong together. Don't hesitate to use some words in several different pairings, and don't worry if some words don't seem to fit with any others.

Reviewing Key Ideas

1. List the three factors that influence communication choices.
2. Explain what being assertive in conversation means.
3. Explain the importance of body language when you speak.
4. Define paralanguage and explain, with examples, how it affects meaning.

Reflecting on Your Project

With your partner, write a paragraph explaining which parts of your project went especially well and which gave you the most trouble. Come up with three strategies for dealing with trouble spots.

Responding to the Essential Question

Use the headings in this chapter to help you write a brief chapter summary that answers the question, "What strategies enhance interpersonal communication?" Compare your summary with your partner's to see if you both covered the main points.

Extending Your Understanding

Everyday Life

1. Brainstorm a list of words and expressions that you and your friends commonly use when you are talking among yourselves. For each one, decide if you would use that word when talking to a four-year-old child. If you wouldn't use it in that situation, explain why you wouldn't.

2. Work with a partner to explore the effects of paralanguage. Read aloud from a phone book, using paralinguistic cues to suggest different feelings and emotions. Choose an emotion—anger, sadness, desperation, elation—and read the phone book in a way that expresses that emotion. See if your partner can guess correctly the emotion you are trying to express.

In the Media

3. Rent a DVD that depicts life in an earlier century. Possibilities include film adaptations of such Jane Austen novels as *Pride and Prejudice* and *Sense and Sensibility* or portions of the TV series *Upstairs, Downstairs* or *The Forsyte Saga.* Take notes about the differences you observe between interpersonal communications conducted in earlier eras and those of today.
4. Watch Oprah, or some other talk-show host, have a conversation with a guest on the show. Analyze it for specific examples of how the host is assertive, courteous, specific, and relevant and how body language supports or detracts from meaning. If possible, record the selection you are analyzing and share it with the class along with your analysis.
5. Use an Internet search engine to research conversation starters. Choose a few that appeal to you. Then try them out with your classmates. Working with a group of three friends, use one of the conversation starters on your list. See how successful it is in getting the conversation going and flowing from one topic to a related topic.

Research

6. Research books on the subject of the art of conversation. Make a list of the recommendations from several of those books that you find most helpful. Apply the CAPS model to your research and present your research to the class.
7. Research historical conversations, such as those that took place during peace talks. Note the participants, setting, purpose, and situation and decide whether or not the conversation went well. Apply the CAPS model to your research and present your research and evaluation to the class.

Interpreting Graphics

Using the map below, explain to a partner how to get from the library to 2nd Street.

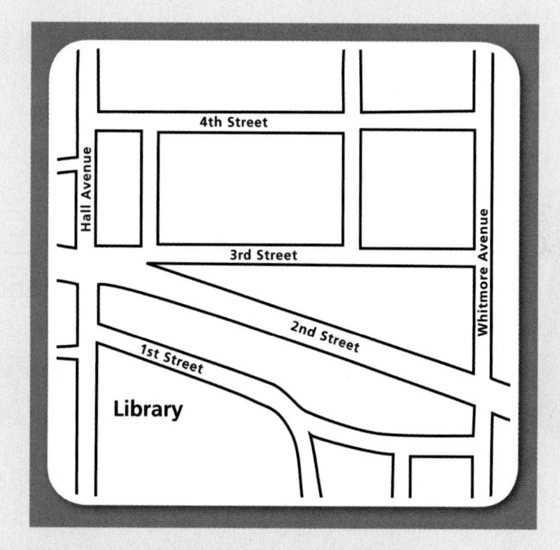

Additional Projects

1. **Group Project:** In a group of 4 or 5, decide on a person you all know who explains complex subjects well. Review the suggestions for giving directions in this chapter. Then show how the person you chose would go about giving directions from school to a destination of your choice.
2. **Individual Project:** With the help of a drama or literature teacher or your school librarian, find a play or novel with a lot of dialogue. Decide whether or not the dialogue is realistic, judging by the standards identified in this chapter.

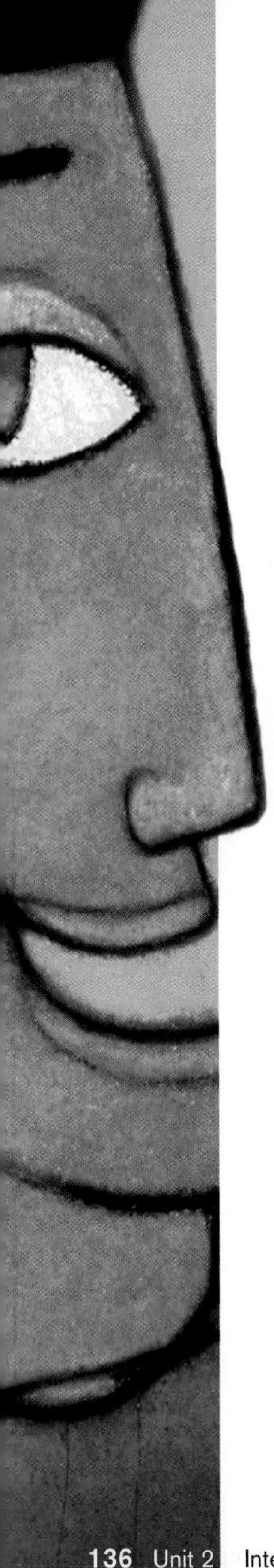

Interpersonal Listening

ESSENTIAL QUESTION

How can skillful listening enhance interpersonal relationships?

Chapter Project: Lend Me Your Ear

The nods, smiles, and caring words of your friends show how carefully they are listening when you talk, just as yours do for them. This project will help you practice three kinds of listening that enhance interpersonal relationships.

With a partner, you will plan and present a two-minute conversation that models critical, empathic, or reflective listening. One of you will act as the main speaker while the other will serve mainly as the listener. The speaker will talk about a made-up problem. The listener will model a specific type of listening. Classmates will then guess which type of interpersonal listening your scene models. They will evaluate how well you complete this activity. Refer to the following CAPS guidelines as you work.

The rubric on page 147 shows the traits on which your presentation will be evaluated.

CONCEPT	critical, empathic, and reflective listening enhance interpersonal relationships
AUDIENCE	a friend with a problem
PURPOSE	model one type of listening
SITUATION	conversation between friends as a demonstration

KEY VOCABULARY

rhetoric	attentive
ethos	supportive
logos	nonjudgmental
pathos	reflective listening

How many times during a school day does listening to classmates help you understand an assignment?

Speak Up!

When your friends laugh at your quips, they are probably using appreciative listening. But when did someone really listen to you? Make notes to yourself about the experience, including the situation, who was involved, and why you felt the other person really listened. Discuss your experience with a partner.

BACKGROUND FOR THE PROJECT

Pages 138–145 will provide the information you'll need to complete this project.

Critical Listening in Interpersonal Relationships

To remember and evaluate something you hear, you use critical listening (see Chapter 4). You use it in conversations when you listen closely before you offer an opinion. You use it with your dad as he gives you a list of chores or with a tutor who's offering tips on taking the SAT. You probably use it in every class every day. In addition, you often use it as part of appropriate audience etiquette. Critical listening helps you:

1. accurately recall information
2. successfully assess information.

KEY POINT

Critical listening requires a clear focus on the message so you can remember and evaluate it.

Strategies for Critical Listening

Suppose that a friend brings you a petition she wants you to sign. It proposes that the school place recycling bins in the classrooms. Currently the school has bins only in the cafeteria and gym. As she talks to you about the issue, you might prepare to use critical listening strategies to help you form an opinion. Four useful critical listening strategies are: 1) keeping track of the information, 2) predicting what comes next, 3) mapping the main ideas, and 4) taking notes.

Strategy 1: Keeping track. Each time a speaker makes a new point, keep the earlier points in mind. As the conversation moves along, you'll have a solid context for all the information you hear. And when you know what's been covered, you can identify issues you'd like the speaker to address. As your friend details the cost of implementing the new recycling program, you might think back to what she told you about the current cost of recycling.

Analyze the interpersonal listening skills of these two people. What is good? What could be improved?

Strategy 2: Predicting. Anticipate what the speaker will say next. Constructing meaning beyond the words the speaker has said actually keeps you engaged. It also helps you listen for holes in logic or missing details. You might predict that your friend will describe the cost of the bins and who will be responsible for buying them.

PROJECT PREP

Describe a favorite activity to your **project partner** while he or she uses critical listening strategy #2. With each new point you make, your partner will try to predict what you will say next. Then switch roles.

Strategy 3: Mapping. Pick out the speaker's main idea. Then identify and evaluate each of the supporting ideas. To decide whether your friend has made a persuasive case for the added recycling bins, evaluate the strength of the supporting ideas. Is her program realistic? Can the school afford it? Will students and staff recycle more items?

Strategy 4: Taking notes. Jotting a few notes while you listen will help you remember main ideas and supporting details so you can evaluate them. Don't try to write everything. Focus on capturing the main idea, major concepts, and important details using phrases, key terms, abbreviations, or your own form of "shorthand." Your notes might look like the following.

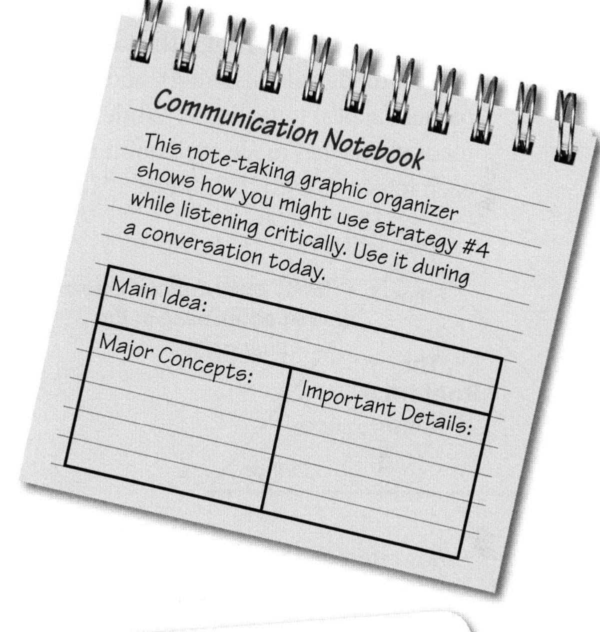

What to Listen For

Aristotle (384–322 B.C.) was a philosopher and scientist—and one of the most influential thinkers in Western civilization. He was also an expert in **rhetoric**, the art of using language effectively, especially in persuasive public speaking. He developed the Rhetorical Triangle to show how a speaker's ability to persuade is based on appeals to listeners in three areas: the **ethos** (appeal to a person's sense of right and wrong), the **logos** (appeal to logical reasoning), and the **pathos** (appeal to feelings). While Aristotle focused on what made each point distinct, each interacts with the others.

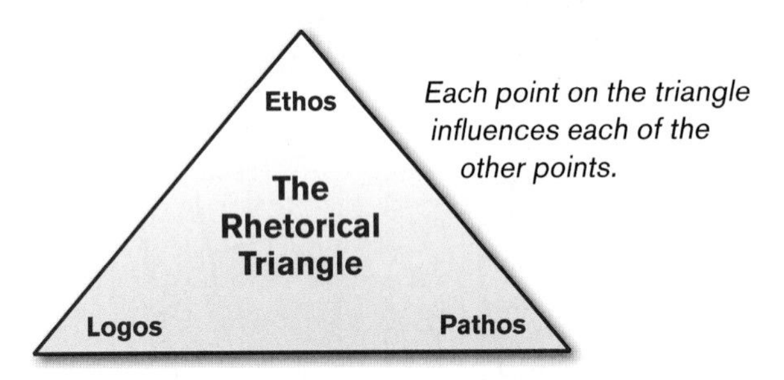

Ethos refers to the speaker's character and credibility—does he or she seem trustworthy and knowledgeable? In the case of your friend's appeal to you to sign her petition, you might ask yourself: *Has she always been upfront with me? Does she have the knowledge or experience to fully understand the school recycling policy? Do I trust what she is telling me?* If you answer yes to these questions, you will probably be inclined to sign the petition.

Logos is the logic of the speaker's message. Ask yourself if your friend has made valid points. *Is her information biased or is it balanced and accurate? Has she done enough research? Has she missed anything?* You might find that you need more information or that the plan as it is doesn't seem workable. You might believe that your friend has addressed all of the important issues and convinced you this is an important petition—in which case you lean toward signing the petition.

Pathos appeals to a listener's emotions and personal interests. Your friend appeals to your feelings by saying, "I know you will sign this petition because you feel strongly about the need for a clean environment." Appeals to emotions are especially important to consider critically, since strong feelings can sometimes get in the way of logical thinking. As a critical listener, decide whether the appeal to your emotions is *all* there is to the argument or if, instead, the argument has logical and ethical merits as well. You will read more about ethos, logos, and pathos and their role in persuasion in Chapter 21.

Summary Chart for Critical Listening
A critical listener keeps earlier points in mind.
A critical listener tries to predict what the speaker will say next.
A critical listener identifies and evaluates the speaker's thesis and supporting ideas.
A critical listener seeks evidence of the speaker's credibility.
A critical listener notices the speaker's use of personal appeals to emotions and needs.
A critical listener seeks the logic of the speaker's message.

Is This Job for Me?

Search: Investigative Journalist

Benjamin sits in a coffee shop, waiting to meet a local businesswoman. She is running for mayor, and Benjamin has set up an interview with her. Benjamin is an *investigative journalist* for a large city newspaper. His job is to keep the community informed. Through his research, he has uncovered information about a voting scandal this mayoral candidate may have been involved in ten years earlier. When two reliable sources told him the candidate was implicated in voting fraud in another city, Benjamin knew he had to investigate further. He must now confront the businesswoman about her past and the accusations. As a journalist, Benjamin has the responsibility to uncover and share information the public needs to form a complete, unbiased opinion about a subject.

The ability to listen closely to and understand others–and then translate all the information he receives into clear, readable text–is crucial to Benjamin's success as a journalist. Before joining his paper, Benjamin earned a master's degree in journalism. He worked his way up from reporting jobs with smaller papers to this job with a major city paper. Benjamin has acquired his occupational skills through education, on-the-job-training, the pursuit of his innate interests, and life experience.

Does a job as an investigative reporter interest you? Measure yourself with this personality inventory to find out if you think you have the required traits. Do you:

- ✓ Have excellent listening skills?
- ✓ Have excellent language skills?
- ✓ Enjoy unearthing information?
- ✓ Work well under pressure?
- ✓ Desire to get the facts straight?
- ✓ Enjoy pulling together information?
- ✓ Manage deadlines well?
- ✓ Know whom to trust?

You might work as an investigative journalist for the following organizations.

Employers	What You Would Do
Traditional print and online news outlets (newspapers, magazines, educational/professional journals, newsletters, Web sites, blogs, and ezines)	Gather information by conducting interviews and research to write in-depth news articles
Broadcast news organizations (radio or television stations; specific broadcasts such as daily news shows, newsmagazines, special presentations, and documentaries)	Gather information by conducting interviews and research to write and present in-depth news stories

Soledad O'Brien contributes to in-depth investigative reports on CNN.

Empathic Listening in Interpersonal Relationships

As you read in previous chapters, when you listen empathically, you put yourself in the speaker's shoes and make an effort to understand his or her feelings. The qualities needed for empathic listening overlap with the qualities needed for strong interpersonal relationships. For example, empathic listening requires that you be **attentive** to what the speaker is saying, to listen with your full concentration. It also assures that you will be **supportive,** providing positive and helpful feedback. Both of these qualities help a speaker feel comfortable confiding in you. You can help a friend sort through a dilemma when you listen closely and don't interrupt with your own commentary. When you really listen—even drawing attention away from yourself—you can focus on helping your friend.

If your friend confides in you about a problem—something serious like possibly failing English or something small like stubbing a toe—you might be tempted to share a similar experience of your own. Usually, though, someone hoping to work through a problem just wants to be heard and to reach his or her own conclusions using a **nonjudgmental** sounding board, someone who will listen without expressing his or her judgments. Those conclusions might include, "I need to find a way to improve my grade before it's too late," or "My toe really hurts, and I'm mad at myself for being barefoot." By listening empathically, you meet the speaker's needs. You may also need to use critical and precision listening strategies. Critical listening can help you evaluate the facts, and precision listening can help you zero in on the speaker's feelings about the facts.

KEY POINT

The empathic listener is attentive, supportive, and nonjudgmental. In conversation, the listener focuses on the speaker's issue and related feelings.

Imagine that your friend Lars has come to you with a serious problem. He has been fighting with his parents about college plans. He wants to apply to a culinary arts school in France, but his parents are insisting that he attend a traditional four-year state university instead. Your goal is to use empathic listening with Lars to support him as he plans his next steps.

If Lars sees himself this way, using empathic listening may help you begin to see him this way, too.

PROJECT PREP

Ask your **project partner**, "What are your plans after high school?" Prompt your partner with relevant questions. Listen to his or her full answers before responding, and resist the urge to insert stories about yourself. Then switch roles.

Strategies for Empathic Listening

As an empathic listener, you can help anyone who comes to you with a problem. Following are strategies that will help you listen empathically.

Strategy 1: Pay close attention. As you listen, identify crucial details, notice tone of voice, utilize context clues and nonverbal cues such as body language, and prepare to give feedback. You want to grasp the facts about Lars's situation, understand his feelings and level of distress, and help him decide what to do.

Strategy 2: Respect the speaker's feelings. You don't have to agree with what the speaker says—just understand and accept what he or she is going through. From previous discussions with Lars, you might think that he doesn't know enough about his dream school to have formed a strong opinion. Yet saying that won't help matters. You can see he's upset, and you should acknowledge that. Allow him to feel what he feels.

Strategy 3: Don't judge. Your role is to be supportive, not to offer unasked-for opinions. Remember, empathy involves putting yourself in someone else's position. Don't tell Lars what you think he should do. Try to help him figure things out based on his interests, needs, and insights.

Strategy 4: Stick to the role of listener—don't interrupt. You are not the focus. Lars needs to talk to someone who will listen, and he has chosen you. Show him that he's made a good choice by letting him say what's on his mind.

Strategy 5: Ask open-ended questions instead of yes/no questions. Open-ended questions encourage the speaker to keep talking and explore thoughts and feelings until he or she reaches a satisfactory conclusion. You might ask Lars, "What do you think about going to State U first and culinary school later?" or "What made you decide that going to culinary school was the right path for you?" or "What reasons did your parents give for going to a state school instead of the culinary school?"

What to Listen For

When using empathic listening, listen for the following:

- major ideas and important details
- verbal expression of feelings
- tone of voice.

Be sure to also look for any nonverbal cues that reveal feelings and attitudes or that add meaning to the words.

Summary Chart for Empathic Listening
An empathic listener serves as a sounding board, even when the speaker is talking about a difficult or emotional subject.
An empathic listener is nonjudgmental; he or she offers opinions only when asked.
An empathic listener respects others' feelings without necessarily agreeing.
An empathic listener respects the role of listener and the speaker's need to talk.
An empathic listener asks open-ended questions to help the speaker clarify thoughts.

Reflective Listening in Interpersonal Relationships

Reflective listening is an active listening process during which you mirror a speaker's thoughts and feelings back for further processing. It often goes along with empathic listening. Your focus stays on hearing and supporting the speaker. You do more listening than talking. And your feedback makes clear to the speaker that you've received the message.

Strategies for Reflective Listening

As Lars talks to you about his dreams and frustrations, you might use reflective listening strategies to help him think things through. The questions you ask and the responses you give Lars should focus on his needs. Use the strategies below.

Strategy 1: Keep the focus on the speaker. With Lars, you might maintain eye contact as he speaks, use body language to express interest (a nod, smile, or raised eyebrow), and base any spoken feedback on his words or feelings.

Strategy 2: Repeat or paraphrase. From time to time, check your understanding by summarizing a speaker's purpose and point of view with questions that repeat the speaker's words. You can also paraphrase, or state the same thing in your own words. To Lars you might repeat, "You want to go to culinary school, but your parents want you to go to the state university." You might paraphrase with "Your parents don't support your wish to go to culinary school."

Eye contact is a key element in reflective listening.

Strategy 3: Use feeling statements. These also help you acknowledge the speaker and check your understanding. Examples include, "Lars, it sounds like you feel . . ." and "You must want to . . . ."

Strategy 4: Clearly express empathy. You want the speaker to feel accepted and supported. You do not want the speaker to feel as though you are marking time, waiting to speak, or pretending to care. You might tell Lars, "This is a big problem. I can see why you're upset."

What to Listen For

To use your reflective listening strategies, listen for the following:

- important details to repeat or paraphrase
- specific expressions of emotion to acknowledge
- major issues to identify.

A reflective listener stays engaged with the speaker and pays close attention to both verbal and nonverbal information.

Summary Chart for Reflective Listening

A reflective listener keeps the focus on the speaker and reflects back information, thoughts, and feelings.
A reflective listener repeats, restates, or paraphrases from time to time to check for understanding and confirm that a message has been received.
A reflective listener uses feeling statements to acknowledge and clarify the speaker's emotions.
A reflective listener expresses empathy for the speaker's situation and feelings.

PROJECT PREP

Listen to your **project partner's** description of a favorite movie. Ask for details about why it's a favorite. Practice repeating and paraphrasing your partner's main points. Then switch roles.

PREPARING THE PROJECT

Begin your project by looking back at the **Project Prep** activities in this chapter and using the directions below.

Make Connections

Discuss with your partner how you connected what you read to what you already knew. Also talk about what you learned about the effect of strong listening skills on interpersonal relationships. Then summarize strategies for using critical, empathic, and reflective listening in interpersonal relationships.

Focus

Turn your attention now to the project, a two-minute conversation that models critical, empathic, or reflective listening in the context of an interpersonal relationship. Think about what you learned in your reading that you can apply to your project.

Plan

Share ideas with your partner for your conversation scene. Choose which type of listening you'd like to model and brainstorm scenarios that would illustrate the skills. Think of three specific strategies that apply to the type of listening you are modeling. These will be the clues for your classmates.

Develop

With your partner, create a draft of your conversation. Try it out by reading it out loud. Have you included plenty of clear examples of how the listening skills you are modeling can enhance interpersonal relationships? Look over the evaluation rubric on page 147 and check to make sure that you have addressed each point.

Practice

Do several practice runs of your conversation. If possible, do one or two in front of an audience of friends or family. Practice together one final time before your classroom presentation. Be sure that you don't go longer than two minutes.

Surefire Listening

While practicing with your partner, take turns giving each other tips for improving the performance. When it's your turn to listen to advice about your role in the scene, use the five strategies for empathic listening outlined on page 143. They will help you better receive, interpret, and implement your partner's suggestions.

PRESENTING THE PROJECT

Use the strategies that follow to help make your presentation as good as it can be.

You should now be ready to share your project: a two-minute conversation that models critical, empathic, or reflective listening. Go over the CAPS guidelines on page 136 and the rubric and visualization technique on page 147 as well as the technique on the next page to help you do your best to meet the project requirements.

Using Visualization

Take a few quiet moments before your presentation to visualize a successful performance. Close your eyes and run through your script in your head. Picture both you and your partner accomplishing everything you set out to do. Visualize your classmates staying interested and engaged.

Evaluate the presentations using the following rubric.

Score the demonstration on each point, with 4 being "outstanding" and 1 being "needs much improvement."

Come up with an overall score and write a brief paragraph that explains your score.

Understanding of Interpersonal Listening Skills	Demonstration of Interpersonal Listening Skills	Creativity and Originality	Preparation and Teamwork
4 Presenters demonstrated a thorough understanding of critical, empathic, or reflective listening.	**4** Presenters gave three or more clear and accurate clues to the kind of listening they were modeling.	**4** Presenters found a creative and unique way to present their conversation.	**4** The presentation flowed smoothly and the partners played off each other well.
3 Presenters demonstrated a good understanding of critical, empathic, or reflective listening.	**3** Presenters gave two clear and accurate clues to the kind of listening they were modeling.	**3** Presenters showed some creative and/ or unique ways to present their conversation.	**3** The presentation progressed fairly smoothly and the partners worked together well.
2 Presenters did not seem to understand some aspects of critical, empathic, or reflective listening.	**2** Presenters gave only one clue to the kind of listening they were modeling.	**2** Presenters showed little creativity or originality in the way they presented their conversation.	**2** The presentation had a few awkward moments and the presenters stumbled over each other at times.
1 Presenters misunderstood much about critical, empathic, and reflective listening.	**1** Presenters gave no clues and it was impossible to know which kind of listening they were modeling.	**1** There was no evidence of creativity or originality in the conversation.	**1** The presentation was not smoothly executed and the partners did not work together well.

Communication *Past* and Present

The Listening Revolution

From Therapy Sessions . . .

In the 1940s and 1950s, most therapists used a directive approach with patients. That is, they listened to a patient's problems and directed them to solutions. Solutions might include behavior modifications, lifestyle changes, or further professional help.

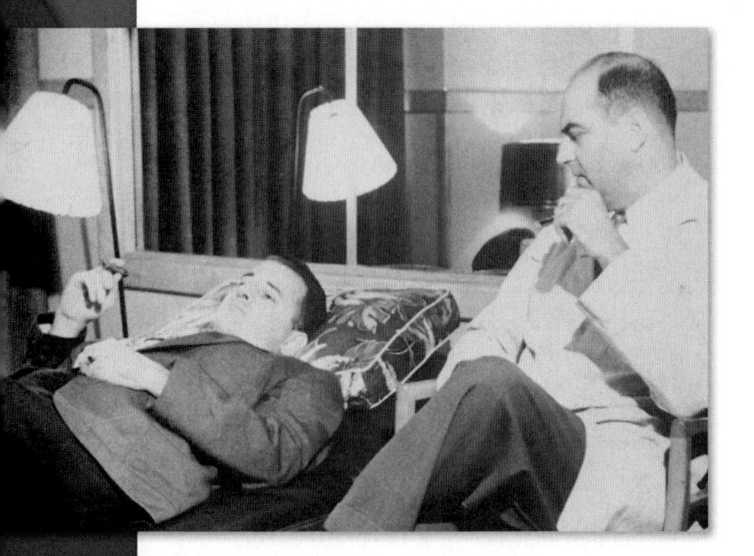

American psychologist Carl Rogers pioneered a nondirective type of treatment approach called Client-Centered Therapy. Rogers wanted to involve his patients in making decisions and changes. To start, he began referring to them as "clients" to signify a partnership between the therapist and the person seeking treatment. Rogers believed that most people already possess the ability to solve their own problems. But sometimes they need the help of an expert listener who guides them to express their needs and find answers.

Critical, empathic, and reflective listening are cornerstones of Client-Centered Therapy. Therapists know what to listen for and when to step in with nonjudgmental feedback that keeps the exchange focused on the client's needs. And, following Rogers, therapists using a nondirective approach try to create a comfortable, accepting environment.

A client-centered therapist:

- treats all clients with respect and compassion
- works to put the client at ease
- seeks to understand the client's perspective without passing judgment
- checks periodically for understanding
- allows the client to thoroughly express feelings and beliefs
- expresses empathy
- helps the client arrive at natural conclusions that result in solutions to problems.

. . . to Everyday Life

Although few therapists today practice strict Client-Centered Therapy, most use the reflective listening practice that Rogers promoted. Reflective listening has also become a routine part of many other interpersonal endeavors. For example, parents use it with their children to ease their way through conflicts. The military uses it to help combat veterans cope with stress. Nurses use it to understand how to help patients. Personal trainers use it to help their clients achieve their exercise goals. Sales representatives use it on business calls. Human resources staff use it to help mediate workplace conflicts.

Reflective listening, while originating in private exchanges, also works well in public areas. For example, reflective listening has become common in the workplace. Reflective listening guards against the all-too-common practice of "hearing what you want to hear." People have a tendency to form preconceptions—judgments based on a variety of impressions before actual evidence is considered. If they don't listen closely to customers or workers or others they do business with—and test their understanding through reflective feedback—they may end up hearing only those points that match their preconceptions. They may then make bad decisions that cost them money. If, instead, they use reflective listening, managers find they can make sound business decisions that lead to moneymaking products and efficiencies.

Many educators have applied Rogers' views in their classrooms, another more public environment. Student-centered education operates on the assumption that students are capable of developing all the skills they need for learning and that the teacher's role is best defined as "coach." Every teacher who supports the "learn by doing" approach pays tribute to the legacy of Carl Rogers.

Chapter 7 Review

Using Vocabulary Words

With a partner, look at the list of vocabulary words at the beginning of the chapter. Find two words that seem related. Tell how you think the two words in each pair are connected.

State your reason by writing a sentence this way: "I would connect _____ and _____ because ______."

EXAMPLE: *I would connect* supportive *and* nonjudgmental *because they are both part of listening empathically in order to help someone.*

Repeat the activity with two more pairs of words.

Reviewing Key Ideas

1. List the four critical listening strategies.
2. Under what conditions would *ethos, pathos,* or *logos* be most important?
3. What are two major goals of critical listening?
4. Describe your role as listener when you are using empathic listening.

Reflecting on Your Project

Discuss your presentation with your partner. How do you think it went? How does your partner think it went? Identify any areas you wish had gone better and discuss strategies for improvement.

Responding to the Essential Question

Use what you learned in this chapter to develop a one-minute speech in response to the question, "How can skillful listening enhance interpersonal relationships?" Present your speech in a small group and ask for feedback on how well you captured the topic.

Extending Your Understanding

Everyday Life

1. The next time you meet someone new, learn a little bit about the person by asking at least two open-ended questions.
2. Go to a quiet place somewhere by yourself. Listening as carefully as you can, make a list of all the sounds you hear. Underline any sounds you hadn't noticed before.
3. At your next checkup, paraphrase your dentist's instructions.
4. While talking with a salesperson who is giving you a sales pitch, listen for his or her appeals to ethos, pathos, and logos.
5. Ask an adult at home to tell you about his or her day. Use empathic listening strategies so the speaker feels understood and supported.

In the Media

6. Watch a celebrity interview on TV or the Web, or listen to one on the radio. List any interpersonal listening strategies from this chapter that the interviewer used.
7. Watch a rerun of *Frasier* or any series or movie that features a therapist. Note any parallels—or contrasts, especially for comic effect—you see between the

therapy sessions depicted and the Client-Centered Therapy approach developed by Carl Rogers.

Research

8. Research the history of investigative journalism, and identify examples of individuals and the impact their reporting has had on forming public opinion or political policies. Present samples of investigative articles to illustrate your thesis. Use a good mix of research sources. Examples might come from books, newspapers, magazines, Web resources, or interviews.
9. Research Aristotle's Rhetorical Triangle of ethos, pathos, and logos. Create a five-minute computer slide show that tracks the concept from its applications in Aristotle's time to clear examples of people using it today. Present the slide show in class, and field questions from classmates afterward.

Interpreting Graphics

Study the flowchart below. Write a brief paragraph explaining the decision described in the flowchart.

Additional Projects

1. **Partnered Project:** Present a scene from a short story or a novel that focuses on a conversation between two characters. Practice the dialogue, and present the scene to the class. Then, lead the class in a conversation analyzing the listening skills of each character in the scene.
2. **Individual Project:** Start an interpersonal listening journal. For three evenings in a row, record instances from the day, both from classes and outside of school, in which you successfully used the strategies covered in the chapter. Note, too, any memorable examples of people using the strategies with you. Write up a one-page summary of your experiences and read it in class. Be sure to include any new insights you've gained about good interpersonal listening skills.

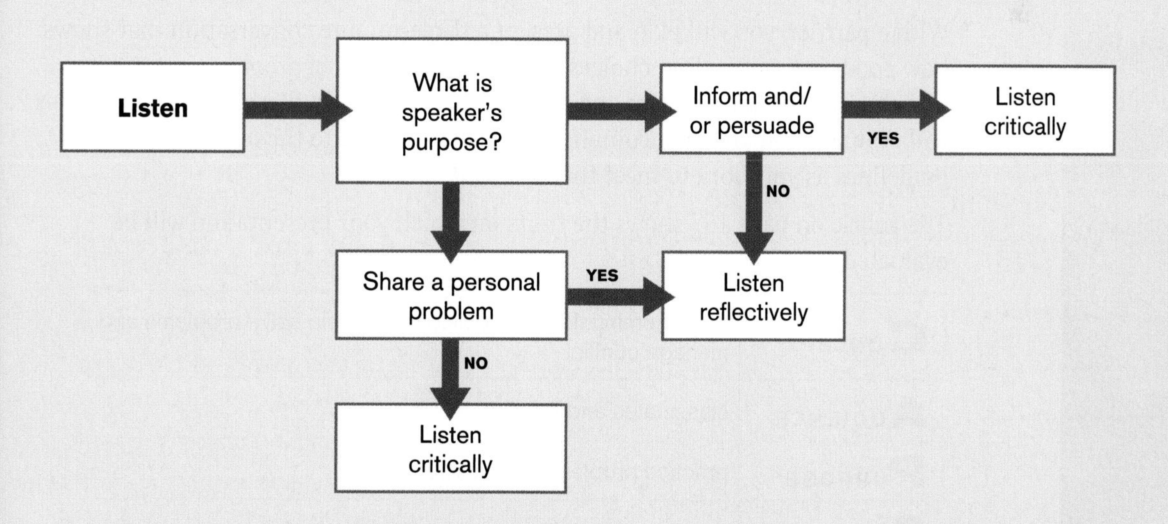

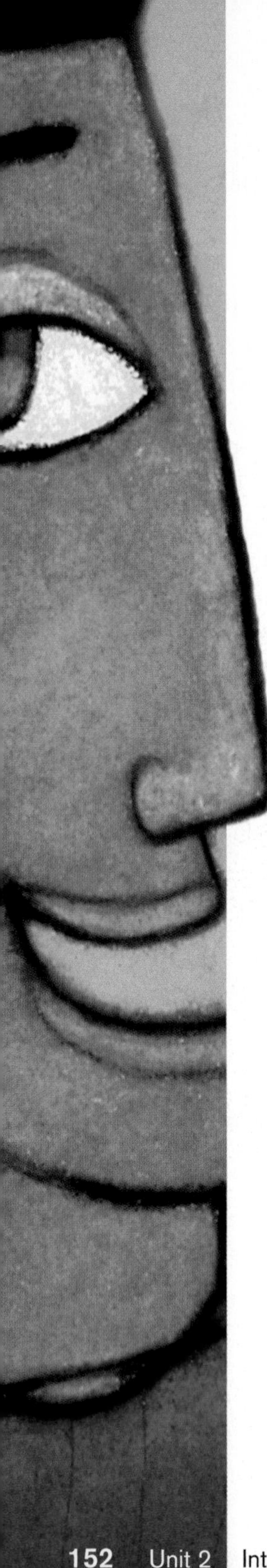

Solving Problems and Managing Conflict

ESSENTIAL QUESTION

What communication strategies are effective for solving problems and managing conflict?

Chapter Project: Work It Out

A conflict with a family member or friend can leave you feeling bad for days. This project will help you learn strategies to solve problems before they become serious conflicts.

With a partner, you will plan and present a three-minute conversation that shows how good communication choices increase the success of problem-solving. You will choose a simple problem and apply what you learn in this chapter. Classmates will evaluate how well you complete this activity. Refer to the following CAPS guidelines as you work to meet this challenge.

The rubric on page 167 shows the traits on which your presentation will be evaluated.

CONCEPT	good communication decisions can help solve problems and manage conflict
AUDIENCE	classmates and teacher
PURPOSE	practice problem-solving strategies
SITUATION	demonstration of interpersonal problem-solving

KEY VOCABULARY

criteria	leading question
strategic questioning	constructive criticism
helping question	defensive climate
rhetorical question	supportive climate
challenging question	"I" comments

What nonverbal cues suggest that these two people have a disagreement?

Speak Up!

Turn to a partner and make a debatable statement about some aspect of your school. You might say, for example, "Our basketball team is the best in the state." Your partner should disagree. Discuss your disagreement for about 30 seconds.

BACKGROUND FOR THE PROJECT

Pages 154–164 will provide the information you'll need to complete this project.

Problem-Solving

Almost every day—maybe even several times a day—people misunderstand and disagree. As you read in Chapter 5, individual differences in perception and self-concept explain why disagreement is so common. Good skills in problem-solving, including effective communication strategies, will help you smooth these rough spots in your everyday interpersonal communication.

How might these two decide which movie to see?

John Dewey, philosopher and educator, believed that problems actually have a benefit. "We only think when we are confronted with problems." In 1910 he created a now-famous problem-solving method. Each step in the process depends on the completion of the step before it. As you read through the sequence, imagine that you and a friend plan to see a movie on Saturday. You want to choose something you'll both like.

Step 1: Identify the "Felt Difficulty." In this step you and your friend decide whether a problem exists. You zero in on a difficulty. You want to see a movie you'll both like, so you'll have to make a choice. The choice itself can be a simple problem, but it becomes more complex if you each have different but strong preferences about what to see and what kind of experience you are looking for.

Step 2: Define the Problem. The next step is to define the problem precisely. As you and your friend pinpoint your problem, you might phrase the problem as a goal. For example, the goal might be to find a movie that suits (a) your wishes to see a lighthearted film and have a social experience, and (b) your friend's wishes to see an action film and avoid having to socialize.

Step 3: Propose Solutions. You and your friend need to generate a list of possible solutions to your problem. Both sides' views should be represented on the list. Proposed solutions might include the following:

A. See the Civil War drama at the campus cinema of a local college, where you're unlikely to run into anyone you know.

B. See the new gross-out comedy at the mall's multiplex, where several classmates said they'd be.

C. Rent a movie to watch at your friend's house with her family.

D. Rent a movie to watch at your house, where your younger sister is having several friends sleep over.

Step 4: Evaluate and Select a Solution. Before you can choose one solution (or combine several) to make a decision, you need to create **criteria**, or standards, for judging the possibilities. Then you can apply the criteria to make your selection. Following are sample criteria.

- Type of movie: it must be a film we think will be worth our time.
- Location: we must both feel comfortable there.
- Company: if we include more people, we must both enjoy seeing them.

Based on these criteria, you can eliminate solutions A and B. Since you both feel comfortable at your friend's house and like her family, solution C seems best.

Step 5: Act on the Solution. Until the two of you act on it, your solution will have no meaning. (No action would bring the same result as no decision.) You might discuss the timing, choose a movie, decide who will go to the rental store, and agree to the time.

PROJECT PREP

Recall a simple problem you've recently experienced. Jot down the steps you used to solve it, and compare them with the Dewey problem-solving method. Discuss the problem with your **project partner**.

How to Solve a Problem

Sequence	You Might Ask . . .
Step 1: Identify the felt difficulty.	What would happen if we didn't discuss this? Why is it bothering me?
Step 2: Define the problem.	What exactly do we disagree about? What is our goal in addressing all sides of the disagreement?
Step 3: Propose solutions.	Should we try this? Do you think this could work?
Step 4: Evaluate and select a solution.	Does this selection meet the goals we identified in Step 2?
Step 5: Act on the solution.	Let's do it!

Communication Strategies for Problem-Solving

When you work through a problem, you make choices about how you communicate at each stage in the process. Some choices can help you resolve the problem, while others might get in the way of resolution.

Effective strategies, good communication choices, and the willingness to find solutions can make many problems solvable.

Asking Questions

You ask questions all the time. It's easy. You think of something you want to know and then you ask: "What time is the game?" or "Where is Mr. Vanich's room?" Those questions have simple answers, and that's that. Some questions, however, are tougher, such as the ones you ask while working to resolve an interpersonal problem. In this case, asking questions often requires skill.

Imagine that Ric thinks he saw his friend Felicia cheating in class by passing a note during a test. He wants to understand what was going on and if she really cheated. Knowing how to ask the right questions will help Ric get at the truth. The following characteristics of good questions grow out of the strategies for effective communication decisions you read about on pages 116–120.

Characteristics of Good Problem-Solving Questions

1. **Assertiveness** Have confidence in the value of your question, and pose it clearly. Felicia may or may not be open to Ric's question. Ric may worry that he's out of line, but he's sure of what he saw and he cares enough to ask Felicia. He might start by simply asking Felicia to confirm what he saw.
2. **Tact** Always be diplomatic. Ric's question is difficult and may be uncomfortable for both of them. He should ask his question when nobody else is around to hear it.
3. **Courtesy** Mind your manners. Say "please" and "thank you," consider the other person's feelings, and choose a good time. If Felicia starts talking about another topic, Ric should courteously wait for a chance to raise his concern.
4. **Specificity** Your question should be clear enough that the person answering understands exactly what you need to know. Felicia needs to know exactly what Ric saw and that he is concerned about why she was passing a note during a test. So Ric's question should include a clarification of both points.
5. **Relevance** Your question should relate to the situation, the person you're asking, and/or a shared task. The person you are asking should be able to answer. For Ric's question, the relevance comes from what he saw Felicia do.
6. **Sincerity** Your question is sincere when you truly want to know the honest answer. Ric's question should assure Felicia that her answer is important to him.

Strategic Questioning People often use **strategic questioning**—questions asked with a purpose beyond getting information—to find solutions to problems. Strategic questioning is based on strategic listening: it leads both speaker and listener to explore new points of view. It often sparks the creativity that forges new strategies for problem-solving. See how many of the following strategic questions are familiar to you.

- **The helping question** A speaker sometimes leaves out important information that would help your understanding. You can ask a **helping question** to bring out that information.

  Example: "You said your note had nothing to do with the test. Why did you pass it during the test, then?" Maybe Felicia will explain that she had forgotten to give Sasha a message earlier and felt bad, so she hurriedly wrote it when she remembered and passed it along.

- **The rhetorical question** When you ask a question to which (a) there is no answer or (b) only one answer fits, you are asking a **rhetorical question**. You use a rhetorical question to make a point, not to uncover information.

  Example: "What do you think it looks like when someone passes a note during a test, Felicia?"

- **The challenging question** You use a **challenging question** to dispute someone else's position in order to make your own point. When you use this strategy, remain tactful and polite.

  Example: "I know you are feeling defensive, but have you thought about how your credibility may be affected if people think you cheat?"

Leading questions can be ruled inappropriate in court, but in interpersonal conflicts they can help someone see things in a new way.

- **The leading question** A **leading question** is one that directs or "leads" the listener to a desired answer. You might want that particular answer for any number of strategic reasons.

  Example: "So, you just wanted to be a good friend and pass someone else's note along?"

Answering Questions

Good answering skills complement good questioning skills. Some of the characteristics of good questions apply to good answers, too. Both can help you solve problems.

Characteristics of Good Answers to Problem-Solving Questions

1. **Tact** Respectfully respond to any question. Remember that asking a question can require some courage.
2. **Courtesy** You may wish to thank a person for asking a strategic question or a question that helps you make your own point.
3. **Specificity** Answer a question in a way that is useful. Specific answers help the questioner more than general answers.
4. **Relevance** Your answers should relate to the question. Provide complete and specific information–but don't give unnecessary information. The better you know your subject, the more specific and more relevant your answers will be.

As you answer questions during problem-solving discussions, you might want to keep the following suggestions in mind.

- **Listen carefully to the question.** Look directly at the speaker. Tell the speaker you think he or she has raised a good question if you believe it to be. Before answering, you might want to repeat the question in your own words.

  Example: "So, are you asking . . . ?"
- **Answer the question directly.** Make your answer brief and to the point. After responding, you may want to check to see if you have really answered the question.

  Example: "Does that answer your question?" or "Was that what you were asking?"
- **Postpone answering a question.** Try to answer questions when they are asked. When time limits or complexities make a quick answer inappropriate, offer to talk to the questioner when you have more time.
- **Never criticize the question.** On occasion you may get a question that you find completely silly and/or counterproductive. In this case, give the speaker a chance to regroup and rephrase by asking that the question be repeated. Never indicate to the speaker that you think it's a silly question. Do your best to answer it or ask for help from others.

What important step in answering a question is this person demonstrating?

PROJECT PREP

Refer to Ric's leading question on page 157. Write an answer for Ric as if you are Felicia. Incorporate two or more characteristics of good answers discussed above.

Constructive Criticism

Criticism can be a negative term, but it often refers to helpful or positive feedback. Helpful feedback is **constructive criticism.** You get it from classmates when they evaluate your project, from your golf coach when she corrects your stance, and from your boss when he suggests a better way to handle customers. Constructive criticism helps someone improve without being negative. Sometimes you give criticism; other times you receive it.

Giving Criticism To give criticism successfully, share your views in a supportive way. Follow these guidelines.

- **Know when to offer criticism.** Make sure that giving criticism is appropriate. For example, are you the right person to provide it? Is this an appropriate time for the listener to hear it? Is this the right place?
- **Be empathic.** Put yourself in the listener's shoes. Be understanding. How would you like to hear the criticism? Your empathy can help you offer supportive, constructive criticism.
- **Mix comments.** "Sandwich" a negative comment between two positive ones. The positive message will help the listener accept the more negative feedback.
- **Be descriptive.** Focus on the behavior, not the person. Instead of saying, "You are unfriendly on the phone," say, "Your phone voice sounds rushed and gruff." By describing the tone of voice, you avoid calling the person unfriendly, which might cause hurt feelings or defensiveness.
- **Offer suggestions for improvement.** When possible, phrase your critical feedback as a positive suggestion for improvement. Instead of, "You're a terrible singer," say, "I'm sure your singing would improve if you talked to a voice instructor."

Novelty headgear never fails to help soften the blow of nasty criticism.

What does the phrase "that's a real feather in your cap" usually mean?

Explain why the man's comments to the woman are not constructive criticism.

Receiving Criticism Few people enjoy hearing criticism. But with the right attitude, you can come to appreciate the help that lies behind it. Let others speak frankly to you without reacting negatively to them. Try to use the suggestions below.

- **Listen.** Even if you think the criticism is unfair, allow the other person to comment.
- **Ask questions.** Make sure you understand the criticism. Check your understanding by asking for more information. Specifics are important. For example, if you've been told to take a word-processing class, ask, "Which course do you think would be best for me?"

KEY POINT

Skillful questions and answers combined with appropriately given and received criticism can go a long way to solving problems.

- **Do a reality check.** You can always check suggestions for improvement with someone else. Maybe that person can help you understand the criticism. Or maybe he or she will have a different opinion.
- **Remember that *you* make the decision.** Unless a criticism comes to you from an authority figure (teacher, parent, boss), you usually can decide whether to accept the criticism or not. Remembering that you have the power of decision-making might help put criticism in perspective.
- **Don't confuse the criticism with how it is delivered.** Even if a critical message is expressed in a clumsy or unsupportive way, consider the content of the criticism. The feedback could be very helpful.

PROJECT PREP

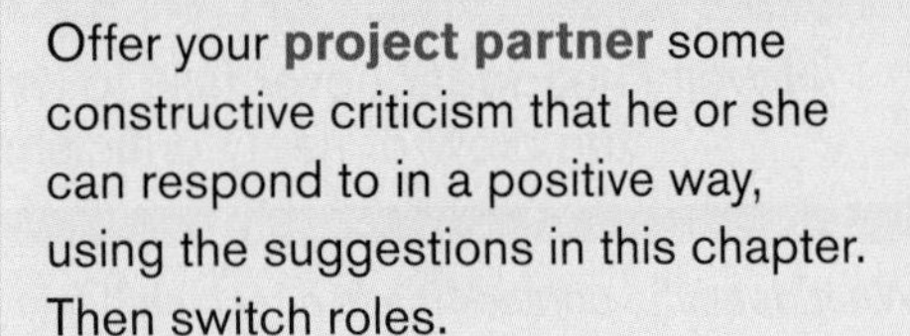

Offer your **project partner** some constructive criticism that he or she can respond to in a positive way, using the suggestions in this chapter. Then switch roles.

Search **Human Resources Manager**

Pat sits in the private office of Maria, the *human resources (HR) manager* of the large advertising firm where they work. Pat has planned a vacation trip, but his boss does not want him to take the time off when Pat has scheduled it. Pat feels this is unfair. As an HR manager, Maria tries to make sure both that employees understand the company's policies and that managers treat employees fairly. She needs excellent listening skills to help her mediate the dispute. She will meet with Pat and his boss to assess the problem, give advice about possible solutions, and facilitate further communication between the two.

Maria's first job out of college was as an HR assistant. Over time, she completed a master's degree in the field, and moved up the HR ladder until she became a manager.

Does a job in human resources interest you? Measure yourself against this personality inventory to determine if you have the qualities of a human resources manager. Are you:

- ✓ Discreet?
- ✓ Attentive?
- ✓ Articulate?
- ✓ Able to put people at ease?
- ✓ Able to analyze problems?
- ✓ Comfortable evaluating others?
- ✓ Calm under pressure?
- ✓ Good at multi-tasking?

You might work as a human resources manager in the following types of organizations.

Employers	What You Would Do
Corporations	Act as a liaison between managers and staff
Law firms	Supervise your own staff and help to create policies on hiring practices, strategic planning, employee benefits, safety programs, and employee relations
Government agencies	Provide information and guidance regarding workplace policies to all employees
Colleges and universities	Provide consulting services as needed to various clients
Independent consulting firms	

Managing Conflict

During interpersonal communication, conflict can arise even when there are no problems to solve. Consider this after-school exchange: Lucinda has been swamped lately. She is studying for midterms, practicing for a recital, and organizing a high school walkathon to benefit a homeless shelter. The pressure has affected her mood, so when Diego asks her for input on a party he's throwing, Lucinda cuts him off and says, "No way can I help with that. Handle it yourself." Her abrupt response affects Diego's mood too. He is hurt and annoyed with Lucinda.

Because of Lucinda's rash remarks, Diego is feeling hurt.

With just a few poorly chosen words, anyone can create a **defensive climate**. In a defensive climate, people hunker down to protect themselves and resist further attacks. Further communication becomes difficult as tensions rise. Creating a **supportive climate,** on the other hand, helps you establish and maintain friendly, productive relationships. A supportive climate will help pave the way for open, positive interactions, even during conflict.

People trying to communicate in a defensive climate often feel threatened, uncomfortable, suspicious, and unfairly judged.

Using Empathy in Positive Communications

In Chapter 4 you read that empathy is an important part of successful communication. Using it consistently, however, can be a challenge. Empathy requires that you temporarily stop thinking about yourself and think of others instead. Lucinda didn't stop to think about how Diego might feel about her negative comments. Putting herself in his place could have helped keep the communication positive.

For more insight into empathy, think about the word *understanding*. You can disagree with someone (or have a different attitude, as in Lucinda's case) and still understand that person's point of view, including the feelings behind it. Using empathy, Lucinda might have picked up on Diego's good cheer and excitement. A response that supported his perspective would have been, "I'm so sorry, Diego, I know the party is important to you, but I'm just too swamped to think about it right now."

Showing empathy is as important as feeling it. The suggestions below will help you show your understanding.

Showing Empathy	
Adopt nonverbal behaviors that show understanding.	Lean forward. Look at the speaker. Nod if you understand. Use silence. It gives the other person time to speak.
Reflect the message.	When appropriate, summarize or paraphrase what you understand. Allow the other person to clarify your understanding by commenting on your paraphrase.
Use think time.	Don't be so busy talking that you don't think about what you are going to say. Consider how the other person will interpret your comments.
Hope for the other person to be empathic–but don't expect it.	Understand when another person is too emotional to be empathic. Give the other person the chance to understand you. Ask if you are understood. Model understanding.
If you don't understand, say so.	Despite your best efforts, sometimes you don't really understand another person's feelings. You can let the person know that.

Using "I" Comments

Sometimes you can help establish a supportive climate using **"I" comments.** These are statements that begin with *I* and express how you feel. Use of *I* helps the speaker describe personal feelings rather than evaluate the other person.

Compare the comments below. Which set will bring out a more positive response from a project partner? Which is more likely to produce a defensive climate?

Comments	
I feel that we are losing sight of our project goal.	You have lost sight of the project goal.
I think we might be better off researching the topic a bit more.	You need to research the topic more.
I would like to consider some alternative ideas.	The second idea is best. That's what we should be talking about.
I feel like my comments aren't really being taken into account.	You aren't listening to me at all.

Evaluating Interpersonal Communication

Have you ever said something you wish you hadn't? Perhaps you've blurted out one friend's secret to another. Or maybe you said something cruel that you really didn't mean. The bad news is that you can't take any of it back. But you *can* work toward improving your future communication by taking a second look at past interactions. Some simple reflection on both successful and not-so-successful communication will help you evaluate what works and what doesn't.

The Basis for Evaluation

In some circumstances, including school, your communication will be evaluated formally. Formal evaluations include critiques, grades, and feedback forms. Far more often, though, you will perform your own informal evaluations of your communication. These help you decide what to improve and what strengths to continue to develop. You can evaluate your communication, and that of your classmates, on the bases shown in the chart below.

PROJECT PREP

Review the chart. With your **project partner,** write a sentence or two telling which basis you find most useful in evaluating your own interpersonal communication.

Basis for Evaluation	Key Question	Use
Results-based	Does the communication accomplish its goal?	This is the "bottom line" evaluation. You reflect on whether the communication transaction achieved the sender's purpose.
Artistic-based	Does the communicator effectively select and use the elements of communication?	This evaluation helps communicators grow. Your teachers use it to point out ways you can improve. When you tell someone to speak more forcefully or to improve eye contact, you are using "artistic" criticism. Be sure your comments are understood to be your opinions, and tie your comment to results. For example: "In my opinion, making better eye contact with your audience will improve your presentation, and you'll probably get a better response."
Content-based	Does the communicator say things that are appropriate to the purpose?	This type of evaluation ignores artistic elements and focuses only on the verbal message. Some communicators need this focused help in constructing meaningful and appropriate information.
Ethics-based	Is the communicator being honest and trustworthy?	This touches on the character of the communicator. It examines the truthfulness or honesty of a message. A key question is, "Does the communicator believe what he or she is saying?" Keep in mind that there is room for honest differences.

PREPARING THE PROJECT

Begin your project by looking back at the **Project Prep** activities in this chapter and using the directions below.

Make Connections

With your partner, summarize these important points:

- the five steps to problem-solving
- how to use strategic questioning
- how to give and receive constructive criticism
- ways to maintain a supportive climate in communication.

Discuss any new information that you found particularly helpful in this chapter. Try to come up with one or two sentences that express your clearest understanding of how interpersonal communication affects problem-solving and conflict management based on your reading of pages 154–164.

Focus

Turn your attention now to the project, a three-minute conversation with a partner that employs problem-solving skills. Decide on a problem. Then reread the five-step problem-solving approach on pages 154–155.

Plan

Spend time with your partner sharing ideas about your problem-solving conversation. Then outline a few scenes. Together, choose the best scene for your presentation.

Develop

With your partner, add details to your conversation outline. The more open-ended and less scripted, the better. In the course of your conversation clearly show how to apply the problem-solving model: identifying the problem, proposing and evaluating solutions, and then indicating how to implement the solution. Check that you have addressed the key points in the evaluation rubric on page 167.

Surefire Outlining

A simple working outline for your presentation should include an attention-grabbing introduction that tells the audience your problem. Your outline should then indicate main points and sub-points that show your steps in solving the problem. The conclusion should specify how you implemented the solution.

Practice

Run through your conversation a few times, but don't memorize it. Make the conflict clear and be as natural in your interchange as possible. Practice one final time before your classroom presentation. Keep it close to three minutes.

What constructive criticism could you give these two people?

PRESENTING THE PROJECT

Use the strategies that follow to help make your presentation as good as it can be.

You and your partner should now be ready to share the project: demonstrating problem-solving and effective communication decisions.

Go over the CAPS guidelines on page 152 and the rubric on page 167 to be sure that your project meets requirements.

Building Self-Confidence

When you walk toward the front of the class to deliver your presentation, you carry more than your notes with you. You also carry your self-confidence—or your lack of it—and it shows in how you walk and look. If your confidence is high, you are likely to deliver your presentation effectively. Your success will reinforce your self-concept: "Yes, I *am* a good presenter." If your confidence is low, you may sound tentative. That experience, too, will reinforce your self-concept: "You see, I am *not* a good presenter."

To boost your confidence as a speaker, ask a friend to let you know if your comments fit the situation.

Fortunately, you can build self-confidence so that you do not need to be caught in a negative cycle if your confidence is low. The following strategies can help.

1. Change the way you think about making a presentation. Instead of viewing it as a performance, think of it as another communication experience. You have a chance to communicate something that matters to you with people you know. If you don't get stage fright talking with your family, you can learn not to get it when talking to a class.
2. Identify the fears that shake your confidence about the presentation. Are you afraid someone will laugh at you? Plan your strategy to respond, just in case they do. "If people laugh, I will ________." Maybe you will join the laughter and make a lighthearted comment. Maybe you will just keep moving. Having a strategy to deal with your fears will increase your confidence.
3. Don't expect perfection–it's impossible to reach. Instead, identify a few areas in which you want to feel you have done your very best. Maybe for the current presentation, you want to avoid looking at your notes as much as you have in the past. Work on that as you practice. Even if other parts of the presentation fall short, congratulate yourself if you looked at your notes less and met that goal.
4. And speaking of practice–be as completely prepared as you can be. Practice until there are no spots at which you feel your confidence tumble.

EVALUATING THE PROJECT

Evaluate the presentations using the following rubric.

Score the demonstration on each point, with 4 being "outstanding" and 1 being "needs much improvement."

Come up with an overall score and write a brief paragraph that explains your score.

Understanding and Conveying the Steps in Problem-Solving	Creativity and Originality	Preparation	Presentation and Use of Time
4 Presenters understood and covered all of the problem-solving steps.	**4** Presenters were very creative and completely original in their presentation.	**4** The presenters were very well-prepared.	**4** The presenters appeared confident and stayed within the time limit.
3 Presenters understood and covered most of the problem-solving steps.	**3** Presenters were somewhat creative and fairly original in their presentation.	**3** The presenters were adequately prepared.	**3** The presenters appeared to use strategies for handling confidence issues and stayed within the time limit.
2 Presenters covered a few of the problem-solving steps with some understanding.	**2** Presenters showed little creativity and originality in the presentation.	**2** The presenters were fairly well-prepared.	**2** The presenters occasionally did not handle confidence issues well, but they stayed within the time limit.
1 Presenters seemed not to understand the steps and did not cover them well.	**1** Presenters did not demonstrate creativity or originality.	**1** The presenters seemed unprepared.	**1** The presenters seemed to let confidence issues get in their way, and they were either over or inappropriately under the time limit.

Communication *Past* and Present

Problem-Solving

From Lao-tzu . . .

Humans have been solving problems for their entire existence. Early humans had to solve problems of how to find food and shelter, how to live together in groups, and how to stay safe in the wild. As social structures and distinct cultures developed, problem-solving methods reflected the beliefs and outlooks of the culture. However, despite many differences, problem-solving methods used through the ages and across cultures have common elements. Following are a few examples of problem-solving stories and approaches from the past.

The following story is from the Taoist tradition. Taoism is an ancient philosophy written down by **Lao-tzu** in the 6th century B.C.

Lao-tzu writing calligraphy

A man who was very good at math needed a new pair of shoes. Before going to the market, he drew detailed diagrams of his foot to get the size exactly right. When he got to the market, though, he realized he'd forgotten his diagrams at home. So he went the long way back home to get them, and by the time he returned, the shoemaker had already packed up all his shoes and was heading home. The shoemaker scolded the man, asking why he didn't just try on the shoes at the market. The man realized his mistake in thinking there was only one way to solve his problem and that his diagrams would be more accurate than his real feet.

A contemporary of Lao-tzu was approaching problem-solving from a different "angle." **Euclid**, a Greek mathematician, is known as the Father of Geometry for his book, *The Elements*, in which he accurately explains physical space. Earlier mathematicians in China and India had also made significant geometric discoveries, especially about triangles. Euclid's book, however, became a standard for solving problems through the method of presenting definitions and assumptions that appear to be obvious and then using them as the basis for proving new ideas that are not at all obvious. This method of problem-solving has been applied in many other areas, including science and philosophy.

Fifteenth century Italian artist, inventor, mathematician, architect, and philosopher **Leonardo da Vinci** revered the accomplishments of Euclid and all of classical Greece. He recorded his thought processes as well as sketches and diagrams in 13,000 pages of notebooks he kept during his life. Because of his soaring accomplishments, many people have studied these pages to learn da Vinci's method of creative thinking. They have found that an unending curiosity and a commitment to testing knowledge—and learning from mistakes—are cornerstones of da Vinci's ability to solve problems far ahead of other thinkers, sometimes by centuries.

. . . to Toyota

John Dewey's 1910 approach to problem-solving (see pages 154–155) was one of many in the 20th century. Other key approaches include the following.

Math Help: The Poyla Method
In 1945 **George Poyla**, called the "Father of Mathematical Problem-Solving," published a book titled *How to Solve It*. In that book he describes a four-step process of solving mathematical problems: 1) understand the problem, 2) make a plan (the hardest step, he feels, since it requires drawing on past knowledge, on pattern recognition, and sometimes on "good luck"), 3) carry out the plan (being sure to check each stage of the process to avoid errors), and 4) look back and reconsider completed solutions.

Dig Through the Mess: Osborn/Parnes Creative Problem-Solving Method
This six-step approach was developed in the 1950s with an emphasis on drawing out people's creativity. The six steps are: 1) mess-finding (become aware of a problem area), 2) fact-finding, 3) problem-finding (turn the general "mess" into a defined problem), 4) idea-finding, 5) solution-finding, and 6) acceptance-finding (making the solution work).

Wish Upon a Star: Disney's Creative Strategy **Walt Disney**, who experienced many business failures before achieving his remarkable success, saw problem-solvers as requiring three different stages. The first stage is the Dreamer—this is the thinker whose imagination is free to go to the "anything's possible" realm and bring back ideas. The second stage is the Critic, whose purpose is to analyze the ideas objectively. Finally, the Realist steps in and says, "Okay, what plan do we need to put in place for that idea to become a reality?"

Toyota Hybrid X Concept Car

Moving Forward: Toyota's A3 Report
This problem-solving tool takes its name from the code for the paper size it is written on (11"x17"). Innovative Toyota Motors developed it to address the root causes of problems, not just their surface-level appearance. The A3 process includes detailed steps within the Plan-Do-Check-Act (PDCA) model developed in the 1930s. The PDCA draws on the scientific method developed by **Francis Bacon** in the 1600s. Bacon's system was to hypothesize (plan), experiment (do), and evaluate (check). The act stage was implied.

Chapter 8 Review

Using Vocabulary Words

For each term listed below, make a box and divide it into four sections. In the top left section, write the word. In the top right section, write the word's definition. In the bottom left section, give an example of what the word means to you. In the bottom right section write a word that you feel is the opposite of that word.

Word	Definition
Example	Opposite

1. challenging question
2. constructive criticism
3. criteria
4. defensive climate
5. helping question
6. "I" comments
7. leading question
8. rhetorical question
9. strategic questioning
10. supportive climate

Reviewing Key Ideas

1. What are five steps in problem-solving?
2. What is strategic questioning?
3. Describe how you might create a supportive climate as opposed to a defensive climate.
4. Give an example of a challenging question.

Reflecting on Your Project

Discuss your presentation with your partner. How do you think it went? How does your partner think it went? Were you able to be spontaneous? Use a problem-solving model to address any issues.

Responding to the Essential Question

Use what you learned in this chapter to write a personal example of a communication strategy that was effective for solving a problem or managing a conflict.

Extending Your Understanding

Everyday Life

1. Make a point to ask one helping question, one rhetorical question, one challenging question, and one leading question today.
2. During dinner at home, answer a sibling's or parent's question courteously and directly.
3. Before offering a piece of constructive criticism to a friend, ask yourself,

"Is it appropriate for me to give the advice in the first place? Is this a good time to do it?"

In the Media

4. Watch an episode of a televised talent competition with a friend. Discuss an individual judge's use of criticism with one contestant. Discuss whether the criticism is constructive and how well the contestant received that criticism.
5. Watch a television interview. Note the host's use of empathy during the interaction.

Research

6. Research the career of school guidance counselor and give a brief presentation detailing how someone would use problem-solving and conflict-management skills in that job. Use a mix of research sources, including books, Web resources, and an interview with your school counselor.
7. Research John Dewey's problem-solving model. Create a brief speech detailing the steps involved, why he developed it, and how it has been used over the years. Present the speech in class and take questions from classmates afterward.

Interpreting Graphics

Dr. Kaoru Ishikawa was a pioneer in quality control and helped spread the now-famous "Quality Circles" that bring workers together in interpersonal groupings to address the challenges and solve the problems they collectively face. The graph below shows Ishikawa's changes to the four-step Plan-Do-Check-Act (PDCA) problem-solving method (see page 169). On a separate paper, explain Ishikawa's changes. Then create a PDCA graph showing how you could apply that method to an issue in your own life.

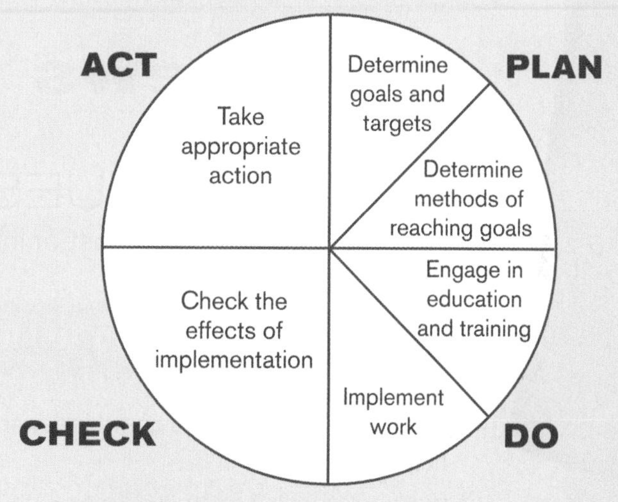

Additional Projects

1. **Partnered Project:** Elaborate on the situation between Lucinda and Diego and write a two-minute scene in which Lucinda apologizes. The only catch is that it must illustrate a concept covered in the chapter. Brainstorm ideas and write the scene together. Perform it in class and ask your audience to provide constructive criticism.
2. **Individual Project:** Write a one-page rhyming poem titled "Showing Empathy." Have fun with it. Read it to the class. Afterward, note any feedback your fellow students offer.

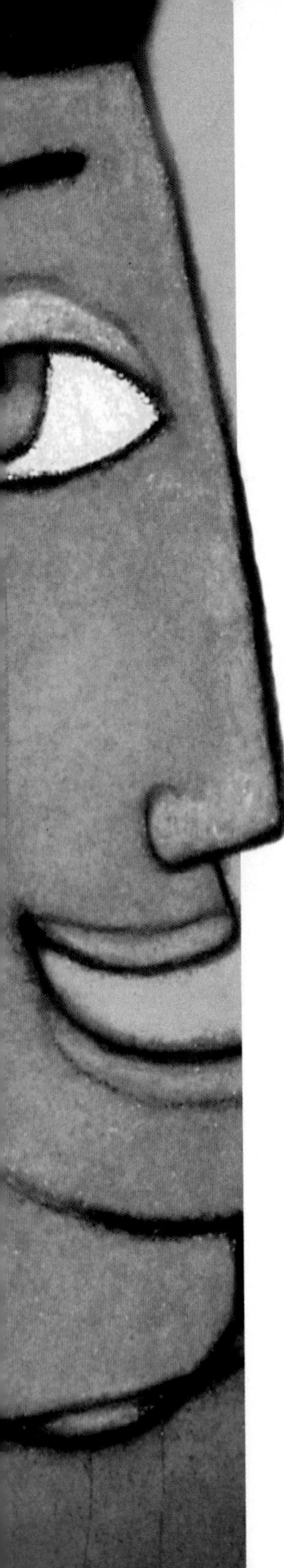

Interviews

ESSENTIAL QUESTION

How can you make the most of interviews?

Chapter Project: "So Tell Me About Yourself . . . "

How would you answer if an interviewer gave you that opening? This project will help you decide.

With a partner, you will plan and present a three-minute interview for a summer job. One of you will play the role of the applicant; the other will play the role of the employer. You will illustrate the steps in the interview process. Classmates will take notes and evaluate how well you complete this activity.

Refer to the following CAPS guidelines as you work to meet this challenge.

The rubric on page 189 shows the traits on which your presentation will be evaluated.

CONCEPT	the standard interview process includes five steps
AUDIENCE	a potential employer
PURPOSE	understand and apply the steps in the interview process
SITUATION	creative classroom demonstration of the interview process

KEY VOCABULARY

- interview
- résumé
- expectations
- conventions
- open question
- closed question
- follow-up question
- hypothetical question

How might the presence of a reporter change how a person responds in an interview?

Speak Up!

Ask a classmate, "What real-life benefits are there in learning how to interview and be interviewed?" Listen carefully to the answer and then share your own reply.

BACKGROUND FOR THE PROJECT

Pages 174–187 will provide the information you'll need to complete this project.

Interview Basics

An **interview** is a structured conversation designed to gather information. Typically, two people meet and one person takes the lead in asking questions. Strong interview skills can help you meet many challenges, from getting a job to being accepted into college.

Types of Interviews

You take part in more interviews than you might realize. Here are just a few everyday instances when interviewing skills might come in handy.

- As a sales clerk in a clothing store, you must ask questions about the return of an item.
- You witness a traffic accident, and a police officer interviews you to help determine what happened.
- You talk with your guidance counselor about colleges, trade schools, and jobs, and he asks you questions about your career goals.
- Before you write an article for the school paper, you interview sources to help shape the story.
- You win a medal at a track meet, and a reporter asks you questions about your victory.
- You visit a new doctor, and she asks you questions about your health history.

Purposes of Interviews

The chart below shows various purposes for interviews.

Interview Type	Purpose
Employment-Related Interviews	
1. Job Interview	To fill a position
2. Instructional Interview	To provide job details to an employee
3. Appraisal Interview	To give feedback about current job performance and set future performance goals
4. Exit Interview	To learn why an employee is leaving a job and ask for feedback about the job
Counseling Interviews	To provide personal or professional advice
Informational Interviews	To gather information (research, news gathering, investigations, medical treatment, problem-solving)
Academic Interviews	To determine admittance into a school or to award a scholarship

The Job or School Interview

Whether you're looking for an after-school job or a full-time position to start your career—or you're trying to gain admission into a school—chances are you will need to have an interview, a challenging and important communication situation. Each interview you have could be a turning point in your life. The person doing the hiring or selecting might speak with dozens, even hundreds, of people vying for the spot you want to fill. Your "job" is to stand out from the pack.

The Screening Process

Your objective is to move from a large pool of applicants, to a small number of candidates, to the winner. The inverted pyramid below illustrates that process.

Letters and Résumés Often, your first communication with an employer or admissions officer is a letter of application. A well-crafted letter helps you stand out in a positive way from all the other applicants. On the other hand, a poor one will probably mark the end of your communication. Consult a good English text or other resource to be sure that you use the formal requirements of a business letter for any letters you include with job or college applications.

Whether in writing, on the phone, or in person, make a good impression so you can move on to the next level in the interview process.

A **résumé,** or brief account of your education, qualifications, and work experience, can take the place of or supplement a job application. Find out what application materials your potential employer expects. A résumé offers an opportunity to show off your assets and set the stage for a successful interview. You can find excellent examples of résumés in the library or on the Internet. This brief example will help you see how important a résumé can be.

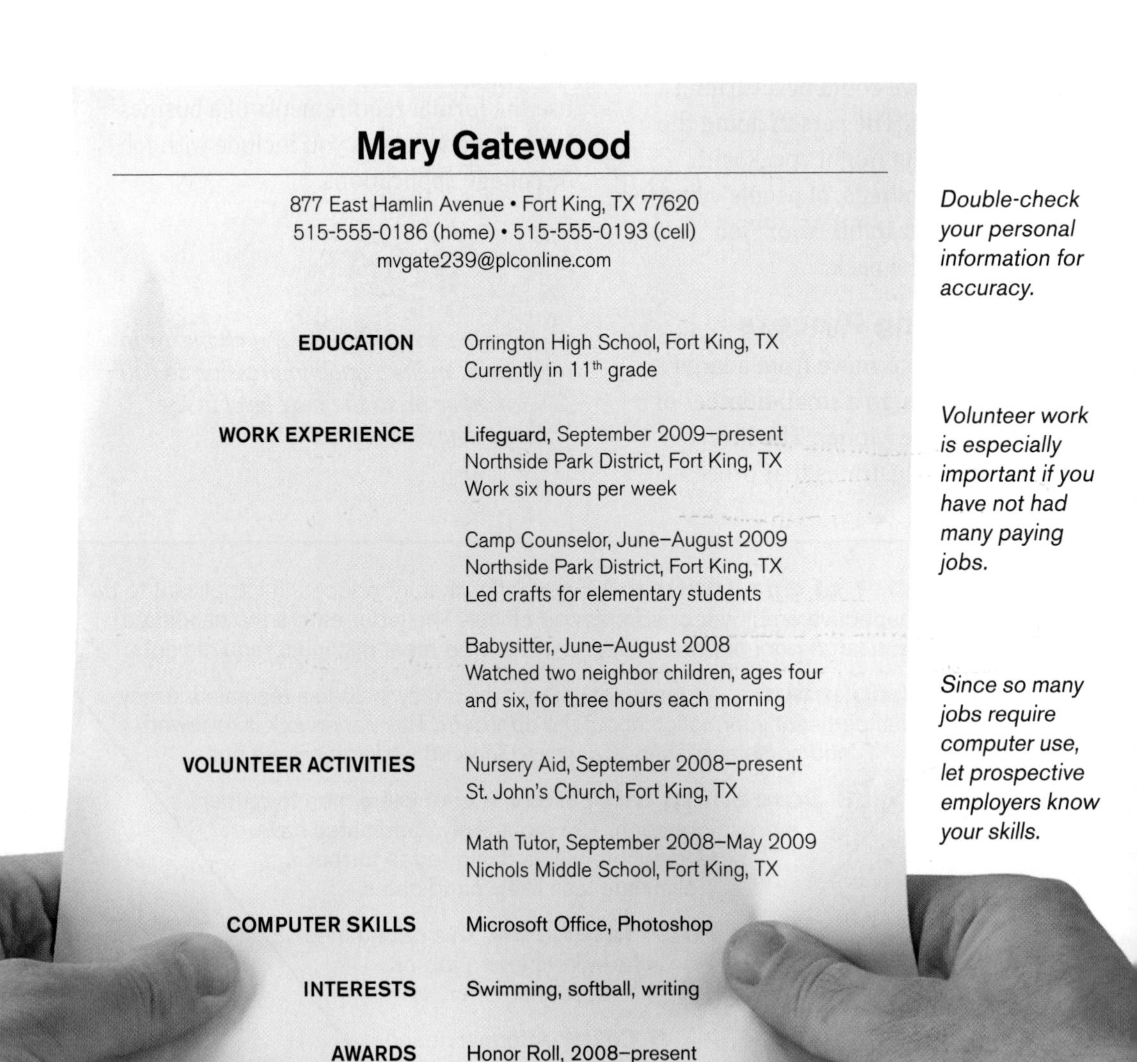
Mary Gatewood

877 East Hamlin Avenue • Fort King, TX 77620
515-555-0186 (home) • 515-555-0193 (cell)
mvgate239@plconline.com

EDUCATION	Orrington High School, Fort King, TX Currently in 11th grade
WORK EXPERIENCE	Lifeguard, September 2009–present Northside Park District, Fort King, TX Work six hours per week
	Camp Counselor, June–August 2009 Northside Park District, Fort King, TX Led crafts for elementary students
	Babysitter, June–August 2008 Watched two neighbor children, ages four and six, for three hours each morning
VOLUNTEER ACTIVITIES	Nursery Aid, September 2008–present St. John's Church, Fort King, TX
	Math Tutor, September 2008–May 2009 Nichols Middle School, Fort King, TX
COMPUTER SKILLS	Microsoft Office, Photoshop
INTERESTS	Swimming, softball, writing
AWARDS	Honor Roll, 2008–present
REFERENCES	Available on request

Double-check your personal information for accuracy.

Volunteer work is especially important if you have not had many paying jobs.

Since so many jobs require computer use, let prospective employers know your skills.

The Face-to-Face Interview

The goal of the letters, résumés, and applications is to get an interview. The interview might be over the phone, or in a group, or face-to-face. Being well-prepared with knowledge of what occurs in a basic face-to-face interview will help you shine in any of these.

Many interviewers consider the handshake a key to understanding character. A handshake that is too forceful seems aggressive, intimidating. A handshake that is too weak indicates lack of resolve or enthusiasm.

Expectations An interviewer's **expectations** involve a strong belief in what he or she expects to see and hear. Use empathy to put yourself in the interviewer's place. What will he or she expect to see and hear from an applicant? How can you exceed those expectations? Anticipating expectations is being sensitive to your audience.

Interviewers' expectations differ depending on the situation. For example, the expectations a store manager has for someone applying for a loading dock position would be different from those for someone applying for a customer service position. An Ivy League admissions officer might have one set of expectations for someone who wants to study acting and another for someone who wants to attend medical school. Learn as much as you can about the company or school and interviewer's expectations before the interview. During the interview, take every opportunity to highlight how you meet or exceed the job expectations.

Conventions Expectations that arise in the interview situation include social **conventions,** or accepted ways of behaving. Most interviewers will expect you to adhere to the following conventions:

- showing up on time
- introducing yourself
- shaking hands
- making "small talk," usually as a transition into or out of the formal interview
- making eye contact
- dressing appropriately
- being well-groomed.

PROJECT PREP

Imagine that you're preparing to interview for a job as a salesperson. With your **project partner**, list expectations and conventions you should be aware of to help you succeed in your interview. Practice the interview with your partner.

What Questions Will Interviewers Ask?

What do interviewers want to see in a candidate? They are almost always interested in your education and training, any work experience you have, your personal habits and character, and your personality type. Most employers develop a list of favorite interview questions they feel elicit these pieces of information.

Standard Questions on a Job Interview

Below are some typical questions an interviewer may ask and tips for handling your answers.

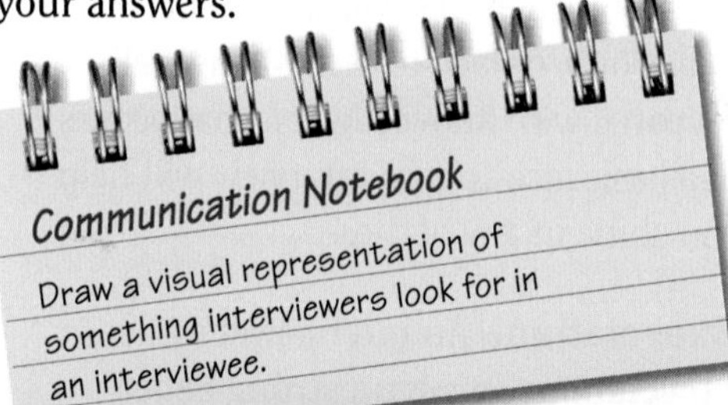

Possible Interview Question	How to Approach the Question
Why are you interested in this job?	Do some research on this job and this employer so you can give a confident, well-informed answer. Give reasons the job would benefit you and list the contributions you can make to the company.
What are your three most important strengths?	Try to tie your strengths to the expectations of the interviewer. If you're applying for a job on a construction crew, talk about the importance of teamwork and your ability to work with others. Be prepared with some ideas about how others see you. Often friends and family can give you ideas you hadn't thought of. Don't brag, but be positive about yourself.
What is your greatest weakness?	Answer honestly, but keep detail to a minimum unless you're asked for more. Don't harm your own interview by being too critical. Use positive phrasing when possible. Instead of saying, "I'm terrible on the computer," say, "I would like to improve my computer skills, and I'd be interested in any training the company offers in that area." This turns your weakness into a strength—your willingness to learn.
Tell me a little about yourself.	Focus your response on areas you'd like to talk about during the interview. Don't include irrelevant information. Your interviewer is probably asking this question to help put you at ease, but use the opportunity to convey truthful, positive messages about yourself.
Why did you leave your last job? (Why are you considering leaving your present job?)	The answer to this question will be of great interest to your interviewer. Whatever you say, be honest. The interviewer is likely to do a reference check. Don't be afraid to say that you are looking for better pay or career advancement if those are true.
Are there any questions you'd like to ask me?	This question is often used to wrap up an interview. Watch for clues that the interview is drawing to a close. Have several questions prepared that show your interest in the company and the job.

A Closer Look at College Interviews

The interview skills needed for college admissions or scholarships are similar to ones used in job-hunting. The tips below will help you focus your preparation and set yourself apart during the interview.

1. **Do your research.** Thoroughly study your chosen school's policies and any specific education programs you're interested in. Be aware of the school's educational philosophies and the campus culture. Your interviewer will be able to tell the difference between an applicant who is genuinely interested and one who's just "winging it."
2. **Anticipate the questions you might face.** Don't script your answers. However, do plan answers for questions such as these:
    - What do you hope to study?
    - What are your plans beyond college?
    - Why do you want to attend this school?
    - How did your extracurricular activities or jobs help you prepare for college?
    - What is your favorite subject and why?
    - What would you like to change about yourself?
    - What personal accomplishments make you feel most proud?
    - Who is a role model for you? Why?
    - What are you reading right now?
    - What do you think about [insert current event]?
    - Are your grades an accurate gauge of your skills and potential? Explain.
    - How do you spend your free time?
    - What advice do you wish you'd had when you started high school?
    - What will you contribute to the learning environment/college community?
3. **Be on time for your interview and stay engaged in the conversation.** You want to impress upon your interviewer that you are responsible, bright, and up to the challenge of succeeding in college. To help yourself remain calm, try some deep breathing exercises before you enter the building.

For both job and college interviews, anticipate the questions and be prepared to ask questions yourself.

4. **Ask questions yourself.** The interviewer will expect you to ask questions along the way. So, speak up with questions that show you are listening carefully. He or she will also end your meeting by inviting questions. Being prepared to ask a few intelligent questions will help you stand out. For example:
    - What qualities are you looking for in new students?
    - How can I find out about scholarships and internships I might be qualified for?
    - Does the college offer orientation and/or organized social activities for incoming freshmen?
    - How does the college rank in my area of study compared to similar schools?

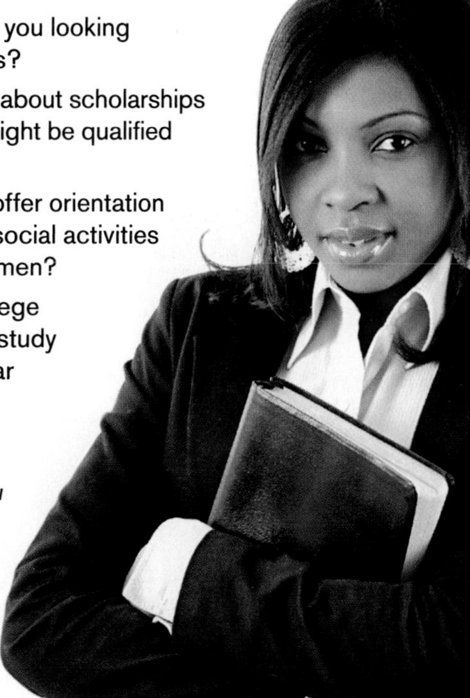

The better prepared you are for an interview, the more confidence you will show. How confident do you think this student is?

Communication in a DIVERSE WORLD

Affirmative Action at the University of Michigan

Many U.S. colleges and universities have affirmative action policies for minority groups who may otherwise have difficulty gaining admission because of circumstances outside their control. Under these policies, such qualities as race, ethnicity, gender, national origin, and social class may take on a special importance in the admissions process. Schools use affirmative action programs to admit more students, or a fair number of worthy candidates who might not have benefited from the same opportunities as those from more privileged backgrounds. Affirmative action policies also create a more diverse student population that realistically represents the world outside the university.

However, affirmative action policies are controversial. For example, the University of Michigan's affirmative action policies came under fire in the 1990s. Some students argued that although they met or exceeded the university's standards of academic excellence, they had been unfairly denied admission because they were not members of a minority group. Many argued that such programs were still unjust and discriminatory.

In 2003, two legal challenges to the school's policies went all the way to the Supreme Court. In *Grutter v. Bollinger,* the court ruled that race could be used as a factor in school admissions decisions.

Another case, *Gratz v. Bollinger*, looked at the "point system" in Michigan's undergraduate admissions policy. According to the point system, applicants with 100 points were guaranteed admission. If an applicant came from one of the identified minority groups, he or she received an automatic bonus of 20 points in favor of admission. That policy was judged to be unconstitutional.

In 2006, Michigan voters passed the Michigan Civil Rights Initiative, which made affirmative action illegal in the state of Michigan. When the law went into effect, many activists and organizations –including Jesse Jackson, Al Sharpton, the American Civil Liberties Union, and the Rainbow/PUSH Coalition–vowed to keep working to change it.

Students from the University of Michigan demonstrate in support of affirmative action.

Answering Questions in a Job Interview

Good answers to the questions that come up in interviews have three main characteristics. They are responsive, specific, and sincere.

Responsive Answers

A responsive answer addresses the question asked. Imagine that a potential employer has asked, "How would your co-workers describe you?" Then look at the sample answers below.

Responsive: "My co-workers would tell you three things. First, they would say I'm organized. They often comment that I know where everything is around the office. Second, they would say I know my job. People come to me when they need to know how to do something. Third, I think they'd say I have a good sense of humor. I enjoy working, and it shows."

Non-responsive: "My co-workers talk about me all the time. They think I work harder than everyone else, and it bothers them. Something's not right there, and everyone is worried about what the boss will do. That's why I want a new job."

Each question an interviewer asks serves a purpose. The responsive answer turns the question into a plus. The non-responsive answer doesn't help the interviewer gather information, and it also hurts your chances of making a good impression.

Specific Answers

Specific answers give the interviewer insight into your knowledge and experience. Something vague such as, "I have experience," tells the interviewer nothing. However, "I worked three summers at Widmer's Market stocking shelves and taking inventory," contains concrete content that the interviewer can use. It also sets you apart as someone who knows how to communicate well. Imagine that an interviewer has asked, "Why are you thinking about leaving your current job?" Then consider the examples below.

Specific: "I am happy with my current job. I have a good supervisor and some great friends. But I recently took some beginning business courses at the community college. I'd like to apply what I've learned to a new sales job at the computer store. I'd like to develop my skills and work my way into a floor manager's position. I'm interested in studying business when I go to college, and I'd eventually like to run my own store. I think this job offers me more chances for career development."

General: "I guess I'm looking for a job that helps me use my skills better. I'm getting bored where I am now. There's no challenge. I know I have more to offer."

A specific answer provides information the interviewer can use to make a decision. A general answer is vague. It does not give the interviewer the information needed to assess the applicant's skills or aspirations.

Sincere Answers

A sincere answer is one that you truly believe. If the interviewer thinks you don't really mean your answer, you won't make a good impression. Your nonverbal communication (gestures, facial expressions, and other visual clues) can make or break the perception of your sincerity.

Behaviors That Communicate Sincerity	Behaviors That Do Not Communicate Sincerity	Analysis of Behaviors
 Direct eye contact	Not looking at the interviewer	Direct eye contact is seen as evidence of honesty and sincerity. A person who avoids eye contact is thought to have something to hide.
 Animated, appropriate gestures	 Emotionless, flat physical delivery	Animated gestures indicate that you are emotionally involved in what you are saying–that you really care. Lack of movement indicates lack of interest, enthusiasm, or passion.
 Fluent, intelligent speech	 Halting, unsure speech	Halting speech sounds as though you don't believe what you are saying–or that you are making it up as you go along. When you speak fluently, you are in command of the situation.

Showing Yourself in the Best Light

Naturally, you want to show yourself in the best light during any interview. If you have an excellent academic record, play that up whether you're trying to get into a great school or trying to land a new job. Interviewers will want to know how you achieved your goals and mastered your studies. On the other hand, if your grades have been average but you've been successful outside of school, you can emphasize your responsibilities and accomplishments on the job. Interviewers will be interested in your work experience and in learning how you think it will benefit you as you meet the challenges of a new school or a new job.

The most important communication strategy for an interview is to be yourself. After all, you don't want to land a job or attend a school that doesn't really suit you. Observe interview conventions, meet expectations, develop strategies for answering and asking questions—and be yourself.

PROJECT PREP

Imagine that you're preparing to interview for college admission. With your **project partner**, choose a real school that interests you and find out as much about it as you can. Then list specific questions the interviewer may ask and prepare strong answers for them.

Conducting an Interview

Sometimes you will find yourself at the other end of an interview, conducting one rather than being interviewed. If you're a tutor, for example, you probably ask the students you work with what they know about the topic. If you are writing a research paper on the Vietnam War, you might interview relatives who took part in it or remember how it affected their lives. If you're the weekend manager at a video rental store, you probably interview job applicants. Like those who interview you, your purpose in conducting an interview is to gather information.

Do you think this person looks prepared for her interview?

Steps in an Interview

Interviews generally follow the same steps. The importance of each step in the process depends on the circumstances of the interview. For example, if you are interviewing an uncle who served in Vietnam, you would probably skip the formal step of introductions and handshakes. On the other hand, if you are a manager looking to hire someone, you would use that step to "break the ice" and begin to get to know one another.

A smile and a handshake help in the nesting process.

Nesting That first step in the interview process is called "nesting" because its purpose is to create a comfortable environment. Good eye contact, a firm handshake, and a smile go a long way to set a relaxed atmosphere. Following are some other helpful nesting tips.

- **Offer the person a seat.** You want the interviewee to feel comfortable, and he or she will appreciate being given a simple instruction. "Assigning" the chair yourself allows you to control the physical setup for the interview.
- **Offer to take the person's coat or bag**. Or, indicate where those items may be left. Holding personal items during an interview can be awkward.
- **Offer water or a soft drink.** People will often decline a drink, but the offer shows thoughtfulness. A glass of water may come in handy if the interviewee coughs or suddenly gets a dry mouth.

Previewing Sharing exactly what's going to happen in the interview will also put the interviewee at ease. First, sketch out the interview itself. You might say, "I'd like to do three things today—explain our hiring process, get to know more about your skills and experience, and give you a chance to ask me any questions you have." Then, give an overview of the hiring process. Tell the interviewee what the next step after the interview is and when the final hiring decision will be made.

Asking Questions The main body of the interview is the part during which you ask questions to gain information. Keep these tips in mind as you plan questions.

- **Start with an easy question.** "Tell me a little about yourself" is a reasonable way to start, but a more precise question can help keep the person–and the interview–focused. For example, say, "Let's begin by reviewing your experience. Tell me about your last job."
- **Stay on topic.** While the tone of an interview is conversational, a productive interview is much more structured than a free-flowing conversation. Resist urges to stray off the topic. If you find that you are doing most of the talking, and not gathering information, politely return to productive questioning.
- **Be encouraging.** Listen closely. Maintain eye contact. Nod to show that you understand. Simple statements such as "I see" and "good point" encourage the person to speak, thereby offering the information you need.

Inviting Questions Good interviewers reserve time for the interviewee to ask questions.

- **These questions add to your information.** If your interviewee asks about details you've already discussed, you know he or she missed something—or perhaps *you* did. If the interviewee asks about management training programs, you know something about his or her ambition. If he or she asks how soon an employee gets vacation time, you might learn something about the candidate's possible focus.

- **These questions help you sharpen your skills.** If your interviewees all seem to ask about the same topic, you might decide to cover it during your nesting, previewing, or questioning phases.
- **These questions provide closure.** An interviewee likes to leave an interview with as few lingering questions as possible.

Making the "Courtesy Exit" Just as nesting helps set the interview on a comfortable course, a courtesy exit helps it end well. A courtesy exit should include the following.

- **An expression of gratitude.** Always thank the person for taking the time to meet with you.
- **An allowance of time for the person to gather personal belongings.** Don't rush an interviewee out the door. Give the person time to retrieve and put on his or her coat, pick up forms, and leave the interview in a relaxed manner.
- **An acknowledgment of the next step.** If the decision will be made in a week, let the person know that. Assure the person that you have all the necessary contact information.

PROJECT PREP

With your **project partner,** review the information about the interview process and discuss how you would apply it to interviewing students for profiles in the school yearbook.

Match the interview process—nesting, previewing, asking questions, inviting questions, and making a "courtesy exit"—to your purpose, audience, and situation.

Productive Kinds of Questions

Different questions will bring out different kinds of answers. Productive interviewers use a mix of the following kinds of questions.

Open Question An **open question** allows your interviewee to answer in any number of ways. For example, a guidance counselor might ask Stephen the open

A coffee shop or even the school cafeteria can be the right place for an informal interview.

question: "Why do you think you are having trouble with math?" Stephen's response could go in many directions. He might define the nature of the problem as one of ability, interest, teaching and learning style, or time management. From the answer, the counselor could also learn something about how Stephen sees his responsibility as a learner. Open questions help the interviewer fulfill the interview's purpose and provide insight into the interviewee's personality and perceptions.

Closed Question A **closed question** is very directed and is limited to a specific piece of information or a simple "yes" or "no." An example is, "How many hours do you spend studying math each night?" This specific information can help the counselor profile Stephen's study habits.

Follow-Up Question A **follow-up question** often comes after a closed question. The counselor could follow up Stephen's answer to how many hours he studies math each night with this question: "How do you think you might make your math study time more efficient?" The open question focuses attention on the subject, and the follow-up gets to the heart of the information you're seeking.

Hypothetical Question A **hypothetical question** is a "what if" question. Answers to these may help you predict behavior. Example: "Imagine that you make the baseball team, Stephen. How would you keep up with your math homework?"

Justification Question You might present a belief and then ask an interviewee to justify or defend his or her opinion about it. The counselor might say, "Some students feel television distracts them from their homework. Do you agree?" After the interviewee agrees or disagrees, you then ask for an explanation.

To get the clearest possible answers, avoid the following problematic question types.

Avoiding Questioning Pitfalls	
Avoid asking leading questions	Keep questions neutral. Do not try to prompt an answer. If the counselor asks, "Don't you think you should study more than two hours a night?" Stephen will feel trapped into giving the answer the counselor seems to want or he may feel he has to disagree with the counselor. A more neutral question would be, "What changes to your study habits might help you do better in math?"
Avoid asking double-barreled questions	Don't use long, complicated two-in-one questions such as: "Were you ever more successful in math, and, if so, what did you do then that you can do now?" This question will lead to a long, complicated answer. A better solution would be to divide the question into two parts and ask appropriate probes in between.
Begin questions with Who, What, When, Where, Why, or How	This structure forces you to ask questions instead of making statements.

Making a Record

For any interview you conduct, keep a record of responses you can refer to as you review the information you gathered. Relying on your unaided memory is risky. You may want to use one or more of the following methods.

1. **Take notes.** Keeping notes as you go helps you track your questions and the interviewee's answers. There is no need to create a word-for-word transcript, but do try to cover the basics.
2. **Use a pre-printed note form.** The form can include spots for names, important information, and notes. It can also list your questions so you don't forget them.

Always let a person know before you begin recording an interview.

3. **Make an audio recording.** This produces a complete record of the interview, and it allows you to share the interview with others. If you plan to record an interview, ask the interviewee at the time you set up the appointment. Use a good microphone, and set it up in an unobtrusive spot.

A recorded interview has drawbacks, however. Your interviewee may feel distracted or inhibited by the recording device. In addition, recorded interviews take a long time to play back and listen to.

Tips for Conducting a Good Interview

A good interviewer is more than someone who just asks questions. The following tips will help you make the most of your interview opportunities.

Prepare Know the kind of information you want and prepare questions that will get you that information.

Listen Listen closely to the answers to your questions. Use the levels of listening discussed in Chapter 4, pages 68–71, particularly informational, critical, precision, and empathic listening. You will receive in a spoken response more information than you can probably ever get from a written answer.

Empathize Think about how the interviewee feels. Recall your own feelings of anxiety before or during an interview. Remember how it feels to be asked a difficult or personal question. Use this empathy as you interview others.

Be Thorough Prepare so that your interview runs smoothly and hits all the important points. If you interview several people, ask the same basic questions of everyone. That way you won't forget to ask anyone an important question and you will be able to make meaningful comparisons.

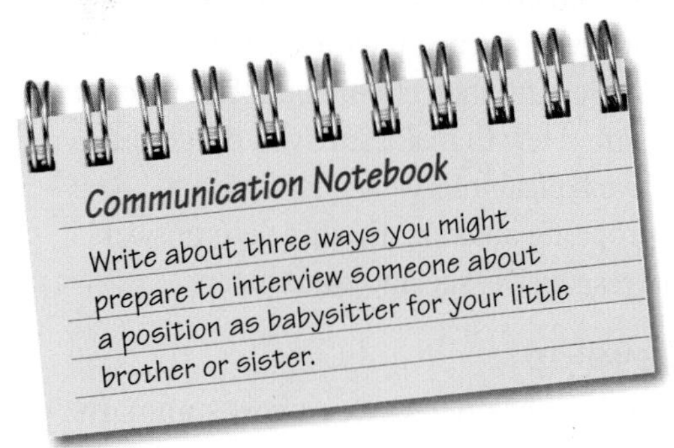

Begin your project by looking back at the **Project Prep** activities in this chapter and using the directions below.

Make Connections

Discuss with your project partner the important points raised in this chapter, such as:

- elements of the interview screening process
- the face-to-face interview
- how to conduct an interview
- productive questions.

Discuss with one another the importance of acquiring good interviewing skills.

Focus

Briefly review the project you and your project partner are working on: planning and presenting a three-minute summer job interview. Go over pages 174–187 to refresh your understanding of the interview process.

Plan

Brainstorm ideas for the interview and decide which one of you will be the interviewer. Come up with a few possible scenarios and then choose one. Talk through the interview to make sure you cover four or five typical interview questions and appropriate answers. Be sure your answers are responsive, specific, and sincere.

Develop

With your partner, write a short summary or outline of your interview. Be sure that you cover all five interviewing steps, from nesting through the courtesy exit. Look over the evaluation rubric on page 189 and be sure you have addressed each point.

Practice

Go through a few practice runs. Do not rehearse so much that your interview seems forced or stiff.

> **Surefire Time Management**
>
> Time your presentation as you practice it together. When you think you are ready, ask a family member or friend to signal when you have two minutes, one minute, half a minute, and then no time left. If your demonstration is running long, agree what needs to be cut and practice again without that part. Time the interview again. It should be at least two minutes long, but no longer than three minutes.

PRESENTING THE PROJECT

Use the strategy that follows to help make your presentation as good as it can be.

You and your partner should now be ready to present your depiction of a summer job interview. Go over the CAPS guidelines on page 172 and the rubric on page 189 to be sure that your project meets requirements.

Metacommunication: You and Your Audience

As you perform your job interview presentation, use metacommunication to adjust any aspect of your performance.

Although your partner is your main audience, as in a real interview situation, your classmates are also watching. Are they laughing when you expect them to? Do they gasp at the blunder one of you has intentionally committed? Or have you lost their attention or inadvertently confused them? Use the signals the class sends you to adjust your performance as needed.

Evaluate the presentations using the following rubric.

Score the demonstration on each point, with 4 being "outstanding" and 1 being "needs much improvement."

Come up with an overall score and write a brief paragraph that explains your score.

Understanding of the Interview Process	Demonstration of a Summer Job Interview	Creativity and Originality	Preparation and Use of Time
4 Presenters showed insight into the interview process.	**4** Presenters' demonstration helped illuminate a typical job interview.	**4** The presentation was attention-grabbing and unique, interesting, and fun.	**4** The presentation was well-prepared, flowed smoothly, and did not go significantly over or under the time limit.
3 Presenters understood the interview process.	**3** Presenters' demonstration was somewhat helpful in illuminating a typical job interview.	**3** The presentation was attention-grabbing, interesting, and fun, but not very original.	**3** The presentation was fairly well-prepared, progressed fairly smoothly, and and did not go significantly over or under the time limit.
2 Presenters did not seem to understand some elements of the interview process.	**2** Presenters' demonstration was minimally helpful in understanding a typical job interview.	**2** The presentation was fairly interesting and fun, but not original or attention-grabbing.	**2** The presentation was not well-prepared, had some awkward moments, and went slightly over or under the time limit.
1 Presenters misunderstood much of the interview process.	**1** Presenters' demonstration did not help in illuminating the typical job interview.	**1** The presentation was not original or attention-grabbing and only moderately fun and interesting.	**1** The presentation was ill-prepared, had many awkward moments, and went considerably over or under the time limit.

Communication *Past* and Present

Equal Opportunity

From Oppression . . .

Look at job ads in the newspaper or online, and you're bound to see these letters: *E.O.E.* They stand for *Equal Opportunity Employer.* An E.O.E. is a company that does not discriminate among applicants based on their race, gender, religion, country of origin, or age. Equal opportunity is a law in the United States, but it hasn't always been.

For example, throughout much of the 1900s, women had a very hard time finding work in fields traditionally dominated by men. They were often denied jobs simply because they were married. Female teachers were expected to quit their jobs if they did get married.

Ethnic and racial discrimination has been very widespread. In the early 1900s, job ads often ended with "NINA"—No Irish Need Apply. Even into the 1960s, a qualified African American or Hispanic might be turned away by a potential employer who had only to gesture to a sign reading "WHITES ONLY."

Laws that required segregation between blacks and whites in all types of economic and social activities, known as Jim Crow laws, were common in the South until the 1950s and 1960s.

President Lyndon B. Johnson signs the Civil Rights Act of 1964 as others look on.

The Civil Rights Act of 1964

An Act to enforce the constitutional right to vote, to confer jurisdiction upon the district courts of the United States to provide relief against discrimination in public accommodations, to authorize the Attorney General to institute suits to protect constitutional rights in public facilities and public education, to extend the Commission on Civil Rights, to prevent discrimination in federally assisted programs, to establish a Commission on Equal Employment Opportunity, and for other purposes.

. . . to Inclusion

June 19, 1964 marked the beginning of real change. That was the day the U.S. Senate passed the Civil Rights Act after a 534-hour debate. Two weeks later, the House of Representatives also passed the bill, and President Lyndon B. Johnson signed it into law. This was a landmark victory, the result of nearly two decades of organizing by people committed to the goal of equal opportunity for all.

Title VII of the Civil Rights Act prohibited employment discrimination based on race, sex, color, religion, and national origin. And it created the Economic Opportunity Act, President Johnson's social and economic initiatives that are also called the "Great Society." From this sprang the Office of Economic Opportunity (O.E.O.). The bipartisan O.E.O. dedicated itself to eliminating unlawful discriminatory employment practices.

Chapter 9 Review

Using Vocabulary Words

For each of the following terms, answer two questions:

- What is it?
- What is an example?

1. closed question
2. conventions
3. expectations
4. follow-up question
5. hypothetical question
6. interview
7. open question
8. résumé

Reviewing Key Ideas

1. Describe a screening interview.
2. With a partner, describe the screening process.
3. List the five-step interview process.
4. Write a paragraph detailing the types and purposes of productive interview questions.

Reflecting on Your Project

Write a paragraph about your experience working on this project. Think of one or two aspects of the presentation that could have gone better. Describe how you would improve them.

Responding to the Essential Question

Write a one-page "Pledge to Practice Good Interview Skills." Share your personal pledge with a partner and get his or her feedback on how well you covered the interview skills discussed in the chapter.

Extending Your Understanding

Everyday Life

1. Conduct a casual interview with a friend about the type of career he or she hopes to pursue. Practice strategic questioning techniques.
2. At home tonight, ask everyone in the house one open-ended question.
3. Engage in some metacommunication the next time someone is interviewing you in an informal situation. Check your own responsive, sincere, and specific answers. See how well you predict upcoming questions.
4. When visiting the sporting goods store, interview the sales clerk about the latest equipment you're interested in. Take notes on his or her responses and review them later to help you decide whether to buy.

In the Media

5. Scan the job ads in your local newspaper. Pick one that interests you and prepare several questions you'd like to ask about the job or the company.
6. Watch a celebrity interview on an entertainment news show and look for the steps in the interview process. How many did the interviewer use?

Research

7. Research historical examples of discriminatory hiring practices. Create a poster timeline that calls out several milestones in equal

opportunity employment in the United States from the early 20th century to today. Display the poster in your classroom.

8. Research the career of an attorney, focusing on the questioning techniques a trial lawyer uses with witnesses during depositions and in the courtroom. Present your findings and your sources in class.

Interpreting Graphics

The graph below was published by the University of Washington Office of Economic Opportunity and Affirmative Action. It shows the race or ethnicity of employees in three job categories: professional (administrators, Web designers, counselors, for example); classified (nurses, trades workers, security guards); and academic (professors, researchers, lecturers). It also shows the breakdown for all the employees put together. Look carefully at the graph and answer the following questions.

1. Which job category has the fewest non-white employees?
2. What is the second largest racial or ethnic group employed at the University of Washington?
3. In which job category do the largest number of Hispanics work?

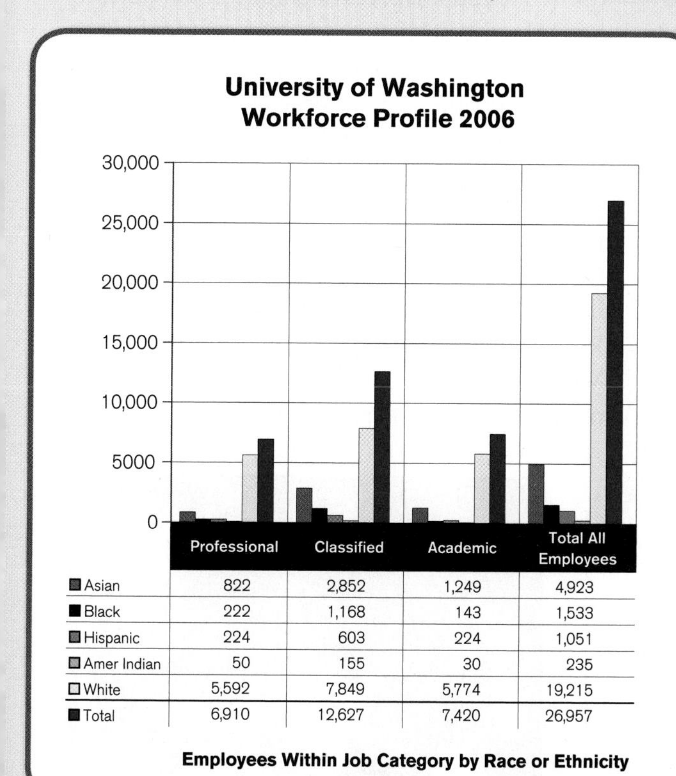

	Professional	Classified	Academic	Total All Employees
Asian	822	2,852	1,249	4,923
Black	222	1,168	143	1,533
Hispanic	224	603	224	1,051
Amer Indian	50	155	30	235
White	5,592	7,849	5,774	19,215
Total	6,910	12,627	7,420	26,957

Employees Within Job Category by Race or Ethnicity

Additional Projects

1. **Small-Group Project:** Select a job that you would like to interview for. With your group, brainstorm a list of questions you would like to ask your potential employer. Select the five best questions and discuss why you think they're winners.
2. **Individual Project:** Write a three-page profile of someone you look up to, whether it's a family member, another student, a teacher, a coach, or a community leader. To prepare, review the Conducting an Interview section starting on page 183. Then set up a time to hold a face-to-face interview. Share your finished profile in class and tell your classmates what worked well.

Unit Two

Culminating Activities

In this unit you have explored interpersonal communication: effective strategies for interpersonal communication, interpersonal listening, solving problems and managing conflict, and interviews. The activities on these pages will help you apply your understandings to situations in everyday life.

Workplace Workout

Josh had never had a job interview before. However, he decided not to give much thought to his upcoming screening interview to be a counselor at Camp Skybridge. After all, he had gone to camp for years. The interview wouldn't present a challenge.

The interview got off to an embarrassing start. Josh had forgotten the list of references he had been told to bring. Looking grave, Ms. Franco, the interviewer, asked Josh why he had applied for the job at Camp Skybridge. Josh shrugged his shoulders and sighed, "I really need a summer job, so I applied to a couple of camps." Ms. Franco then asked why he wanted to work in a camp instead of in a store or an office. Josh looked around the room. "I guess because I went to camp for like four years," he said. "Camp is fun."

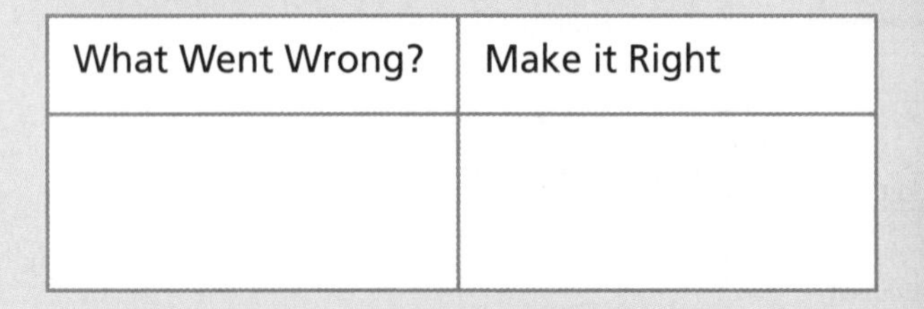

What Went Wrong?	Make it Right

At the end of the interview, Ms. Franco explained that she would call selected candidates to set up a final interview. She did not contact Josh.

What Went Wrong? With a partner, use what you have learned about interviews and effective strategies for interpersonal communication to analyze what went wrong in Josh's interview. Record notes in the left-hand column of a T-chart like the one here.

Make it Right With your partner, complete your T-chart to determine ways to improve Josh's performance in the interview. Then, in front of the class, re-enact the interview to show how Josh could have made a better impression on Ms. Franco. Ask your classmates to identify what made Josh's performance better.

GenderJourney

With a small group, create a scenario about a conflict between two friends. Ask an equal number of boys and girls how they would go about resolving the conflict. Then, in your group, discuss whether the responses point to any differences between the ways in which boys and girls resolve conflicts. With your group, research the topic of gender differences in conflict resolution. Present a brief oral report to the class comparing the group's conclusions with the research findings.

Media Master

Listen critically to the ads during a TV show. Write down the product names, and identify the types of appeals—to ethos, logos, and/or pathos—used in each ad. Then, for a product of your choice, create a storyboard for an ad. The show's viewers should be the target audience for the product and the ad. Use all three types of appeals in your ad.

OWN IT!

Think about the Deborah Tannen quotation at the beginning of Unit 2: "Each person's life is lived as a series of conversations." With a partner, discuss what you think this quotation means. Then, on your own, reflect on what you learned in Unit 2 and on your own real-world communication. Do you agree with the quotation? If so, why? If not, how would you complete the statement, "Each person's life is lived as a series of . . ."? Write a paragraph expressing your opinion. Discuss your opinion with your partner.

Group Communication

Never doubt that a small group of thoughtful, committed citizens can change the world; indeed, it's the only thing that ever has.

– Margaret Mead

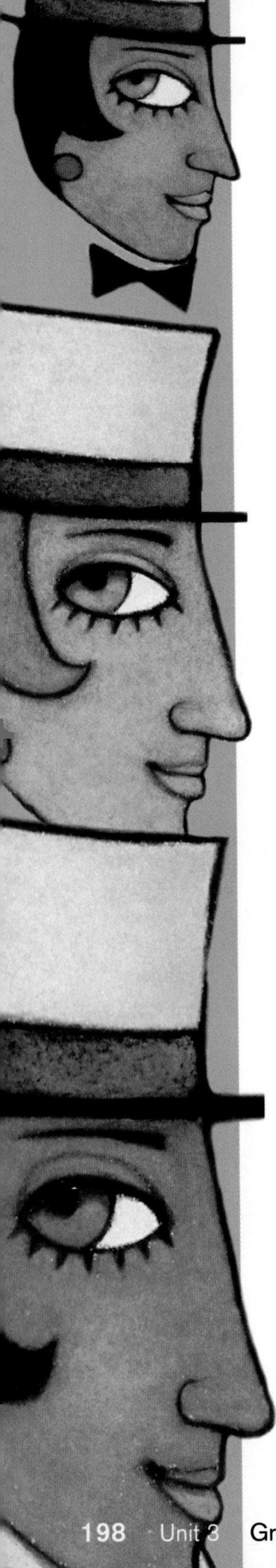

The Power of Groups

ESSENTIAL QUESTION

What purposes and functions of groups make them so important?

Chapter Project: Power to the Group!

Think of the many groups you are a part of: your family, your class, maybe school government, a club, or a team. You will continue to belong to groups your whole life. This project will help you understand how a group is greater than the sum of its individual parts.

You will form a group with several classmates. You might be a group of diplomats debating responses to global warming, a committee to plan an all-class party, or any other type of group. Together, you will determine the group's purpose, the type of group it is, and how it qualifies to be that type of group. Your group will present a three-minute description of all the aspects of your group. Refer to the following CAPS guidelines as you work to meet this challenge.

The rubric on page 209 shows the traits on which your presentation will be evaluated.

CONCEPT	the ability to function effectively in a group is a fundamental life skill
AUDIENCE	classmates, teacher, and other group members
PURPOSE	practice effective group communication
SITUATION	cooperative classroom discussion

KEY VOCABULARY

civic groups
political groups
group norms
formal group
informal group
social group
task group
public group
private group
committee
subcommittee

Several friends who go out for a snack make up one type of group.

Speak Up!

What groups do you interact with in a typical week? Write a quick list of as many as you can think of. Then, taking turns, share your list aloud with the class. Do you have similar ideas about the definition of the word *group*? Think about your list, and the lists of others, as you read this chapter.

BACKGROUND FOR THE PROJECT

Pages 200–207 will provide the information you'll need to complete this project.

Groups in a Democratic Society

Alexis de Tocqueville, a French political thinker, visited the United States when it was still very young. He observed American society closely and in 1835 published a book called *Democracy in America.* He believed Americans' drive to form groups, or associations, set them apart from others. He wrote, "Americans of all ages, all stations of life, and all types of disposition are forever forming associations." He went on to say that knowing how to form groups is what makes progress possible.

Purposes of Groups

Americans do have a long history of forming groups that fulfill a variety of *purposes*. For example, people come together in book groups, scout troops, congregations, bowling leagues, block parties, and many other local associations. These kinds of associations are called **civic groups**. Membership is voluntary and based on shared interests, concerns, and goals. When people feel connected to one another, they are more invested in their communities than if they remain isolated. People united in concern about their neighborhoods or social problems can bring much positive change.

Some groups are organized quickly to attack immediate, specific problems. The civil rights movement of the 1960s included powerful civic organizations, such as the Southern Christian Leadership Conference, led by Dr. Martin Luther King Jr. In addition, the movement included many lesser known, short-lived groups. These groups were organized by people who donated their energy and risked their lives to integrate the South's lunchrooms, movie theaters, and public transportation. In small groups, they carried out their mission of nonviolent protest. Eventually their hard work brought sweeping changes to the country.

In August 1963, a group of 200,000 people marched on Washington in support of jobs and civil rights. There they heard Martin Luther King Jr.'s "I Have a Dream" speech. The speech is reprinted in Chapter 18.

Americans also form **political groups**. One purpose of political groups is to create power. The Democratic and Republican parties represent one kind of political group. Members of these and other political parties use their strength in numbers to elect candidates to office. Another purpose of political groups is to accomplish the work of government. Groups that are an official part of government, such as the Supreme Court and Congress with all its committees, depend on vigorous communication among members to make and interpret laws.

Presidential candidates John McCain and Hillary Clinton

Groups and Individual Needs

While some groups serve democratic society, other types of groups provide other benefits to individuals. The chart below shows some of the needs that groups fulfill.

Individual Needs and Group Purposes	
Individual Needs	**Group Contribution to Meeting Individual Needs**
Belonging	A group can give individual group members a sense of being a part of something. Families often help us meet the need for belonging, as can clubs and other organizations. Many groups that advocate for social change give their members a sense of belonging to a larger movement for justice.
Accomplishment	Some groups are set up to allow individuals to achieve specific goals. A music group in which people share songs, play instruments, and learn from each other is an example. Members can feel both accomplishment and a sense of belonging in such a group.
Therapy	Sometimes individuals become members of a group to meet highly personal emotional needs. For example, many groups help people deal with grief or substance abuse problems.
Learning	A learning group satisfies individual needs for gaining new knowledge and skills. Book clubs give members an opportunity to discuss what they've read. Computer user groups help members understand and learn more about the newest technology.

People who study groups use a precise definition of them. They have determined that a group must meet one or more of the individual needs listed in the chart on page 201. In addition, a group must have each feature listed in the chart below.

Defining Features of a Group

A Group Is	Explanation
a number of people . . .	Groups are made up of three or more people.
who interact with each other . . .	Members of a group must be able to talk to each other directly, often face-to-face. With a large number of members, this isn't possible. Hence groups, or the subgroups within larger groups, usually don't get much larger than 20 people.
who have standards and values that determine an individual's behavior . . .	The members of a group must share some standards for behavior. If they don't, the group will likely dissolve, or members who do not follow the group's standards will leave.
who share common interests or goals . . .	Members of a group share ideas, goals, or activities that keep them together.
and who see themselves as a group.	Even if people meet daily to communicate, if they don't perceive themselves as a group, they will not function as well as they could.

This family—like all families—has the defining characteristics of a group.

PROJECT PREP

With your **project group** look at the groups you listed for the Speak Up! activity. Assign each group the need or needs it meets: belonging, accomplishment, therapy, or learning. Then choose one group and explain how it has all the defining features of a group.

Types and Functions of Groups

All groups share defining features and fulfill certain individual needs. All groups also have **group norms**, standards of behavior expected from group members. Any group that has been together for a while is likely to have clearly defined norms, and some of them can be fairly strict. Groups differ in the extent to which their norms are formally expressed.

Formal and Informal Groups

A **formal group** is one in which group norms are often verbalized. Often, the norms are written down so that they remain stable over time, and members can refer to them. Consider a group formed by the school activities council. This group probably has written norms.

- One person puts together the agenda for each meeting and runs it.
- Anyone who will be absent must let group members know in advance.
- Everyone must bring paper and pen to the meeting.
- Everyone will get an opportunity to share his or her views and opinions.

These norms might be part of the group's rules or bylaws. They might have developed over time, or they could have been set up when the group first formed.

Now imagine another type of group—say, five students that eat lunch together every day. Here are some of the group norms that could develop.

- Members bring their lunches so they don't have to wait in the cafeteria line.
- Members do not talk about classroom-related topics.

What norms might be part of this group's behavior?

- Members always sit in the same order around the table.

The group might follow this pattern every day and never specifically talk about their group norms. That is, they could informally develop a set of behaviors, follow them closely, enforce them, and do so entirely through nonverbal communication. Such norms can develop, and change, naturally over time. A group without clearly expressed group norms is called an **informal group.**

Group norms govern the way people in groups interact in both formal and informal groups. Some are clearly stated policies and others develop without any formal action.

Imagine being newly introduced to either the student activities council or the lunch group. How would you know how, when, and what to communicate? You would "read" the norms of the group.

1. **Listen.** By listening to a group critically, you can notice the norms they follow in expressing themselves. How long do they speak at a time? Do they tell jokes or personal stories?
2. **Ask.** Most groups have a norm that allows new members to break in with questions. You might want to ask an established member questions outside a group gathering.
3. **Observe.** Watch how others act within the group. Before they speak, are they recognized by the group leader? When speaking, do they make eye contact with everyone in the group, or just one person?
4. **Do research.** Formal groups might have written documents you could read, such as meeting records or a mission statement. People who are not part of the group may also give you background on the group.

A group's level of formality also affects its language, leadership, size, meeting time, and organization. The chart below shows some of these differences. Where would groups you belong to fit in?

	Very Formal	**Somewhat Formal**	**Somewhat Informal**	**Very Informal**
Example	• Jury • School board	• Business committee • Community group	• Study group • After-school writing club	• Post-game pizza party • Neighborhood picnic
Language	Tendency toward formal oral speech	⟵	⟶	Tendency toward informal nonstandard speech
Leadership	Tendency toward formal titles and assigned duties	⟵	⟶	Tendency toward various people casually filling roles as needed
Group Size	Tendency toward a fixed size or range	⟵	⟶	Tendency toward a varying size as situations or occasions change
Time	Tendency toward regular meeting times and lengths	⟵	⟶	Tendency toward more flexible use of time
Order and Organization	Tendency toward use of rules and procedures, agenda	⟵	⟶	Tendency toward following common-sense rules of polite society

Social and Task Groups

In The Jane Austen Book Club, *the participants form a social group that meets their needs.*

Groups can also be classified by their functions. One function of a group is to fulfill social needs. Another is to accomplish tasks. Many groups serve both functions for group members. Either type can be formed intentionally by someone who says, "Let's get organized." Many, though, just evolve.

Social Groups As social creatures, most people enjoy regular interactions with others. A **social group** forms around the needs of the individual members for attention, entertainment, a sense of belonging, or some other social purpose. People might form a group to play cards, attend plays, or read books together.

Members of social groups develop norms to help meet their social needs. If the purpose of the group is to have fun, for example, its members will develop norms that encourage informality and relaxed get-together times.

Task Groups There's always work to do at school, at home, and on the job. A **task group** forms around doing some of that work or around solving problems. For example, imagine that members of the student council want to reduce littering in the halls. If the council appoints a group of students to study the issue and propose solutions, those students are a task group. Task groups tend to value members who are focused, informed, and involved. Norms for task groups promote confronting issues and solving problems.

Many groups serve as both task and social groups. Consider clubs at your school. They provide students the chance to meet in small groups with people who share their interests. The members work on projects together, tell stories, and develop friendships. Or suppose a group organizes itself around a purpose, but its members discover they like each other enough that they want to continue meeting after their purpose is ended. All task groups have some social dimension, because members naturally use such groups to meet their own social needs.

PROJECT PREP

With your **project group** create a list of group norms that might govern a social group. Then create another set of norms for a task group. Share your lists with the rest of the class and discuss similarities and differences between the two sets of norms.

Communication in a DIVERSE WORLD

Our Town in Compton

The low-income, racially diverse southern California community of Compton had long been known as one of the most violent areas in the United States. Drive-by shootings were almost routine. But in 2002 at Dominguez High School, something special was happening.

The school hadn't put on a play in more than 20 years. It didn't even have an auditorium. However, English teacher Catherine Borek had a plan. She worked with a group of untrained students as they became a cohesive task group dedicated to presenting a play. She chose Thornton Wilder's 1938 play *Our Town,* which explores social relationships in a tight-knit town, Grover's Corners, New Hampshire.

Functioning as a cohesive task group was challenging. Students who barely knew one another suddenly found themselves playing each other's boyfriends or girlfriends or family members. Some students got frustrated at the amount of time and discipline required. Many saw little similarity between the fictional town and their own very real community.

Soon, though, the group took on a new life. Working together, members redefined their task. Instead of simply performing the play, they decided to personalize it to make it *their* town. They selected contemporary music to play under some scenes. They brought in photographs of family members and locations in Compton, including the graves of classmates who had been murdered, to project on the walls during the show. Through establishing group norms, the students began to know each other as individuals. And despite setbacks, their rousing production of *Our Town* opened on schedule and sold out every performance. The result was a spectacular success. And, it brought a new auditorium—and a drama department—to Dominguez High School.

Our Town *is a documentary film about Dominguez High School's production. Putting on a play can challenge the group communication skills of a cast.*

Public and Private Groups

If you're like most people, your behavior in private situations differs from your public behavior. Groups, too, have different characteristics depending on whether they are public or private. A **public group** meets in public, and its information is widely available. It often meets in front of an audience and has minutes, or written records, for people to review. Public groups are usually formal and include school boards, city councils, and public hearings. A **private group** meets in private, and information about its meetings is not widely shared.

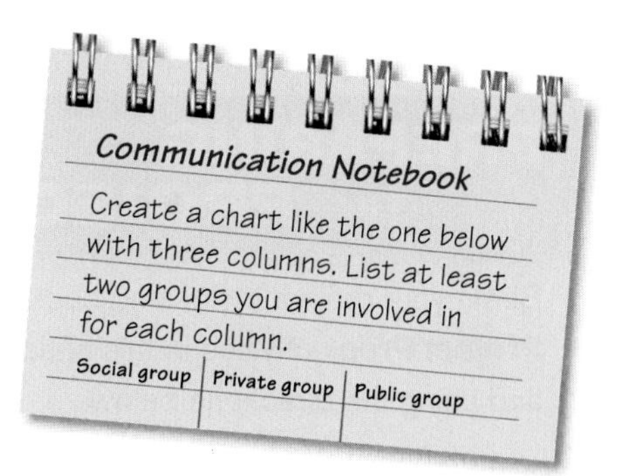

"All right—who stole my gavel?"

Public groups function differently and tend to have more rigid norms than private groups.

Some groups include both the private and the public levels. For instance, a **committee** is a small group of members within a group who come together to carefully consider a particular subject. A **subcommittee** is a smaller group formed within a committee. Often, a subcommittee meets in private and then reports its findings to the committee. These findings usually become public as soon as they are reported. The larger committee would normally then present the findings of their meetings publicly.

When a private group meets in public, the members' behavior may be different. In these situations, the give and take of a private group might seem confusing and disorganized to a larger audience, so public groups usually have a written agenda and a set of rules. Imagine meeting privately with a group of classmates to discuss the plans for an upcoming school dance. You will probably spend time brainstorming and chatting about decorations, music, and so on. But when you present your ideas to school officials, your communication will be focused on fully formed ideas and decisions.

PROJECT PREP

With your **project group** see how many different types of public groups you can name. Then try the same thing with private groups. Keep track of all the groups you name.

PREPARING THE PROJECT

Begin your project by looking back at the **Project Prep** activities in this chapter and using the directions below.

Make Connections

Discuss with your classmates the new information you learned about groups. Share your personal accounts of roles you have played in group communication. Then talk about and summarize:

- the definition of *group*
- the needs that groups fulfill
- the differences between groups that are formal and informal, task and social, and public and private.

Focus

Review your group project: forming a type of group and identifying its defining features.

Plan

Brainstorm ideas about what type of group you and your classmates will form. Ask yourselves:

- What is our group's purpose? Who do we each represent?
- What specific task will we perform?
- Where and how often will we meet?
- What are some of the group norms of behavior we will use?

Surefire Planning

Create a graphic organizer to help map out your project. Visualizing its parts will help you see each part in relation to the others.

Develop

Divide the tasks of the presentation among group members. Figure out who will identify the group and introduce members, who will explain the group's purpose, and who will describe the group's norms. Give each group member a role.

Practice

Practice until each group member feels comfortable with his or her part. Time the presentation and if you are running long, work together to cut back.

PRESENTING THE PROJECT

Use the strategy that follows to help make your presentation as good as it can be.

Your group should now be ready to present the project: forming a group and describing its basic operations. Go over the CAPS guidelines on page 198 and the rubric on page 209 to make sure that your project meets the requirements.

Recovering from Stumbles

Mistakes can happen in performance that don't happen during rehearsal. You might suddenly stumble over words or draw a blank. Don't panic. Take a deep breath and relax your face. In a moment you're likely to be fine. If someone else has an attack of nerves, be supportive! Don't gesture or whisper comments: just help your team member get back on track.

EVALUATING THE PROJECT

Evaluate the presentations using the following rubric.

Score how well the group described its basic operations, with 4 being "outstanding" and 1 being "needs much improvement." Come up with an overall score and write a brief paragraph that explains your score.

Understanding of the Group Communication Process	Demonstration of the Group Communication Process	Creativity and Originality	Preparation and Use of Time
4 Presenters showed insight into the group communication process.	**4** Demonstration helped illuminate the group communication process.	**4** Presentation was unique and interesting.	**4** Presentation flowed smoothly and stayed within the time limit.
3 Presenters understood the group communication process fairly well.	**3** Demonstration helped illuminate the group communication process somewhat.	**3** Presentation was unique and fairly interesting.	**3** Presentation progressed fairly smoothly and stayed within the time limit.
2 Presenters did not seem to understand some elements of the group communication process.	**2** Demonstration helped little in understanding the group communication process.	**2** Presentation was not unique but was fairly interesting.	**2** Presentation had a few awkward moments and went a bit over or noticeably under the time limit.
1 Presenters misunderstood much of the group communication process.	**1** Demonstration was not helpful in understanding the group communication process.	**1** Presentation was neither unique nor interesting.	**1** Presentation was not smoothly executed and went well over or significantly under the time limit.

Communication *Past* and Present

Individuals, Groups, and Government

From the Voice of the Monarch . . .

When George III became king of England in 1761, some American colonies had already experienced more than a century of local self-rule. In 1620, the Pilgrims had written the *Mayflower Compact* to define themselves as a group with the power to "enact, constitute and frame such just and equal Laws . . . as shall be thought most . . . convenient for the general good of the Colony." As most members of groups do, the Pilgrims traded some of their individual concerns for the benefits that the group provided. For the Pilgrims and later colonists who also established local self-rule, those benefits included just and orderly villages and colonies and a clear, strong voice in local government.

At the higher levels of government, however, the colonists' voices were drowned out by the booming voice of George III. In proclamation after proclamation, the king and British Parliament silenced—or tried to—the voices of the colonists. For example, against the wishes of the colonists, the British government issued the Stamp Act of 1765 to raise money for its military costs in America. The Stamp Act required the colonies to pay taxes to England directly rather than to their local legislatures—something they had never done before. Under the Stamp Act, all printed materials were taxed, including newspapers, bills, leaflets, legal documents—even playing cards. The American colonists protested the Stamp Act, asserting that Parliament did not have the right to impose this tax upon them without their consent.

Like most royalty in his day, King George III thought his voice was more important than that of anyone else.

. . . to the Voice of the People

Individual protests to the Stamp Act went unheard, but when colonists formed a group called *Sons of Liberty*, they discovered the power of their voices. Through their choice of name, the protesters defined the group and its purpose. For patriots, the name *Sons of Liberty* conveyed an image of unity and self-determination. It also probably gave its members a sense of righteous power.

In response to colonial protest led largely by the Sons of Liberty, Parliament did finally repeal the Stamp Act in 1766. By this time, however, many colonists were not prepared to lower their voices anymore. Tom Paine and others were writing essays insisting that people should act upon their own beliefs. Others urged colonists to remain stalwart against the assaults of the British Parliament. After the creation in 1771 of the Committee of Correspondence, the Sons of Liberty had a network through which to spread their often fiery words from colony to colony.

Parliament continued to pass acts that the colonists resisted. As it did, the voices of the colonists grew stronger.

Finally on July 4, 1776, these voices rose above the king's proclamations. Thomas Jefferson expressed the power of these protests in the Declaration of Independence, a document that sharply criticized King George III. The United States of America came into being as a republic, a government that guarantees a voice to its citizens through the representatives the people elect. It also guarantees that both individuals and groups are free to express their views and to support what they believe is right and protest what they think is wrong.

Jefferson's statement in the Declaration of Independence that "all men are created equal" implied that every person's voice was equal to that of the most powerful ruler in the country.

Chapter 10 Review

Using Vocabulary Words

For each of the following terms, answer these questions:

- What is it?
- What is an example?

1. civic groups
2. committee
3. formal group
4. group norms
5. informal group
6. political groups
7. private group
8. public group
9. social group
10. subcommittee
11. task group

Reviewing Key Ideas

1. Explain the importance of civic groups and political groups.
2. What are the necessary elements for individuals to be considered a group?
3. What are group norms and how do they influence communication decisions?

Reflecting on Your Project

Groups allow face-to-face interaction. What part did direct communication play in your group's ability to present your project?

Responding to the Essential Question

Use the headings in this chapter and your understanding to help you write a concise one-paragraph response to the question, "What purposes and functions of groups make them so important?"

Extending Your Understanding

Everyday Life

1. Classes are group meetings. Some function as formal groups with norms established by the teacher. Others are less formal with few teacher-established norms. Hold a group discussion to determine which of these class formats is more likely to lead to learning. Identify advantages and disadvantages of each approach.
2. Identify the functions that groups serve in your life. Focus your answer on how these groups meet your needs and the needs of other group members.
3. Generalize about the kinds of groups you belong to now. Then make predictions about how your group memberships might change as you get older.

In the Media

4. Observe one of the group discussions that usually are broadcast on Sunday morning news programs or on C-SPAN. Notice the roles played by

the individuals. Based on what you see, determine why you feel the individuals have been invited to participate in the group.

5. Pay attention to the group communication in the movies or TV shows you see. Make a list of the different types of groups.

Research

6. Use a variety of sources such as Web sites, books, and encyclopedias to research the definition of *group communication*. Then write a complete definition to present to the class.

7. Interview a family member about the groups he or she belongs to or has belonged to in the past. Ask questions to find out these groups' types and purposes, as well as their norms. Ask your interviewee if all the norms were verbalized. Take notes or use a tape recorder. Then write up your interview using a dialogue format. For example:

   Carmen: What was your favorite group of all-time?

   Aunt Jo: It was probably the other nurses I worked with when I was in the army.

Interpreting Graphics

On a separate sheet of paper, fill in the blanks at the bottom of the chart to the right with an example of a group activity that fits into each category.

Additional Projects

1. **Group Project:** Act out a first meeting of the group you created in this chapter's project. For the class, have a discussion to establish your group's norms both verbally and nonverbally. Ask your classmates to identify the nonverbalized norms.

2. **Individual Project:** Attend a meeting of the student council, the school newspaper, or another formal group within your school. Write a summary of the communication that takes place, paying special attention to the impact of the formal nature of the group.

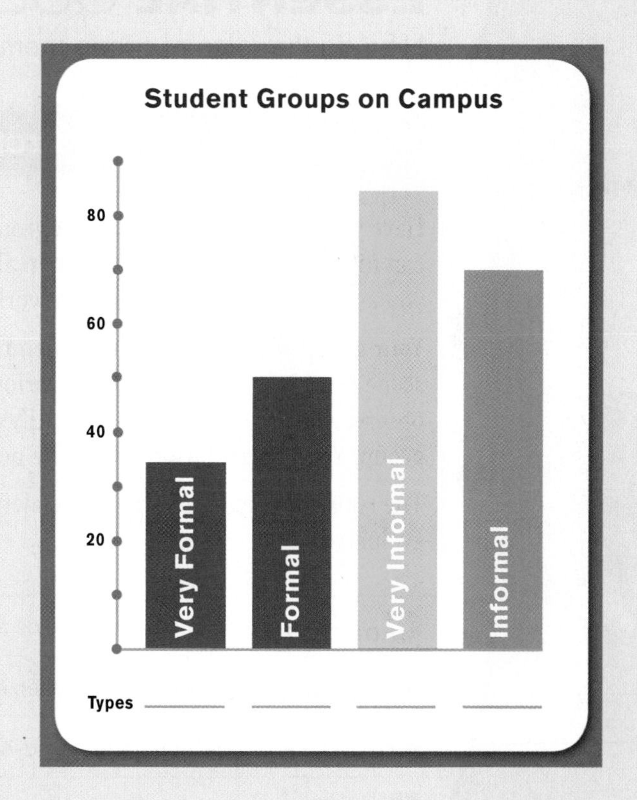

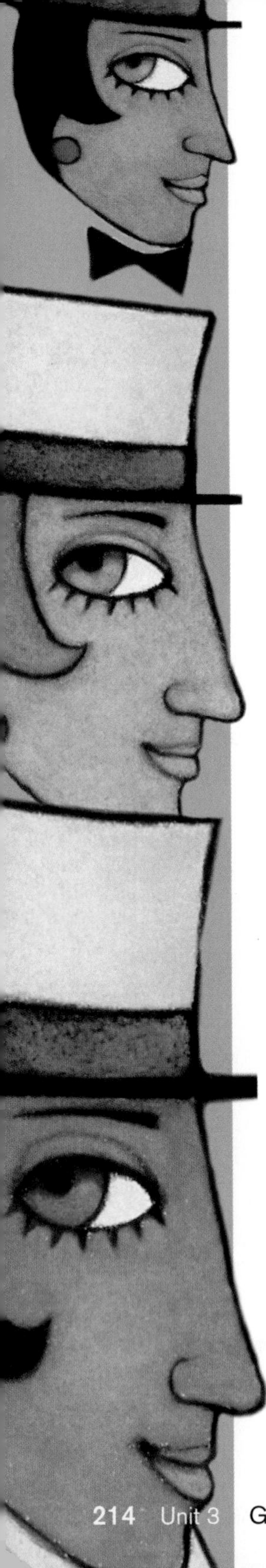

Group Dynamics and Roles

ESSENTIAL QUESTION

How do the roles of group members influence a group's effectiveness?

Chapter Project: The Group Roles On

Have you ever had to work with a group that just couldn't get it together? Groups can function at their best only when all the members pitch in. This project will help you appreciate group roles as you work with others.

Your group will have four to six members. You will work together to present a short scene in which you demonstrate various roles of group members. Classmates will observe your scene and try to identify the different roles and their influence on the group. Your presentation should be no longer than three minutes.

The rubric on page 225 shows the elements on which your presentation will be evaluated.

CONCEPT	group member roles are a key part of group dynamics
AUDIENCE	classmates, teacher, and other group members
PURPOSE	illustrate effective use of group member roles
SITUATION	cooperative classroom presentation

KEY VOCABULARY

group dynamics	group maintenance roles
group member roles	self-centered roles
task roles	

Each individual's facial expressions, gestures, and posture are clues to how well a group is working together.

Speak Up!

Study the photo above and think about what might be going on among the members of this group. Write a comment you think each character might make. Then take turns with your classmates to share your interpretations with the class. As you read this chapter, think about what these responses reveal about each group member in the photo.

BACKGROUND FOR THE PROJECT

Pages 216–223 will provide the information you'll need to complete this project.

Group Dynamics

You've probably been in a group that worked smoothly to accomplish its goals. You've probably also been in a group that got bogged down and sputtered to a halt. Why was one successful while the other one failed miserably? Looking into the behaviors among group members might help you understand the reasons.

How groups function—how they attempt to solve problems and develop personal interactions—is called **group dynamics**.

Group dynamics are the interactions among members that distinguish group members from a random collection of individuals.

Many different theories try to explain how groups function. Two of these (see below) analyze the stages groups go through before they are fully functional. One is by social psychologist Brian Tuckman. Another is by psychiatrist Scott Peck.

PROJECT PREP

With your **project group** choose one of the two sets of stages in the chart. Make a list of five words or phrases that describe an individual's behavior in each stage. Share your lists with the class, and discuss whether everyone interprets the stages in the same way.

Stage	Tuckman	Peck
1	**Forming** In the first meeting of any group, members tend to make a very strong effort to get along.	**Pseudocommunity** The prefix *pseudo-* means false or fake. At this stage, members attempt to ignore or deny their differences and at least appear to get along.
2	**Storming** At some point, though, members may begin to sacrifice getting along or "being nice" in order to get down to the issues even if feelings are hurt.	**Chaos** When pretending to get along fails to work, members voice their differences. Although this stage can be tense, it is necessary to create a cohesive group.
3	**Norming** Members begin to get used to each other and build trust.	**Emptiness** In this stage, members give up self-centered behavior that will get in the way of the group's progress. Ideally this leads them to stronger interactions.
4	**Performing** Members reach a point of working cooperatively together if they have succeeded in building trust.	**True Community** Members have moved past their frustrations and are able to work effectively as parts of a whole. Even when they disagree, members keep communicating.

Member Roles

Think again about groups you've been in. If you analyze a successful group, you'll see that the work was divided so that the group worked efficiently. You will also notice patterns of interactions and roles.

Patterns of behavior tend to emerge in all groups. These roles don't come about because a group decides some members must behave in certain ways. Yet with or without verbalization, certain **group member roles** emerge anyway. Not every group exhibits every role. More than one person can play the same role, and one person may play more than one role. People switch in and out of roles during group interactions, and their roles fall into two categories: task and maintenance.

All groups function by using group member roles, whether the participants acknowledge those roles or not.

Task Roles

Pilar, Justin, Miranda, and LaShawn are members of their school's yearbook committee. The yearbook committee is a task group (see page 205) created to see that the yearbook is published on schedule. Members of a task group can have fun and enjoy themselves, of course, but their primary purpose is to meet their goal. To do so, the group has **task roles**, communication behaviors that help the group address the issue, solve any problems, and perform the task.

TechConnect The yearbook budget allowed the committee to buy new computer software that included more design options. It allowed the use of more type styles, ways to wrap text around images, and options for enhancing photographs. The use of new technology changed how the committee worked. With more design options, the committee recruited two students with graphic design skills, Jackie and Todd.

TechConnect *The yearbook staff may have to play many different roles as they learn how to use software to create their product.*

The chart on the next page identifies eight of the task roles common to well-functioning task groups. The third column illustrates how a committee member with this task role might speak. (The group member roles in this chart are based on ones first identified by John K. Brilhart.)

Task Role	Influence on Group Dynamics	Verbal Cue That Role Is Being Met
Initiator	Proposes new ideas, new goals, procedures, methods, solutions	Miranda: Besides doing what we did last year, let's think about new ways to really improve the yearbook.
Information seeker	Asks for facts, opinions, or clarification from members when more information is needed	Todd: Since I'm new to the committee, can you talk about what didn't work last year?
Information giver	Offers relevant facts and information, personal experiences, evidence, and opinions	Justin: My friend at King High said they doubled their yearbook sponsors last year.
Clarifier	Elaborates on ideas by giving examples and by noting the relationships among them	Miranda: The photo deadline is February 15. To make this date, we need to do what both Justin and Miranda suggest.
Orienter	Keeps the group focused on its goal and summarizes the direction of the discussion	Miranda: These ideas are great, but will they result in a yearbook that gives students what they really want?
Energizer	Prods the group to greater activity or to a decision, and warns the group to act while there is still time	LaShawn: We've talked about doing a survey for the past two meetings. If we're going to set that up, we should do it now.
Procedure developer	Suggests how-to tasks such as seating arrangements, handing out papers, and making copies	Todd: If everyone will give me their email addresses, I will make a list we can all use to keep in touch between meetings.
Recorder	Keeps written record and serves as the group's "memory"	LaShawn: Could you repeat that? We should take that comment down word-for-word.

Maintenance Roles

As the yearbook committee assumes its task roles, it operates on another level as well. The members also take on **group maintenance roles** which are centered around team-building. These roles help establish and maintain positive, cooperative relationships and group-centered interaction. Think of the task roles as the engine that moves the group and the group maintenance roles as the lubrication for the engine. By assuming group maintenance roles, members help everyone get along as they are busy accomplishing the group's task. The following chart identifies the four group maintenance roles often seen in well-functioning groups. No one individual is formally designated to fill each of these roles. Rather, several people fill each role, and each person usually fills several roles. The third column shows sample comments from yearbook committee members.

You can see from the verbal cues that task and maintenance roles often work together. For example, an information giver can comment in a humorous way that relieves tension. Those who are effective in their task roles will judge the impact of their remarks and actions on the group's social dimension. Even a good idea might not help if it is presented in an offensive way.

Group Maintenance Role	Influence on Group Dynamics	Verbal Cue That Role Is Being Met
Supporter	Praises, agrees, indicates warmth and solidarity with others, or goes along with them	Justin: That's a great idea, Miranda. I think you've found the key to the whole situation.
Harmonizer	Mediates differences between others and reconciles conflicts	Pilar: Hold on a second. Todd's and LaShawn's opinions aren't that far apart. They both want what's best. Just because they have different approaches doesn't mean there's a problem.
Tension reliever	Tells jokes or brings out humor in a situation; reduces formality and status differences; relaxes others	LaShawn: I'm glad Miranda and I are on the same side. With as much experience as she's had with this yearbook, she should have a full-color section dedicated just to her!
Gatekeeper	Opens channels of communication; brings in members who otherwise might not speak; sees that everyone has a fair chance to be heard	Miranda: We've heard from everyone here except Jackie. So, Jackie, what do you think about Justin's idea?

Nonverbal Communication and Group Member Roles

The charts on the previous pages illustrate only the verbal cues of group roles. Nonverbal cues can be even more important. A smile by someone in the role of tension reliever might break the tension more than any words could.

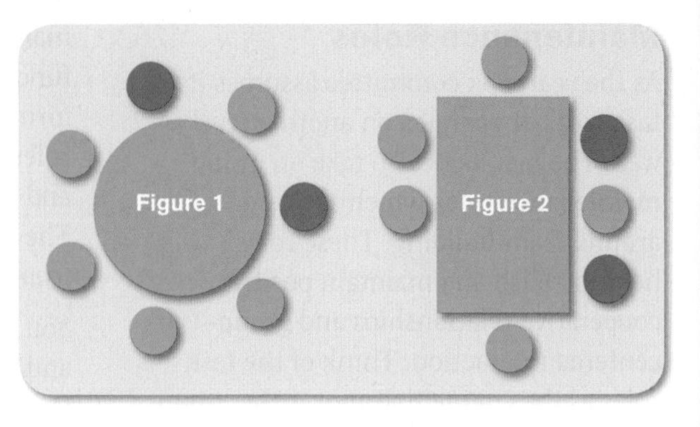

Noting other group members' posture, gestures, and expressions will help you understand the *entire* discussion, not just what you hear. Suppose a group member separates herself from the others by moving her chair, crossing her arms, and frowning. Clearly something is wrong. Someone in the role of gatekeeper could try to bring her back into the group.

Consider your own nonverbal signals. What are you conveying? If your verbal and nonverbal messages conflict, people are likely to believe the nonverbal.

Space and Group Member Roles

Another dimension of nonverbal behavior is seating arrangement. In the following figures, the large shapes represent tables. The small circles represent people. The darker circles represent people whose interactions with each other you are trying to encourage. Which seating arrangement promotes better participation?

Figure 1 provides greater opportunity for interaction than figure 2. In both figures, the dark dots are separated by one other group member. The rectangular table hides them from each other while the circular table allows eye contact.

The amount of physical space between members also affects how people act. A space of a foot and a half to four feet between members is ideal for most smaller group meetings. If members sit any closer, they may feel inhibited from speaking. If they sit any farther apart, they may find the space impersonal and empty.

PROJECT PREP

With your **project group** sit in a circle with about four feet of open space in the middle. Discuss your project and what you have learned so far about task and maintenance roles in group dynamics. As you talk, slowly move your chairs back until there is a space of about ten feet in the middle. Afterward, discuss the ways in which the communication changed.

Communication in a
DIVERSE WORLD

In a Japanese Classroom

Have you ever wondered about the life of students in other countries? You would probably find a typical Japanese school day very different from what you're used to.

The group dynamics of a traditional Japanese classroom emphasize being quiet and respectful. Japanese culture values education highly, and students take pride in representing their school well, even when they are away from school. Inside, everything is geared toward learning–about both school subjects and what it means to be Japanese.

Instead of going to a different room for each class, Japanese students stay together in the same room throughout the day as various teachers arrive to instruct them. This practice allows students to become familiar with one another and to form more cohesive learning groups. In each class, one student is assigned to help the incoming teacher with any necessary setup before instruction begins. According to Japanese tradition, this same student is charged with the duty of formally inviting the teacher to begin teaching.

From an early age, Japanese students learn effective group dynamics.

High school classroom instruction begins at 8:30 A.M. in Japan, as it does in many American schools. But a Japanese school day doesn't end at 3:30 P.M. as most American school days do. Japanese students remain at school to take part in one of the many culture clubs–where they receive further instruction in calligraphy, math, science, or English–or sports teams. Their teachers serve as after-school club leaders, coaches, and tutors. The after-school atmosphere is more social than that of the regular school day.

These procedures reflect the somewhat stricter policies of the Japanese educational system. They also serve as evidence of highly effective group dynamics. Students get to know and work very closely and cooperatively with their classmates and teachers. Each student's daily routine includes working in a group to clean the school–the classrooms, the halls, and the bathrooms. In Japanese society, schools are reflective of the larger community, and students quickly develop a sense of responsibility toward and pride in both their schools and communities.

Group norms govern the way people in groups interact in both formal and informal groups.

Evaluating Group Performance

You can use a chart like the one below to evaluate the roles of group members. The chart represented shows an evaluation of the yearbook task group over a short period of time. Each check mark represents a comment or action that fits in the designated role. What conclusions can you draw about their group dynamics?

As you can see from the chart, Jackie seems pretty uninvolved. She hardly participates in any of the group's task activities and not at all in maintenance. Finding out why could be a first step in improving group dynamics. LaShawn is functioning as both energizer and tension reliever, but both tension relief and hamonizing efforts seem to be coming up short. Perhaps these results help explain why the group hasn't been getting along—not enough attention is being paid to the lighter side of things or cutting down on the friction.

PROJECT PREP

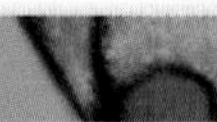

With your **project group** discuss what other information you can read from the chart that would help explain the group's dynamics. Share your ideas with the rest of the class.

	Justin	LaShawn	Pilar	Jackie	Todd	Miranda
Task Role						
Initiator	✔✔		✔			✔
Information seeker		✔			✔✔	
Information giver	✔		✔			✔
Clarifier					✔	✔
Orienter	✔					✔✔
Energizer		✔✔				
Procedure developer					✔	
Recorder		✔	✔			
Group Maintenance Role						
Supporter	✔				✔	✔
Harmonizer			✔			
Tension reliever		✔				
Gatekeeper			✔			✔

Self-Centered Roles

Group members may sometimes assume roles that don't work well for the group as a whole. Such roles are known as **self-centered roles**. These roles meet the needs of that individual while harming the task or maintenance dimension of the larger group. The influence of self-centered roles on group dynamics can be very negative. You'll find a partial list of self-centered roles in the chart below.

Self-Centered Role	Representative Actions	Verbal Cue That Role Is Assumed	Possible Response
Blocker	Constantly raises objections and insists that nothing can be done	LaShawn: These kinds of plans never work.	Ask the blocker for feedback on this particular plan. Point out that this is a new group, one that is tackling problems successfully.
Aggressor	Expresses disapproval, jokes at the expense of others, expresses ill will or envy	Todd: That is the stupidest thing we've discussed yet.	Defend the person who proposed the idea. Ask people to keep their comments supportive, directed to the topic, and constructive.
Recognition seeker	Boasts, calls attention to self, seeks sympathy or pity	Miranda: If they'd listened to me when this first came up, we wouldn't have this problem now.	Ask everyone to focus on the task that exists for this committee now, and how to succeed.
Confessor	Uses the group as audience for personal mistakes and feelings irrelevant to the task	Justin: My classes are killing me this year, I have no time and just can't do all this work, I'm sorry.	Respond that, though everyone is busy, each person has committed to working on this project, and the committee is making good progress.
Class clown	Avoids involvement in the task by making jokes and cynical comments	LaShawn: Move this meeting along, or I'm ordering pizza. This girl is interested only in cheese versus sausage.	Note that distractions don't get decisions made. The sooner the group focuses, the sooner everyone can order pizza.
Dominator	Tries to run the group by giving directions, interrupting and insisting on his or her own way	Pilar: It's time to vote. The rest of you can talk more if you want to, but we need to vote by secret ballot.	Note that people want to discuss other possible solutions, and that hearing everyone will lead to a good decision. Request that the group make decisions as a group.
Special-interest pleader	Acts as the representative of one group to the detriment of the group process	Jackie: Devoting four pages to the forensics club is a lot, but we won the state championship this fall.	Say that the committee has to balance the demands of all student organizations, and note that only the largest ones, such as the band, get more than one page.

Begin your project by looking back at the **Project Prep** activities in this chapter and using the directions below.

Make Connections

Discuss with your group the important points raised in this chapter, such as:

- the characteristics of group dynamics
- the difference between task roles and maintenance roles
- the importance of nonverbal communication in group dynamics
- the effects of physical space on group dynamics.

Focus

Review your group project: acting out group roles for the class to identify.

Surefire Collaboration

Collaborate throughout your planning to be sure you all are in agreement about your goal. Make a list of who does what, dividing work clearly and fairly. Then create an outline or a script and refer to it often, revising as needed. Address all disagreements right away and come to a compromise.

Plan

Decide whether you will demonstrate a task or maintenance group. If your group is a maintenance group, what is its focus? If it is a task group, what is the task? Create a chart of your group's roles, following the model on page 222. Decide how to divide the tasks. Will individuals outline dialogue for their roles or will the group collaborate? Together, visualize how you will behave and interact so that your roles in the group will be clear to the class.

Develop

Use the collaborative method you chose during the planning stage to refine your script. As you read through it, work together to add humor and emotion.

Practice

Remember to time the presentation to keep it between three and four minutes. Go through the material several times so you feel relaxed enough to look up from the script. Encourage one another.

PRESENTING THE PROJECT

Use the strategy that follows to help make your presentation as good as it can be.

Your group should now be ready to present the project: demonstrating group dynamics, maintenance and task roles, and self-centered roles. Go over the CAPS guidelines on page 214 and the rubric on page 225 to make sure that your project meets the requirements. Arrange your chairs to illustrate the proper use of physical space.

Harnessing Communication Apprehension

Anxiety and apprehension are natural reactions. You can learn to use these feelings and the energy they give you to strengthen your presentations. They can give you the boost you need to rehearse effectively and to connect to what you say.

EVALUATING THE PROJECT

Evaluate the presentations using the following rubric.

Score the demonstration on each point, with 4 being "outstanding" and 1 being "needs much improvement."

Come up with an overall score and write a brief paragraph that explains your score.

Understanding of Group Dynamics	Demonstration of Roles in Group Dynamics	Creativity and Originality	Preparation and Use of Time
4 Presenters fully grasped the various aspects of group dynamics.	**4** Demonstration fully illuminated the roles played in group dynamics.	**4** Presentation was unique and interesting.	**4** Presentation flowed smoothly and was within the time limit.
3 Presenters understood the most important aspect of group dynamics.	**3** Demonstration helped in understanding most roles in group dynamics.	**3** Presentation was interesting but not unique.	**3** Presentation was smooth but went over the time limit.
2 Presenters did not seem to understand all aspects of group dynamics.	**2** Demonstration was somewhat helpful in understanding the roles in group dynamics.	**2** Presentation was fairly interesting, but not unique.	**2** Presentation had awkward moments and went over or noticeably under the time limit.
1 Presenters did not understand many aspects of group dynamics.	**1** Demonstration did not help in understanding roles in group dynamics.	**1** Presentation was neither interesting nor unique.	**1** Presentation was very awkward and went well over or significantly under the time limit.

Communication *Past* and Present

Group Dynamics

From the 20th Century . . .

In 1945, Kurt Lewin set up the Research Center for Group Dynamics as part of the Massachusetts Institute of Technology. Lewin had been delivering lectures and seminars on the subject of the behavior of individuals in group situations since the early 1920s. Now he wanted to use scientific thinking and research to better understand the processes that influenced this behavior in many different types of groups.

Lewin and his staff pioneered this brand new field of study. Not only did they conduct research into this new discipline, but they also did fieldwork, experimenting with and evaluating the behavior of workers in a variety of U.S. corporations and organizations. In one study, they evaluated the extent to which the minority members of an auto workers' union were accepted by others. This study led them to further fieldwork, and experiments on group morale and productivity in the face of discrimination. At a major communications company, they explored the role of status and the perception of social power among employees. In most cases they dealt directly with groups of employees, doing face-to-face interviews, and collecting other types of data.

Lewin died in 1947, but the work of his center continued. As knowledge of group dynamics became a valued aspect of nearly every workplace environment, the center flourished. The work of Lewin's students and colleagues at the center has influenced generations of researchers in the fields of experimental and applied social psychology.

How is the making of a car both an individual and a group activity?

. . . to the High-Tech 21st Century

What do you think Kurt Lewin would have thought about the vast selection of Internet groups—ranging in size from just a few people to several million—that are a growing part of today's world? The chances are good he would have been fascinated. He would almost certainly have recognized some similarities between actual and virtual group behavior. And many of Lewin's classic principles of group dynamics in face-to-face situations could be applied to understanding and improving the way these cyber groups work—aspects such as leadership, group boundaries, problem-solving, and patterns of communication.

But think about the many *differences* Lewin would encounter! Subtract nonverbal communication and add members' ability to hide or alter their identity. How does this relative anonymity affect group relations? After all, even those virtual members who use their real names usually feel more or less anonymous. Sometimes anonymity can foster negative communication—allowing group members to engage in rude and aggressive behavior without fear of punishment.

But would Lewin have interpreted such anonymous interaction as a totally negative aspect? Perhaps not. Many recent studies claim that anonymous communication in cyber groups *can* be a positive thing. Members often feel more comfortable sharing deeply held beliefs and personal thoughts and feelings than they would if they were meeting other members face to face. And if there is unity and a fair amount of cohesion within the group, virtual members are more likely to conform to group norms than their counterparts in the face-to-face world.

Today, millions of teens interact daily with one or more online groups.

Chapter 11 Review

Using Vocabulary Words

For each term listed below, make a box and divide it into four sections. In the top left section, write the word. In the top right section, write the word's definition. In the bottom left section, give an example of what the word means to you. In the bottom right section write a word that you feel is the opposite of that word.

Word	Definition
Example	Opposite

1. group dynamics
2. group maintenance roles
3. group member roles
4. self-centered roles
5. task roles

Reviewing Key Ideas

1. Explain the importance of group dynamics.
2. In what way are task roles and maintenance roles different? How are they similar in some cases?
3. Define self-centered roles and give an example.
4. Re-read the section on page 216, which covers the theories of group dynamics developed by Brian Tuckman and Scott Peck. In your own words, explain how these theories are similar and different.

Reflecting on Your Project

In what ways was your group most successful at revealing its various roles? What part did communication play in the dynamics of your group?

Responding to the Essential Question

Think about the groups you have belonged to in terms of the roles you assumed within those groups. Use your experience and what you have learned in the chapter to help you write a concise one-paragraph response to the question, "What types of roles do members of groups play?"

Extending Your Understanding

Everyday Life

1. Would you say that in groups your roles are typically more task-centered or maintenance-centered? Compare your impressions with those of a classmate.
2. Why do you think the same kinds of roles tend to emerge in most groups?
3. Describe the group dynamics of a group you currently belong to. By the standards you learned about in this chapter, would you say that this group functions well or poorly? Explain your position.

In the Media

4. Observe one of the panel discussions that usually are broadcast on Sunday morning news programs or on C-SPAN. Notice the roles played by the individuals. How healthy are their group dynamics? Based

on what you see, determine why you feel the individuals have been invited to participate in the group.

5. Many television shows are set within a workplace environment—for example, a police station, a law office, or a hospital. Watch one of these shows and see if you can spot task roles, maintenance roles, and self-centered roles. Write a summary of your observations.

Research

6. Use a variety of sources such as Web sites, books, and encyclopedias to research the definition of *group dynamics*. Then, in your own words, write a complete definition to present to the class.
7. Interview a family member whose job requires him or her to work within a group. Ask questions to find out what type of roles are common in the group and which ones your relative typically takes on. Draw your interviewee out by asking about the other group members. Try to get a sense of how many of the roles from the chapter are played out within the group during a typical workday.

Interpreting Graphics

Copy the image of the library table and chairs on a separate sheet of paper. Put an X on the chairs that you think would be chosen by a group of three of your peers. Base your decision on what you have learned about group dynamics in this chapter.

Additional Projects

1. **Group Project:** Illustrate the life cycle of the group you created in your project. In other words, use your creativity to come up with an imaginative way to illustrate Brian Tuckman's forming, storming, norming, and performing model. You can do a group performance or create a graphic organizer or poster.
2. **Individual Project:** Sit in on a public meeting in your community. Observe the group dynamics and the roles assumed by the group members. Write an essay about what you notice. In a final paragraph, list suggestions you would make to the group to enable it to function at the highest level of productivity.

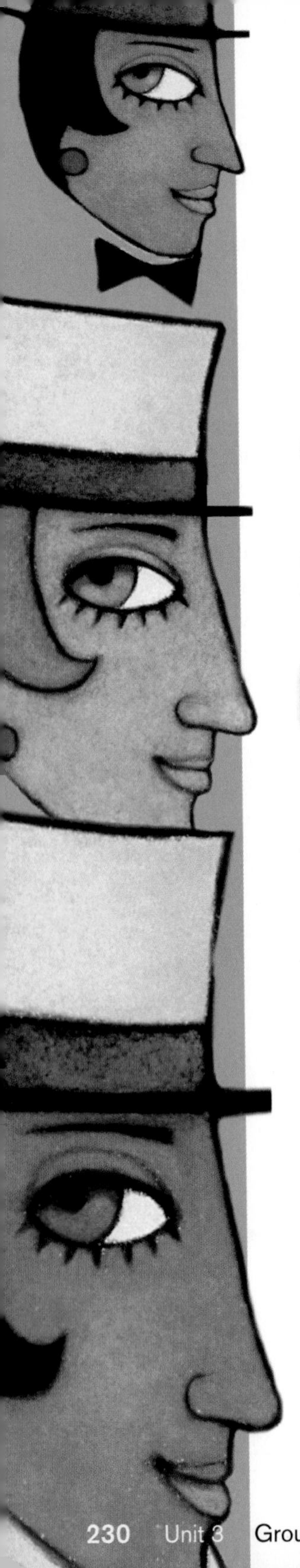

Group Discussions

ESSENTIAL QUESTION

What are the elements of effective group discussion?

Chapter Project: Got a Problem? Here's the Solution.

You've probably had your share of problems. Some of them you solved on your own. Others might not have been so easily managed.

For this project, you will work with a group to address a problem and try to solve it. As a class, you will choose and define the problem. Then you will divide into three or four groups. Each group will present a three-minute discussion proposing solutions to the problem and the action to be taken.

The rubric on page 249 shows the traits on which the presentations will be evaluated.

CONCEPT	discussion leads to accomplishment of group goals and purpose
AUDIENCE	classmates and teacher
PURPOSE	take part in a group discussion that offers solutions to a problem
SITUATION	collaborative classroom presentation

KEY VOCABULARY

group discussion	group leadership
panel discussion	formal leadership
symposium	informal leadership
town hall meeting	authoritarian leadership
roundtable	democratic leadership
question of fact	laissez-faire leadership
question of value	impromptu
question of policy	consensus

When a group is functioning well, everyone focuses on the same topic.

Speak Up!

Think about a group discussion you recently participated in. Quickly write a list of words that describe the experience. Then take turns sharing your words with classmates. Were any of the words repeated by several people? If so, what might the repetition tell you about the nature of group discussions?

Pages 232–248 will provide the information you'll need to complete this project.

Planning for Group Discussion

A **group discussion** is an exchange of views on a topic. Interacting with other students, family, and neighbors, you take part in various group discussions without thinking about their formats. When you plan for a group discussion, however, the format shapes your preparations. If the topic is complex, you may want to outline a schedule for a series of meetings.

Discussion Formats

Discussions fall into two main categories: public and private. Within either category, discussions can be formal or informal.

Public Discussions Discussions that are open to the public take many forms. A **panel discussion** is a formal task group that meets in front of an audience. Panel members are experts on a specific topic, and the discussion is structured to provide information to the audience. Most panels are run by a moderator who asks questions and moves the discussion along.

In another type of formal public discussion, the **symposium,** each speaker has prepared a presentation to address the topic. When all the speakers have had their say, the moderator or the audience members address questions to them.

A third format is a **town hall meeting**, in which the people of a community are invited to voice opinions or ask questions of public figures. These are typically informal meetings set up to hear from as many community members as possible.

Private Discussions A private discussion takes place out of view of an audience. Typical formats include committees and roundtables. Committees, as you may remember from Chapter 10, feature generally free-flowing discussions, but they sometimes have a chairperson or moderator. A **roundtable,** on the other hand, is an open-forum discussion in which all participants have equal status and the freedom to speak candidly and informally.

Politictians often hold town hall meetings as part o their election campaigns.

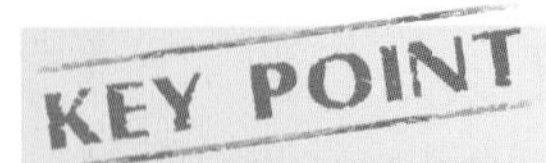

When planning for group discussion, follow the conventions of your chosen format. If the discussion will be public, remind participants of this.

Identifying the Purpose of Group Discussions

As in any kind of communication, knowing your purpose is vital when planning a group discussion. One way or another, however, the goal of most group discussions is problem-solving.

Imagine that several members of your school band have been asked to form a committee to look into buying new band uniforms. Take another look at the problem-solving sequence you read about in Chapter 8. Notice how the group works through each stage of the process.

Group vs. Individual Problem-Solving Solving problems in groups has some advantages over individual problem-solving. For one, group members collectively have more ideas and a broader background and knowledge than a single individual. They also have more resources to implement solutions. How could one individual do all of the tasks in Step Five?

Group problem-solving also has disadvantages, however. It may take longer because meetings need to be scheduled and everyone's voice needs to be heard. And if some group members play self-centered roles or the group dynamics are off in some other way, the group can get bogged down in interpersonal squabbles.

The Problem-Solving Sequence	How the Group Works Through the Problem
Step One: Determine if a problem exists.	The committee members agree that the old uniforms are in bad shape. How will they get new ones?
Step Two: Analyze and describe the problem.	The school does not have the money to replace the uniforms, so fundraising will be needed.
Step Three: Generate a list of possible ways to solve the problem.	The group brainstorms and comes up with several ideas: (1) Sponsor a weekly student-run car wash, (2) Ask band members to pay for their own uniforms, (3) Ask alumni for donations, and (4) Ask local businesses for donations.
Step Four: Evaluate solutions and choose one.	After discussing the pros and cons of each solution, the group combines two ideas. They will try to get alumni to match or double any money band members raise from a weekly car wash.
Step Five: See that the solution is turned into action.	The group splits up into two teams. One team will gather an alumni list, create a letter asking for funds, gather responses, and do follow-ups. The other team will find out the details of holding a weekly car wash, and get the process moving.

Framing a Discussion Question

Even within fairly cohesive groups, interpersonal conflicts, ambiguous language, and misunderstandings can derail discussion. One way to avoid these problems is to frame the discussion question carefully.

Effective discussion questions share several characteristics. These are shown below:

Precise Language Vaguely worded discussion questions diffuse the group's energy and concentration. Use wording that keeps things focused and moving forward.

Vague: *What shall we do about the band uniforms?*

Precise: *How do our current uniforms compare in style, durability, and cost to those of other schools?*

Focus on the Problem, Not the Solution Questions that focus on the solution instead of on the problem tend to limit discussion and squelch participants' creativity by suggesting that there is only a very narrow field of possible answers.

Solution-based: *How can we get the school to pay for our new uniforms?*

Problem-based: *What strategies can we adopt to provide funding if needed in the future?*

The problem-based question ensures a broader discussion by opening up a range of possible solutions that go beyond simply getting the school to pay for new uniforms.

Open to Objective Discussion
Subjective or biased wording can push a group toward a solution that is buried in the question.

Subjective wording: *Should our old, gross band uniforms be replaced?*

Objective wording: *What are the benefits and disadvantages of getting new uniforms?*

If the uniforms are gross, who wouldn't support getting new ones? That choice of word pushes the group toward getting rid of the uniforms at almost any price. The objective wording, in contrast, broadens potential discussion to examine both the pros and cons of replacing the uniforms.

Public demonstrations often answer questions with a clear "yes" or "no." However, "yes/no" questions will shut down small group discussion.

Types of Discussion Questions

Most discussion questions can be divided into three major categories: questions of fact, questions of value, and questions of policy. Understanding these three categories can help groups keep their focus on the question at hand.

A **question of fact** can be answered by obtaining evidence from outside sources or direct observation.

Unlike a question of fact, a **question of value** is subject to interpretation. Value-based questions ask whether something is good or bad, needed or not needed, better or worse. This type of question usually contains judgment words, such as *good, better, best, effective, worthwhile, bad,* or *unworthy*. The answers to value-based questions depend upon group members' personal beliefs and cultural values.

A **question of policy** is also subject to interpretation. It attempts to discover what action should be taken in a given circumstance. The word *should* is an important part of most policy-based questions. In this type of question, *should* is nearly always either stated or implied. These are also the most common kinds of questions in group discussion formats.

PROJECT PREP

With your **project group**, identify an issue to discuss, such as standardized testing. List questions of fact, value, and policy that you could use in the discussion.

Fact, Value, or Policy?

Questions of fact deal in provable facts.	• What percentage of high school band members later play professionally? • What percentage of teenagers work at fast-food jobs during high school? • What jobs earn the highest annual salaries? • Has the rate of domestic violence in Michigan increased in the past year?
Questions of value are based on individual and cultural beliefs.	• Does the contemporary U.S. economy offer equal opportunity for all? • How should young people be educated about the use of alcohol? • Is the contemporary television news media biased? • How should Americans treat undocumented immigrants?
Questions of policy try to find out what action *should* be taken.	• Should high schools require three years of foreign language study? • Should undocumented immigrants be granted amnesty? • Should the U.S. government provide universal health care for all citizens? • Should the United States intervene militarily where genocide is reported?

Leading a Group

In many cases, a group's success depends on strong leadership. **Group leadership** is the ability to influence group members to meet the group's goals and/or to develop positive communication. Sometimes leadership duties are assigned, but often they simply evolve as needed. The type of leadership a group needs will depend on several factors, including whether such leadership is formally recognized.

Types and Styles of Leaders

Formal leaders are appointed, elected, designated, or assigned through some formal process. **Formal leadership** is leadership that is designated as a norm of the group. The captain of the basketball team, the chairperson of the Spanish club, the mayor of a city, and chief executive of a company are all formal leaders.

Informal leadership, in contrast, emerges from the natural functioning of the group. For example, if a member of the band uniform committee is especially dynamic and insightful, he or she might develop influence over the group. In the process, he becomes an informal leader. Groups of friends often have an informal leader.

Some groups have both types of leadership. A formal leader (the group's chairperson, for example) might have responsibility for the group's task behaviors and the talent to manage these activities well. Sometimes, however, a person who excels at task behavior is not as good at group maintenance behavior. Another leader could emerge who can help the social dimension of the group. This leader—without any official title—could be vital to the group's success.

Group leaders typically work in one of three styles: authoritarian, democratic, or laissez-faire. These styles can produce radically different group experiences and results. Often, however, the same leader will use different styles in different situations.

Authoritarian leadership involves a single leader who dominates and dictates processes to group members. This leader is aggressive and directive, often defining tasks and challenging others. This kind of leadership may make decisions quickly.

With **democratic leadership**, one or more leaders attempt to help the group develop its own identity based on input from all the members. This leader is friendly and sociable and this style is effective in groups with long-term goals.

What style of leadership is probably most effective for these firefighters? Why?

Laissez-faire leadership is marked by a leader who allows the group to figure out its own processes with little interference. (*Laissez-faire* is a French term meaning "to allow to do.") The laissez-faire leader is patient and passive and especially effective when other group members are willing to take on leadership roles.

> **PROJECT PREP**
>
> With your **project group**, write an exchange among members of a group working under authoritarian, democratic, and laissez-faire leadership styles. Discuss the differences among the styles.

Qualities of Effective Leaders

No matter what their style, leaders who are effective in small groups tend to be:

- **unaffected by the role.** You may know people whose personalities seemed to change after they took on a leadership role. Effective leaders usually feel comfortable and act naturally in the role.
- **organized.** Effective leaders establish and maintain protocols such as setting agendas, notifying members of meeting dates and times, and supplying any necessary background materials.
- **sensitive to the group's needs.** Leaders cannot ignore the interpersonal needs of group members. To be effective, even authoritarian leaders must empathize and make an attempt to understand member needs. Democratic leaders can empathize and act with authority when the group needs firm leadership.
- **good listeners.** Good group leaders follow group discussion closely. Through listening, they are able to assume necessary roles, summarize group activities, and report to others. They ask people to expand on responses to clarify their ideas.
- **flexible.** Even the best plans can go off track. Strong, flexible leaders don't let the unexpected disrupt group processes.
- **open to learning from experience.** No one masters all leadership traits the first time he or she is placed in a leadership position. But with practice, just about anyone can become a better leader.

How does leadership vary by situation?

Guidelines for Leading a Group

If you are the leader of a group, you will be expected to see the meeting through from planning to adjournment. Suppose you were appointed leader of the band uniform committee. The guidelines below could help you lead the meeting effectively.

Plan Start by determining what needs to be done before the meeting. Locate a meeting place—maybe the band room—and arrange for its use. Set a start and end time for the meeting. Send emails or text messages or make phone calls to notify everyone about the meeting, and prepare an agenda. If a committee member is an especially good writer, you might ask him or her to help you frame the tasks as clearly as possible. (See page 234.)

Develop Procedures When the meeting begins, review the group's task and present the carefully worded discussion question. Try to get the discussion going on a positive note. Keep in mind whether this group needs an authoritarian, democratic, or laissez-faire leader.

Keep the Discussion Moving Fill roles not being filled by others. If tensions flare, and no one is relieving it, say something to help. Insert an appropriate comment, put the discussion in perspective, or even say something appropriately funny. Also, if no one is encouraging comments from other members, do so yourself. Encourage other group members to assume roles by directing questions or comments to them. Try to build on the ideas of each speaker, so the discussion moves in a positive direction. If someone gets off the subject and starts talking about football uniforms, get the group to refocus without offending anyone. Getting everyone involved, even those who seem reluctant to participate, will help ensure that you have a fair and productive meeting.

Close the Meeting When the meeting is close to being over, summarize the suggestions offered for fundraising and the decisions that were made. Review the tasks that need to be accomplished before the next meeting and go over what each team is supposed to do. Ask for questions or comments. Finally, set a time, date, and location for the next meeting.

Effective leaders conduct orderly, well-planned meetings and exert a positive influence on the group's ability to achieve its goals.

Is This Job for Me?

Search: Group Facilitator

It wasn't like Angie to be so cross with the other group members. Damon, too, snapped at a comment. The group at Benson Industries that met to tap employee creativity was bogging down. A round of layoffs had made people worried about their jobs, and the tension made them less creative.

In just a few months, though, Angie, Damon, and the committee were again working well. Good, new ideas were flowing again. What happened? Benson hired a *group facilitator*, a professional whose job is to remove obstacles to effective group functioning and bring out the best in group members. The person they hired had a strong background in communication, sociology, and psychology. A facilitator is typically hired from outside to guide task groups to understand their common objectives and help them find processes to achieve them. Because the facilitator is not a company employee, he or she can be objective. Instead of taking an active part in the group's discussion or trying to solve any task issues, the facilitator focuses on healthy group maintenance.
A large part of the facilitator's job is helping the group negotiate disagreements and move forward.

Does being a facilitator sound attractive to you? Measure yourself with this personality inventory to find out if you have the required traits. Do you:

- ✓ Have excellent organizational skills?
- ✓ Know how to establish group trust?
- ✓ Have expertise in drawing people out?
- ✓ Know how to use teamwork exercises?
- ✓ Know how to help others meet goals?
- ✓ Have the ability to keep meetings on track?
- ✓ Know how to interpret and paraphrase ideas?
- ✓ Have excellent time-management skills?

If you were to become a professional facilitator, your job opportunities could take you to many different kinds of work environments.

Employers	What You Would Do
Hospitals	Help employees discuss and act on goals and long-range plans; run meetings in which groups brainstorm ways to improve service to patients
Banks	Develop agendas that represent a bank's attempts to help debt-ridden clients, entrepreneurs, or local business people
Schools	Help groups of teachers as they work to implement school and district policies; organize and preside over in-school meetings
Corporations	Help plan and present seminars to groups, focusing on both the personal and organizational levels

Participating in Group Discussions

A good leader can have a strong influence, but a group's success depends on all the participants, not just the leader. To get the most *out* of your group, you need to put your best *into* the group and participate as fully as possible.

Creating a Supportive Climate

You read in Chapter 8 that your behavior within a group can help create either a supportive climate, in which people trust each other, or a defensive climate, in which they do not. Defensive communication occurs when a member perceives or anticipates a personal threat and responds in a defensive manner.

For example, imagine the second meeting of the band uniform committee. Everyone is supposed to be bringing up ideas. But Carla has started to feel as if no one respects her. In fact, several of her ideas have been ridiculed. She feels threatened and makes defensive remarks like the following.

- "Oh yeah? Well, my ideas are better than the stupid ideas you come up with." She defends herself by attacking others and increases tension in the group.
- "You guys don't like me. That's why you don't appreciate my ideas." She expresses her feelings of rejection.
- Silence. This "comment" expresses withdrawal.

With good teamwork, the band uniform committee was able to buy new uniforms.

You might recognize these behaviors (aggressiveness, self-criticism, and withdrawal) as self-centered (see Chapter 11). They are unlikely to contribute to the group task or to group maintenance.

Group members affect the meeting by their responses to others. Suppose Carla heard the responses shown in the chart below. Which would encourage her to participate? Which would keep the discussion going positively? Which might make her angry or embarrassed?

You probably noticed that the remarks on the left are supportive and positive while those on the right seem critical and unfriendly. Use the following strategies to keep your comments supportive.

Supportive or Critical Responses?	
"That idea seems really complex. Can you explain it further?"	"That's not a very good idea."
"That's something we haven't tried yet. It just might work."	"Can't you wait until it's your turn?"
"That's interesting. You're thinking outside the box."	"That idea really doesn't fit into our plans, does it?"
"OK. Let's consider it. We should put everyone's ideas on the list of possible solutions."	"You know, for a new member that's not a half-bad idea. But we've all heard it before."
"That's not how I see the problem, but let's consider it. I'm willing to look at this from a different angle."	"I'm sure that the other plan is better. As far as I'm concerned, there's no point in going on with this."

Describe, Don't Evaluate "That's not a very good idea" might score points for honesty, but it doesn't help group discussion. It's a comment that will shut almost anyone down. The person can either fight for the idea or drop it. Either way, the group is likely to stall, because dropping ideas, even those that aren't very good, may soon become normal behavior. If every idea risks immediate attack, few people will want to propose an idea. If, however, you describe instead of evaluate, you can keep the discussion moving: "That idea seems really complex. Can you explain it further?"

Focus on the Problem, Not Who's in Control

If members of a task group feel that other members are addressing the task, the discussion is likely to be productive. But if someone says, "Can't you wait until it's your turn?" that member is focusing on controlling the group rather than addressing the problem. Controlling comments can lead to resentment and can sour group relations. Spending time on ideas you may not agree with is part of the give-and-take in groups. The discussion's focus should always be on the task. Considering lots of ideas is the best start for getting to the best ideas.

If a meeting feels like a boxing match, it probably isn't working well.

Use Other Supportive Strategies

Here are some other approaches to positive discussions.

- **Keeping an open mind** ("Let's think outside of the box") will welcome further discussion. Relying too much on a set plan for the discussion ("That idea doesn't really fit into our plans") will shut out new and possibly intriguing points.
- **Recognizing equality among members** ("Let's put everyone's ideas on the list") will make all members feel that their input is valued. Focusing on status ("For a new member that's not a bad idea") may inhibit group members from making their fullest possible contribution.
- **Withholding final judgment** ("I'm willing to look at this from a new angle") will leave the doors open for more discussion. Conveying superiority ("I'm sure the other plan is better") will close those doors.

Use Empathy and Group Roles

You take on various roles in a group to help accomplish task and maintenance needs, and so do other group members. If you can understand what the other members are doing and empathize, you can help make their task as easy as possible. The easier their task, the easier your task, and the more efficiently the group achieves its goals.

Using empathy to take on different group roles is also effective. Suppose, for example, that Keesha, another member of the band uniform committee, wants to make a comment but is having trouble breaking into the discussion. A group member with empathy will recognize her difficulty and might use any of the following group roles to help her and the group out.

- **Gatekeeper:** "Can we hear from some people who haven't spoken yet?"
- **Information seeker:** "Anyone have any facts or data to add?"
- **Opinion seeker:** "I think Keesha has something to say. How do you feel about this issue?"
- **Procedure developer:** "Maybe we can get more information out if we go around the table and ask everyone to share his or her feelings about the topic. That way, no one will be left out."

With empathy, you can recognize when someone wants to be heard, and you know how to get others to listen considerately.

Empathy can even help you deal with group members who are assuming self-centered roles. If someone is seeking attention, ask yourself, "Why?" If you can identify the source of those feelings, you will know what to work on to improve the group dynamics.

Use supportive responses, empathy, and appropriate contributions to keep the discussion positive.

Imagine you are a member of this group. What might you say to them as they shared their ideas?

Working Toward a Resolution

A supportive climate encourages individual creativity, a key to solving problems. At the same time, the group as a whole can come up with ideas and solutions that even the most creative individuals might not have developed on their own. One process for working toward resolution that promotes both individual creativity and group participation is brainstorming.

Brainstorming When you brainstorm as a group, ideas come tumbling out quickly. You can then evaluate each of them and further explore the most promising ones. Brainstorming is a task skill, but it requires supportive maintenance norms to encourage useful, imaginative contributions.

- **Share all ideas with the group.** Even if an idea seems strange or unworkable at first, it might turn out to be the answer to the problem.
- **Withhold evaluation until all the ideas have been given.** Immediate evaluation can squelch creativity.
- **Reward group members for voicing ideas.** A simple "good idea" or "good job" often encourages even shy group members to continue contributing.
- **Write down all ideas before you forget them.** If you don't write them down, they may be lost. Worse, a person who suggests an idea that is ignored may withdraw from the group.
- **The more ideas the better.** Be open to rearranging, reworking, or combining ideas. Be creative.

TechConnect *Laptops are great for taking notes while brainstorming.*

Gathering Information Brainstorming can point the way to a fresh solution, but sooner or later a group will need to gather information to resolve its problem. Groups generally use three sources.

- **Knowledge and experience of individual group members.** One of the benefits of a group is that it combines the knowledge and experience of a number of individuals, giving the group a broader base of information than any one individual has.
- **Research in the library or on the Internet.** Groups can divide the research into topics for each individual to explore. If your group is looking at a problem faced by other schools, each student could investigate how one other school has responded. Students should bring any important information to the attention of all members.
- **Opinions, beliefs, and values researched directly by the group.**

The last source is one of the most important. Groups often conduct their own surveys of the opinions, beliefs, and values of others. They often use the following strategies to get data for problem-solving.

Strategy #1: Asking Questions and Listening If a group develops a list of questions, all members can collect the same information to share with the group.

Strategy #2: Using Questionnaires Groups can determine the attitudes, beliefs, and opinions of large numbers of people through thoughtfully worded surveys. With that information the group can design appropriate solutions.

TechConnect Groups can use an online survey service to distribute questionnaires efficiently to many people. Respondents can go to the site and complete the survey. The site then compiles the information.

PROJECT PREP

With your **project group,** discuss what you would do if you were a member of a club trying to raise money for a local pet shelter by selling t-shirts. Which strategy would you use to gather information—direct interviews with students or a questionnaire? Come up with three questions that you would use in your strategy.

Goals and Compromise

Sometimes in the process of discussing an issue, group members lose sight of their group purpose and get sidetracked by differences of opinion. Consider the committee charged with buying new uniforms for the school band. The group received a generous donation from a community organization and is discussing how to use it. Some members want to spend the money on radio ads to advertise their weekly fundraising car wash. Others want to save the money for the uniforms and create handmade posters for advertising. Their differences of opinion might cause them to lose sight of their goal: new uniforms. How can they get past this deadlock?

A well-functioning group would try to come up with a compromise, an agreement requiring each side to give something up in order to get something else it wants. In this case, the committee came up with a compromise in which they paid for one well-timed radio ad, followed it up with poster advertising, and put the remainder of the donation toward the new uniforms.

Impromptu Contributions and Speeches At times during group discussions, especially when compromises are being considered, you may have to speak up without invitation or preparation. This kind of speaking is called **impromptu**, which means given on the spur of the moment. For example, you might see that the tone of a group discussion is becoming negative, so you decide on the spur of the moment to make a few comments that focus the group's attention on the negative tone so it can be remedied. Such a contribution might well restore a supportive climate and hasten the process of reaching a compromise. At other times you might feel that your thoughts have crystallized and the group would benefit from an extended impromptu contribution from you. In such an impromptu speech, you rely on your ready knowledge of the subject as you state your case, perhaps in support of a proposed compromise, or to offer a modified compromise. An impromptu speech can sometimes pave the way to a solution of the group's problems.

KEY POINT

A compromise focused on achieving the group's goal will resolve the group's problem and promote ownership among group members.

Decision and Ownership

Effective compromise helps members feel ownership of the group's final decision. Ownership is the commitment by group members to support a decision publicly because they have been part of making it. Group members who feel ownership will be likely to help carry out the group's decisions.

A handshake is a traditional way to recognize that two people have compromised to reach an agreement.

A good discussion before a vote can help all members of a group feel comfortable with the final decision.

Communication Notebook

Write about an experience you have had in coming to an agreement with others in a group.

Voting At some point in the group decision-making process, members usually vote. Voting has the advantage of moving the group toward a decision. It also allows the majority to have its way. In some groups, voting is the only legitimate way to make important decisions.

When is voting *not* a good idea? Consider what happens when the group votes before recognizing objections from a minority of group members. When a vote buries problems instead of resolving them, it can hurt group process.

Consensus Groups can avoid taking difficult votes by attempting to reach **consensus**, or general agreement. In some ways consensus is like a compromise; its goal is a decision that everyone can live with. Reaching consensus requires more than persuading the majority of the group to vote for a decision. Here are strategies for reaching consensus:

1. **Allow others to talk.** When group members feel they have been heard, they are much more likely to join a consensus decision.
2. **Take time.** Allowing people to talk will take time. Rushing a vote will bring about a decision, but consensus will bring about ownership.
3. **Word the decision carefully.** A decision can be expressed in a way that divides or unifies the group. Spending some time on wording can help achieve general agreement and ownership.
4. **Remember the strategies for generating a supportive climate** (see pages 240–242). If communication within the group is supportive, group members will be more likely to cooperate in reaching consensus.

PREPARING THE PROJECT

Begin your project by looking back at the **Project Prep** activities in this chapter and using the directions below.

Discuss with your group the following:

- the definition of leadership
- different types of leadership
- the five steps of the problem-solving sequence
- methods of gathering information for problem-solving.

Make Connections

What connections to your own experience in groups can you make with the information in this chapter? Share your connections with your group.

Focus

Review the group project you are working on: presenting a three-minute discussion proposing solutions to a problem and the action to be taken.

To begin this project, your group will take part in a whole-class discussion to select an issue for the presentation. For example, you might select a topic such as the need for academic standards for high school athletes. Once the class decides on the topic, each group will then present its own problem-solution sequence and recommend an action.

Plan

With your group, review the problem-solution sequence on page 233. Then discuss the issue the class chose to focus on. Sketch out a framework for how you will complete your problem-solving task.

Surefire Listening Skills

Working with other group members calls for careful listening. Listen not only for the messages expressed but also for what might be going on underneath a person's comments and behavior.

Develop

Brainstorm for ideas and use the problem-solving sequence to work toward a solution. As you develop your presentation, consider the leadership or task roles each of you takes on. Use task roles and take leadership action if necessary to make sure every group member has input as you work through the five problem-solution steps. Brainstorm with your group about the best way to present the material for these steps. For example, maybe each of you will take one of the steps. Or maybe you will all pitch in at each step with reasons and explanations. Also, decide whether you will create a script for the presentation or improvise. If you improvise, create and follow a scenario that guides you through the main points you need to cover.

One way to brainstorm is to let your mind focus far away so that you can see a topic from a new perspective.

Practice

Once your group has developed the material you will be presenting, talk through it together. Look for areas where the discussion might be unclear and make them stronger. Also, consider the physical aspects of your project. Where will each presenter stand or sit? Practice using volume, posture, and eye contact to convey meaning. If you are reading from scripts, mark areas where you will look up, pause, or emphasize a word.

Use the strategy that follows to help make your presentation as good as it can be.

Your group should now be ready to present the project: demonstrating each step of the problem-solution sequence and suggesting an action to resolve the problem. Go over the CAPS guidelines on page 230 and the rubric on page 249 to make sure that your project meets the requirements.

Using Improvisation

Like brainstorming, improvising is based on the notion of accepting the ideas of others and adding something to them. It is used in many different contexts, from live theater performances to corporate board meetings. The simple guideline for improvisation is that instead of shutting down someone else's idea with a response of "No," improvisers inspire one another by responding with "Yes, and . . . . " When improvisation is working well, a presentation sparkles with excitement and mutual respect among the improvisers. If your group is planning to improvise the presentation instead of preparing a script, remember that improvisation is:

- a way of working cooperatively, creatively, and flexibly
- based on the idea that all participants will really listen to one another
- nonjudgmental—everyone's input is important and "No" is not an option
- a way to involve everyone and come up with new ideas and solutions.

Improvisational comedy works well when team members say "Yes" to the ideas of others.

EVALUATING THE PROJECT

The rubric below will help you assess your own and your classmates' presentations.

Score the demonstration on each point, with 4 being "outstanding" and 1 being "needs much improvement."

Understanding Group Discussion in Problem-Solving	Demonstration of the Steps in the Problem-Solving Sequence	Creativity and Originality	Preparation and Use of Time
4 Presenters fully grasped how groups use problem-solving in discussions.	**4** Presenters clearly demonstrated all steps in the problem-solving sequence.	**4** The presentation was strikingly original.	**4** The presentation was well prepared and stayed within the time limit.
3 Presenters understood many elements of how groups use problem-solving in discussions.	**3** Presenters demonstrated the steps in the problem-solving sequence, some more clearly than others.	**3** The presentation was fairly inventive.	**3** The presentation was fairly well prepared and stayed within the time limit.
2 Presenters did not seem to understand many of the elements involved in how groups use problem-solving in discussions.	**2** Presenters missed a step or two when demonstrating the problem-solving sequence.	**2** The presentation was somewhat predictable.	**2** The presentation showed some lack of preparation and went a bit over or noticeably under the time limit.
1 Presenters misunderstood all elements involved in how groups use problem-solving in discussions.	**1** Presenters did not demonstrate the steps in the problem-solving sequence clearly.	**1** The presentation seemed to repeat ideas used by others.	**1** The presentation was neither well-prepared nor an appropriate length.

Communication *Past* and Present

Leadership Styles

From the Transactional . . .

Imagine you are the casting director for a movie. The script calls for an "old-fashioned, gruff, World War II Army general." The person you picture in your mind is probably a great example of a transactional leader, or at least the stereotype of one.

The transactional leadership style starts with the belief that a group functions most efficiently with a clear hierarchy of command. Decisions start at the top, and work their way down the organization. Leaders motivate people by offering reward for success and punishment for failure. Subordinates understand that their job is to carry out the directions from above. Thinking about whether one agrees with the decision or not, or whether it is good for the subordinate, feels like a waste of time.

Communication takes the form of orders or task-focused directions. Discussions between people of different status are rare. Complaints are almost unheard of. The most important listening skill is the ability to follow directions.

A graphic image of transactional leadership might look like this:

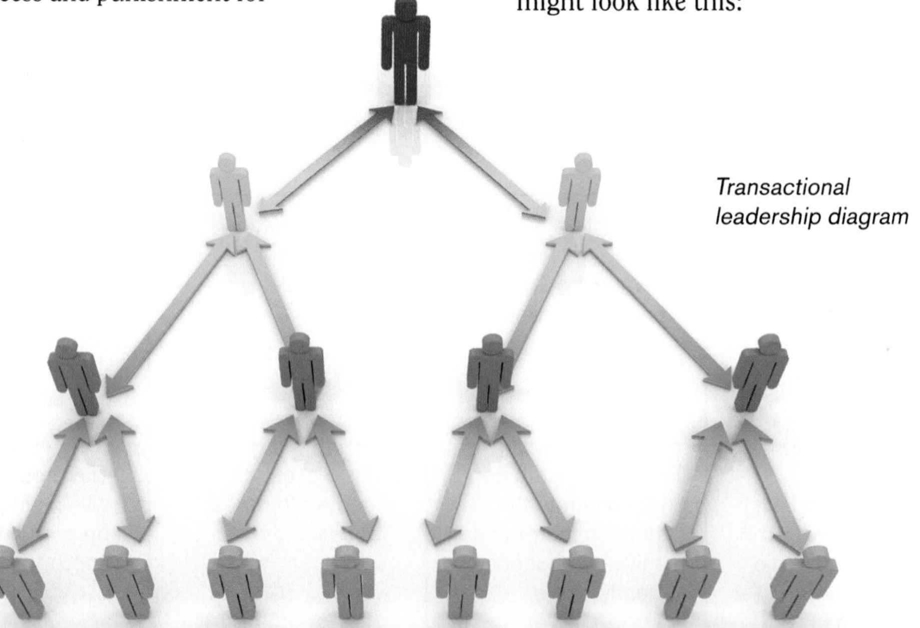

Transactional leadership diagram

. . . to the Transformational

A transformational leader starts from a different assumption than a transactional leader. A group will work best if the members can develop themselves to their fullest potential. As a result, transformational leaders try to create an environment in which others enjoy working and contributing. Many elementary school teachers follow a transformational leadership model. Their goal is to help their students develop as individuals.

Transformational leaders communicate quite differently than do transactional leaders. They emphasize discussions rather than orders. They consider listening to the subordinates, providing feedback, and allowing dissent important.

The theories of American psychologist Abraham Maslow can help explain why both types of leadership can be effective. Maslow wrote a very influential paper called "The Theory of Human Motivation." In it, he categorized all human needs and motivations and represented them within a pyramid. His theory held that at the most basic level—the bottom of the pyramid—human beings are motivated by physiological needs such as food, water, and sleep. After people have met these needs, they are motivated by higher ones: safety and social interactions, which includes love.

The two highest levels of motivation are esteem and self-actualization. Esteem refers to the human need to feel good about ourselves. Self-actualization motivates us to "be all we can be," to realize our unique potential. Graphically, Maslow's hierarchy looks like this:

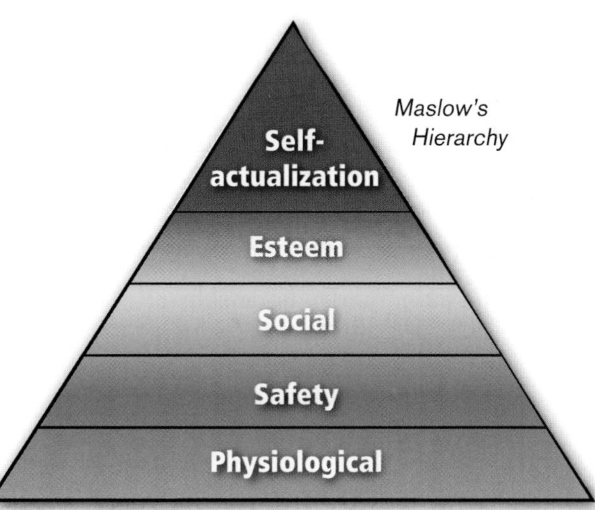

Maslow's Hierarchy

The transactional leader focuses on meeting people's lower-order needs on the hierarchy. For a soldier in battle, survival is a real issue. The transformational leader, in contrast, appeals to the highest motivations: esteem and self-actualization. In an elementary classroom, students can build their esteem as they develop their academic skills.

Chapter 12 Review

Using Vocabulary Words

Create a chart like the one below on a separate sheet of paper, making sure the last column is the largest. Choose six vocabulary words from the list that you find most challenging and write them in the left column. Then write a definition of the vocabulary word in the middle column. Finally, create a memory aid in the form of a drawing in the right column.

Vocabulary Word	Definition	Memory Aid Drawing

1. authoritarian leadership
2. consensus
3. democratic leadership
4. formal leadership
5. group discussion
6. group leadership
7. impromptu
8. informal leadership
9. laissez-faire leadership
10. panel discussion
11. question of fact
12. question of policy
13. question of value
14. roundtable
15. symposium
16. town hall meeting

Reviewing Key Ideas

1. Define *group leadership*. Be sure to explain the role of communication in the definition.
2. What is a panel discussion? How does it differ from a symposium?
3. Identify traits commonly associated with effective leaders.
4. Distinguish among authoritarian, democratic, and laissez-faire leadership styles.

Reflecting on Your Project

What aspects of your group presentation were most successful? What did you admire most about the other presentations?

Responding to the Essential Question

Consider a group that you currently belong to or one you have belonged to in the past. How effective are this group's discussions? Write an essay describing the group's discussions and leadership.

Extending Your Understanding

Everyday Life

1. Think about the emergence of informal leadership in classrooms. Explain how student leaders emerge to fill informal leadership positions.
2. You are a member of many groups. Identify the leadership functions that you are comfortable performing.

3. People in many countries tend to prefer a democratic leadership style. Using terminology from this and the previous chapters on group communication, listening, and member roles, explain why you think people might have this preference.

In the Media

4. Many plays and TV shows examine group activities. One of the most famous is *Twelve Angry Men*. View or read the play. Evaluate the leadership styles of the formal and the informal leaders. Select specific lines from the play that reveal the leadership qualities of each.

5. Bookstores typically feature sections devoted exclusively to books on leadership. Select one of these books for review. Read the book and present your review in a speech to the class.

Research

6. Select a well-known leader from contemporary times or from the past. Research this person's leadership style. Write a brief report in which you analyze that style in terms of the concepts you learned in this chapter.

7. Interview an older family member who remembers the presidencies of several different American leaders. Ask questions to compare and contrast those leadership styles with that of the current American president.

Interpreting Graphics

Copy this diagram of Maslow's hierarchy on a separate sheet of paper. Make sure you copy it on a large enough scale that you can write a few words in each area of the pyramid. Then fill in your personal hierarchy identifying the ways in which you fulfill each of the need categories.

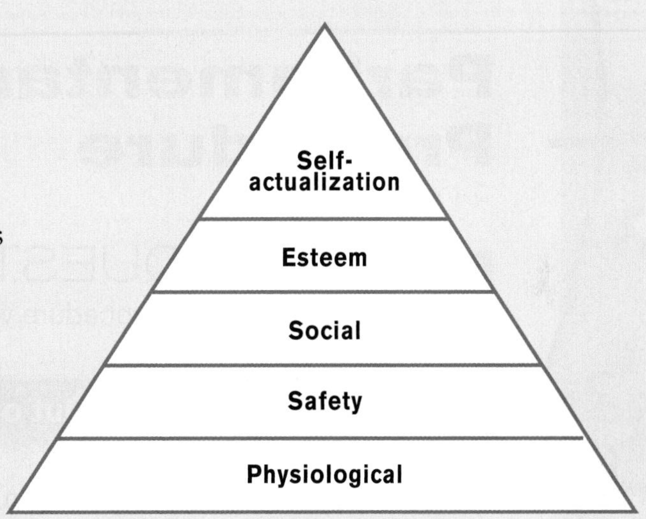

Additional Projects

1. **Group Project:** Conduct a panel discussion on leadership. Allow enough time for research. Then establish each panel member as an authority on one leadership theory or style. Develop a set of questions for the panel to address.

2. **Individual Project:** Visit a town hall meeting or panel discussion in your area. Take notes on the quality and purpose of the presentation. Then, in a one- or two-page essay, analyze the discussion using the concepts you learned in this chapter.

Parliamentary Procedure

ESSENTIAL QUESTION

How does parliamentary procedure work?

Chapter Project: You're Out of Order!

Have you ever been involved in a meeting in which everyone was talking, no one seemed ready to listen, and you couldn't calm the situation? This project will help you understand how to apply guidelines for conducting formal meetings.

In a small group of four to six you will hold a mock meeting using parliamentary procedure, including at least three "out of order" exchanges. Your classmates will call out, "You're out of order!" whenever these occur.

The entire presentation should take no more than three minutes. Refer to the CAPS guidelines below as you work.

The rubric on page 267 shows the traits on which your presentation will be evaluated.

CONCEPT	standardized rules of order can facilitate group communication
AUDIENCE	classmates, teacher, and other group members
PURPOSE	understand and use elements of parliamentary procedure
SITUATION	creative classroom demonstration

KEY VOCABULARY

- parliamentary procedure
- chair
- agenda
- motion
- adjourn
- secretary
- minutes
- quorum
- executive session
- main motion
- incidental motion
- subsidiary motion
- table
- amend
- privileged motion
- parliamentarian
- abstain
- rescind
- reconsider

How much business would get done if all the people at this meeting tried to talk at once?

Speak Up!

Take a moment to think about speaking in public, such as in a class or a meeting. Then, when your teacher says "Go," begin speaking aloud your thoughts on the subject. Try to make yourself heard over the other people talking. While you are talking, try also to hear what others around you are saying. When your teacher gives you a sign, stop talking. Discuss your response to this exercise with your classmates. Were you able to understand what the others were saying?

Pages 256–265 will provide the information you'll need to complete this project.

Rules of Order and Parliamentary Procedure

The meeting of the new Green Team club was a disaster. Kelly repeated complaints about an earlier decision, Jake rolled his eyes and sighed, and everyone talked at once. Finally, Carlos stood up and said, "We need Robert's Rules of Order."

Robert's Rules of Order

In 1876, General Henry M. Robert was asked to lead a public meeting. He had no experience at this, and it showed. At the meeting, he was so embarrassed by his failure to maintain order that he vowed never to preside over another meeting until he could be effective. So he studied the rules used by the American Congress and the British Parliament, and wrote *Robert's Rules of Order.* His work became the most widely used source for **parliamentary procedure,** a recognized procedure for conducting a formal meeting in an orderly manner.

The Principles of Parliamentary Procedure

The Green Team at Evergreen High School has a great idea for the new club. Its mission will be to think globally and act locally to help the environment. But as Carlos pointed out, the club needs an effective way to run meetings. Parliamentary procedure has advantages that promote effective meetings.

Advantages of Parliamentary Procedure

1. The main purpose of parliamentary procedure is to facilitate business while maintaining group cooperation.
2. All parliamentary members share the same rights and obligations. The responsible behavior of each member is vital to the group's overall effectiveness.
3. The group can consider only one issue at a time. This ensures focused discussion and forces members to stick to the point.
4. Every member's vote counts equally.
5. In a vote, the majority always rules. The minority must accept the decision. This policy not only saves time, but it also ensures that the overall judgment of the collective membership prevails.
6. The minority has the right to be heard. Parliamentary rules ensure that every minority opinion gets a fair hearing before a vote can be taken.

All this sounds good to the Green Team group members. They decide to go for it.

KEY POINT

The rules of parliamentary procedure ensure orderly and fair meetings.

Parliamentary Roles

Parliamentary groups are very different than social groups. The leadership is more formal, and the roles are more defined.

Duties of the Chair

The presiding officer in a parliamentary group is called the chairperson or **chair**. The chair might be elected by the group, appointed from outside the group, or elected by voters. The chair runs meetings following parliamentary rules and group norms. The chair must (1) enforce the right of the majority to prevail, (2) protect the right of the minority to receive a fair hearing, and (3) remain impartial.

The Green Team elects Jenna to the position of chair. To fulfill her duties, Jenna will:

1. prepare the **agenda**, or outline, of the issues and proposals at least two days before each meeting.

Clear rules of order lead to efficient meetings.

2. call the meeting to order, get the group's attention, and work step by step through each agenda item.
3. call for reports to the group from the treasurer and other officers.
4. call for old business (issues remaining from previous meetings) and then move on to new business.
5. recognize individuals to speak. Speakers must be recognized by the chair, who keeps the discussion focused. Whether the chair participates in the discussion varies from group to group.
6. rule on each parliamentary motion, a proposal for action suggested by a member. If a motion is not relevant to the discussion, it is ruled "out of order." If a motion is approved, the group must act on it. (For more on motions, see pages 262–264.)
7. appoint committees as needed. These usually focus on one particular task.
8. conduct votes following a debate on a motion. Those in favor say "aye" and those opposed say "no" or "nay."
9. report the results of all votes by saying "The ayes have it. The motion is carried" or "The motion is defeated." Votes can be carried out by voice, or by roll call, in which case members state their votes as their names are called.
10. call to **adjourn**, or close, the meeting and set the time for the next session.

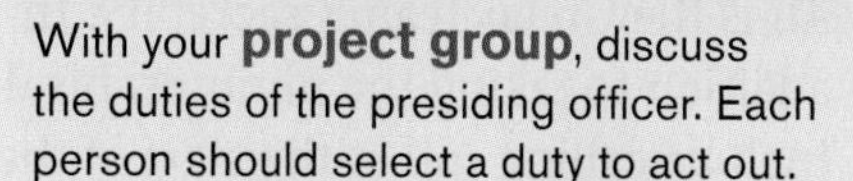

PROJECT PREP

With your **project group**, discuss the duties of the presiding officer. Each person should select a duty to act out.

Duties of Members

In a parliamentary group, each member has valuable contributions to make. In addition, each has guidelines to follow.

1. **Never talk out of turn.** You must receive permission from the chair to speak.
2. **Stick to the discussion topic.** Members who wander off the point sidetrack the meeting. Motions must be approved by the chair.
3. **Abide by the rules of the group.** Parliamentary procedure works only if members follow the rules.
4. **Be courteous.** Respect the views others, and use empathy and group problem-solving techniques. Do not interrupt a speaker, except in unusual circumstances.
5. **Be on time** for all meetings.

In some political groups, members use techniques of parliamentary procedure to avoid issues or block discussion. But the fundamental purpose of a parliamentary group is to achieve a fair hearing for all.

Duties of the Secretary or Recorder

Another key role in the parliamentary group is the **secretary**, sometimes called the recorder. This person can be either appointed or elected. The secretary takes notes and keeps written record, known as the minutes, of each meeting's discussion points, motions, votes, and outcomes. The **minutes** serve as the official documentation of the meeting.

Ali is the Green Team's secretary. In addition to taking the minutes, his duties include calling roll at the start of the meeting, making any corrections to the minutes of the previous meeting, calling member names during roll-call votes, keeping accurate counts and breakdowns of all votes, and making the minutes of the meeting accessible to members.

TechConnect Some secretaries print out copies of their minutes and distribute them to members. Being a serious conservationist, however, Ali wants to create a paperless environment. He types up all minutes on his laptop and circulates them to all members via the file transfer protocol (FTP) site on the Green Team server. If people have corrections, they use the "track changes" feature to highlight them and return them to Ali. He takes digital photographs, when necessary, and incorporates them into his reports along with helpful diagrams or spreadsheets. He has, on occasion, projected important ecological images, films, and news stories using data projectors which are connected to his laptop. He can also record meeting discussions and votes for everyone to share. Ali figures he has avoided photocopying hundreds of pages over the time he has served as secretary.

What advantages does electronic distribution of minutes have over traditional means? What disadvantages might it have?

Minutes

Because minutes are the formal, written record of what took place during the meeting, they are usually straightforward. They include:

- the physical details of the meeting, such as the time, date, and location where it took place
- the names of those present
- a summary of reports from officers
- all major motions and a notation of which member made each one, as well as whether or not it was passed
- all major discussion points
- any major announcements.

The Quorum and Executive Session

Conducting a parliamentary meeting requires the presence of a **quorum**, the minimum number of members necessary to be present for the group to vote on its issues. Organizations can establish their own quorums. In some cases—for example, the U.S. Congress—no votes can be approved without a majority (more than half) of eligible member voters present. But many groups, particularly large ones with a pattern of low attendance, set their quorums much lower.

If a quorum is not present, the meeting must automatically adjourn. If there is a quorum at the beginning of the meeting and a number of members leave during the course of the proceedings, the quorum may be lost. Then, the presiding officer has no choice but to adjourn the meeting.

Although guests are often welcome at many parliamentary meetings, only members are allowed in an **executive session**. Executive sessions give members the opportunity to discuss personnel or disciplinary issues within the group. For the sake of privacy, issues discussed in executive sessions are confidential.

PROJECT PREP

With your **project group**, discuss the kinds of issues that might call for an executive session. Make a list of your ideas.

"We have no quorum, Ms. Hedgely. I'm here, and that's all that matters."

Communication in a DIVERSE WORLD

The Power of the Talking Stick

For centuries cultures around the world have attempted to find methods to provide for fair and impartial communication in groups. In many Native American traditions, important meetings were often ruled by means of a simple yet effective communication tool known as the talking stick. Used at tribal councils, the talking stick regulated the flow of discussion with a single unbreakable rule: Anyone wishing to address the council had to first have his or her hands on the talking stick. When one person finished speaking, he or she held out the stick for another group member to take. Whoever took it next had the right to speak. In this way, anyone who wished to speak eventually got the chance. And when all had spoken, the talking stick was handed back to the leading elder for safekeeping.

Symbols of Communication

This talking stick, sometimes called a ceremonial stick, was usually decorated with materials from nature that symbolized an aspect of communication. For example, an eagle feather tied to one end symbolized bravery and wisdom, encouraging the speaker to say only the truth. Sometimes one end of the stick was covered with rabbit fur, which meant the speaker's words should be soft and warm. A blue stone affixed to it symbolized the Great Spirit who would watch the proceedings and hear the speaker's message. Some Native American groups used a feather, a shell, or a peace pipe instead of a stick. Whatever the chosen object, it conferred on the speaker a special power: the power to speak.

Whose Turn to Speak Today?

The talking stick is still used today in some Native American communities. It helps teach children how to interact socially and is used in conducting ceremonies, solving disputes, and in storytelling circles.

In modern parliamentary meetings, an object is not handed back and forth among speakers. But each speaker must still wait until he or she "has the floor," which means the chair has granted that person the right to speak.

A Parliamentary Meeting

The members of the Evergreen High School Green Team have now had several meetings and they are growing accustomed to using parliamentary rules. Below is a breakdown of their process.

The Order of Business

Under parliamentary procedure, groups follow a standard order for conducting a meeting. This order allows group members to anticipate the group's progress and plan for the discussion. This is Green Team's order of business:

The Evergreen High School Green Team Meeting	
1. Call to order	The chair, Jenna, raps her gavel and says: "The formal meeting of the Evergreen High Green Team is now in session."
2. Roll call	The secretary, Ali, calls out the names of the group members and makes note of who is present at the meeting.
3. Reviewing the minutes of the previous meeting	Ali asks if everyone received the minutes he distributed, and if anyone has any changes. No one has any corrections, so the minutes are approved.
4. Officers' reports	Jenna requests reports from the parliamentary officers. The treasurer, Holly, says the school has approved her request for free meeting space in the community center after school.
5. Special committee reports	Jenna next asks for reports from any committees on special issues. Devon, head of the public relations committee, reports that the local paper wants to do a story on the Green Team.
6. Old or unfinished business	The group then discusses an unresolved issue from previous meetings—whether to meet in the community center. A motion is made, seconded, and passed to meet there.
7. New business	Then the group discusses a new issue—the idea of the newspaper story. Devon asks for a publicity committee member to act as point person for the story. Rachel volunteers.
8. Announcements	This includes issues any member finds pertinent to group business. No one has any announcements to share today.
9. Date, location, and time for next meeting	The new meeting location at the community center is announced as well as the time of the regularly scheduled meeting—the second Tuesday of each month at 4:00 P.M.
10. Adjournment	Jenna says, "The meeting of the Evergreen High School Green Team is now closed," and raps the gavel.

Conducting Business

The most important parliamentary tool is the motion. A motion is a statement of the topic under discussion. Motions are always introduced by a member addressing the chair. The member begins the motion by saying "I move that . . ." and states the motion. For example, after Rachel volunteered to work on the newspaper story about the Green Team, Eric made this motion: "I move that Rachel be our liaison for the *Newton City Gazette* article." The chart below describes the four types of motions.

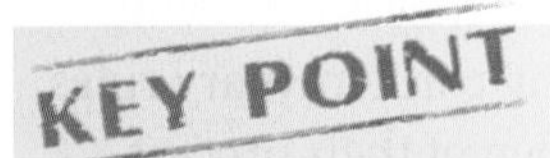

Of the four kinds of motions in parliamentary procedures, only the privileged motion is unrelated to the main motion.

The Motion	How It Works	Examples
Main motion It brings up business matters before the group.	• Only one main motion may be considered at a time. • Before being considered, a main motion must receive a second, an endorsement from another member: "I second the motion." • One main motion must be voted on before another is introduced.	• "I move that we hold future meetings at the community center." • "I move that we spend $100 on publicity for recruiting new members."
Incidental motion It is related to the main motion and must be introduced immediately after a main motion.	• An incidental motion may or may not require a second. (See the chart on page 264 for examples of each.) • It must be discussed or dispensed with before resuming discussion on the main motion.	• "I object to considering this motion now. We first need to vote on the motion that is already on the floor." • "Point of order." When recognized by the chair, the speaker continues: "I believe that the chair forgot to ask for a second for this motion."
Subsidiary motion It modifies, delays action on, or disposes of a main motion.	• A subsidiary motion always requires a second. • Some are debatable, others aren't. • Some require immediate action. They must be resolved before resuming discussion of a main motion.	• "I move to lay this motion on the table." To **table** means to put aside until later. • "I move to amend this motion by substituting $300 for $100." To **amend** means to alter.
Privileged motion It is not related to the main motion.	• Privileged motions take precedence over main motions because of their importance or urgency. • They may or may not require a second.	• "I move to recess for 15 minutes." To **recess** means to take a break. • "I move to adjourn this meeting."

Sequence of a Motion

The following sequence of actions shows how a motion can move through the parliamentary process.

1. A motion has been made. Eric has moved that Rachel be named the point person for the *Newton City Gazette* story about the Green Team.

2. The motion must be seconded or discussion does not move forward. "I second the motion," says Andrew.

3. Now the motion must be stated by the chair. This is to make sure everyone understands it and so the secretary may make an accurate note of it. Jenna says, "There is a motion to appoint Rachel the new point person for the newspaper article about us in the *Newton City Gazette*."

4. The motion can now be debated. Holly mentions that Rachel doesn't have a cell phone or a home email account and indicates this will be a problem for ongoing communication with the *Gazette*. Others agree. The discussion goes on for a few minutes. Then Justin suggests a two-person contact team: Rachel and himself. He has both a home email account and a cell phone. Rachel and several others respond that splitting the duties might create more problems than it solves.

5. At this point, Rachel herself has decided that Justin is the better choice for the job. She proposes an amendment that makes Justin the appointee. The amendment is seconded, voted on, and passed.

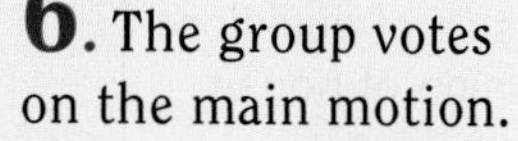

6. The group votes on the main motion.

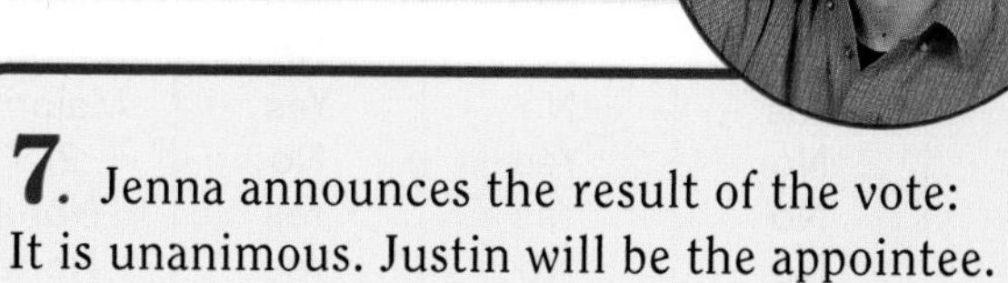

7. Jenna announces the result of the vote: It is unanimous. Justin will be the appointee.

Parliamentary procedure can be complicated. So, many groups appoint or elect a person as **parliamentarian**, someone to help the presiding officer follow the rules. Despite the complexity, however, almost any group can use the procedure to get business done quickly, fairly, and effectively.

The table below gives an overview of the rules of motions. The first twelve motions are ordered by precedence, or rank. A higher ranked motion takes priority over a lower ranked or unranked one. The person who seconds a motion must be someone other than the person who made the motion. Some motions can be debated before voting; others cannot. Some motions can be changed, or amended, and others cannot.

Precedence of Motions

Kind of Motion	Rank	Second Required	Can Be Debated	Can Be Amended	Can Interrupt Speaker	Vote Required
Privileged Motions						
Adjourn	1	Yes	No	No	No	Majority
Recess	2	Yes	No	Yes	No	Majority
Question of privilege	3	Yes	No	No	Yes	Majority
Call for orders of the day	4	No	No	No	Yes	No
Subsidiary Motions						
Lay on the table	5	Yes	No	No	No	No
Previous question	6	Yes	No	No	No	Majority
Limit or extend debate	7	Yes	Yes	Yes	No	2/3
Postpone definitely	8	Yes	Yes	Yes	No	Majority
Refer to committee	9	Yes	Yes	Yes	No	Majority
Amend	10	Yes	Yes	Yes	No	Majority
Postpone indefinitely	11	Yes	Yes	No	No	Majority
Main Motions						
Main motion/resolution	12	Yes	Yes	Yes	No	Majority
Reconsider		Yes	Yes	No	No	Majority
Rescind		Yes	Yes	Yes	No	2/3
Take from table		Yes	No	No	No	Majority
Incidental Motions						
Suspend the rules		Yes	No	No	No	2/3
Withdraw a motion		No	No	No	Yes	Majority
Object to consideration		No	No	No	Yes	2/3
Rise to point of order		No	No	No	Yes	None
Reopen nominations		Yes	No	Yes	No	Majority
Appeal decision of chair		Yes	Yes	No	Yes	Majority
Close nominations		Yes	No	Yes	No	2/3
Call for division of question		No	No	Yes	Yes	None
Call for division of house		No	No	No	Yes	None

In this vote in the United Nations in 1955 on the admission of new members, the United States abstained.

Communication Notebook

Draw a cartoon depicting a person voting "aye," "nay," or "abstain" on a motion. Make the cartoon humorous by including some contradiction between how the person votes and the person appears.

Voting

Voting is how members pass motions. Besides "aye" or "nay," a voting member can **abstain**, meaning he or she can choose to neither support nor oppose the motion.

The method of voting can take a number of forms. Depending on the group norms, members may vote by voice (the "aye" and "nay" way), by raising their hands, by rising from their seats, by filling out a secret ballot, or by answering a roll call. No matter what form the vote takes, the chair or the secretary makes an official count. There are some circumstances in which a two-thirds majority vote is required. However, most motions require only a majority. In the case of a tie, the chair has the right—but not the obligation—to cast the tie-breaking vote. If the tie remains unbroken, the motion cannot pass.

Sometimes a vote is too close to call, and in this case members have the right to ask that the vote be repeated. The chair will then call for a second vote. If the first vote was a voice-only vote, the second vote will typically take another form—one that can be more accurately counted.

The outcome of a parliamentary vote is not set in stone, however. Members are free to make a motion to **rescind**, or cancel, an earlier motion. A member may also move to **reconsider**. When a group reconsiders, it takes a second look at a motion that has passed. But what if a member who voted against a motion moves to reconsider it, thereby slowing down the group's discussion of other points? Parliamentary procedure screens this action by allowing reconsideration only by members who voted on the winning side of the question.

Begin your project by looking back at the **Project Prep** activities in this chapter and using the directions below.

Make Connections

Share ways that you have interacted in formal groups. Then discuss:

- your understanding of the roles involved in parliamentary procedures
- the four kinds of motions
- the process of parliamentary voting.

Focus

Briefly review the group project you are working on: a demonstration of parliamentary procedure.

Plan

Brainstorm a list of meeting events, such as making a motion and debating a motion, for your project. They should illustrate (1) effective parliamentary procedure and (2) behavior that would be considered out of order, such as:

- talking without first being recognized by the chair
- arguing in an unruly manner
- making a rude or inappropriate motion
- interrupting another speaker
- demanding a vote on a motion that is still being discussed.

Surefire Team Building

To get the best results in meetings:

- listen more than you talk
- brainstorm without judging the results
- respect your classmates' opinions and ideas
- learn and abide by your group's rules of order.

Develop

Decide who will act as chair, who will be secretary, and who will make a motion. If you include a parliamentary vote in the presentation, decide how the voting is to be done: by voice or roll call. If you select a voice vote and the vote is uncertain, how will you resolve the vote?

Practice

Practice as often as it takes to make all group members feel confident. Stay within the time limit.

Use the strategy that follows to help make your presentation as good as it can be.

Maintaining and Directing Focus

When presenting in a group, some of the time you will *take focus*, or be the center of attention. When you take focus, be as clear as possible and try to sound natural. When you *give focus* to other group members, use your eyes and body language to point the audience toward the person speaking.

EVALUATING THE PROJECT

Evaluate the presentations using the following rubric.

Score the project on each point, with 4 being "outstanding" and 1 being "needs much improvement."

Come up with an overall score and write a brief paragraph that explains your score.

Understanding of Parliamentary Procedure	Demonstration of Parliamentary Procedure	Creativity and Originality	Preparation and Use of Time
4 Presenters showed insight into parliamentary procedure.	**4** Presenters' demonstration helped illuminate parliamentary procedure.	**4** The presentation was attention-grabbing and unique, interesting, and fun	**4** The presentation flowed smoothly and was neither too short nor too long.
3 Presenters understood the basics of parliamentary procedure.	**3** Presenters' demonstration was fairly helpful in understanding parliamentary procedure.	**3** The presentation was attention-grabbing, interesting, and fun, but not very original.	**3** The presentation progressed fairly smoothly and was neither too short nor too long.
2 Presenters did not seem to understand some elements of parliamentary procedure.	**2** Presenters' demonstration was minimally helpful in understanding parliamentary procedure.	**2** The presentation was fairly interesting and fun, but not original or attention-grabbing.	**2** The presentation had a few awkward moments and went a bit over or noticeably under the time limit.
1 Presenters misunderstood much of parliamentary procedure.	**1** Presenters' demonstration did not help in understanding parliamentary procedure.	**1** The presentation was not original or attention-grabbing and only moderately fun and interesting.	**1** The presentation was not smoothly executed and went well over or well under the time limit.

Communication *Past* and Present

Setting the Record Straight

From Ancient Egyptian Scribes . . .

For as long as humans have conducted business and known how to write, some individuals have had the task of keeping records of the transactions. In ancient Egypt, where education separated the rulers from the ruled, record-keeping was the special duty of a class of intellectuals known as scribes.

Egyptian leaders valued accurate records highly, so scribes were well-respected.

Highly educated, scribes were elite members of society. They were in charge of other people's most important information. That duty not only won the respect and admiration of the public, but it also endowed them with an enormous amount of social power. Their tasks included writing up wills, contracts of all kinds, and private and business letters. They kept track of amounts of crops and goods for sale. They kept records about changes in the weather and in government policies. They maintained lists of births and deaths. With the knowledge and information scribes possessed, they held the keys to the lives of entire communities.

Scribes created one of the earliest forms of shorthand, a system of syllable and word stems they used in place of complete words. This system allowed them to take down complicated information quickly and accurately.

The occupation of scribe was so important and so prized that it was typically handed down within families—from father to son. Only rarely were the sons of men from other professions allowed to become scribes. Unlike many other professionals, scribes had tremendous career stability. They always had work because they were needed to record meetings and business activities at all levels of society.

With the use of laptops and microphones, meeting minutes can be more accurate than ever.

. . . to Microphones and Computer Chips

Now imagine how an ancient Egyptian scribe might respond to this business meeting scenario: A group of people sits around a table. At each end of the table is a very small, powerful microphone. In front of one person is a laptop computer. It is equipped with a sound card that allows the voices in the room to be recorded directly into the computer by means of the table microphones. It's not necessary to keystroke while the meeting is in process. As the meeting continues, the information that the computer gathers is stored in a computer data file.

Changes in technology have meant that contemporary secretaries can take part in meetings virtually hands-free! Later the secretary can transcribe the meeting from the sound card and create a hard copy of the meeting minutes. The secretary listens through a headset and types with his or her hands. To start, stop, and repeat the tape, the secretary controls the recording with a foot pedal. Just like the Egyptian scribes, getting the information down accurately is still the most important goal.

Chapter 13 Review

Using Vocabulary Words

Choose ten of the following terms and describe what each one means and how it would be used in a meeting.

1. abstain
2. adjourn
3. agenda
4. amend
5. chair
6. executive session
7. incidental motion
8. main motion
9. minutes
10. motion
11. parliamentary procedure
12. parliamentarian
13. privileged motion
14. quorum
15. reconsider
16. rescind
17. secretary
18. subsidiary motion
19. table

Reviewing Key Ideas

1. What are some of the characteristics of an effective agenda?
2. List several tasks that members can perform before a parliamentary meeting to help the meeting run more smoothly.
3. How does parliamentary procedure help a meeting run smoothly?
4. Identify several types of information that should be included in the minutes of a parliamentary meeting.
5. Explain the four types of motions used in parliamentary procedure.

Reflecting on Your Project

With your small group, discuss which parts of your project went especially well and which gave you the most trouble. Come up with two or three strategies for dealing with problem areas in future projects and presentations.

Responding to the Essential Question

Create a brief chapter summary that answers the question, "How does parliamentary procedure work?" When you finish, compare and contrast your summary with that of a partner.

Extending Your Understanding

Everyday Life

1. What friend or family member would make a great presiding officer in a parliamentary group? List the communication and leadership skills this person possesses that make him or her right for the job.
2. Sit in on a meeting of your student council. Take detailed notes on how the agenda governs the progress of the meeting. Report back to the class with your observations.
3. Visit a public meeting and take notes as if you are providing meeting minutes. Limit your notes to a single typed page, but summarize all group activities and discussions.

In the Media

4. C-SPAN broadcasts the proceedings of Congress, including debates, committee hearings, confirmation hearings, etc. Watch one of the broadcasts that is parliamentary in nature. Maintain a list of motions and votes. Compare their process with the chart of motions on page 264.
5. Check out a courtroom drama on TV, and identify the different aspects of procedure used there.

Research

6. Use your research skills to find out more about parliamentary procedure. Give a short informative speech on your findings.
7. Using this chapter as a jumping-off point, use the Internet and other sources to provide further background for a report on General Henry M. Robert, author of Robert's Rules of Order.
8. Reread the Communication in a Diverse World feature on page 260. Do further research to find out more about the purpose and appearance of various talking sticks. Then use found materials to create a talking stick of your own.

Interpreting Graphics

Copy the diagram on the right on a separate sheet of paper. Make the scale large enough to allow you to write inside the circles easily. Then fill in the circles to identify the various kinds of motions, how they function, and how they relate to one another.

Additional Projects

1. **Group Project:** Working with your project group, imagine that you are all members of your state's legislative body. Come up with three possible laws your group will discuss during a meeting. Write up an agenda. As you discuss the proposed laws, use all four types of parliamentary motions.
2. **Individual Project:** Create a poster or graphic organizer depicting the role of parliamentary procedure in American democracy. Begin with Internet research to give yourself enough information for an informative graphic. Try to create eye-catching visuals using colorful drawings, stylish lettering, or images cut from magazines. When you have finished, display your work for the class.

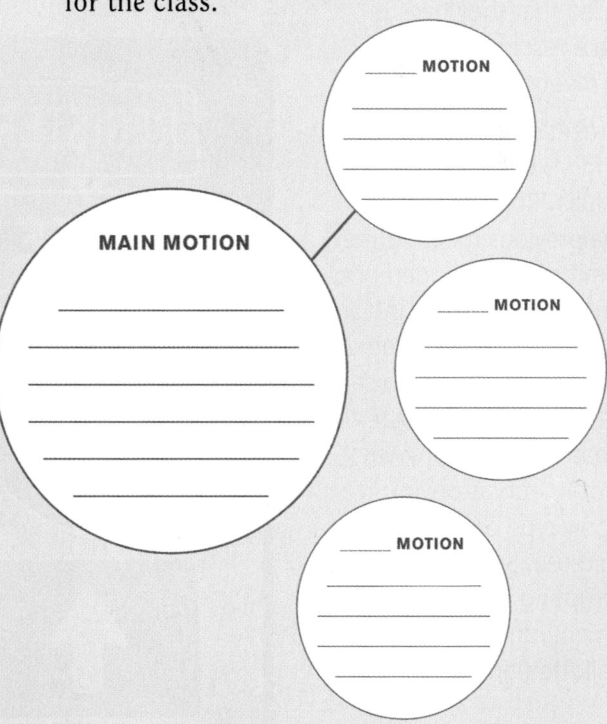

Unit Three

Culminating Activities

In this unit you have explored group communication: the power of groups, group dynamics and roles, group discussions, and parliamentary procedure. The activities on these pages will help you apply your understandings to situations in everyday life.

Workplace Workout

Planning a media campaign to encourage young people to vote, the interns at the advertising agency faced a conflict. They could not agree on which types of media to use in the campaign. Amber, the committee leader, decided that they had to reach a resolution in their next meeting.

The meeting began with an argument between Rokeem and Julia. Rokeem said that in the previous meeting the committee had decided not to produce radio ads, but Julia claimed that no such decision had been reached. Zach said it was ridiculous to waste time on that argument anyway; the Internet was obviously the only type of media they should use. Soledad kept interrupting everyone. When the meeting had run over the allotted time, Amber exclaimed, "We're using the Internet and TV. And that's final."

"And you can count me out," said Julia and Rokeem simultaneously.

What Went Wrong? With a partner, reread the scenario aloud, keeping in mind what you have learned about group roles, effective leadership and participation in group discussions, and working toward a resolution. As you read, stop after each sentence, and discuss what the committee member(s) did wrong. Take notes on your discussion.

Make it Right With your partner, create an action plan for the committee to help the members hold effective meetings and reach a resolution in the future. Present your action plan to the class, and explain the reasons for each element of your plan.

GenderJourney

The merits of single-sex versus coed education have been the subject of much research and discussion. Hold a class debate about the issue. To develop reasons and gather evidence for your argument, your team should create a questionnaire and ask an equal number of males and females whether they think boys and girls tend to play different roles and behave in different ways in groups. Research the issue using library and Internet sources as well. To present a strong argument, be sure to support all of your reasons with evidence.

Media Master

Choose a local, state, or national leader, and analyze the way this leader is portrayed in the media. Do you think the media's image of this leader is fair and accurate, or is it biased? Write a script for a short documentary aimed at a middle-school audience in which you communicate your image of this leader. Focus on how effectively the leader motivates his or her group to function productively. (See page 576 for documentary guidelines.)

OWN IT!

Think about Margaret Mead's statement at the beginning of Unit 3: "Never doubt that a small group of thoughtful, committed citizens can change the world; indeed, it is the only thing that ever has." (See page 197.) Reflect on what you have learned in this unit, and think about groups that have brought about change. Could one person have produced these results? Then, imagine that you and some friends are starting an organization dedicated to an important cause. Write the "About Us" page for the organization's Web site. Use Mead's statement to explain the organization's purpose.

Unit Four

Public Speaking

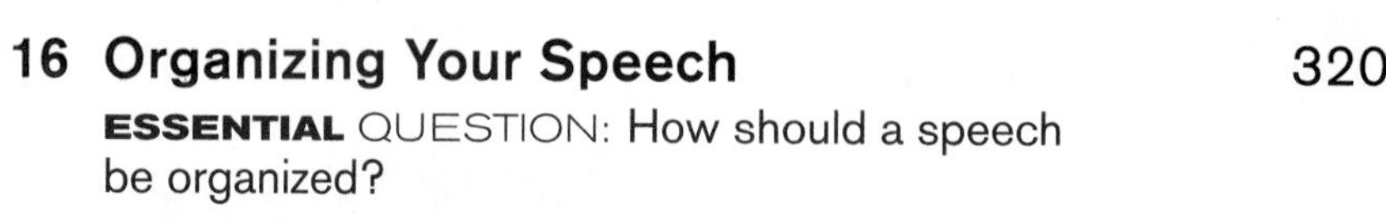

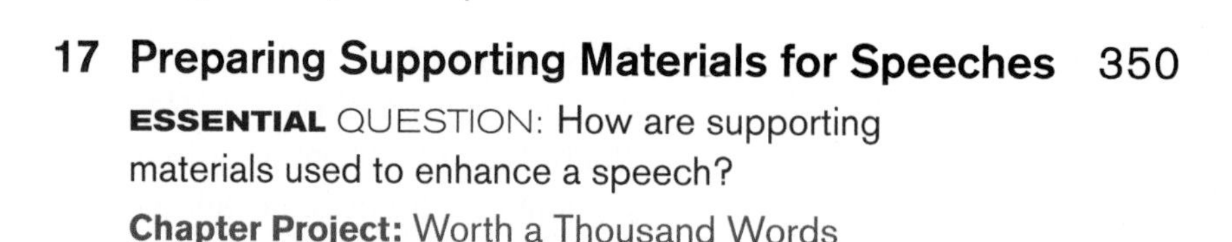

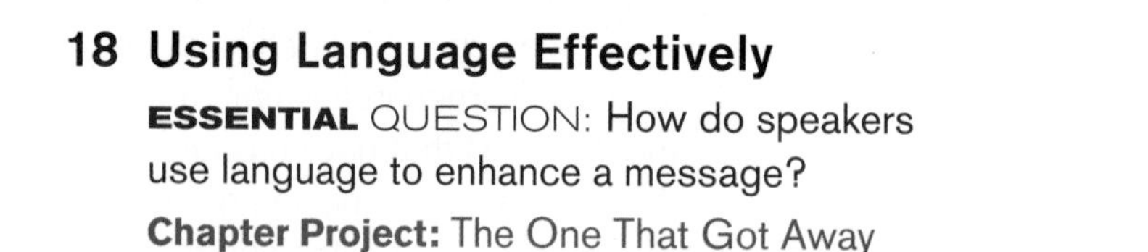

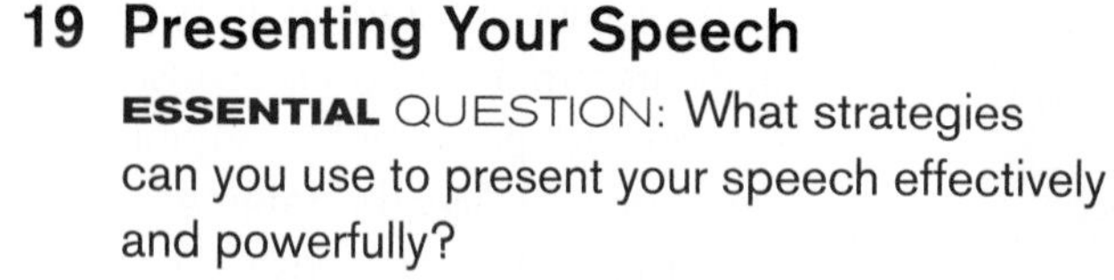

There are always three speeches for every one you
actually gave. The one you practiced, the one you
gave, and the one you wish you gave.
– Dale Carnegie

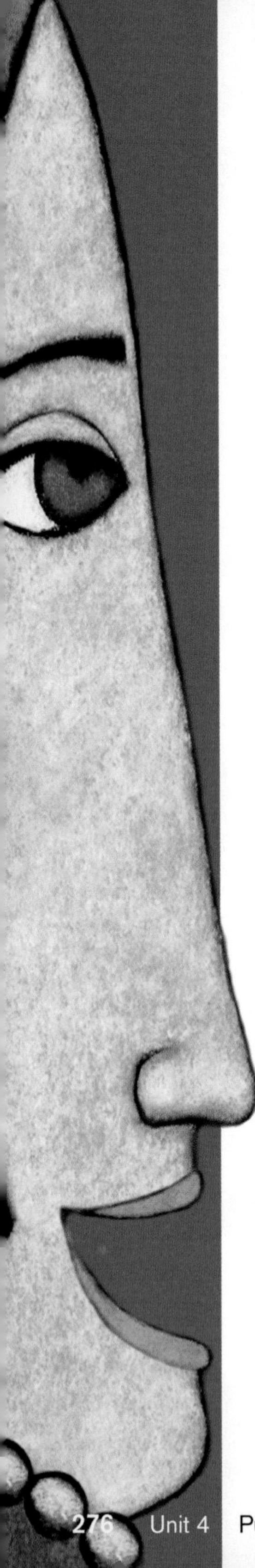

Preparing to Speak

ESSENTIAL QUESTION

What can you do to prepare for a speech?

Chapter Project: Get to the Point!

Have you ever been concentrating on one thing when someone tried to talk to you about something else? If so, you probably appreciate a speaker who gets to the point. This project will help you "get to the point" that will best suit your audience, speaking purpose, and occasion.

Your teacher will pair you with a partner and assign you a very broad topic, such as music or home safety. You and your partner will choose an audience, purpose, and occasion and then work together to limit your topic and write a thesis statement and short outline of a speech. You will then take no more than two minutes to discuss with your classmates how you kept your audience, purpose, and occasion in mind when you limited the topic. Your classmates will consider how effectively you "got to the point." Refer to the CAPS guidelines below as you work.

The rubric on page 291 shows the traits on which your presentation will be evaluated.

CONCEPT	preparation is critical in making an effective presentation
AUDIENCE	classmates and teacher
PURPOSE	understand the important aspects of preparing a speech
SITUATION	classroom presentation

KEY VOCABULARY

purpose statement
controlling purpose
thesis statement

Since DNA is such a broad subject, these students had to zero in on a specific aspect of the subject so their speech for science class would have a clear point.

Speak Up!

You and your friends play soccer in a city park almost every evening. Recently other residents of the city have complained that your games are interfering with their enjoyment of the park. They have asked the city council to ban all sports from the park. You want to present your side to the council. How would you prepare your arguments? Discuss your ideas with your classmates and keep these thoughts in mind as you read this chapter.

BACKGROUND FOR THE PROJECT

Pages 278–289 will provide the information you'll need to complete this project.

Analyzing Audience, Purpose, and Occasion

When preparing to speak before a group of people, you consider three factors: your audience, your purpose for speaking, and the occasion of the speech. You think about the age of your audience as well as their interests and attitudes. You are clear about your purpose, or reason, for speaking and what you hope to accomplish. You also think about the occasion—is it a birthday party, a pep rally, a town council meeting? Keeping these three factors in mind helps you prepare your speech.

Suppose you are planning a speech about the benefits of a new wing of the public library. How would you plan to address an audience of adults? How might your planning differ if you were speaking to your own classmates? Your purpose in speaking would likely be somewhat different, as would the details and language of your presentation. The chart below shows how different audiences would influence your decisions when speaking about a new library wing.

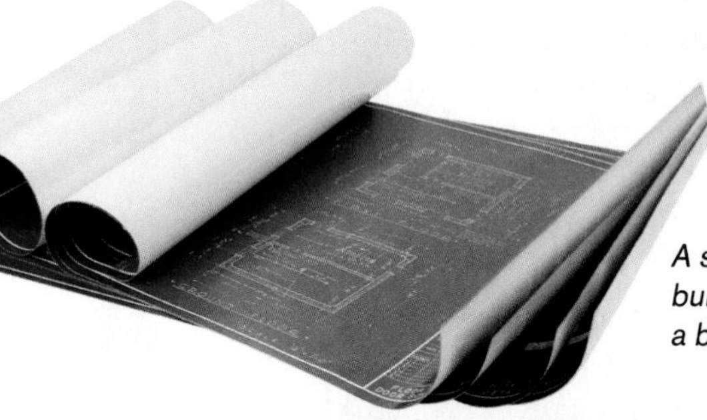

A speech, like a building, needs a blueprint.

KEY POINT

As you prepare a speech, keep in mind whom you are speaking to, why you are speaking, and when and where you are speaking.

	Audience: High School Students	Audience: Adults
Purpose	Inform them about the new library wing and the many ways they could use it	Inform them about the new library wing and encourage them to support it financially
Occasion	A free screening at the library of a popular comic film that takes place in a library	A lecture at the library by a well-known local author
Decisions	• Keep it lighthearted and fun: the audience came to see a funny movie. • Stress the services of the new wing useful for students–computers, help with research, discussion groups, places to study with friends. • Hand out a library calendar of events especially designed for teens.	• Keep it brief: people came to hear the author. • Focus on the civic pride this wing will create. • Stress the vital contribution to community life the wing will offer the community. • Make an appeal for support. • Hand out a brochure about the new wing with an envelope for contributions.

Understanding Your Audience

The first step in preparing a speech is to think about your audience and what you know about them. Develop a profile of your audience by asking yourself the questions below.

- **What are your audience's assumptions and values?** Knowing these will help you prepare a presentation that will appeal to them and win their respect.
- **What do they know, and what do they need to know?** Don't refer to things that are unfamiliar to your audience or bore them with facts they already know. Give them only useful information.
- **What is your relationship to the audience?** Knowing this will help you use the appropriate level of language.
- **What effect do you want to have on them?** Do you want the audience to do something as a result of what you say or to change the way they think about a certain issue?

PROJECT PREP

With your **project partner**, discuss the kinds of audiences to whom you might present a speech on the topic your teacher has assigned you. Then decide on the audience and discuss the issues raised above.

Understanding Your Purpose

After you have chosen your topic and profiled your audience, next ask yourself: "What do I hope to accomplish with my speech?" Your answer will fall within one of these basic communication purposes.

Entertain	
interest amuse	please enliven

Inform	
teach educate	familiarize introduce

Persuade	
convince win over	influence cause to act

Many speeches combine purposes. Suppose, for example, you were giving a speech on how humor can help people recover from illness. While your main purpose would be to inform, you would probably also sprinkle your speech generously with humor, which would also entertain your listeners. Too much humor, though, might distract listeners from your main purpose of informing.

Understanding the Occasion

Finally, when preparing a speech, consider the occasion. Why will everyone be gathered at this time and place? What do they expect? What does the occasion call for? Considering the occasion will help you select the appropriate content and tone for your speech.

Humor in the right amount can be appropriate for many different kinds of speeches.

Choosing Your Topic

The topic you choose should be appropriate for the audience and the occasion. It should also suit you. That is, it should be something you already know about or genuinely want to learn about. After you have come up with several possible topics, use the questions below to help you choose one that takes all three considerations into account.

Consider Your Audience

- What does your audience already know about the topic?
- What does the audience need to know?
- How can you make your topic fresh, original, and interesting?
- Will your audience expect to be entertained, informed, or persuaded? Will the topic allow you to meet your audience's expectations?

A speech about volunteering at an animal shelter could make good use of photos of the animals.

Consider the Occasion

- Can you speak on this topic in the amount of time allotted?
- Will developing the topic give you a speech that is long enough but not too long?
- Is the topic appropriate for the occasion?
- How might the occasion influence what the audience considers an appropriate topic?
- Are you comfortable speaking about the topic on this occasion?

Consider Yourself

- What topic interests you?
- Is there a topic you already have some information about through experience or study?
- Do you have enough time to prepare adequately to speak about the topic?
- Will you enjoy speaking about this topic?
- Does the topic allow you to be entertaining, informative, or persuasive?

What if the topic has already been determined—either by the situation or by someone else? For example, imagine that your basketball team won the state championship and your principal asked you to talk to community groups about the experience. Or perhaps you're a volunteer at an animal shelter, and the director asks you to tell other students about the shelter and its work. The topic has been chosen for you, but you must make it your own. Use the lists above to help you adjust the topic to your audience and situation as well as your own interests.

Limiting Your Topic

If you are going to talk about the local animal shelter, your broad topic is clear, but what aspects of the animal shelter will you focus on? You can't possibly tell the audience everything. So you narrow the topic and zero in on the points that are most appropriate for your audience and occasion and that will achieve your purpose. The following questions can help you sift through a broad topic and find a narrow topic within it that will be suitable for your audience.

- What is it? Define your topic.
- What are examples of your topic? Which are most interesting? Most typical? Most unusual? Most controversial?
- What are the topic's features? Can you break the topic down into subtopics, parts, or groups?
- What is the most important feature of the topic for your audience?
- What is the nature of the topic? Is it a process, a series of steps, or part of a series of steps?
- Is your topic part of a larger topic? Will the audience be aware that it is?
- What are the results or consequences of the topic?
- What have others said about the topic?
- Does investigation into the topic reveal a need for change? If so, what kind?

PROJECT PREP

Discuss with your **project partner** how to focus more closely on the topic your teacher has assigned you. How can you limit your topic? Use the points above to help you.

Focusing on one dog might unify a speech covering several topics related to an animal shelter.

Occasionally, you may be asked to make a speech that covers more than one topic. For example, the director of the animal shelter asks you to talk about three specific things—the animal adoption requirements, the shelter's volunteer dog-walking program, and the pet surrender policies. To accomplish all of these purposes, you would look for ways to connect the topics. The approaches below should help.

- Look for a unifying principle that connects the different topics.
- Use organization and style to help create unity.
- Tell your audience you are going to discuss three different topics. Then speak on each topic.

Limiting Your Purpose

As you read on page 279, speeches tend to fulfill one or more of three broad purposes—to entertain, to inform, and to persuade. A strong speech, though, has a focused purpose within one of those categories. One way to focus your purpose is to create a **purpose statement**, a written account of the specific outcomes you want your speech to achieve. The limited purposes in the second column of the chart below show specific purposes *beyond* the general purposes of entertaining, informing, or persuading. Notice that both these purpose statements mention the audience as well as the purpose.

Keeping your purpose statement in mind as you prepare your speech will help you stay focused on your goal and determine what information is relevant to your goal and what is not.

Topic	Purpose Statement
Basketball team's victory at state finals	to inform the community about the basketball team's success in order to inspire pride and good feeling about the achievements of its young people
Animal shelter's volunteer dog-walking program	to persuade other teens to volunteer to walk dogs at the shelter

Controlling Purpose

Your limited purpose is also called your **controlling purpose**. This name shows how important a focused purpose is to a speech: it controls all your choices about what to include and what to leave out. It steers your speech, keeping it from taking unnecessary side roads.

Your purpose statement may or may not be included in your speech. You might include it because you want to avoid surprising anyone with a request for help: "I'd like to tell you about my experience with the dog-walking program at the animal shelter in the hope that some of you will want to help out." However, consider a purpose statement such as, "I'm here to talk about our basketball team's victory so you can all feel good about what's happening at our school." Including this would not add much to your presentation.

What might be the purpose of a speech about a basketball victory?

Thesis Statement

A **thesis statement** is a way of concisely and gracefully expressing the essential idea of your speech. A thesis statement is your message reduced to a single sentence. Unlike the purpose statement, it doesn't mention the audience or the effect you hope your speech will have on them. The examples below show how a thesis statement differs from a purpose statement. You could work either of the two thesis statements into the introduction to a speech.

Three reasons justify including a thesis statement early in your speech. First, audiences usually expect it. They want a statement that not only states the topic but also grabs their attention. They want more than just, "My topic is the volunteer dog-walker program at the animal shelter." Second, a thesis statement helps the audience follow your speech closely. For example, if you promise to reveal a way to get great exercise while having fun, your audience will probably be very interested. Third, a well-written thesis statement can ease the audience into the content and purpose of your speech. An audience who hears, "I'm going to try to persuade you to volunteer at the shelter," might tune you out before you have a chance to tell them how much fun someone can have walking the dogs there.

Topic	Purpose Statement	Thesis Statement
Basketball team's victory at state finals	to inform the community about the basketball team's success in order to inspire pride and good feeling about the achievements of its young people	Winning the state championship was an achievement not only for our team but for our school and our community.
Animal shelter's volunteer dog-walking program	to persuade other teens to volunteer to help walk dogs at the shelter	Walking a dog is great fun and good exercise. I'm going to tell you how you can do it even if you don't own a dog!

A Good Thesis Statement . . .			
Creates Interest	**Is Precise**	**Is Concise**	**Is Reasonable**
When the audience hears a good thesis statement, they want to know more.	It uses exact words–words that appeal to the audience and tell exactly what your speech is about.	It is brief. It leaves out fillers such as "I believe" or "in my opinion."	It doesn't overstate the case or promise things that can't be proven. It avoids words such as *never, all, always, totally.*

The chart below can help you turn a weak thesis statement into a strong one. Read the weak statement and think about how to improve it. Then read the improved thesis statement and the reason it is better.

Weak Thesis Statement	Improved Thesis Statement	Why It's Better
I'm going to tell you about walking dogs at the animal shelter. Walking dogs at the animal shelter is a good thing.	Walking a dog is fun and great exercise, and I'm going to tell you how you can do it even if you don't own a dog.	The audience will want to hear about something that promises to be fun and good exercise. Avoid phrases such as *a good thing*. They are vague and boring.
If you ask me, walking a dog is wonderful way to get exercise, superior to running or skating, because you don't have to get all sweaty, you don't have to wear kneepads, and you don't have to be all by yourself–you can be with a dog.	Walking a dog is an excellent way to get exercise, and walking dogs at the animal shelter is the perfect way to help animals in need.	Using fewer words makes your message clear and focused. Avoid phrases such as *if you ask me* or *in my opinion*. Avoid unnecessary references (such as *running or skating*, *getting sweaty* and *kneepads*).
Volunteering to walk dogs at the animal shelter will make you a totally fit and happy person.	Walking dogs at the animal shelter is a good way to keep fit and feel good about what you're doing.	The first statement is unsupportable and rings false. The improved statement is reasonable.

What would you include in a thesis statement for a speech about walking dogs?

Clarify a controlling purpose and create an effective thesis statement for each speech you give.

PROJECT PREP

With your **project partner**, write a thesis statement for the topic your teacher has assigned you, taking into account how you have limited the topic.

Analyzing a Speech to Understand Purpose

Following is an excerpt from a speech by Richard W. Riley, former Secretary of Education. One of his annual "back-to-school" addresses, this speech had special relevance in the wake of several incidents of school violence. Analyzing this excerpt can help you understand how a speaker can take a broad subject, narrow it, develop a purpose and a thesis, and create a unified presentation in which all the details support the controlling purpose.

Two Key Transitions: Ninth and Twelfth Grades

> The title focuses audience attention on the chosen subject. He limits his topic to "transitions."

1 Two very important transition points take place in the American adolescent experience: when young people first enter high school; and when they graduate. These transitions really amount to rites of passage, as they come at key moments in adolescent development. We need to see them in a new light.

> This paragraph identifies the transitions and advances the simple thesis: "We need to see them in a new light." The audience is invited to hear new ideas about two critical moments in adolescent development.

2 The typical eighth grader, for example, leaves a much smaller elementary or middle school and suddenly finds himself in a very big and, at times, impersonal high school. The transition can, at times, be overwhelming. The result is that some students become low achievers, some drop out, and some decide that they are not college material.

> The speech focuses first on the first transition–into ninth grade. The style is simple and straightforward. This paragraph outlines the problems.

3 And suicide prevention experts tell us that ninth grade is the most troubling year. So this first transition deserves our attention. Several recommendations come to mind.

> This short paragraph both highlights the urgency of the problem and moves the audience toward a solution.

4 Schools can create a smoother transition in a number of ways, such as freshmen academies, regular contact with the same group of teachers and advisors, and transition courses that address new challenges from study skills to understanding other cultures. The key is to create smaller and more personalized learning environments for these young people.

> The organization of the speech breaks the solution down to what schools can do . . .

5 Parents need to stay very involved with their children when they enter high school. This is so important and goes against the common assumption that parents should give their teenagers more independence. The truth of the matter is that teenagers want to grow and

> what parents can do . . .

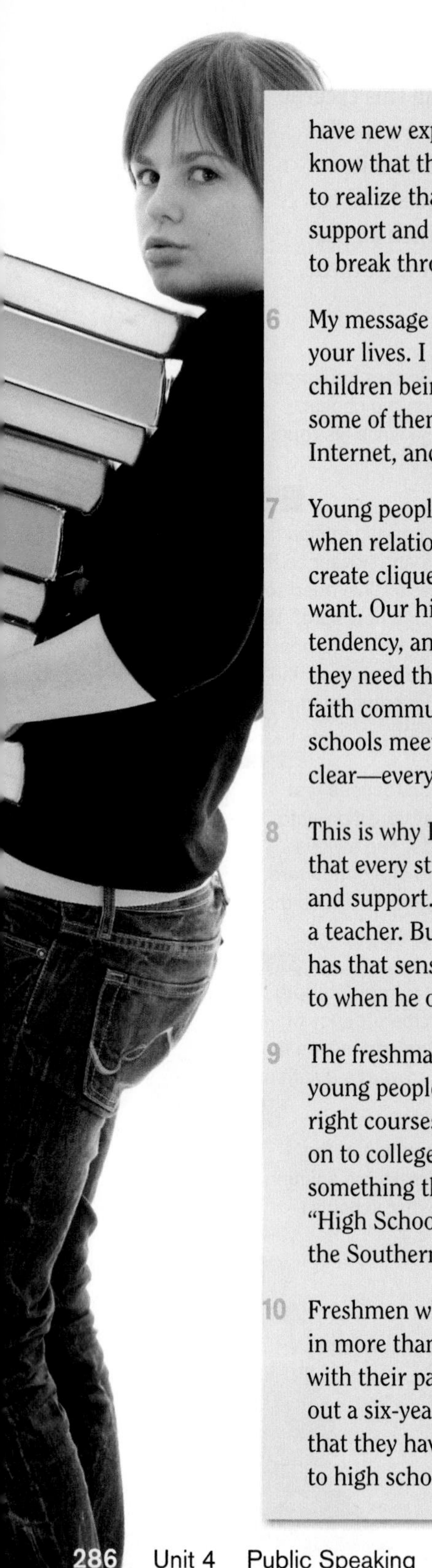

have new experiences; at the same time, they want to know that their parents are there for them. Parents need to realize that they are still the most important source of support and guidance for teenagers. Sometimes it is hard to break through.

6 My message to parents is to stay involved. Slow down your lives. I hear a real concern from parents about their children being bombarded by a multitude of messages—some of them harmful—from television, movies, the Internet, and even from their children's best friends.

7 Young people can be very tough on each other at a time when relationships are so important to them. They create cliques, groups, and select out those they do not want. Our high schools have to push back against this tendency, and students are telling us that this is where they need the most support. Community groups and faith communities can also play a positive role in helping schools meet this challenge. The message should be very clear—every teenager matters.

what communities can do . . .

8 This is why I believe that schools should set a real goal that every student has some adult to turn to for advice and support. It may be a counselor, a mentor, a coach, or a teacher. But the key is to make sure that every teenager has that sense of security about knowing whom to turn to when he or she is struggling.

and what adults in general can do.

9 The freshman year is also a crucial year for getting young people on the right track in terms of taking the right courses and getting them thinking about going on to college. This is why I want to recommend highly something that Gene Bottoms is doing as part of his "High School That Works" initiative that is supported by the Southern Regional Education Board.

In this paragraph, the speech prepares the audience for a new idea–the "High School That Works" initiative.

10 Freshmen who participate in this program, which is now in more than 500 high schools across the South, sit down with their parents and a high school advisor and sketch out a six-year plan. The young people get the message that they have a new and higher horizon and that going to high school has a larger purpose.

In this paragraph, the speech is more specific about the program that is achieving the desired results.

11 We can also do more to create new pathways to learning and to adulthood. In a world exploding with knowledge, with teenagers hooked on the Internet as never before, the traditional seven-periods-a-day way of learning may not be the best or the only way to educate our young people.

At this point, the speech uses this organization pattern to focus on the second transition: moving beyond high school and into adulthood.

12 New pathways to learning and adulthood mean new connections to colleges and universities, new connections with other institutions in the community, whether it is a hospital, a bank, a zoo, or a museum. Close to 230,000 high school students, for example, are now taking college-level courses across the country. Tech Prep courses and School-to-Work programs, for example, are great ways to link high school students to community colleges.

The speech addresses the need to link high schools with the outside world, including other institutions in the community . . .

13 High schools of the future need to see themselves as the starting place where young people launch themselves into other learning experiences, and then come back to their high school to integrate what they have learned.

. . . and opportunities for other types of important learning experiences.

14 I also encourage schools to do some creative thinking about the senior year experience. Some high school seniors start "checking out" once they have filled out their last college application or received an early acceptance notice from college. The young people tell us in a very direct way that they want to move on.

The speech focuses on the senior year specifically. This is one of the "transitions." Notice how the speech's purpose is reflected in the phrase, "I also encourage schools to do some creative thinking." This is the language of gentle persuasion.

15 Senior year should be a well-thought-out transition into adulthood with students being given increasing responsibility. They should be given many more opportunities to be out in the community in structured internships, apprenticeships, or service-learning opportunities. By treating these young men and women as adults, we send a powerful message that we expect adult behavior from them as well.

The words *adulthood* and *adults* are repeated here. The focus on transition is reflected in the use of the terms internships, apprenticeships, and service-learning.

16 I end now with this thought. Believe in our young people. I say that again—believe in our young people. Please help me give them a message of hope, promise and possibilities. I am tired and weary of the worn-out nostalgia and pessimism that seems to haunt American thinking when it comes to our young people.

Although the speech is about schools, the conclusion focuses on young people.

17 Let us reject the twin belief that once there was a time in American education when all things were better; and the negative assumption that this generation of young people can't quite cut it. Our young people don't buy that and neither do I.

The language now becomes more inspirational and less political. The speech switches focus—from problems to a solution involving what good schools can accomplish for everyone.

18 Surely, in this time of peace and prosperity, in this great nation—the world's best democracy and hope—we can send a more positive message than that to our nation's young people.

19 I believe in America's young people. They are optimistic and ambitious and they are looking for direction. If you don't know a high school student, go out and meet one.

20 The high school student you meet will be full of possibilities and bored at the same time; extraordinarily creative and, at times, absolutely clueless. High school students will be full of themselves, and scared to death about what people are thinking about them. They are our children and grandchildren. And in a few years, when all of us are in our rocking chairs, they will be our leaders.

21 Let's give them hope and promise for the coming times, and let's create high schools that are exciting, exploring, creative, and challenging, high schools that spark all of our young people to see the full value of their God-given potential.

Thank you.

Is This Job for Me?

Search: Speechwriter

The job of John F. Kennedy's speechwriters was made easier by Kennedy's own gift with words.

Every four years, usually on January 20, on the steps of the Capitol in Washington, D.C., a President of the United States takes the Oath of Office. After the swearing in, the newly inaugurated President delivers the first speech of the new term. Every President strives to make this inaugural address memorable. Some have been exceptionally inspiring. In 1933, Franklin Roosevelt spoke these words to a nation suffering the hardship of the Great Depression: "Let me assert my firm belief that the only thing we have to fear is fear itself–nameless, unreasoning, unjustified terror which paralyzes needed effort to convert retreat into advance."

In his inaugural address in 1961, John F. Kennedy energized the country when he said: "And so, my fellow Americans: Ask not what your country can do for you–ask what you can do for your country."

With the exception of Abraham Lincoln, who wrote all of his own speeches, American Presidents have always had help writing their speeches. Calvin Coolidge was the first to hire a full-time *speechwriter*, and every President since then has done the same. Many speechwriters were English majors in college.

Does speechwriting interest you? Measure yourself with this ability inventory to find out if you have the basic traits you need. Do you:

- ✓ Listen carefully?
- ✓ Research thoroughly?
- ✓ Think in an organized way?
- ✓ Have superior writing skills?
- ✓ Find creative solutions to problems?
- ✓ Have a broad vocabulary?
- ✓ Work well on a one-to-one basis?

As a professional speechwriter, you might have job opportunities in the following areas.

Field	Who Would Need Your Services
Government/Politics	Politicians in federal and state government, mayors of major cities, candidates for important offices
Corporations	Company presidents, CEOs, high-level corporate officers
Academics	Presidents of colleges and universities
Not-for-profit organizations	Organization presidents and professional fundraisers

Begin your project by looking back at the **Project Prep** activities in this chapter and using the directions below.

Make Connections

Discuss with your partner the following skills for preparing speeches.

- how to analyze and understand your audience, your purpose, and the occasion
- how to select a topic and give it focus
- how to determine your controlling purpose and use it to unify your presentation
- how to analyze a speech and understand its structure and organization.

Focus

Review your project description. You and your partner will limit a topic your teacher has assigned to you; determine your audience, purpose, and occasion; and write a thesis statement.

Surefire Focusing

To help you narrow your thesis statement, rewrite it using only half the number of words. Notice what information you think is most important to keep.

Plan

You should have already limited your topic and decided on your audience, purpose, and occasion. Now you can refine your planning.

- Are you writing primarily to inform, persuade, or entertain?
- What are the expectations of your audience?
- Write a purpose statement and refine your thesis statement to share in class.
- Write a short outline of the speech.

Develop

Remove anything that is not relevant to your audience, purpose, and occasion. Talk with your classmates and teacher about the reasons behind your plan.

Practice

Read your thesis statement and run through the discussion of your topic and the audience, purpose, and occasion of your speech.

Use the strategy that follows to help make your presentation as good as it can be.

You and your partner should now be ready to discuss your ideas for a speech by explaining how you limited the topic; determined the audience, purpose, and occasion; and created your thesis statement.

Thinking On Your Feet

Sometimes a listener may throw you for a loop with a question. To stay on track, ask the person to rephrase the question. Then you and your partner can try to answer it to the best of your ability.

EVALUATING THE PROJECT

Evaluate the presentations using the following rubric.

Score the demonstration on each point, with 4 being "outstanding" and 1 being "needs much improvement." Come up with an overall score and write a brief paragraph that explains your score.

Understanding the Importance of Preparation	Discussion of Audience, Purpose, Occasion, Thesis Statement	Creativity and Originality	Preparation and Use of Time
4 Presenters showed insight into speech preparation.	**4** Presenters' discussion helped illuminate the speech preparation process.	**4** Choice of audience and purpose was creative and interesting.	**4** The discussion showed careful preparation and stayed within the time frame.
3 Presenters demonstrated understanding of the speech preparation process.	**3** Presenters' discussion was fairly helpful in understanding the speech preparation process.	**3** The discussion was interesting, but choice of audience and purpose was weak.	**3** The discussion was fairly well-prepared and stayed within the time frame.
2 Presenters did not demonstrate a clear understanding of speech preparation.	**2** Presenters' discussion was minimally helpful in understanding the speech preparation process.	**2** The discussion was fairly interesting, but choice of purpose was poor.	**2** The discussion showed little preparation but was within the time frame.
1 Presenters misunderstood much of the speech preparation process.	**1** Presenters' discussion did not help in understanding the speech preparation process.	**1** The discussion was not interesting. Choice of audience and/or purpose was misguided.	**1** The discussion showed no preparation and ignored the time frame.

Communication *Past* and Present

Finding a Public Voice

From True Womanhood at Home . . .

For much of the nation's history women were generally not allowed to speak at public gatherings. In the early 1800s, "true womanhood" required that women stay in their "rightful" sphere—the home—and not venture into the masculine public world of business and politics. Some women were nonetheless committed to having their voices heard and sometimes tried to disguise the nature of their comments. For example, to avoid the appearance of public speaking, educator Emma Hart Willard stayed in her seat as she spoke before an assembly in New York in 1819.

By mid-century, many women were drawn to the anti-slavery movement. Some anti-slavery leaders did not want women speaking out in public on the subject, since the furor over the women's public presence would detract from anti-slavery efforts. In the 1830s, for example, Sarah and Angelina Grimké—white Southerners who took up the anti-slavery cause—were booed when they tried to speak in public, especially before gatherings that included men. Reactions such as these often served to raise awareness among women that their own rights were also limited.

One woman, Sojourner Truth, embodied the legacy of both enslaved and repressed women. By the time she delivered her most famous speech in 1851 at the Ohio Woman's Rights Convention in Akron, more and more women were speaking out in public. Few, however, touched their listeners as deeply as Sojourner Truth in her "Ain't I a Woman?" speech. The entire speech is reprinted in the Communication Sourcebook (see page 609).

That man over there says that women need to be helped into carriages, and lifted over ditches, and to have the best place everywhere. Nobody ever helps me into carriages, or over mud-puddles, or gives me any best place! And ain't I a woman?

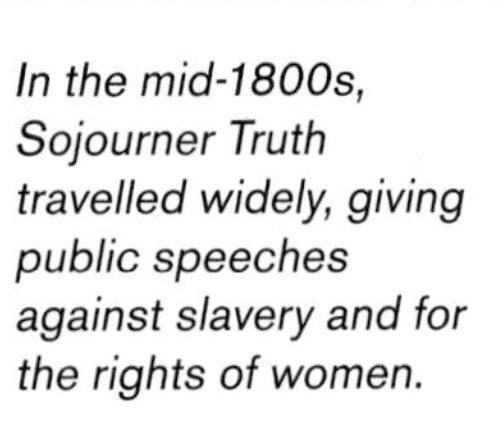

In the mid-1800s, Sojourner Truth travelled widely, giving public speeches against slavery and for the rights of women.

Queen Rania follows in a long tradition of advocates for the rights of women.

. . . to the Public Spotlight

Women in the United States are now welcome in the public spotlight. In some other cultures, however, many women are still expected to refrain from public speaking. In some Arab countries, for example, women are expected to keep not only their faces hidden but also their thoughts and words—at least from men who are not relatives. Yet great role models are helping to bring change. Queen Rania of Jordan, for example, travels the world speaking out on behalf of women's and children's rights. She encourages creating counseling centers to reduce child abuse. She speaks strongly against "honor killings," the murders of female family members believed to have brought dishonor to the family. Speaking both English and Arabic, Queen Rania gracefully disarms hurtful stereotypes about the Arab culture wherever she goes. Following is an excerpt from a speech she gave at the United Nations Foundation.

You all know the old saying, give a man a fish and you feed him for a day; teach a man to fish and you will feed him for a lifetime. Well . . . when you teach a woman to fish, everybody eats. Study after study shows that investing in women's leadership and development is one of the smartest investments societies can make . . . Today, women in the Middle East and North Africa have the world's lowest rate of economic participation. But the landscape is changing. We've made real strides in closing gender gaps in health and education. In Jordan, we have 89 percent of children in primary school . . . studies show that Arab girls perform better than boys in school—which makes me suspect that if you teach an Arab woman to fish, it won't be long before she invents a better fishing pole!

Queen Rania seeks audiences wherever she can find them, often using current technology to share her message. You can watch her on YouTube to appreciate her powerful presence.

Chapter 14 Review

Using Vocabulary Words

Read the terms below. Write your own definition of the term and then use it in a sentence.

1. controlling purpose
2. purpose statement
3. thesis statement

Reviewing Key Ideas

1. List the three factors you should consider when you are preparing to speak to a group and explain how each influences what you say and how you say it.
2. List the three basic purposes for a speech and tell how a successful speech might have more than one purpose.
3. Tell what a *thesis* is and explain why having a thesis will help you narrow down your topic.
4. Explain the importance of a purpose statement as you prepare your presentation.

Reflecting on Your Project

With your partner, discuss whether your experience preparing for your presentation illustrates the saying, "It takes one hour of preparation for each minute of presentation time." Discuss which parts of the preparation were most difficult and which you thought were most important to the success of your project.

Responding to the Essential Question

Use the headings in this chapter to help you write a brief chapter summary that answers the question, "What can you do to prepare for a speech?"

Extending Your Understanding

Everyday Life

1. Think about purpose for speaking as you carry on your everyday conversations. Try to be aware of times when you are speaking to inform, to entertain, or persuade. Then draw a conclusion about what is the most frequent purpose of your part of conversations.
2. While watching a TV show, think about the dialogue. As each new person speaks, decide what the purpose for speaking is and note it on a piece of paper, using *I* for inform, *E* for entertain, and *P* for persuade. Review what you recorded and determine which is the most frequent purpose for each character.
3. Compare two conversations you have with your friends or your family. Think about the topics you talked about in each situation and your most frequent purpose for speaking. Then draw some conclusions about the effect audience has on topic and purpose in personal conversation.

In the Media

4. Listen to a political speech on television. As you listen, try to identify the topic and the purpose. Also try to map or outline the speech to show how the information and ideas are organized.
5. Find an example in a newspaper of writing that is meant to inform, writing that is meant to entertain, and writing that is meant to persuade. Analyze each piece to identify the parts that are meant to serve a secondary purpose. For example, in a sample of writing that is meant to persuade, identify the sentences or paragraphs that inform.

6. Watch a TV interview. As each question is asked, decide what the interviewer's purpose was in asking the question. Make a note of that, and then listen to see if the answer to the question recognizes and addresses that purpose or if it introduces a purpose of its own.

Research

7. The following inaugural addresses are often mentioned as being the best examples of the genre: Abraham Lincoln's second inaugural address, delivered in 1865; Franklin Roosevelt's first inaugural address, delivered in 1933; and John F. Kennedy's inaugural address, delivered in 1961. You can find them online at www.yale.edu/awweb/avalon/presiden/inaug/inaug/htm. Read the three speeches and write a brief analysis that explains the purpose of the speech and why it is effective.

8. Every American president except Abraham Lincoln has sought help from others in preparing speeches. Choose a favorite President and use the Internet to do some investigative research on who his speechwriters were and how he worked with them. Present your findings to the class in a brief report.

Interpreting Graphics

Supppose you are giving a speech on the broad topic of the importance of education. Using the information in the chart at the right, develop a controlling purpose, purpose statement, and thesis statement you could use as the basis of your speech.

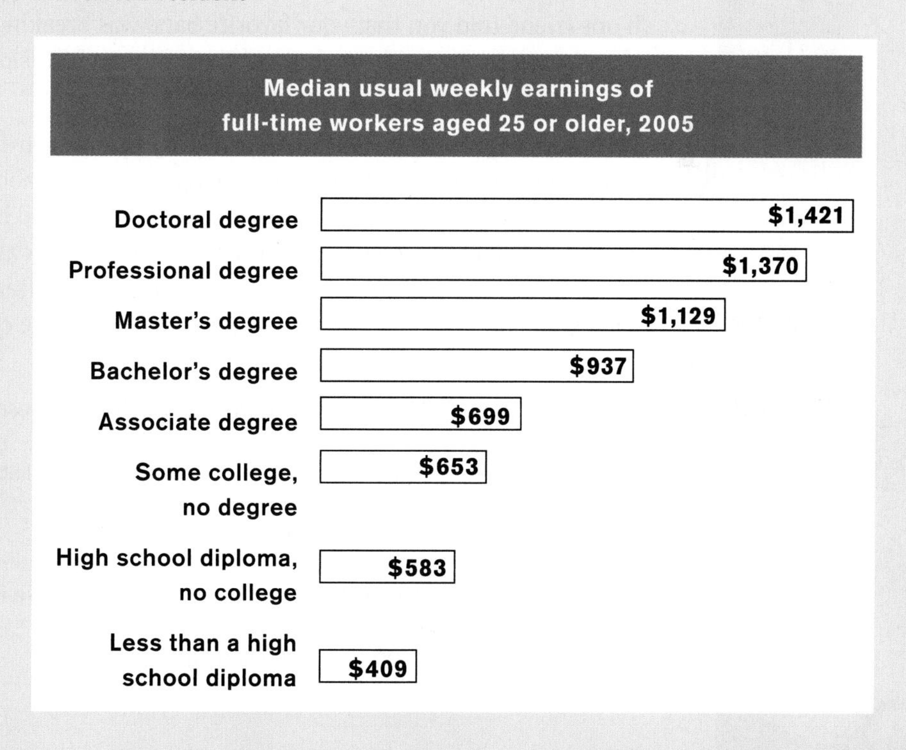

Additional Projects

1. **Group Project:** The Web site www.americanrhetoric.com allows you to listen to great speeches from the past. With a small group of classmates, visit the site, select a speech from the top 100, and listen to the speech together. Discuss why you believe this speech was ranked in the top.

2. **Individual Project:** Create a diagram that illustrates the process a speaker must go through to prepare to make a presentation. Include in your diagram all the elements of preparation described in this chapter. Try to be both accurate and inventive in your diagram. Display your finished diagram in class.

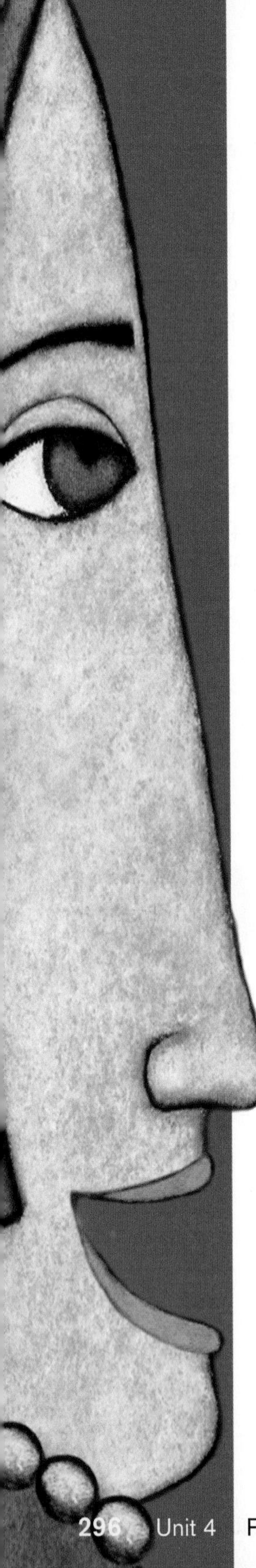

Researching Your Speech

ESSENTIAL QUESTION

How can I find and use the information necessary for my speech?

Chapter Project: Says Who?

If one friend told you that your favorite band was breaking up and another said that wasn't true, how would you find out the real story? This project will help you know where to turn to get reliable information.

With a small group, you will think of a story you've heard that may or may not be true—perhaps one about a dolphin saving a person or about e-mail chain letters promising cash back if you forward a message. It should be something strange but possibly true. When you've chosen your story, work as a team to find sources that prove the story to be true or expose it as a hoax. After finishing your research, you will take two minutes to report your findings to the class. Refer to the CAPS guidelines as you work.

The rubric on page 315 shows the traits on which your presentation will be evaluated.

CONCEPT	true accounts can be confirmed by reliable sources
AUDIENCE	classmates and teacher
PURPOSE	locate sources that confirm or disprove information
SITUATION	report research findings

KEY VOCABULARY

- primary source
- secondary source
- database
- call number
- Dewey Decimal System
- Library of Congress System
- online catalog
- claims
- proof
- testimony
- analogy
- false analogy
- statistics

What tips on using computers for research could you share with your classmates?

Speak Up!

Your cousin doesn't want people to throw rice at her wedding. She says that when birds eat the rice, it swells in their bodies and can kill them. Is your cousin right or not? How would you go about proving or disproving her claim? Share your ideas as your teacher writes them on the board. Keep these ideas in mind as you read this chapter.

BACKGROUND FOR THE PROJECT

Pages 298–313 will provide the information you'll need to complete this project.

The Need for Research

Some speeches don't require research. If you've just returned from an Outward Bound wilderness expedition and are invited to give a talk about the experience, research would not be necessary. You would have to organize your material and plan your main points, but you wouldn't have to do research or cite sources. You would be speaking from personal experience.

In some situations, however, even when you know the topic well, you will have to do some research to find just the right information to make a speech entertaining, informative, or persuasive. In speaking about your wilderness experience, you might start by giving background information about the origins of Outward Bound. That's not something you learned on the expedition, so you would have to do some research.

There are many reasons to do research when preparing a speech. For example:

- Research imparts knowledge, and knowledge is power. Knowing all you can about a subject gives you confidence. You speak with authority and skill. And when the audience asks questions, your depth of understanding helps you answer with ease.
- Research provides material to help you vividly illustrate the points you are making.
- Research can give you helpful ideas for ways to begin and conclude your speech.
- Research can offer a new angle or a fresh insight into the topic.

If you rely only on what you already know when you're preparing a speech, you'll be working with a relatively limited amount of information. If you research your topic well, you'll have a broader base of information and can assemble the supporting details that will make your speech clear and effective.

Research helps you find the most effective information for your situation, audience, and purpose.

Credibility and Research

Speakers who establish credibility, or believability, are likely to be well received. Speakers gain credibility by demonstrating expertise, showing good intentions, and appearing trustworthy. Research plays a key role in supporting all of these qualities.

Expertise

Audiences want speakers who are experts on the topic. In-depth research can help you turn familiarity with a topic into expertise. It can help assure the audience that you know your subject and that your words are true. Suppose while telling about your Outward Bound experience you want to point out that experiencing nature firsthand has a positive long-term effect on young people. Since you are not an expert in adolescent development, you personally will probably not convince your audience. However, if you add to your personal comments by quoting experts in the field, your audience will probably accept this statement. Research can help you borrow the expertise you need to support your beliefs.

Good Intentions

Audiences need to feel that speakers are trying to accomplish something positive. Doing responsible research can help you convince your audience of your good intentions. A speaker who has made the effort to research and understand the available information will be perceived as open-minded, hardworking, and helpful. A speaker who doesn't make the effort will be perceived as apathetic, indifferent, and even devious. If you don't care enough about the topic to do the research, the audience probably won't care what you have to say.

Trustworthiness

Audiences need to feel they can believe in the speaker. Accurate and responsible research plays an important role in establishing a speaker's trustworthiness. If a speaker says one thing that the audience knows to be untrue or questionable, then everything the speaker says is called into question. A speaker who consistently presents information that is well-researched and accurate, in contrast, will build trust. Your speech is more likely to accomplish its purpose if the audience believes you are trustworthy.

You can speak about your wilderness expedition from experience, but by doing research you can give it more punch.

Former Vice-President Al Gore is not a scientist himself, so he relies on research from well-respected experts as he presents his slide show, An Inconvenient Truth, *on global warming.*

PROJECT PREP

With your **project group**, talk about the sources you use to verify information. Which do you find are the more reliable–primary or secondary? When might a primary source be unreliable?

Primary and Secondary Sources

There are two kinds of sources that are used for research: primary sources and secondary sources. A **primary source** is an original source of information. A **secondary source** comments on or develops information found in a primary source.

Both primary and secondary sources can be useful to a public speaker. Suppose you were preparing a speech about the founding of your school. The primary sources might be materials prepared at the time of the school's opening, early school yearbooks, newspaper articles reporting on the opening, old school records, and old photographs of the school. A book about the history of the school written years after it opened would be an example of a secondary source. Often secondary sources will contain primary source material. For example, a book on your school's history (a secondary source) might quote speeches or reproduce photographs from the past (primary sources).

Primary Sources	Secondary Sources
• original documents • diaries and letters • autobiographies • video and audio recordings • period photographs • artifacts	• books about original documents • article explaining or interpreting textbooks • biographies • copies or reproductions of artifacts
The Benefits of Primary Sources	**The Benefits of Secondary Sources**
provide an authentic, firsthand account of what was stated or written	help to interpret primary sources, which are sometimes confusing
rely on original documents rather than another's interpretation to give speaker credibility	allow the borrowing of respected author's expertise
help answer follow-up questions about the topic	broaden speaker's knowledge by exposure to varied points of view on the topic

Research Efficiency

The suggestions below should help you research a subject with a minimum of wasted effort. Remember, too, that librarians are expert researchers and are always willing to help.

Narrowing Your Topic

You could never read all the information there is on almost any topic on the Internet and in the media. You have to narrow your topic and focus your research to avoid being overwhelmed. In Chapter 14 you learned how to use a purpose statement to narrow and focus your topic. You can also limit your topic using the following research strategies.

First, find and read a general article about your topic. You might find it in an encyclopedia, a magazine, or on a Web site. This general article will contain lots of ideas about the topic. One of them may spark your interest and imagination and engage your audience.

Next, use an online or print index of periodicals to note the subtopics listed for your subject. These might give you ideas for narrowing your topic. Then find magazine and journal articles on specific subjects that interest you. You may want to research the material available before you narrow your topic.

TechConnect Use the Internet or your public library to find books devoted to your subject. Most libraries now make use of technology to catalog books by title, subject, author, and location within a network of libraries. Certain Web sites store information and will allow you to print out articles on various topics.

Preparing for Research

Whether researching online or at the library, prepare by thinking about the purpose of your speech as well as the situation and audience. If you don't know much about your audience, do some research about them to understand their expectations.

Be sure to bring along what you'll need when taking notes at the library: pencil or pen, paper, note cards, a computer. Keep all research materials in a folder.

Give yourself enough time to get into your research and follow up on leads. One long research session can be more valuable than several shorter ones. It gives you time to settle in, focus on what you need to do, and answer such questions as *Where do I look? What do I write down? How much information do I need?*

TechConnect *Use your public library's technology to locate books or magazine articles on any subject.*

Images also help you gather information. What information can you take away from this photograph of men waiting in a bread line during the Great Depression?

Using Indexes and Tables of Contents

Many books have indexes and tables of contents to help you locate information. To find out quickly if a book might be useful, check the table of contents in the front. You might discover a whole chapter on the very topic you're researching. In the index at the back of the book, look for the key words related to your topic. For example, if you are researching the stock market crash of 1929, look under *depression, Great Depression,* and *Black Thursday.*

Skimming the Material

Skim your sources to locate useful information. Following are tips to improve this skill.

- Look at the headings, which serve as "mini-titles" that announce the content of each section. You will then know which sections you can skip and which call for your concentration.
- Look for key words and transition words. Keep your eye out for terms that are related to your topic, and when you find them give that section a closer read. Transition words such as *in other words* indicate an explanation, while *for example* may introduce just the example you're looking for.
- Skim at different rates. The faster you skim, the less content you take in. When you come to a section that looks promising, slow your skimming down to get more information.

Taking Notes

Write down any useful information. Here are some tips for taking notes.

- Write down the book's title, the author's name, the page number, and other relevant source information. Summarize or paraphrase what you read. These strategies will help you avoid inadvertent plagiarism. If you plan to use the exact words of the source, they must be in quotes and credited.
- Use symbols and abbreviations. Create an abbreviation for your topic and for terms that will appear often in your notes. Use symbols for common words—+ or & for *and* and *w/* for *with.*
- Keep all research notes in a folder. Keep the folder in a handy spot.

Using the Internet

The Internet as a research tool has many advantages. It is available almost anywhere and it never closes. It provides an enormous amount of information on just about any subject, and it is indexed in different ways. By using a search engine, you can find information about your topic very easily. Many Web sites are updated daily, so you can be fairly sure your information is current. And because the Web is immediate and interactive, you can share knowledge with people miles away and in real time.

The World Wide Web

The Internet does have some drawbacks, though. One of the biggest is reliability. How do you know if what you learn at a Web site is accurate? Printed materials, such as books, magazines, and newspapers, as well as their related Web sites, usually go through a process of evaluation. The authors and editors have credentials and are held to account for what they write. Fact-checkers often go over a piece to assure its accuracy. Most material in any library has gone through review and evaluation before being purchased. However, many independent Internet sites are never evaluated or checked. You must gauge the reliability of the text yourself.

Evaluating Web Documents

Here are three questions to ask yourself about Web materials.

- **Who sponsors the Web site?** The reputation of the institution or organization that sponsors a Web site can help you evaluate the material. You can probably trust the Web site of a recognized university, a government agency, or a reputable newspaper. If you've never heard of the Web site's sponsor, find out about its reputation before using it as a source.
- **Who wrote the content?** Is an author identified? Are any credentials for the author provided? Is the site, like Wikipedia, open to editing by users? Knowing the author's qualifications will help you judge the reliability of the site's information and opinions.
- **When was this written?** While most Internet information is updated often, some isn't. A report written in the present tense can sound current even if it is not. Always look for a copyright date, a publication date, or an indication of when the material was last revised.

How reliable do you think the information on a university Web site might be?

Culling Information One advantage of the Internet can also be a big problem: extensive information. A topic search can yield thousands of results. How do you find the exact information you need? Search engines typically arrange the results by relevance. If you've used the right key word for your search, the results that appear first will probably be the most useful ones. Sometimes a search engine will suggest related topics. Review those and click one that seems promising.

Search engines also have the capacity to do an "Advanced Search." Click "Advanced Search" and the screen looks something like this: an advanced search allows you to specify which aspects of a topic you are interested in. For example, if you wanted to learn about the history of chess, but you weren't interested in learning about game rules or former chess champions and tournaments, you would enter the words *chess history* in the field after "Find results with all of the words," and the words *tournament, champion, competition* in the field after "Find results with none of the words." An advanced search also lets you specify:

- where the key words should appear (anywhere on the page, in the page title, or in the Web address)
- which domain or part of the World Wide Web you want to search (commercial sites, which are indicated as .com; not-for-profit organizations, which are .org; schools, colleges, and universities, which are .edu)
- the language you want your Web sites in
- the country where the sites originate
- how recent the information should be.

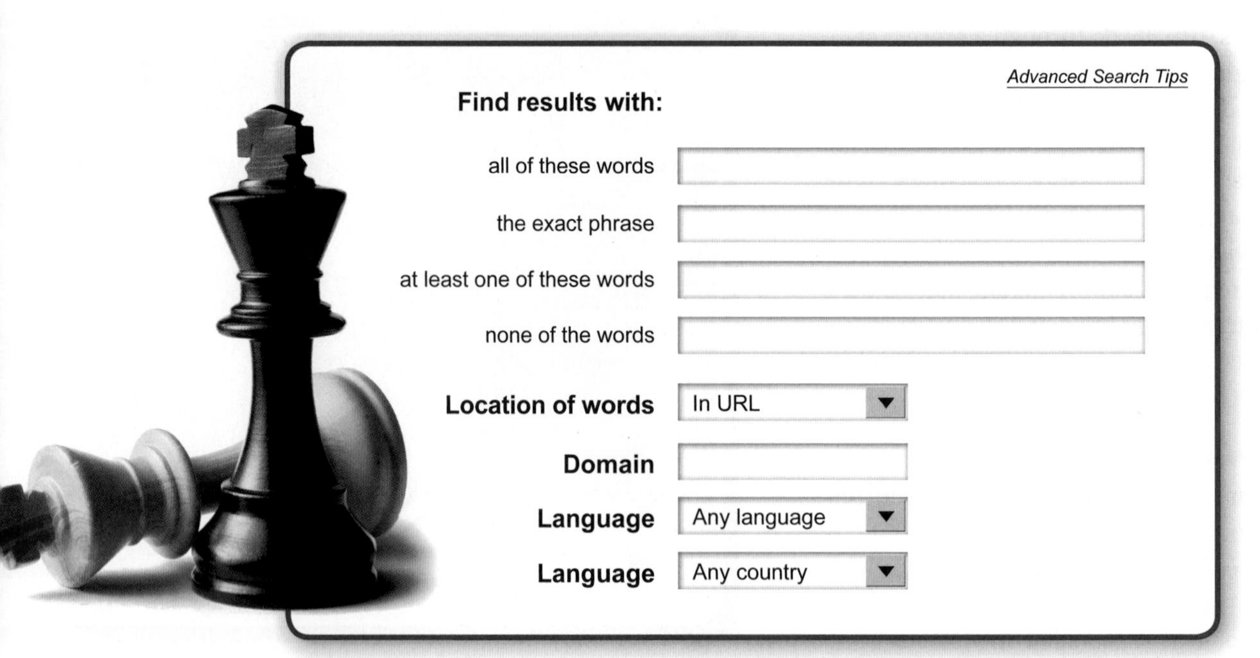

Advanced searches increase the probability that you will find the information you want.

Many Web sites yield fascinating information on the history of chess. This image is of a medieval couple playing at chess, circa 1550.

Searching Effectively

Here are some tips to make the most of your Internet research.

- **Try out more than one search engine.** Different search engines often yield similar results, but sometimes one search engine will help you find something that the others don't.
- **Use the right key words.** For example, if you want to find sample speeches, you'll be more likely to find what you want if you use the key words "public speeches" than if you simply use the word "speech."
- **Use the summaries.** When you use a search engine, each of the results appears with a very brief summary of the content. Use that information to decide which of the results you want to pursue.
- **Copy and paste.** When you're doing Internet research on your own computer, you can "copy" and "paste" to make notes of your research. Highlight the information you want, use the copy command to copy it, and then paste it into a blank document in a word processing program. Copy or bookmark the Web address where you found the material. You can save your notes as an electronic file or print them out to store in your research folder.
- **Use links.** Sometimes a document you are reading on the Internet will contain links to other material. It's easy to recognize a link. It is type that appears in color, usually blue, and clicking on it takes you to another Web page. Explore the links that promise to offer useful information on your topic.
- **Use other sources.** Internet documents often direct you to print materials. Record the recommendations and head for the library to check them out.

Other Internet Sources

An online **database**, a collection of related information, can offer excellent research options. Most databases require that you subscribe in order to use them—paying a monthly or yearly fee for the service. However, your public library may subscribe to certain databases to give patrons access to a broader range of information than is available in their book collections. You may be able to access these databases from the library's computers or your home using the barcode number on your library card.

A database exists for just about any area of interest. One helps people find interpretations of hundreds of literary works. Another provides the latest news on the hottest new careers. Others provide information about health and fitness, help people trace their ancestors, or view great art.

Libraries also give their patrons greater access to research materials by subscribing to digital libraries, which offer online versions of printed materials. Some digital libraries provide access to reference books, such as specialized encyclopedias and dictionaries. Others let users read articles in current and back issues of a variety of magazines, journals, and newspapers.

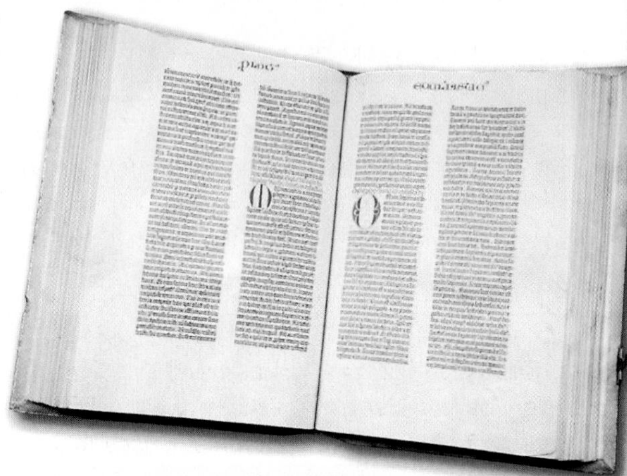

A Gutenberg Bible, the first printed European book, opened to Ecclesiastes.

Most digital libraries are subscription services available only to libraries and schools. Other sites allow anyone to read books online or download and print them. For example, Project Gutenberg (www.gutenberg.org) offers more than 20,000 books absolutely free. These books are in the public domain—they were either never copyrighted in the United States or their copyrights have expired. Project Gutenberg is maintained by volunteers who identify eligible books and proofread the online versions.

The combination of laptops and digital libraries means that people can read books anywhere, anytime.

Is This Job for Me?

Search: Digital Librarian

Starting the day by scanning her e-mail, Elena sees several complaints from users about problems accessing a database. The users are students in an online graduate program, and access to the database is critical to an assignment. Elena is a *digital librarian* who works in a state-of-the-art library for a large university. She immediately analyzes the students' complaints and prepares a detailed report for the people in the Information Technology (IT) department. She marks the report "urgent": this problem should be solved as soon as possible.

After sending the report, she checks usage for the previous day. She keeps track of how many people use the online public access catalog, the database, and the digital research center every day, as well as how many people visit the library and check out books. Every month she uses this data to write a report that helps her director evaluate the library's effectiveness.

Digital librarians are information experts.

Does a job as a digital librarian interest you? Measure yourself with this personality inventory to find out if you have what it takes. Are you:

- ✓ Good at listening?
- ✓ Organized?
- ✓ Tech savvy?
- ✓ Flexible?
- ✓ Creative?
- ✓ Good with languages?
- ✓ Able to multitask?
- ✓ Good at problem-solving?
- ✓ Analytical?
- ✓ Interested in information?

If you become a digital librarian, you might find job opportunities with the clients below.

Clients	What You Would Do
Academic library	Manage digital library, troubleshoot systems issues, track usage of databases and general library use, help design online learning systems, market digital library to students and faculty
Public library	Manage digital library, troubleshoot systems issues, track usage of databases, digital resources, and general library use, generate reports, market digital library to the public
Medical library	Manage databases, troubleshoot systems issues, analyze data needs, keep users informed of available resources

Many publishers are offering electronic versions of their texts, or e-books. Still, they produce more than 150,000 new printed titles and editions each year.

Print Sources

Even with today's high-speed electronic access to information, print materials remain the most important research tool. Two reasons are their reliability and their use of copyrights. For serious scholars and authorities in given fields, writing is a source of income. Their published works are copyrighted to protect their intellectual property rights, assuring them payment for the use of their ideas. Copyrighted material is available on the Internet, but usually for a fee. You can find it for free only at a library.

Finding Books

Libraries are full of books that offer valuable information when you are researching a speech, but how do you locate the ones that can help you? The task is not as overwhelming as it may seem. Libraries use one of two systems to organize and identify books. One is the Dewey Decimal System, developed by Melvil Dewey in 1876. The other is the Library of Congress system. Both organize books by subject matter and use a **call number**, identifying numbers and letters, which indicate a book's location in its system.

The Dewey Decimal System

The **Dewey Decimal System,** as its name suggests, categorizes books into ten general subject areas, each of which is assigned a range of numbers:

000 General Works
100 Philosophy and Psychology
200 Religion
300 Social Sciences
400 Language
500 Nature Sciences & Mathematics
600 Technology
800 Literature
900 History & Geography

In the Dewey Decimal System every nonfiction book has a call number. Online, the call number appears like this: 599.884 FOS. On the spine of a book, it appears like this:

The number indicates the subject of the book, with each number indicating a more specific subcategory. The letters are the first three letters in the author's name. You would find this book in the 500 section. Then you would use numerical order to find the books numbered 599.884 and alphabetical order to locate the book.

The Library of Congress System

The **Library of Congress System** uses letters instead of numbers to indicate major subject areas. The call number for *Gorillas in the Mist* would appear this way online: QL737 P96 F67. It would appear this way on the spine of the book:

The first line defines the subject matter. The second and third represent the particular item and the author.

The Library of Congress System uses letters to represent twenty basic subject areas:

- A General Works
- B Philosophy, Psychology, Religion
- C History–Auxiliary Sciences
- D History
- E–F American History
- G Geography
- H Social Sciences
- J Political Science
- K Law
- L Education
- M Music
- N Fine Arts
- P Language
- Q Science
- R Medicine
- S Agriculture
- T Technology
- U Military Science
- V Naval Science
- Z Bibliography, Library Science

Using an Online Catalog

Finding a book using an **online catalog** is a lot like using a search engine to find information on the Internet. You can search for a book by its title, the name of the author, or by a key word. You can also do an advanced search that allows you to search for whole phases, use "and" or "or" to specify more than one word and "and not" to exclude words. An advanced search also lets you specify the language you want the materials to be written in and the type of material you're looking for—a book, periodical, book on tape, or book on CD, for example. You can also specify when the materials were published. For example, you may not be interested in any material over two years old. An advanced search will limit your search to materials published after a given date or within certain dates.

The library is the only access to the Internet for many low-income patrons.

With practice, you'll soon be comfortable searching online for books. From your home computer, you have access to your public library's Web site and their online catalog. You can search at home for the research materials you need, then pick them up at the library.

Using Reference Books

Reference books provide researchers easy access to lots of information. You've probably used encyclopedias in the library or online to get information about different topics. But there are many other kinds of reference books that can help when you are preparing a speech.

One especially helpful reference work is a dictionary of quotations. Here you can find what famous speakers and writers had to say about the topic you're researching. An apt quotation can be an excellent way to begin or end your speech or to help you illustrate a point.

Periodicals

A periodical is a work published at regular intervals, or periodically. Magazines and newspapers are periodicals. Journals that publish poetry, short works of literature, essays, and scholarly articles are also periodicals.

Why do hippos look like this? You could probably find a periodical article that would tell you.

The Reader's Guide to Periodical Literature

One useful index for finding recently published articles in magazines and journals is the *Reader's Guide to Periodical Literature,* available in book form and electronically. The online version has a high-powered search feature. In the book, topics are arranged in alphabetical order. Under each topic heading is a list of articles about that topic. Here's a typical entry:

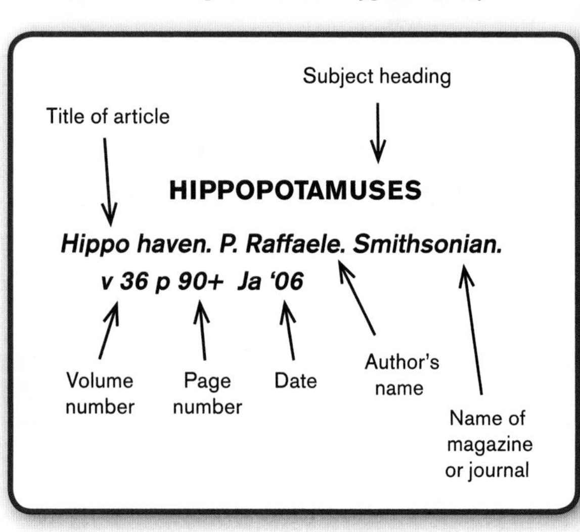

This article, called "Hippo Haven," was written by P. Raffaele and appeared in the January 2006 issue of *Smithsonian* magazine, beginning on page 90.

PROJECT PREP

With your **project group**, work up a "game plan" for doing research. Consider all the resources at your disposal. Then make a list of the resources you would use to verify the truth of a story in the order in which you would use them.

Supporting Your Thesis

When you're working on a speech, the purpose of your research is to clarify or broaden your understanding of a topic and to gather support materials to help you make the points you want to make. Your thesis determines what kind of research you need to do. To show that your thesis is valid, you use **claims**, the conclusions or ideas you want your audience to accept. Claims need to be supported by **proof,** or evidence. For example:

Thesis: Fairy tales like "Little Red Riding Hood" and "The Three Little Pigs" have given us a false impression of wolves.

Claim 1: Wolves do not kill human beings.

Proof: There is no documented evidence of a healthy, wild wolf killing a human in the United States.

Proof: There is more threat to humans from dogs than wolves—4.7 million people in the U.S. are attacked by dogs each year.

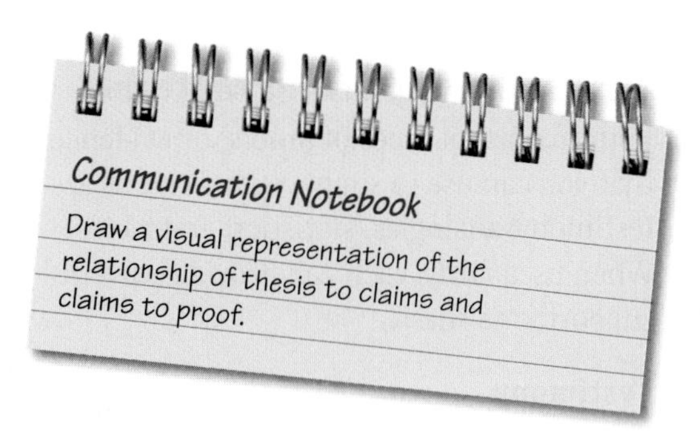

Claim 2: Wolves do not kill off populations of elk, deer, and moose.

Proof: Wolves and the animals they prey on survived together for thousands of years.

Proof: Wildlife conservationists report that wolves help make herds stronger by killing off weaker animals, leaving the strongest animals to reproduce.

This example shows the relationships among the thesis, claims, and proof: the thesis is supported by claims, and the claims are supported by proof.

You may want to also include images of the fairy tales to support your thesis.

Types of Supporting Material

Four important types of proofs, or evidence, that you can use to support your claims are testimony, analogies, statistics, and facts. When used fairly, each can provide powerful support for a thesis.

Testimony

When you use another person's words or ideas to support your claims, you are using **testimony**. Testimony is particularly valuable when your audience might doubt your experience or expertise with the topic. Firsthand experience might make you an expert on your school lunch program. However, if you are describing how wolves live, you may want to cite a wildlife conservationist.

You can find testimony in written works by recognized authorities on a topic. You can also find it in works in which other writers draw on experts to support their argument, just as you will.

Analogies

An **analogy** is a comparison between two things, ideas, or situations. Analogies are often used to explain an unfamiliar subject by comparing it to a more familiar one which has some but not all of the same features as the unfamiliar one. Analogies are also used to prove a point. In this use, the two subjects, though different, are presented as being alike in most ways because they are alike in some key ways. For example, in the 2008 presidential race, the candidates disagreed over whether the United States should negotiate with Iran, a nation hostile to the United States. One candidate, Senator John McCain, said no. He made an analogy between present-day Iran and Germany in the 1930s, arguing that negotiations failed then so they would likely fail now. The other candidate, Senator Barack Obama, said yes. He made an analogy between present-day Iran and the Soviet Union in the 1960s and 1970s, arguing that since negotiations succeeded then, they would succeed now as well.

Watch out, though, for the **false analogy,** an analogy between two cases that are not alike enough to be compared meaningfully. A candidate who said, "Don't bother negotiating; you can't get dogs to talk to cats" would be making a comparison without basis.

Statistics

Statistics are numbers presented as facts. Statistics can effectively add emphasis to your speech and help listeners visualize important points. The chart on the next page shows how to use statistics successfully.

Most of the statistics you use will come from the research of others. An almanac contains statistics on many different topics from many different sources. If you use statistics from an almanac, be sure to credit the original source, which will be indicated in the almanac.

You can also develop your own statistics. For example, you might want to poll your classmates about their attitudes toward wolves, gather the information, and supply a statistic that is easy to formulate and just as easy for your listeners to understand. For example: "Of the fifty classmates I asked, 'Do wolves kill human beings?' forty answered, 'Yes.'" Be fair when gathering information about controversial issues. Don't select just people who already agree with you.

Facts

Because facts can be confirmed as true, audiences respond well to them and often retain the information they give. Remember these tips when working with facts.

- **Facts need to be developed.** If you say, "Wolves use a 'coursing' technique to cull a herd and ensure that genetically weak animals do not reproduce," that is a fact. Most audiences, however, will need to be told what coursing means as well as how wolves go about doing it.
- **Present facts that are interesting.** Your research will probably uncover lots of facts. Use the most interesting ones—those that will draw in the audience and support your points.
- **Tell how you learned the fact you are citing.** Do you know it from your own experience? Did you read it in a book or magazine article? Did you find it at a credible Web site on the Internet? Confirm for your audience why they should accept what you are saying as fact.

Good, thorough research can make the difference between a powerful speech that will engage your audience and a mediocre speech that will leave your audience yawning. At the beginning of the process, when you've chosen your topic, general research helps you explore the possibilities and find a fresh approach to the topic. After you've determined your thesis and are structuring your presentation, more specific research helps you find the facts, quotes, and statistics to support your points and enliven your speech.

Facts can help end myths about wolves.

Type of Proof	Definition	Example
Testimony	The opinions of others, usually experts, quoted in support of a claim	Wildlife conservationists report that wolves help make herds stronger by killing weaker animals, leaving the strongest to reproduce.
Analogy	A comparison between two things, ideas, or situations often to show that what is true about one is true about the other because they are alike in some ways	The wolf pack structure requires that wolves work together for their survival in much the same way that members of human families take roles to assure the welfare of the family.
Statistic	Information that is presented numerically	There is more threat to humans from dogs than wolves: 4.7 million people in the United States are attacked by dogs each year.
Fact	Statements that can be proven true	Wolves and the animals they prey on have survived together for thousands of years.

PREPARING THE PROJECT

Begin your project by looking back at the **Project Prep** activities in this chapter and using the directions below.

Make Connections

Discuss the importance of making research part of the process of planning a speech. Summarize these points:

- the benefits of primary and secondary sources in research
- the practices that make research efficient and effective
- the advantages of the Internet and traditional research tools.

Focus

Review the group project you are working on: researching to find sources that prove a story true or false.

Plan

Agree on the story you want to research. Discuss the sources you might consult and make a list of primary and secondary sources, Internet sites, magazines, and reference books. Divide up the work so that each member of the group has a specific assignment. Decide on a time when you will get back together to compare your findings.

If you can't find the right information, revise the way you're searching. Try different key words or an advanced search using the search engine. A reference librarian or media specialist can help you identify and locate the materials also. If you are working on a speech, your difficulty finding information may mean you need to change your topic or try to focus on an angle that might yield better results.

Surefire Cooperation

Be supportive, fair, and understanding in your dealings with one another. Talk about any disagreements right away. Check in with one another periodically to see how things are going.

Develop

Meet again and report on and evaluate your findings. If you still aren't sure if the story is true or false, check more sources. When you are sure, divide up the presentation so that everyone has a role. One member explains what you set out to prove or disprove. Others summarize the research and explain the conclusion you came to.

PRESENTING THE PROJECT

Use the strategy that follows to help make the presentation of your research as good as it can be.

Practice

When you've assigned the "parts" of the presentation, practice it as often as necessary to feel comfortable. Once you are comfortable, consider ways to add creativity and sparkle to the presentation.

EVALUATING THE PROJECT

Evaluate the research reports using the following rubric.

Score the demonstration on each point, with 4 being "outstanding" and 1 being "needs much improvement."

Come up with an overall score and write a brief paragraph that explains your score.

Understanding of the Research Process	Demonstration of the Research Process	Creativity and Originality	Preparation and Use of Time
4 Presenters showed insight into the research process.	**4** Presenters' report helped illuminate the research process.	**4** The research report was interesting and original.	**4** The research report flowed smoothly and was within the time limit.
3 Presenters understood the research process fairly well.	**3** Presenters' demonstration was helpful in understanding the research process.	**3** The research report was fairly interesting and somewhat original.	**3** The research report progressed fairly smoothly and was within the time limit.
2 Presenters did not seem to understand some elements of the process of researching.	**2** Presenters' demonstration was minimally helpful in understanding the research process.	**2** The presentation was fairly interesting, but not original.	**2** The research report had a few awkward moments and went a bit over or noticeably under the time limit.
1 Presenters did not understand how to do research.	**1** Presenters' demonstration did not help in understanding the research process.	**1** The presentation was neither interesting nor informative.	**1** The research report was not smoothly executed and went well over or under the time limit.

Communication *Past* and Present

Public Libraries

From the Library Company of Philadelphia…

Benjamin Franklin—a founding father of the United States and a signer of the Declaration of Independence—was completely self-taught. He believed that "the doors of wisdom are never shut," and he educated himself by reading. Getting access to books in America of the 1730s, however, wasn't easy. Books were rare and expensive, and people of moderate means could not easily afford them. This circumstance inspired Franklin to create America's first public lending library in 1731: the Library Company of Philadelphia.

Benjamin Franklin

The scheme for the library grew out of a discussion group Franklin organized called "the Junto." The Junto was made up of "like-minded aspiring artisans and tradesmen who hoped to improve themselves while they improved their community." They could not achieve their goal without books, and none of the members owned very many. So Franklin came up with the idea of pooling their resources to buy books that would be available to all. Each of the fifty members invested forty shillings to pay for the books that became the basis of the library's collection. These books were then available to all the members. Every year after that, each member paid another ten shillings to improve and maintain the collection.

Imitating the success of Franklin's Library Company of Philadelphia, subscription libraries appeared in many early American cities, but a hundred years passed before the first genuinely public library was established. That library was the Peterborough Town Library, founded in Peterborough, New Hampshire, in 1833. The library started out as a subscription library. Only months after the library was established, the town voted to put a portion of its tax revenue toward the purchase of library books, thus creating the world's first free public library supported by taxation.

Soon after the founding of the Peterborough Town Library, Boston became the first large city to follow its example. The Boston Public Library was established by city ordinance in 1852 and opened its doors in 1854. Public lending libraries, where anyone could borrow books to take home, was an idea whose time had come.

But perhaps no one contributed more to the creation of public libraries in the United States than Andrew Carnegie. A Scottish immigrant to the United States, Carnegie educated himself by reading, just as Franklin did. The books he read as a boy in Pittsburgh came from a small library.

Andrew Carnegie constructed his first steel mill in the mid-1870s, and as he started accumulating wealth, he also started building public libraries. Between 1883 and 1929, Carnegie donated about $50 million to create 1,689 public libraries across the United States. He believed that in the United States, people with the desire could educate themselves, and that public libraries could help them do just that. Carnegie wrote: "It was from my own early experience that I decided there was no use to which money could be applied so productive of good to boys and girls who have good within them and ability and ambition to develop it, as the founding of a public library."

. . . to Your Local Public Library

Today, there are more than 16,500 public libraries in the United States. They carry on the traditions of Franklin and Carnegie by providing the tools people need to educate themselves. In addition to the books that can be borrowed and the reference books and materials that can be consulted, today's libraries offer universal access to computers and the Internet. They also serve as literacy centers, where people who need to improve their reading skills and people learning English as a second language can connect with tutors who can help them.

Andrew Carnegie

More than ever before, today's libraries offer, in the words of Edward Rothstein of *The New York Times*, an "alluring mix of enlightenment and entertainment." Not only can you borrow books from the library, you can also borrow video games and DVDs. Many libraries encourage their users to think of them as community gathering places where books are read and discussed and where you can also get a cup of coffee or a snack, see a movie, hear a lecture, meet an author, or learn a craft.

Chapter 15 Review

Using Vocabulary Words

Use the following terms in pairs to complete this sentence:

I would connect ________ and ________ because ____________________.

1. analogy
2. call number
3. claims
4. database
5. Dewey Decimal System
6. false analogy
7. Library of Congress System
8. online catalog
9. primary source
10. proof
11. secondary source
12. statistics
13. testimony

Reviewing Key Ideas

1. List four reasons why you should do research when preparing a speech.
2. What three qualities help a speaker gain credibility? Explain how research plays a role in each of them.
3. Explain the difference between primary sources and secondary sources. Give examples of each type of source.
4. Compare using the Internet as a research tool with using print materials available at the library. Explain the advantages and disadvantages of each.

Reflecting on Your Project

With your small group, discuss which research tools you found most useful and which caused you some problems. Discuss what you could do to eliminate similar problems in future research projects.

Responding to the Essential Question

Use the headings in this chapter to help you write a brief chapter summary that answers the question, "How can I make my speech effective and believable?" Compare your summary with a partner's to see if you both covered the main points.

Extending Your Understanding

Everyday Life

1. The saying goes: "You learn something new every day." Select from the new things you learned in this chapter one thing you would like to learn more about. What research tool would you use to do that?
2. Identify a topic that interests you. Discuss how you would go about researching it—not in preparation for a speech but simply to learn more about it for your own satisfaction and enjoyment.
3. Pick an object at random in your home. Define something you would like to learn about it. Then use research tools to do that.

In the Media

4. Listen to a political speech on the radio or TV. Listen for statements that you would like to have verified. What questions would you ask the speaker?
5. Watch a documentary on TV. Discuss the kinds of research that you think the documentary filmmakers needed to do in order to create the film.
6. Read a magazine article on a topic that interests you. Highlight the statements that make you ask, "How do you know that?" Compare the statements you underlined to those of a classmate. Speculate on the answers to your questions together.

Research

7. Do a research project in which you find out how much time, on average, students at your school spend at the computer—doing homework, connecting with friends, or just having fun. Work with a classmate to design the project, deciding what would be a representative sampling of the student body and how you will carry out your research. Report the findings of your research to the rest of the class.
8. Choose something you learned about in this chapter that you would like to learn more about. It might be the work of digital librarians or the role of libraries in the next 50 years. It might be Benjamin Franklin's Library Company of Philadelphia. Or it might be something else altogether. Spend one hour researching your topic. Then report your findings to the class.

Interpreting Graphics

Study the diagram of a floor in a library (below) and describe what you see. How might this floor be used?

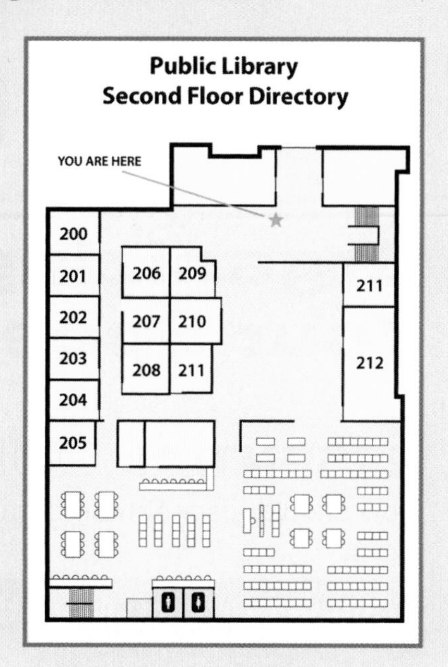

Additional Projects

1. **Group Project:** Prepare to play a variation of "Fictionary." Each player must come up with four "facts"—three that can be documented as true and one that is false. Each player writes down the four "facts" and the source used to document whether it's true or not. To play the game, each player in turn reads a "fact" aloud. All guess which one is false. Players must cite the source used to confirm a true statement.
2. **Individual Project:** Create a model that shows all the steps you would go through in preparing a speech. Begin with identifying your topic and end with rehearsing for the presentation.

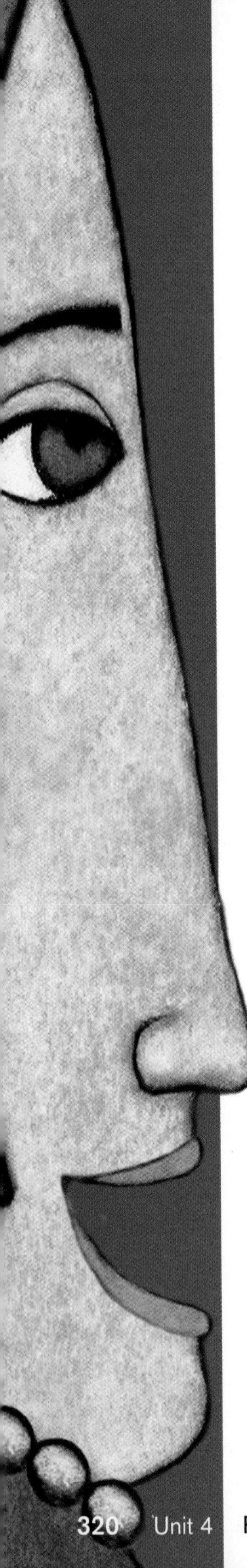

Organizing Your Speech

ESSENTIAL QUESTION

How should a speech be organized?

Chapter Project: Map It!

If you're lost, you can look at a map to see how the roads are organized and to find where you are in relation to where you are going. Graphic organizers, like maps, show relationships and provide direction. This project will help you "map" the structure of a speech.

With a partner, you will create a graphic organizer to help you structure a speech. You will then creatively present your graphic to the rest of the class so that they will understand your organizational pattern. Your presentation should last between two and three minutes. As you work, refer to the CAPS guidelines below.

The rubric on page 345 shows the traits on which your presentation will be evaluated.

CONCEPT	an effective speech has a logical and organized pattern
AUDIENCE	classmates and teacher
PURPOSE	to develop clear and logical organization for a speech
SITUATION	creative classroom presentation of a graphic organizer

KEY VOCABULARY

- climactic order
- topical order
- chronological order
- spatial order
- classification order
- problem-solution order
- cause-effect order
- mnemonic
- transition

A clear organization makes a speech easier to write—and listen to.

Speak Up!

Think about effective speeches you have heard. What about them stands out? Share your ideas as your teacher writes them on the board. Are certain characteristics mentioned more than others? Keep these in mind as you read this chapter.

Pages 322–344 will provide the information you'll need to complete this project.

The Importance of Organization

If someone says to you, "I want you to do four things," you are prepared to hear four things. These things might be presented in the order in which they need to be done, in the order of their importance, or in some other logical order. But what if the four tasks were presented in no particular order? You'd probably have a harder time remembering all four, and you would most likely not perform your task well.

A speech works in much the same way—if it isn't organized, it can't properly perform its task. A well-organized speech helps the audience see how things are connected so they can understand the speaker's meaning.

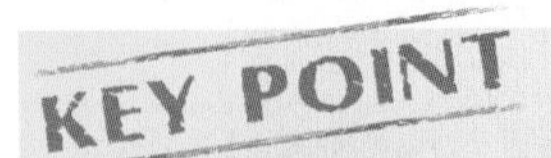

Organization conveys meaning and helps the audience understand the substance of a speech.

The Introduction of the Speech

The word *introduction* comes from the Latin verb meaning "to lead in." A good introduction leads the audience into the speech and gives them a good reason for listening. It prepares them for the main part of your message, serving the seven purposes below.

1. **Getting the audience's attention.** A good introduction will get the audience to focus on what you are saying.
2. **Introducing the topic.** The introduction prepares the audience for the message. By the end of the introduction, they should know why you are speaking, why they should listen, and why the topic has merit.
3. **Stating the thesis.** An introduction should state the thesis, or main idea. This concise statement helps the audience prepare to hear your position on the topic.
4. **Previewing the major ideas.** A good introduction outlines the major ideas that will be developed in the body of the speech. It alerts the audience to what is coming.

A good introduction draws in the audience.

5. **Establishing credibility.** The introduction is important in establishing your credibility, especially if the audience doesn't know you. By showing expertise and good intentions, you build trust, align yourself with your audience, and create credibility. The audience is then open to receiving your message.
6. **Setting the tone.** You want the audience to understand your views, and tone is a way to share your attitudes with them. If you want the audience to laugh and have a good time, the tone of your introduction should let the audience know that. On the other hand, a somber, serious introduction lets the audience know this will be a serious speech.

Read the introduction below to "Cyberbabble and Other Facts," a speech by communication expert Greg Farmer. Note how it prepares the audience for what will follow.

The U.S. economy has undergone dramatic and fundamental changes in its communications infrastructure. Those changes have recast the very foundations that our country rested on—but what has emerged today offers more potential for working together, living longer, and enjoying life more than anyone might have dreamed early on in our history, or for that matter a few days ago.

You may have heard the stunning story of a Russian sailor [Viktor Yazykov] who had to practice telemedicine—on himself. This sailor was participating in a race in South Africa. He was alone in his boat when he injured his arm and it became infected. In true Internet style, he communicated his symptoms through satellite e-mail to an emergency room doctor in Boston. The Boston doctor became alarmed, concerned that the sailor was in [imminent] danger. So he guided the sailor—via satellite e-mail—through surgery that the sailor performed on himself. He drained his abscess, stopped his bleeding, and managed to survive all this and then, for good measure, he won the race. As astonishing as this story is, we have only just begun.

What Does This Introduction to "Cyberbabble" Do?	
Gets the audience's attention	The story of the Russian sailor captures the attention and focuses it on the topic.
Introduces the topic	The topic—the dramatic changes in life brought about by technology—is illustrated in the introduction.
States the thesis	The second sentence is the thesis. As the speech continues, the body deals specifically with the impact of the dramatic communication changes.
Previews the major ideas	This introduction hints at the ideas to come but does not preview them entirely. A preview lets the audience see that the body of the speech will expand on the topic.
Establishes credibility	As the vice president of a major communication firm, the speaker's credibility was established. If the audience didn't know him, his insider's knowledge about the Russian sailor might impress the audience and give him credibility. Showing his surprise regarding the story assures the audience that he is like them.
Sets the tone	The tone—surprise at what can happen—makes it clear that the speech will be one of amazement at the advances communication will continue to make.

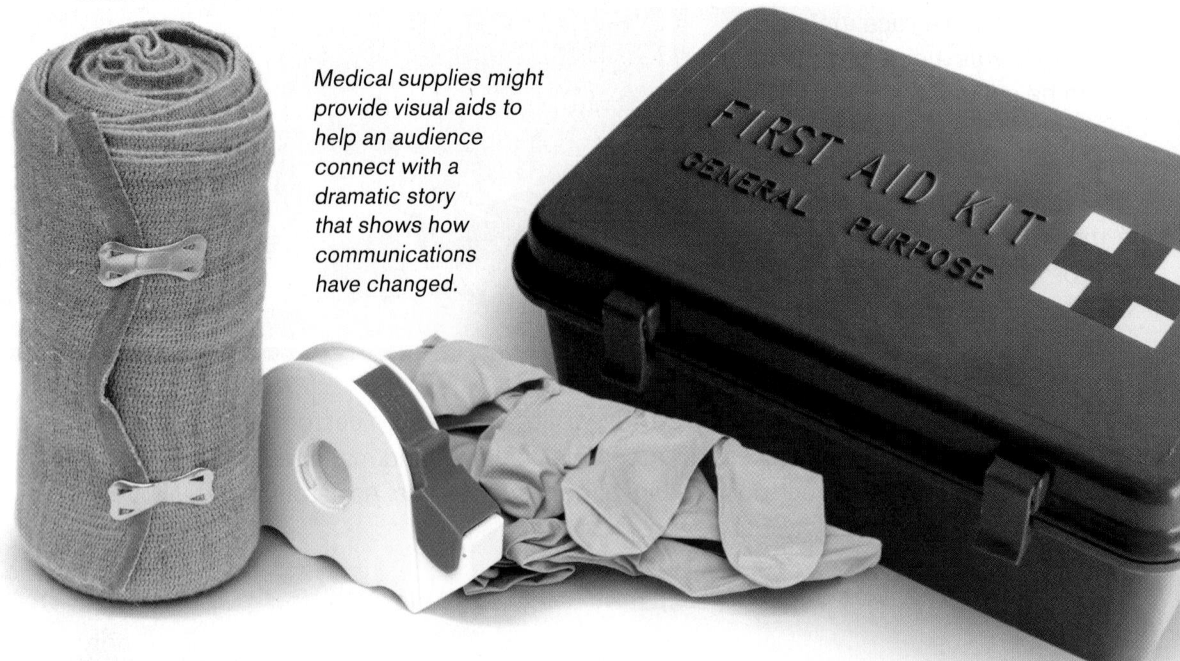

Medical supplies might provide visual aids to help an audience connect with a dramatic story that shows how communications have changed.

Introductory Devices

Speakers have many effective ways of constructing an introduction that will draw in the audience. Following are a few common introductory devices.

Incident

Farmer's introduction recounts an unusual yet true incident—a lone sailor treats his own injury guided by a doctor half a world away. This introduction is effective for several reasons.

- People enjoy hearing a well-told, true-life incident. When used in an introduction, it engages the audience.
- A true story appeals to the audience's emotions. They are curious about what will happen and often identify with the main character.
- An interesting incident is memorable. The audience will remember it and its relevance to the topic as they listen to your speech and long after you've finished speaking.

Quotation

Speakers often use a quotation in the introduction to a speech. A well-chosen quotation has several advantages.

- A quotation is typically an idea eloquently expressed. When you use a quotation, your speech is enhanced as much by the language as by the idea expressed.
- A quotation can bolster your credibility. Quoting someone who is respected and admired by the audience can gain respect for you.
- A quotation in the introduction gives you an opportunity to unify your speech since you can refer back to it when you reach your conclusion.

In the "Cyberbabble" speech, the introduction includes a quotation and the speaker's assessment of it: "By means of electricity, the world of matter has become a great nerve, vibrating thousands of miles in a breathless point of time." Sounds contemporary doesn't it? Nathaniel Hawthorne said this 150 years ago when describing a new invention, the telegraph.

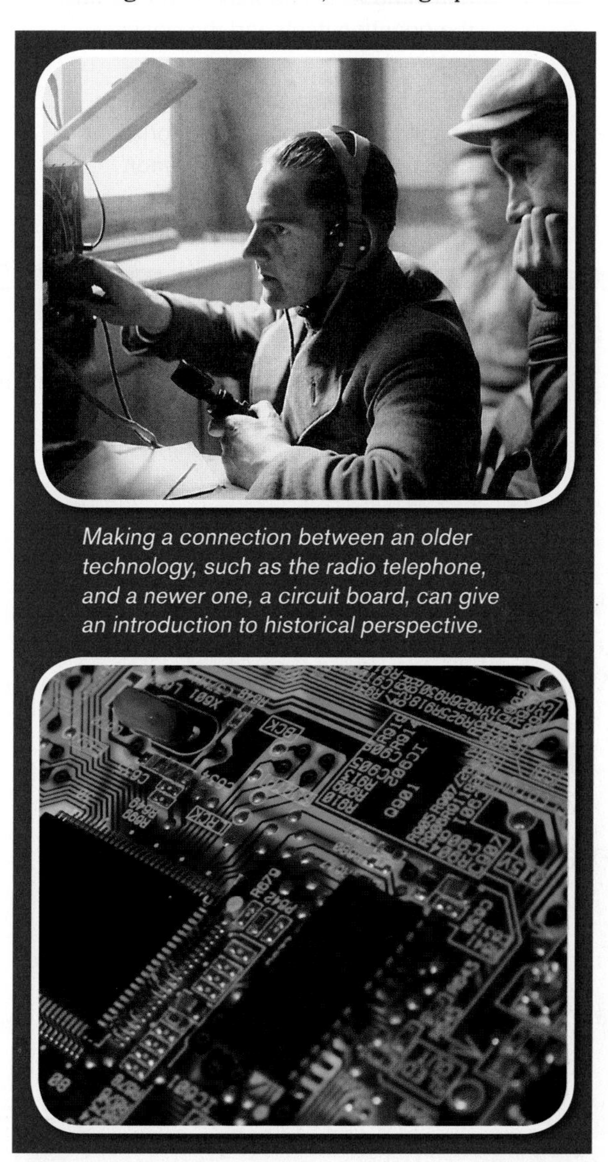

Making a connection between an older technology, such as the radio telephone, and a newer one, a circuit board, can give an introduction to historical perspective.

Rhetorical Question

You read in Chapter 8 that a rhetorical question is asked for effect rather than to obtain an answer. Even if a speech does not answer a rhetorical question it raises in the introduction, the question is still useful for the reasons listen below.

- A well-stated rhetorical question can intrigue the audience–with both the question itself and the possible answers.
- If it is a question that the audience has wondered about, a rhetorical question can establish common ground between the audience and the speaker.

A rhetorical question should not seem contrived or too simple and is most effective when used sparingly.

References to History, Audience, or Self

References can be very interesting, especially if you capture a familiar event in history in a fresh way. For example, the "Cyberbabble" introduction goes on to refer to the invention of the telephone: "Who would have dreamed communications would have so far to go back in 1876 when Alexander Graham Bell spoke those famous first intelligible words into his 'talking machine': *Mr. Watson, come here. I want you*?"

Humor

In some cases, humor is inappropriate, but for many speeches it is both appropriate and effective. Humor gets attention, sets a comfortable tone, can relieve tension, and can build credibility. To be effective, a joke or humorous story should:

- relate to the situation, the audience, the speaker, or the topic. If it doesn't, it will not focus the audience's attention in a favorable way.
- be tasteful. If humor is off-color, it will make the audience uncomfortable and may alienate them. You can lose credibility as a result of tasteless humor.
- be amusing. The story or joke must make the audience chuckle or laugh, or there is no point in using it. A joke that falls flat will not serve your introduction well.

References to famous historical moments make a connection between the event, your topic, and the audience.

Startling Statement

A startling statement challenges the perceptions, knowledge, and opinions of the audience by shaking them up. It prompts the audience to pay attention. Consider the example:

> I'd like you all to think about everything you know about computers. Think about the programs you know; think about the tricks and shortcuts you've learned; think about how you troubleshoot problems. Recall all the creative ways you know to achieve certain things with the computer. Think about the music downloads, the screensavers, the databases and games. Do you have all that in your head? Now do one more thing. On that desktop inside your head, find the icon that looks like a recycle bin. Take everything you know about computers and drag it all into the recycle bin. In five years—maybe less—the things you know now will be as out of date as a Model T or a buttonhook. You've just taken the first step in preparing for the new millennium of technology.

Asking your audience to forget what they understand can startle them. The introduction presented above may be overstated, but it dramatically illustrates the concept that technology is changing.

What could you say about the speed of technological change that would startle your audience?

Communication in a

DIVERSE WORLD

Culture and Public Speaking

Niini Vartia-Paukku at the University of Helsinki in Finland analyzed how public speaking styles reflect cultural values. The study looked at public speeches delivered at Chamber of Commerce meetings in Finland; Singapore, an island nation in the Malay Peninsula; and the United States. Following are some of the findings.

In the United States, speakers often use topic sentences that express personal opinions and experiences. This pattern is rare among speakers in Singapore. There, speakers present topics in terms of the group, rather than the individual. The Finnish speakers, like those in Singapore, usually do not express individualistic views on their topics.

Speakers in Singapore often begin a speech with a look back at history.

Rhetorical questions are often used to introduce an issue by U.S. speakers. They use them to prompt the audience to think. They are hardly used in speeches in the two other countries. In Singapore and Finland, the introduction to a speech is far more formal than in the United States.
In Singapore, speeches often begin with in-depth historical context. This technique occurs less often in the other two countries.

How speakers state their topic and give their thesis statements varies among the countries. In the United States and Finland, these are commonly part of the introduction. However, in Singapore, a speaker may provide various perspectives on the general topic before clearly stating the specific topic for the speech.

Vartia-Paukku concluded that the differences in speaking style reflect differences in attitudes and values. The United States and Finland are more "individualistic" cultures and Singapore is more "collectivist." In the United States, and to some degree in Finland, individual initiative, action, and interests came across as highly prized. In Singapore, the group was seen as having more value and being more worthy of recognition than the individual.

The studies of Vartia-Paukku may help people speaking outside their culture. They can provide insight into ways to create the right speeches for audiences around the globe.

The Body of the Speech

Most of the information you want to communicate to your audience, such as claims, evidence, and development, is contained in the body of a speech. If the introduction draws the audience's attention, the body is what holds them. Organizing the information must be done in a way that makes the substance of the speech meaningful. This involves three steps:

1. Choose an organizational pattern.
2. Outline the speech.
3. Connect the ideas.

Organizational Patterns

The most effective organizational patterns are variations on the way people think. When you provide the audience with a natural and recognizable pattern, they can easily follow your speech from one point to the next. See the basic organizational patterns in the chart below.

Gestures and expressions can give the audience cues about the organization of a speech.

Organizational Pattern	How to Use It
Climactic order	The body of the speech builds to a climax, leading the audience from the least important point to the most important point.
Topical order	When the ideas in the body of your speech seem to flow naturally from one to the other, you present them in this logical order.
Chronological order	This is the order in which things happened. Use chronological order to present ideas in a clear sequence.
Spatial order	Spatial order organizes ideas according to physical space–top to bottom, left to right, west to east. It is useful when describing something.
Classification order	Use this order when grouping ideas. The groups must then also be ordered, so classification order is typically used with another organizational pattern.
Problem-solution order	This organizational pattern is useful in persuasive speeches. The first part of the body of the speech explains the problem; the second part presents the solutions.
Cause-effect order	Using this pattern, you first establish a cause (or causes) and then explain the effects. This pattern is related to chronological order since both follow a sequence.
Combination patterns	Combining patterns often works well. Present a problem-solution pattern chronologically to discuss the problem as it developed. Combine classification order with climactic order going from least to most important group.

The nature of a topic helps determine the most logical order for presenting it. For example, a speaker orienting new student volunteers at the public library might use different organizational patterns for different orientation sessions. While the audience is always new volunteers, and the situation is always an orientaton session, the purpose of the orientation might vary.

Climactic Order The presenter uses this pattern to emphasize the most important part of the job. For many volunteers, this is working at the circulation desk.

Topic: A Volunteer's Duties

1. Keeping the library tidy
   a) Removing things patrons leave on tables and desks
   b) Removing old notices from bulletin boards
   c) Returning books and magazines left on tables to their proper places
2. Reshelving books
   a) Sorting books by location in library
   b) Organizing books by call number
   c) Using call numbers to return books to their proper spots
3. Working at the circulation desk
   a) Checking in returned books
   b) Checking out books
   c) Requesting books from other libraries

Topical Order This pattern covers a variety of tasks. Volunteers often help patrons find or checkout books. Sometimes, they respond to complaints.

Topic: Patron Service

1. Helping patrons find books
   a) Determining their needs

   b) Using the electronic card catalog
   c) Directing them to the proper stacks
2. Checking out books
   a) Scanning the patron's library card
   b) Scanning the bar code on the book
   c) Printing the due date
3. Handling dissatisfied patrons
   a) Listening to patrons
   b) Defining the problem
   c) Solving the problem or referring to staff librarian

Chronological Order The presenter uses this pattern to show the order of completing steps in a task.

Topic: Reshelving Books

1. Dividing books by destination

a) Pulling out books going back to other libraries
b) Sorting books into carts by location in library
2. Organizing returned books by call number
   a) Grouping books in the same major categories
   b) Ordering books within categories
   c) Alphabetizing fiction by the author's last name
3. Using call numbers to return books to their proper spots
   a) Finding the shelf where a book belongs
   b) Finding the exact spot to reshelve a book

The task volunteers do will determine how their training will be organized.

Spatial Order This pattern asks the volunteers to see the how the library is organized physically while they get information about where things are located.

Topic: The Layout of the Library

1. West wing
   a) Children's library
   b) Lecture room
   c) Café
   d) Stacks: L–P
2. Central building
   a) Information desk
   b) Circulation desk
   c) Reference room
   d) Public access computers
3. East wing
   a) Periodical room
   b) Stacks: A–K
   c) Stacks: Q–Z

Classification Order The speaker takes the patron services and groups them by type.

Topic: Patron Services

1. Answering inquiries
   a) Suggesting books
   b) Using the electronic catalog
   c) Finding titles
   d) Locating books on shelves

2. Providing assistance
    a) Issuing library cards
    b) Checking out books
    c) Collecting overdue fines
    d) Accepting returned books
    e) Requesting books for other libraries
3. Dealing with complaints
    a) Responding to claims that missing books were returned
    b) Listening to protests about fines
    c) Listening to criticism of the library collection
    d) Resolving complaints about other patrons

Problem-Solution Order This pattern explores aspects of a problem and the nature of the solution.

Topic: Providing Quality Service

1. Problem: Volunteers are the "face" of the library for patrons.
    a) No orientation can help you deal with every situation.
    b) Examples of problems you might encounter
        i) Patrons breaking library rules
        ii) Patrons misusing public access computers
        iii) Patrons abusing library resources
        iv) Patrons angry about perceived offenses
2. Solution: Knowing how to deal with problems
    a) Listening to patrons
    b) Defining problem
    c) Referring issues to library staff members

Checking out books for patrons may be a key part of volunteers' jobs–or it might be a task they don't do at all.

Treating patrons with respect and politeness is probably expected of every volunteer.

Cause-Effect Order The presenter describes the causes of patron complaints. In these cases, one effect should be an appropriate response from the volunteer.

Topic: Dealing with Complaints

1. Reasons for patron complaints
   a) Library policy
   b) Inability to find what they need
   c) Other patrons
   d) Perceived unfair treatment
2. Rules for responding to complaints
   a) Never criticize library policy
   b) Listen and be patient
   c) Be helpful and try to solve the problem
   d) Refer patrons to library staff as needed
   e) Always be polite

Combining Patterns This problem-solution pattern makes use of both climactic order and chronological order.

Topic: Providing Quality Service

1. Problem: Volunteers are the "face" of the library for patrons.
   a) No orientation can help you deal with every situation.
   b) Examples of problems you might encounter
      i) Patrons breaking library rules
      ii) Patrons misusing public access computers
      iii) Patrons abusing library resources
      iv) Patrons angry about perceived offenses
2. Solution: Know how to deal with problems.
   a) Listening
   b) Defining problem
   c) Deciding when a problem should be referred to library staff
   d) Identifying the appropriate staff person

PROJECT PREP

With your **project partner**, think of a problem with a simple solution. Then outline the solution using one of the organizational patterns described.

Library volunteers use the mnemonic LEARN in working with patrons.

Mnemonics and Logical Order

There are times when using a **mnemonic** will help you relate your ideas to the audience more effectively. A mnemonic is a memory aid that uses associations or patterns to help people remember information. If you were giving a presentation to library volunteers about dealing with patrons' complaints, you could use this mnemonic device:

L Listen to what the patron is saying.

E Explain relevant library policy.

A Apologize for the problem.

R Remedy the problem if you can, or refer the patron to a staff person.

N Notify library staff about the problem.

This mnemonic works because it covers the steps of the process in a logical order. Mnemonics won't work if they are phony or forced.

Outlining

Outlining your speech helps you organize your ideas. The brief outlines on the previous pages illustrate how the body of a speech can be organized. Experienced speakers often speak using only an outline.

A good outline shows order and relationship. When your outline you use in your speech presents ideas in a meaningful order and makes the relationship between those ideas clear, the audience will readily understand your message.

Standard Outline Form

A traditional outline uses Roman numerals for major points, capital letters for subpoints, and Arabic numerals for items that support subpoints. A subpoint relates directly to a major point; information under a subpoint relates directly to the subpoint. If ideas are developed further, lowercase letters with parenthesis are typically used. An outline also uses indentation to show some ideas are subordinate to others.

Standard Outline

I. Major point
    A. Subpoint
        1. Development
        2. Development
    B. Subpoint
        1. Development
        2. Development
            a) Further development
            b) Further development
        3. Development

II. Major point
    A. Subpoint
        1. Development
        2. Development
        3. Development
            a) Further development
            b) Further development
        4. Development
    B. Subpoint
        1. Development
        2. Development
            a) Further development
            b) Further development

Rules of Outlining

Outlining is all about order and relationships. Following simple rules can make your thinking more focused and your speech more organized.

Rule One: *Express only one idea at each level of an outline.*

WRONG	RIGHT
1. Scanning the patron's library card and the bar code on the book	1. Scanning the patron's library card 2. Scanning the bar code on the book

Rule Two: *Maintain distinct levels.* In the example below, if returning materials to their proper places is part of keeping the library tidy, it should be included in that category.

WRONG	RIGHT
1. Keeping the library tidy a) Removing things patrons leave on tables b) Removing old posters and notices 2. Returning books and magazines to their proper places	1. Keeping the library tidy a) Removing things patrons leave on tables b) Removing old posters and notices c) Returning books and magazines to their proper places

Rule Three: *Express each item in a level in a similar way.*

WRONG	RIGHT
3. Examples of possible problems a) Patrons breaking library rules b) Misuse of public access computers c) Abuse of library resources d) Offenses	3. Examples of possible problems a) Patrons breaking library rules b) Patrons misusing computers c) Patrons abusing library resources d) Patrons angry about perceived offenses

Rule Four: *Use complete sentences for major points only.* Using sentences would make the outline cumbersome.

Rule Five: *Create three separate outlines for a long speech.* Write one outline for the introduction, one for the body, and one for the conclusion.

Order is useful in many ways. In what order are the books this student is carrying? How does this make handling them easier?

Connecting Ideas: Using Transitions

A **transition** is a word, phrase, or sentence that connects ideas in order to move the audience from one point to the next. External transitions move from one major point of the speech to the next. Internal transitions connect words or subpoints that are part of a major point. Transitions are important because:

1. **They create unity.** They help the audience see the speech as a whole.
2. **They help the audience know where they are in a speech.** They mark important divisions in the speech, signaling when one point has been made and another is coming.
3. **They reveal relationships** by showing how one idea is connected to the next.

Two common techniques are using "transition words" and repeating a word or idea. Transition words show how parts of the speech relate to one another. They connect sentences, ideas, or major parts of a speech. The following chart shows some common transition words.

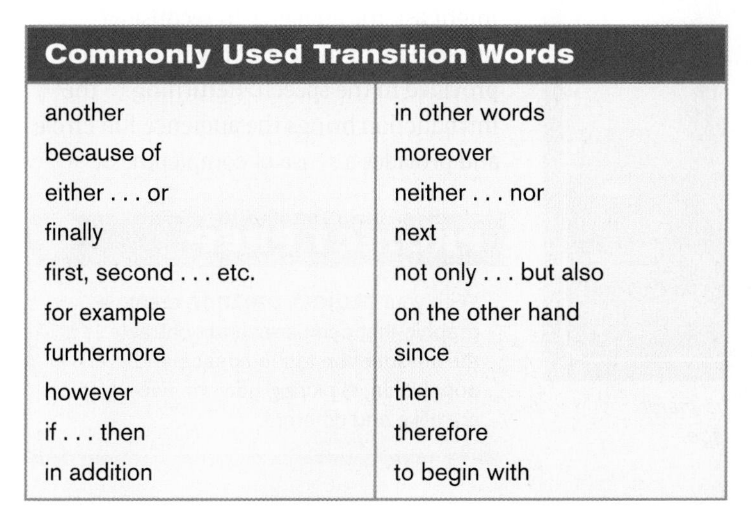

Commonly Used Transition Words	
another	in other words
because of	moreover
either . . . or	neither . . . nor
finally	next
first, second . . . etc.	not only . . . but also
for example	on the other hand
furthermore	since
however	then
if . . . then	therefore
in addition	to begin with

A successful speaker uses transitions and key words to help the audience follow the flow of ideas.

Repeating a key word can also make an effective transition from one point to another. For example:

. . . When you've activated the new *library card*, have the patron sign his or her name on the back of the card.

The *library card* gives the patron access to all the library's resources and services, and the patron must present it whenever checking out a book. . . .

The term *library card* is the repeated idea that helps the audience move smoothly from the topic of issuing a library card to checking out a book.

The Conclusion of the Speech

When a well-organized speech comes to an end, the audience knows it. There is no need for an awkward statement such as "That's it" or "I guess I'm done." As with other parts of the speech, what you say in the conclusion should reflect the situation, the purpose, and the audience. Most conclusions accomplish these three goals:

1. **Signaling the audience that the speech is coming to an end.** Audiences appreciate a tidy wrap-up at the end of a speech. If they get the signal that this is happening, they may pay closer attention to be sure they grasp the message of the presentation.
2. **Summarizing the major ideas.** This is the wrap-up that the audience wants. You don't have to review everything you said, but a short recap reminds the audience of what is most important.
3. **Leaving the audience with something to remember.** A good conclusion should be the climax of the speech. It should restate the main message of your presentation in a way that will help the audience remember it.

A strong conclusion includes a summary of the major points and a restatement of the primary message.

Concluding Devices

Just as there are devices commonly used by speakers in the introduction to a speech, there are devices that can be used in the conclusion. In fact, many of the same devices used in an introduction can be used effectively in the conclusion. For example, a quotation can summarize the speech's content and leave the audience with something to remember. An incident can apply the content communicated in the body of the speech to a specific and memorable example. Humor, too, can be as effective in the conclusion as it is in the introduction.

One effective technique for a conclusion is actually to return to the speech's introduction. For example, if the speech started with a rhetorical question, the conclusion could return to the question and answer it. If the speech began with a startling statement, the speaker, in the conclusion, might ask the audience to reconsider the statement in light of the information provided in the speech. Returning to the introduction brings the audience full circle and provides a sense of completeness.

PROJECT PREP

With your **project partner**, create a graphic that compares and contrasts the introduction to the speech and the conclusion, exploring how the two parts are alike and different.

Analyzing Speech Form: Organizational Principles

"Mending the Body by Lending an Ear: The Healing Power of Listening" was presented by Carol Koehler, Ph.D., Assistant Professor of Communication and Medicine, in 1998. The audience was made up of attendees of the International Listening Association Business Conference held at the Ritz-Carlton Hotel in Kansas City, Missouri.

1 I would like to start this morning by telling you two different stories. Each story has the same two characters and happens in the same location. Both stories occur within a twenty-four hour period.

The first paragraph of the introduction tells the audience what to expect from the introduction. This helps the audience know there will be a two-part introduction.

2 Over the Christmas holidays, my husband and I were invited to a formal black-tie wedding. This was to be an elegant event, so we put on our best evening clothes. Adding to that, I wore my mother's diamond jewelry and this fabulous mink coat that I inherited. Just before we left the house, I telephoned my 86-year-old mother-in-law for her daily checkup. When she answered, her voice sounded a little strange so my husband and I decided to stop at her apartment to make sure she was all right before we went to the wedding.

Both parts of the introduction are incidents, so they are sequential. Narration, by its very nature, is usually organized according to time sequence. Note that this speaker often begins sentences with *When* or *While*. This helps the audience understand that some things happened in sequence (*when*) and some things happened simultaneously (*while*).

3 When we arrived she seemed slightly disoriented (she was 86 years old but wonderfully healthy, sharp-witted and self-sufficient). We called her physician to ask his advice, and he said to bring her to the local Emergency Room and have her checked out. We did that. This was a Saturday night so the Emergency Room was pretty active. When we arrived, I in my mink and my husband in his tux, we looked noticeably different from the general population in the waiting room. While my husband filled out the forms, the doctors took my mother- in-law into a makeshift curtained room.

This part of the introduction builds suspense. Is the mother-in-law going to be all right? Will they still get to the wedding? Why is the way they were dressed important?

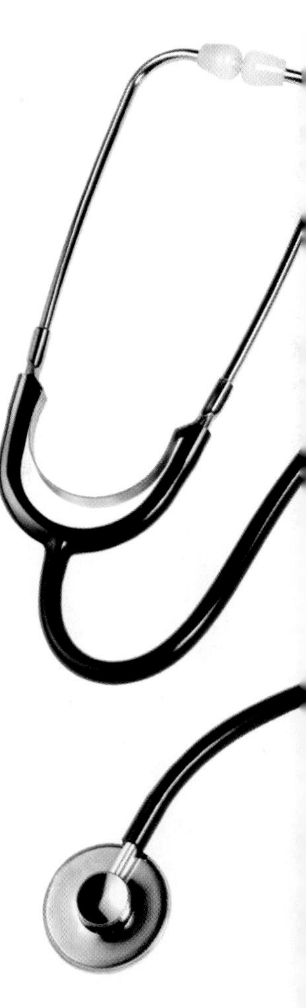

4 When I noticed that the staff had removed both her glasses and her hearing aid, I realized she would experience some anxiety, so at that point I decided to stay with her to keep her from being frightened. As I went into the room, a young doctor said, “Ma'am, you can't go in there.” Without missing a beat I said, “Don't be ridiculous.” With that I went and found a chair in the waiting room, brought it into the examination room and sat down. I remember thinking the staff looked a little bewildered but no one challenged me at any time. When my mother-in-law's hands felt a little cold, I asked for a heated blanket and one was brought immediately. So it went for the entire evening. We missed the wedding but finally got my mother-in-law in a permanent room about 2 A.M.

5 The next morning I went to the hospital about 10 o'clock in the morning, dressed in tennis shoes, a sweat suit, and no makeup. As I arrived at my mother-in-law's room, an unfamiliar doctor was just entering. I introduced myself and asked him to speak up so my mother-in-law would be aware of why he was there and what he was doing. I told him that she tends to be frightened by the unexpected and without her glasses or hearing aid, she was frightened enough. This thirty-something male doctor proceeded to examine my mother-in-law without raising his voice so that she could hear, and without acknowledging me or my request in any way. Actually, he never really looked at either one of us.

“The next morning” makes the transition from the first story to the second by indicating the passage of time.

6 In both scenarios, I was listened to not by ears alone, but by eyes, by gender, by age judgments, and by social status assessments. That started me thinking.

This paragraph calls attention to the similarities and differences in the two situations and provides a transition to the topic of the speech.

7 Why did a recent article in the *Journal of the American Medical Association* indicate high dissatisfaction in traditional doctor–patient appointments? Why is it the *Wall Street Journal* claims that perception of physician concern and not physician expertise is the deciding factor in

The author introduces the specific topic of the speech with a series of rhetorical questions.

the rising number of malpractice suits? Why did the *New England Journal of Medicine* report that the care and attention quotient is causing "alternative" medicine practices to grow by leaps and bounds? Given this litany of events, what does it really mean to listen? And why, in the name of science, don't we produce better listeners in the medical profession?

The final rhetorical question summarizes the speaker's topic and implies the thesis of the speech: better listeners make better doctors.

8 The reasons are so obvious that they are sometimes overlooked. First, listening is mistakenly equated with hearing, and since most of us can hear, no academic priority is given to this subject in either college or med school. This, by the way, flies in the face of those who measure daily time usage. Time experts say we spend 9% of our day writing, 16% reading, 30% speaking, and 45% listening—just the opposite of our academic pursuits. Second, we perceive power in speech. We put value on those who have the gift of gab. How often have you heard the compliment, "He/she can talk to anyone"? Additionally, we equate speaking with controlling both the conversation and the situation. The third and last reason we don't listen is that we are in an era of information overload. We are bombarded with the relevant and the irrelevant and it is easy to confuse them. Often it's all just so much noise.

The body of the speech begins with reasons why people don't generally listen well. The statement "The reasons are so obvious" is the transition from the general nature of the introduction to the specifics of the body.

The speech's basic organization is problem-solution. Along with the illustrations in the introduction, these reasons establish the nature of the problem.

The speaker enumerates the points–first . . . second . . . third–to help the audience track her analysis.

9 How can we address this depressing situation? Dan Callahan, a physician and teacher, argues that primacy in health care needs to be given to the notion of care over cure. Caring as well as curing humanizes our doctor–patient relationships.

The speaker uses a rhetorical question to move the audience from problem to solution. She uses the contrast of *care* and *cure* as an effective memory anchor for the audience.

10 Let's talk about what that might mean for health care. What comes to mind when someone is caring? [The audience responded with the words *giving, interested, genuine,* and *sincere.*] Now, what comes to mind when you think of the opposite of care? [The audience volunteered *cold, uninterested, egotistical, busy, distracted,* and *selfish.*]

The speaker involves the audience by asking them to suggest synonyms and antonyms for *care.* In the remainder of the speech, she will explore the connection between *care* and *listening.*

11 What might a caring doctor be like? If we take the word CARE and break it down, we find the qualities that are reflective of a therapeutic communicator—in other words, someone who listens not with ears alone.

Another rhetorical question. Then the speaker introduces a mnemonic device to identify four things doctors can do to become better listeners.

12 **C** stands for *concentrate*. Physicians should hear with their eyes and ears. They should avoid the verbal and visual barriers that prevent real listening. It may be as simple as eye contact. (Some young doctors have told me they have a difficult time with looking people in the eye, and my advice is when you are uncomfortable, focus on the patient's mouth and as the comfort level increases, move to the eyes.) In the placement of office furniture, try and keep the desk from being a barrier between you and the patient. Offer an alternative chair for consultations—one to the side of your desk and one in front of your desk. Let the patient have some control and power to decide their own comfort level.

The speaker uses a repeated pattern: "**C** stands for . . ., **A** stands for . . ., **R** stands for . . . , **E** stands for . . . ." The pattern makes any other transitions unnecessary.

Notice that the repeated pattern always includes an imperative verb.

13 **A** stands for *acknowledge*. Show them that you are listening by using facial expressions, giving vocal prompts, and listening between the lines for intent as well as content. Listen for their vocal intonation when responding to things like prescribed medication. If you hear some hesitation in their voice, say to them, "I hear you agreeing, but I'm getting the sound of some reservation in your voice. Can you tell me why?" And then acknowledge their response. Trust them and they will trust you.

The speaker moves on to **A.** Because the audience already knows that she is going to break down the word CARE, they are prepared to follow her through the major points of the body of the speech.

14 **R** stands for *response.* Clarify issues by asking, "I'm not sure what you mean." Encourage continuing statements by saying "and then what" or "tell me more." The recurrent headache may mask other problems. Provide periodic recaps to focus information. Learn to make cryptic notes and then return your attention to the patient. (Note-taking is sometimes used as an avoidance tactic, and patients sense this.) Use body language by leaning toward the patient. Effective listening requires attention, patience, and the ability to resist the urge to control the conversation.

The speaker repeats the pattern. The repetition establishes a clear and reliable way for the audience to understand and remember the speaker's suggestions.

15 **E** stands for *exercise emotional control.* This means if your "hot buttons" are pushed by people who whine, and in walks someone who does that very thing, you are likely to fake interest in your patient. With your mind elsewhere, you will never really "hear" that person. Emotional blocks are based on previous experiences. They are sometimes activated by words, by tone of voice, by style of clothes or hair, or by ethnicity. It is not possible for us to be free of those emotional reactions, but the first step in controlling them is to recognize when you are losing control. One of the most useful techniques to combat emotional responses is to take a long, deep breath when confronted with the urge to interrupt. Deep breathing redirects your response, and as a bonus it is impossible to talk when you are deep breathing.

The speaker repeats the pattern.

16 Who of us would not choose the attentive, caring physician?

This rhetorical question provides a summary and signals the audience that the speech is coming to an end.

17 As it nears time for me to take a deep breath, I would just like to reiterate that listening is a learned skill and learning to listen with CARE has valuable benefits for health care professionals and patients. As a wise man named J. Isham once said, "Listening is an attitude of the heart, a genuine desire to be with another, which attracts and heals."

The conclusion begins by repeating something the audience just heard: *deep breath.* This repetition is another signal that the speech is ending, since the speaker just made the point that a person can't talk while deep breathing. She then reiterates her message and ends with an inspiring quotation that relates to her message.

18 Thank you very much.

Her final words do two things: (1) They express her gratitude to the audience for their attention. (2) They are the official signal that the speech is over, and the audience is free to stop listening.

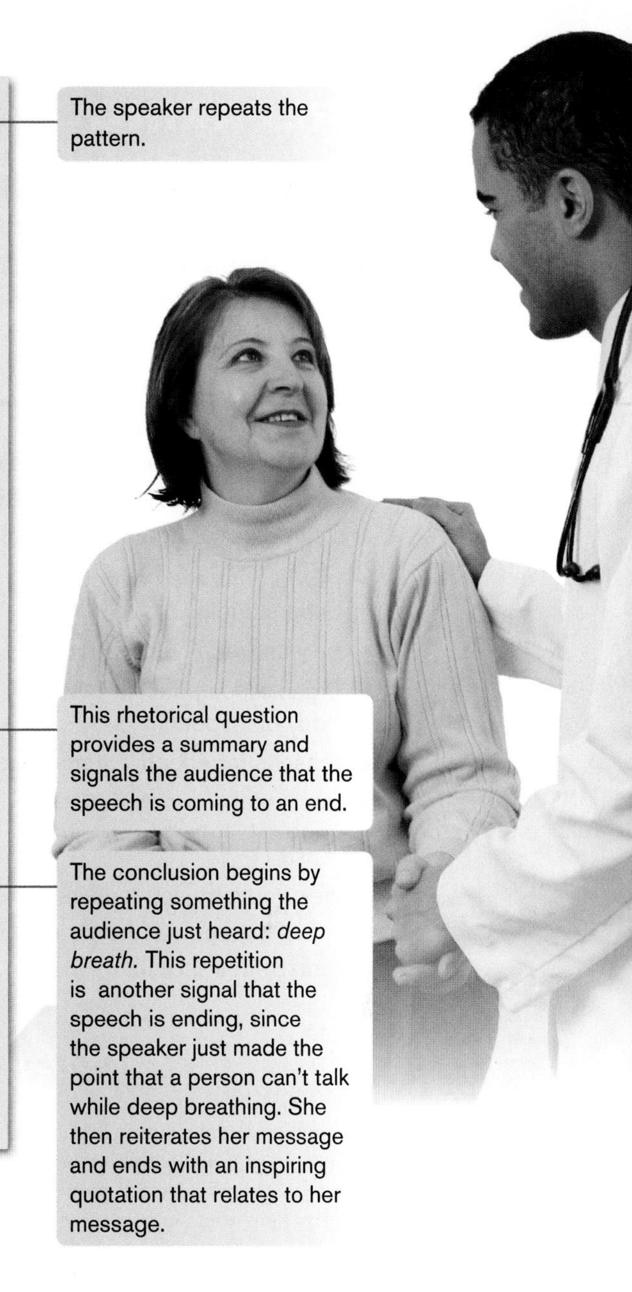

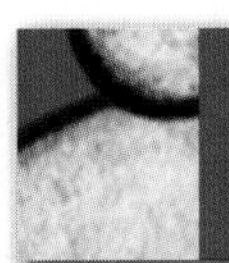

PREPARING THE PROJECT

Begin your project by looking back at the **Project Prep** activities in this chapter and using the directions below.

Make Connections

Discuss with your partner your understanding of how effective speaking depends on good organization. Discuss and summarize these key points:

- how organization affects understanding
- purposes of an introduction
- organization patterns in the body of a speech
- reasons for effective transitions
- goals of the conclusion.

Focus

Review your project: a presentation showing a graphic of how ideas are organized in a speech.

Surefire Graphics

To make a great graphic organizer:
- make a graphic that suits the subject
- let your ideas drive the graphic
- represent ideas in a fresh way.

Plan

Work with your partner to create a graphic representing the three parts of a speech. Show how the three parts function separately and in relation to one another.

Develop

With your partner, outline your presentation. Discuss your graphic. Will it be large enough for all to see or will you just describe it? You may wish to create the graphic as you speak.

Practice

If things are not going smoothly in practice, you can refine your plan. If your presentation is too long, cut it to three minutes.

PRESENTING THE PROJECT

Use the strategy that follows to help make your presentation as good as it can be.

Using Visual Aids

One of you should speak while the other points out or creates items on the graphic. The person responsible for the visual must coordinate with the speaker. Be sure everything is operating properly. Your markers should have ink and your laser pointer should work. Have your projector ready to go. Display your graphic organizer before you begin.

Use clear gestures to direct the audience's attention to your graphic.

EVALUATING THE PROJECT

Evaluate the presentations using the following rubric.

Score the demonstration on each point, with 4 being "outstanding" and 1 being "needs much improvement."

Come up with an overall score and write a brief paragraph that explains your score.

Understanding How to Organize a Speech	Presentation of a Graphic Organizer	Creativity and Originality	Preparation and Use of Time
4 Presenters showed thorough understanding of speech organization.	**4** Presenters' graphic helped illuminate speech organization.	**4** The presentation was very original and creative.	**4** The presentation was well-prepared and stayed within the time limit.
3 Presenters showed a basic understanding of speech organization.	**3** Presenters' graphic was fairly helpful in explaining speech organization.	**3** The presentation was original and fairly creative.	**3** The presentation was well-prepared but went slightly over the time limit or was noticeably under.
2 Presenters showed some understanding of speech organization.	**2** Presenters' graphic was minimally helpful in explaining speech organization.	**2** The presentation was fairly original but not creative.	**2** The presentation was ill-prepared and went slightly over the time limit or was noticeably under.
1 Presenters showed little understanding of speech organization.	**1** Presenters' graphic was not helpful in explaining speech organization.	**1** The presentation was neither original nor creative.	**1** The presentation was ill-prepared and went significantly over the time limit or was significantly under.

Communication *Past* and Present

Getting Organized

From Cicero . . .

Rhetoric—the art of persuasion—was the subject of intense thought and theorizing in the classical world. Plato, Aristotle, and other influential Greeks wrote books about rhetoric. Cicero, one of the greatest Roman orators, helped introduce to the Roman world Greek theories about effective speaking. In *De Inventione*, he defines and describes the six parts of an oration. He sums up the classical tradition of how to organize a speech. Although the terms might be unfamiliar, you are likely to find many familiar ideas in the following descriptions.

Cicero spoke to the Roman Senate about the corruption of one of his political rivals, Catiline. Cicero's opening words–his exordium–have rung through history ever since: "How long, O Catiline, will you abuse our patience? How long is that madness of yours still to mock us?"

I. The Exordium This is the introduction to the speech. The name comes from a Latin word that means "to urge forward." The exordium gets the audience in the right frame of mind to listen to the rest of the speech. It makes the audience favorably disposed toward the speaker and the subject. It should also make the purpose of the speech clear.

II. The Narration The narration is the statement of the case. It explains the issue to be dealt with clearly and concisely. If the topic is new or unfamiliar to the audience, the narration must help the audience understand its importance. If the topic is one that is very familiar to the audience, the narration can sometimes be omitted.

III. The Partition The partition outlines the arguments that the speaker will present. It states what will be covered and in what order.

IV. The Confirmation The confirmation presents all the arguments that support that case. It gives greatest attention to the strongest arguments.

V. The Refutation The refutation anticipates opposing arguments and refutes them. It responds to all possible objections to the speaker's position before they can be voiced.

VI. The Peroration The peroration is the conclusion of the speech. In the peroration, the speaker sums up the arguments, arouses indignation or pity, and motivates the audience to action.

These six parts comprise the classical model for the organization of a speech. Since the time of Cicero, many great serious speeches about war, taxes, and morality have followed this model. So have many great comic ones.

. . . to Dave Barry

In 2004, humorist Dave Barry wrote a spoof of a commencement address, titled "One Degree of Separation." This short speech, intended for a college graduation ceremony and meant to be funny, displays the structure described by Cicero. It begins with an **exordium**, which grabs the audience's attention by stating the main idea of the oration: "Now you're leaving college and embarking upon the greatest adventure—and the biggest challenge—of your young lives: moving back in with your parents." He engages the audience with humor.

After the exordium, Barry delivers the **narration**. He states the case that, while his generation would have undergone the equivalent of torture rather than move back in with their parents, today it's OK. For today's graduates, moving back home is an acceptable alternative to going "straight from college into a harsh and unforgiving world fraught with unbearable hardships, such as no free high-speed Internet."

Barry skips the **partition**—even classical orators knew that the pattern allowed a certain amount of flexibility depending on audience, purpose, and situation. He also reverses the order of the **confirmation**, where he presents the arguments, "Your parents don't mind!" and "It's only temporary, right?" with the **refutation** of this idea: "Does the fact that you, a grown adult, are moving back with your parents mean that you're a sponging loser?"

Barry's **peroration** is one that the classic orators would have considered ideal. It sums up the arguments and arouses indignation and pity ("Yes, graduates, as much as you love your mom and dad, you're realistic enough to understand, deep down inside, that they are the two most annoying human beings on the planet"), and it motivates the audience to action ("If you set your goals high, and you never, ever give up, I guarantee you that one day you will find yourself working for a huge impersonal corporation run by morons").

Classic oratory lives on!

Dave Barry begins his exordium with: "This is your big day–the day when you jam four years' worth of unlaundered underwear into a Hefty bag and leave college . . . ."

Chapter 16 Review

Using Vocabulary Words

For each term listed below, make a box and divide it into four sections. In the top left section, write the word. In the top right section, write a situation in which you might use the word or an example of it. In the bottom left section, give an example of what the word means to you. In the bottom right section, write a word that you feel is a non-example or opposite of that word.

Word	Situation
Example	Non-example

1. cause-effect order
2. chronological order
3. classification order
4. climactic order
5. mnemonic
6. problem-solution order
7. spatial order
8. topical order
9. transition

Reviewing Key Ideas

1. Explain why organization is important for an effective speech.
2. Identify and explain the six devices speakers commonly use in their introductions and indicate those that can also be used effectively in the conclusion.
3. Identify and explain the eight organizational patterns for the body of a speech.
4. Compare and contrast the content and goals of the introduction and the conclusion of a speech.

Reflecting on Your Project

With your partner, discuss which aspect of the project you were more successful with: designing the graphic or presenting it to the class. Talk about what you would do differently if you had the project to do all over again.

Responding to the Essential Question

Use the headings in this chapter to write a brief chapter summary that answers the question, "How should a speech be organized?" Compare your summary with a partner's to see if you both covered the main points.

Extending Your Understanding

Everyday Life

1. Listen to people as they speak to you and others and try to detect and identify the organization patterns in everyday communication.
2. Think about if and how you use introductions and conclusions in your

everyday speech. Try to identify the communication situations in which you are most inclined to introduce a topic or issue you want to talk about and wrap up what you say with a conclusion.

3. Think about something interesting or amusing that happened to you. Share it with a partner. Together, brainstorm topics for speeches in which you could use your story in the introduction.

In the Media

4. Listen to someone delivering a speech on television. It might be the president or the governor of your state. It might be someone running for office. See if you can identify the organizational pattern used in the speech.
5. Watch an interview on a television news program. Listen for examples of one of the six devices used by speakers in introductions: incident, quotation, rhetorical question, humor, startling statement, references to history, audience, or self. Discuss how the device was used in the interview and how it compares with the way it might be used in a speech.
6. Read an editorial opinion piece in your local newspaper. Compare the organization of this work with what you have learned about the organization of a speech.

Research

7. Visit www.americanrhetoric.com and listen to a speech that interests you. Take notes about the organization of the speech and the use of devices discussed in this chapter.
8. The term *rhetorical question* comes from the classic word *rhetoric*. Use online sources to research the definition of *rhetoric*. Present your findings to the class.

Interpreting Graphics

This image is an example of "visual rhetoric." Study it and explain in a brief paragraph the message it conveys.

Additional Projects

1. **Group Project:** With a small group, agree on a topic for a speech. Then each of you individually decide on a thesis sentence for your speech and a device you would use in your introduction. Get back together and compare your ideas. Discuss how your different decisions might lead to very different speeches.
2. **Individual Project:** Select a topic and find some quotations from famous people about the topic. Select your favorite quotations and create a poster to display them.

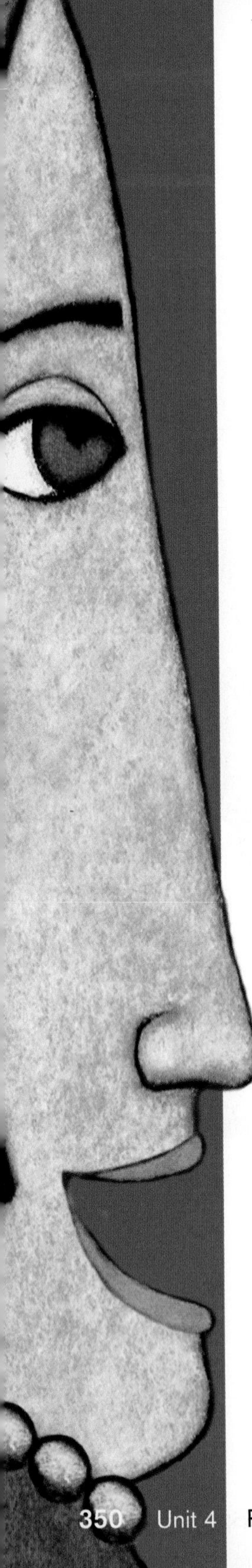

Preparing Supporting Materials for Speeches

ESSENTIAL QUESTION

How are supporting materials used to enhance a speech?

Chapter Project: Worth a Thousand Words

If someone describes an animal that is part mammal and part reptile and that looks something like a beaver but has a duck bill and webbed feet, you might begin to get a fuzzy image of this creature in your mind. But if someone shows you a picture of a platypus along with that description, your mental image becomes crystal clear. This project will give you practice in preparing visual and other kinds of supporting materials for your speeches that will help you get your point across clearly and forcefully.

In a group of four, you will research something that you all find interesting—how your favorite band got its name or a baseball player's career batting average, for example. You will then create a four-minute speech about your topic and develop four visual and/or audio aids to add interest. Each group member will be responsible for one item. As you prepare your presentation, refer to the CAPS guidelines below.

The rubric on page 367 shows the traits on which your presentation will be evaluated.

CONCEPT	supporting materials add interest and value to speeches
AUDIENCE	classmates and teacher
PURPOSE	practice using supporting materials with a speech
SITUATION	group presentation with audio or visual aids

KEY VOCABULARY

manuscript	Q & A
digression	storyboard
memorized	multimedia
extemporaneous	font

Visual aids such as the diagram being used above help your audience get a clear mental image.

Speak Up!

With a partner, quickly brainstorm different types of visual aids you might want to use when giving your speech. What have you used in the past? What other aids would you like to use?

Pages 352–364 will provide the information you'll need to complete this project.

Speech Delivery Formats

Speeches can be delivered in four different ways: impromptu, manuscript, memorized, and extemporaneous. Each of the four methods has special usefulness for certain purposes, situations, and audiences.

Impromptu

You learned in Chapter 12 that some situations, such a group meeting, call for impromptu speaking—sharing your views with no preparation. There are many other times when you may have to make an impromptu speech, such as when your English teacher asks you to update the class on research you are doing. In these situations you need to develop your speech on the spur of the moment.

Tips for an Effective Impromptu Speech

Even with mere seconds to prepare, make decisions about your message, audience, and purpose. Think about the tips that follow.

1. Your audience knows that your speech is impromptu, so they will not expect a fully structured speech. They will not be judging your technique.
2. Use whatever time you have—even the time it takes to walk to the front of the room—to think up a thesis and simple outline.
3. Speak clearly, briefly, and to the point.
4. Present a conclusion—even if it is just a brief comment saying you have finished.

Ginny was asked to give an impromptu talk about global warming. Does she seem ready for the challenge?

Manuscript

Reading a speech from a prepared document, or **manuscript**, is called a manuscript delivery format. Its use is often limited to situations in which speakers must have a complete and accurate record of their statements. Examples include the President's State of the Union address, statements to the press, or a speech made in response, point by point, to someone else's speech.

Tips for an Effective Manuscript Speech

1. **Do your best to anticipate audience reaction.** Consider your listeners' potential needs for explanation and clarification and build those into your script. Because the manuscript format is so inflexible, you must deal with these issues at the writing stage.

2. **Have someone else read your speech before you give it.** Ask your reader to make suggestions for improving language, content, and style.

3. **Rehearse aloud.** This helps you gauge the length and timing of your speech, hear how the language sounds, and polish your delivery style. Strive for vocal variety. Listen for your use of pauses and a variable rate of speech to enhance your meaning and keep your audience interested.

Avoid simply reading a manuscript speech—put expression into your delivery.

Written Style vs. Oral Style

When writing a manuscript speech, you draw upon your knowledge of good composition—using organization and transitions and supporting your thesis. There are, however, differences between oral style and written style (some of which are covered in Chapter 2). Try to "hear" these differences to achieve a natural oral style. Remember the following points.

1. Oral style is more casual than written style, and it draws on a smaller vocabulary. When speaking, people use about half the number of words they use in writing.

The teacher seems happy with Maria's writing style, but what can she do to make her oral style equally impressive?

2. Oral style prefers contractions, something you typically avoid in formal writing.

3. Oral style uses incomplete sentences, but a more formal written style typically does not. As you speak, you can use tone and gestures to convey meaning with fewer words.

4. Oral style uses more repetition. Repetition is awkward in writing. On the page, a repeated word looks like an error. Speakers enhance repeated words through voice and gesture, making them sound natural and fresh.

5. Oral style sometimes contains a **digression**, an idea that departs from the main message. If you can keep your listener engaged during a brief but relevant bit of information, a digression can serve your speech well. Digressions are avoided in written style, which relies on a more structured presentation.

Read the two announcements below and think about how one functions well for a reader while the other is better suited for a listener.

Notice in the School Paper (Written Style)

IMPORTANT NOTICE
TO ALL STUDENTS

We experienced a disruption in our normal school year due to persistent severe weather conditions this past winter. As a result we had an unusual number of school closures. The School Board, therefore, has voted to add three full days to the end of the school year. Instead of being dismissed for the summer on Wednesday, May 28, we will extend the year to Monday, June 2. Please see your teachers for information about how this affects your end-of-year academic responsibilities.

Announcement over the PA System (Oral Style)

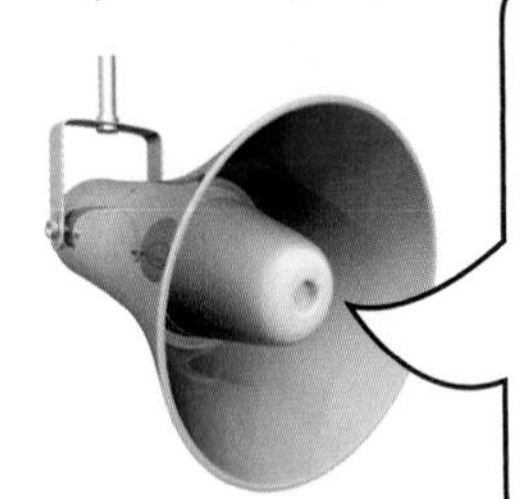

Just a quick announcement from last night's School Board vote. I know you're all waiting to hear it! Unfortunately, we are required to make up three snow days this spring. That puts the last day of school at June 2 instead of May 28. Your teachers will fill you in on further details related to your coursework.

Memorized

All the suggestions for manuscript speeches also apply to the **memorized** format. Although you might participate in a classroom assignment or a speech competition that asks you to memorize a speech, the format is uncommon because it carries the risk of memory failure. You may forget your next important point or realize you've skipped an entire portion of your speech. When preparing a memorized speech you must rehearse, rehearse, rehearse and know your subject well enough to play it by ear if you must.

Extemporaneous

An **extemporaneous** speech has some preparation and rehearsal time, but not much. You will have to make speaking decisions as you go. Prep time involves writing key words and phrases that you will use to track your ideas so you can hit the important points. The actual words will be spoken as they come to you. This delivery format is quite flexible and very common in academic and professional situations.

Tips for an Effective Extemporaneous Speech

1. Use your preparation time to concentrate on making communication decisions based on your understanding of situation, purpose, and audience.
2. Any outline or notes you use should be reminders, nothing more. An outline that simply shows the order and relationships of your ideas can help you achieve a natural and lively delivery style.
3. Concentrate on using your prep time wisely and maintaining a spontaneous feel to your speech.
4. Consider using the extemporaneous style whenever you feel very familiar with your subject.

PROJECT PREP

What visual aids might you use with each speech-delivery format? Discuss your reactions with your **project group**.

Preparing Notes for Extemporaneous Delivery

The extemporaneous style is one that speakers use most often, with good reason. See the chart below.

Advantages of Extemporaneous Style
Less preparation time is needed than for most other prepared speeches.
It is less nerve-wracking than the impromptu or memorized style.
It offers the chance to use a more natural speaking style than either manuscript or memorized style.
It offers a more carefully considered message than the impromptu style.
It is more flexible than either manuscript or memorized style.

You can create memory prompts for your extemporaneous speech. Here are some simple guidelines.

1. If you want a feeling of security, write out a few key elements of the speech entirely. You might write out your introduction, a few crucial points or transitions, and a conclusion.
2. Use large printing or oversized type and lots of white space so you can easily find your place when you look down at your notes.
3. Number your note cards or outline pages to keep them organized. Keep your outline and notes in a folder.

Joe is giving a speech about the German club's visit to Hamburg. He wrote a short introduction and outline as a memory prompt.

Outline Format

Introduction

Thank you for attending the German Club's annual program. We are just back from our fall trip to Hamburg. We had a wonderful time seeing the sights, meeting new people, and learning new things. We'll take turns sharing the highlights. We hope you enjoy them. Feel free to ask questions.

I. The Road to Hamburg
- A. Fundraising
  1. Car wash
  2. Plant sale
- B. Planning the Trip
  1. Creating an itinerary
  2. Working around school schedules
- C. Travel details
  1. Securing passports
  2. Effective packing strategies
  3. The bumpy plane ride

II. We Made It!
- A. First night
  1. Speaking German—in Germany!
  2. Youth hostel
- B. The next day
  1. Sightseeing
  2. Eating brats

Joe might have decided to use note cards for his speech. They would look like the ones below.

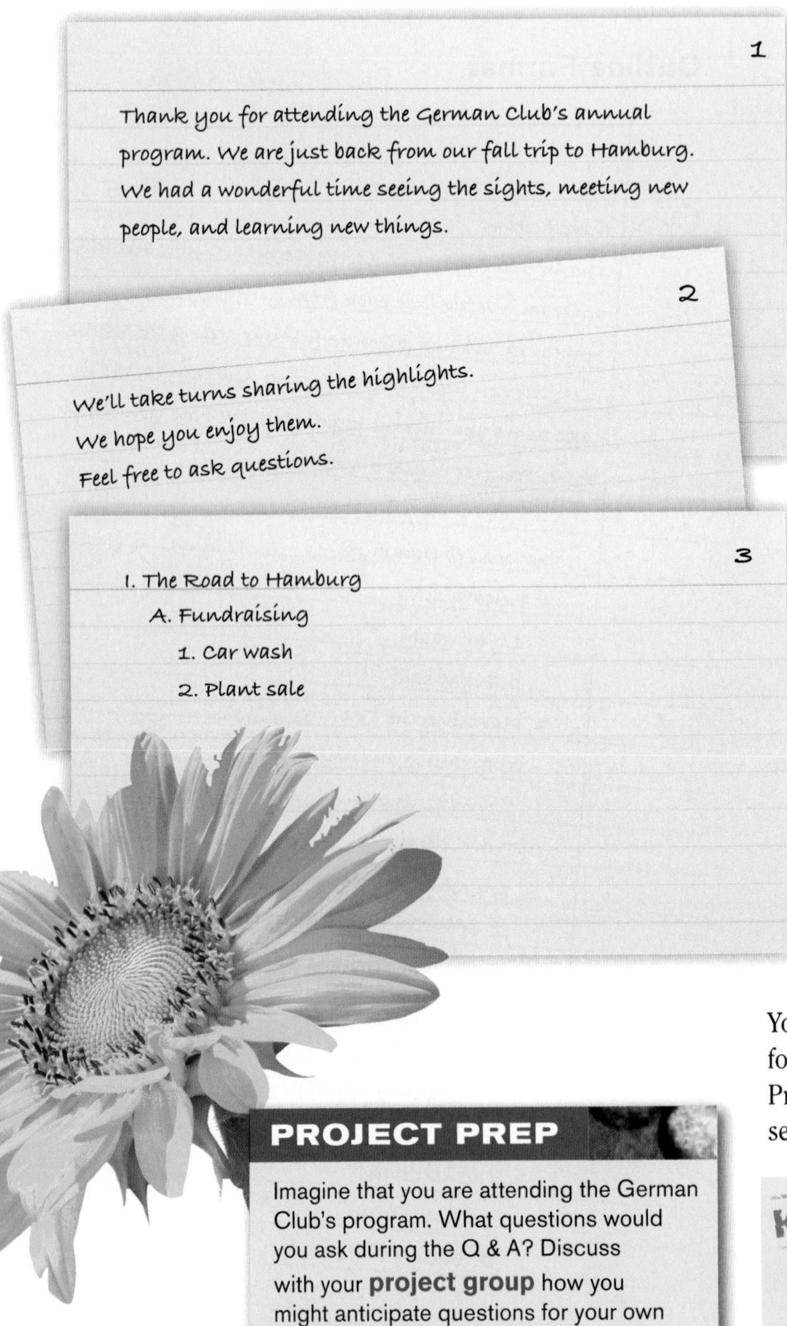

PROJECT PREP

Imagine that you are attending the German Club's program. What questions would you ask during the Q & A? Discuss with your **project group** how you might anticipate questions for your own presentation.

Note Card Format

Longer statements such as your introduction or transitions can be written onto note cards, but space is limited. Don't put too much information on a note card. You want to be able to quickly find your memory prompts. Rehearse using your note cards or outline so you know exactly where to look for information.

Anticipating Questions and Answers

No matter which delivery format you use for your speech, you will likely be faced with a question-and-answer period, or **Q & A.** Audiences will appreciate having the opportunity to ask questions or clarify information. The Q & A helps you sharpen and focus your communication techniques.

In many ways, the Q & A is like an impromptu speech. You can't know for sure which questions your listeners will ask, but you can try to anticipate them. Whenever you prepare a speech, think about places where the audience may want to know more—and be prepared to answer their questions. You may even want to have note cards ready for responding to some possible questions. Proper preparation will make your Q & A sessions run smoothly.

The Q & A helps you refine your message for your listeners—it is feedback at its best.

Producing Standard Visual Aids

Visual aids can help you reinforce information in your speech. If you make a point by sharing statistics, for example, your audience may benefit by seeing a chart or a graph that illustrates them. If you present a sample of courtroom testimony, the text might pack more punch if you project an artist's image of the defendant.

Visual aids address a variety of learning styles. They help those who learn best by reading, those who find that listening has the greatest impact, and those who learn best by seeing an image. Sometimes a visual aid is the best way to convey a message—better than spoken words. For example, if you are describing a boundary dispute between countries, you could *talk* about latitudes and longitudes. Nothing though, would convey the idea better than a map. Suppose you are describing a film you want to make. You might use a **storyboard**, a series of sketches that shows the sequence of scenes in a video.

Chalkboards and Marker Boards

The classroom chalkboard was a prominent visual aid in classrooms for many years. Today erasable white marker boards are also common. Professional meeting rooms are also equipped with marker boards or easels with poster paper to draw or write on. They are all handy and easy to use.

A valuable feature of these boards is that they promote interaction between speaker and audience. For example, you might ask your listeners to do some brainstorming with you and use a board to write down their ideas. Or if you are explaining how to do something, you might sketch the process like the different images on a storyboard.

Following are ways you can make your interactivity as clear as possible.

1. Be sure your printing is readable and large enough for everyone to see.
2. Don't let your board work get in the way of gestures and other movements that enhance your presentation.
3. Avoid writing too high or too low on the board. The audience will have to strain to see, and you will have to strain to reach.
4. Avoid blocking the board. Stand to the side of what you've written and use a pointer if necessary.
5. Don't talk when writing. Talk first, then write, or write and then speak. Try to write while glancing at the audience to maintain eye contact.
6. Keep it simple. Don't create long sentences or intricate drawings. Use abbreviations to save time.
7. Erase frequently or you'll have a jumble of information on the board that will confuse your audience.
8. When using a chalkboard, avoid wearing dark colors. The white chalk dust can spoil your appearance.

Writing on a marker board is an excellent way to show the relationships among ideas.

Posters

Posters are visually appealing and have the following advantages:

- You can prepare them ahead of time.
- They can be colorful and interesting.
- They can help you preview the organization of your presentation.
- They can summarize material; show charts; and present new terms.

Tips for Using Posters

1. Use dark markers.
2. Use clear, large letters.
3. Feature just one idea on each poster.
4. Tape posters to the wall or an easel.
5. Show a poster only when discussing its content.

Objects and Models

Objects and models can be particularly useful as visual aids. If you are discussing classic Greek architecture, bring in a model. Pass around a replica of Lindbergh's *Spirit of St. Louis* for a speech in history class.

In 1927, Charles Lindbergh became an international hero when he became the first person to fly solo across the Atlantic Ocean.

Tips for Using Objects and Models

1. Be safe—don't use models that produce high heat, electrical currents, or chemical reactions.
2. Keep it simple enough that your audience will benefit from seeing it.
3. Keep it out of sight until you are ready to use it. Occasionally, you will want to use a model as a focal point before the speech starts to help build curiosity.
4. Keep it visible once you've introduced it. The audience needs to see it as you continue to talk.

Handouts

Audiences love handouts because they get to take something away to look at later. Handouts allow you to provide the audience with concrete reminders of your message.

Tips for Using Handouts

1. Always prepare enough handouts. Anticipate the size of your audience and make extra copies.
2. Use your understanding of situation, purpose, and audience to decide when to make the handouts available to your audience. If you want people to follow along with your speech, distribute them ahead of time. Pass out handouts when you'd like the audience to focus on them. If you want the focus on you, distribute handouts after your speech.
3. Plan how you will distribute the handouts. Will you stack them on a table at the entrance? Will you hand them out during the speech or send an e-mail before or after the event?

Using Presentation Software

TechConnect By now you've likely seen many speeches that incorporate some kind of presentation software. You may have even given a few yourself. Today's software options—as well as other audio-visual tools—have made **multimedia** presentations easier than ever. When skillfully used, these tools can help make your speech visually interesting, entertaining, and memorable. Sophisticated audiences respond well to up-to-date technology that engages their intellect.

Examples of presentation software and audio-visual aids include:

- "slides" created on a computer and shown on a monitor or projected onto a screen
- handouts picturing the slides for audience members to follow and take with them
- video clips
- audio recordings
- overhead transparencies.

KEY POINT

Presentation software includes computer programs and applications that help a speaker add interesting audio-visual elements to a speech.

Ask yourself the following questions to help you decide whether these tools are right for your speech.

Is it appropriate to the situation? A slide show using cartoons might be a great way to present Walt Disney's life and work, but it wouldn't be appropriate for a talk about wars or famine.

Will it help my speech's purpose? Ask, for example, "Will the video clip of swallows returning to San Juan Capistrano help me meet my speech purpose?" If the answer is yes—because your purpose is to inform the audience about this annual phenomenon—use the video. But if the answer is no—because it doesn't address your purpose of illustrating the migration habits of wrens—don't use it.

How will it benefit the audience? Your audience's needs must be your priority. The various presentation tools discussed give you many options for adding audio-visual elements, from sound effects to Web access to slide shows. Will your audience benefit from this, and how? Will it help them understand your message or distract them from it? Take what is useful, and forget the rest.

TechConnect *A media presentation can include slides, audio, and video–all in one session.*

Design

Your design decisions will shape the appearance of your visual aids. If you are creating a slide show using presentation software, for example, you can use a pre-designed template or create your own. Either way you will want to craft a clear, cohesive, and easy-to-follow presentation.

A good tip is to use the same template throughout your speech. Frequent changes in the look or color scheme will distract your audience and cause them to lose sight of, or interest in, your message.

Keep the elements of your visual aids in the same location throughout the presentation. Keep the headings in the same place on slides, transparencies, or handouts. Use standard formatting for text and bullets. And, when using pictures and graphs, use the same location—left or right, top or bottom—throughout. Consistency helps an audience stay focused and interpret information quickly.

Content

The purpose of visual aids is to support the content of your speech. If you decided to use text-based slides for your speech, for example, the following guidelines could help you assure that your multimedia supports your content rather than detracts from it.

Let your situation, purpose, and audience guide you in deciding what multimedia presentations to use.

Use the chart below to help you organize your thoughts about whether to use multimedia and other audio-visual aids when giving a speech.

Should I Use a Multimedia Presentation?

Situation	Purpose	Audience
Give yourself time to work with the tools. Don't wait until the last minute to learn the operating system.	Be sure that your purpose will be well served by multimedia or visual aids.	Will your audience benefit? Will the visual or audio help them understand your message or will the technology detract from the message?
Consider whether the tools fit the tone you need to achieve.	Know which purpose(s) these tools will help you meet.	Will your audience like this type of presentation?
Be sure the room has the proper setup for your tools. Keep in mind the space, audience vantage point, lighting, outlets, and available equipment such as a projection screen, computer, or VCR.	Tools should help (not hinder) in adapting to changing situations and audience needs. Anticipate ways you can react to the unexpected. For example, what if the monitor won't work or some audience members can't hear you?	Does the audience expect a multimedia presentation? If other speakers are using these tools, your decision to use them–or not–might help you "blend in" or "stick out." Which will the audience perceive as more positive?

1. Keep it simple. Slides are meant to support and clarify your speech, not function as a script. Keep text to a minimum.
2. Think of your slides as a simplified outline. Text should refer only to your main points.
3. Ask yourself, "What do I want my audience to remember?" Provide key points. If the text is explanatory or in any way "extra," it doesn't belong on a slide.
4. Limit the number of bullets per slide. Three or four should be the maximum for this use. You want your audience to spend more time listening to you and less time reading information.

Images

When using clip art, photos, and other images that come with your presentation software or that you download from the Internet, be sure they address the speech's situation, audience, and purpose.

> **PROJECT PREP**
>
> Discuss the content tips with your **project group**. How might they apply to visual aids such as transparencies and handouts that you will use in your presentation?

Tips for Using Images

1. Use images that clarify and support the content of your speech. If you had a photo of Walt Disney drawing Mickey Mouse, for instance, you wouldn't add it to a slide that corresponds to your talking about his childhood in Missouri. Instead you might find a photo of Disney as a boy.

Mickey and Minnie may be appealing but their image should be used only if relevant.

2. With clip art, always use a consistent style. When graphic elements match, your speech appears polished and prepared.
3. Don't toss in decoration just because you can. Graphic elements should always reinforce your message.

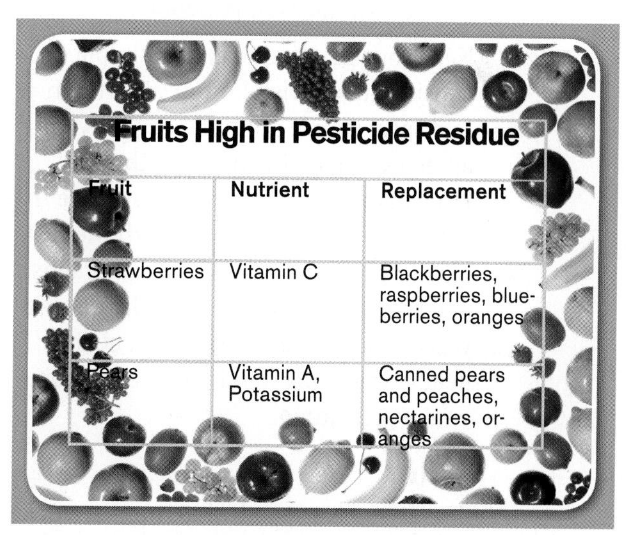

Fruits High in Pesticide Residue

Fruit	Nutrient	Replacement
Strawberries	Vitamin C	Blackberries, raspberries, blue-berries, oranges
Pears	Vitamin A, Potassium	Canned pears and peaches, nectarines, or-anges

What's wrong with this slide?

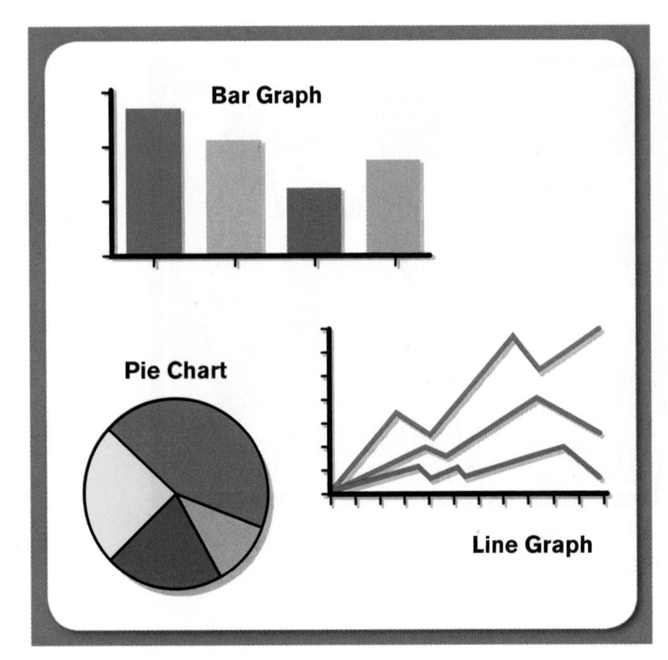

Bar graphs, line graphs, and pie charts help the audience visualize information.

Charts and Graphs

Presentation software typically includes graph and chart modules. You can add these to slides or reproduce them for use on transparencies or handouts.

Keep your graphs and charts simple, consistent, and visible. You want them to display clearly onscreen so that your audience can easily interpret them. Keep information to a minimum. See that your color scheme fits well with the rest of your presentation and that all graphs and charts follow a similar style. Be sure your audience can clearly see a chart's details and understand the information you're presenting.

Color

The days of black-and-white transparencies are gone. Color presentations are more attractive and interesting—and they are a breeze to create.

Tips for Using Color

1. **High contrast makes your text readable** from the audience. Use a light background with a dark font, and vice versa.
2. **Use appropriate color schemes** for your format. For example, with transparencies use colored fonts and other design elements over a clear background.
3. **Use color for emphasis.** A shot of color will draw people's attention to key words, phrases, and data.
4. **Use a consistent color scheme.** Resist the urge to "play" by throwing in every possible color and design. You want the end result to look polished.

Fonts

A **font** is a typeface of a particular size. A good presentation font is clear and easy to read. A poor font choice can quickly frustrate an audience trying to read your message. Readability is the theme for all the following tips.

Tips for Using Fonts

1. **Heavy fonts are easier to read** from a distance than light ones. Most presentation software templates use appropriate fonts, but be sure to check yours.
2. **Fancy fonts are hard to read**, so choose a simple one.
3. **Font size is important for readability** and structure. Headings should be larger than the rest of the text to show their importance.
4. **Limit your presentation to two font styles.** More than that can create a cluttered look.

Language

All of the following tips flow from the "keep it simple" philosophy. Any text you incorporate into your visual aids must be clear, to the point, and understandable. Your speech is the message, and the visual aid is the support.

Tips for Using Language Effectively

1. **Limit the number of words you use.** Limiting bullets and using a large font will help you keep your words brief.
2. **Use parallel language.** For example, the bullet points on a single slide should exhibit similar phrasing. If the first one is a complete sentence, all should be.
3. **Each sub-point you include should relate to the bullet directly above it.** This clear visual organization keeps you and your audience on track as you present a clearly structured speech.

Creating Your Own Audios and Videos

Use of homemade audios and videos has exploded in recent years. You may have created your own sound and video clips to share with friends through DVD or MP3 players, your own Web site, blog, or social networking sites. You can use your skills (or develop new ones) to add interesting audio and video elements to classroom, community, or work-related speeches.

Creating a PowerPoint presentation is not difficult, and it can help your audience understand and remember many of the important points in your speech. PowerPoint works well when you need to present charts, graphs, lists, or outlines.

By creating your own video, you can include exactly the information you feel is important.

Your school may have programs available for student use. If not, you can look on the Internet for more information.

You can also download audio and video images from your computer for use in your speeches by scanning them or transferring them to a disk. You can manipulate images and edit videos to serve your purposes. You can then program the material you have gathered to appear onscreen at just the right intervals as you speak, leaving you free to interact with your audience.

Audio and Video Examples at a Glance

- movie scene or other Internet video
- snippet from a recorded speech, interview, or public event
- TV ad
- home movie or video blog
- sound effects such as rain, a birdcall, or a creaky door
- live music or a song sample from a CD

Is This Job for Me?

Search: Graphic Designer

Did you ever receive one of those glossy brochures whose vibrant images drew you in and set your imagination whirling? If it caught your eye and communicated a message to you, then someone like Antonia can take the credit. Antonia is a *graphic designer.* Her job is to visually communicate her client's mission, values, or product. She works on all kinds of newsletters, brochures, and pamphlets, and her customers include local theatres, TV stations, and newspapers.

Antonia creates stand-alone graphics and images and also turns prepared text into a variety of visually interesting presentations. She uses an up-to-date computer outfitted with the latest design software and may even use tools as simple as a pencil and sketchpad. She pursued this career after studying art and graphic design in college and acquired her skills through education, on-the-job training, and personal experience. She worked in a design firm for a few years but then decided to work for herself in her home studio.

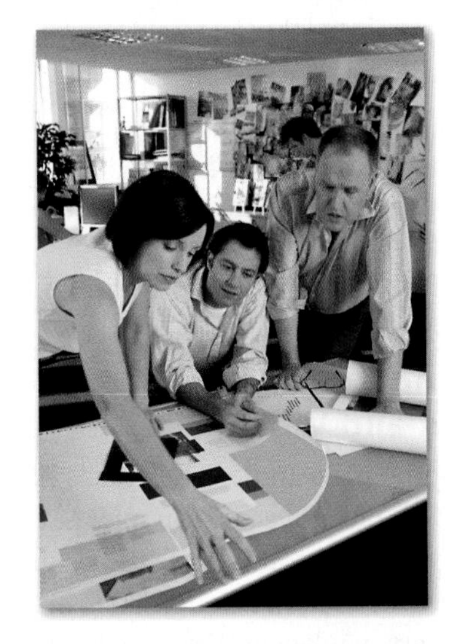

Does a job as a graphic designer interest you? Measure yourself with this personality inventory to find out if you think you have the traits. Do you:

- ✓ Have a strong interest in art and design?
- ✓ Possess excellent computer skills?
- ✓ Have the ability to express complex ideas with simple visual elements?
- ✓ Work well with others and on your own?

You might work as a graphic designer in the following types of organizations.

Employers	What You Would Do
Ad agencies **Book publishers** **Magazines or newspapers** **Internet-based companies** **Corporations** **Colleges and universities**	Design print, Web, TV, and other types of visual ads (billboards, signs, etc.) Design book, magazine, and other print layouts Create logos/designs used on mugs, tee-shirts, pencils, cereal boxes and other promotional objects Create brochures, booklets, books, and newsletters
Freelance business (self-employed)	Provide specialized graphic-design services to businesses or individuals on a contract basis

PREPARING THE PROJECT

Begin your project by looking back at the **Project Prep** activities in this chapter and using the directions below.

Make Connections

Discuss with your group the most valuable insights you gained from this chapter. Talk about any new information that surprised or inspired you. Talk about how you connected what you read to what you have observed or experienced when using supporting materials to enhance a speech. Be prepared to share your ideas with the rest of the class at a later time. With your group, discuss and summarize these important points from the chapter:

- the four speech-delivery formats
- preparing notes for extemporaneous delivery
- types of visual aids and presentation software
- using presentation software.

Focus

Briefly review with your group the project assignment you are working on: to research a topic of interest and create a four-minute speech that uses four visual and/or audio aids. With your group, brainstorm ideas for the topic you will explore in your presentation.

Plan

Having chosen your topic, assign research tasks to each group member and decide the order in which each will be presented. Together, come up with a different visual aid for each of you to use while giving that specific portion of the presentation. Take the time to divide the work thoughtfully: if one group member is a computer wiz, he or she might create a technology graphic; if another is artistic with pen and paper, that person might create a poster. Agree to a timetable that allows each individual the same amount of time to present his or her portion of the speech.

Surefire Decision-Making

As you develop your portion of the project, remember to base communication decisions on your understanding of situation, audience, and purpose. Your visual or audio aid should help the audience fully understand your portion of the presentation.

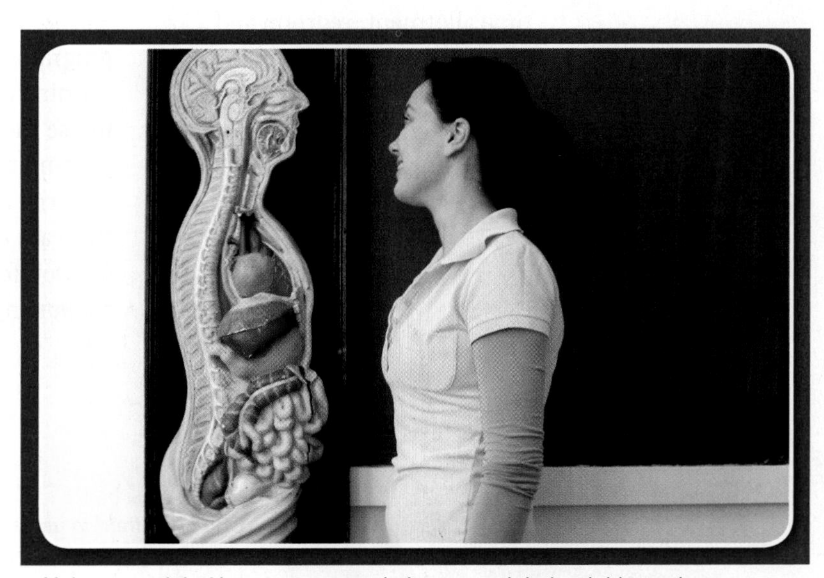

Using a model of human anatomy in her speech helped this student explain how singers like her support their breath.

Develop

With your group, write a short introduction to your presentation. Agree who will present the introduction and the order in which you will follow. Then each individual should write a draft of his or her part and find or create a visual aid. Be sure that your visual aids are distinct from one another and really help the audience understand and appreciate your topic. Practice your part on your own before your first group practice.

Practice

Practice with your group until each portion of the presentation moves seamlessly to the next. Practice in front of family and friends to get the feel of a "live" audience. Ask one of them to time your presentation to be sure that it isn't longer or significantly shorter than four minutes. If you are over or under your time allotment, regroup and reconfigure your presentation. Also be sure to practice using any technical equipment that you will employ during your presentation.

Use the strategies that follow to help make your presentation of your research as good as it can be.

Your group should now be ready to share the topic you have researched using visual and/or audio aids. Your presentation should be no longer than four minutes, and each of you should be ready to speak and then smoothly offer a transition to the next speaker.

Go over the CAPS guidelines on page 350 and the rubric on page 367 to be sure that your project meets all the requirements.

Using Supporting Materials Effectively

Be sure to review any chapter information about using visual aids and presentation software. If you are using such tools as videos, slide projectors, or computer programs, be sure they are up and running and that you know exactly how to use them effectively. Recall other presentations you've seen, the supporting material that grabbed your attention, and the ways in which the speaker used them. Get comfortable using and discussing your supporting materials.

Don't be afraid to use any supporting materials that you think will help you connect to your listeners.

EVALUATING THE PROJECT

Evaluate the presentations using the following rubric.

Score the demonstration on each point, with 4 being "outstanding" and 1 being "needs much improvement."

Come up with an overall score and write a brief paragraph that explains your score.

Understanding of Supporting Materials	Demonstration of Supporting Materials	Creativity and Originality	Preparation and Use of Time
4 Presenters showed insight into the use of supporting materials.	**4** Presenters' use of supporting materials greatly aided in understanding the topic.	**4** The presentation was attention-grabbing and original.	**4** The presentation flowed smoothly and stayed within the time limit.
3 Presenters understood the use of supporting materials.	**3** Presenters' use of supporting materials helped in understanding the topic.	**3** The presentation was fairly attention-grabbing and original.	**3** The presentation progressed fairly smoothly and stayed within the time limit.
2 Presenters did not seem to understand some elements of the use of supporting materials.	**2** Presenters' use of supporting materials was minimally helpful in understanding the topic.	**2** The presentation was attention-grabbing but not original.	**2** The presentation had a few awkward moments and went a bit over the time limit or was noticeably short.
1 Presenters misunderstood much about the use of supporting materials.	**1** Presenters' use of supporting materials did not help in understanding the topic.	**1** The presentation was not attention-grabbing or original.	**1** The presentation was not smoothly executed and went well over or under the time limit.

Communication *Past* and Present

A Visual History of Presentation Equipment

From "Back in the Day" . . .

Prehistoric Times — cave drawings (Acacus, Libya)

1826—photography invented by Louis Daguerre

1943—overhead projector

1801— blackboard introduced in U.S.

1891—corkboards

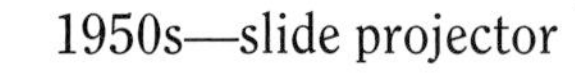

1950s—slide projector

. . . to Our Day
1962—audiocassette
1971—videocassette recorder
1990s—LCD projectors, DVDs, and computer presentation software
1970—floppy disk
1980s—white boards
2000s—Internet video sharing sites
STOP
PAUSE
START
CASSETTE

Chapter 17 Review

Using Vocabulary Words

For each term listed below, make a box and divide it into four sections. In the top left section, write the word. In the top right section, describe a personal association with the word. In the bottom left section, give an example of what the word means to you. In the bottom right section, write a word that you feel is the opposite or non-example of that word.

Word	Personal Association
Example	Opposite

1. digression
2. extemporaneous
3. font
4. manuscript
5. memorized
6. multimedia
7. Q & A
8. storyboard

Reviewing Key Ideas

1. What is an impromptu speech?
2. Describe the function of notes used for an extemporaneous speech.
3. List several ways in which oral style is more casual than written style.
4. Briefly discuss how the speaker benefits from the Q & A.

Reflecting on Your Project

Jot down some notes about which parts of your project went especially well and which gave you the most trouble. Share your thoughts with your group. Does everyone agree? Come up with two or three strategies for dealing with trouble spots in future projects.

Responding to the Essential Question

Use what you've learned in this chapter to write a brief answer to the question, "How are supporting materials used to enhance a speech?" Compare your response with a partner's to see if you covered similar points.

Extending Your Understanding

Everyday Life

1. Recall the last speech you gave. What delivery format did you use? What information from this chapter do you wish you'd known then?
2. Some people think the impromptu speech is the most difficult type to pull off because there is no time for preparation. Others think it's the easiest—for the same reason. In which camp do you fall? Discuss your position with a classmate.

3. Write and memorize a short speech detailing the best hour of your day. Present it at home during dinner, and ask your audience for feedback on your oral style.

In the Media

4. Plan to watch an academic lecture on a cable channel. Before it begins, think about your own expectations for the types of supporting materials you'd like to see. Why do you think you have those expectations? As you watch the speech, note which aids are used. Were they appropriate to the situation, audience, and purpose? Why or why not?
5. Watch the weather forecast on a local news station. List at least two additional audio-visual aids you can imagine the forecaster using. Note how you as the audience would benefit from them.
6. Watch a memorized speech from a political figure, a lawyer, or some other person making a prepared public statement. Discuss with another viewer how the speaker made use of effective oral style.

Research

7. Choose a famous speech from history such as Abraham Lincoln's Gettysburg Address. Imagine it as a five-minute extemporaneous speech. Present it to the class, being sure to include appropriate visual aids.
8. Research the current use of multimedia technology in business presentations. Use a variety of sources, such as books, articles, videos, and Web sites. Apply the CAPS model to your research and present your findings to the class.

Interpreting Graphics

A student giving a research speech on income taxes used the pie chart below. Answer the following questions about this visual aid.

- Where does the bulk of collected income taxes go?
- What amount of money is spent on physical resources?

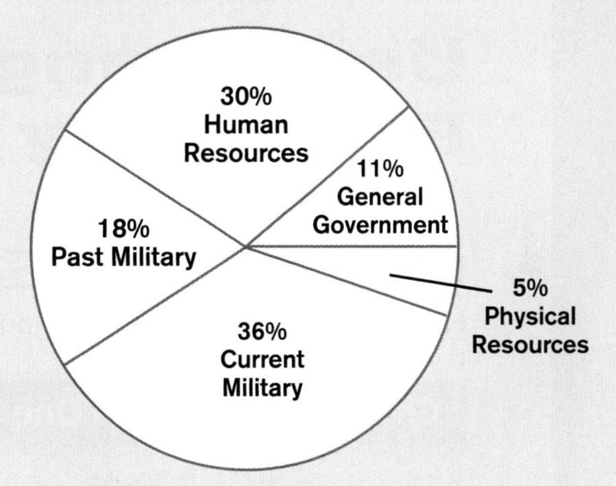

Additional Projects

1. **Group Project:** With a small group, plan a one-hour workshop in which you offer tips for using a specific type of presentation software. Work together to research, write, and rehearse your workshop. Present it in class and ask your classmates to identify what went right and what went wrong.
2. **Individual Project:** Imagine the future of presentation software and other audio-visual aids. Create a drawing or other artwork that captures your predictions for what might come next.

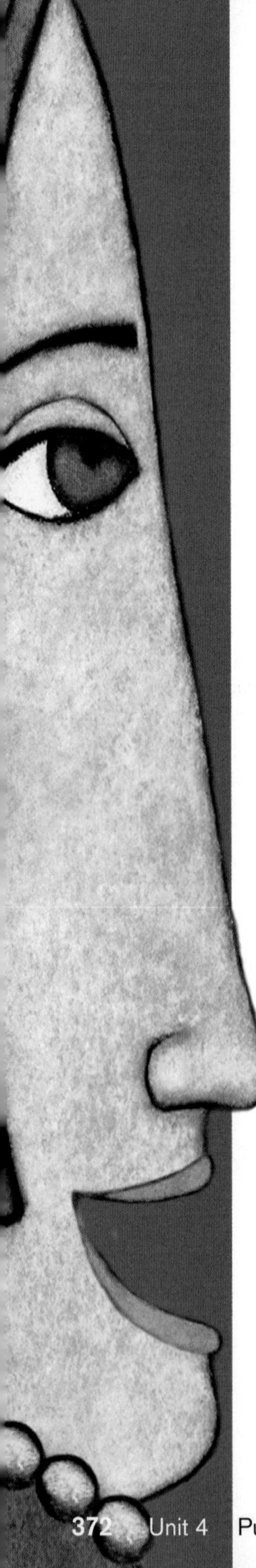

Using Language Effectively

ESSENTIAL QUESTION

How do speakers use language to enhance a message?

Chapter Project: The One That Got Away

Have you ever heard a fisherman talk about the fish he fought for hours until it snapped his line? That fish was tough as old boots and faster than lightning. Even though the outcome was apparent, the fisherman's story was suspenseful, intense, and delightfully descriptive. Now is your chance to create a similarly expressive tale.

You will write a 100-word story that includes as much expressive language as possible. You'll make the language memorable by using metaphors, personification, exaggeration—whatever might grab the audience. You will present your story to the class, and classmates will evaluate how well you completed the assignment. Refer to the CAPS guidelines as you work.

The rubric on page 389 shows the traits on which your presentation will be evaluated.

CONCEPT	using expressive language requires skill
AUDIENCE	classmates and teacher
PURPOSE	practice using different types of expressive language
SITUATION	classroom reading of an expressive story

KEY VOCABULARY

- simile
- metaphor
- allusion
- hyperbole
- understatement
- irony
- personification
- characterization
- alliteration
- assonance
- consonance
- cliché
- euphemism

Sportscasters search for vivid and fresh words to describe plays and motions that occur often in the sports they call.

Speak Up!

Think of some phrases you've heard that describe something or someone "to a T." Share them with the class. Refer to them when you are working on your project.

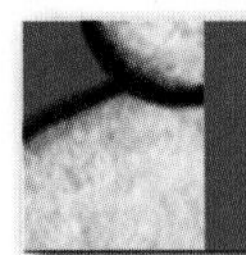

BACKGROUND FOR THE PROJECT

Pages 374–387 will provide the information you'll need to complete this project.

The Right Words at the Right Time

You read about selecting and organizing your language to fit a specific situation, purpose, and audience in Chapter 2. Every situation is unique and will carry with it a set of expected behaviors and communication standards. For example, you make certain choices about communication style and language during a pizza party with friends and others during trigonometry class.

At the party, you are in a situation where chatting with friends is your main purpose. In trig class, the situation is different. You have to answer or ask questions in a specific way to meet your learning objectives. The two audiences are very different. One consists of friends you know and choose to spend time with. The other includes classmates you may not know well and a teacher in a structured environment. In both situations, you want to find "the right words at the right time."

On the following pages are two speeches that seem—on the surface—similar in situation, purpose, and audience. Read through both with an eye toward identifying the differences and recognizing how each speaker's word choice enhanced his speech.

What can you tell about the situation, purpose, and audience for each photo? How might the speaker need to adapt her language in order to maximize the effectiveness of her speech?

One of the most famous farewell speeches in American history was given by General Douglas MacArthur to Congress on April 19, 1951. One of the greatest generals during World War II, MacArthur later clashed with President Truman over the division of power between the president and the military. Truman removed MacArthur from command. Here are excerpts from MacArthur's speech.

1 Mr. President, Mr. Speaker, and distinguished members of the Congress:

2 I stand on this rostrum with a sense of deep humility and great pride—humility in the wake of those great American architects of our history who have stood here before me, pride in the reflection that this forum of legislative debate represents human liberty in the purest form yet devised. Here are centered the hopes, and aspirations, and faith of the entire human race. . . .

3 I am closing my fifty-two years of military service. When I joined the Army, even before the turn of the century, it was the fulfillment of all of my boyish hopes and dreams. The world has turned over many times since I took the oath on the plain at West Point, and the hopes and dreams have long since vanished, but I still remember the refrain of one of the most popular barrack ballads of that day which proclaimed most proudly that
"Old soldiers never die;
they just fade away."

4 And like the old soldier of that ballad, I now close my military career and just fade away—an old soldier who tried to do his duty as God gave him the light to see that duty.

5 Good-bye.

MacArthur was a skillful public speaker who considered entering politics after his military career ended.

Baseball great Cal Ripken Jr. retired from the Baltimore Orioles after playing his last game on October 6, 2001. One of the best all-around shortstops ever, Ripken earned the nickname "Iron Man" for his longevity. He played an amazing 2,632 straight games across 16 seasons. After his final game, he gave the following farewell speech to the fans.

1 As a kid, I had this dream.

2 And I had the parents that helped me shape that dream.

3 Then, I became part of an organization, the Baltimore Orioles—the Baltimore Orioles, to help me grow that dream. Imagine playing for my hometown team for my whole career.

4 And I have a wife and children to help me share and savor the fruits of that dream.

5 And I've had teammates who filled my career with unbelievable moments.

6 And you fans, who have loved the game, and have shared your love with me.

7 Tonight, we close a chapter of this dream—my playing career.

8 But I have other dreams.

9 You know, I might have some white hair on top of this head—well, maybe on the sides of this head. But I'm really not that old.

10 My dreams for the future include pursuing my passion for baseball. Hopefully, I will be able to share what I have learned. And, I would be happy if that sharing would lead to something as simple as a smile on the face of others.

11 One question I've been repeatedly asked these past few weeks is, "How do I want to be remembered?" My answer has been simple: to be remembered at all is pretty special.

12 I might also add that if, if I am remembered, I hope it's because, by living my dream, I was able to make a difference.

Thank you.

Ripken played his entire major league career with the Baltimore Orioles. He was 41 years old when he retired.

The Right Words for the Situation

Both MacArthur and Ripken were saying farewell, but their situations were different. MacArthur had shaped the outcome of two of his era's most significant events, World War II and the Korean War. His job involved making life and death decisions. Ripken was retiring from playing the nation's favorite pastime. His job was to entertain the public—to take their minds off the type of serious issues that MacArthur confronted.

It made sense for MacArthur to refer to history, human liberty, and the "faith of the entire human race." It was equally appropriate for Ripken to talk about living his dream and joke about his white hair.

The Right Words for the Purpose

The purpose of both speeches was to say good-bye. Each speaker intended to end one significant chapter in his life and move on to the next. Each affected a serious, respectful tone that showed how much the preceding portion of their careers had meant to them. Both men made frequent use of the pronouns "I" and "we" to create speeches that were intimate and personal.

Speaking in the first person and deliberately using the words "I" and "we" will connect with your audience and draw them in. The audience will feel as though you are speaking directly to them.

The Right Words for the Audience

Consider the two audiences for these speeches. MacArthur was speaking to Congress, while Ripken was speaking to baseball fans. What differences between the two groups come to mind?

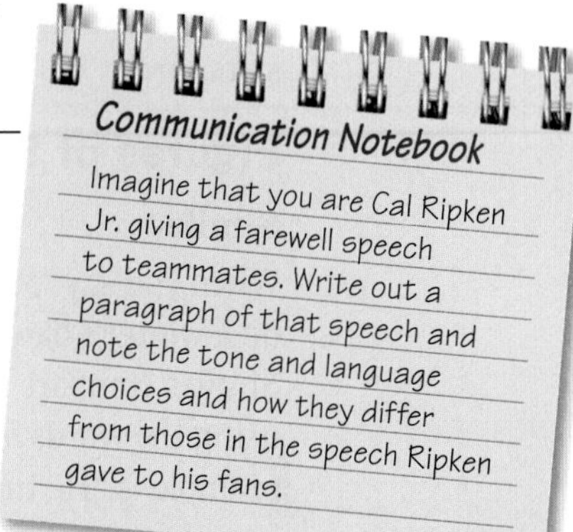

Ripken's casual opener—"As a kid, I had this dream"—likely put his audience at ease and hinted at the informal, easygoing nature of the speech to come. His joke about his age beginning with "You know" is an example of how informal usage and tone can relax and draw in an audience. He knew his listeners were baseball lovers and he spoke to them as a friend.

The opening phrase from MacArthur's speech immediately set a formal tone, one reflecting his role as a military commander: "I stand on this rostrum with a sense of deep humility and great pride." His formality and use of Standard English reflected his position of responsibility.

PROJECT PREP

Scan your local newspaper and plan to attend a government meeting, club activity, or other event in your community involving a speaker. Take notes about how the speaker uses the right words at the right time–how the language choices affect the presentation's mood and tone. Refer to these notes as you prepare your project.

Expressive Language

Expressive language—words and phrases that create especially vivid images—adds depth and interest to your topic. Following are descriptions of expressive language elements, including figures of speech, sound effects, and parallel structure.

Figures of Speech

Simile

When you say "My hands are like ice" on a winter's day, you are using a **simile**. Similes compare one thing to another using the words *like* or *as*. Another example is "He turned as white as a sheet."

Metaphor

A **metaphor** is similar to a simile—it draws a comparison. It does not use *like* or *as*, however. If you see someone chowing down lunch, you might think, "What a pig!" If your friend won't go along with your plans, you might tell her, "You're a wet blanket." Metaphors and similes add interest to your speeches by engaging the imaginations of your listeners.

Allusion

An **allusion** is an indirect reference to something or someone. It refers to a well-known event, place, literary work, artwork, or person. Calling someone a "Benedict Arnold" is an allusion to the most famous traitor in American history. If you use it in a speech, be sure your audience understands that you're alluding to someone who betrayed a cause. Choose your allusions carefully. If your audience doesn't understand the allusion, they may lose the point of your message.

Hyperbole

You probably use **hyperbole**, deliberate and obvious exaggeration, for effect in your everyday speech. "I could eat a horse" or "I'm so embarrassed I could die" use hyperbole to make a strong point. Use hyperbole to make an important point and to "grab your audience by the throat" (another hyperbole).

"I don't suppose I need to remind anyone that when I use the term 'bite the bullet,' I mean it metaphorically."

Understatement

Understatement is a way to deliberately express an idea in a less dramatic way than your audience might expect. You make the situation sound less important, usually to add humor or to give a weighty topic a light touch.

The title of former Vice-President Al Gore's movie on global warming, *An Inconvenient Truth*, is an example of understatement. The movie explains how the very fate of the planet is at stake, a problem far more serious than just "inconvenient." Understatement works best when you want to subtly suggest something to the audience.

Irony

When you use **irony**, you choose language that suggests the opposite of the literal meaning. For example, an ironic description of a lazy guy who sits around playing video games all day might be, "He's a real go-getter." "That's as subtle as an axe to the skull" is an ironic simile used to suggest that the situation is not subtle at all.

Personification

Personification involves suggesting that objects, animals, or ideas possess human qualities. You might call a favorite book "an old friend" or say "Love knocked on my door." The phrases "whispering wind" and a "smiling daisy" also employ personification. A speech using personification helps engage the audience in visualizing a scene or experiencing an emotion.

Figures of speech are used to create an effect—they are not meant to be interpreted literally.

Characterization

Speakers who use **characterization** provide details about a person's words and actions in order to make the person real. Characterization can also refer to the identification of the defining characteristics of a subject. For example, a speaker could characterize the conditions in which tornadoes might spawn, or characterize a style of fashion. Characterization helps listeners fill out their understanding of a subject.

One way to portray character is to include dialogue. For example, consider an anecdote you are using as supporting material. You might want to keep it lively by sharing actual dialogue between characters rather than just a summary of their exchanges. Like so many other examples of effective language, dialogue gives listeners something concrete and specific to charge their imaginations.

Sound Effects

In addition to thinking about well-chosen figures of speech and characterization, also consider how your speech sounds to a listener. Sound effects, which are patterns of vowel and consonant occurrence, can help you emphasize certain points. When used sparingly, they add flair to your delivery.

Alliteration

Alliteration is the repetition of an initial consonant sound. It is used to brighten sentences and to add emphasis and humor. "Peter Piper picked a peck of pickled peppers" uses alliteration. So does "Barney, the big bad beast" and "A woefully worthless worker was William."

Assonance

Assonance is the repetition of stressed vowel sounds within words to create internal rhyming. The ending consonant sounds are different, distinguishing assonance from rhyme. Examples include "stone cold killer," "make the grade," "joyful noise," and "light a fire." Both alliteration and assonance can add zing to your message.

Consonance

Consonance is the focused repetition of stressed consonant sounds. Vowel sounds in this instance differ. Examples include "think tank," "she hugged the great big dog," and "the broken clock struck ten."

Parallel Structure

Parallel structure in speech is a way to show that two or more ideas have the same level of importance by expressing them in the same grammatical pattern. Sentences are structured so that one part agrees with another.

Use your knowledge of grammar to employ consistent verb tense, sticking to either active or passive voice. MacArthur, for example, presented his feelings of humility and pride using parallel phrases in his first sentence. Following are sentences whose structures are parallel and not parallel.

Parallel: The students quickly put down their pencils and quietly handed in their tests.

Not Parallel: The students quickly put down their pencils and were quiet as they handed in their tests.

Parallel: J. P. wants to play football, shoot hoops, and run track.

Not Parallel: J. P. wants to play football, hoops, and run track.

Parallel: Caroline cried, moped, and sat around all day.

Not Parallel: Caroline cried, moped, and she was sitting around all day.

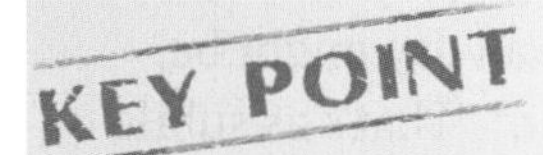

Consistency is the key to parallel structure. Stick to one language pattern in the sentence so your listener follows what you saying.

How does this student's shirt represent parallel structure?

Language Dos and Don'ts

If you expect your audience to give serious attention to your comments, be aware of their values and expectations. Always use language that is culturally sensitive and that considers people's individual differences. If you detect resistance and feel that your words or message may be viewed as inappropriate or ineffectual, change strategies. Restate your ideas in a more tactful, constructive way. Always avoid jargon, clichés, euphemisms, and sexist language. The chart below provides examples of these.

Kind of Language	Definition	Samples
Jargon	Jargon is technical and specialized terminology characteristic of a certain profession or group.	• "O neg" is medical jargon for the blood type O Negative. • In legal jargon, to "execute" a document means to sign it.
Cliché	A **cliché** is an overused phrase or expression.	• "hit the nail on the head" • "better late than never" • "needle in a haystack"
Euphemism	A **euphemism** is a word or phrase used as a substitute for an unpleasant or disturbing expression.	• *Passed away* is a euphemism for *died.* • *Downsizing* is a euphemism for *laying off employees.*
Sexist Language	Sexist language uses sexism, gender-based stereotypes, or the generic use of *man* or *he* as universal references.	• Using *girl* instead of *woman* for adult females in formal situations • Using *male nurse* or *lady doctor* when the gender is irrelevant • Using *man* or *mankind* instead of *humans* or *humankind*

PROJECT PREP

Write a piece of "bad prose" about your school using all the clichés, jargon, and euphemisms you can. Then rewrite the piece without the bad prose.

Euphemisms are often longer and less clear than the words they replace. Some might euphemistically and humorously call a window washer a "transparent-wall maintenance officer."

Pulling It All Together

On August 28, 1963, Rev. Martin Luther King Jr. delivered one of the most influential speeches in American history, his "I Have a Dream" speech. King was addressing 200,000 people in Washington, DC in support of jobs and civil rights. Note how he uses language to craft a compelling speech that fits the situation, purpose, and audience.

1 Five score years ago, a great American, in whose symbolic shadow we stand, signed the Emancipation Proclamation. This momentous decree came as a great beacon light of hope to millions of Negro slaves who had been seared in the flames of withering injustice. It came as a joyous daybreak to end the long night of captivity.

Allusion to Abraham Lincoln's Gettysburg Address

2 But one hundred years later, we must face the tragic fact that the Negro is still not free. One hundred years later, the life of the Negro is still sadly crippled by the manacles of segregation and the chains of discrimination. One hundred years later, the Negro lives on a lonely island of poverty in the midst of a vast ocean of material prosperity. One hundred years later, the Negro is still languishing in the corners of American society and finds himself an exile in his own land. So we have come here today to dramatize an appalling condition.

Parallel Structure

3 In a sense we have come to our nation's capital to cash a check. When the architects of our republic wrote the magnificent words of the Constitution and the Declaration of Independence, they were signing a promissory note to which every American was to fall heir. This note was a promise that all men would be guaranteed the inalienable rights of life, liberty, and the pursuit of happiness.

4 It is obvious today that America has defaulted on this promissory note insofar as her citizens of color are concerned. Instead of honoring this sacred obligation, America has given the Negro people a bad check which has come back marked "insufficient funds." But we refuse to believe that the bank of justice is bankrupt. We refuse to believe that there are insufficient funds in the great vaults of opportunity of this nation. So we have come to cash this check--a check that will give us upon demand the riches of freedom and the security of justice.

Alliteration

5 We have also come to this hallowed spot to remind America of the fierce urgency of *now*. This is no time to engage in the luxury of cooling off or to take the tranquilizing drug of gradualism. *Now* is the time to make real the promise of democracy. *Now* is the time to rise from the dark and desolate valley of segregation to the sunlit path of racial justice. *Now* is the time to open the doors of opportunity to all of God's children. *Now* is the time to lift our nation from the quicksands of racial injustice to the solid rock of brotherhood.

Metaphor

6 It would be fatal for the nation to overlook the urgency of the moment and to underestimate the determination of the Negro. This sweltering summer of the Negro's legitimate discontent will not pass until there is an invigorating autumn of freedom and equality. Nineteen sixty-three is not an end, but a beginning. Those who hope that the Negro needed to blow off steam and will now be content will have a rude awakening if the nation returns to business as usual. There will be neither rest nor tranquility in America until the Negro is granted his citizenship rights. The whirlwinds of revolt will continue to shake the foundations of our nation until the bright day of justice emerges.

Assonance

7 But there is something that I must say to my people who stand on the warm threshold which leads into the palace of justice. In the process of gaining our rightful place we must not be guilty of wrongful deeds. Let us not seek to satisfy our thirst for freedom by drinking from the cup of bitterness and hatred.

Personification

8 We must forever conduct our struggle on the high plane of dignity and discipline. We must not allow our creative protest to degenerate into physical violence. Again and again we must rise to the majestic heights of meeting physical force with soul force.

9 The marvelous new militancy which has engulfed the Negro community must not lead us to a distrust of all white people, for many of our white brothers, as evidenced by their presence here today, have come to realize that their destiny is tied up with our destiny and their freedom is inextricably bound to our freedom. We cannot walk alone.

Alliteration

10 And as we walk, we must make the pledge that we shall march ahead. We cannot turn back. There are those who are asking the devotees of civil rights, "When will you be satisfied?"

11 We can never be satisfied as long as the Negro is the victim of the unspeakable horrors of police brutality.

12 We can never be satisfied as long as our bodies, heavy with the fatigue of travel, cannot gain lodging in the motels of the highways and the hotels of the cities.

13 We cannot be satisfied as long as the Negro's basic mobility is from a smaller ghetto to a larger one. We can never be satisfied as long as a Negro in Mississippi cannot vote and a Negro in New York believes he has nothing for which to vote.

14 No, no, we are not satisfied, and we will not be satisfied until justice rolls down like waters and righteousness like a mighty stream.

Allusion to the Bible; Simile

15 I am not unmindful that some of you have come here out of great trials and tribulations. Some of you have come fresh from narrow cells. Some of you have come from areas where your quest for freedom left you battered by the storms of persecution and staggered by the winds of police brutality. You have been the veterans of creative suffering. Continue to work with the faith that unearned suffering is redemptive.

16 Go back to Mississippi, go back to Alabama, go back to South Carolina, go back to Georgia, go back to Louisiana, go back to the slums and ghettos of our Northern cities, knowing that somehow this situation can and will be changed. Let us not wallow in the valley of despair.

Consonance

17 I say to you today, my friends, that in spite of the difficulties and frustrations of the moment I still have a dream. It is a dream deeply rooted in the American dream.

18 I have a dream that one day this nation will rise up and live out the true meaning of its creed: "We hold these truths to be self-evident; that all men are created equal."

19 I have a dream that one day on the red hills of Georgia the sons of former slaves and the sons of former slave owners will be able to sit down together at a table of brotherhood.

King's effective use of expressive language inspired his listeners to advocate for civil rights.

20 I have a dream that one day even the state of Mississippi, a desert state, sweltering with the heat of injustice and oppression, will be transformed into an oasis of freedom and justice.

Metaphor

21 I have a dream that my four children will one day live in a nation where they will not be judged by the color of their skin but by the content of their character.

22 I have a dream today.

23 I have a dream that one day the state of Alabama, whose governor's lips are presently dripping with the words of interposition and nullification, will be transformed into a situation where little black boys and black girls will be able to join hands with little white boys and white girls and walk together as sisters and brothers.

24 I have a dream today.

25 I have a dream that one day every valley shall be exalted, every hill and mountain shall be made low, the rough places will be made plain, and the crooked places will be made

straight, and the glory of the Lord shall be revealed, and all flesh shall see it together.

26 This is our hope. This is the faith with which I return to the South. With this faith we will be able to hew out of the mountain of despair a stone of hope. With this faith we will be able to transform the jangling discords of our nation into a beautiful symphony of brotherhood.

27 With this faith we will be able to work together, to pray together, to struggle together, to go to jail together, to stand up for freedom together, knowing that we will be free one day.

Parallel Structure

28 This will be the day when all of God's children will be able to sing with a new meaning, "My country, 'tis of thee, sweet land of liberty, of thee I sing. Land where my fathers died, land of the Pilgrim's pride, from every mountainside, let freedom ring."

29 And if America is to be a great nation, this must become true. So let freedom ring from the prodigious hilltops of New Hampshire. Let freedom ring from the mighty mountains of New York. Let freedom ring from the heightening Alleghenies of Pennsylvania!

30 Let freedom ring from the snowcapped Rockies of Colorado! Let freedom ring from the curvaceous peaks of California! But not only that; let freedom ring from Stone Mountain of Georgia! Let freedom ring from Lookout Mountain of Tennessee!

31 Let freedom ring from every hill and every molehill of Mississippi. From every mountainside, let freedom ring.

32 When we let freedom ring, when we let it ring from every village and every hamlet, from every state and every city, we will be able to speed up that day when all of God's children, black men and white men, Jews and Gentiles, Protestants and Catholics, will be able to join hands and sing in the words of the old Negro spiritual, "Free at last! Free at last! Thank God Almighty, we are free at last!"

PROJECT PREP

Reread the King speech and identify examples of effective language in addition to those noted. Look for the right words at the right time, figures of speech, sound effects, and parallel structure.

Is This Job for Me?

Search **News Writer**

Everyone expects Bradley to use language effectively–because it's part of her job description. She's a *news writer* at a local television station. She writes everything from news stories to headlines to tidbits called "teasers" to be read by various on-air personalities. In addition, she helps with investigations by researching facts and situations, interviewing sources, and formulating a story.

Sometimes Bradley uses another reporter's material as the basis for the story she writes. She also writes and posts items to the station's Web site. Bradley has to write clear, engaging copy and must have command of the language and the techniques needed to craft news stories for her audience.

Bradley earned a bachelor's degree in journalism. While still in school she gained real-life experience through summer internships. Before landing this position, she honed her skills and proved her abilities through a series of lower-level jobs in the industry.

Does a job as a television news writer interest you? Measure yourself with this personality inventory to find out if you think you have the traits of a news writer. Do you:

- ✓ Possess excellent writing and language skills?
- ✓ Communicate effectively?
- ✓ Have a strong interest in current events?
- ✓ Have a strong work ethic?
- ✓ Have the ability to target your message to a specific audience?
- ✓ Work well both independently and as part of a team?
- ✓ Work well with regular deadlines in a high-pressure field?
- ✓ Quickly synthesize and distill information?

Employers	What You Would Do
Television stations Radio stations Newspapers	Investigate leads to find facts in local news stories Work on your own to complete writing tasks Work closely with the rest of the news team to accomplish reporting and promotional goals

Begin your project by looking back at the **Project Prep** activities in this chapter and using the directions below.

Make Connections

Use a notebook to summarize this chapter, including the following concepts:

- adapting language to purpose, audience, and situation
- using expressive language
- avoiding certain language.

Write one or two sentences about using language effectively in a speech.

Focus

Review your project assignment: Writing a 100-word story that includes as much expressive language as possible. Think of three specific ideas that you can apply to the project.

Plan

Spend some time thinking about your project. Determine the topic and begin planning the kind of expressive language you will use. Try to use two figures of speech and one sound effect. If you'd like to give your audience a chance to find a mistake in your writing, add jargon or a cliché.

Develop

Write a first draft of your story. Edit and revise until you are satisfied with your piece. Look over the evaluation rubric on page 389 and be sure you have addressed each point.

Surefire Proofreading

Here are a few tips for proofreading your own work.

- Find a quiet place to work where you can concentrate.
- Read slowly and out loud–one word at a time.
- Remember that punctuation usually indicates pauses. Listen to the pauses as you read out loud to know where to place punctuation.

Practice

Read your story aloud several times in front of an audience of friends or family, if possible. Be sure that you meet—but don't exceed—the 100-word limit. Go over the CAPS guidelines on page 372 and the rubric on page 389 to be sure that your project meets the requirements.

PRESENTING THE PROJECT

Use the strategy that follows to help make your presentation be as good as it can be.

Reading Your Work

You've written, edited, and proofread your piece, so you should now feel that it is as good as it can be. The story is well written and uses expressive language. Now all you have to do is read it. But wait—don't *just* read it. Tell it with enthusiasm and eagerness. You are sharing something important. Be sure your audience understands that.

Evaluating THE PROJECT

Evaluate the presentations using the following rubric.

Score the evaluation on each point, with 4 being "outstanding" and 1 being "needs much improvement." Come up with an overall score and write a brief paragraph explaining your score.

Understanding of Using Language Clearly and Well	Demonstration of a Story with Expressive Language	Creativity and Originality	Preparation and Length
4 Presenter showed insight into using language.	**4** Presenter used figurative language, parallel structure, and several other types of expressive language throughout the story.	**4** The story was attention-grabbing, unique, and fun.	**4** The story was well-prepared, flowed smoothly, and was just the right length.
3 Presenter understood how to use language fairly well.	**3** Presenter used some types of expressive language throughout the story.	**3** The story was attention-grabbing and fun but only fairly original.	**3** The story was fairly well-prepared, progressed fairly smoothly, and seemed to be the right length.
2 Presenter did not seem to understand some aspects of using language well.	**2** Presenter used some expressive language in a few places in the story.	**2** The story was fairly fun, but not unique or attention-grabbing.	**2** The story was not well-prepared, had some awkward moments, and was either too long or too short.
1 Presenter had no understanding of effective language use.	**1** Presenter used little or no expressive language in the story.	**1** The story was not attention-grabbing, unique, or fun.	**1** The story was ill-prepared, had many awkward moments, and was far too long or short.

Communication *Past* and Present

Memorable Commencement Speeches

From the 1800s . . .

In the mid 1800s, college commencements were lengthy proceedings with many formal speeches. The 1842 commencement at Kenyon College in Ohio, for example, lasted three hours. It began with a prayer, included a guest speaker and eight student speakers whose presentations were punctuated by musical entertainment, and ended with a benediction. The final speaker was graduating senior Rutherford B. Hayes, who later became the nation's 19th president, serving from 1877 to 1881. A local newspaper reporter described the speech in glowing terms: "This oration was rich, and splendid, chaste, beautiful and sublime, pure in diction, unique in arrangement and lofty in sentiment, and was delivered with a flow of animation that struck like peals of music upon the soul." His speech used language expressively to reflect on college life, to lay out the obligations of the students, and to thank the faculty and university president for their leadership.

After winning an extremely close vote, Hayes used his speaking skills to deliver an inaugural address in 1877 that helped unify the nation.

Commencement speakers have frequently warned graduates of the troubles in the world. In 1937, the storm clouds of World War II darkened. Journalist William Allen White addressed the graduates of Northwestern University, creating a metaphor between national hostilities and a spreading wildfire: "Today, as never before, nationalism in small geographical areas is pulling men into bitter disunion and controversy. Some flame of envy and rancor is abroad in the world. We see it moving across the face of Europe in various tyrannies, each exalting its own nationalism, each challenging liberty in its own way—Italy under fascism, Germany under the Nazis, Russia under communism, Spain boiling with confusion . . . ."

. . . to the 20th Century and Beyond

One of the best-known commencement speeches was never actually given. On June 1, 1997, *Chicago Tribune* newspaper columnist Mary Schmich wrote what she would say if she were speaking to graduates. Somehow the speech was attributed to a famous writer, Kurt Vonnegut, and sped around the Internet under his name. It even inspired a successful song. Here are the introduction (paragraphs 1 and 2) and conclusion:

1 *"Ladies and gentlemen: Wear sunscreen. If I could offer you only one tip for the future, sunscreen would be it. The long-term benefits of sunscreen have been proved by scientists, whereas the rest of my advice has no basis more reliable than my own meandering experience. I will dispense this advice now.*

2 *Enjoy the power and beauty of your youth. Oh, never mind. You will not understand the power and beauty of your youth until they've faded. But trust me, in 20 years, you'll look back at photos of yourself and recall in a way you can't grasp now how much possibility lay before you and how fabulous you really looked. You are not as fat as you imagine. . . .*

3 *Be careful whose advice you buy, but be patient with those who supply it. Advice is a form of nostalgia. Dispensing it is a way of fishing the past from the disposal, wiping it off, painting over the ugly parts and recycling it for more than it's worth.*

4 *But trust me on the sunscreen.*

On June 7, 2007, Bill Gates gave a real speech at Harvard University that challenged the graduates to take on the wider world. Following is his conclusion.

1 *Don't let complexity stop you. Be activists. Take on the big inequities. It will be one of the great experiences of your lives.*

2 *You graduates are coming of age in an amazing time. As you leave Harvard, you have technology that members of my class never had. You have awareness of global inequity, which we did not have. And with that awareness, you likely also have an informed conscience that will torment you if you abandon these people whose lives you could change with very little effort.*

3 *You have more than we had; you must start sooner, and carry on longer. Knowing what you know, how could you not?*

4 *And I hope you will come back here to Harvard 30 years from now and reflect on what you have done with your talent and your energy. I hope you will judge yourselves not on your professional accomplishments alone, but also on how well you have addressed the world's deepest inequities or how well you treated people a world away who have nothing in common with you but their humanity.*

5 *Good luck.*

Gates combined clear language, frequent use of parallel structure, and a personal focus. Like every successful commencement speech, it inspired his audience.

Review Chapter 18

Using Vocabulary Words

From the list below, choose three sets of two terms that you think are connected. Write a sentence for each set explaining the connection between the terms. Example: *A simile makes a comparison using* like *or* as, *while a metaphor also makes a comparison.*

1. alliteration
2. allusion
3. assonance
4. characterization
5. cliché
6. consonance
7. euphemism
8. hyperbole
9. irony
10. metaphor
11. personification
12. simile
13. understatement

Reviewing Key Ideas

1. List the different elements of using the "right words at the right time."
2. Describe the purpose of Cal Ripken's speech.
3. What is a figure of speech?
4. List three figures of speech and two sound effects.

Reflecting on Your Project

If you could start your project again from scratch, what would you do differently? What went particularly well for you as you worked on the project?

Responding to the Essential Question

With a small group, discuss your response to the essential question from page 372.

Extending Your Understanding

Everyday Life

1. Keep a running list of clichés you say and hear during one full day. Did they come up more often than you expected?
2. While on the phone with a friend, use hyperbole to describe an event from your day.
3. Give two examples of jargon you heard at school the past week.
4. Practice adding personification to your everyday speech to give it greater punch.

How do people talk differently on a cell phone than in person?

In the Media

5. While reading the newspaper, identify five similes and convert each one to a metaphor.
6. Listen for examples of alliteration, assonance, and consonance in radio ads.

Research

7. Research Douglas MacArthur's career as a military leader. Write a one-page report discussing events from his life that likely influenced the tone and content of his farewell speech.
8. Find a famous historical speech online. Give a presentation about how the speaker used language effectively to enhance the speech.

Interpreting Graphics

Imagine that all language is made up of these examples from the chapter: figures of speech, sound effects, and language to avoid. The graph shows a hypothetical breakdown of how much of daily speech comes from each category. Based on this graph, what conclusions can you draw about the difficulty of incorporating figures of speech and sound effects into a speech versus the difficulty of steering clear of language to avoid?

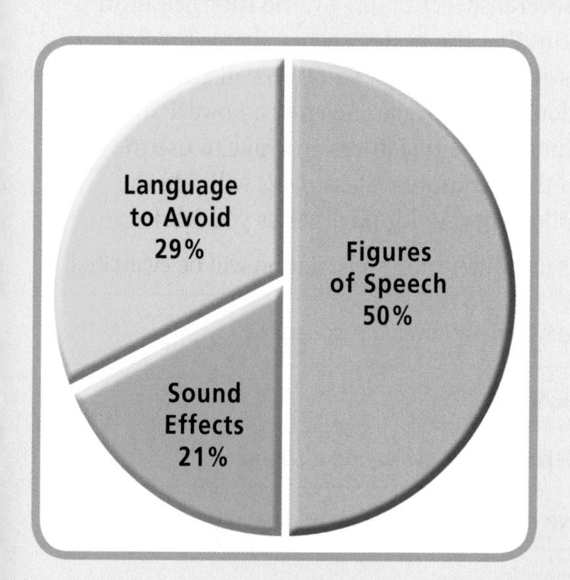

Newspapers, especially the opinion pages, are a great source of colorful writing.

Additional Projects

1. **Partnered Project:** Rehearse your next assigned speech in front of a partner. Have him or her provide feedback on how effectively you used language to enhance your speech. Did your words suit the situation, purpose, and audience? What types of expressive language did you use? How well did they work? Incorporate your partner's feedback as necessary. Then switch roles.
2. **Individual Project:** Look up the Bulwer-Lytton Fiction Contest online. Try writing a contest entry and submit it online. Report on the process in class.

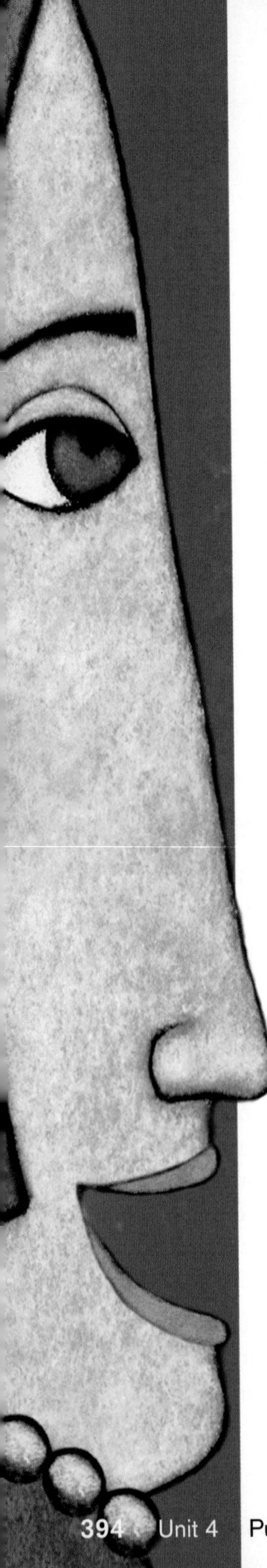

Presenting Your Speech

ESSENTIAL QUESTION

What strategies can you use to present your speech effectively and powerfully?

Chapter Project: Check It Out

Suppose you want the best possible summer job you can find. To make the best choice, you might develop a checklist of features that are important to you: good pay, close enough to ride your bike to, flexible hours, for example. In the same way, to make the best possible speech, you may want to have a checklist of important features and qualities. This project will help you develop such a checklist, or rubric.

With a small group, you will observe several speeches (on TV, the Internet, or in person) and then determine the qualities that the best speeches share. Together you will develop a rubric that includes specific qualities you think all good speeches should have. You will then make handouts (or transparencies or a PowerPoint presentation) explaining why you included certain features and how to use the rubric. This should take no more than three minutes. Classmates will rate the effectiveness of your rubric. Use the following CAPS guidelines as you work.

The rubric on page 413 shows the traits on which your presentation will be evaluated.

CONCEPT	a rubric helps you develop and evaluate speeches
AUDIENCE	classmates and teacher
PURPOSE	gain insight into the process of evaluating a speech
SITUATION	three-minute creative demonstration of an original rubric

KEY VOCABULARY

delivery	framing
diaphragm	pitch
generators	monotone
resonators	self-confidence
articulators	stage fright
projecting	revise

Your presentation can make last night's meal sound ordinary or fantastic.

Speak Up!

Turn to a partner and share what you ate for dinner last night. Give all the details. When you've finished, have your partner comment on your delivery style. Was your anecdote easy to follow and understand? Did you seem comfortable giving your account?

Pages 396–412 will provide the information you'll need to complete this project.

Qualities of Effective Delivery

When discussed in the context of speeches, **delivery** refers to the speaker's manner, or speaking style. Whatever the speech's subject or situation, audiences appreciate a good delivery. The following five qualities of an effective delivery are based on what the audience sees.

The way a message is delivered is often as important as the message itself.

When Kimberley Aiken became Miss America, she knew she would be called upon to give speeches. What qualities do you think she sought to develop in her delivery?

Qualities of Effective Delivery	
It is natural.	A natural delivery helps the audience believe in the sincerity of your message (and you). It makes the audience feel you are talking directly to them. It is free flowing–without distracting interruptions.
It is lively.	A lively delivery gains and keeps the audience's attention and increases your credibility with them.
It suits the situation.	If a delivery style matches the situation, the audience will feel that the speaker is making appropriate communication choices. The audience will take cues from your delivery to readjust their perceptions of the situation if necessary.
It aligns with the message.	Your delivery must help convey your message. Tone is important. For a serious topic, your audience will expect a serious delivery. An audience can become confused or lose interest if your message and delivery do not align.
It is clear.	Your delivery should allow your message to come through without clutter or distraction.

Voice

Like a fingerprint, your *vocal quality* is distinctly your own. No one has exactly the same range of voice or texture—that's why people know exactly who you are when you call on the phone. If there are aspects of your vocal quality you might want to change—maybe you feel you are too nasal or twangy, or too whispery and soft, you can work on addressing those when you understand voice production. Understanding vocal production will also help you polish your vocal delivery to make your speeches and presentations as effective as possible.

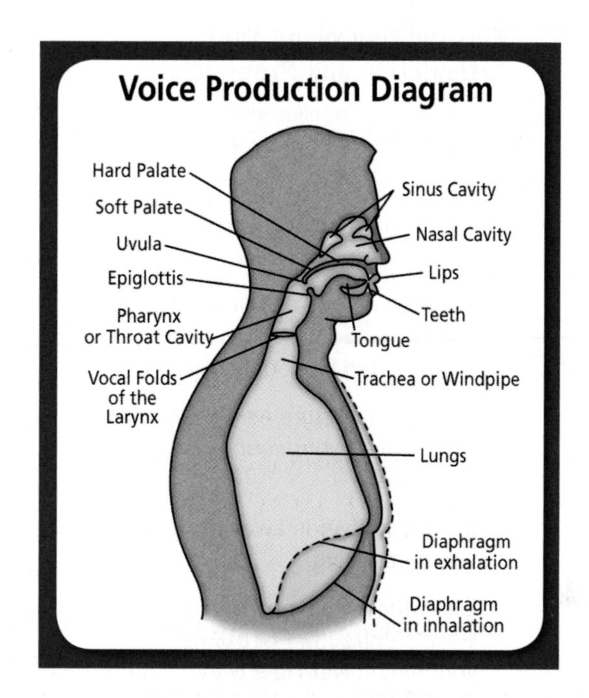

Voice Production

A simple utterance like "Hello" is actually the result of a complicated vocal process. The word is produced by air forced through the lungs by the muscles of the ribs and **diaphragm,** an organ that separates the chest from the abdominal cavity. The exhaled air vibrates the muscles that make up the larynx, which are also called vocal cords (or folds) or **generators**. Air is pushed out in a way that vibrates these vocal folds, producing sound. The sound is then modified by **resonators** (head, throat, nose, mouth, and sinuses) and formed into vowels and consonants by **articulators** (tongue, jaw, teeth, cheeks, lips, and the hard and soft palate).

Resonators

Areas in your head resonate by picking up sound vibrations. To experience resonance, first relax the jaw, lips, throat, and tongue. Then say *m-m-m-m-m-m* with your lips just touching. You should feel a vibration in your head. This is the air resonating in your head and sinuses. To achieve better resonance in your speech and give your voice a rich, mellow tone, relax your throat so that lower tones resonate well. Also try opening your mouth so that vowel sounds do not resonate through the nose. This will eliminate any twang in your voice.

Articulation Problem Examples		
Dropping syllables or word endings	"zamination" instead of "examination" "accidently" instead of "accidentally"	"speakin" instead of "speaking" "galrey" instead of "gallery"
Running words together	"didja" instead of "did you" "gonna" instead of "going to"	"kinda" instead of "kind of" "couldya" instead of "could you"

Tips for Improving Your Articulation and Pronunciation

1. Practice unfamiliar words. Use a dictionary to help you with pronunciation.
2. Listen to how other people use words, especially new terms.
3. Record yourself as you read a prepared speech or passage from a book. Listen back critically.
4. Use good posture as you speak to help project your sound toward the audience.
5. Keep your hands away from your face when speaking.
6. Use your tongue and mouth to shape vowels correctly. For example, open your mouth wide to say the *o* in *hot.* Bring your tongue forward with your mouth closed just a bit to say the *e* in *teeth.*

Communication Notebook

List examples of any articulation problems you notice today. Pay particular attention to your own speech. Also write down problems you hear as others speak in person, on TV, or on the radio.

Using Vocal Variety

Most outstanding public speakers know how to use vocal variety to keep the audience engaged. You learned about the importance of volume and rate in Chapter 6. Along with pitch these vocal qualities can convey meaning and provide good vocal variety.

Volume

At times you want your voice to ring out. At other times you want your audience to lean in to hear you. Varying your volume adds interest to your speech.

- In general, you want to speak loudly enough for the entire audience–front row to back–to hear your voice.
- Vary the volume of your voice according to your message. To make an exciting point, speak loudly. To draw in your audience to a tender scene, speak softly.
- Increasing your volume is also called **projecting.** When you need to raise your voice, never make it harsh and unpleasant. A good tip is: "Project to connect. If you yell, you repel."
- Volume variety is key to keeping your audience listening. Emphasize key words and phrases. Look for natural spots to let your volume rise and fall.

Projecting your voice assures that the audience hears it no matter where they are seated.

Projecting DOES NOT mean yelling.

Below is the conclusion to a speech by Geneva B. Johnson, printed twice. Each excerpt has different italicized words to indicate volume and emphasis. Compare the differences.

Conclusion A

We humans have *shown* ourselves capable of nobility, of kindness, and of generosity. We must *draw* on our strength from those who exhibit the best that is *in* them. And, let us remember, "to everything there is a *season*, and a time to every purpose under heaven." And if this be not your *season*, it will *come*. At least, let them say of you in the future—you cared enough to do the very best. This was the time you planned to serve: this was your *seed* time for reform. And remember—"Man is the *only* animal that laughs and weeps, for he is the *only* creature that is struck with the *difference* between what things are, and what they *ought* to be." Peace be with you.

Conclusion B

We humans have shown ourselves capable of *nobility*, of *kindness*, and of *generosity*. We must draw on *our* strength from those who exhibit the *best* that is in *them*. And, let us remember, "to *everything* there is a season, and a time to *every* purpose under heaven." And if this be not *your* season, it *will* come. At least, let them say of *you* in the future—you *cared* enough to do the very *best*. This was the time you planned to serve: *this* was your seed time for reform. And remember—"Man is the *only* animal that laughs and weeps, for he is the only creature that is struck with the difference between what things *are*, and what they *ought* to be." Peace be with you.

One of these versions is more effective than the other. When you compare the first sentence of A to the first sentence of B, what differences do you see?

First Sentence A

We humans have *shown* ourselves capable of nobility, of kindness, and of generosity.

First Sentence B

We humans have shown ourselves capable of *nobility*, of *kindness*, and of *generosity*.

The Sentence A delivery suggests that, above all, it is important that humans are capable of showing the qualities mentioned. In Sentence B, the vocal emphasis on the qualities of nobility, kindness, and generosity indicates the importance of those qualities.

Rate

The speed or rate at which you speak also adds interest and liveliness to your speech. A steady rate is often desirable. If you speed through a presentation, you will be seen as nervous, excited, or impatient. If you speak too slowly, you may seem too cautious or unsure of what to say. Vary your rate as you do during conversation. Consider the points that follow.

- Pauses are an important part of your speaking rate. They break up a speech into meaningful portions. Use well-placed, meaningful pauses for emphasis or a logical transition, but don't use extended or random pauses.

Pauses with no purpose can make you seem unprepared, uncommitted, and unskilled.

- In a manuscript, periods and commas are markers for pauses, so it is logical to pause when you end a sentence or a phrase. Periods and commas exist in an extemporaneous (unwritten) speech only when you put them there—in the form of pauses.
- Use of **framing,** or pauses on either side of a word or phrase for special emphasis, can work well. Your audience will automatically understand the pauses as vocal directions to pay special attention to whatever you say within the "frame." An example would be if you said, "Michael Jordan, the greatest basketball player of all time, says, 'I've failed over and over and over again in my life and that is why I succeed.'" You'd pause with the commas in order to frame "the greatest basketball player of all time" and emphasize the high level of Michael Jordan's success.
- Speaking too fast can be problematic. It becomes hard to control your speech and speak clearly. If your listeners have to struggle to keep up with your rapid-fire, unclear speech, they might get lost or give up entirely.
- The rate at which you speak impacts the timing of your delivery. A "pause for dramatic effect" or the use of "comic timing" can add immeasurably to your presentation. Subtle changes in rate can change the meaning or the effect of a word or phrase.

On this and the next page is a passage from a speech by James W. Compton, president of the National Urban League of Chicago, delivered to an audience composed of young African-American males. This passage is marked with italics for *emphasis*, with / for pauses, and // for long pauses. As you read the passage, note how the emphasized words and pauses contribute to the meaning.

1 Future men, / it's *rough* out here. Just when you think you've got things under control, / something else happens. You have to learn to accept adversity as just another part of this puzzle called life. Every time you're knocked down, / you need to be thinking of how you're going to *get up,* / even before you hit the ground. And then *get up* and move on.

2 Don't dwell on the bad times, because there are always more out there waiting for you.

3 Also, don't dwell too long on the good times, because there are always more challenges to meet.

4 No matter how smart or talented you are, / remember there's always someone out there smarter and more talented. Take what gifts you have and *improve* on them. We all are gifted at *something.* Use your talents to help someone else, and you too will prosper.

Comedian Chris Rock has perfected his volume, rate, and pitch to create perfect comic timing.

5 And above all else, // be *proud* of who you are. As young African-Americans / you are unique. Look at how others imitate you. And because of all of the sacrifices of your elders there is nothing in this world that you cannot do.

6 Never fear to fail. And as a famous song once said, / 'Never walk in someone else's shadow.' / I'm saying, / be great enough that others will want to trail you and walk in your shadow. / You *can* be just that great.

The pauses, along with the added emphasis, help convey meaning. Consider the drama in this sentence: And above all else, // be proud of who you are. The pause builds a sense of suspense. The speaker has given his audience several pieces of advice. The transition "and above all else" tells his audience that he is giving his most important advice. The long pause sets up the advice, and sets it apart from the words around it. The advice "be proud of who you are" stands out.

Pitch

The relative highness or lowness of the voice is called **pitch**. A speech delivered in a flat **monotone**, or expressionless pitch bores your listener. Any speaker can vary pitch to build interest and convey meaning.

The easiest way to note how pitch is used to convey meaning is to take an easy question such as, "Are you going on a trip?" The voice naturally goes up at the end of questions. Such inflection signals a question to the listener.

Read the next passage from Compton's speech aloud to hear the pitch and inflection. Try it once in a monotone. Then try it again using a normal pitch.

7 The truth is that it doesn't matter *how* old you are if you have *not* learned some of the basics / of what it takes to be a man. It's *not* automatic. There is a *necessary* and *continuous* period of development, / nurturing, / and mentoring. Too often / our children are just left to raise themselves, / and never learn how to assume the *awesome* responsibility that goes with being a *real* man in this society.

8 Being a man means that you learn to accept *responsibility* for your actions. It means being able to say / 'I'm sorry' / when you are wrong. It's learning how to reach *down* / and help someone else make a way. It's understanding that you can gain *more* in this life by being *cooperative* / rather than competitive.

9 It's being *respectful* to the women in your life. It's being willing to *clean up* and *build up* your community. It means contributing to your *household,* / rather than always taking. It's understanding that being *respectful* and *courteous* are examples of strength, / not weakness. It's understanding that it takes *courage* to feel so strongly about something that you cry. That's simply giving into the spirit that's inside all of us.

10 It's understanding that our community has raised up some *sorry* 40-year-old boys, as well as some *magnificent* 15-year-old men. Which will you be?

What are the differences in the two vocal deliveries? How might an audience receive one versus the other?

Vocal Delivery and Manuscript Format

Plan your vocal delivery by using the manuscript speech-delivery format found in Chapter 17. Try italicizing the words you want to emphasize and marking the spots where you will pause for effect. You may wish to use your own handwritten markings to indicate pitch.

Following is a passage from Sue Suter's speech "Disability Is No Big Deal." Suter, formerly of the World Institute on Disabilities, spoke to people who make products for the severely disabled. As you read, identify places where pitch variation could add to the meaning.

1 A 1995 Mason-Dixon poll revealed that *87 percent* of businesses that reported hiring people with disabilities said that they would encourage *other* employers to do the same. And a Harris poll reports that *75 percent* of managers surveyed said they were *likely* to make *greater* efforts to hire qualified people with disabilities in the next three years.

2 Yet the key word here is // *"qualified."* // If the people you serve are to take advantage of these opening doors, / we'll need to focus much greater effort on training. What are the benefits to those who are ready? The benefits go well beyond a good paycheck. A job gives a person with a disability the chance to make a difference in the world, // "I matter."

Vocal Delivery and Extemporaneous Format

You remember from Chapter 17 that the extemporaneous speech format can help your delivery sound fresh and spontaneous. Below are some tips for varying your delivery.

Tips for Developing Vocal Variety in an Extemporaneous Speech

1. Get experience speaking. The more experience you have, the more comfortable and expressive you'll be.
2. Rehearse your speech. Get confident with your content so you can spend rehearsal time on vocal delivery.
3. Record yourself so you can hear what others will hear.
4. Take advice. Practice in front of an audience and use their feedback.

PROJECT PREP

With your **project group**, choose one of the paragraphs above. Take turns reading it aloud using vocal variety. Assess one another's readings.

How would you deliver the line, "Disability Is No Big Deal"?

Using Supporting Tools Appropriately

Chapter 17 offered suggestions for using effectively such supporting materials as notecards, chalkboards, posters, presentation software, and other visual and audio aids. In addition to these, you might find yourself using a microphone and rostrum. Getting comfortable with these tools will help your speech go smoothly.

Using a Rostrum and Microphone

TechConnect A rostrum gives you a solid base from which to present your speech. The microphone enhances your speech by assuring that you can be heard in any sized room. The tips below will help you get comfortable with the microphone and rostrum.

1. Be sure the rostrum is the right height. You should be able to adjust it so that you can look at your notes comfortably and be seen clearly by the audience.
2. Rehearse with the microphone so you know what to expect.
3. Always adjust the microphone to suit your height and posture.
4. Establish a good microphone distance. Words with *p* and *b* explode into the microphone if you are too close. If you're too far away, it can't do its job.
5. Check the microphone before starting your main presentation. No need to tap on it or say "Is this thing on?" Instead, use a simple greeting such as "Hello." You'll know right away if the microphone is working.

TechConnect *Properly used, a microphone and rostrum will enhance your presentation.*

6. Practice dealing with microphone and speaker feedback. To stop the annoying sounds of feedback, back away slightly from the microphone and reduce your volume. If that doesn't work, you may need to move the microphone.
7. If you are seeking a more intimate atmosphere, step away from the rostrum and speak directly to your audience.

Interacting with Your Audience

Every speaking situation carries with it the expectation that you will interact with your audience in some way. Effective nonverbal strategies, responding to listener feedback, and handling Q & A after you have finished your speech are all important parts of interacting with your audience.

Nonverbal Strategies

You've already learned about the many types of visual aids available to you. When you think about it, though, the ultimate visual aid just might be you. You don't need special equipment or artistic talent to "use" yourself to your best advantage. All you need is your ability to use nonverbal strategies to convey your message.

To emphasize that you'll cover three points, you might hold up three fingers. To illustrate the contrast between a very tall person and a much shorter person, you might hold your hand up high and then position it down low as you talk. Of course you can also use nonverbal behaviors in conjunction with other supporting materials. You can gesture toward a poster, hold up a stack of handouts you're about to pass out, or smile when you present a funny slide. Following are a few ideas for using nonverbal behavior as you speak.

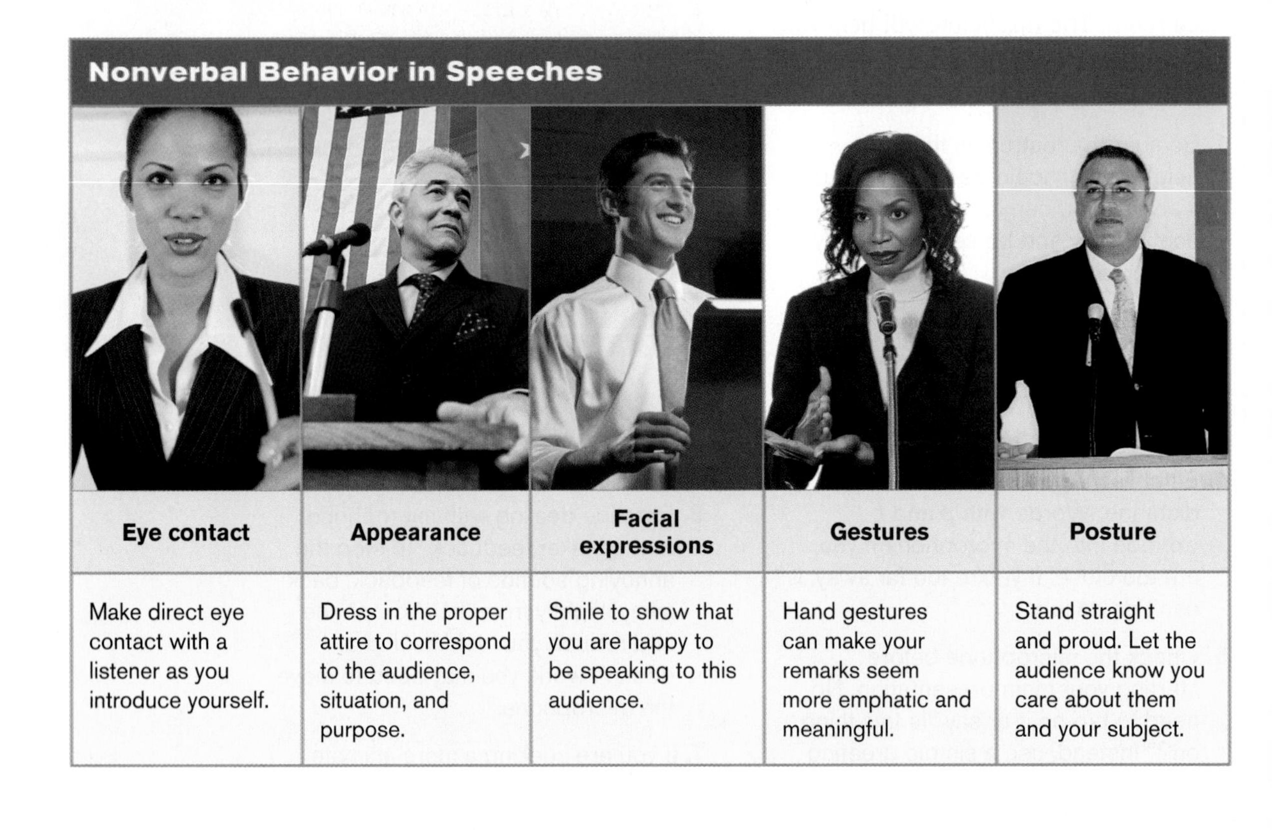

Nonverbal Behavior in Speeches

Eye contact	Appearance	Facial expressions	Gestures	Posture
Make direct eye contact with a listener as you introduce yourself.	Dress in the proper attire to correspond to the audience, situation, and purpose.	Smile to show that you are happy to be speaking to this audience.	Hand gestures can make your remarks seem more emphatic and meaningful.	Stand straight and proud. Let the audience know you care about them and your subject.

Responding to Feedback

As you speak, audience feedback helps you gauge how things are going. Stay flexible so you can react to that feedback as needed. Are they paying attention or do they seem bored and restless? Expect the unexpected. Be ready for whatever comes up. You may have to:

- Vary your volume, rate, or pitch to re-engage your audience.
- Shorten an anecdote when you seem to be losing your audience.
- Add to a topic your audience is clearly enjoying.
- Restate a concept that seems to confuse your audience.
- Pause for a beat when people laugh.
- Stop to ask whether everyone is "with you."
- Allow a question during your speech.
- Ask an audience member to close a window if a distraction crops up.
- Reposition a poster or TV monitor if anyone is straining to see it.
- Acknowledge an audience member who is vigorously nodding in agreement with a point you've made.
- Politely ask listeners with hands in the air to hold their questions until the end.

Give listeners time to laugh before continuing your message.

Handling the Q & A

The Question and Answer period can be one of the most enjoyable parts of a presentation. Keep these tips in mind.

1. Restate the question to gain time and help other listeners understand the question. Ask a questioner to clarify, illustrate, or expand on a question so that you and others understand it well.
2. Address the entire audience, not just the person asking a question. This will keep everyone involved.
3. Always be polite, even when your message is being challenged. This helps you build a strong relationship with your audience.
4. Questions give you an opportunity to clarify and refine your message. Add a new explanation or example, or expand your message with additional material.
5. Be less formal during the Q & A than during your actual speech.
6. When you don't know something, say so. Volunteer to look into the question and get back to the questioner.
7. Respond to the last question by saying, " time for one more question." This lets the audience know that time is up.
8. Thank your audience.

Building Self Confidence

When you trust your own abilities and judgment, you exhibit **self-confidence.** Self-confidence is important when communicating. Giving a speech can be nerve-wracking, but the more you practice, the more strategies you'll learn and the more confident you will become.

Managing Stage Fright

Stage fright is a feeling of apprehension or dread when speaking to an audience. Many famous people admit to having stage fright. Stage fright can actually work to your advantage by causing you to prepare well and practice often. And for many, the extra energy you feel just before a speech can enhance your performance. You'll stay sharp and focused.

But what if you get so nervous you don't think you'll be able to speak, or breathe, or face your audience? Luckily, there are strategies to help you manage your fear.

Remember, your audience will want you to do well.

- Prepare. Prepare. Prepare. Thoroughly research and review your content. Know it backwards and forwards.
- Rehearse. Rehearse. Rehearse. Know exactly what you plan to say—and how you plan to say it.
- Practice in front of trusted listeners. Intentionally put yourself in practice situations that test your nerves.
- Take a few deep breaths. Inhale through the nose. Exhale through the mouth. Relax the neck and shoulders.
- Make tight fists and relax your hands several times.
- Move around. If you have time, take a short walk to burn off nervous energy.
- Think about how you feel as an audience member. Remind yourself that audiences are usually understanding and eager to support the speaker.
- Keep your speech in perspective: You are ready. It will be fun. Nothing bad will happen. It's just a few minutes out of your life, so make the most of it.
- Remove negative thoughts from your mind and picture yourself succeeding.

For more on managing nerves, see page 18.

KEY POINT

To build self-confidence, learn as much as you can and practice often.

Revising Your Speech

Through plenty of practice, any speaker will gain command of his or her ideas and information. Knowing your content is the first key. Imagine that you're about to give a talk about the spinal column in biology class. You need to know your subject so well that a small case of nerves won't make you forget important information. You also need to understand your situation, audience, and purpose in order to craft an appropriate speech.

Your rehearsal time helps you identify unnecessary or inaccurate content. It also helps you see if you're short on information, or if your speech is far too long for the situation. In any of those cases, you know it's time to **revise**, or rework your speech. By now you've likely revised many reports, essays, and other projects, so you probably are aware of the following strategies for revising.

1. Identify parts of your speech that need revision. Decide whether you need to add, delete, rearrange, or substitute information. For a speech about Abraham Lincoln's life, you might use the revision examples below.

- **Add content.** Add more details about Lincoln's childhood to balance other information.
- **Delete content.** Remove one of two anecdotes about Lincoln's reading habits; one will make the point.
- **Rearrange content.** Correct the order of his jobs.
- **Substitute content.** Replace a passage from the Gettysburg Address with text from the Emancipation Proclamation to better fit information you present on either side of it.

Before presenting information on your subject to others, know it inside and out.

2. Next, make all of your revisions.
3. Rehearse your speech next to get comfortable with the changes.
4. Then present your speech to a classmate, friend, or family member; ask for feedback about your content and delivery style.
5. Incorporate additional feedback that you feel is necessary.
6. Finally, practice until you feel ready to present your speech for real.

PROJECT PREP

With your **project group**, write a thorough definition of the word *revise* as it applies to preparing an effective speech.

Is This Job for Me?

Search: Pharmaceutical Sales Rep

Marilee arrives at the medical plaza thirty minutes before her appointment. She collects her thoughts, sets up for her presentation, and does a few deep-breathing exercises. Marilee is a *pharmaceutical sales representative* presenting several of her employers' products to a group of pediatricians.

She's giving a multimedia presentation about a medicine for treating infections. Most doctors prescribe another drug for this purpose. Her goal is to sell them on this new drug. She needs to be fully prepared to answer any questions and address any concerns the physicians have about the product. She must appear professional, self-confident, and knowledgeable about her subject.

Marilee obtained work in pharmaceutical sales after earning a bachelor's degree in communications. She acquired her job skills through education and on-the-job training. Measure yourself with this skills inventory. Do you:

- ✓ Have an interest in medicine?
- ✓ Have excellent speaking skills?
- ✓ Possess strong self-confidence?
- ✓ Have the ability to target a message to a specific audience?
- ✓ Stay calm under pressure?
- ✓ Feel comfortable responding to listener feedback?
- ✓ Have an aptitude for persuading others?

Employers	What You Would Do
Large, medium, or small drug manufacturer	As a sales representative for a drug manufacturing company, you would work closely with researchers and salespeople to learn about the pharmaceuticals you sell, develop messages about their benefits, and create individual and group sales goals.
Self	You would work to develop sales and marketing perspectives for drug companies and present your message to various clients.

Evaluating Your Speech

Throughout this book you've been using evaluation checklists, or rubrics, to assess classroom presentations for each chapter's main project. You've probably also referred to the rubrics while planning your presentation to keep in mind the elements others will be evaluating. When the learning objectives are clear, there should be few surprises for anyone at the end of a project. This holds true even when you're evaluating your own speech.

Those involved in evaluating someone else's work must practice critical listening. An evaluator has a responsibility to pay attention, gather the necessary information, and judge that information according to the criteria laid out in the rubric. Below are a few basic rubrics you might use to evaluate speeches. Keep in mind that these are not comprehensive. One checklist is geared toward evaluating others' speeches. You can use the other sample to evaluate your own speech.

Sample Checklist 1		
This Speech...	**Yes**	**No**
Accomplished the main assignment		
Was engaging		
Included a clear beginning, middle, and end		
Incorporated appropriate research		
This Speaker . . .	**Yes**	**No**
Used an effective vocal delivery		
Seemed thoroughly prepared		
Made good use of eye contact and gestures		
Handled audience feedback well		
Hints I'd give the speaker for next time:		

Sample Checklist 2		
My Speech...	**Yes**	**No**
Accomplished the main assignment		
Kept the audience engaged		
Included a clear beginning, middle, and end		
Incorporated appropriate research		
As a Speaker, I . . .	**Yes**	**No**
Used an effective vocal delivery		
Was thoroughly prepared		
Made good use of eye contact and gestures		
Handled audience feedback well		
What I'd like to improve for next time:		

The difference between checklists and rubrics is that rubrics actually contain a scoring guide. In addition to listing the key traits of a successful presentation, rubrics define varying degrees of achieving those traits, as the graphic below shows.

	Key Traits			
	Trait 1	**Trait 2**	**Trait 3**	**Trait 4**
Achievement Level	**4** Trait achieved completely	**4** Trait achieved completely	**4** Trait achieved completely	**4** Trait achieved completely
	3 Trait mainly achieved	**3** Trait mainly achieved	**3** Trait mainly achieved	**3** Trait mainly achieved
	2 Trait somewhat achieved	**2** Trait somewhat achieved	**2** Trait somewhat achieved	**2** Trait somewhat achieved
	1 Trait not achieved	**1** Trait not achieved	**1** Trait not achieved	**1** Trait not achieved

PROJECT PREP

Refer to the discussions on pages 138–140 to refresh your memory about the impact critical listening skills have on communication. Then with your **project group**, develop a statement about the application of critical listening skills in the process of evaluating a speech.

A rubric contains a set of rules or instructions for evaluating the success of a classroom assignment. It helps an evaluator assess how well a student has met the intended learning objectives.

PREPARING THE PROJECT

Begin your project by looking back at the **Project Prep** activities in this chapter and using the directions below.

Make Connections

Discuss with your group your understanding of how a rubric works and what it helps you do. Share any experiences you've had working with a rubric. Then, discuss information you learned in this chapter, including:

- the qualities of effective delivery
- using the voice
- using supporting materials appropriately
- interacting with the audience
- building self-confidence
- evaluating your speech.

Write one or two sentences about strategies you can use to help you give a good speech.

Focus

Briefly review the group project you are working on: observing speeches and developing a rubric that assesses qualities good speeches should have and then presenting a rubric and explaining how it is used. Think of three specific qualities you've learned that you can apply to your rubric.

When planning your group presentation, create an outline that covers the important points.

Think about the type of rubric your project group needs to create. Ask and answer these questions as a group:

- Which rubric elements do we want to include for our project?
- How specific should a speech-evaluation rubric be?

Plan

Meet with your group to select speeches for review, choose roles, and assign tasks for your presentation. You'll want to begin gathering information for your rubric now. Work together to reach consensus about your rubric's format and contents. Make a date to watch and/or listen to the speeches as a group.

Develop

Use your rubric to evaluate the speeches you have watched. Meet with your group to plan your presentation. Write an outline that includes all the points you'll cover. Look over the evaluation rubric on page 413 and be sure you have addressed each point.

Practice

Do several practice runs of your presentation in front of an audience of friends or family, if possible. Be sure that you don't exceed the time limit of three minutes.

Surefire Rehearsal

Follow these tips to help your group rehearsal run smoothly:

- Know what you want to achieve during the rehearsal.
- Keep all group members informed.
- Make sure everyone has a part and feels comfortable with it.
- Stay focused and avoid getting bogged down in details.
- Create and maintain good discipline.
- Try to finish the rehearsal with a positive comment.

PRESENTING THE PROJECT

Use the strategy that follows to help make your presentation as good as it can be.

Your group should now be ready to share the project: creating and sharing a speech-evaluation rubric. Go over the CAPS guidelines on page 394 and the rubric on page 413 to be sure that your project meets the requirements.

Boosting Self-Confidence with Positive Self-Talk

Self-talk refers to the ideas you tell yourself about yourself. Ideally, your internal self-talk is overwhelmingly positive. Be your own cheerleader: send yourself encouraging messages. For this project, you might tell yourself, "I'm ready for my speech"; "The group did a great job of preparing"; or "The audience is really going to enjoy this presentation."

If all group members feel they are contributing, the rehearsal should run smoothly.

EVALUATING THE PROJECT

Evaluate the presentations using the following rubric.

Score the evaluation on each point, with 4 being "outstanding" and 1 being "needs much improvement."

Come up with an overall score and write a brief paragraph explaining your score.

Creating a Speech-Evaluation Rubric	Creativity and Originality	Preparation	Time Limit
4 Presenters created an outstanding rubric for evaluating speeches.	**4** Presenters found a creative and original way to complete the project.	**4** Presenters were very well-prepared.	**4** Presenters used all of the time well, with no empty spaces, and did not go over or under the time limit.
3 Presenters created a good rubric for evaluating speeches.	**3** Presenters showed creativity and originality in presenting most parts of the project.	**3** Presenters were well-prepared.	**3** Presenters used the time well, with only one or two awkward spots, and did not go over or under the time limit.
2 Presenters created an adequate rubric for evaluating speeches.	**2** Presenters showed creativity and originality in some parts of the project but not others.	**2** Presenters were fairly well-prepared.	**2** Presenters used the time well, with only one or two awkward spots, but went over or under the time limit.
1 Presenters created a poor rubric for evaluating speeches.	**1** Presenters did not demonstrate creativity or originality.	**1** Presenters seemed unprepared.	**1** Presenters did not use the time well and went considerably over or under the time limit.

Communication *Past* and Present

Inspiring Deliveries

From Yesteryear . . .

In 1588, England's Queen Elizabeth I gave one of the most memorable speeches in recorded history. She spoke to her troops as they prepared to battle the Spanish Armada. Though brief —(only 310 words)—her stirring language and passionate delivery are said to have inspired the British victory.

[I] think foul scorn that Parma or Spain, or any prince of Europe, should dare to invade the borders of my realms: to which, rather than any dishonor should grow by me, I myself will take up arms; I myself will be your general, judge, and rewarder of every one of your virtues in the field. . . . we shall shortly have a famous victory over the enemies of my God, of my kingdom, and of my people.

Nearly three centuries later, Abraham Lincoln gave his Gettysburg Address at a dedication ceremony for a Civil War burial ground. Like Elizabeth's speech, Lincoln's was short—274 words delivered in less than 2 minutes—but it was especially meaningful to his audience. Accounts estimate that about 20 thousand spectators hung on his every word that bleak November day in 1863. Lincoln expressed what so many Americans were feeling about the deep loss the country had suffered during the deadly, divisive war.

The brave men, living and dead, who struggled here, have consecrated it, far above our poor power to add or detract. The world will little note, nor long remember, what we say here, but it can never forget what they did here.

. . . to Modern Day

In 1997, another passionate speaker, Republican Senator Olympia Snowe of Maine, delivered a speech like Queen Elizabeth's in its resolve but worlds apart in its intent. She asked Americans to rise above politics and called for cooperation and unity among foes. Following is a portion of her speech.

It seems that we live in a time where partisanship and ideology are held in greater value by many of our nation's elected officials in service to the American people. We live in a time when the campaigning never stops, and the governing all too frequently never begins. When public disenchantment with politics runs high. In an age where issues and outcomes are spun often by spin doctors. I go back far enough in politics, where I remember a world without spin.

The enduring fact is we are a great nation with resilient citizens who have overcome the most powerful trials of the 20th century. Our success in the 21st century will require cooperation, not confrontation. Civility not hostility. Vision not division. In short, it will require the restoration of confidence in our nation's leaders and our political institutions. And that confidence I believe, will only be secured by evidence of a new and lasting bipartisanship among our leaders.

In 2008, another strong speaker took center stage. During his bid for the Democratic nomination as a presidential candidate, Senator Barack Obama delivered a speech called "A More Perfect Union." He'd been under pressure to clearly state his views on the issue of race in 21st-century America. Here is a glimpse of that speech:

This was one of the tasks we set forth at the beginning of this campaign—to continue the long march of those who came before us, a march for a more just, more equal, more free, more caring, and more prosperous America. I chose to run for the presidency at this moment in history because I believe deeply that we cannot solve the challenges of our time unless we solve them together—unless we perfect our union by understanding that we may have different stories, but we hold common hopes; that we may not look the same and we may not have come from the same place, but we all want to move in the same direction—toward a better future for our children and our grandchildren.

Obama's words were carried live on TV, radio, and Internet channels worldwide. Millions of people had instant access not only to his words but to his thoughtful delivery and rhetorical style.

Chapter 19 Review

Using Vocabulary Words

Choose five vocabulary words to help you complete this chart. Write the term in the left-hand column and a definition in the center column. Draw a simple sketch in the right-hand column to use as a memory aid to help you remember the meaning.

Vocabulary Term	Definition	Memory Aid

1. articulators
2. delivery
3. diaphragm
4. framing
5. generators
6. monotone
7. pitch
8. projecting
9. resonators
10. revise
11. self-confidence
12. stage fright

Reviewing Key Ideas

1. List five qualities of effective delivery.
2. List and define the three basic variables in vocal delivery.
3. Identify common problems with articulation.
4. What's the number-one tip for using a microphone for your speech?

Reflecting on Your Project

Can you use a rubric to evaluate a rubric? Give it a try! Create a short rubric to help you think about the effectiveness of the one your group developed for the project. Answer the questions and discuss them with your group.

Responding to the Essential Question

Give an impromptu speech that answers the essential question from page 394. Ask for audience feedback on how well you covered the material discussed in the chapter.

Extending Your Understanding

Everyday Life

1. Listen for good use of vocal variety in conversations with friends or family, during classroom lectures, or anywhere you happen to be. Start a list of tips for yourself based on examples you find effective.
2. Practice projecting your voice outside. Have a friend be your audience. As you talk, your friend should gradually increase the distance between you and stop when he or she starts having trouble hearing you. Without resorting to shouting, experiment with volume to ensure that your listener can hear you.
3. Read aloud the back of a cereal box and experiment with using pauses and word emphasis to affect meaning.

4. During your normal conversations today, emphasize a point using framing three different times.

In the Media

5. With a friend, watch a speech delivered in manuscript format on the cable television channel C-SPAN. What advice would you give the speaker for improving vocal delivery?
6. Watch a portion of a TV movie and look for common articulation problems. Stop when you've caught ten examples.

Research

7. Research the events leading up to Abraham Lincoln's Gettysburg Address. Focus on events from just the month prior to the speech. Write a one-page report discussing the circumstances surrounding Lincoln's presence at the cemetery that day.
8. Research the career of a well-known speaker of any era. Investigate the person's education, training, and day-to-day job duties. Present your findings and your sources in class.

Interpreting Graphics

Consider this graphic representation showing the length of some famous speeches. What conclusions can you draw about the speech lengths relative to what you know about the situation of each one?

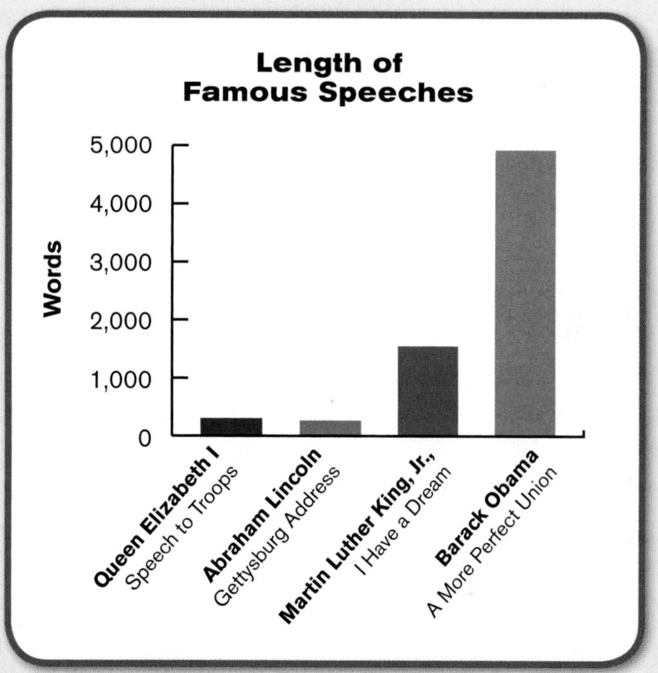

Additional Projects

1. **Partnered Project:** With a partner, identify five famous figures that possess an appealing voice. Develop a list of qualities you think every pleasing voice has and share that list in class.
2. **Individual Project:** Arrange to give a speech or read a piece of literature in your school auditorium using a rostrum and microphone. Practice standing at the rostrum and turning on the microphone. Adjust the height of each as needed. Speak into the microphone, correcting for feedback.

Unit Four

Culminating Activities

In this unit you have explored public speaking: preparing to speak, researching and organizing your speech, preparing supporting materials, using language effectively, and presenting your speech. The activities on these pages will help you apply your understandings to situations in everyday life.

Workplace Workout

Emily had to give a speech to create enthusiasm among the sales reps for the new video game her team was creating. She was very nervous, so she decided to read a manuscript of her speech.

Emily began by describing the team's efforts to solve technical glitches in the video game because her team was most proud of this work. Using presentation software, she showed the audience a series of flowcharts to illustrate the team's solutions. When she sensed that the audience was getting restless, she began to read her speech faster. In precise, technical language, she concluded by explaining how the game worked.

In the Q & A session, the managers wanted to know what the most attractive features of the game were and what distinguished the game from the others on the market. Emily spent as much time answering these questions as she had in making her speech.

What Went Wrong?

Reflect on what you have learned about preparing and presenting a speech. Then, imagine that you are Emily's supervisor. What feedback would you give her so that she can revise her speech before presenting it to the entire sales force? Write down notes for a discussion with Emily.

Make it Right

Keeping in mind the feedback you would give Emily, prepare the introduction to Emily's revised speech. Then, present the introduction to your classmates. Ask your classmates for feedback.

Media Master

With a partner, identify the elements of a typical TV news story. Then, using information from primary and secondary sources, write a script for a two-minute news story. Present your informational story to the class. As a follow-up, discuss how you could use your story's subject in different kinds of presentations. Create a storyboard or write a sketch of each of the following based on your story's subject.

Types of Media Presentations	Example
Expressive (artistic)	A dialogue between people in the story
Argumentative (persuasive)	A video editorial
Critical (analytic)	A brief documentary

Gender Journey

As a class, study the effects of gender and age on the use of language. List pairs of job titles in which one term is gender neutral and the other term is gender marked, such as *police officer* and *policeman.* Survey an equal number of males and females in different generations to determine which term in each pair they would most likely use. Record the findings in a class chart. Discuss any conclusions you can draw about the use of gender marked or gender neutral language among males and females in different generations.

OWN IT!

Unit 4 began with Dale Carnegie's statement, "There are always three speeches for every one you actually gave. The one you practiced, the one you gave, and the one you wish you gave." (See page 275.) Reflect on what you have learned in this unit and the differences between the speeches you practiced and ultimately gave. List goals for the speeches you *wish* you gave. Then, present one of your speeches again to a partner. Use your list of goals to prepare. Did you meet your goals? Keep your list for the future.

Public Speaking: My Goals

1. Create an engaging introduction.
2. Use pauses effectively.

Types of Presentations

When a heart is on fire, sparks always fly out of the mouth.
– Anonymous

The Speech to Inform

ESSENTIAL QUESTION

How can you make speeches to inform as effective as possible?

Chapter Project: Here's How

If you've ever relied on someone's information to get out of a tight spot—a parent's directions by phone when you are lost, for example—you know how clearly information must be conveyed to be helpful. This project will help you learn how to present information clearly and effectively.

With a partner, you will create a short, entertaining presentation that informs your audience how to make something, perform an activity, or follow a specific process. The presentation can be comic or serious, but it should take no more than two to three minutes. Refer to the CAPS guidelines below as you work.

The rubric on page 445 shows the traits on which your presentation will be evaluated.

CONCEPT	explanations require clear organization and useful details
AUDIENCE	classmates and teacher
PURPOSE	speak informatively about an activity, task, or process
SITUATION	in-class speech

Julia used a map as a visual aid during her speech on the National Park Service.

KEY VOCABULARY

- informative speech
- expository speech
- process speech
- demonstration speech
- exposition
- narration
- diction

Speak Up!

Write down a quick set of directions to or from a place you know well. Try to be specific but brief. When your teacher calls on you, read your directions to the class. Were your classmates able to understand how to get to the place you described? Discuss why you did or did not get your information across.

Pages 424–443 will provide the information you'll need to complete this project.

Types of Informative Speeches

An **informative speech** presents information or explains a process. Examples of informative speeches in school include oral reports, announcements at meetings, and class lectures. Beyond high school, informative speeches may take the form of college- or employment-orientation speeches, scientific reports, public-safety speeches, or critical commentary by reviewers. There are two basic types of informative speeches—those designed to give information about a topic, known as expository speeches, and those explaining a process, or a process speeches.

Expository Speeches

An **expository speech** offers information about an object, place, person, event, or idea.

- **Object informative speech.** This kind of speech informs the audience about a specific object. Imagine a doctor speaking to a group of first-year medical students about the function and necessity of a blood pressure monitoring device.
- **Place informative speech.** This kind of speech tells the audience about a specific place. An example might be an orientation speech for new students telling them how the school is laid out and where the classrooms and other facilities are located.
- **Person informative speech (biographical).** This type of speech gives a verbal snapshot of a person. For example, you might want to inform club members about the background and personality of a friend who has just joined. The information helps everyone feel comfortable when your friend first attends a meeting.
- **Event informative speech.** This type of speech summarizes the activities that took place or will take place. A recap after a baseball game is an event informative speech.
- **Idea informative speech.** Idea informative speeches inform an audience about a concept, book, movie, or other product of creativity. The challenge of this type of speech is to make an abstract idea such as democracy understandable to others. Concrete examples will help the audience relate the concept to their own experiences.

Process Speeches

A **process speech** has one of the following purposes:

- **To show how something works.** For example, what happens in the engine of a car when you turn the key in the ignition? A process speech would tell you step by step.
- **To show how to do something.** Some process speeches demonstrate the process. A flight attendant showing how to pull down the oxygen mask is giving a **demonstration speech**.
- **To show how something was done or made.** A speech about how the Grand Canyon was formed would cover the geological processes that formed this deep gorge in Arizona.

Steps for Preparing an Expository Speech

Before you go on a trip, you identify your destination. In the same way, before preparing an expository speech, learn what you are aiming for. The following chart, using the example of a speech about zippers, shows the features you will want in your expository speech. Which of these features are unique to expository speeches?

Features of Expository Speeches	
Attention-grabbing beginning It's inspired a harrowing carnival ride, a ceramic sculpture, even performance art, but most of us know it more simply as the item that keeps the cold out: it's the zipper. **Thesis statement** The zipper is a device most of us take for granted, but in fact it has a rich and complicated history that parallels the history of American industry.	**Introduction** • grabs attention with startling detail, anecdote, or quote • makes the purpose clear • includes the thesis statement so the listener will know just what to expect
First main point In 1893, Whitcomb Judson of Chicago began to sell a newfangled kind of fastener. **Second main point** However, the zipper did not catch on right away. Judson showed off his device at the World Columbian Exposition in Chicago in 1893, but another invention at the fair–the Ferris Wheel–got all the attention. **Third main point** Though the zipper itself existed since the 1890s, it was not called the zipper until much later. According to the Massachusetts Institute of Technology's Lamelson-MIT Web site, the term *zipper* was coined by B.F. Goodrich, who first used the fastener on galoshes in 1923.	**Body** • states main points • uses supporting details such as researched facts, examples, reasons, and comparisons to develop the main points • links the points through transitions such as *however, though, first of all, most important* • follows a clear organizational pattern, such as chronological, as shown here. See pages 430–431 for more organizational patterns. • uses lively language
Wrap-up Judson died in 1909 never knowing that his invention became successful and revolutionized the fashion industry. **Strong ending statement** So if you ever encounter The Zipper at a carnival, or come upon a zipper sculpture in an art museum, you might want to take a minute to remember the history of this fastener and the way it reflects the changing nature of American industry.	**Conclusion** • pulls ideas together • presents ideas in new light • often refers back to attention-grabbing beginning

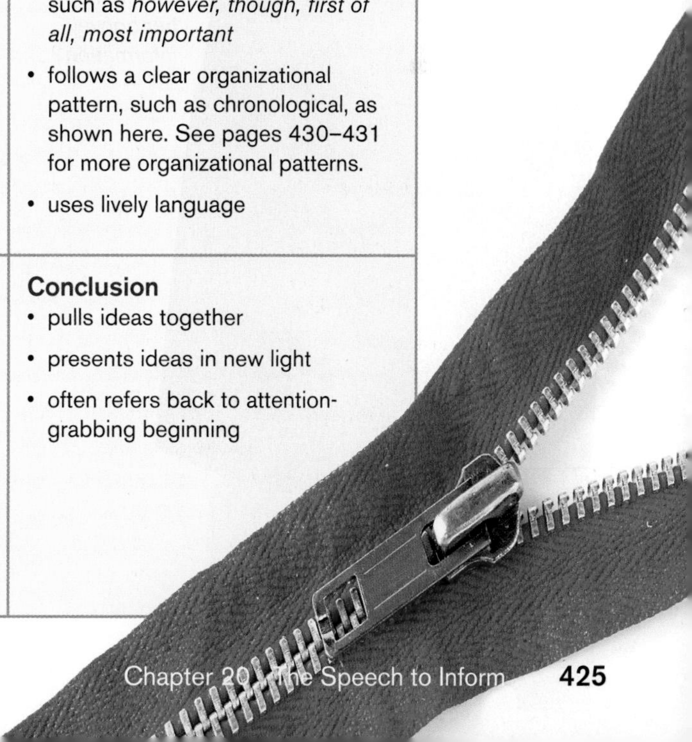

roduct	Amount of Caffeine
Coffee, brewed	40 to 180 milligrams (mg) per cup
Coffee, instant	30 to 120 mg per cup
ffee, decaffeinated	3 to 5 mg per cup
, brewed American	20 to 90 mg per cup
Tea, brewed imported	25 to 110 mg per cup
Tea, instant	28 mg per cup
Tea, canned iced	22 to 36 mg per 12 ounces
Cola and other soft drinks with caffeine	36 to 90 mg per 12 ounces
Cola and other soft drinks, decaffeinated	0 mg per 12 ounces
Cocoa	4 mg per cup
Chocolate, milk	3 to 6 mg per ounce
Chocolate, bittersweet	25 mg per ounce

How does Andrea's poster help her convey information?

Choose a Subject

The best speeches are those that connect your genuine interests with the interests and needs of your audience and the situation. For example, Andrea is trying to narrow her list of topics for a speech she will present in her communication class. She's considered some topics in the news—global warming, the spread of certain viruses—but since she does not feel excited about any of them right now, she wisely decides to tackle those another time. She is, however, genuinely curious about why drinking caffeinated cola makes her jittery, and she wonders if improving what she eats and drinks might benefit her health. She knows that some of her classmates drink quite a lot of caffeinated diet soda, so she figures that a large percentage of her audience will be interested in her topic.

Of course each public speaking situation is different. Be sure that your topic and its presentation are appropriate to the situation and audience. When you can see the importance of a topic from both your perspective and your audience's, then you can feel secure in your selection.

Research

Informative speaking requires a working knowledge of the subject at hand. To gather her information, Andrea will look at three general sources:

- **herself:** her experiences, knowledge, and background
- **immediate sources:** the people she is close to, sources within her school or work environment, and information she already has on file
- **outside sources:** books, magazines, documentaries, and the Internet.

Here are some questions that can help Andrea focus her research in all three types of research materials.

- What is the subject?
- How is it defined? Do people agree on its definition? If not, where are the disagreements?
- Why is it important to your audience? (Or why should it be important to your audience?)
- What does the audience already know? Does the audience have misconceptions?
- What important terms relate to the subject? Does the audience need to know their meaning as part of gaining understanding?
- What are the parts or features of the subject?
- Are any parts or features more important than the others? Why or why not?
- Is it like something else? In what ways? Are these similarities important? Why or why not?
- Is it unlike something else? In what ways? Are these dissimilarities important? Why or why not?
- Are there causes and effects related to the topic? Which are important for your purpose?
- What have others said about the subject or topic?
- Are there any statistics that will help the audience understand the subject or topic?

As Andrea begins her research process, she may find such strategies as interviewing, note-taking, and summarizing very useful for locating and synthesizing the information she needs.

Interviewing Asking interview questions about various perspectives on your topic can be very helpful for informative speeches. For example, as part of her research, Andrea could interview several people standing in line to buy drinks at the school's vending machine, as well as a nutritionist at the community health center. Through these interviews she can find out what others think or know about her topic. The nutritionist might supply her with valuable definitions and the latest scientific theories. The interviewees in the line might reveal important information such as misconceptions, negative or positive responses to caffeine, and purchasing trends.

Note-taking Whether she does interviewing or Internet research, Andrea must take notes on the information she finds and keep track of its source. For written materials she will need to note the author, title, page number, and/or Internet site. As always, when quoting a person or text directly, Andrea will put quotation marks around the beginning and end of the quote to avoid plagiarism. She will also put her notes in a special folder to keep her materials organized.

Summarizing When talking to an interview subject or taking notes, Andrea uses summarizing to recap what she has heard or read. This practice allows her to take in a large amount of information and distill it down to its essential elements—its main idea and major supporting details. Ideally, this will help her to locate the most interesting and appropriate information from her research.

Search: Teacher

It's the final hour of the state achievement test and Elora is in a panic. She is just starting the math portion and that's the part she worried most about. However, once she gets going, she starts to relax. She remembers how to solve the problems, in large part because her *teacher* explained the concepts so clearly. Explaining clearly is one of a teacher's most important jobs.

Teachers spend a good part of their workday talking, always adjusting for the purpose, situation, and audience. The obvious purpose teachers have for speaking is to inform: to teach, to educate, to introduce, and to familiarize. But teachers also speak to entertain when they enliven the instruction to keep students interested in a topic. They speak to persuade when they try to convince students that something is important or to motivate them to try harder.

Teachers need to be excellent extemporaneous and impromptu speakers. Sometimes they deliver lectures organized and prepared in advance, but most teachers speak in response to on-the-spot questions and comments from students. Good teachers organize answers immediately and offer alternative ways of answering if students need more help in understanding.

Does a job as a teacher interest you? Measure yourself with this ability inventory to find out if you have the basic traits needed to be a teacher. Do you:

- ✓ Explain things clearly?
- ✓ Find creative solutions?
- ✓ Think effectively on your feet?
- ✓ Think in an organized way?
- ✓ Listen well?
- ✓ Like sharing information and ideas?

If you became a teacher, you might have job opportunities in these areas.

Educational Setting	Students You Would Teach
Schools	Children and teenagers
Community centers	All ages who want a wide range of classes
Colleges and universities	Students preparing for professional and academic careers
Corporations	Employees who want to improve/ learn skills

What communication skills does a great teacher possess?

Develop Support

The support materials for informative speeches are the same as those for any speech. Their function is to lend credibility to the speech. It's not enough for Andrea to develop a theory about soft-drink consumption and health, she must support her thesis with proof, using:

- **facts:** statements that can be proven true
- **statistics:** information presented in numbers, such as "Thirty-one percent, or 7.6 million, of American teens say they drink caffeine-laden energy drinks regularly."
- **testimony:** statements by experts, such as "Pinecrest Hospital's chief nutritionist finds that caffeine consumption among teenagers has reached an all-time high."

To develop your proof and make it as clear as possible, you can use the types of support listed below.They all support **exposition,** the presentation of information.

- **incident:** an example in the form of a story. For example, Andrea might include a brief anecdote about a person trying to give up caffeinated soda and going through withdrawal.
- **comparison/contrast:** Andrea might compare the effects of drinking one soda per week with those of drinking one soda per day. Or she might use an analogy: "Just as habit-forming drugs contain FDA warnings on their labels, so too should caffeinated drinks."
- **description:** vivid details that bring a subject to life. Andrea might describe the mood effects of caffeine.
- **definition:** special terms defined for the audience. Andrea might define the word *stimulant*, for example.

Even though the main purpose of Andrea's speech is expository, she is likely to have other purposes in the service of that larger purpose. For example, she may use **narration**, the recounting of the events in an incident, to add support and liveliness. She might place herself at the center of the story and speak from the first-person point of view.

Andrea might also use persuasion. For example, she may encourage students to change their buying and drinking habits.

Product	Amount of Caffeine
Coffee, brewed	40 to 180 milligrams (mg) per cup
Coffee, instant	30 to 120 mg per cup
Coffee, decaffeinated	3 to 5 mg per cup
Tea, brewed American	20 to 90 mg per cup
Tea, brewed imported	25 to 110 mg per cup
Tea, instant	28 mg per cup
Tea, canned iced	22 to 36 mg per 12 ounces
Cola and other soft drinks with caffeine	36 to 90 mg per 12 ounces
Cola and other soft drinks, decaffeinated	0 mg per 12 ounces
Cocoa	4 mg per cup
Chocolate, milk	3 to 6 mg per ounce
Chocolate, bittersweet	25 mg per ounce

Statistics can help support your thesis.

Organize

You can unearth lots of fascinating research material, but unless you present it in an organized way, your speech will not feel like a unified whole. Try to find the strongest possible organization method for your subject, and craft a thesis statement that suggests that order. Following are some of the most useful methods for expository speeches.

Chronological Order With a thesis statement like the following, Andrea might use chronological order and arrange her speech according to what happened first, second, third, and so on. *Thesis statement:* Over the years, scientists have learned much about the effects of caffeine on people.

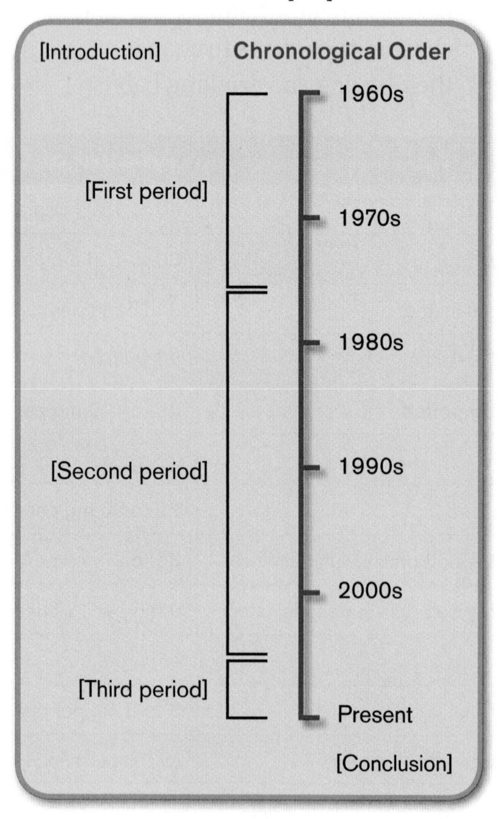

Topical Order With a different kind of thesis statement, Andrea would more naturally use topical order, in which each main idea flows logically from the one before. *Thesis statement:* To draw conclusions about the use of caffeine, you need to understand three different issues.

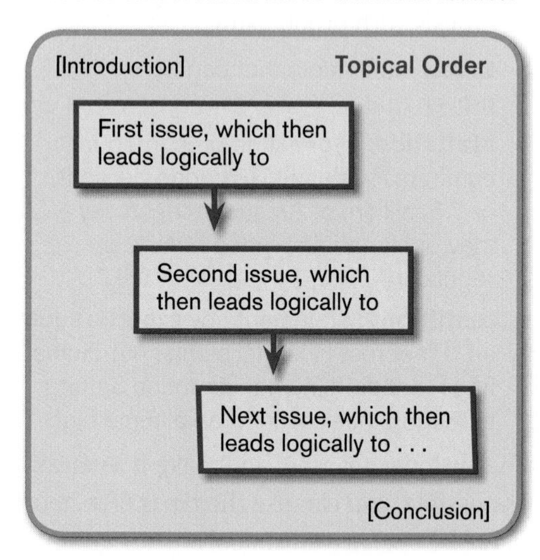

Order of Importance Sometimes your ideas are best presented in order of importance. Andrea might place her information so that it builds to a climax, beginning with less important material and building to the most important or dramatic information. *Thesis statement:* Caffeine affects the body in several ways, some more serious than others.

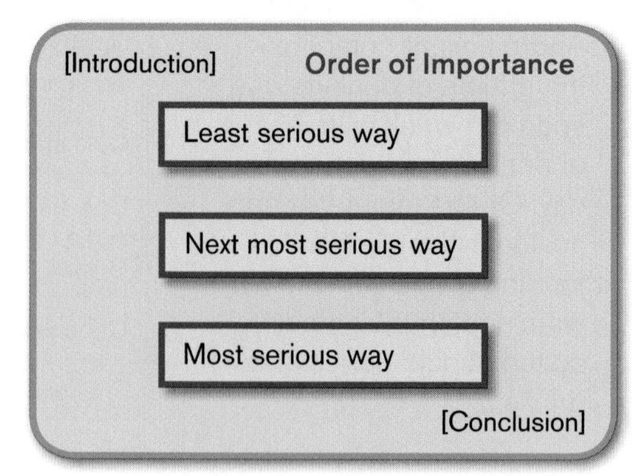

Cause-Effect Order The focus of your expository speech might be to explain a cause-effect relationship. Andrea might establish a cause and follow it with an effect—a variation on chronological order. *Thesis statement:* The way caffeine acts on the nervous system results in the possibility of developing cravings for it.

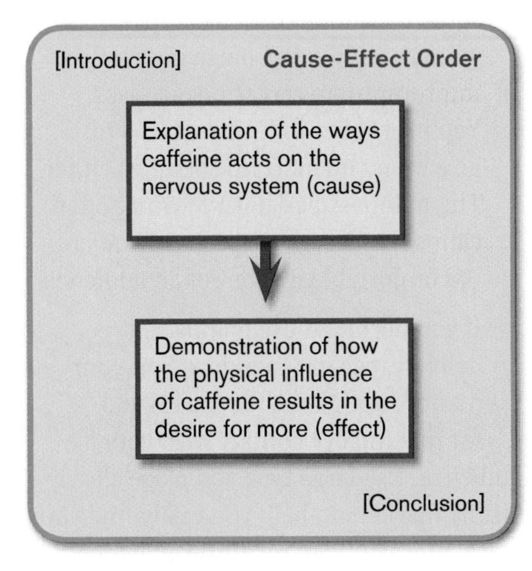

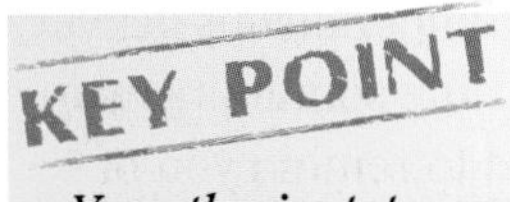

Your thesis statement will help you determine the best order in which to present your ideas.

Problem-Solution Order This format is common in both informative and persuasive speaking. To use it, Andrea would focus on the problem in the first part of the body of her speech and use the second part to develop solutions. *Thesis statement:* Wise consumers will limit their use of caffeine.

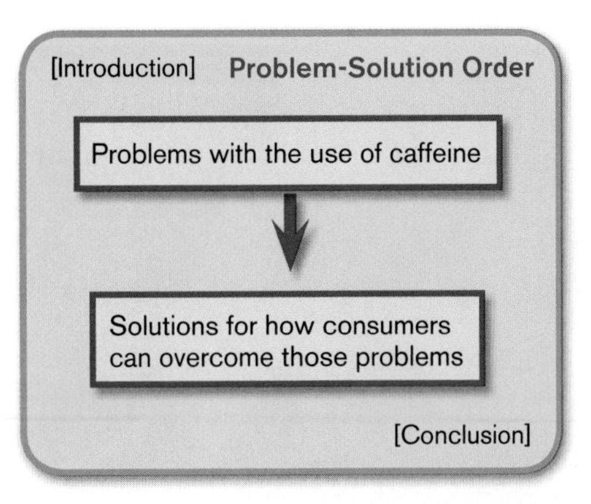

To convey these organizational patterns, some speakers create an outline similar to the one below.

I. Major point
  A. Subpoint
    1. Development
    2. Development
  B. Subpoint
    1. Development
    2. Development
      a) Further development
      b) Further development
II. Major point
  A. Subpoint
    1. Development
    2. Development
  B. Subpoint
    1. Development
    2. Development

TechConnect *A PowerPoint presentation is a good supplement to informative speeches.*

Prepare Visual or Multimedia Aids

TechConnect A visual aid can neatly synthesize some of the ideas in your speech. You can use computer graphics or you can create a hard-copy chart, graph, or poster by hand or using a computer for images. You can bring in objects for classmates to hold and use.

Visual aids must be logical and, above all, visible to everyone in the audience. No matter what type of visual or multimedia aid you choose, make sure that it amplifies the information in your speech. A visual aid that introduces brand new information that is not in the speech may distract your listeners from your main points.

Prepare Notes or Manuscript

In Chapter 17 you learned about four common delivery formats for effective public speaking: impromptu delivery, extemporaneous delivery, manuscript delivery, and memorized delivery. Most often, you will have some time to prepare for a speech, so you probably won't be giving many impromptu presentations in class. You probably won't be required to give many memorized speeches either. The manuscript delivery format often calms the nerves of speakers who are uncomfortable in front of an audience.

If you decide to use manuscript delivery, be sure to indicate on your manuscript places for pauses and for making eye contact with your audience. Use large type and place clearly visible markers to help you easily find your place after you look up at the audience.

If you choose the extemporaneous delivery format, create an outline containing words and phrases designed to remind you of the ideas and organization of your speech. Rehearse your speech to get comfortable with delivering the points in your outline. Try not to get tied down to wording the ideas in the speech the same way each time. When speaking extemporaneously, try to stay fresh and spontaneous.

PROJECT PREP

With your **project group**, begin to think about the thesis statement you may develop for your speech, the kind of order that thesis statement suggests, and some possible visual aids for your speech.

Steps for Preparing a Process Speech

You use the same basic steps for a process speech as you would for an expository speech. But what sets the process speech apart is that it always focuses on how something works, how to do something, or how something developed.

Features of Process Speeches	
Attention-grabbing beginning You're riding along with the sun on your back and the wind on your face. Then it happens. The pop. The hiss of air. That sinking feeling. That's right–your bike got a flat tire. If you know how to fix it, it takes fifteen minutes. If you don't … there's no telling how long it'll take. That's why if you ride often, you want to learn this skill sooner rather than later. **Thesis statement** So you'll always be ready if *you* get that sinking feeling, here's what you need to know to fix a flat tire.	**Introduction** • grabs attention with startling detail, anecdote, or quote • uses lively language • makes the purpose clear • includes the thesis statement so the listener will know just what to expect
First step in the process If you think you have a flat or a puncture, you'll first need to inspect the tire. The puncture may be on the outside of the tire, so turn the bike upside down so it balances on the seat and handlebars. **Second step** Once you have found the puncture, remove whatever object might have made the hole. **Further steps** After you have made certain the surface of the tube is clean and dry, use a small piece of sandpaper to scuff up the area where you want to apply the patch.	**Body** • states each step in process • links the steps with transitions such as *first, next, once, after, finally* • follows a clear organizational pattern. For steps in a process, chronological order is the most logical. • presents adequate research support, with properly cited sources, such as www.ehow.com
Wrap-up In a very short time your repaired tire is ready to take you wherever you want to go. **Strong ending statement** So don't get stranded on the open road without the knowledge you need to keep your wheels rolling. Learn how to fix a flat tire. It's easy, quick, and painless, and you'll be back in the saddle while the sun is still shining.	**Conclusion** • pulls ideas together • presents ideas in new light • often refers back to attention-grabbing beginning

A process speech can tell you how to sew on a button, how a lawn mower motor works, or how stalagmites are formed.

Choose a Subject

When choosing a subject, recall that a process speech can come in three forms:

- **Speeches that tell how to do something.** Sample topics include how to sew on a button, how to write a haiku poem, or how to program a DVR.
- **Speeches that tell how something works.** Sample topics include the inner mechanism of a lawn mower motor, the steps in the legislative process, and how a fax machine operates.
- **Speeches that show how something was done or created.** Sample topics include how stalagmites are formed and how a bird develops inside an egg.

A process speech on the zipper might focus not on its invention, but on how it works or how it is made.

Todd's process speech is about how to write a haiku poem. Todd is eager to share his interest in this poetic form. He has an idea that he could show the class how to write a simple haiku and then have the class create one together.

Research

When presenting his process speech, Todd will likely use some of the same research techniques that Andrea used for her expository speech. Like every speaker, Todd already has valuable sources: his personal experience; sources such as people he knows and information he has on file; and outside sources such as books, periodicals, and the Internet.

The questions below can help you inventory all three sources to find what you need for a process speech.

- What process are you going to discuss?
- Why is it important to you?
- How is the process defined?
- Why is it important to your audience?
- What does the audience already know? Do they have misconceptions?
- What terms are part of the subject? Must the audience know their meanings to understand the process?
- What are the stages or steps in the process?
- Are any stages or steps more important than the others?
- In what way is the process like or unlike something else?
- Are there causes and effects related to the topic? Which are important for your purpose?
- Are there statistics that will help others understand the process?

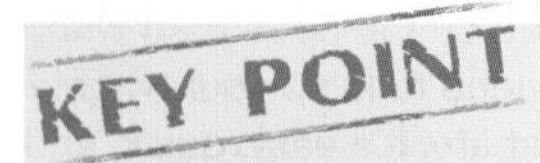

Steps involved in preparing an informational speech include choosing a subject, developing support, using visual aids, and using notes or a manuscript.

Develop Support

While you can use the types of support other speeches use (see page 429), process speeches rely mainly on the clear explanation of the stages or steps in the process.

Organize

Because of the content and purpose of process speeches, most of them use chronological order to show the steps in sequence. Below are a list of steps Todd might include in his speech on how to write a haiku poem.

- Brainstorm ideas.
- Choose a theme from nature.
- Choose a place and a time or a season of the year.
- Organize ideas into three lines.
- Make sure syllable count is correct.
- Revise to refine syllables and wording.

His audience might not know what haiku is, so Todd plans to begin the speech with an example and a definition.

Prepare Visual or Multimedia Aids

Many speeches benefit from visual or multimedia aids. Demonstration speeches, a type of process speech in which the process is actually acted out, rely on these aids more than most other speech forms. Todd has decided to use the chalkboard to demonstrate the process of writing haiku. He will be creating the poem on the spot so he won't need much preparation. He will need only chalk and legible handwriting.

Prepare Notes or Manuscript

You will recall the four different delivery formats of public speaking: impromptu, extemporaneous, manuscript, and memorized. Todd decides he will present his process speech extemporaneously. He creates a series of note cards, each one featuring a briefly stated step in the process. He will expand on those ideas as he presents his speech.

Consider what visual aids will strengthen your presentation.

Presenting Your Informative Speech

Whether you are making a speech to give information or to explain a process, you will need the same set of skills.

Practice, Practice, Practice

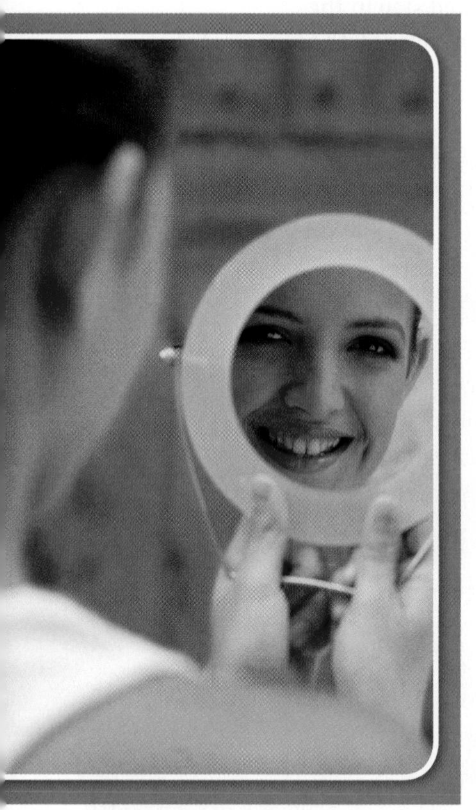

If no one is available to hear you practice, use a mirror.

There are three keys to delivering a great speech: Practice, practice, practice. If you are very familiar with the ideas and structure of your speech, you've done the proper preparation. Giving the speech can then actually be fun.

Managing Nerves
Just about everyone gets nervous before giving a speech. In fact, many people rate public speaking as their number-one fear. A shaky voice, trembling, and other physical stress can be alleviated with a few deep breaths. Standing up straight, with your shoulders back, will help you to breathe deeply. Sometimes pausing for a moment is all you need to start feeling more balanced. For further tips on managing nerves see page 406.

Building Self-Confidence Sometimes your self-confidence might feel a bit shaky too. Perhaps you begin to think your topic is stupid or that your audience won't understand you. Try practicing your speech in front of friends or relatives to get their feedback. Chances are good that they will find your topic interesting and perhaps give you some ideas about how to make your speech even better.

Imitating a speaker you admire can also help build your confidence. Think about what that person does, and practice doing the same. Novice speakers often lapse into monotonous delivery, so monitor your rhythm, pitch, volume, and pace when you rehearse. You might try tape-recording your speech. Videotaping allows you to see both your verbal and your nonverbal communication.

Gaining Command of Information
Nothing will build your confidence like knowing your subject inside and out. Remember that no research is really wasted. Even if you didn't plan to use certain ideas and facts in your speech, you have them to draw upon. Often speakers add details from their research on the spot or use those details to answer listeners' questions at the end.

Knowing When to Revise Listen critically to yourself and then practice your speech in front of others. Take to heart any constructive criticism. Acknowledge and improve sections that you know are not quite right or not the best they can be.

Use Language Clearly and Appropriately

Good public speakers use clear, understandable language appropriate to themselves, the audience, and the speaking situation. Don't use fifty words when ten well-chosen ones will do. Avoid repetition and unfinished sentences.

Following are a few additional tips.

- Use appropriate word choice, or **diction**, to suit the audience. Avoid jargon or run-on sentences.
- Vary your syntax, or sentence structure, to keep listeners interested. If you use too many sentences of the same length and structure, your audience will get bored and tune out.
- Make sure your tone is appropriate to the situation. If you are giving a speech about high infant mortality in parts of the world, avoid joking or sarcasm. Audiences are offended by what they see as a careless tone.

Use Nonverbal Strategies Well

Observers estimate that 90 percent of human communication is nonverbal. Use its power to strengthen the clarity of your speech. For example, if are you making three points about the history of zippers, you may want to take a step or two before you start each one, so you are standing in a slightly different spot as you explain each point. Those movements will alert listeners to each main point. If you are giving a demonstration speech, let your gestures help you explain the procedure. No matter what your speech is about, make eye contact and keep your head high. For more on nonverbal communication strategies, see Chapter 3.

Use Supporting Materials Well

Set up your supporting materials before you begin to speak. No one will mind if you take a few seconds to place your notes on the rostrum, adjust the microphone, and get comfortable. If possible, make sure any special equipment or non-handheld visual aid is set up and ready to go in advance. Try to make the transitions from speaking to using support materials seamless.

Interact in a Lively Way with Listeners

Of course your language, nonverbal strategies, and visual aids are important to present an effective speech. But a part of each speech will always be dependent on audience response. When presenting a speech, you receive constant audience feedback. It may not always be the kind of feedback you want or expect, but even negative feedback helps you keep your speech on track. If you notice people in the back row looking unhappy or puzzled, try raising your voice. If the puzzled, disturbed looks disappear, you have found the source of the back row's frustration—their inability to hear you. Use audience feedback to guide your presentation.

Question-and-Answer Sessions

Treat the question-and-answer portion as though it were just another part of your speech. Use it to clarify, illustrate, and expand your points. Ask your questioners to expand on and clarify their questions. When you are an audience member, ask any questions that you feel have not been answered. Your questions should clarify how the speaker feels about the subject.

PROJECT PREP

With your **project partner**, give each other a set of simple instructions; then give each other feedback on steps in the process that may need further clarification.

Analyzing Speeches to Inform

Read the following speeches and think about how well they meet the goal of informing the audience.

The Expository Speech

Caffeine: Villain or Hero?

1 How many of you here consider yourself caffeine addicts? How many caffeinated beverages—and that includes coffee, tea, most types of soda, and energy drinks—do you consume in a day? Recently I started noticing that I was jittery and my stomach kept churning. I also realized that I was up to three caffeinated diet sodas a day.

2 Caffeine is pervasive in contemporary society, and every few months we hear about a new study that has shown that it is bad for us or good for us. Which story are we supposed to believe?

3 Today I'd like to give you some of the facts about caffeine and its effects on your body. It may not cause you to change your caffeine consumption but at least you'll be better informed about what you are taking in. I'm going to talk about the positive and negative effects of caffeine and discuss what are considered safe levels of caffeine consumption.

4 Let's start with the good news. Caffeine, which comes from the leaves, seeds, and fruits of about 63 different plants, is well-known as a stimulant. That's why people drink coffee in the morning, right?

5 Caffeine *does* help you wake up and feel more alert and it has been shown to increase attention spans. This is a beneficial effect for people who are driving long distances and people who are doing tedious work. Calling this a health benefit may be stretching the point, though staying awake while you are driving a car is definitely a benefit to your well-being.

6 Caffeine also contains antioxidants, which have been shown to have cancer-prevention qualities.

7 The negative effects of caffeine are largely dependent on how much you consume. When consumed in small quantities—for example, one cup of coffee or one soda—caffeine can cause an increase in your heart rate, more frequent urination, which can cause dehydration, and increased acid production in the digestive system.

8 In larger amounts, caffeine can cause headaches, restlessness and nervousness, insomnia, and even, when consumed in very large quantities, hallucinations. Don't try that at home! Consumption of amounts of caffeine over 600 milligrams per day used over long periods of time has been linked to depression, insomnia, and digestive disturbances.

According to a Medline article on the National Institutes of Health Web site, having caffeine in your diet is not of any benefit to your health, but moderate consumption is not considered harmful. This article claims that up to three 8-ounce cups of coffee a day or 250 milligrams of caffeine is considered "average or moderate." Drinking ten cups of coffee a day is considered excessive. Also, remember that the amount of caffeine per cup can vary depending on the type of beans that are used and the strength of the brew.

Most sodas with caffeine, unless they are specially enhanced, have about 35 milligrams of caffeine per 8 ounces, so you don't have to worry too much unless you are drinking several 2-liter bottles per day. Also, the effect of caffeine on you personally will depend on a number of factors like your weight, general health, mood, and personal sensitivity to caffeine.

You can see that caffeine can have both positive and negative effects on our health and well-being, but the bottom line is that if you drink your caffeinated beverages in moderation, you don't have to worry too much. So, the next time you are wondering whether you should drink that soda to perk yourself up, relax. At least now you know what it is and isn't doing to you!

The Process Speech

Before the speech begins, Todd writes a haiku poem on the chalkboard. As the speech progresses, he creates another one, following the steps in the process he outlines.

How to Write a Haiku Poem

Gently the snow falls

White against my windowpane

Winter comes again

I wrote that haiku this morning after checking the weather outside our kitchen window. I like to write haiku because it helps me capture in a few words an image of some aspect of my life.

Haiku is a traditional poetic form, developed in the mid-15th century in Japan where to this day it is revered. Even so, just about anybody can learn to write a haiku poem. I wrote my first one when I was eight. My mother was trying to keep me occupied one day when I had to stay home from school. She got out a pad of paper and a pencil and sat me down at the kitchen table. In ten minutes she had taught me how to write haiku. It was simple and fun. And today I'd like to show *you* how.

Nature has inspired many poets to compose haiku.

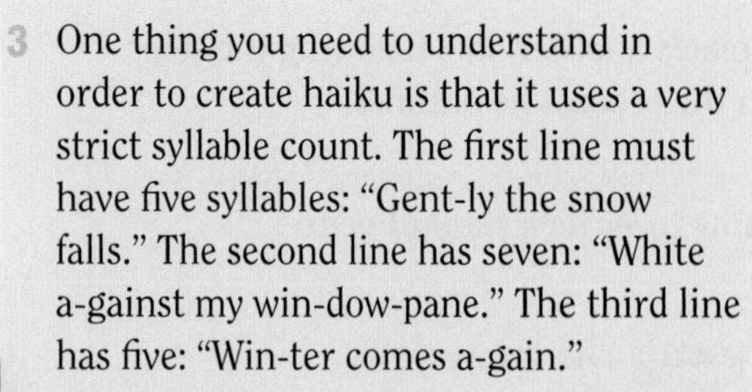

3 One thing you need to understand in order to create haiku is that it uses a very strict syllable count. The first line must have five syllables: "Gent-ly the snow falls." The second line has seven: "White a-gainst my win-dow-pane." The third line has five: "Win-ter comes a-gain."

4 The first step is to brainstorm ideas about your subject. For our purposes here, we'll focus on times of day or times of the year. I'm just going to write a few ideas here on the board. Late autumn. Sunset. Dusk. Dawn. Midnight. Indian summer. That's a start. I'm going to choose midnight.

5 Next I consider what I think I know about midnight. What are some of its characteristics? Well, it's completely dark. It's quiet. My family is sleeping. The house makes sounds I don't hear during the day. It's hours until morning. I'm sleepy. Maybe I wake up and I don't know where I am at first. Then slowly I recognize I'm in my bed.

6 Obviously we don't have a lot of space to work with, but at this point I can create a first line: "Darkness like velvet." Check the syllable count. Five syllables. Perfect.

7 On to line two. Remember, this is the big line—we've got a whole two extra syllables to work with. Still going with ideas from my brainstorming, I want to amplify the phrase, "darkness like velvet," to say something I think is true about midnight. I go back to the idea of the strange noises a house sometimes makes late at night. What does that sound like? The refrigerator hums. The heating sometimes chugs or clicks. The old floors creak. I've got it now. "The house creaks, groans, like an old man." But wait a minute. It turns out I don't have it after all because now I've got eight syllables instead of seven. I could rewrite the whole line. But instead I'm just going to remove the word "like." I think that way is even better because then I don't use "like" twice within two lines. So far we have "Darkness like velvet. The house creaks, groans, an old man."

8 Now we can move on to line three. We have only five syllables to go. I want to end with something that either crystallizes the idea of midnight or says something a bit surprising, or both. How about: "Midnight, my good friend." Five syllables.

9 So now we have "Darkness like velvet / The house creaks, groans, an old man / Midnight, my good friend." So midnight becomes a creaking old man who turns out to be a friend.

10 If I keep at it, I'm sure I'll get better at writing haiku. Maybe now you will too. Seventeen syllables and an idea. That's really all it takes. Thank you.

Did you find these speeches effective? Did the expository speech explain all the aspects of caffeine consumption you expected it to? Did the second speech include all the steps in the process? Which one did you enjoy more? Which fulfilled its function better? Discuss these questions with your classmates.

Communication Notebook

Write a paragraph about an area of communication in which you feel you excel. Then write a second paragraph about a communication area in which you feel you could use improvement.

Evaluating Informative Speeches

The first and most important aspect of evaluating informative speeches is to listen to them carefully by:

- staying focused on the topic
- looking at the person who is speaking and trying to put yourself in his or her place. Empathy is important in making you a more active listener.

Also use such critical listening skills as the ones listed below.

Prepare to Listen

One effective way to ensure that you listen well is to prepare yourself for each listening experience. Seat yourself where you can see and hear. If you know the speaker's topic, ask yourself what you already know about it and what you would still like to know. Clear your mind of other thoughts so you can receive the message without barriers. Have paper and pen or pencil handy so you can take notes and jot down any questions you may have when the speech begins.

Listen for Main Idea and Supporting Details

One good focus technique is to actively listen for the speaker's main idea and the details that support that idea. Main ideas are usually signaled by key words and phrases, such as *first, a second point to remember, finally*. Supporting details are usually signaled by a different set of words and phrases, including *for example, in contrast, additionally, another*. Some listeners construct a mental outline of what a speaker is saying by listening for main ideas and identifying the details that support them.

Listening attentively goes a long way when trying to evaluate informative speeches.

Use Context Clues and Nonverbal Cues

Listen for other key words as well. Speakers usually clue you in when they are about to say something important. For example, the word *however* is a clue that the person is about to state an exception to whatever was just said. The word *although* prepares you to listen for information that the speaker will counter in some way. Speakers also give nonverbal cues. Sometimes a speaker will pause, clear his or her throat, or make eye contact with several people before making a point. Learn to pick up on these moments.

Make Predictions

Another way to keep your focus as a listener is to make predictions about where the speaker is headed. Whether your predictions end up being accurate or not doesn't really matter. Either way, you will listen more attentively.

Read Between the Lines

Making a speech is a collaboration between the speaker and the audience. Listeners make a nonverbal contract with the speaker, offering their attention and intelligence. The speaker, in turn, shares an idea. If listeners pay attention, they hear what is said, certainly, but they must interpret and read between the lines to get the most out of a speech. Ask yourself questions as you listen to a speech. What does he mean by that example? How does the anecdote the speaker just shared expand on the goal and purpose of her speech? This type of questioning allows you to construct meaning and remain an active participant in the listening process.

Offer Formal Critiques

Offering a critique of someone's speech is a good way to lock in your understanding and appreciation of it. You can provide either oral or written critiques. The evaluation form below can help you measure excellence in informative speaking.

Recognizing Excellence in Informative Speeches

	Needs Improvement	Satisfactory	Excellent
1. Audience analysis	• speech leaves many audience questions unanswered	• speech responds to audience's needs • speech is appropriate to audience's level of understanding	• speech anticipates needs of the audience, needs they might not even be aware of
2. Understanding of situation	• speech doesn't acknowledge the needs of the situation • speech is not appropriate for the situation	• speech responds adequately to the situation • speech is appropriate for the situation	• speech helps the audience understand the situation better
3. Purpose	• audience largely unaware of the importance of the topic	• audience understands the importance of the topic	• audience develops an appreciation for the speech topic
4. Substance and content	• audience confused about the information • audience receives no new information relevant to topic	• audience receives new information appropriate to the topic • audience understands information clearly	• audience receives new information that it highly values • audience understands the information well enough to pass it on to others
5. Introduction	• the introduction confuses the audience • the introduction fails to gain the audience's attention	• the introduction gains audience attention and focuses it on the topic	• the introduction creates enthusiasm for the topic

	Needs Improvement	Satisfactory	Excellent
6. Body	• the body of the speech is disjointed	• the body of the speech is organized for clarity	• the body of the speech is organized for clarity and facilitates understanding
7. Conclusion	• the conclusion of the speech leaves the audience uncertain	• the conclusion effectively wraps up the speech	• the conclusion effectively wraps up the speech and sustains audience interest and enthusiasm for the topic
8. Language	• the diction, syntax, mood, sentence patterns, and tone are inappropriate for the situation • the language is unclear • the language is unnecessarily wordy	• the diction, syntax, mood, sentence patterns, and tone are appropriate for the situation • the language is clear and economical	• the diction, syntax, mood, sentence patterns, and tone are strong and appropriate for the situation • the language is clear and economical • the language is graceful
9. Verbal delivery	• delivery does not flow smoothly • inadequate control of rate, inflection, pitch, volume, quality, and articulation	• delivery is fluent and easy to listen to • adequate control of rate, inflection, pitch, volume, quality, and articulation	• delivery is fluent and easy to listen to • excellent control of rate, inflection, pitch, volume, quality, and articulation • audience enjoys the delivery
10. Nonverbal delivery	• few meaningful gestures • poor posture • poor eye contact • little or no movement	• gestures, posture, eye contact and movement are appropriate for the situation	• in addition to being appropriate, gestures, posture, eye contact, and movement significantly contribute to speech's effect
11. Visual aids	• visual aids ineffective • visual aids inappropriate	• visual aids help audience understand the speech content	• visual aids significantly contribute to audience's understanding of the speech
12. Question and answer	• questions unanswered	• questions answered to audience satisfaction	• answers reinforce and extend the message

Begin your project by looking back at the **Project Prep** activities in this chapter and using the directions below.

Make Connections

Discuss with your partner your definition of informative speaking. Summarize these important points:

- the types of informative speeches
- how to consider audience and situation when preparing an informative speech
- the differences and similarities between expository speeches and process speeches.

Focus

Briefly review the group project you are working on: a presentation telling how to make or do something or how to follow a specific process.

Plan

Brainstorm ideas for your presentation with your partner. Come up with five strong possibilities. Choose the one you like best. Be sure the process can be explained in three minutes and that the audience will be able to repeat the process after hearing your speech.

Surefire Brainstorming

To get the best results from brainstorming:

- work cooperatively toward a goal
- don't judge ideas–just let them flow
- try looking at things in a fresh way
- build on ideas; try unlikely combinations.

Develop

Create note cards or an outline that you can follow during the presentation. Decide which parts of the speech will be delivered by each of you. Be sure you have a strong introduction, body, and conclusion. Also make sure to describe each step in the process clearly. Use visual aids that everyone can see or perform an easy-to-follow demonstration.

Practice

Practice your speech together until you feel that you will have no trouble presenting it. Ask someone to time you to be sure that you do not go over three minutes. If your demonstration is running long, decide what you can afford to cut. Then, practice again without that part. Be prepared to answer questions. Go over the CAPS guidelines on page 422 and the rubric on page 445.

PRESENTING THE PROJECT

Use the strategy that follows to help make your presentation as good as it can be.

Looking Your Best

When giving a speech, you don't want to worry about how you look. So spend a little time in advance thinking about how you would like to present yourself when speaking. You needn't dress up, but do dress appropriately, with your hair combed. Your presentation starts the moment you walk to the rostrum.

EVALUATING THE PROJECT

Evaluate the presentations using the following rubric.

Score the demonstration on each point, with 4 being "outstanding" and 1 being "needs much improvement."

Come up with an overall score and write a brief paragraph that explains your score.

Understanding of the Informative Speaking Process	Demonstration of the Informative Speaking Process	Creativity and Originality	Preparation and Use of Time
4 Presenters showed insight into the informative speaking process.	**4** Presenters' demonstration helped illuminate the informative speaking process.	**4** The presentation was attention-grabbing and unique, interesting, and fun.	**4** The presentation flowed smoothly and stayed within the time limit.
3 Presenters understood the informative speaking process.	**3** Presenters' demonstration was helpful in understanding the informative speaking process.	**3** The presentation was attention-grabbing, interesting, and fun, but not very original.	**3** The presentation progressed fairly smoothly and stayed within the time limit.
2 Presenters did not seem to understand some elements of the informative speaking process.	**2** Presenters' demonstration was minimally helpful in understanding the informative speaking process.	**2** The presentation was fairly interesting and fun, but not original or attention-grabbing.	**2** The presentation had a few awkward moments and went a bit over or noticeably under the time limit.
1 Presenters misunderstood much of the informative speaking process.	**1** Presenters' demonstration did not help in understanding the informative speaking process.	**1** The presentation was not original or attention-grabbing and only moderately fun and interesting.	**1** The presentation was not smoothly executed and went well over or under the time limit.

Communication *Past* and Present

The State of the Union Address

From George Washington . . .

On a cold January morning in 1790, George Washington rode in a horse-drawn carriage to Federal Hall in New York City. He was on his way to do what the new Constitution dictated he must—report to Congress about how things were going in the new nation.

> *The President shall from time to time give to Congress Information of the State of the Union and recommend to their Consideration such Measures as he shall judge necessary and expedient.*
>
> Constitution, Article II, Section 3

George Washington and his successor, John Adams, reported to Congress by delivering an informative speech. Thomas Jefferson, the third U.S. President, thought that making an oral presentation was too formal and kingly. So, in 1801, as President, he wrote a report and sent a copy to each house of Congress. For the next 112 years, all presidents followed Jefferson's example and presented written reports. Newspapers printed excerpts from the report so that the public could read what the President had to say.

George Washington

Woodrow Wilson

Woodrow Wilson revived the practice of making an oral address to Congress in 1913. When he did so, Theodore Roosevelt, who had been president from 1901–1909, is said to have complained that he wished he had thought of delivering the address in person.

The address—oral or written—was known as "the annual message to Congress" until Franklin Roosevelt used the phrase "State of the Union" in his 1935 speech, quoting the words of the U.S. Constitution. Since then, the annual message has been known as the "State of the Union address."

From George Washington on, presidents have used their message to Congress to outline national priorities and to present their legislative agenda. In his first address, Washington focused on the concept of union and made recommendations for the economy, education, and a uniform currency. In 1823, James Monroe used his seventh annual address to Congress to present the foreign policy known as the Monroe Doctrine, declaring that European powers were no longer to colonize the Americas or interfere with their affairs. Abraham Lincoln spoke to Congress in 1862 to express his desire that slaves be emancipated.

. . . to George W. Bush

In the 20th century, the State of the Union address became an informative speech delivered not only to Congress but also to the American people. In 1923, Calvin Coolidge's speech was the first to be broadcast on the radio, and the State of the Union address delivered in 1947 by Harry Truman was the first to be broadcast on television. In 1941, Franklin Roosevelt delivered a famous State of the Union, now popularly known as the "Four Freedoms" speech.

In the future days which we seek to make secure, we look forward to a world founded upon four essential human freedoms. The first is freedom of speech and expression—everywhere in the world. The second is freedom of every person to worship God in his own way—everywhere in the world. The third is freedom from want . . . everywhere in the world. The fourth is freedom from fear . . . anywhere in the world.

President Roosevelt was alerting Congress and the American people to the possibility of entering the war against Germany. His speech appealed to the American vision of a world in which freedom was shared by all.

In 2001, nine days after the terrorist attack on the World Trade Center and the Pentagon, George W. Bush delivered a special State of the Union address. He began by saying he did not need to report on the state of the Union because recent events had proven that the state of the Union was strong. Instead he used the speech to declare war on terrorism and express resolve to seek justice.

Harry Truman

George W. Bush

Chapter 20 Review

Using Vocabulary Words

Divide a box into four sections. In the top left box, write the word to be defined. In the top right box, draw an illustration of that word. In the bottom left box, give an example of the word. In the bottom right box, write the opposite of the word.

Word	Illustration
Example	Opposite

1. demonstration speech
2. diction
3. exposition
4. expository speech
5. informative speech
6. narration
7. process speech

Reviewing Key Ideas

1. What are the two main types of informative speeches?
2. Describe at least three kinds of expository speeches.
3. Explain why most process speeches use chronological order as their organizational pattern.
4. What are the three types of research sources available to speakers?

Reflecting on Your Project

With your partner, discuss which parts of your project went especially well and which gave you the most trouble. Come up with two or three strategies for dealing with trouble spots in future projects.

Responding to the Essential Question

Use the headings in this chapter to help you write a brief chapter summary that answers the question, "How can you make speeches to inform as effective as possible?" Compare your summary with that of a classmate and discuss any discrepancies in the two interpretations.

Extending Your Understanding

Everyday Life

1. As a student, you are frequently the audience for informative speeches from your teachers. List the speeches (or lectures) you've heard in the past two weeks. Use the list of types of informative speeches to classify them.
2. Teachers frequently attend training sessions, many of which are made up of one or more informative speeches. Get permission from your teacher to attend a portion of the training. Take notes and evaluate the presentation.
3. Present an ideal informative three- to five-minute speech in which you explain how to analyze situation, purpose, and audience to select appropriate methods in public speaking.

In the Media

4. Watch a television program designed to inform the audience. Examples include shows about cooking, crafts, home design, and gardening. What do the hosts do to increase the effectiveness of their informative presentations? What can you as a speaker learn from them? Discuss your findings in small groups.

5. Listen to a radio news program and write down each example of an informative speaking technique you hear. Look for object informative speaking, place informative speaking, person informative speaking, event informative speaking, and idea informative speaking. Note which organizational patterns are used and whether the language is lively and interesting. Write a review of the news show and rate it in terms of at least five categories.

Research

6. Using an Internet search engine, research speeches from recent political campaigns. Find one you think is particularly compelling. Copy the speech and annotate its various features. Prepare a display, with illustrations, of your annotated speech and share it with your class. Be prepared to explain why you felt it especially compelling.

7. Find a well-known informational speech from history. Research to find out the situation in which the speech was delivered. What was happening in history and society at the time? Using this information and any pertinent quotes from the speech, write an essay on why you believe the speech affected the audience the way it did.

Interpreting Graphics

Copy the model below on a separate sheet of paper. Make the circles large enough to allow you to write in them. Fill in the circles with examples of the different types of support needed for informative speeches.

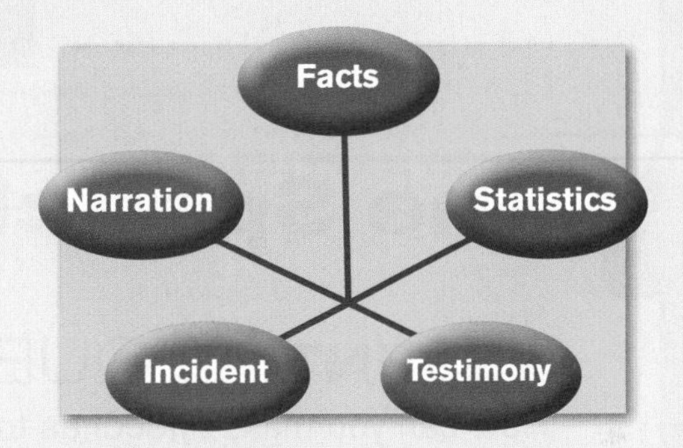

Additional Projects

1. **Group Project:** Have a panel discussion in which you and a small group of classmates identify topics that you believe people need to be informed about. Before the discussion select your topics. Use the discussion, to explain why your group made the choices it did. Identify an appropriate audience for each topic and give reasons why that audience would particularly benefit.

2. **Individual Project:** Create a poster to illustrate an idea for a speech about a simple process, such as burning a CD, making a hot fudge sundae, or ironing a shirt. Make sure you choose a process that you are very familiar with. You can use a process diagram, a flowchart, or any other graphic presentation of your idea. Letter your poster clearly and use drawings or photographs to decorate and/or clarify the action of the process. Display and discuss your finished poster in class.

The Speech to Persuade

ESSENTIAL QUESTION

How can you make speeches to persuade as effective as possible?

Chapter Project: The Triple Play

Have you ever been committed to a cause that you wanted others to become involved in also? Presenting a solid, persuasive argument can change minds and hearts, and move people to action.

For this project, you will work in a group of three to make persuasive appeals on a simple topic. One person will spend a minute offering an appeal based on logic; another will present a one-minute appeal based on emotion; and the third will give a one-minute appeal based on ethics or credibility. The entire presentation should take no more than three or four minutes. Refer to the CAPS guidelines below as you work.

The rubric on page 473 shows the traits on which your presentation will be evaluated.

Concept	persuasive appeals come in three basic varieties
Audience	classmates and teacher
Purpose	understand and use the three kinds of persuasive appeal
Situation	cooperative classroom demonstration

Who is persuading in this picture?

KEY VOCABULARY

- persuasion
- motivation
- syllogism
- fallacy
- false syllogism
- slippery slope
- hasty generalization
- post hoc ergo propter hoc
- ad hominem
- bandwagon
- circular reasoning
- red herring
- motivated sequence

Speak Up!

When do you use persuasion? Think of times when you have attempted to persuade a friend, family member, teacher, coworker, or classmate to change his or her mind about something. Repeat in one or two sentences the persuasive argument you used—for example: "Can I please stay at my friend's house past curfew? Her parents will be there the whole time." Share your sentences with a classmate. Did you find one another persuasive? Why or why not? Discuss your responses with the class.

Pages 452–470 will provide the information you'll need to complete this project.

Persuasion

If you have ever tried to convince your parents to let you go on a trip, you've used **persuasion,** a form of communication that tries to change attitudes, opinions, or behaviors. A persuasive speech might focus on a proposition of fact, value, problem, or policy (see page 235).

Persuasive, or argumentative, public speaking can be demanding, especially if your audience may disagree with you. In this chapter you'll learn how good speakers can persuade even resistant audiences.

Situation and Persuasion

Preparing a good persuasive speech requires that you understand the audience and the situation. To persuade others to change, you must understand their circumstances from *their* point of view. If your audience thinks you lack empathy for them, you will never get them to change their minds or their actions.

Purpose and Persuasion

Convince, defend, encourage, motivate, discourage, support: These words signify an intent to change the attitudes and/or the behavior of others. For example, when you *encourage*, you try to build positive feelings and get people to act on those feelings. To *discourage*, you attempt to make them leave behind an attitude or behavior. When delivering a persuasive speech, you often work from a purpose statement in which you use many of the words listed above. Below are a few examples.

- The purpose of this speech is to *support* the proposal to upgrade our existing computers.
- The purpose of this speech is to *convince* drivers to wear seatbelts.
- The purpose of this speech is to *discourage* the school board from cutting funding to our school's arts programs.

"I can't give you a raise Kimble, but your speech was so convincing I'm transferring you to our sales dept."

Explain whether a persuasive speech can be effective even if it does not achieve its goal.

Audience Motivation and Persuasion

In some instances, persuasion is about **motivation**, the forces that cause people to act certain ways. If you want to persuade people, you have to understand what motivates them. If you were an advertiser promoting a new hybrid car, you would use information and ideas to motivate buyers to choose your hybrid. The chart below identifies some common ways that companies market cars.

Motivating Factors for Car Buyers	
An ad about fuel economy shows how to save money.	The advertiser expects the audience to be motivated by the *economics* of buying a car that *saves money.*
An ad about luxury stresses the comfort of the car.	The advertiser expects the audience to be motivated by a *desire for comfort.*
An ad showing the car on a race track displays the car's speed and power.	The advertiser expects the audience to be motivated by a *need for excitement.*
An ad showing a family driving and camping reflects the fun they can have with the car.	The advertiser expects the audience to be motivated by a *sense of family values and togetherness.*

What motives could an advertiser appeal to in trying to sell this model of car?

You may recall Maslow's hierarchy of human needs (see page 251). Maslow's theory holds that humans must have their most basic needs met before they can respond to higher order needs. It's a theory that persuasive speakers can make good use of. In the model below, the basic needs (physiological and safety) are followed by the higher order needs (social, esteem, self-actualization).

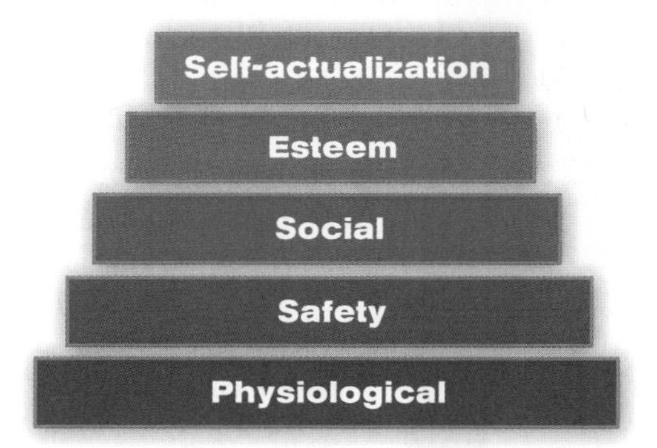

Imagine that you are speaking to the school board about funding new computers at your school. New computers might not seem related to students' physiological needs. However, you might convince the board that updating the computers will help students get jobs and earn money that will provide them food and shelter. If you do, then you've accomplished your mission. You can also persuade the board by appealing to higher order needs. For example, newer computers might create even better training, which could lead to higher-status jobs. These jobs could solidify the graduates' esteem and lead to self-actualization, for them and the school board.

No matter which needs you appeal to, when you speak persuasively, your goal remains the same. You want to motivate your audience to change their minds or their behavior.

Now imagine you are giving a speech about the benefits of using seat belts. If your goal is to persuade others to use seat belts, you will have to understand the issue from their perspective. Your research may indicate that a person who uses a seat belt and is injured in a car accident will have medical expenses two thousand dollars lower than those of a person who doesn't wear a seat belt. You may see this cost savings as an excellent reason for changing behavior. But the speech isn't about *you*. The speech is about your *audience*. These facts may not motivate them. They may think, "I'm insured. I won't have to pay the bill."

Do you find this ad for using a seat belt persuasive?

A friendly smile can help a person be persuasive.

A different approach may work better. Perhaps an emotional description of a family's tragedy when the father is thrown through the windshield because he isn't wearing a seat belt will have greater impact. Any time you are trying to make a persuasive appeal, be aware of your audience's beliefs and attitudes.

Analyze Your Audience

To succeed at persuasive speaking, align yourself with your audience as much as possible. Never approach them as adversaries to be overwhelmed. Some audiences will be more supportive than others, but never count on winning over everyone in the audience. Your goal is simply to win over as many of them as possible. Audiences typically fall into four general categories: supportive, neutral, indifferent, or hostile. Most audiences are made up of a blend of these.

The Supportive Audience

Most speakers enjoy talking to supportive audiences—they are predisposed to like what you have to say. Imagine you are a candidate delivering a speech at a fundraising dinner for your election. The crowd is predisposed in favor of your address—because they paid to be there. As a persuasive speaker, your job is half done, since your audience is supportive. Your main goal then becomes to make your listeners even more enthusiastic about you and your goals. Supportive audiences need less information than other types of audiences because they have already bought in to your idea. Still, it's important speak with vigor. Even the most supportive audiences don't like to be taken for granted.

PROJECT PREP

With your **project group**, discuss experiences you have had as part of a supportive audience. How did the speaker use the audience's supportive energy?

Neutral Audience

A neutral audience is one that has no strong belief about your idea one way or the other. They are not on your side the way a supportive audience is; however, they aren't against you either. They are potentially very good listeners, but they still need to be convinced. Think about courtroom dramas you have seen. The jurors are neutral, unbiased listeners who try to weigh the evidence fairly. Each lawyer tries to persuade the jurors to view the evidence a certain way. That is also *your* job as a persuasive speaker.

Persuasive speakers love a supportive audience.

Indifferent Audience

The term "captive audience" refers to an audience that has no choice but to listen to the speaker. Chances are that most captive audiences are indifferent; they didn't choose to hear this speaker and they don't care what he or she has to say. Naturally, an indifferent audience is not ideal for a persuasive speaker because they are hard to motivate. As a speaker, your job is to grab their attention and draw them in. Conveying why the topic is personally significant—to yourself and to your audience—is one way to connect with the audience at a fundamental level. Only by engaging them will you be able to move them beyond their apathy.

What can a speaker do facing an audience such as this one?

Knowing as much as you can about the attitudes and beliefs of your audience will help you develop the most effective persuasive appeals.

Hostile Audience

The audience that is the most difficult to persuade is the one that rejects your point of view. A hostile audience is against you, what you have to say, or both. Most speakers will tell you that all they want from a hostile audience is a fair hearing—and even that is often hard to achieve.

To manage a hostile audience, try to find out where their objection lies. Are they opposed to your subject matter or do they simply not like you and what you stand for? If you can determine the cause of their hostility, you can try to neutralize their objections and get them to lower their listening barriers. The most effective way to do this is to show them that you're willing to compromise. Assure them that you know you don't have all the answers but that you need their support. Let them know you see some merit in their point of view—or at least that you understand why they feel the way they do. Avoid unnecessary confrontation, and use humor to ease tensions.

PROJECT PREP

With your **project group**, discuss the situations in which an audience might be hostile to the speaker. Can you think of other effective techniques a speaker might use in order to be heard by a hostile audience?

Persuasion and Ethics

Ethics is the understanding of right and wrong. As a speaker attempting to persuade others to change their attitudes and behavior, you need good motives and strong ethical values.

History provides a long list of leaders who used their speaking skills to deceive others. Some leaders persuaded people to do things they knew were wrong. Some believed that to gain the result they sought, any means were acceptable, even deceit and manipulation. Adolf Hitler is the twentieth century's leading example of a powerful but unethical speaker who persuaded vast numbers of people to carry out monstrous acts.

On a smaller scale, a speaker's ethical stance often rests on the day-to-day right and wrong of buying and selling or self-promotion. How can a speaker check his or her own ethics? Use the chart on this page to help answer that question.

An ethical speaker will admit when he has made a mistake.

Persuasive Appeals Based on Reason: Logos

A rational appeal is a speaker's attempt to change attitudes and behavior by using clear and well-reasoned thinking. The ancient Greeks' word for appeals to reason was *logos*. Along with ethos and pathos, logos is one of three modes of persuasion used in classical Greek rhetoric (see, page 140). A speaker using a rational appeal targets the intellect and thinking of the audience. How can you change the way someone thinks? Some workable approaches follow on the next page.

Ethics Check	
What are my motives?	Does my audience understand my motives?
Why am I trying to persuade the audience?	Am I telling the truth?
Am I comfortable with my own motivation?	Am I exploiting prejudice to accomplish my goal?
Am I proud of what I am saying?	Am I willing to accept the consequences of everything I am saying?
Do I have an obligation to present the "other side" of the argument and can I represent it accurately?	Am I omitting important information that the audience needs to know to make a good choice?

New Information

If your audience lacks information, you'll need to provide them with that information and explain it in a way that shows the topic in a new light. Imagine, for example, that you are trying to convince the student council at your school to organize an Internet campaign to attract people to the school's upcoming fundraising event. In the past, the student council has always used posters and flyers. The other members are dubious about your idea because they haven't used the Internet for promotional purposes in the past. So, you might gather new information that will show the Internet's effectiveness for this type of mass-marketing effort. You might share quotations about groups that raised an events' attendance numbers by 50 percent after posting on an Internet message board. That information might change some minds about Internet promotion because the members have a motive: to make sure as many potential attendees as possible find out about the event.

New Context for Old Information

Maybe your fellow council members already have this information. How can you get them to think about it differently? If they already know that Internet posting can bring in more people, they might need to be shown what that means. Have them see the information in a new context. For example, you might break it down in terms of dollars and cents. The admission fee is $5 per person. Last year, three hundred people attended the event and it made $1,500. But if six hundred people attend this year, the school stands to make $3,000—twice as much money.

TechConnect You might also bring up that people who look for things to do on the Internet can do so at their convenience any time of the day or night. People who see a poster in a store window or grab a flyer from the windshield won't find out much about the organization hosting the event—in this case, your school. However, when they see an Internet posting, they can click on a link to the school's Web site and access more details. By offering the information in a new context, you will help council members make a more thoughtful decision.

TechConnect *People can find out about an event any time of the night or day on the Internet.*

You might persuade people to post information on the Internet just by reminding them of the advantages of this form of communication.

Logic

Logic is the structure of reasoning. If you structure your arguments soundly, you can lead your audience to sound conclusions. Think about the following rational appeal which uses a logical structure common in mathematics (if *a* is true, and *b* is true, then *c* must also be true). This construction is called a **syllogism**, a tool for reasoning by which a conclusion follows from premises.

Premise 1:
People who use the Internet regularly at home are likely to be financially comfortable.

Premise 2:
People who are financially comfortable are in a position to make donations.

Logical Conclusion:
Therefore, advertising on the Internet is a reasonable way to reach likely donors.

The logic of these three statements is compelling. That is, if you can convince the council the first statement is true (and it is almost inarguable, since there is a cost involved), and if you can convince them that the second statement is true (and you can show that from studies or surveys about charitable giving), then the third statement is also true. From that conclusion, it's a short jump to "We should use the Internet more to recruit guests at fundraisers, because those guests are likely to become donors."

Logical Fallacies

Speeches may sometimes contain a logical **fallacy**, a statement that sounds logical but is not true. As a speaker, you should learn to avoid fallacies. As a listener, you should know how to recognize them. Eight common types of fallacies are the **false syllogism**, **slippery slope**, **hasty generalization**, **post hoc ergo propter hoc**, **ad hominem**, **bandwagon**, **circular reasoning**, and **red herring**. See the definitions and examples of each in the chart on next page.

Logical Fallacies

Type	Description	Example
False syllogism	a fallacy in which two true statements are put together to reach a false conclusion	True: Crows are black. True: Crows are birds. False syllogism: Therefore all birds are black. (Although the premises are true, the conclusion does not follow logically from them.)
Slippery slope	a fallacy in which a proposed course of action is presented as leading inevitably (but illogically) to a particular conclusion	"If you relax the dress code at all, you can forget about having any dress code at all." (Relaxing one part of the dress code does not inevitably lead to other changes.)
Hasty generalization	a fallacy in which a conclusion about an entire population is drawn using too small a sample; also called overgeneralization	"Everyone is staying healthier longer these days. My grandfather is 92 and he works every day." (Just because your grandfather is healthy doesn't mean everyone is.)
Post hoc ergo propter hoc	a fallacy of questionable, or false, causation (*A* happened, then *B* happened, so *B* must have been caused by *A*.)	"People who go outside without a coat will catch a cold. I've seen it happen time and time again." (Just because a person goes outside without a coat does not mean that doing so results in catching a cold. Colds are caused by germs.)
Ad hominem	a fallacy in which a person replies to a factual claim by attacking a belief or characteristic of the person who made the claim	"My opponent accuses me of being elitist and ignoring ordinary working Americans, but it might surprise you to know that he actually went to Harvard."
Bandwagon	a fallacy built on the idea that because a lot of people think something is true, it must be	"Millions of teenagers share copyrighted images and music, so there's nothing illegal about that."
Circular reasoning	a fallacy in which an idea is just repeated in different terms rather than proved	"Sports stars are overpaid because their incomes are greater than their worth."
Red herring	a fallacy that attempts to divert attention from the real issues by interjecting a related topic	"The defendant is guilty. Crime is out of control here." (Crime rate has nothing to do with the guilt or innocence of the defendant.)

Evidence

Just about any persuasive argument relies on some form of evidence. You will recall three basic kinds of evidence discussed in chapter 15:

- **Facts** Audiences respond well to evidence that is factual. In general, audiences are most comfortable with information that can be proved.
- **Testimony** Using another person's words as evidence for your claims can be useful. This is a good technique when you (1) don't have much firsthand information on your subject, (2) feel your audience might doubt your credibility, or (3) are speaking to a hostile audience.
- **Statistics** Presenting numbers as evidence can be effective, provided you obtain your statistics through careful research and present the information clearly and honestly.

Persuasive Appeals Based on Credibility: Ethos

In earlier chapters, you learned about credibility, what the Greeks called *ethos*. If you and your sources are seen as credible, the audience is likely to believe what you say. An audience probably won't trust what you say if they don't trust you personally. The following characteristics are strong factors in persuading an audience.

- In the past, the speaker or source has been proven right about similar issues.
- In the past, the speaker or source has provided reliable information.
- The speaker or source has been shown to have the audience's best interests in mind.
- The speaker or source has the type of information that is the basis for a good decision.

Once you have established yourself as a credible speaker, you will still have to provide some motive for people to accept your ideas. It is a rare speaker who can persuade people on personal credibility alone. You can, however, borrow credibility. You might not be an authority on the subject, but if you can quote someone who is, that person's credibility can help you persuade your audience.

Persuasive speaking using logic and credibility can be highly effective, but there is a third strategy that can also help persuade audiences: an appeal to their emotions.

Persuasive Appeals Based on Emotion: Pathos

The Greeks knew well that emotions play an important role in attitudes and behaviors. Their third mode of persuasion, *pathos*, calls these emotions into play. Logic often won't overcome fear or anxiety, nor will honesty. People who are afraid can't absorb statistics or honest appraisals. A good persuasive speaker knows that appealing to human emotion can alter an individual's thinking.

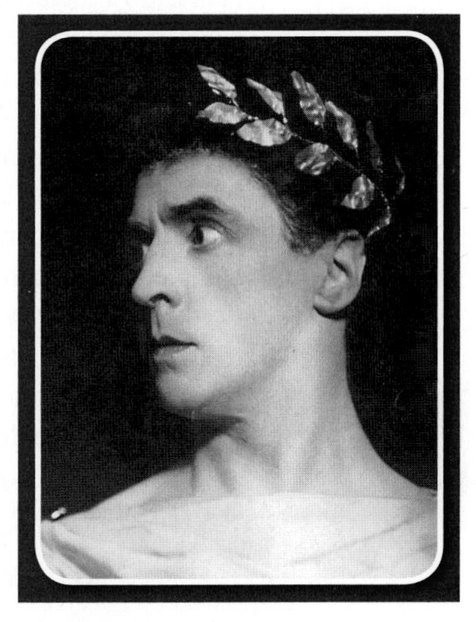

The word pathos *can be translated as "instructive suffering." Ancient Greek drama was, in part, intended to persuade audiences to follow the right path.*

Appeal to Pride

Pride is a powerful motivator. Sometimes a speaker can use the audience's sense of pride to help change their minds and behavior. For example, if your fellow student council members remain reluctant to use the Internet to advertise your fundraising event, you might appeal to their pride to convince them. By showing that other top-rated schools use the Internet for the same basic types of promotion, you can illustrate for them that Internet advertising could make your school appear more competitive. Your fellow council members will feel they are part of an organization and an event they can be proud of.

Appeal to Fear

Fear is another powerful motivating emotion. Think about fear in terms of Maslow's hierarchy. If an audience believes they have something to lose—safety, self-esteem, social standing—fear becomes a motive. However, if you are successful in causing the audience to respond emotionally, you risk having the intended response veer off course. It could even spin completely out of control. Unlike logic, fear can cause people to react irrationally. Using fear as a persuasive device can lead to an audience response you never anticipated.

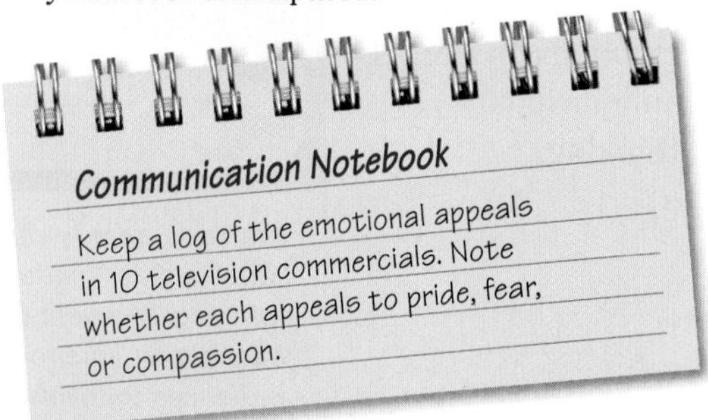

Appeal to Compassion

Compassion—empathy for the condition of others—is one of the best motivators. Many charities appeal to compassion to generate contributions. Often, a speaker can build compassion with specific stories or descriptions of other people's problems. For example, a speaker trying to persuade the audience to donate to hurricane victims might focus on the lives and daily struggles of a single particularly hard-hit family.

Persuasive speakers use appeals to credibility, reason, and emotion.

Appeals to compassion helped raise funds for victims of Hurricane Katrina.

Organizing the Persuasive Speech

One of the best ways to organize a persuasive speech is the **motivated sequence**, a five-step speaking process developed by speech professors Alan Monroe and Douglas Ehninger. It uses a problem-solution method to organize information. Read the steps below.

The Motivated Sequence

1. **The Attention Step.** Start with an effective introduction to get the listener's attention. For more detailed information on writing a good introduction, see Chapter 16.
2. **The Need Step.** Let the audience know that the problem is *their* problem. Give them a good reason for adopting new opinions and behaviors. Using Maslow's hierarchy, ask which type of need will get them to respond personally to the problem. You will use appeals based on logic, credibility, and emotion. Developing the substance of the need step is covered in Chapter 18.
3. **The Satisfaction Step.** Once you've identified the audience's need, clarify how you will help them change their attitude or behavior. This often means you will share your plan for what they can do to bring about that change.
4. **The Visualization Step.** With this step you show how the proposed solution to the problem will work. This is where you explain how your proposal will reduce or eliminate their problem.
5. **The Action Step.** Finally, tell your listeners how to apply the solution. This is where you make your pitch to vote a certain way, buy a particular product, or write a letter of support. Encourage the audience to feel personally responsible for the solution. The action step empowers them to go forward with the plan on their own.

There is some overlap between the motivated sequence and John Dewey's problem-solving method, which you first learned about in Chapter 8. See the chart below.

Dewey's Steps Compared to Motivated Sequence

Problem-Solving Steps	What Each Step Does	Motivated Sequence Step
1. Identify Felt Difficulty	Determines that there is a problem	Attention Step
2. Define Problem	Focuses on the scope of the problem–its causes and effects	Need Step
3. Propose Solutions	Lists the number of possible ways to solve the problem	Satisfaction Step
4. Evaluate/Select Solution	Chooses the best solution	Visualization Step
5. Act on Solution	Takes steps to see that the solution is turned into action	Action Step

Analyzing the Characteristics of Persuasive Speech

Analyze the following speech, "Responding to Land Mines: A Modern Tragedy and Its Solutions," by Princess Diana of Wales. She delivered it on June 12, 1997.

1 Ladies and Gentlemen, I must begin by saying how warmly I welcome this conference on land mines convened by the Mines Advisory Group and the Landmines Survivors Network. It is so welcome because the world is too little aware of the waste of life, limb and land which anti-personnel land mines are causing among some of the poorest people on earth. Indeed, until my journey to Angola early this year—on which I am going to speak this morning—I was largely unaware of it too.

Introduction

Purpose statement

2 For the mine is a stealthy killer. Long after conflict is ended, its innocent victims die or are wounded singly, in countries of which we hear little. Their lonely fate is never reported. The world, with its many other preoccupations, remains largely unmoved by a death roll of something like 800 people every month—many of them women and children. Those who are not killed outright—and they number another 1,200 a month—suffer terrible injuries and are handicapped for life. I was in Angola in January with the British Red Cross—a country where there are 15 million land mines in a population, Ladies and Gentlemen, of 10 million—with the desire of drawing world attention to this vital, but hitherto largely neglected issue.

Body text

Appeal based on credibility

3 Some people chose to interpret my visit as a political statement. But it was not. I am not a political figure. As I said at the time, and I'd like to reiterate now, my interests are humanitarian. That is why I felt drawn to this human tragedy. This is why I wanted to play down my part in working towards a world-wide ban on these weapons. During my days in Angola, I saw at first hand three aspects of this scourge. In the hospitals of Luanda, the capital, and Huambo, scene of bitter fighting not long ago, I visited some of the mine victims who had survived, and saw their injuries. I am not going to describe them, because in my experience it turns too many people away from the subject. Suffice to say, that when you look at the mangled bodies, some of them children, caught by these mines, you marvel at their survival. What is so cruel about these injuries is that

Princess Diana

they are almost invariably suffered where medical resources are scarce.

4 I observed for myself some of the obstacles to improving medical care in most of these hospitals. Often there is a chronic shortage of medicine, of pain killers, even of anaesthetics. Surgeons constantly engaged in amputating shattered limbs, never have all the facilities we would expect to see here. So the human pain that has to be borne is often beyond imagining. This emergency medical care, moreover, is only the first step back to a sort of life. For those whose living is the land, loss of an arm or leg is an overwhelming handicap which lasts for life. I saw the fine work being done by the Red Cross and other agencies to replace lost limbs. But making prostheses is a costly as well as a complicated business. For example, a young child will need several different fittings as it grows older. Sometimes, the severity of the injury makes the fitting of an artificial limb impossible. There are never enough resources to replace all the limbs that are lost.

Rational appeal

Princess Diana met with land mine victims in Angola.

5 In Angola, one in every 334 members of the population is an amputee! Angola has the highest rate of amputees in the world. How can countries which manufacture and trade in these weapons square their conscience(s) with such human devastation? My third main experience was to see what has been done, slowly and perilously, to get these mines out of the earth. . . . Much ingenuity has gone into making some of these mines. Many are designed to trap an unwary de-miner. Whenever such tricky mines appear, the de-miner will call in one of the supervising team, who will then take over. That is what keeps their lives perpetually at risk. It might be less hazardous, I reflected, after my visit to Angola, if some of the technical skills used in making mines had been applied to better methods of removing them. Many of these mines are relatively cheap—they can be bought for 5 pounds apiece, or less. Tracing them, lifting them, and disposing of them, costs far more—sometimes as much as a hundred times more. Angola is full of refugees returning after a long war. They present another aspect of this tragedy. The refugee turns towards home, often ignorant of conditions in his homeland. He knows of mines, but homeward bound, eagerness to complete the journey gets the better of him. Or he finds mines on what was once his land, and attempts to clear them. There were many examples of that in Angola. These mines inflict most of their casualties on people who are trying to meet the elementary needs of life. They strike the wife, or the grandmother,

Emotional appeal

A pound is the British unit of currency. At the time of the speech, one pound was worth about $1.63.

gathering firewood for cooking—they ambush the child sent to collect water for the family.

6 I was impressed to see the work being done by many of the world's agencies on "Mine Awareness." If children can be taught at school, if adults can be helped to learn what to do, and what not to do in regions that have been mined, then lives can be saved and injuries reduced. . . . Even if the world decided tomorrow to ban these weapons, this terrible legacy of mines already in the earth would continue to plague the poor nations of the Globe. "The evil that men do, lives after them." And so, it seems to me, there rests a certain obligation upon the rest of us. One of my objectives in visiting Angola was to forward the cause of those, like the Red Cross, striving in the name of humanity to secure an international ban on these weapons. Since then, we are glad to see, some real progress has been made. There are signs of a change of heart—at least in some parts of the world. For that we should be cautiously grateful. If an international ban on mines can be secured it means, looking far ahead, that the world may be a safer place for this generation's grandchildren. But for this generation in much of the developing world, there will be no relief, no relaxation. The toll of deaths and injuries caused by mines already there will continue.

Satisfaction Step

7 This tracing and lifting of mines, as I saw in Angola, is a desperately slow business. So in my mind a central question remains. Should we not do more to quicken the de-miners' work, to help the injured back to some sort of life, to further our own contribution to aid and development?

Conclusion

8 The country is enriched by the work done by its overseas agencies and nongovernmental organizations who work to help people in Africa and Asia to improve the quality of their lives. Yet mines cast a constant shadow over so much of this work. Resettlement of refugees is made more hazardous. Good land is put out of bounds. Recovery from war is delayed. Aid workers themselves are put at risk. I would like to see more done for those living in this "no man's land" which lies between the wrongs of yesterday and the urgent needs of today.

9 I think we owe it. I also think it would be of benefit to us, as well as to them. The more expeditiously we can end this plague on earth caused by the land mine, the more readily can we set about the constructive tasks to which so many give their hand in the cause of humanity.

Wearing protective armour, Princess Diana visited sites being cleared of land mines.

Presenting Your Persuasive Speech

When speaking to an audience—no matter what type of speech you are making—you need to use certain basic public speaking techniques. Many of the techniques you learned about in Chapter 20 on informative speaking apply to persuasive speaking as well as to other kinds of speeches.

Gain Command of Your Information

Have the facts of the issue well in hand so you will appear—and actually be—credible. Use proper research techniques and citations. Organize your speech logically and know it well enough that you can look up from your notes and make eye contact with your audience.

Use Language Clearly and Appropriately

When speaking persuasively, get your point across clearly and concisely. Here are a few simple techniques that can help you.

- Vary your sentence length. Inserting an occasional very short sentence, or even a phrase, can give your speech impact and punch.
- Use pauses for dramatic effect or to let a particular idea sink in.
- Use sensory language that helps the audience visualize and mentally experience your ideas.
- Avoid loaded language, or word choices tinged with emotional bias. The student council members might tune you out completely if you said that not using the Internet to advertise was "irresponsible," which carries a strong negative judgment. Saying it is "ineffective" is less harsh.

When listening to your persuasive speech, the audience will note how you dress and behave.

Use Nonverbal Strategies

Use movement wisely, avoiding excessive moves and mugging. Maintain eye contact and stand up straight. Dress appropriately. If you are making an emotional appeal, let your facial expression, movements, stance, and gestures reflect your feelings.

Interact in a Lively Way with Listeners

Be aware of any signs of confusion in the audience. Puzzled expressions, questioning looks, or shaking heads alert you that you are not hitting the target. Stay in the moment so that you can respond effectively and provide clarification when needed.

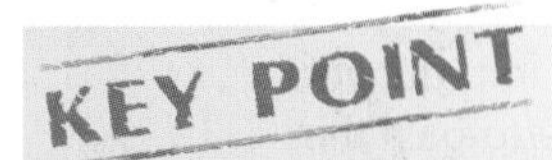

An effective delivery supports your ideas with appropriate language, thoughtful nonverbal communication, and animated interaction with the audience.

Evaluating Persuasive Speeches

To improve your own public speaking, pay attention to the public speaking of others. An evaluation form can help you appreciate the qualities of a good persuasive speech.

Recognizing Excellence in Persuasive Speeches

	Needs improvement	Satisfactory	Excellent
Audience analysis	• speech leaves many audience questions unanswered	• speech responds to audience's needs • speech matches audience's level of understanding	• speech anticipates needs of the audience, needs they might not even be aware of
Understanding of situation	• speech doesn't acknowledge the needs of the situation • speech is not appropriate for the situation	• speech responds adequately to the situation • speech is appropriate for the situation	• speech helps the audience understand the situation better
Purpose	• audience is not sure what is being asked of them	• audience thoroughly understands what is being asked of them	• audience develops appreciation for the speech topic
Substance/content	• audience is confused about the information being told them	• audience understands information clearly	• audience receives new information or old information in a helpful new context • audience grasps the information well enough to pass it on to others
Introduction	• the introduction confuses the audience • the introduction fails to gain the audience's attention	• the introduction gains audience attention and focuses it on the topic	• the introduction creates enthusiasm for the topic

	Needs improvement	Satisfactory	Excellent
Body	• the body of the speech is disjointed	• the body of the speech is organized for clarity	• the body of the speech is organized clearly and facilitates understanding and memory
Conclusion	• the conclusion of the speech leaves the audience uncertain	• the conclusion effectively wraps up the speech	• the conclusion effectively wraps up the speech and sustains audience interest and enthusiasm in topic
Language	• the language is inappropriate for the situation • the language is unclear • the language is unnecessarily wordy	• the language is clear and economical	• the language is clear and economical • the language is graceful
Verbal delivery	• delivery does not flow smoothly	• delivery is fluent and easy to listen to	• delivery is fluent and easy to listen to • audience enjoys the delivery
Nonverbal delivery	• few meaningful gestures • poor posture • poor eye contact • little or no movement	• gestures, posture, eye contact, and movement are appropriate for situation	• gestures, posture, eye contact, and movement contribute significantly to the overall effect
Visual aids	• visual aids ineffective • visual aids inappropriate	• visual aids help audience understand the speech content	• visual aids contribute significantly to audience's understanding of the speech
Question and answer	• questions left unanswered	• questions answered to audience satisfaction	• answers actually reinforce and extend the speech's message

Communication in a DIVERSE WORLD

Global Persuasion

You know that there are many different kinds of persuasive tactics, but are some better than others? The answer depends on where in the world you are. Research shows that many cultures favor certain persuasive tactics over others.

In the United States, one of the most popular forms of persuasion operates on the principle of *reciprocation,* or *reciprocity*. People obligate themselves to one another in terms of favors done and returned. This form of persuasion operates on the principle that, "If you do me a favor, then I owe you a favor." This is why you get "free samples," or why salespeople will often begin a pitch with, "What can I do for you?" Eventually, of course, they want to get to what the customer can do for them: buy a product or service.

In many Asian cultures the power of persuasion to a large extent turns on the concept of *authority*. This means that "the voice of the expert" rules in persuasive encounters. The person making a persuasive request is likely to get satisfaction provided he or she is closely connected to an authority of some kind–or is the authority.

In Spain and Latin America, the most powerful form of persuasion tends to be based on the concept of *liking*. In other words, people are most easily persuaded by those they like or those they feel are most like them. They also tend to support persuasive messages that make them feel that they play a vital role in the success or failure of the transaction or endeavor.

In Germany, people have a tendency to favor persuasive tactics that place *consistency* and fairness above other values. They are also more likely to respond to persuasive appeals that refer to rules and regulations–whether written or implied.

None of these persuasive methods is the "right" one. Each of them can be highly effective depending on the audience, the situation, and the place.

PREPARING THE PROJECT

Begin your project by looking back at the **Project Prep** activities in this chapter and using the directions below.

Make Connections

Discuss with your group how your understanding of persuasion may have changed as you read pages 452–470. Discuss and summarize these important points:

- the types of persuasion you use every day
- the similarities and differences between persuasion and other types of speaking
- the four types of audiences
- the ethical issues in persuasive speaking
- the motivated sequence.

Focus

Briefly review individual and group aspects of the project you are working on: "The Triple Play" presentation demonstrating three different types of persuasive appeal.

Plan

Work collaboratively to select a topic for your presentation. You might choose a product, such as a new energy drink. Or you could decide to speak about a charity or relief organization. As you discuss potential topics, keep the following questions in mind:

- Are there ethical problems associated with this product or organization?
- Will this product or organization work as the topic for all three appeals?
- Who would be the ideal audience for this presentation?
- In what circumstance might you deliver an appeal for this topic?
- Do you need to do any research on this topic?
- How do you want your audience to change as a result of your presentation? Would you like them to (1) think or believe as you do, (2) change their existing attitude about your topic, or (3) take action such as buying a product, donating money, or supporting a cause?

Decide which person will deliver each type of appeal. Discuss each type of appeal in detail as it relates to your topic.

Surefire Transitions

In this project, you work with two other people to deliver a cohesive three-way presentation. To bridge the three sections, you will need to create transitions to maintain the flow of the presentation and keep the audience engaged. You can create bridges using one of these techniques:

- Speaker one, upon finishing his or her speech, introduces speaker two. Speaker two delivers his or her part and introduces speaker three.
- Speaker one introduces the overall presentation, and introduces and presents the logical appeal. Speaker two then introduces and delivers the appeal to credibility. Speaker three introduces and delivers the emotional appeal. Speaker one then ends the presentation by summarizing the three types of appeals.

Develop

Work individually to shape your appeal. An outline can help you keep your thoughts on track; sometimes a list of bullet points or detailed notes works well. Make your transition copy as brief as possible, and write it out word for word. Try for wording that will engage the audience. For example, you might begin your appeal with a question or a surprising statement.

Practice

Once you have developed your part of the project, collaborate with your fellow presenters to decide on the "look" of your presentation. For example, will you stand the whole time, sit the whole time, or stand only when speaking? Whatever you decide, make it consistent.

Next, rehearse the presentation as a group until you are confident that you can perform it smoothly for the class. Time yourselves so that your group stays under four minutes. If your presentation is running long, make appropriate cuts. Be sure you can get through all the material at a measured pace. Speaking too quickly is a sure way to lose the audience.

Use the strategies that follow to help make your presentation as good as it can be.

You should now be ready to share the project. Go over the CAPS guidelines on page 450 and the rubric on page 473 to be sure that your project meets the requirements.

Offering Strong Team Support

Imagine that you are acting in the school play. You are in the midst of an important scene—really putting your heart and soul into your performance—when you notice that your scene partner is staring off into space. He looks bored. Yet when it's time for him to deliver his lines, he comes in right on cue.

Has your scene partner done a good job in the scene? No. When you collaborate, you are part of a team. Your individual performance is important, but it's only one aspect of the overall effort. When you present a speech in three parts, you have to stay engaged in the presentation even when you're not speaking. Here are a few ways to support your team:

1. **Body Language.** You don't have to stare at the speaker the whole time he or she is talking, but do incline your body or your head toward the person. Stand straight and stay engaged.
2. **Listening.** If the speaker before you slows down or speeds up the rhythm of the presentation too much, you can get that rhythm back on track. But you can only do so if you are paying attention to what the other person is saying and the way he or she is saying it.
3. **Eye Contact.** If you are in the midst of speaking and you happen to glance at your co-presenters, it will give you confidence to know that they are watching and listening. They will feel the same way when it is their turn to speak.

EVALUATING THE PROJECT

Evaluate the presentations using the following rubric.

Score the presentation on each point, with 4 being "outstanding" and 1 being "needs much improvement."

Come up with an overall score and write a brief paragraph that explains your score.

Understanding of Persuasive Speaking	Demonstration of Persuasive Speaking	Creativity and Originality	Preparation and Use of Time
4 The presenters revealed insight into many elements of persuasive speaking.	**4** The presenters were adept at demonstrating the three forms of persuasive speaking.	**4** The presentation was attention-grabbing, unique, interesting, fun, and imaginative.	**4** The presentation flowed smoothly and stayed within the time limit.
3 The presenters revealed insight into some elements of persuasive speaking.	**3** The presenters were adept at demonstrating most forms of persuasive speaking.	**3** The presentation was attention-grabbing, interesting, and fun, but not very unique or imaginative.	**3** The presentation progressed fairly smoothly and stayed within the time limit.
2 The presenters did not seem to understand some of the aspects of persuasive speaking.	**2** The presenters were minimally adept at demonstrating some forms of persuasive speaking.	**2** The presentation was fairly interesting and fun, but not attention-grabbing, unique, or imaginative.	**2** The presentation had a few awkward moments and went a bit over or was noticeably under the time limit.
1 The presenters did not seem to understand very much about persuasive speaking.	**1** The presenters were not helpful in demonstrating any forms of persuasive speaking.	**1** The presentation was not attention-grabbing, unique, fun, or interesting.	**1** The presentation was not smoothly executed and went well over or significantly under the time limit.

Communication *Past* and Present

The Art of Persuasion

From Aristotle . . .

Back in 350 B.C., the Greek philosopher Aristotle wrote a book called *Rhetoric.* This book has had an enormous influence on speech-making for over two thousand years. For Aristotle, rhetoric, or the art of effective speaking, was all about persuasion. He defined three ways to achieve this goal.

Aristotle was one of several Greek thinkers who analyzed what made a speech persuasive.

The first and most important way is based on the speaker's character. According to Aristotle, when listeners view the speaker as credible, the speech is most likely to be persuasive: "We believe good men more fully and more readily than others; this is true generally whatever the question is, and absolutely true where exact certainty is impossible and opinions are divided." He then says that "personal goodness revealed by the speaker . . . may *almost* be called the most effective means of persuasion we possess."

The second way persuasion is achieved, according to Aristotle, has to do with the audience. To be effective, a speech must stir the emotions of the listeners. The reason for this is that "emotions have the power to modify our judgments." Aristotle continues: "When people are feeling friendly and placable, they think one sort of thing; when they are feeling angry or hostile, they think either something totally different or the same thing with a different intensity." The emotions the speaker tries to arouse will be different depending on the desired outcome. If the speaker wants the audience to embrace an idea, the speech should stir warm and friendly feelings. If the speaker wants the audience to take action against something, the speech should arouse feelings of anger and outrage.

The final mode of persuasion for Aristotle has to do with the speech itself. It must be logical and reasonable. It must demonstrate or seem to demonstrate that something is true. It must "prove a truth or an apparent truth by means of the persuasive arguments suitable to the case in question." For Aristotle, these persuasive arguments could be either inductive—proceeding from the specific to the universal—or deductive—beginning with a general premise and supporting it with specific evidence. The true test of the persuasiveness of an argument is its effect on the audience.

. . . to Advertising

For Aristotle, there were also three kinds of oratory. Political speaking urges the listeners to do or not do something. Forensic speaking either attacks or defends someone in a court of law. Ceremonial speaking either praises or criticizes someone. Today, in addition to these three, we have a genre of persuasive communication that Aristotle never imagined: advertising. Although advertising often has strong graphic and visual elements, at heart it is persuasive speech with a flair. It employs the same three modes of persuasion that Aristotle talked about: credibility, emotion, and logic.

Think about a few advertisements you've seen recently. How many used as a spokesperson someone famous, or someone whose demeanor immediately won your trust? These advertisements tapped into what Aristotle recognized as the first mode of persuasion: the speaker's personal character. If we believe in the credibility of the speaker, we will be more inclined to believe the message. That's why celebrity testimonials are used so often in advertising.

Now think about ads that stir your emotions. Ads for products try to make listeners feel comfortable and amiable and receptive to the idea that the product will benefit them and improve their lives in some way. Ads for not-for-profit causes and organizations may try to arouse either friendly or angry emotions to inspire listeners to take action. For example, an environmental group might try to persuade the audience to support their cause either by making them feel good about a safe and clean environment or by making them feel angry about the threats to the environment. Either way, they are utilizing Aristotle's second mode of persuasion.

Now think about Aristotle's third mode of persuasion: logical argument. Is that mode of persuasion ever used in advertising? Remember that Aristotle said a speech must demonstrate or seem to demonstrate that something is true. There are definitely ads that use this method of persuading their audience. Can you think of an example?

What type of appeal do you think this advertisement might have?

Chapter 21 Review

Using Vocabulary Words

For each term listed below, make a box and divide it into four sections. In the top left section, write the word. In the top right section, draw an illustration of the word. In the bottom left section, give an example of what the word means to you. In the bottom right section, write a word that you feel is the opposite or non-example of the word.

1. ad hominem
2. bandwagon
3. circular reasoning
4. fallacy
5. false syllogism
6. hasty generalization
7. motivated sequence
8. motivation
9. persuasion
10. post hoc ergo propter hoc
11. red herring
12. slippery slope
13. syllogism

Reviewing Key Ideas

1. When presenting a speech to persuade, what is your primary goal or purpose?
2. List and describe three categories of persuasive appeal.
3. List five key points that can help a speaker determine whether or not a speech is ethical.
4. Why is motivation such an important factor in persuading others to change their attitudes or behavior?

Reflecting on Your Project

With your partners, talk about the work you all did to prepare this project. Are you happy with the roles you played? Explain what you might do differently next time.

Responding to the Essential Question

Do you feel that you now understand the important elements in giving a persuasive speech? Write a short essay about a persuasive speech you see yourself giving twenty years from now.

Extending Your Understanding

Everyday Life

1. Present a five-minute speech in which you attempt to persuade your audience to feel as you do about an issue or idea. After you've researched the situation, write a statement expressing your purpose with a specific audience in mind. Prepare your speech as if you were speaking to this audience. Use two of the three types of appeals identified in this chapter. Use the motivated sequence as your organizational pattern.
2. Interview a family member or friend about a time when he or she used persuasion to achieve a goal. What kinds of appeals were used? Create a dramatic or comic sketch based on this scenario.
3. In general, what kind of audience member do you think you are? Write a one-page analysis of your own

audience behavior. Give examples from recent persuasive speeches you have heard.

4. Think about the people you trust. Identify common characteristics that link these people in terms of their credibility.

In the Media

5. Select a current advertising campaign. Analyze the campaign's appeal to the motives of the audience. Prepare a presentation for your class in which you show what kinds of motivation the advertiser is relying on to change attitudes or behaviors.

6. In a group of three, compose your own thirty-second radio spot. Based on a current event or issue of your choice, make one logical appeal, one emotional appeal, and one appeal based on credibility. Present all three to your audience. After your presentation, discuss which one was most effective.

Research

7. Research a recent political campaign. Use the Internet, newspapers, and magazines to find out about persuasive statements or speeches used by the candidates. Analyze each side for effective use of persuasion.

8. Do historical research to find a persuasive speech from the past. Deliver a particularly persuasive excerpt from it for the class.

Interpreting Graphics

Copy the flowchart on this page on a separate sheet of paper. Be sure the scale is large enough to allow you to write inside the boxes. Then fill in the boxes with a fictional example of each step in the motivated sequence.

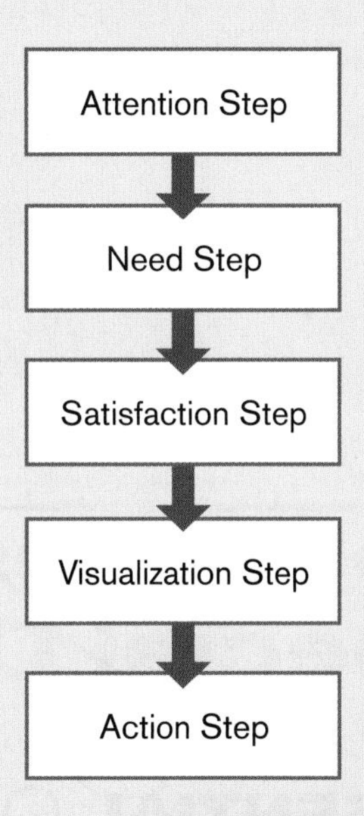

Additional Projects

1. **Group Project:** Work together in small groups to research an issue such as underage alcohol consumption or fraternity hazing. Use an Internet search engine such as Google to find statistics, quotes, recent news stories, and legal cases having to do with your chosen topic. Use the information to create a brief persuasive speech.

2. **Individual Project:** Create a poster or graphic organizer or comic strip illustrating the various kinds of logical fallacies. Try to create eye-catching graphics. Use your imagination; as long as the graphic depicts a logical fallacy you can make the situations or subjects as unusual as you like. When you have finished, display your work for the class.

Speeches for Special Occasions

ESSENTIAL QUESTION

How do speeches for special occasions differ in content and organization?

Chapter Project: And the Winner Is . . .

One of the nicest occasions for making a speech is when you accept a prize or an award. In this project, you'll get some impromptu practice doing just that.

This project involves the whole class. Half the class will be presenters, and the other half will be recipients. The presenters get to dream up silly awards to give out. The recipients, chosen at random for each award, get to make speeches accepting their awards. Presenters' and recipients' speeches can be humorous, but they should follow the models for these kinds of speeches presented in this chapter. As you think about how you're going to prepare for this project, refer to the CAPS guidelines below.

The rubric on page 503 shows the traits on which your speech will be evaluated.

CONCEPT	presentation and acceptance speeches have expected elements
AUDIENCE	classmates and teacher
PURPOSE	practice making presentation and acceptance speeches
SITUATION	informal classroom presentation

Reese Witherspoon gave a gracious speech upon accepting the Academy Award for her leading role in Walk the Line in 2006.

KEY VOCABULARY

tone	anecdote
valedictory	theme
dignitary	testimonial
auspicious	eulogy

Speak Up!

If you've ever watched the Academy Awards, you've witnessed some great, and some awful, acceptance speeches. Some are focused and memorable. Others ramble on until the award-winner is escorted off the stage.

Think about what makes a good acceptance speech and write down your ideas. Then take turns sharing your ideas as your teacher writes them on the board. Keep these ideas in mind as you read the chapter.

BACKGROUND FOR THE PROJECT

Pages 480–500 will provide the information you'll need to complete this project.

Understanding Special Occasion Speeches

Audience, purpose, and situation influence every public speaking situation. In special occasion speeches, the situation dominates. The situation determines not only the audience for the speech but also the purpose.

Special occasion speeches may be the most familiar kinds of speeches. They mark important moments in life. Some are serious, such as a commencement address at a graduation. Some are somber, such as a speech at a funeral. Some are joyful, such as at the opening of a new library. You have probably heard one or two already, and you will probably deliver one or more sometime in your life.

The basic structure of a special occasion speech is the same as the structure of any other speech. There's an introduction, a body, and a conclusion. The nature of the occasion, however, dictates the kinds of things that are appropriate for each part as well as the speech's overall **tone,** or spirit. This chapter will explore each unique type of special occasion speech.

KEY POINT

The occasion itself, which is often a social gathering that marks an important life event, sets the tone and determines what is appropriate content for a special occasion speech.

What special tone would you expect the speaker to adopt at your graduation?

The Graduation Speech

Each spring, thousands of speakers give commencement addresses to the millions of students graduating from high school and college. In general, these speeches combine congratulations on graduating with advice about where to go next in life.

Purpose and Audience

Graduation ceremonies usually involve several speeches—by students, members of the faculty, school officials, and special guests. One of these is usually a **valedictory**, delivered by the student graduating with the highest grade-point average, or some other student leader. Another longer speech is usually a commencement address, delivered by an invited **dignitary**, or famous person. The audience is made up of the graduating class, the faculty of the school, and the families and friends of the graduates. Although some of the comments in these speeches may be directed to teachers and parents, the principal audience is the graduating class.

Valedictory The valedictory speech is meant to be a farewell address. Graduation marks the end of one significant phase of life and the beginning of the next. The members of the graduating class, who have been in school together for four or more years, are about to go their separate ways. It's an **auspicious** moment, and a valedictory speech should acknowledge the promise of the day. Valedictory speeches usually recall shared experiences, celebrate the students' accomplishments, and reflect on their expectations for the future. Sometimes they motivate and inspire. Still, since the speaker is a student talking to his or her classmates, the tone is often personal and intimate.

Commencement Address The commencement address differs from the valedictory in purpose because the person delivering it has a different relationship with the audience. Commencement speakers are invited to speak because of their achievements in world. They may be graduates of the school, but they are not contemporaries of the graduating students and don't share common experiences with them. They are adults who speak to the students from their own perspective on the world. Commencement speeches focus less on the past and more on the future. They reflect on the graduating class's place in history, but they focus more on motivating and inspiring their future attitudes and behavior.

A valedictorian says farewell.

Developing Ideas

If you are asked to deliver a valedictory for your high school class, you will face a big challenge but have an enormous opportunity. Can you make your fellow students feel good about their high school experience and inspire them to look to the future? Planning just the right graduation speech and delivering it effectively will require a lot of thought and a lot of time.

Begin by thinking about the experiences that the students in your class share. Make a list of the highlights from the past school year. Did anything dramatic or important happen? Did anything exceptionally funny happen? Did your class establish any records? Did it have a special reputation with teachers? Making a list will help you reflect on your school experience and formulate in your mind what you want to say. Identify any **anecdote**, or brief story, that demonstrates your main points. The anecdote might be funny or touching. It will make your speech more entertaining and memorable.

Another way to develop ideas for your speech is to look for quotations that are relevant to what you want to talk about—high school, the future, the nature of success, parting with friends. Many speakers use quotations to begin or end their speech. Think of how you might use one of these quotations in a graduation speech:

> We all take different paths in life, but no matter where we go, we take a little of each other everywhere.
>
> Tim McGraw, singer

> True terror is to wake up one morning and discover that your high school class is running the country.
>
> Kurt Vonnegut Jr., writer

> In order to succeed, your desire for success should be greater than your fear of failure.
>
> Bill Cosby, comedian

As you develop your ideas, take enough time to explore various ways to express what you really want to say. A graduation speech is your opportunity to speak to your classmates and say something memorable, appropriate to the occasion, and worthy of the accomplishment being celebrated. Your speech should be formal and dignified, but that doesn't mean it can't be entertaining and even amusing. Share a funny story, but avoid being silly or disrespectful.

Graduation Speech Framework

Like any other speech, a graduation speech needs to have an introduction, a body, and a conclusion, but the content of each of these parts is specific to a graduation speech.

Introduction Graduation ceremonies can involve several speeches, all given before the diplomas are handed out. The graduates, and their families, are likely to be excited and restless to get to the part where the graduates receive their diplomas. You will need an amusing anecdote or compelling quotation to grab their attention and give them a reason to listen to you. Your introduction should identify your theme and summarize the points you will make in the body of your speech.

A graduation speech requires that you inspire fellow students to look to the future.

Body In a graduation speech, you want to reflect on the past, acknowledge the significance of the occasion, and express encouragement for the future. So, it makes sense to think of the body of your speech in three parts: past, present, and future. You can tell about important shared experiences in the past. You can congratulate your classmates for their achievements in the present. You can contemplate how your classmates will move forward in the future. What you say in each part of the body needs to relate to and support your overall **theme** or message.

Conclusion The conclusion of your speech should summarize the points you made in the body and bring the audience back to your central message. In a graduation speech, you want to leave the audience with inspiring words about the future. A quotation that expresses the idea you want to share can be a very effective way to bring your speech to an inspiring and memorable conclusion.

Graduation Speech

Introduction

- Acknowledge the people you are addressing, including teachers, family members, and fellow graduates.
- Grab the audience's attention with an amusing anecdote or quotation.
- Introduce your theme, or central message.
- Preview the points you will make.

Body

- Reflect on the **past**—the experiences your class has shared that relate to your theme.
- Discuss the significance of the **present** moment, as it relates to your theme.
- Connect your theme to the **future.**

Conclusion

- Summarize the points you made and return to your theme.
- Inspire your audience with a quotation or a memorable statement of your theme.

The Speech of Introduction

Mark Twain was famous as both a writer and speaker. Once, he was in the audience for a speech by actress Clara Morris when the person who was supposed to introduce her did not show up. Twain was asked to fill in. His comments provide guidance to anyone preparing a speech of introduction:

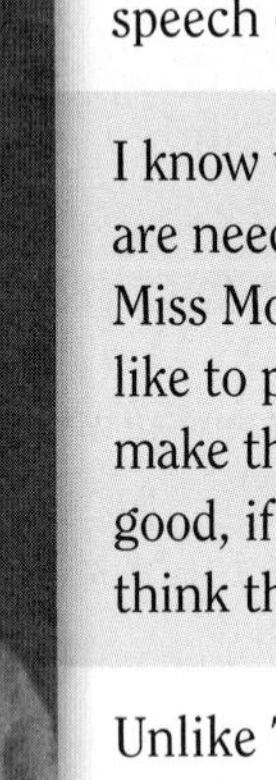
Mark Twain

> I know that no compliments are needed in the case of Miss Morris yet I should like to pay her a few, and to make them real strong and good, if I only had time to think them out.

Unlike Twain, you will probably never be asked to introduce someone without preparing for it. You will probably have time to think out a few "real strong and good" compliments. And you should. These form the core of a good speech of introduction.

Purpose and Audience

When you introduce people you know to each other, you want them to feel comfortable with the other person. Introducing a speaker has a similar purpose. You want the audience to feel friendly toward the speaker and receptive to the speech. To succeed, you will want to know something about the speaker and the subject of the speech, and the audience and its expectations.

Imagine you are introducing Stephanie Meyers, a famous science fiction/fantasy author. Will she be talking about the content of her latest book? Or her life as a writer? Will the audience consist of fans who already know all about her? Or people unfamiliar with her work? You need to tailor your introduction according to the context.

In the introduction, present the speaker's credentials to make the audience confident that the speaker is qualified to speak on the subject. Establish the tone of the occasion. For a formal speech, give a formal introduction. For an informal speech, give an informal introduction.

Developing Ideas

When you're delivering a speech of introduction, remember that your speech is not the main event. Keep it short. You don't want to bore the audience before the main speaker even gets started.

To help you with introductions, speakers often provide background information on themselves. You should also do your own research using other sources. Warning: if you use other sources, let the speaker know what you plan to say. Besides being courteous, this can save you and the speaker embarrassment if you found information that isn't actually true.

When you contact the speaker for background information, also ask about the topic of the speech. Knowing the topic will help you decide what's important to tell the audience about the speaker's background. You should also mention the topic in your speech of introduction. You don't need to speak at length about it. The speaker will do that. Your job is simply to let the audience know what the speaker will be talking about.

Introductory Speech Framework

The speech of introduction takes about a minute—and should never exceed three minutes. Short as it is, a speech of introduction still has the same three parts that any other speech contains.

Introduction Begin your speech with a statement or idea that grabs the audience's attention and includes the name of the speaker. An appropriate beginning might be something like this: "'Grow up and get serious!' is something we teenagers hear often, but that's not the sort of advice you'll get from writer and teacher Sarah Wedrychowics." When you say this speaker's name, make certain that you pronounce it correctly. You may not be familiar with, so write it out phonetically and practice it. Here's how your spelling might look: *"ven duh HAH vitch."*

Body The body of a speech of introduction should tell four or five interesting and relevant things about the speaker. What you say in the body needs to build on what you said in the introduction. The speaker introducing Sarah Wedrychowics would want to tell things about her life that provide clues to why she would never admonish someone to "grow up and get serious!" For example, the body of the speech might include this information about her:

- While in law school, she and a friend opened a pet-sitting service.
- She kept a journal of her pet-sitting adventures.
- Friends who read parts of her journal thought it was hilarious.
- Her journal became the book *Claws and Whiskers.*

When you've given some specifics of your speaker's background and experience, tell what he or she is going to talk about. For example: "Today, Ms. Wedrychowics is going to speak to us about the very real dangers of taking yourself too seriously."

Conclusion The conclusion needs to transfer the audience's attention to the speaker. Often this can be accomplished in a single sentence. For example, the person introducing Sarah Wedrychowics might say something like: "Since I really hate it when adults tell me to 'grow up and get serious,' I'm eager to hear what she has to say." The final sentence of the speech of introduction welcomes the speaker to the podium: "Please join me in welcoming writer, teacher, and humorist Sarah Wedrychowics."

Speech of Introduction

Introduction

- Get the attention of the audience.
- Tell them the speaker's name.

Body

- Tell four things about the speaker's background that qualify him or her to speak to this audience on this topic.
- Identify the topic or title of the speech.

Conclusion

- Transfer attention back to the speaker.
- Finish with a sentence of welcome such as, "It's my honor to present your guest for today, Sarah Wedrychowics."

The Presentation Speech

Whenever an award or prize is given, someone makes a presentation speech. Like a speech of introduction, a presentation speech is usually short. Typically it tells the audience who is bestowing the award, what its significance is, who is receiving the award, and why the person was selected to receive it. Following is a typical opening to a presentation speech. It is the first paragraph of a speech made by Professor Ole Danbolt Mjes, chairman of the Norwegian Nobel Committee, when he presented the Nobel Peace Prize for 2007:

Al Gore and R. K. Pachauri, representing the IPCC, share the 2007 Nobel Peace Prize.

> The Norwegian Nobel Committee has decided that the Nobel Peace Prize for 2007 is to be shared, in two equal parts, between the Intergovernmental Panel on Climate Change (IPCC) and Albert Arnold (Al) Gore, Jr., for their efforts to build up and disseminate greater knowledge about man-made climate change, and to lay the foundations for the measures that are needed to counteract such change.

The speech then elaborates on the significance of the award, and what the IPCC and Al Gore had done to deserve it. Because of the formality of the occasion, the Nobel presentation speech is longer than most presentation speeches. Still, if you are asked to present an award, you can use it as a model.

Purpose and Audience

One common presentation you might be asked to make is an award. Perhaps the students in your school select a teacher of the year each spring. To present the award, you would first explain its significance. Then, you'd want to explain what the recipient has done to deserve the award. Sharing a story that reveals something significant about the recipient and his or her qualifications for the award is always a good idea. Remember that the audience may include people who hoped to win the award, but didn't.

Another presentation you might make is a gift. When a gift is presented, the audience is often comprised of friends and family. Rather than dwelling on the gift, you should focus on the recipient. Your comments about the gift should be limited to what it is and why it's appropriate for the person. If a teacher were retiring, for example, and you knew that he planned to spend time gardening, you might give him a horticultural encyclopedia. You would simply name the gift and explain why it's fitting. If the award or gift is a trophy or plaque, read the inscription aloud. This will help the audience understand its significance.

Developing Ideas

When you are preparing a presentation speech, think about the following:

- how your words represent the thoughts of the group you're representing
- the significance of the award or gift (you may want to read a statement about the award in your presentation)
- who is receiving the award or gift.

The person receiving the gift must be your focus. Gather your own impressions as well as anecdotes from others who know the person. List four reasons why this person deserves the honor. It may be appropriate to ask the recipient what life experiences led to this achievement.

Presentation Speech Framework

Like a speech of introduction, a presentation speech should be fairly short—never more than five minutes and usually much shorter. It should have an introduction, a body, and a conclusion.

Introduction Your introduction should make it clear to the audience what the award or gift is, what group or organization is presenting it, and who the recipient is. Make it clear that you are speaking on behalf of a group.

Body If you are presenting an award or prize, the body of the speech is where you explain the significance of the award and why the recipient is deserving of the award. The nature of the award will help you determine which aspect deserves greater attention. For example, the chairman of the Norwegian Nobel Committee devoted considerable attention to answering this question:

"Why have the IPCC and Al Gore been awarded a Nobel Prize for *peace*?"

The Norwegian Nobel committee has always had a broad approach to peace. Its opinion has been that there are many different paths to peace. . . .

Environmental problems certainly affect human security in this broad sense. When low-lying areas are flooded, their inhabitants will no longer have any form of security. . . . Melting glaciers, and rivers which first overflow and then have their rate of flow reduced or dry out, mean dramatic changes in people's everyday lives. . . .

The Nobel committee bestows its awards. How would you prepare a speech to accept this prestigious honor?

Often, the accomplishments of the individual receiving the award are already well-known. Try to share a little-known anecdote that illustrates a quality that makes the recipient the perfect person to be honored with the award.

If you're presenting a gift, the body of the speech is where you want to talk about the reason the recipient is being honored. If it is for one specific act, focus on that. If it is for a long history of achievement, talk about how the person's qualities make him or her unique and deserving. Beginning this kind of tribute with an anecdote about the person's approach to a challenge or to life in general is usually quite effective.

Conclusion Always conclude a presentation speech by inviting the recipient to join you. Say the person's name clearly and pronounce it correctly. Then read the inscription on the award before giving it to the person. Shake hands or perhaps offer a hug, if appropriate. After you have made the presentation, join the rest of the audience in applauding the recipient. Then take your seat, and let the recipient deliver his or her acceptance speech.

Presentation Speech

Introduction

- Name the group for which you are speaking.
- If it's an award, tell what the award is and who the recipient is.
- If it's a gift, explain the occasion—retirement, special achievement, or contribution.

Body

- If you're presenting an award, explain the award's significance and why the recipient is deserving.
- If it's a gift or other tribute, explain why the recipient is being so honored.
- Share anecdotes that illustrate the recipient's personal qualities.

Conclusion

- Invite the recipient to join you.
- If appropriate, read the inscription on the plaque or trophy.
- Give the person the award or gift and shake the person's hand or exchange a hug.

The Acceptance Speech

In 2002, the Hollywood Foreign Press Association awarded its Cecil B. DeMille Award to Harrison Ford for his "outstanding contribution to the entertainment field." In accepting the award, Harrison Ford made the following speech:

In anticipation of tonight, I wrote two speeches, a long one and a short one. I'll give you the short one: "Thank you." But it seems there might be enough time for the long one as well, which is: "Thank you very much."

Harrison Ford accepts one of many awards he has been given in his long career.

This speech captures what an acceptance speech is all about: saying thank you.

PROJECT PREP

In the project, you and a **partner** will practice presenting and accepting awards. Get ready for it now by dreaming up some outlandishly silly awards. With a partner, think up humorous award titles. Write an "official description" of each award and define the criteria to be used for selecting a recipient. For each of the awards, create an appropriate "trophy" to present.

Purpose and Audience

The main purpose of an acceptance speech is to express appreciation for an award or gift received. The audience for an acceptance speech usually includes people who know the recipient—friends, family, and colleagues—and people who are connected with the organization giving the award. In some situations, the audience may also include people who were nominated for the award but didn't get it. In these situations, it's especially important for the recipient to be gracious.

The length of an acceptance speech depends on what is being accepted. When a candidate is accepting his party's nomination for President, the speech might run 45 minutes. Besides thanking the party, the candidate needs to explain his or her philosophy and positions on issues. At the other extreme, winners of the Academy Awards have only 45 seconds to make their acceptance speech, so saying "thank you" is about all that can be said. The appropriate length for most acceptance speeches falls between 45 seconds and 45 minutes. Most are only two or three minutes.

Developing Ideas

Sometimes you know in advance that you are getting an award, and you have time to prepare an acceptance speech. Sometimes you might go to an awards event not knowing if you've won or not. If that's the case, it's a good idea to plan what you're going to say beforehand, just in case you win.

An effective acceptance speech needs to have the right tone. You need to convey the sense that you are grateful and honored, but you should avoid false modesty. You can say you're surprised to receive the award, but you shouldn't insist that you don't deserve it. A statement like that implies that the people giving the award made a bad decision.

Besides thanking the group giving the award, a good acceptance speech does two other things. First, it tells the importance of the award to you. Whoopi Goldberg accomplished this in only three sentences in her speech accepting the Best Supporting Actress Award for her role in *Ghost* in 1991. Speaking to the actors and actresses assembled for the Academy Awards, she said: "As a little kid, I lived in the projects and you're the people I watched. You're the people who made me want to be an actor. I'm so proud to be here." Second, it gives credit to the people who helped you achieve this recognition. Give some thought to whose names you will mention.

By all means include everyone whose help or support was critical to your success, but try to avoid reeling off a laundry list of people in your life, going back to early childhood, whose names mean nothing to the audience.

Whoopi Goldberg's Academy Award acceptance speech gives credit to those who inspired her.

Acceptance Speech Framework

Even a two-minute speech should have the same structure of all speeches— an introduction, a body, and a conclusion.

Introduction Thank the group who presented the award. That is adequate introduction for a speech of acceptance.

Body The body of an acceptance speech is where you should tell what the award means to you, either now or for the future. In accepting the ALAN Award for literature for young people from the National Council of Teachers of English in 1997, author Mildred D. Taylor explained the significance of the award to her in this way:

> Many years ago when I first started writing the stories told by my family about our family history and about neighbors and friends and the community in which my family lived, I envisioned presenting an aspect of American history which during my own childhood was not presented in history books.
>
> I envisioned presenting a family united in love and self-respect, and parents, strong and sensitive, attempting to guide their children successfully without harming their spirits through the hazardous maze of living in a discriminatory society. I wanted readers to know this family, based upon my own, and I wanted them to feel akin to them and to walk in their shoes.
>
> The presentation at the National Council of Teachers of English Convention of the 1997 ALAN Award signifies to me that perhaps I have achieved some of these goals I set so long ago, and I sincerely thank you for this great recognition.

Talking about the award's significance provides the opportunity to share an anecdote. This gives the speech a personal tone.

The body of an acceptance speech is also the place to acknowledge the people who contributed to your success. You may feel like saying, as Maureen Stapleton did when she accepted an Academy Award in 1982:

> "I want to thank . . . everybody I have ever met in my entire life."

Still, you will probably want to limit your list so that the audience does not get tired of listening. Focus on the handful of people whose support was most important. You can interject warmth and humor into your acknowledgments by making comments about the people you name that tell what they did or reflect how you feel about them.

J.K. Rowling was given an honorary degree from Harvard University in June 2008. She began her commencement address with these words accepting the honor: "The first thing I would like to say is 'thank you.' Not only has Harvard given me an extraordinary honor, but the weeks of fear and nausea I've experienced at the thought of giving this commencement address have made me lose weight. A win-win situation! Now all I have to do is take deep breaths, squint at the red banners and fool myself into believing I am at the world's best-educated Harry Potter convention."

Robin Williams accomplished this masterfully in his acceptance speech when he won an Academy Award in 1998 for his role in the film *Good Will Hunting*. Williams begins his speech by thanking younger actors Matt Damon and Ben Affleck, who wrote the screenplay, and the director, Gus Van Sant:

> Thank you, Ben and Matt—I still want to see some ID. Thank you, Gus, for being so subtle you're almost subliminal. Most of all, I want to thank my father, up there, the man who when I said I wanted to be an actor, he said, "Wonderful. Just have a back-up profession like welding."

Conclusion To conclude an acceptance speech, you need a simple statement that reiterates your thanks. You might say: "I am grateful for this honor, and I thank you all very much."

Acceptance Speech

Introduction

- Thank the group that gave you the award.

Body

- Tell what the award means to you.
- Thank the people who helped you succeed.

Conclusion

- Thank everyone again with a line that wraps everything up: "I am honored to receive this, and I thank you all so much."

PROJECT PREP

At the Academy Awards, the time limit for an acceptance speech is 45 seconds. With a **partner**, practice making an acceptance speech in that length of time. As one of you gives your speech, the other will use a stopwatch to time 45 seconds. When you've both had a chance to make a 45-second acceptance speech, discuss the things you think are critical to include when you have so little time to speak.

Robin Williams gives thanks with good humor at the 1998 Academy Awards.

Reverend Bernice King, daughter of Martin Luther King, Jr. and Coretta Scott King, delivers a eulogy at her mother's funeral in 2006.

The Commemorative Speech

A commemorative speech may be given to celebrate a special event or place, or to honor an individual. For example, at a college opening of a new fine arts building, the dean might give a commemorative speech celebrating how the building enhances the college. The president of the college might give a commemorative speech honoring the generous alumnus who donated money for the building. Commemorative speeches about people are of two types. A **testimonial** honors a living person while a **eulogy** honors a person who has recently died.

Purpose and Audience

The primary purpose of a commemorative speech is to honor someone or something. In addition, a commemorative speech should be inspiring. It should heighten the audience's esteem for the subject and leave the audience with a sense of hope for the future.

The audience for a commemorative speech is made up of people who have a connection to the event or person being honored. For example, the people attending the dedication of a new fine arts building would be people connected with the college. They might include college officials and faculty, alumni and current students, and local elected officials. The audience at a memorial service where a eulogy is presented will be people who knew, admired, and loved the person.

As a speaker giving a eulogy, you can assume that the audience is open to hearing praise about the subject. Even with a supportive audience, however, it's important that a commemorative speech not go on for too long. Often, more than one person will speak on these occasions, so each speaker should be brief.

Developing Ideas

Whether the subject of a commemorative speech is a place, an event, a group, or a person, your speech needs a theme. Decide what aspect of your subject is the most important and the most compelling. If your subject is a place, the controlling idea of your speech might be the effect it has on people who spend time there. If it's an event, you might focus on the meaning it has to the people who participated in it. If the subject is a group, you could highlight the group's role in the community. If your subject is a person, the theme might be the person's most memorable quality. Once you've defined your theme, think about examples and experiences that illustrate it.

In her eulogy for Sonny Bono, Cher developed a theme, disputing misconceptions about the man who was her former husband and singing partner:

> Some people thought that Son wasn't very bright, but he was smart enough to take an introverted 16-year-old girl and a scrappy little Italian guy with a bad voice and turn them into the most successful and beloved couple of this generation.

Sonny and Cher during the height of their popularity

Sometimes when you're developing your ideas, the process can work in reverse. You might start with a favorite memory that seems to capture the essence of your subject. You can analyze what it reveals about the subject and discover the theme for your speech. Senator Edward Kennedy's eulogy for his nephew John F. Kennedy, Jr., may have developed this way. It begins with a memory that held special meaning to the speaker, and it goes on to explore the kind of person his nephew was:

> Once, when they asked John what he would do if he went into politics and was elected president, he said, "I guess the first thing is call up Uncle Teddy and gloat." I loved that. It was so like his father.

Senator Edward Kennedy

Once you've decided on your theme, think of examples that illustrate it. At your parents' 25th wedding anniversary, your theme might be their belief in their children. Your examples could include statements made by your parents and family anecdotes that illustrate this.

After you have developed your theme, return to the theme for a conclusion that reiterates the values or achievements being honored. Try to think of one effective statement—perhaps a quotation—that expresses the whole idea and will help your audience remember your message.

Commemorative Speech Framework

All commemorative speeches need an introduction, a body, and a conclusion.

Introduction In your introduction you should introduce yourself and explain your connection to the person or thing being celebrated. Describe the subject of your speech in a way that identifies a significant aspect of your subject—a quality, a characteristic, an effect, an achievement—and give the audience some idea of what the theme of your speech will be.

Body In the body of the speech, you should state your theme and develop it. Here you can share anecdotes, memories, experiences, or examples that illustrate the important aspect or quality of your subject that you have chosen as your theme. Organize your comments so that you are making three or four strong points that support your theme and bring it home to your audience. Remember that a commemorative speech should have the effect of increasing the audience's respect for your subject and inspiring the audience with some message of hope.

Conclusion The conclusion of a commemorative speech returns to the theme and restates it in a way that provides hope for the future. When President Bill Clinton dedicated his Presidential Library on the Arkansas River in Little Rock, the theme of his speech was that the library represented "a bridge to the 21st century." The speech's conclusion returns to the theme to deliver a message of hope for the future:

Yes, this library is the symbol of a bridge, a bridge to the 21st century. . . . What it is to me is the symbol of not only what I tried to do, but what I want to do with the rest of my life: building bridges from yesterday to tomorrow, building bridges across racial and religious and ethnic and income and political divides, building bridges. . . .

We all do better when we work together. Our differences do matter but our common humanity matters more.

Former New York City Mayor Rudy Giuliani gives a commemorative speech to those attending the World Trade Center memorial service.

Commemorative Speech

Introduction

- Introduce yourself and explain your connection with the person or thing being celebrated or honored.
- If appropriate or necessary, acknowledge dignitaries present, welcome people, and thank those who contributed to the achievement.
- Introduce your theme.

Body

- Develop your theme by sharing three or four examples that illustrate your theme or making three or four points that support your theme.
- Use anecdotes, personal stories, and memories to develop your theme.

Conclusion

- Return to your theme and restate it in a way that is memorable and gives the audience some hope for the future.

The After-Dinner Speech

An after-dinner speech is the entertainment at many banquets. A successful after-dinner speaker is part speaker and part performer.

One of the most famous recent examples of an after-dinner speech was given by comedian Stephen Colbert in 2006. He was speaking to the White House Correspondents' Dinner, a prestigious annual event attended by politicians and influential journalists. His humorous comments about politics and the press were immediately sold as an audio download. Within a few weeks, Colbert's speech was a best-seller among downloads, a category normally dominated by music.

For Colbert and other writers and celebrities, making after-dinner speeches is a source of income. But what if you're not a professional entertainer and you're invited to speak at a special dinner? What do you need to know to succeed?

Purpose and Audience

The primary purpose of an after-dinner speech is entertainment. The audience has just finished a meal. They are relaxed and ready to listen. But they have also been sitting still for a long time, which explains an old joke about after-dinner speeches. When invited to speak, the after-dinner speaker asks, "What would you like me to talk about?" The answer: "About ten minutes." If more than one person will be speaking, each speech may be no more than five minutes.

The members of the audience for an after-dinner speech usually have something in common. They may be supporters of the same charitable cause or participants in the same sport or club. As the after-dinner speaker, you can use this common interest to guide what you say.

Developing Ideas

After-dinner speakers often can choose their own topic. If you are brainstorming for a topic, think about the audience and the occasion. What will appeal to this audience's experience and concerns at this event? For example, if your audience is a group of incoming freshman, your topic might be "Surviving High School," mixing humor with serious advice. If your audience is made up of people who support pet rescue programs, you might choose the topic "Dogs I Have Known" and share stories about rescued dogs.

After choosing your topic, decide what you want to say about it. What is your main message, your thesis? If your subject is "Dogs I Have Known," your thesis might be "There are no bad dogs."

After settling on your thesis, identify three or four supporting points or examples. Think carefully and do research as needed so you have facts and examples to support your viewpoint. The best after-dinner speeches are more than a series of funny stories strung together. They have structure and ideas that make a point.

After-Dinner Speech Framework

An after-dinner speech follows the same basic format as any other speech: introduction, body, and conclusion.

Introduction Mark Twain never prepared a speech. Instead he always asked to be placed at the end of the program and would use what speakers before him said as inspiration for his own speech. According to him, he had "lived so long, and had so many and varied experiences" that no one could talk for five minutes without suggesting to him "a train of thought and a consequent number of pertinent anecdotes and important points."

Don't try to follow Mark Twain's example of preparing a speech only minutes before you deliver it. However, be ready to revise your opening remarks if you are inspired by something that happens or is said just before you start speaking. This is a great method of grabbing the attention of your audience. After your impromptu opening, return to your planned remarks. State your topic and why it is important to you and the audience.

Body In the body of the speech, you should present the support for your thesis. In an after-dinner speech, the support for your thesis should include amusing anecdotes, odd statistics, or humorous props. For example, gardener and humorist Cassandra Danz, while making an after-dinner speech about garden design, was making the point that fences are important garden elements. To prove her point, she snatched a floral arrangement from the banquet table and pulled a cardboard picket fence out of her clothing. She held the fence behind the flowers, and declared, "There! Isn't that much better?"

After-Dinner Speech

Introduction

- Begin with a funny remark or a joke.
- Introduce your topic and your thesis.

Body

- Develop your thesis.
- Present three or four examples that support your thesis.
- Use anecdotes, amusing personal stories, funny statistics, or humorous props.

Conclusion

- Reiterate your thesis.
- Review your supporting points.
- Thank the audience and wish them well.

Conclusion The conclusion of an after-dinner speech should restate the message of your speech in a new and memorable way. Then you should wish the audience well and thank them for their attention. At a White House Correspondents' Dinner in 2005, Laura Bush, the wife of President George W. Bush, concluded her remarks with three reasons for her appreciation of the correspondents:

> So George and I thank you for inviting us, thank you for all of the good work that you and the press do, and thank you for your very kind hospitality this evening.
>
> *Laura Bush*

Presenting Your Special Occasion Speech

A speaker's interaction with the audience is particularly important for special occasion speeches. For these speeches, the audience has usually come together to witness something important, such as the awarding of a diploma or the honoring of someone who has died. You must be sensitive to the mood of the audience. The following factors affect the speaker's interaction with the audience. (See the chart to the right for the issues to keep in mind on when speaking on special occasions.)

Language The words and expressions you use can be formal—the language of most writing—or informal—the language of most conversation. Using one when the other is called for is inappropriate. The use of slang is almost always a mistake in public speaking.

Tone A big part of the way an audience perceives a speaker is the tone used. Tone is the manner in which something is said. Besides choice of words, inflection, pitch, intonation, modulation, and phrasing all help create the tone. Tone reveals the speaker's attitude and expresses how he or she feels about the subject. Using the right tone is particularly important for special occasion speeches.

Voice The way a speech is presented is shaped by voice. Some of the aspects of voice affect the audience's ability to hear and understand what the speaker is saying. Volume, rate, and articulation are particularly important for outdoor speeches. The audience must be able to hear clearly. If you are using a public address system, you should speak into the microphone and stand in one place. Moving around can result in some words not being picked up by the microphone. Speak slowly enough to articulate all words clearly. The audience is eager to hear and understand you.

Inflection and timing are also important aspects of voice. Inflection involves changes in pitch that create expressiveness in speech and signal questions. Inflection makes speech interesting and engaging to listen to. Without inflection, a speech is a monotone. Timing involves pausing at appropriate times. It is critical. A pause after something important is said allows the audience time to take in its significance. When telling a joke, pause to give the audience time to react and laugh before you go on.

Gestures Gestures are a way of interacting with the audience and enhancing the meaning of the speech. They can provide visual cues to help the audience follow the speech. Standing motionless reduces a speaker's effectiveness. However, too much movement can distract the audience, so be sure your gestures are natural and necessary.

	Language	Tone	Voice	Gestures
Graduation Speech	Formal and dignified	Intimate and personal but not casual	Use appropriate inflection	Stress only the most important points
Speech of Introduction	Formal or informal, depending on the speaker to follow	Serious or humorous, depending on the speaker to follow	Pronounce speaker's name correctly	Direct attention to the speaker as he or she approaches
Presentation Speech	Formal	Respectful, but can be personal if the speaker knows the recipient well	Read any inscriptions with inflection; pronounce the recipient's name correctly	Use appropriate gestures with anecdotes to congratulate the recipient
Acceptance Speech	Formal or informal depending on the award	Warm and personal	Speak clearly so that the audience can understand each word	Use appropriate gestures to express thanks
Commemorative Speech	Formal	Respectful but appropriately warm and personal	Pause after important statements	Use gestures when they are natural and appropriate
After-Dinner Speech	Informal	Lighthearted and amusing	Pause for reaction to humorous comments	Use gestures more freely, but not to distraction

Communication in a DIVERSE WORLD

Know Your Audience

The word *audience* derives from the Latin verb *audire,* "to hear," which helps define what an audience does. The speaker speaks; the audience listens. Speakers expect, or at least hope for, rapt attention, laughter at appropriate moments, and a sprinkling of spontaneous applause. What speakers don't expect is for the audience to talk back—at least not in most public speaking situations. Some African American audiences form the exception.

When Barack Obama was campaigning In 2008, an interviewer asked him this question: "Do you try to talk in the same way to a black audience as a white audience?" His answer reveals some differences in Americans that are rooted deep in history:

There's a certain black idiom that it's hard not to slip into when you're talking to a black audience because of the audience response. It's the classic call and response. Anybody who's spent time in a black church knows what I mean. And so you get a little looser; it becomes a little more like jazz and a little less like a set score.

African influence shows in both English- and French-speaking Christian churches in the Americas.

In call and response, the audience talks back to the speaker. The speaker's statements are punctuated by oral responses from the listeners. In many black churches, members of the congregation commonly respond aloud to statements made in the sermon with comments such as "Amen, brother," "Speak the truth," and "Praise the Lord." Prayers offered aloud are similarly enhanced with responses from others, such as "Yes, Lord," "Have mercy, Lord," and "Amen."

The tradition of call and response was brought to America by enslaved people from Africa. Over the centuries, this tradition influenced various forms of culture—most notably music. Gospel, blues, rhythm and blues, and jazz all have their roots in African music, and all show the influence of the call and response pattern.

Barack Obama's statement suggests that the call-and-response tradition influences audience interaction in situations well beyond the church. Speakers new to this type of response might do well to adapt to the interaction and vary a bit from the "set score."

PREPARING THE PROJECT

Begin your project by reviewing the award ideas you and your partner came up with in the first **Project Prep** activity in this chapter and by using the directions below.

Make Connections

Discuss with your project partner how your ideas about special occasion speeches may have changed as you read pages 480–500. Share your personal understanding of what sets special occasion speeches apart from other kinds of public speaking. Discuss and summarize the nature and characteristics of these types of speeches:

- graduation speeches
- speeches of introduction
- presentation speeches
- acceptance speeches
- commemorative speeches
- after-dinner speeches.

Focus

Briefly review the discussion of presentation speeches and acceptance speeches on pages 486–491. Think particularly about the basic elements of these kinds of speeches.

Surefire Acceptance

To be gracious when accepting an award:

- keep your comments simple
- be sincere
- feel proud and honored
- thank the people who helped you.

Plan

With your partner, select the best idea from the ones you came up with in the **Project Prep** activity. Create a name for your award, a description of the achievement for which it is given, and a name and purpose for the group who gives the award. Offer this idea when your teacher requests it. The class will need half as many award ideas as there are students in the class. Your teacher may ask everyone to share their best ideas with the class to see if any awards duplicate others. If your favorite award is too much like another, you may need to select an alternative.

When your award has been accepted, write the information about the award—the name, the purpose, the group making the award—on a piece of paper. Your teacher will collect these for distribution to the students who are designated presenters.

Develop

Your teacher will divide the class into presenters and recipients. In this project, the presenters will know what award they are presenting, but the recipients will not know what award they have received until the presenter announces it. The names of all the recipients will go into a hat, and each presenter will draw out a name before making a presentation speech.

Practice

Your teacher will distribute the award descriptions to the presenters. Then presenters will have five minutes to plan and practice their two-minute presentation speeches. Since the recipients will not know exactly what award they will be given, their one-minute acceptance speeches will have to be impromptu. While the presenters are preparing their speeches, the recipients should use the time to plan some words of thanks that they can use with any award.

Both presenters and recipients should review the format of the type of speech they will be making—a presentation speech or an acceptance speech. Presenters should jot down what they are going to say in the introduction, the body, and the conclusion of their speech. Presenters may have time to run through their speech once, to make sure it fits the time limit, but recipients won't be able to prepare as thoroughly because they won't know exactly what award they're getting until the presenter announces it. They should, however, think in general terms about what they will say in the introduction, body, and conclusion of their speech and about the people they will want to thank. Recipients might want to run through a trial speech to get a sense of how much can be said in one minute.

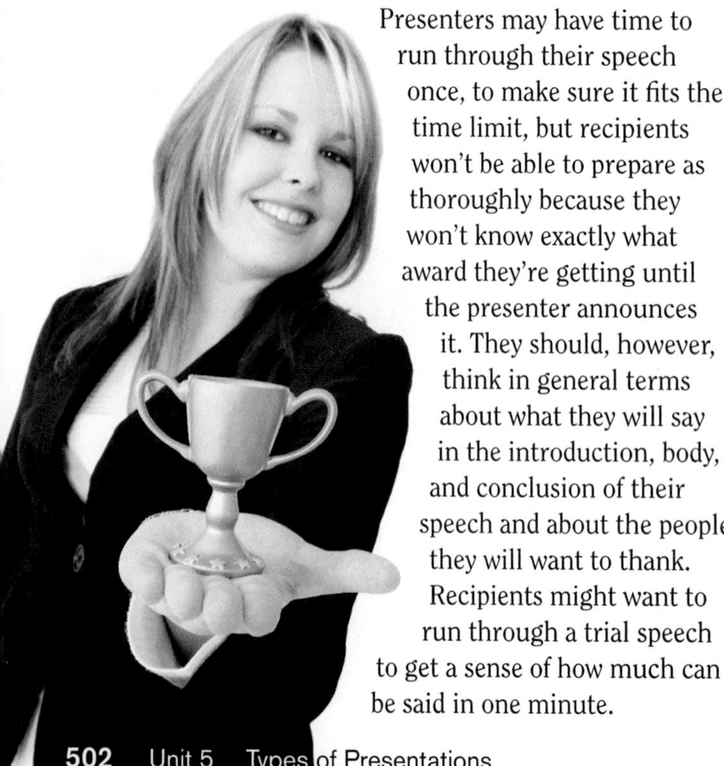

PRESENTING THE PROJECT

Use the strategies that follow to help make your speech as good as it can be.

Now it's time for the "awards ceremony." Your teacher will call on the presenters, one at a time. Each presenter will select the name of a recipient and make a presentation speech announcing the award, revealing the recipient, and introducing that person. The recipient will then deliver his or her acceptance speech.

Your teacher will time each speech. Award presenters will have two minutes. Recipients will have one minute for their acceptance speech. Speakers will be stopped at the end of their allotted time. Your teacher and your classmates will be evaluating your performance using the rubric on the right.

"And the Winner Is . . ."

This project has some of the features of a real awards presentation. There's even a little element of suspense, since the recipients don't know what award they receive. Presenters have an advantage over recipients because they know in advance which award they will be presenting, but they also have more information to include in their speeches. Both presenters and recipients will be presenting impromptu speeches, but the experience should be fun. The awards are goofy. Your audience should be sympathetic—they have to do the same thing you do. So, whether you're a presenter or a recipient, have fun with it!

EVALUATING THE PROJECT

Evaluate the presentations using the following rubric.

Score the presentation and acceptance on each point, with 4 being "outstanding" and 1 being "needs much improvement."

Come up with an overall score and write a brief paragraph that explains your score.

Understanding of Presentation or Acceptance Speech	Demonstration of Presentation or Acceptance Speech	Creativity and Originality	Preparation and Use of Time
4 The speaker clearly understood the format of a presentation or acceptance speech.	**4** The speech followed the format of a presentation or acceptance speech.	**4** The presentation or acceptance speech was original, creative, and fun.	**4** The speaker was poised and delivered a well-structured speech within the time limit.
3 The speaker seemed to understand the format of a presentation or acceptance speech.	**3** The speech more or less followed the format of a presentation or acceptance speech.	**3** The speech was fun and original but not very creative.	**3** The speaker was fairly poised and the speech stayed within the time limit.
2 The speaker did not seem to recognize the format of a presentation or acceptance speech.	**2** The speech did not have the three elements of a speech: introduction, body, and conclusion.	**2** The speech was moderately amusing but not very creative or original.	**2** The speech had some awkward moments and was not completed within the time limit or was noticeably short.
1 The speaker did not follow the format of a presentation or acceptance speech.	**1** The speech rambled and had no explicit organization.	**1** The speech was not original, creative, or fun.	**1** The speech was not delivered well and went beyond the time limit or was significantly short.

Communication *Past* and Present

Praising the Dead

From Ancient Greece . . .

In about 430 B.C., at the end of the first year of the Peloponnesian War, Athenians held a public funeral to honor those who had died defending their city. Such public funerals were customary in ancient Greece. On this occasion, the well-known politician and orator Pericles delivered the funeral oration. Praise for the dead was a major element of the eulogy. In addition, though, Pericles included praise of Athens for its civic values and their importance:

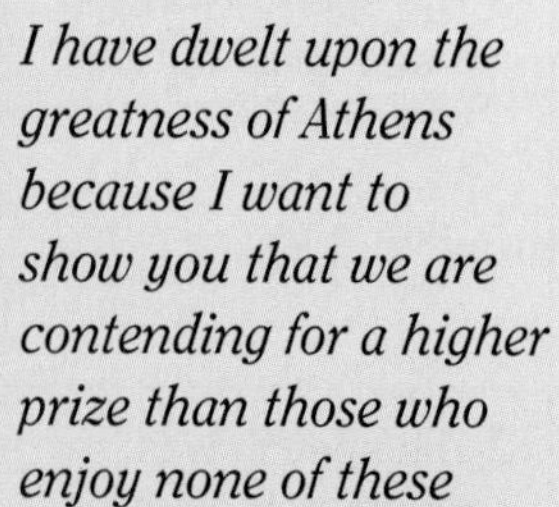

I have dwelt upon the greatness of Athens because I want to show you that we are contending for a higher prize than those who enjoy none of these privileges, and to establish by manifest proof the merit of these men whom I am now commemorating. Their loftiest praise has been already spoken. For in magnifying the city, I have magnified them, and men like them whose virtues made her glorious.

The classical tradition was continued in the Roman funeral oration. As in the Greek tradition, speakers' praise of individual deeds and virtues was always set in the context of celebrating the greater glory of Rome.

In the Middle Ages, however, there was a change in emphasis. The medieval funeral oration was based more on religion than politics. Speakers still praised the deceased's virtues and achievements; however, the celebration of the individual became a vehicle not for praising the state but for praising God. This is evident in Gregory of Nazianzus's funeral oration for his sister, Gorgonia:

Gorgonia's native land was Jerusalem above [heaven], the object not of sight but of contemplation . . . her nobility consisted in the preservation of the Image, and the perfect likeness to the Archetype . . . in things pertaining to God.

In the sixteenth century, the era of the Protestant Reformation and the Catholic reaction to it, funeral orations shifted again. The idea of praising the virtues and achievements of the deceased was all but abandoned. Speakers at funerals praised God and attempted to console the congregation.

By the late eighteenth century, funeral orations and eulogies were more secular. Once again funeral orators praised the personal qualities of the departed. This is reflected in Henry Lee's famous eulogy for George Washington, delivered on December 26, 1799:

First in war, first in peace and first in the hearts of his countrymen, he was second to none in the humble and endearing scenes of private life. Pious, just, humane, temperate and sincere—uniform, dignified and commanding—his example was as edifying to all around him as were the effects of that example lasting. . . . Correct throughout, vice shuddered in his presence and virtue always felt his fostering hand. The purity of his private character gave effulgence [brightness] to his public virtues.

. . . to John Cleese

Contemporary eulogies, like classical ones, usually praise the dead and celebrate their lives. President Ronald Reagan's eulogy in 1986 for the seven *Challenger* astronauts who died in an accident is a good example.

The sacrifice of your loved ones has stirred the soul of our nation and, through the pain, our hearts have been opened to a profound truth—the future is not free, the story of all human progress is one of struggle against all odds . . . .

Today, the frontier is space and the boundaries human knowledge. Sometimes, when we reach for the stars, we fall short. But we must pick ourselves up again and press on despite the pain. Our nation is indeed fortunate that we can still draw on immense reservoirs of courage, character and fortitude—that we are still blessed with heroes like those of the Space Shuttle Challenger.

However, some contemporary eulogies break from tradition. They don't always portray the deceased as models of virtue. They don't focus only on the traits that everyone admired and praised. Rather, some eulogies today celebrate the qualities that made the person special and beloved. An extreme example of this was comedian John Cleese's eulogy for his colleague Graham Chapman. Both men were part of the famous comedy group, Monty Python. Cleese praised Chapman's love of the outrageous:

Well, I feel that I should say, "Good riddance to him! . . . I hope he fries."

And the reason I think I should say this is, he would never forgive me if I didn't, if I threw away this opportunity to shock you all on his behalf. Anything for him but mindless good taste . . . . And that's what I'll always remember about him—apart, of course, from his Olympian extravagance. He was the prince of bad taste. He loved to shock.

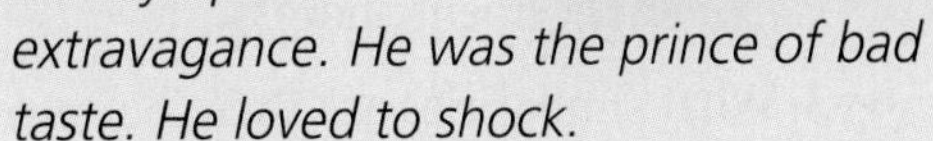

The shift from praise by Pericles to shock by Cleese is dramatic. However, eulogies continue to honor individuals in their own way.

Chapter 22 Review

Using Vocabulary Words

Use a four-part box like this to analyze each of the vocabulary words.

Word or Term	Personal Association
Definition	**Something Completely Different**

1. anecdote
2. auspicious
3. dignitary
4. eulogy
5. testimonial
6. theme
7. tone
8. valedictory

Reviewing Key Ideas

1. List six different kinds of special occasion speeches.
2. Explain the differences between a valedictory speech and a commencement address.
3. What similarities are there between a speech of introduction and a presentation speech?
4. What tone is appropriate for most commemorative speeches? Why?
5. What advice would you give someone who has been asked to give an after-dinner speech?

Reflecting on Your Project

Think about the presentation or acceptance speech you delivered. What do you wish you'd done differently?

Responding to the Essential Question

Use the headings in this chapter to help you write a brief chapter summary that answers the question, "How do speeches for special occasions differ in content and organization?" Compare your summary with that of a partner.

Extending Your Understanding

Everyday Life

1. Use a local newspaper to review the events that took place in your community last week. List events that involved speakers and, if possible, note the speech topics. Share your observations about how the occasion determined the topic with a partner.
2. Take turns with classmates proposing special occasions and topics for a speech for that occasion. One person suggests an occasion and another suggests a speech topic. Then someone else thinks up another special occasion and calls on someone else to suggest a topic, and so on.
3. Plan a banquet for a group of which you are a part. Select a person from the present or past that you would like to have deliver the after-dinner speech. Explain why you chose this person.

In the Media

4. Analyze a special occasion speech that you find on the Internet. Discuss the speaker's theme.
5. At www.oscar.com, you can watch videos of the winners of the most recent Academy Awards backstage speaking to the "Thank-you Cam." Analyze two of them.
6. In the listing of upcoming events in your local newspaper, find an event that would probably involve speech-making. Decide who would be likely to speak at the event and select a topic for that speaker.

Research

7. Select a famous person who is no longer living. Use the Internet to locate an excellent eulogy for that person. Read it to the class and explain why it is a good eulogy.
8. The Gettysburg Address by Abraham Lincoln was not the featured speech at the dedication of the Soldiers' National Cemetery in Gettysburg, Pennsylvania. The featured speaker was Edward Everett, a famous orator known for his eloquence. Everett gave a speech that lasted for two hours. You can find it at http://en.wikisource.org/wiki/Gettysburg_Oration. Read Everett's speech. Then read Abraham Lincoln's speech (page 592), which was billed on the program as "Dedicatory Remarks" and took only two or three minutes. Prepare and present a one-minute speech explaining why Lincoln's speech is so well-remembered.

Interpreting Graphics

One recommendation for a successful after-dinner speech is to use humorous props. The visual aid below was employed by a speaker giving an after-dinner speech to a parents' group. What do you think the topic of the speech was? What does this chart show and how does it relate to what the speaker had to say? Jot down your ideas and then share them with the rest of the class.

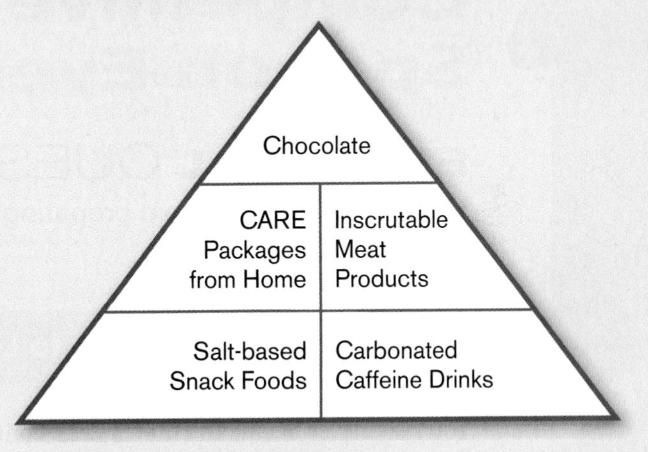

Additional Projects

1. **Group Project:** With your group, plan and carry out a mock dedication. Decide what will be dedicated, how many speeches there will be, and who will deliver them. Create a program for the dedication. Then have the speakers prepare their speeches and deliver them for the rest of the class.
2. **Individual Project:** Pretend that you have been asked to deliver the valedictory at your high school graduation. Make a list of the important experiences you and your classmates have had in your four years that would help you prepare your speech. Then write a short valedictory speech.

Competitive Speech Events

ESSENTIAL QUESTION

What can you learn from preparing for competitive speech events even if you never compete?

Chapter Project: Bring It to Life

You may never decide to enter speech contests, but think of how many times you've already presented your ideas to a group, debated a point, and read aloud to others. This project will help you gain some skills of competitive speaking so you can enrich your ability to communicate in any setting.

With your class, you will decide on a broad theme—perhaps friendship, patriotism, or public service—then you and a partner will create a presentation that brings that theme to life. Your presentation can take the form of an extemporaneous speech that you deliver together, a debate, or an oral interpretation of a poem, a piece of literature, or a scene in a play. Time limits may vary, depending on the type of speech. Use the CAPS guidelines as you work.

The rubric on page 533 shows the traits on your speech will be evaluated.

CONCEPT	an effective oral presentation brings a subject to life
AUDIENCE	classmates and teacher
PURPOSE	practice using the forms of competitive speaking
SITUATION	informal classroom presentation

How many times in your school years have you been called on to speak in front of your class?

KEY VOCABULARY

- forensic
- analytical
- oral interpretation
- narrative
- excerpt
- dialogue
- resolution
- proposition
- affirmative position
- negative position
- rebuttal

Speak Up!

Speaking in public without time to prepare and practice may worry you, but the truth is you have experiences every day that prepare you to do just that. Think about what those everyday experiences are and write down your ideas. Then take turns sharing your ideas as your teacher writes them on the board. Keep these ideas in mind as you read the chapter.

Pages 510–531 will provide the background you'll need to succeed with this project.

Competitive Speaking

Chapter 17 noted that there are four speech-delivery formats: manuscript, memorized, extemporaneous, and impromptu. The first two formats allow the speaker time to prepare a speech and write it out word for word, to be either read or recited from memory. The other two formats—extemporaneous and impromptu—don't give the speaker much time to prepare. All four formats are used in **forensic** competitions—public speaking tournaments.

Extemporaneous Speaking

In extemporaneous speaking, the speaker is assigned a topic and given a limited period of time to prepare a speech. The goal is to appear well-prepared yet conversational while speaking. Even though competitive extemporaneous speaking may not be something that interests you at all, the skills needed to think on your feet and express your ideas clearly and confidently will be useful throughout your school years and beyond. For example, suppose your English teacher asks the class to compare two works of literature, and he pauses briefly before calling on someone. During that pause, you think about how the two works are alike and different. If he calls on you, you share your ideas. In doing so, you are speaking extemporaneously.

Now imagine that you are ten years older, and working in a job. You are sitting in a meeting with your coworkers, trying to solve a problem. As you listen to the other people in the room share their ideas, you jot down your own thoughts. When the time is right, you present your idea for solving the problem. That's another example of extemporaneous speaking.

Extemporaneous speaking is a useful skill in most jobs.

Extemporaneous speaking, or "extemp," is a regular part of high school and college forensic competition. In speech competitions, extemporaneous speakers, or "extempers," speak informatively or persuasively about current events. They are knowledgeable about current events and can speak on many issues with very little preparation time. In a competitive situation, extempers are usually given a choice of three specific topics, often in the form of questions about current events. They choose one and have a limited time to prepare their speech. Prep time can be from 30 to 45 minutes. During prep time, extempers can use any magazines and newspapers they have with them. They are sometimes permitted to use laptops for retrieving stored information but not to do any new research. At the end of the prep time, extempers present their speeches before a judge and an audience. The rules of the competition also indicate the length of the speech, which can range from four minutes to seven minutes. Some competitions allow speakers to use several note cards. Others allow only one card, or no notes at all.

Extemporaneous speaking requires confidence, knowledge of current events, and the ability to think on your feet.

TechConnect *Extempers watch a wide range of news programs to get a full spectrum of ideas.*

Building A Knowledge Base

TechConnect

For an extemper, preparation starts before the tournament. Extempers work at building their knowledge base all the time. Because the questions used in extemporaneous speaking are all about current events, extempers read several news sources. Popular ones include the *New York Times,* the *Washington Post,* the *Economist, Foreign Affairs, Financial Times,* and the *Christian Science Monitor.* Many of these can be accessed online. Analyzing this information keeps them up to date on critical current issues and helps them with their **analytical** thinking, or logical reasoning, and their organization skills.

Extempers also watch many different news shows on network and cable television and visit Internet news sites to keep themselves informed. These all provide different "takes" on current events and demonstrate how professionals analyze situations and present their views.

Five-Point Plan for Extemporaneous Contests

Suppose you are a contestant in a tournament. You've chosen your question, and you've got thirty minutes to get ready to speak. Here's what you do:

1. **Prepare** Start by thinking about the question. What do you know about this subject? Where can you find the information you need? You can use only the periodicals you brought with you or the information you have stored on your laptop. So, a well-organized collection of articles, anecdotes, and practice speeches are helpful in planning what you will say. Next, decide how you will answer the question. Be ready to cite your sources.

Practicing in front of a mirror is helpful. The more you see yourself, the more eye contact you will make with your real audience.

2. **Organize** Use one of these five organization patterns: order of importance, logical order, chronological order, problem-solution order, or cause-effect order. With any of the patterns you choose, your speech must have a clear three-part structure: introduction, body, and conclusion. (See chapter 16 for effective techniques for crafting a speech.)

3. **Outline** In some tournaments, extempers are not allowed to use notes at all. However, usually presenters may use an outline that fits on one index card. Be concise in your introduction, including only key words and phrases you want to use. List the main points for the body of your speech, including facts and sources to which you will refer. List the main points of your conclusion. Also note key transitions. Your outline should be easy for you to read and you should leave space to add notes when you rehearse your speech.

4. **Practice** Your prep time will probably be limited to thirty minutes. Save at least the last ten minutes so that you can run through your entire speech. Pay special attention to length. In most tournaments, extemporaneous speeches have a time limit of seven minutes. The judge has a stopwatch. Although you won't be asked to stop when you've spoken for seven minutes, going over the time limit will lower your score. Consider whether adding notes to your outline might help you polish your delivery. Spend any last minutes brushing up on rough spots.

5. **Present** As you present your speech, keep these points in mind:
    - Speak loud enough to be heard, especially by the judge and any listeners in the back row.
    - Pronounce words clearly and correctly. If you're not sure how to pronounce a word, don't use it.
    - Avoid adding the word *like* as a filler in sentences or using vocal pauses in the form of *ums* and *ahs.*
    - Vary the pitch, tempo, and tone of your voice. Use pauses to help you introduce new ideas and give emphasis to important points. Monitor your speed: don't talk too fast.
    - Make eye contact with the judge in particular and audience members in general. Use any feedback you receive from your listeners.
    - Use gestures that are effective but not distracting.
    - Use movement wisely. Some extempers like to a take a step with each main point. This practice is sometimes called the "extemp dance."

Many fine speakers believe that nothing is more effective in developing speaking and writing skills than competing in extemporaneous speaking. Additional positive effects are the building of organizational and analytical skills along with greater awareness of political, economic, and social issues that make for a well-rounded citizen.

Speaking in front of groups at work, in voluntary organizations, or just among friends, is a skill you will use the rest of your life. The more practice you get, the more confidence and poise you will have.

To become a better extemporaneous speaker, try to prepare for topics you might be discussing. Organize your comments in a clear pattern and outline the details that support each main point. Practice before you present, and use good speaking skills when you deliver your speech.

Analyzing an Extemporaneous Speech

The question chosen by this extemper was: "What can be done to curb global food prices?" Read the sample speech and commentary that goes with it.

1 You've probably heard the story of Marie Antoinette, the queen of France during the French Revolution, who when told that the poor of Paris were rioting because they had no bread allegedly replied, "Let them eat cake."

The speaker uses the device a story about a real person as an attention-getter.

2 Historians aren't sure if Marie Antoinette actually said that, but the part of the story that cannot be disputed is that hunger can lead to riots and social unrest. It's happening today. In 2008, the prime minister of Haiti was forced to resign when hungry mobs staged violent protests.

This paragraph connects the historic account to current events.

3 Haiti isn't the only country facing a food crisis. The president of the World Bank says that the rising cost of food is forcing 100 million people into hunger and malnutrition and pushing thirty countries toward social upheaval. Even food-rich countries like the United States are being affected by the rising costs of staples like wheat, rice, and milk. It's a crisis that is making world leaders ask: "What can be done to curb global food prices?"

This paragraph elaborates on the problem, quotes an authority, and ends with the topic question.

The speaker might pause before stating the question and then say it quite deliberately.

4 In order to solve the problem, we need to understand what caused it. Most analysts point to three factors that have contributed to the current food crisis: greater demand for higher quality food—especially meat—from emerging economies like China's; rising oil prices; diverting food resources to make biofuels. Let's think about each of these factors.

The introduction indicates that the problem is complex. It previews the problem–solution organization of the speech.

The last sentence is a transition to examining the causes.

5 China is the most populous country in the world. A diet that includes a lot of meat is not very economical in terms of food resources because in raising animals you use food to produce food. With

beef, for example, it takes 700 calories of grain to produce a 100-calorie piece of beef. What happens when you have more people demanding a diet that requires more food resources? We're starting to see what happens.

The speaker uses a question to engage the audience and get them to think about the consequences of the two things just mentioned.

A question is used as a transition.

6 How do rising oil prices affect food prices? Oil and petroleum products are involved in every step of modern agriculture, but let's think about the most obvious connection. The countries that are most severely impacted by the global food crisis—countries like Haiti, Mauritania, Senegal, and Cameroon—are countries that import more than half their food. As the price of oil goes up, the price of food goes up, and the situation gets worse when some food-exporting countries decide to stockpile food and keep it at home.

The speaker comments on each of the three factors cited as causes of the food crisis.

The speaker might move one hand up when mentioning rising oil prices and the other when mentioning rising food prices.

7 Then there's biofuel. It seemed like such a good idea—easing America's dependence on foreign oil by growing our own fuel. What a perfect example of American ingenuity and self-sufficiency! But is it really? American farmers are getting paid more than twice as much for selling their corn to ethanol distilleries as they were selling it as food. The *Washington Post* reports that in 2008, about a quarter of the corn crop in the United States went to make ethanol. This diversion of a food crop to produce fuel comes at a time when the global demand for grain is growing. World Bank President Robert Zoellick put things into perspective when he said, "While many are worrying about filling their gas tanks, many others around the world are struggling to fill their stomachs, and it is getting more and more difficult every day."

The speaker might pause for a bit after saying *biofuel.*

This question is used to engage the audience and make them think.

The speaker cites a source of information and then quotes a recognized authority.

The speaker would probably slow down and stress the last part of this quote.

8 So, what's to be done? I don't have a quick fix, although hungry people around the world deserve one. What I do see is a problem that is not going away but one that can be solved if we are willing to make the effort to change. My solution to the global food crisis has three parts.

A question is used as a transition and to introduce the solution part of the speech.

There are three parts to the solution to correspond with the three factors causing the problem. The speaker might take a step as each part of the solution is presented and hold up fingers to indicate *first, second, third.*

9 First, we as individuals need to adopt a more plant-based diet and stop using up so many food resources to raise animals for meat. A plant-based diet is healthier for us, and it is certainly more humane to the animals.

10 Second, as individuals, we need to eat locally—that is, we should try to eat only foods that are grown within 50 miles of where we live. For people in northern states, that would mean giving up things like strawberries in winter. It would mean rethinking what we eat and how we plan and provide for non-growing seasons. But it can be done. Also, as a nation, we need to help revive the ruined agricultural economy of Haiti and figure out ways to help countries like Mauritania become more self-sufficient agriculturally.

The speaker would probably stress *can* in the sentence "It can be done."

11 Third, we need to admit that oil reserves have peaked, our excessive use of oil to power cars and airplanes has harmed the planet, and we are not going to find a magic alternative that will allow us to keep on the way we're going. We simply must conserve.

The first two points related to demand for higher quality food and rising oil prices. This one relates to using food crops to produce biofuel.

12 For decades Americans have enjoyed a high standard of living that other countries envy and aspire to, but our standard of living consumes an enormous amount of the Earth's resources, and we are coming to realize that the Earth cannot support everyone living the way we Americans do.

Having presented the three-part solution, the speaker begins the conclusion.

13 As individual Americans, it seems to me we have a choice. We can say of the 100 million people in the world struggling with hunger and malnutrition, "Let them eat cake," or we can make the changes in our own diets and habits that conserve food and energy resources. By doing so, we will make our lives more sustainable and will benefit the rest of the world.

In the conclusion, the speaker refers back to the story used at the beginning.

In the final sentence, the speaker might gesture toward herself on "our lives" and make an open gesture on "benefit the rest of the world."

Communication in a
DIVERSE WORLD

"Chinese Bridge" Speech Competition

"Chinese Bridge" is a speech competition that has more to do with language proficiency than with analysis and delivery. It is an annual contest sponsored by the China National Office for Teaching Chinese as a Foreign Language. It is coordinated by Chinese embassies in countries where Chinese is not the first language. The primary purpose of the competition is to inspire interest in learning the Chinese language and to enhance understanding of Chinese culture.

Chinese Bridge competitions have been held in the United States since 2002. The first were intended for college and university students. College contests are open both to students learning Chinese as a second language and to "heritage students" for whom Mandarin Chinese or some other Chinese dialect is their native language. To make the competition fair, contestants are divided into six groups according to their year level in studying Chinese and their native language. For example, a non-heritage student studying Elementary Chinese, would be in Group 1. A heritage student studying Intermediate Chinese might be in Group 5. Winners are selected to go to the finals in Beijing. One hundred students from all over the world come together to compete in this final contest.

In 2006, Chinese Bridge competitions were started for high school students. At the high school level, only contestants who are learning Chinese as a second language can enter.

A Chinese Bridge speech competition consists of two events, which are meant to demonstrate a contestant's knowledge of Chinese language and culture. Each contestant first presents a three-minute prepared speech delivered in Chinese. The topic of each contestant's speech must relate to that year's theme. In 2008, for example, the theme was "Fervor with Olympics, Fun with Chinese" to tie into the Beijing Olympics. When all the speeches have been presented, each contestant presents a Chinese cultural talent, such as singing a Chinese song, doing a Chinese dance, demonstrating Chinese painting, or performing martial arts or a puppet show.

College student Casey Thomas Kerian, the 2007 winner of the midwestern regional Chinese Bridge competition, believes that learning Chinese creates better East-West understanding. "Nothing can give you more insight into a culture than its language."

The Chinese Bridge Competition helps American students share Chinese language and culture.

Competitive Impromptu Speaking

Impromptu speaking involves the least amount of preparation—usually none at all. People engage in impromptu speaking all the time at school and at work. If you are asked to report on the progress of a class project or have to answer a reporter's question about an upcoming game, you're engaged in impromptu speaking. Developing ease and poise in spontaneous and straightforward speaking is always worth the effort.

Reading on a wide variety of topics helps impromptu speakers keep useful information in their mental libraries.

In impromptu speech contests, students are usually given a choice of two topics and a few seconds in which to read them and make their choice. The topic may be a quotation, a famous person, an ordinary thing, a proverb, or an abstract word. Impromptu topics give speakers the opportunity to be creative and imaginative and use their own knowledge to interpret a subject. Once they've chosen a topic, they must prepare and deliver their speech in the judge's presence. The time given to prepare and deliver the speech differs from competition to competition. The National Forensic League allows each impromptu contestant five minutes for prep and five minutes for speaking. Some competitions allow only three minutes of prep time while others combine prep and speaking time.

Broader Background Knowledge Building a knowledge base is as important for impromptu speakers as it is for extempers, but the reading material differs. Extempers focus on current events. Impromptu speakers read everything, from history and philosophy to movie reviews. You never know what information will be helpful in an impromptu speech.

Three-Point Plan for Impromptu Contests

Imagine that you are a competitive impromptu speaker. You've chosen your topic, and the clock has started ticking. You have five minutes to prepare your speech and five minutes to deliver it. What will you do?

Prepare The first thing you must do is decide on a thesis. Your thesis will determine everything else you say. Following are just a few ways of arriving at a thesis.

Quotation: "The only real mistake is the one from which we learn nothing."
—John Powell
Thesis: If we are thoughtful, all life's experiences can be learning experiences.

Person you admire: Rachel Carson
Thesis: Rachel Carson was a biologist and writer who helped launch the environmental movement.

Ordinary thing: MP3 Player
Thesis: An MP3 player is an important tool for any student.

Abstract word: Sustainability
Thesis: Sustainability means meeting the needs of the present without compromising the ability of future generations to meet their needs.

The development of the MP3 player might make for a good impromptu speech.

Organize Like all good speeches, an impromptu speech needs an introduction, a body, and a conclusion. In an introduction, you arouse the audience's attention, state your topic and thesis, and preview the support provided in the body of the speech. Typically two or three reasons are offered in the body, and each one is supported by examples that illustrate your point. While extempers support their reasons with references to books and magazines, most impromptu speakers illustrate their points with personal references and anecdotes, real stories from their own lives or the lives of others. The conclusion should restate the topic and the thesis and wrap things up, sometimes by referring back to an idea from your introduction.

Deliver In impromptu competition, notes are not permitted. You speak "off the cuff." Judges look for a natural and spontaneous delivery. You need to speak clearly, varying the pitch, tempo, and tone, and use pauses to make your presentation interesting and effective. You must make eye contact with your audience and engage them in what you have to say. Use their reactions as an indicator of how you're doing and adjust your presentation accordingly.

A good impromptu speech involves a certain amount of animation. Your gestures and movements should enhance and punctuate your message.

KEY POINT

Impromptu speaking relies on personal references and stories and calls for a natural and spontaneous delivery.

PROJECT PREP

Interpreting quotations is something that impromptu speakers are often expected to do in competitive situations. With your **project partner**, help one another practice this technique. Check out a book of quotations or use a Web site such www.quotationspage.com to find quotations that have to do with the theme the class has chosen for the project. Find a quotation you both like and discuss what you think it means. How would you interpret it for your listeners?

Competitive Dramatic Events

Dramatic events are another category in speech competitions. Dramatic events include dramatic interpretation, humorous interpretation, and duo interpretation. In dramatic interpretation, one person presents aloud a selection from a piece of literature that is dramatic in nature—a novel, short story, play, or poem. Humorous interpretations focus on selections that are amusing or lighthearted. A duo interpretation involves two people who present a selection together—dramatic or humorous.

In all of these events, the presentations must be memorized and performed without costumes or props. For each event, there is usually a ten-minute time limit. The time limit includes an introduction that sets the mood and gives the audience the information they need to understand the selection.

Oral Interpretation

Oral interpretation is a performance art that blends theatre and public speaking. People use it when they read from letters at weddings, poems at funerals, or scripture at religious services.

This art involves using the voice, facial expressions, and gestures to communicate the meaning of any written work, particularly of literature. It enhances the understanding and appreciation of literature for both the interpreter and the audience. The interpreter learns more about the work through study and preparation for a performance, and this understanding is passed along to the listener in the performance.

Oral interpretation can be an expressive monologue done by one person. Or, it can be done by two people or a group. Dramatic interpretation, humorous interpretation, and duo interpretation are all forms of oral interpretation. The process of preparing and presenting a selection is the same for all three forms of oral interpretation.

Choosing Your Selection

Oral interpretation begins with choosing the right selection. Begin by thinking about literature you know—a favorite poem or story that lends itself to being read aloud. Consider too the quality of the literature. It should be well-written and interesting and should offer you and your listeners something to think about and interpret. It should also relate to the human experience. Some students prefer to choose a **narrative**, or story, rather than a selection that is primarily description or explanation.

Oral interpretation blends public speaking and theatre.

The selection you choose should be something that affects you in a meaningful way. It should move you or challenge you, and it should have significance for you that you are eager to share with the audience. Your selection should be something that is both appropriate to the occasion and interesting to the audience. If you're struggling to find the right selection, ask your English teacher or librarian for suggestions.

Adapting and Cutting Your Selection

Once you have decided on a work of literature, you need to determine how much of it you will be able to present within your time limit. If you have chosen a poem, you might be able to read the entire thing within the time allowed. However, if you're working with a short story or a scene from a novel or play, you have to decide which **excerpt**, or portion, you will read. This decision can be challenging because what you read must be able to stand alone. It has to tell a story that hangs together and makes sense to the listeners and can be performed in less than ten minutes. You may have to read through a number of excerpts before you find a selection that will be meaningful to your audience.

On the other hand, you don't want to do so much cutting and adapting that you destroy the integrity of the work or the character of its language. The idea is to change as little as possible while also presenting a piece that reads well and has structure and unity. You will want to cut any confusing or distracting references to characters or events that don't play a part in the excerpt. You may also want to cut material that doesn't further the thread of the plot that your excerpt focuses on. When you're reading **dialogue**, or conversation, particularly when there are two or more of you presenting, you will want to leave out words that identify who's speaking and any descriptive adverbs. For example, you can omit words such as *Algernon said* or *said Martha with a grin.*

Presenting Your Selection

Your approach to interpreting and presenting your literary selection will be different depending on the nature of the literature you choose. What you need to consider as you prepare for your presentation will be different if you are reading prose, poetry, or drama.

Prose The first thing you need to think about when interpreting prose is whose voice is telling the story. Identify who is narrating the sequence of events and communicating their importance to the audience. Is it a character in the story? Or is it a narrator who isn't part of the story but is observing and reporting?

When reading an excerpt as a group, take time to discuss how each person should present each line.

If the story is being told by a character who uses the pronoun *I* in the narration, the story is a *first-person narrative*. First-person narratives are often good choices for oral interpretation because the whole story is told in one voice and from a single point of view. The following paragraph from "Fish Cheeks" by Amy Tan is an example of first-person narrative.

> I fell in love with the minister's son the winter I turned fourteen. He was not Chinese, but as white as Mary in the manger. For Christmas I prayed for this blond-haired boy, Robert, and a slim new American nose.
>
> When I found out that my parents had invited the minister's family over for Christmas Eve dinner, I cried. What would Robert think of our shabby Chinese Christmas? What would he think of our noisy Chinese relatives who lacked proper American manners?

Amy Tan's writing draws on her experience growing up as a Chinese American.

When interpreting a first-person narrative, ask yourself these questions: Who is the narrator? Is this person young or old? What does his or her voice sound like? How does he or she feel about the story being told? How does the narrator expect you to react to the story? By answering these questions, your interpretation will be true to the voice of the narrator.

In a *third-person narrative*, the story is told by a narrator who is not a character in the story. If the narrator knows everything that happens and how all the characters feel about things, the narrator is spoken of as omniscient. The passage below from "The Legend of Sleepy Hollow," by Washington Irving, is an example of third-person narrative.

> The schoolmaster is generally a man of some importance in the female circle of a rural neighborhood; being considered a kind of idle, gentlemanlike personage, of vastly superior taste and accomplishments to the rough country swains, and, indeed, inferior in learning only to the parson. His appearance, therefore, is apt to occasion some little stir at the tea-table of a farmhouse, and the addition of a supernumerary dish of cakes or sweetmeats, or, peradventure, the parade of a silver teapot. Our man of letters, therefore, was peculiarly happy in the smiles of all the country damsels.

When analyzing a third-person narrative, be aware of the narrator's attitude toward the characters and the story. Is it sympathetic? Is ironic or amused? You will then reflect this understanding in your interpretation.

A selection with dialogue involves an additional challenge. You must use different voices so that listeners can distinguish the characters and what they are saying.

Poetry The three qualities that make poetry different from prose—meter, rhythm, and rhyme—also make interpreting poetry more challenging. Be careful not to read in a sing-song fashion, which may obstruct the poem's grace and meaning.

Meter is the pattern of rhythm in a poem. Poetry is measured in metric feet, in which every syllable gets a weak or strong stress. In the sonnet below by Shakespeare, each line has five feet, and each foot is made up of two syllables: the first unaccented, the second accented. When interpreting poetry, always try to balance meter and meaning.

Several Web sites include all of Shakespeare's 154 sonnets. He wrote most of them between 1591 and 1598.

Shall I compare thee to a summer's day?
Thou art more lovely and more temperate;
Rough winds do shake the darling buds of May,
And summer's lease hath all too short a date;
Sometime too hot the eye of heaven shines,
And often is his gold complexion dimm'd;
And every fair from fair sometime declines,
By chance or nature's changing course untrimm'd;
But thy eternal summer shall not fade
Nor lose possession of that fair thou owest;
Nor shall Death brag thou wander'st in his shade,
When in eternal lines to time thou growest;
So long as men can breathe or eyes can see,
So long lives this and this gives life to thee.

Rhythm is the musical quality produced by the repetition of stressed and unstressed syllables. Rhythm occurs in all language, but it is especially important in poetry. Rhythm is closely connected with meter; in fact, meter is the regular rhythm in poetry. The meter of Shakespeare's sonnet is iambic pentameter: *iambic* because each foot is an *iamb,* an unaccented syllable followed by an accented syllable; and *pentameter* because each line has five feet.

Rhyme is the occurrence of words that sound the same at the end. Many poems have rhyming words at the end of lines. When a rhyme appears in the middle of a line, it is called an *internal rhyme.* The *rhyme scheme* is the pattern of rhyme in a poem. Letters are used to indicate rhyme scheme. The rhyme scheme for most sonnets is *abab cdcd efef gg.*

Drama Interpreting drama may not involve costumes, sets, props, or entrances and exits, but the essence of theatre is still there. Body movement, facial gestures, tone and volume of voice convey much meaning. In dramatic interpretation, presenters *become* the characters through voice and articulation rather than appearance and action.

Unless a presenter is doing a long monologue or soliloquy, interpreting drama often involves two people. Performers select an excerpt from a play that focuses on an exchange between two characters and interpret it for an audience. These presenters work together to agree about how the selection should be interpreted. They react to one another's words, emotions, and rhythm.

Readers Theatre

Readers Theatre, also known as interpreters theatre, is a dramatic interpretation or adaptation of a play or narrative fiction. It involves as many presenters as there are characters. In narrative fiction, one person reads the narration while the others read the dialogue of the characters. Presenters stand or sit in one place and create the scene vocally.

In Readers Theatre, a group of people work together to bring out the meaning of an excerpt.

Readers Theatre is a form of oral interpretation. Like any other form of oral interpretation, it involves communicating the presenters' understanding of a work of literature to the audience. If an individual's understanding of a character changes as he or she grows more familiar with the selection, this new understanding can be incorporated into the group's interpretation of the work.

PROJECT PREP

Work with your **project partner** to explore oral interpretation. Choose a brief selection from your literature book or some other source. Each of you should prepare and present to one another an interpretation of the same selection. Discuss how each of you interpreted the characters, the tone, and the mood of the work.

Storytelling

As long as there has been language, there has been storytelling. Every culture has stories that have been passed down from generation to generation by storytellers. Before there was written language, storytellers were revered as important sources of a community's culture. Today, the tradition of storytelling is alive and well, and the ability to tell a good story is a skill you can nurture. It will make you a more effective speaker as well as an interesting thinker and conversationalist.

In a storytelling competition, presenters don't memorize their stories. Instead they internalize a traditional story and tell it in their own way, using their voice, facial expressions, body language, and gestures to bring the story and the characters to life. Stories told by storytellers are usually fairy tales, folktales, or fables. Storytellers practice by telling a story over and over again, often in front of a mirror so they can see their facial expressions and gestures as they tell the story. The more they practice their stories, the more they refine their technique and the more familiar they become with the story's meaning and mood.

KEY POINT

Competitive dramatic events help both listeners and performers gain a deep appreciation of literature.

Storytellers may never tell a story in exactly the same way twice. When they perform for an audience, good storytellers use eye contact and audience feedback to gauge the success of their delivery. Storytellers respond to how the audience is receiving the story. Interaction with the audience helps to make every storytelling performance unique.

A great storyteller is a great speaker, and vice versa.

Competitive Debate

Debate is the process of examining an issue or question by looking at both sides and weighing the evidence to solve a problem, establish truth, or understand opposing viewpoints. Debate is often associated with politics, but it actually takes place in many contexts. A school board might debate the pros and cons of rehabbing the gym or building a new one. A family buying a new car might debate the advantages and disadvantages of different models. When you analyze your options before making a decision, you're debating.

Competitive debate is formally structured. It can help you develop critical thinking skills, research strategies, and public speaking skills. As an academic area of study, debate is a training ground for business, government, and community leadership. The topics that are debated in academic settings deal with current events. Like extemporaneous speaking, debate helps prepare students to be participating citizens in their communities.

What Do Debaters Debate About?

Competitive debate involves two teams or two individuals. They debate a position statement, called a **resolution** or **proposition**. One side takes the **affirmative position,** which argues in favor of the resolution. The other side takes the **negative position**, which argues against the resolution. Resolutions or propositions for debate are of three types: fact, value, and policy (see Chapter 12). A fourth type of resolution, the problem statement, is typically presented as a question—for example, "What should be the role of the federal government in public education?" (See Chapter 8 on Solving Problems and Managing Conflict and Chapter 12 on Group Discussions.)

Proposition of Fact A proposition of fact makes a statement that can be proved to be true or false. You may wonder why something that can be proved needs to be debated, but the typical proposition of fact concerns things that are not easily proved or disproved. An example might be this statement: "The United States is winning the war on terrorism." If you were to debate this, you might first have to define what winning would be and then use a series of facts to demonstrate that the United States is winning.

Vice-presidential candidates Senator Joe Biden and Governor Sarah Palin debated each other in 2008. How is a political debate like the debate you might have when trying to choose a new car? How does it differ?

Proposition of Value A proposition of value suggests that one idea, belief, or action is preferable to another. A value is neither right nor wrong. Rather it is something that is held dear by an individual or a society. A proposition of value that might be debated in an academic setting is "National security is more important than transparency in government." In this proposition, the values being debated are "national security" and "transparency in government."

Proposition of Policy Propositions of policy are usually broad and complex, and they cover current problems facing the country or the world. An example of a proposition of policy is "The federal government should guarantee comprehensive health insurance to all U.S. citizens." There are four standards for a proposition of policy. These are:

1. There should be sufficient information on each side.
2. The wording of the proposition should take a position so that the affirmative and negative positions are clear.
3. The resolution should address one central idea.
4. The wording of the proposition should be neutral.

Types of Debate Events

Competitive debate follows different formats: policy debate (also called team debate), Lincoln–Douglas debate (also called individual debate), parliamentary debate, public forum debate, student congress, and mock trials. The purpose of competitive debate is to give students the opportunity to discuss some of today's most important social, political, and moral issues in a contest setting. In the process, important critical thinking skills are developed that will remain with them throughout their lives.

Policy Debate Also called team debate, this competitive debate event involves teams of two that focus on policy topics. The same topic is used for the policy debate in speech competitions throughout the country. Every August, representatives of the nation's debate coaches meet to select five topics. In the fall, these five topics are voted on by all the debate coaches, and the choices are narrowed down to three. The three choices are voted on by each state to determine the national topic for the year, which is announced in early January.

Lyndon B. Johnson taught high school debate in Texas. When he became president, he appointed several of his debaters to important government positions.

The format of a policy debate is carefully structured so that each team has an adequate opportunity to present its side of an issue. One team takes the affirmative position; the other takes the negative position. Both members of each two-person team deliver two speeches: a constructive speech and a **rebuttal**, or statement countering the other's position. The speeches are usually delivered in this order:

First Affirmative Constructive

First Negative Constructive

Second Affirmative Constructive

Second Negative Constructive

First Negative Rebuttal

First Affirmative Rebuttal

Second Negative Rebuttal

Second Affirmative Rebuttal

The Lincoln-Douglas debates were accompanied by brass bands and cheering crowds.

There is a time limit for both the constructive speeches and the rebuttals. In addition, each constructive speech is followed by limited period of cross-examination during which one person from the opposing team may ask questions of the speaker. At the end of the entire round, a judge decides which team has done a better job of debating.

Lincoln–Douglas Debate In 1858, Abraham Lincoln, then a virtual unknown running for senator from Illinois, challenged his opponent, Stephen Douglas, to a debate. Douglas accepted, and a series of seven debates took place in seven cities throughout Illinois. Occurring just three years before the beginning of the Civil War, the debates were dominated by the issues of states' rights and slavery, and they drew national interest. Today, any debate between two individuals on a proposition of importance is named for these historic debates.

In a Lincoln–Douglas, or LD, debate, each debater gets to speak for a total of thirteen minutes, but how the time is divided up is different for the affirmative debater and the negative debater. Each debater presents a constructive speech (an affirmative and a negative constructive) and a rebuttal (an affirmative and a negative rebuttal). The affirmative gets two short rebuttals while the negative gets one longer rebuttal. An LD debate also involves cross-examination. The chart on the next page shows how the debate is formulated.

The values debated in LD events may have to do with achievement, democracy, equality, freedom, justice, liberty, privacy, progress, the pursuit of happiness, and security. Resolutions for competitive LD debates change every two months. Following are some recent examples of debate topics from National Forensic League tournaments:

- Secondary education in America should value the fine arts over athletics.
- Hate crime enhancements are unjust in the United States.
- A just society ought not use the death penalty as a form of punishment.
- It is just for the United States to use military force to prevent the acquisition of nuclear weapons by nations that pose a military threat.

The goal of the debate is to persuade the judge of the merit of your argument. Because LD debate involves propositions of value, debaters rely more on persuasion, logical analysis, and speaking skills than they do on statements of fact and the presentation of evidence.

Lincoln-Douglas debaters try to convince the judge that their arguments are sound.

Total Time Limits for Lincoln-Douglas Debates	
Affirmative Constructive	6 minutes
Cross-examination of Affirmative by Negative	3 minutes
Negative Constructive	7 minutes
Cross-examination of Negative by Affirmative	4 minutes
First Affirmative Rebuttal	4 minutes
Negative Rebuttal	6 minutes
Second Affirmative Rebuttal	3 minutes

Parliamentary Debate Parliamentary debate is another academic debate event. Since the format is based on British parliamentary procedure, the two sides are are called the Government and the Opposition. Each side has two speakers. For the Government, there is the Prime Minister and the Minister of the Crown. For the Opposition, there is the Leader of the Opposition and a Member of the Opposition. The chart below shows the typical format used in the United States.

Total Time Limits for Parliamentary Debaters	
Prime Minister	7 minutes
Leader of the Opposition	8 minutes
Minister of the Crown	8 minutes
Member of the Opposition	8 minutes
Leader of the Opposition Rebuttal	4 minutes
Prime Minister Rebuttal	5 minutes

Parliamentary debates can be about propositions of fact, value, or policy. Most parliamentary debates, however, have a policy focus. Here are some sample resolutions from recent National Parliamentary Debate Association tournaments:

- The federal government should enact a comprehensive water policy.
- This House prefers fair trade to free trade.
- The federal government should eliminate prison sentences for non-violent offenses.
- The federal government should significantly increase space exploration.
- When in conflict, United States politicians should value their personal conscience over the will of the people.

British Parliament's debate format is the basis for parliamentary debate as practiced in the United States. This format is more common in college than in high school.

Other Debate Formats

Policy debates, Lincoln–Douglas debates, and parliamentary debates have spawned other types of debates. In different ways, the formats listed below have made debating accessible to more students.

Public Forum Debate This debate format is sometimes known as Ted Turner debate or Crossfire debate, because it is a hybrid based on the TV current events show *Crossfire*, which aired from 1982 to 2005 on CNN, the network founded by Ted Turner. This is a relatively new debate format. The judges for public forum debates are "lay" judges who are unfamiliar with traditional forms of debate, so communication skills are very important. Cross-examination plays a much larger role in public forum debate than it does in traditional debate formats. Participants also need to be very good at asking questions and often prepare their questions in advance.

Student Congress This debate format is also known as Congressional debate. In this event, students imitate members of the U.S. Congress and debate bills and resolutions. The debate usually takes the form of three-minute speeches given by speakers who support the legislation and those who oppose it. The goal of each speech is to persuade others to embrace the speaker's point of view. When the speeches have been delivered, the participants vote on whether or not to adopt the legislation.

Mock Trial In a mock trial, teams of students—one on the side of the plaintiff, the other aligned with the defendant—act out a courtroom trial. Some members of each team are attorneys, the others witnesses. The teams are given all the information about the case, and they must prepare their arguments and testimony. They go through all the steps of a trial: opening statements, direct examination and cross-examination of witnesses, and closing statements. Mock trials have scoring judges, who decide which team gives the best performance, as well as the presiding judge, who delivers the verdict. Consequently, the team that wins the case may not be the team that ends up winning the event.

Ted Turner founded the Cable News Network, the first full-time news channel, in 1980. Since then, cable news has developed a reputation for featuring intense debates on current events.

Debate events help build skills for effective participation in the business world and in public life.

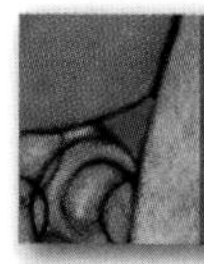

PREPARING THE PROJECT

Begin your project by looking back at the **Project Prep** activities in this chapter and using the directions below.

Make Connections

Think about how best to present your theme as related to the following:

- characteristics of extemporaneous speaking
- characteristics of impromptu speaking
- characteristics of oral interpretation
- characteristics of debate.

Focus

Briefly review your group project: exploring a broad theme by using either extemporaneous or impromptu speaking, oral interpretation, or debate.

Plan

You and your partner must decide how you plan to approach the theme your class has chosen. What element of friendship, patriotism, or public service do you want to discuss? Once you have decided this, you have to agree on the format—an extemporaneous speech that you deliver together, a debate, or an oral interpretation with each of you taking a part.

Develop

If you choose to present an extemporaneous speech, how will you develop your thesis and construct the introduction, body, and conclusion? If you choose oral interpretation, what piece of literature will you use? If you plan to debate, what will be your proposition and who will take the affirmative position and who the negative? Time limits may vary, but your teacher may want to adjust them so that everyone speaks for about the same length of time.

Practice

Run through your presentation once or twice to see if you can get through it in the allotted time. If you are debating, each of you should practice your constructive speech and rebuttal.

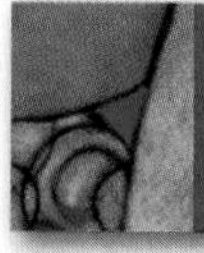

PRESENTING THE PROJECT

Use the strategies that follow to present your project.

Your teacher will establish time limits for the presentations. If you are doing oral interpretation, one of you should introduce the selection. If you are debating, one of you should state the proposition of value you are debating—for example, "Resolved: It is easier to forgive an enemy than it is to forgive a friend."

Offering New Ideas

This project allows you to speak on a broad theme that is important to you and your classmates. It should be interesting and enlightening to be both a presenter and listener—you will see how many different ways a theme can be approached. So relax, have fun, and show just how creative and persuasive you can be.

Surefire Persuasion

To be a moving and persuasive speaker, you first must establish credibility and pull in the audience. Then present thought-provoking questions and answers and build to a logical conclusion.

EVALUATING THE PROJECT

Evaluate the presentations using the following rubric.

Score the impromptu speech on each point, with 4 being "outstanding" and 1 being "needs much improvement."

Come up with an overall score and write a brief paragraph that explains your score.

Understanding of the Speech Event	Demonstration of a Form of Speech	Creativity and Originality	Preparation and Use of Time
4 Presenters understood requirements of the speech event they chose.	**4** Presenters' demonstration was true to the form and well organized.	**4** The presentation was creative, original, and compelling.	**4** The presentation was well-planned and did not exceed the time limit.
3 Presenters had a basic understanding of the speech event they chose.	**3** Presenters' demonstration was true to the form and fairly well organized.	**3** The presentation was creative and original but not very compelling.	**3** The presentation was fairly well-planned and stayed within the time limit.
2 Presenters did not fully understand the speech event they chose.	**2** Presenters' demonstration was fairly true to the form but not organized.	**2** The presentation was fairly creative and original but not compelling.	**2** The presentation lacked planning but stayed within the time limit.
1 Presenters had scant knowledge of the speech event they chose.	**1** Presenters' demonstration was not true to the form or organized.	**1** The presentation was neither creative, original, nor compelling.	**1** The presentation was not well-planned and went over or considerably under the time limit.

Communication *Past* and Present

The Story of Debate

From Disputation . . .

Like most things having to do with oratory and rhetoric, debate got its start in ancient Greece. Protagoras (487–411 B.C.) is considered the "father of debate." He helped his students hone their oratorical skills by having them argue the pros and cons of issues important to Greek society. There were two schools of thought about debate at that time. One school, made up of paid teachers of philosophy and rhetoric, taught students how to argue effectively in court debates. They emphasized the importance of an argument's effect on the audience. Protagoras had a broader view. Rather than offer specific training in public speaking, he instructed students to formulate a general philosophy. He wanted them to have a reasoned understanding of a wide range of issues. He believed that understanding both sides of an issue would reveal the truth.

Greek historian Plutarch relates a day-long conversation between Pericles and Protagoras debating this question: "In an athletic contest a man had been accidentally hit and killed with a javelin. Was his death to be attributed to the javelin itself, to the man who threw it, or to the authorities responsible for the conduct of the games?"

Through the Middle Ages and the Renaissance, the tradition of debate was an essential part of education. In fact, it's been said that education between the 11th century and the 17th century consisted mostly of "disputations" in which students practiced presenting and defending their own ideas and arguing against the ideas of others. In the colonial period in America, debate continued to be the principal instructional method in institutions of higher learning.

Midway through the 19th century, however, debate began a transition. It went from serving as the primary means of education to providing an enjoyable supplement to the regular course of study. Students on many campuses founded debating societies. Among the first was the Jefferson Literary and Debating Society, which was founded at the University of Virginia 1825. The members met every Friday when school was in session at 7:29 P.M. "to engage in spirited debate on matters ranging from current events to philosophy and law to humorous topics."

The end of the 19th century saw the beginning of intercollegiate debate competitions. The first was between Harvard and Yale in 1892. In the next two years, the new tradition moved west. Similar competitions were held between the University of Michigan and the University of Wisconsin and between Stanford University and the University of California.

. . . to Debate Camp

In the 20th century, debate evolved into a popular academic competition for both college and high school students. What started as a debating contest between Harvard and Yale has become a series of tournaments conducted by forensic leagues involving hundreds of schools. Today, at the college level, the American Forensic Association sponsors the annual National Debate Tournament. Debating teams from 286 colleges and universities participate.

At the high-school level, the National Forensic League conducts an annual tournament that involves competitors from all fifty states. Policy debate, Lincoln–Douglas debate, and public forum debate are all regular events in this tournament. In recent years, debates have included the following topics:

- whether to increase federal subsidies for alternative energy (policy)
- whether felons should be allowed to vote (Lincoln-Douglas)
- whether the United States should have a draft (public forum).

Every summer, debate camps are held at colleges and universities across the country. Debate camps are training workshops that last from two to seven weeks. Debate camps often focus on a single type of debate—policy, Lincoln-Douglas, or public forum.

At the present time, public forum debate may be the most popular form for debate camps. Working closely with experienced debate coaches, high school and collegiate debaters learn to analyze debate resolutions, construct a compelling case, and find resolutions to conflicts. Throughout a camp session, debaters develop their delivery skills and rebuttal strategies. A mini-tournament usually caps off the camp experience, and students receive individual speaker and team awards for their achievements.

Harvard Hall

Yale University

Chapter 23 Review

Using Vocabulary Words

Use two of the following terms to complete this sentence and explain how they are connected: "I would connect _____ and _____ because _______________." Use at least three pairs of the words.

1. affirmative position
2. analytical
3. dialogue
4. excerpt
5. forensic
6. narrative
7. negative position
8. oral interpretation
9. proposition
10. rebuttal
11. resolution

Reviewing Key Ideas

1. Tell how an impromptu speech differs from an extemporaneous speech.
2. Explain what oral interpretation is.
3. Tell why quality is an important consideration when selecting literature for oral interpretation.
4. Explain the differences among the three major types of debate: policy debate, Lincoln–Douglas debate, and public forum debate.

Reflecting on Your Project

Think about the presentation you made. Were you satisfied with your performance? Decide on two or three things you will do differently the next time you are asked to make a presentation about a broad theme.

Responding to the Essential Question

Use the headings in this chapter to help you write a brief chapter summary answering the question "What can you learn from preparing for competitive speech events even if you never compete?" Compare your summary with a classmate's to see if you both covered the main points.

Extending Your Understanding

Everyday Life

1. During the course of a week, keep a list of the situations that required you to make an impromptu speech. Compare your list with a classmate's list. Be prepared to explain why you think each item on your list qualifies as an impromptu speech.
2. As a class, brainstorm professions or jobs in which a person would directly benefit from having experience in competitive debate. For each example listed, explain how and in what circumstances a person in that profession or job would use debating skills.
3. Identify a major issue currently being discussed in your community. Prepare positions of fact, value, or policy that are related to the issue.

In the Media

4. Watch a news talk show on TV, such as "Face the Nation" or "Meet the Press." Listen to the participants and analyze the way they organize their comments. Make a list of the organizational patterns you recognize.

5. Watch a press conference on TV. Typically at such an event, there is a prepared statement and then questions from the press are answered. Listen and note differences in tone and delivery.
6. Watch a Congressional debate on C-SPAN or watch a city council meeting on your local public access cable channel. Decide what is being debated and prepare a proposition of fact, value, or policy that states the essential issue of the debate.

Research

7. Spend some time exploring the speech and debate videos on SchoolTube. Watch tournament rounds. Listen to interviews with the competitors. View the promos for various speech tournaments. Then prepare a two-minute description of what it's like to be involved in competitive speech and debate. Present your description to the class.
8. Visit the National Forensic League Web site at www.nflonline.org and click on "Alumni" to find out the names of some famous people who were members of the NFL when they were in high school. Select one of those people and do some further research about that person's life. Then prepare and present a three-minute speech about that person, explaining how being involved in speech and debate may have contributed to that person's success in his or her adult life.

Interpreting Graphics

Impromptu speaking topics often involve interpretation. Usually what's interpreted is a quotation or an abstract word, but it could just as well be a graphic. Imagine that you were asked to deliver a two-minute speech about this graphic. What would you say? Jot down your ideas.

Additional Projects

1. **Group Project:** With your group, act out a press conference. Work together to select a current events issue you want to deal with. Think up a recent event or breakthrough related to that issue. Then choose one group member to make an official announcement of that news. That person will make a prepared statement to the rest of the members of the group who will act as reporters and ask questions. Perform your mock press conference for the rest of the class.
2. **Individual Project:** Look in news magazines for photographs of people taken when they are in the act of speaking. Note who the people are and what communication act they are engaged in. Create a montage of these photographs to illustrate the importance of public speaking skills in daily life.

Culminating Activities

In this unit you have explored different types of presentations: speeches to inform and to persuade, speeches for special occasions, and competitive speech events. The activities on these pages will help you apply your understandings to situations in everyday life.

Workplace Workout

Sarah, a young doctor, welcomed the opportunity to introduce educator Beth Vega as the keynote speaker at the conference on science education. At the same time, the importance of the occasion weighed heavily on her. Standing stiffly at the podium, she spoke slowly, and her tone was very serious.

Sarah decided to focus on her own love of science. She began by describing her career as a doctor. She then explained that Beth, her high-school biology teacher, had first sparked her interest in science. Becoming Sarah's mentor, Beth gave Sarah the confidence to pursue her interest. For ten minutes, Sarah spoke about her poor performance in middle school, her new motivation in high school, and her achievements as a doctor. She concluded by explaining that she was currently a volunteer mentor to students interested in a medical career. Later in the day, Sarah overheard someone say, "Sarah seemed to think that *she* was the keynote speaker."

What Went Wrong?

Reflect on what you have learned about the speech of introduction and about presenting special occasion speeches. Then, with a partner, create an evaluation form for a speech of introduction. (See page 485 for a summary of the traits of a good introductory speech.) Use the form to evaluate Sarah's speech. Write a paragraph explaining your evaluation.

Make it Right

Using your evaluation form as a guide, prepare a new speech of introduction for Sarah to deliver. Make up details about Sarah, Beth, and the situation as necessary. Present your speech to your partner, and discuss his or her evaluation of it.

Media Master

As a class, compare and contrast informative speeches and commercials. What are your expectations of each genre? Next, prepare a two-minute informative speech on a subject of your choice. Then, create a script for an infomercial based on your speech, using the Ethics Check chart on page 457 to monitor your ethics. Present your speech and script to the class. Discuss the ethical issues raised by blurring genres to create an infomercial.

Gender Journey

With a small group, use library and Internet sources to research gender differences in competitive speech events. Explore men's and women's different levels of participation and success rates, as well as the possible reasons for and consequences of these differences. (For example, consider how debating can help students prepare for future careers.) In addition, interview at least two people who have participated in competitive speech events. Then, explore the subject in a panel discussion presented in front of your classmates.

OWN IT!

Think about the anonymous quotation at the beginning of Unit 5: "When a heart is on fire, sparks always fly out of the mouth." (See page 421.) Reflect, too, on what you have learned in this unit and from speeches you have heard. Do you think the best speakers are motivated by the heart or the mind—or by both? Deliver an extemporaneous speech to the class in response to this question.

Unit Six

Mass Communications

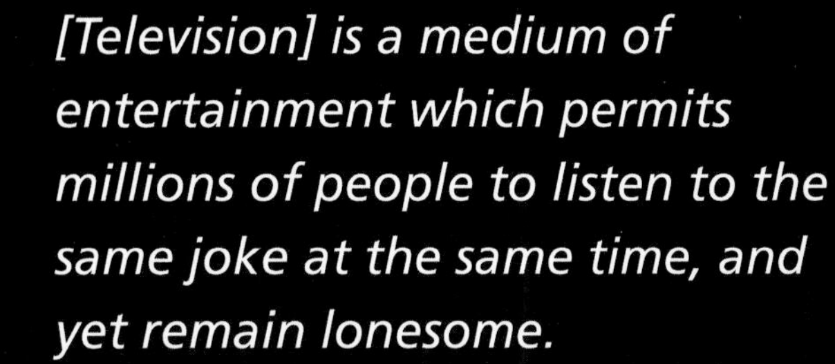
[Television] is a medium of entertainment which permits millions of people to listen to the same joke at the same time, and yet remain lonesome.
– T. S. Eliot

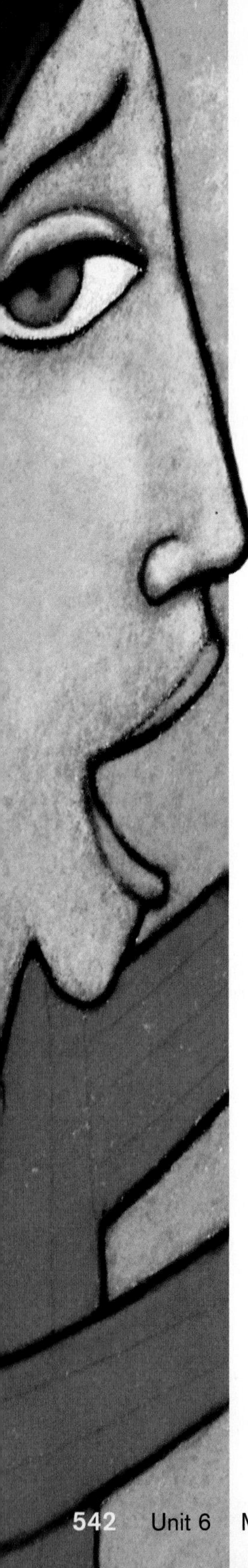

Mass Communications in Society

ESSENTIAL QUESTION

What are mass communications?

Chapter Project: Media Crystal Ball

You're probably aware of the changes in mass media just since you were born: the Internet, cable TV stations for every interest, cell phones that can take videos. Try to imagine what changes another 15 years might bring. This project will help you understand the role of mass communications in your life—now and in the future.

You will keep a log of the media you are in contact with for a whole day. In groups of three, you will then think about the role of each form and imagine how it will change in the next 15 years. Your group will choose three future mass communications to report on to the rest of the class. The entire presentation should take no more than two to three minutes. Refer to the CAPS guidelines below as you work.

The rubric on page 557 shows how your presentation will be evaluated.

CONCEPT	media exposure is a part of American life
AUDIENCE	classmates and teacher
PURPOSE	identify and understand elements of mass communications and their rapid rate of change
SITUATION	creative classroom demonstration

KEY VOCABULARY

- mass communications
- mediated communication
- synchronous media
- asynchronous media
- narrowcasting
- socialization
- media literacy
- cultivation analysis
- misinformation
- disinformation
- media piracy
- propaganda
- plagiarism

Times Square in New York City advertises various media offerings.

Speak Up!

How do advertising, television programming, music, and other media offerings affect you? Jot down examples of slang, slogans, or catchphrases that you have picked up through media exposure. When your teacher says "go," take turns calling out a few of these words and phrases. Discuss your responses with the class.

Pages 544–554 provide the information you'll need to complete this project.

Mass Communications and Mass Media

Mass communications come in many formats. Mass media are so much a part of daily life that you may not even be aware of their impact. Knowing what mass communications are and how they differ from interpersonal communication will help you interpret the media's message.

Definition of Mass Communications

Mass communications are messages sent by some form of technology to masses of people at the same time. Radio, television, books, newspapers, magazines, online news, Internet sites, photographs, movies, and videos are all mass communications.

Many years ago, the printing press enabled thousands of people to receive the same message. Electronic media later allowed millions of people to receive the same message simultaneously. Today, the Internet allows a mass audience to not only receive the message in an instant but also to interact directly with the developer of the message.

As you learned in Chapter 1, mass media are the forms of technology used to transmit mass communications. The methods for communicating the message to the masses are referred to as media. Mass media make up the distribution system for mass communications. Mass communications are media controlled—they are a **mediated communication.**

Characteristics and Forms of Mass Communications

Unlike interpersonal communication, mass communications depend on technology to produce and transmit messages. With interpersonal communication, you can adjust your gestures, tone of voice, or vocabulary level if your listener doesn't understand you. Or you can restate your idea to get your point across. A person giving a speech to a crowd watches the audience and reacts to them. Mass communications can't make these adjustments because they're not interactive. The sender of mass communications has no idea who the receivers are or what they understand.

Mass communications are filtered—someone decides what goes on a newspaper's front page and what television story gets the most coverage. Most of what you read, listen to, or watch has been packaged to create a certain message. What you end up receiving is the result of what was left out as well as what was put in.

Live telecasts occur in real time. They are called **synchronous media. Asynchronous media**, in contrast, let the individual choose when to receive the communication. CDs, movies, and books are examples of asynchronous media.

A Model of the Mass Communications Process

Mass communications, like other forms of communication, can be simplified to three vital elements: the sender, the message, and the receiver.

Key Elements in the Mass Communications Process	
Sender	the initiator of the message
Message	the information the sender is communicating to the receiver
Receiver	the target of the message

The characteristics that follow are what separate mass communications from interpersonal communication.

One-way Communication

Because mass communications flow in one direction, the message is transmitted outward from one sender to many receivers. The receivers in this vast audience are similar to a single passive receiver. They are consumers rather than interactive participants in the communication process. Media organizations try to create content they think people will want, but their audiences have little opportunity to communicate whether they believe that content is worthwhile. Delayed feedback in the form of letters to the editor or turning off a show is all that is available.

Also, different receivers have differing interpretations of the message. Every receiver brings personal factors such as past experiences and preferences into play while interpreting a message. Nonverbal cues in the mass media, such as photographs, illustrations, and video footage, evoke varying responses as receivers interpret and filter the meaning through their own perspectives. Consider, for example, the now famous drawing of Abraham Lincoln with his head in his hands that first appeared in 1963 after the assassination of John F. Kennedy. To a young child, or to people unfamiliar with American history, the drawing would convey sadness, but it would not have the depth of meaning it does for those who recognize Lincoln from the Lincoln Memorial and understand his important role in U.S. history.

Political cartoonist Bill Mauldin drew this famous cartoon in just an hour, racing against a deadline. It was published in the Chicago Sun-Times, *which devoted the entire back page to it.*

Courtesy of the Bill Mauldin Estate LLC.

Two-Way Communication

Two-way communication does take place to a limited extent within some forms of mass communications. One example is the talk-radio show in which the host takes calls from listeners and alternately argues and agrees with them. Another is the mass text message asking you to support an issue to which you can respond immediately. Many online newspapers also feature blogs where readers can share their opinions.

TechConnect *How has new technology changed the role of newspapers?*

Multi- and Single-Channel Media

TechConnect Technology can be broken down into single-channel and multi-channel media. For example, radio is an example of a single-channel mass communications technology. It is strictly an audio device. Print media, such as newspapers, books, and magazines, are also single-channel communication tools. Television and film employ both visual and audio media. And the Internet is developing more ways to bridge the gap between single- and multi-channel media.

Interpersonal communication is two-way—it flows back and forth between the sender and the receiver. Mass communications flow one way—to a mass of receivers who interpret it anonymously.

Reaching the Audience

Mass communications can be general or targeted. Targeted mass communications are known as **narrowcasting,** meaning that the sender is trying to reach a specific portion of the population—for example, teenagers or retirees. If you have ever been to a shop that sells magazines, you know that there are periodicals marketed to just about every special-interest group. Many cable television networks gear their programming for people with specific interests also.

PROJECT PREP

With your **project group**, brainstorm some ideas for a public-service message, such as the importance of wearing seat belts or getting regular exercise. Select a target group for your message. Determine their common interests and their expectations. Share with the class how you would create a message using visual media that would appeal to this audience.

Purposes of Mass Communications

Each day many millions of people interact with various media in all kinds of ways for all kinds of reasons. Nearly all mass communications transmissions attempt to inform or educate, persuade, entertain, or transmit culture. Many transmissions combine two or more of these goals.

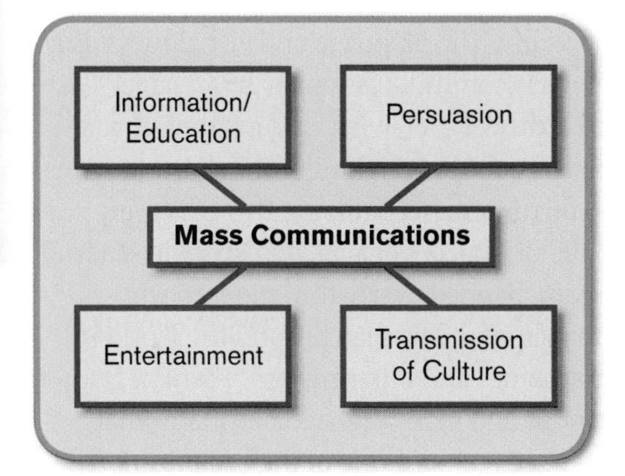

Inform or Educate

Have you ever read a pamphlet or magazine article about HIV/AIDS education and awareness or the dangers of using drugs? Perhaps you've seen a television special outlining statistics and other information about the increasingly urgent problem of global warming. The purpose of these types of mass communications is to inform or educate audiences about pressing issues. You encounter informative mass communications many times a day.

Entertain

Another major function and purpose of mass communications is to entertain. Some entertainment mass communications also feature elements of persuasion or education.

Do you think these TV viewers are watching to be informed, entertained, or persuaded? Why?

Others, such as reality TV, are created strictly for the purpose of providing entertainment.

PROJECT PREP

With your **project group**, discuss the phenomenon of reality TV. Why do you think this form of entertainment media is popular?

Persuade

Imagine a commercial for a brand of bottled water. Music blares as athletic-looking teens skateboard up and down curving ramps. One of them performs a particularly awesome move, then catches the bottle in midair, pops the top, and guzzles it. Then the water's name appears, clear and blue. Viewers understand the commercial's message: people who drink this product will have fun and be active. To whom, in your opinion, is the commercial geared? What emotional response is it trying to create?

The attempt to persuade audiences to do something specific, such as buy a particular brand of water, is a large part of how mass communications operate. The HIV/AIDS-awareness pamphlet and the global-warming documentary mentioned previously might very likely feature elements of persuasion as well; in other words, these communications attempt to educate and inform but also to persuade receivers to behave in specific ways. You will find persuasive techniques in many mass communications.

Transmit Culture

Mass media can also transfer cultural information from place to place and from generation to generation. In today's increasingly global environment, this aspect of mass communications has gained great significance. It is particularly important in terms of **socialization**, the process by which people learn and adapt to the rules of society.

The reach of mass media can bring any new concept, any offbeat viewpoint, any ancient culture into the lives of people who had no idea such concepts, viewpoints, or cultures existed. It can open people's minds and hearts to entirely new experiences (good and bad). The world's cultures (how they are perceived, misused, or preserved) can be deeply affected by how the mass media portray them. Following are a few issues that nations must come to terms with regarding culture and the impact of globalization:

- How does economic globalization impact the production of cultural goods and services?
- How does treating culture as a commodity enhance or harm a culture?
- How can investment, production, distribution, and consumption of cultural goods and services help or hurt cultures?
- How can the delicate balance between culture and consumerism be maintained to everyone's benefit?

Shape Perceptions of Reality

Mass communications have a profound effect on how people construct their views of reality. The language and visual messages of mass communications have an effect on attitudes, behavior, understanding, and beliefs about everything from clothing styles to terrorism. Recognizing this effect, in 2006 organizers of a fashion show in Madrid, Spain, banned overly thin models, whose images would be seen around the world in magazines and other media. "Fashion is a mirror and many teenagers imitate what they see . . ." said one of the organizers. The "reality" created in large part by the fashion industry was that only the very thin are beautiful. Cigarette ads were banned from TV for a similar reason—the suggestion that smoking was desirable.

How would the Madrid fashion show organizers react to the cultural influence of these models?

Potential Drawbacks

Mass communications provide many benefits to society, but they also create plenty of potential pitfalls.

Stereotypes

A nerdy high school teacher in a bow tie and white socks stands droning in front of a class. A precocious five-year-old rolls her adorable eyes and makes cute, clever quips at the expense of her clueless parents. A police officer, red-faced and sputtering, can't even order a cup of coffee without yelling, "Give me one of dem doughnuts too!" These and other stereotypes have entered American mainstream media culture and when they are broadcast all over the world, there is vast potential for confusion between fact and fiction.

The messages sent by mass media exert great influence on consumers about social roles and what constitutes appropriate behavior. Television and film can provide young people especially with early signals about gender roles and expectations, which then influence their self-perceptions. Studies have shown that television has traditionally assigned the roles of "good guy" and "bad guy" according to race. In fictional shows, more drug lords, gang members, and murderers are played by people of color; while lawyers, doctors, and police officers are white (and often male). The situation has been improving, but there is a long way to go before television catches up to the real world.

Stereotyping often takes very subtle forms, which in turn can work themselves into people's belief systems. Many experts believe that courses in **media literacy** help students develop lasting skills in interpreting mass communications and sorting the real from make-believe.

The nerd is a common stereotype in popular entertainment.

Globalization Issues

Although cultural transmission by means of mass communications is considered a positive thing by many, some experts express concern that the predominance of American mass communications could eventually lead to a dull, media-saturated planet in which all cultures would become homogenized—a world in which people all over the globe would dress, eat, and speak like everyone else.

Consumers of mass communications need to weigh the drawbacks against the advantages and approach media messages with a critical mind.

Distraction from Learning

Have you ever gotten behind on your homework because you were chatting online with friends or watching a favorite TV show? While mass communications have limitless potential as learning tools, they can also *distract* you from learning. For some, mass communications get in the way of the learning processes. Consider the following exchange between two classmates.

Stefan: Hey, did you finish your report on *Native Son* for American lit?

Terri: I didn't have time to read the novel. I went to litnotes.com, though, and it had all the information about the book I needed to write my paper.

In order to write her report, Terri read about the novel online. What would you say to Terri about this decision?

Terri's use of this mass communications tool provided her with a way to get through her assigned reading. It was a quick solution to her problem, but in the long run it works against her. In reading the novel, she would be able to differentiate the voice of each character, understand the author's purpose through description and exposition, and appreciate the flow of the text. Someone else's analysis of the book may supply her with the plot but not the depth and breadth of this American classic. She gets no more out of it than someone who tries to satisfy hunger by listening to a description of a wonderful meal. The Internet offers easy shortcuts like the one Terri took. However, true learning, now as ever, depends upon the individual. Using mass media as a learning aid is great—replacing more meaningful types of learning with it can be a costly mistake.

Violence and Children

Does watching violent television programs or films make people, particularly children, more apt to commit violent acts? This question has been hotly debated for nearly as long as these media have been in existence. Research has led to a much-discussed theory known as **cultivation analysis,** a theory that proposes a link between habitual television watching and one's perception of the real world. It is thought that long-term viewing of physical and psychological violence may bring about not only aggressive real-world behavior but also a perception of the world as a much more dangerous place than it actually is. More recent research suggests that while there may be a correlation between violence on TV and violence in the real world, the one does not actually cause the other. A key factor is this: if children can discuss what they watch with parents and other elders, they are more likely to be able to differentiate between the world of entertainment and the world in which they live.

With your **project group**, identify issues that have become important to you because you heard about them via the media. Then discuss ways in which the media shape the kinds of topics people think and talk about.

Communication in a DIVERSE WORLD

Freedom of the Press

The United States boasts constitutionally mandated freedom of expression–both for its citizens and for its mass communications organizations. However, there are many places throughout the world where freedom of expression–including the right to seek information from all kinds of media sources–as well as freedom of the press are severely hindered. Much of the Middle East is struggling against powerful odds to enter the age of information. For some of these Middle Eastern nations, authoritarian governments, feeble economies, and religious or cultural systems work against modernization.

The forces to limit a free press can work from a variety of angles. According to the Committee to Protect Journalists, a nonprofit organization based in the United States, attacks against the press include:

- government-mandated dismissal of controversial journalists
- news blackouts on politically controversial topics
- government condemnation of journalists who criticize existing power structures
- religious leaders' condemnation of journalists who criticize religious practices
- government hiring of editors to ensure the government will not be criticized
- in extreme cases, the threatening, abducting, and even killing of journalists.

Al Jazeera Amidst the volatile nature and limited press freedoms in many areas of the Middle East, tucked away in the tiny Arab emirate of Qatar is the headquarters of one of the world's most controversial satellite television channels–Al Jazeera. This 24-hour Arabic-language news channel was founded in the mid-1990s to supply Arabic-speaking audiences around the world with coverage of some of the world's most war-torn places. Over the years, Al Jazeera has won a huge and loyal audience around the globe. It has also been the subject of international debate and sharp criticism. It is often charged with sensationalism for airing footage of the carnage of war zones and for giving a platform to those considered by many governments to be violent and extremist. The intense scrutiny from–and frequent criticism by–international governments has helped Al Jazeera resolve to maintain its credibility as a strong voice in the Arab community.

The headquarters of Al Jazeera

Ethical Issues

New technologies have brought remarkable changes in mass communications within a relatively short period of time—and the innovations just keep coming. Along with more media alternatives come the age-old questions about ethics in communication.

Misinformation and Disinformation

Misinformation is wrong or inaccurate information passed along under the assumption of truth. **Disinformation** is false information spread knowingly. For example, if a candidate for public office accidentally quotes an incorrect statistic about her political record in a televised interview, this is a form of misinformation. However, if the candidate uses the statistic repeatedly even though she knows it to be false, she is guilty of disseminating disinformation. If a newspaper ignores certain facts in a controversial story it runs and chooses instead to focus on only one side of the story, this is a form of misinformation. If the reporters or editors at the newspaper know they have left out facts that would refute the story, this is disinformation.

TechConnect *Millions of songs are available legally for downloading at very little cost.*

Pirated DVDs, music CDs, and books illustrate the case against China over copyright piracy.

Pirating

Media piracy is the illegal copying of music, video, or computer software. It has existed for nearly as long as these technologies themselves and has become a huge industry. Many people don't think of copying music and software CDs, videotapes, or other media as an illegal act because they plan to keep the copied material for their own use rather than sell it. No matter what the purpose may be, however, piracy is piracy.

TechConnect A few years ago, if you were downloading music, you were probably doing it illegally. These days, legal downloads are offered by several companies. These stores have libraries that offer a wide range of music, although some musicians will not allow their music to be sold online.

Editing

Because the mass communications you see and hear have been carefully packaged, editing of the content has been an integral part of the process. Good editing can draw in and inform readers. It can also unite scenes to create a fast-paced adventure film. However, editing can distort the quality and integrity of the information. If a newspaper editor favors one presidential candidate over another, for example, he could choose to publish a flattering picture of his favored candidate and an unflattering picture of the opponent to accompany a news story. Even though the words in the story itself might be fair and accurate, the chosen photographs, filtered through the political preference of the editor, convey certain attitudes. A television producer might present snippets from a candidate's speech that express only the most controversial views and leave out the ideas that might be much more widely accepted. In that way she might portray the candidate as risky or undesirable. As a consumer of mass communications, try to discern when a piece of information has been edited in a way that distorts its content. This will give you a balanced understanding of the information.

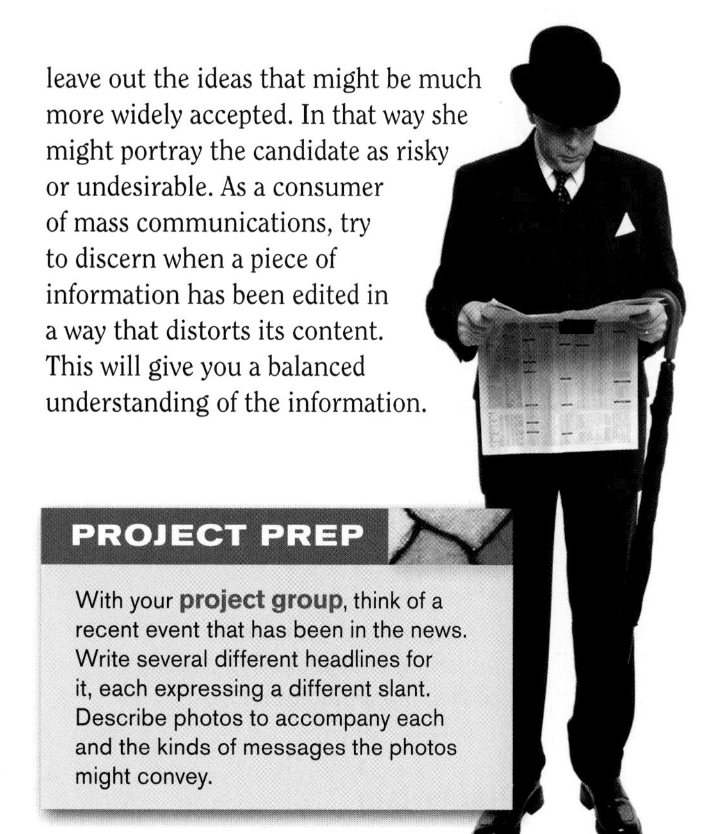

PROJECT PREP

With your **project group**, think of a recent event that has been in the news. Write several different headlines for it, each expressing a different slant. Describe photos to accompany each and the kinds of messages the photos might convey.

"All the News That's Fit to Print."

The New York Times.

NEW YORK, TUESDAY, APRIL 16, 1912—TWENTY-FOUR PAGES. ONE CENT

TITANIC SINKS FOUR HOURS AFTER HITTING ICEBERG;
866 RESCUED BY CARPATHIA, PROBABLY 1250 PERISH
ISMAY SAFE, MRS. ASTOR MAYBE, NOTED NAMES MISSI

Col. Astor and Bride, Isidor Straus and Wife, and Maj. Butt Aboard.

"RULE OF SEA" FOLLOWED

Women and Children Put Over in Lifeboats and Are Supposed to be Safe on Carpathia.

PICKED UP AFTER 8 HOURS

Vincent Astor Calls at White Star Office for News of His Father and Leaves Weeping.

FRANKLIN HOPEFUL ALL DAY

Manager of the Line Insisted Titanic Was Unsinkable Even After She Had Gone Down.

HEAD OF THE LINE ABOARD

Biggest Liner ... to the Bo... at 2:20 A. M.

RESCUERS THERE T...

WOMEN AND CHILDR...

SEA SEARCH FOR ...

OLYMPIC SENDS TH...

ST. LOUIS POST-DISPATCH

Only Evening Paper in St. Louis With the Associated Press News Service.

HOME EDITION

Last Sunday's Count of Want Ads: Post-Dispatch....7149; All....6011; Post-Dispatch Gain 384

ST. LOUIS, TUESDAY EVENING, APRIL 16, 1912—28 PAGES. PRICE ONE CENT

1302 LIVES LOST WHEN "TITANIC" SANK; 868 SAVED

Carpathia Steaming to New York With Survivors; None on Other Ships

NEW YORK, April 16.—Wireless from Capt. Rostron of Carpathia, to Cunard line here, reads: "Proceeding to New York with about 800. Consulted with Mr. Ismay. So much ice about, considered New York best. Large number icebergs and twenty miles field-ice with bergs amongst."

MONTREAL, April 16.—The Allan Line issues the following statement: "We are in receipt of a Marconi via Cape Race, from Capt. Gambell of the Virginian, that he arrived on the scene of the disaster too late to be of service and is proceeding to Liverpool."

HALIFAX, N. S., April 16.—The Allan Liner Parisian reports by wireless, via Sable Island, that she has no passengers from the Titanic on board.

CAPE RACE, April 16.—Olympic reports by wireless "Carpathia reached Titanic position at daybreak FOUND BOATS AND WRECKAGE ONLY. Titanic sank about 2:20 a. m. in 41:16 n. 50:14w. ALL HER BOATS ACCOUNTED FOR, containing about 675 souls saved, crew and passengers included. Nearly all saved women and children. Californian remained searching exact position of disaster.

2-THIRDS WOMEN IN PARTIAL LIST OF THOSE RESCUED

Astor, Butt, Guggenheim and Many Other Famous Men Who Were on Board Not Mentioned Among Survivors---Money Loss Is $20,000,000.

7 ST. LOUISANS ARE REPORTED SAFE ON BOARD CARPATHIA

Mrs. Robert, Misses Madill and Allen, Hays and Wife Rescued and

ABOUT 2200 PERSONS WERE ABOARD TITANIC.

Lifeboats for Only One-Third on Board

How did the editors' choice of headlines and graphics affect the focus of these newspapers' coverage of the sinking of the Titanic?

Propaganda and Misleading Information

Propaganda is the systematic output of information that reflects and promotes a certain cause or point of view. Propaganda presents its information selectively, so it can distort the truth by leaving out pertinent facts. Nearly every country uses the mass media to disseminate propaganda to promote its governmental, social, and cultural interests, and the United States is no exception.

Mass communications raise important ethical questions because of their immense power.

Plagiarism

Plagiarism is the act of passing off as one's own the written words of someone else. This practice is unethical and, in many cases, illegal as well. There have been several high-profile cases of journalistic plagiarism in recent years. The Internet, with its vast array of readily available—and sometimes dubious—information, has created a sharp spike in the number of cases of plagiarism around the world.

Plagiarism can often be avoided with the application of a few simple rules:

- Never copy the words or ideas of another without crediting your source. If you are in any doubt about whether or not something might be plagiarism, cite your source.
- Provide complete source citations. Always credit your sources correctly—supplying erroneous or misleading information about a source is a form of plagiarism.
- Always use quotation marks to enclose direct quotes.
- If you are claiming a fact or idea as common knowledge, make sure you can back it up with five different sources.

Is This Plagiarism?	
YES	**NO**
Scanning images from electronic or print media and using them without citing your source	Using illustrations you drew, photos you took, or digital artwork you created
Using information you took from a personal interview without citing your source	Writing about events and ideas from your own life
Reusing specific information from electronic media	Using common sense or common knowledge about history, society, and so on

How is a remote control a good symbol for changes in mass communications?

PREPARING THE PROJECT

Begin your project by looking back at the **Project Prep** activities in this chapter and using the directions below.

Make Connections

Discuss with your group how your understanding of mass communications may have changed as you read pages 544–554. Discuss and summarize these important points:

- the difference between mass communications and mass media
- the link between television violence and the real world
- synchronous and asynchronous media
- single-channel and multi-channel media
- ethical issues in mass communications.

Focus

Briefly review individual and group aspects of the project you are working on: a description of how three of today's technologies may be different in 15 years.

Surefire Projection

To plan your projection, ask yourself:

- What purpose does this communication fulfill today?
- How will people's need to fulfill that purpose change over time?
- How might mass communications adjust to fulfill that purpose?

Plan

This project requires you to make projections. The most likely projections are those that demonstrate an understanding of the purpose of a communication today and extend it logically into the future. Make a list of the television shows, films, advertisements, newspapers, magazines, blogs, CDs, Internet sites, and other media you have seen recently. Write as quickly as you can. Try to come up with several examples of each type of media. Then go through your list and consider the following questions with regard to each item:

- Did you encounter any media stereotypes?
- Did you think any of the media provided misinformation or disinformation?
- Did you encounter anything that smacked of propaganda?
- Were there many instances of violence?
- How might you answer each of the above questions in the future?
- Why would the future answers be what they are?

Develop

Come up with names for your future mass communications. Then plan a brief explanation of how they developed from what they are now to what they will be in 15 years. Include a logical extension of the purpose each serves today and the media used to transmit it. Divide up the work in a way that makes sense to you.

Practice

Rehearse your presentation until you are confident that you can perform it smoothly for your classmates. Ask someone to time you to be sure the presentation is under three minutes. If your presentation is running long, decide what needs to be cut and practice again without that section.

Be creative! Maybe you want to set your presentation 15 years in the future. If so, how would you dress? What might be the fashionable slang terms? Try to make your presentation as original and creative as possible.

How will people be dressing 15 years from now?

PRESENTING THE PROJECT

Use the strategies that follow to help make your presentation as good as it can be.

You should now be ready to share the project. Go over the CAPS guidelines on page 542 to and the rubric on page 557 to be sure that your project meets the requirements.

Maintaining Spontaneity

You have rehearsed your presentation thoroughly. You know it backward and forward. You have it timed right down to the second. You're not the least bit nervous . . . . But what if something goes wrong? What if you drop your notes, lose your train of thought, or trip on your way to the front of the room? Rehearsal is great for polishing a performance. But maintaining a sense of spontaneity once you're in front of the audience is important as well. Here are two tips that should help:

1. **Use your head.** You may feel more at ease if you have your notes, but if you have practiced well you should know your material inside and out. So just let it come out naturally if your notes become jumbled or otherwise unusable.
2. **Use humor.** What if instead of looking sheepish about losing your train of thought, you make a joke: "In the future, there will be a chip you can implant in your brain to keep you from losing your train of thought."

EVALUATING THE PROJECT

Evaluate the presentations using the following rubric.

Score the presentation on each point, with 4 being "outstanding" and 1 being "needs much improvement."

Come up with an overall score and write a brief paragraph that explains your score.

Understanding of Mass Communications	Discussion/ Description of Mass Media	Creativity and Originality	Preparation and Use of Time
4 The presenters revealed insight into many elements of mass communications and offered logical extensions.	**4** The presenters were helpful in illuminating the various forms of mass media and their extensions.	**4** The presentation was attention-grabbing, unique, interesting, fun, and imaginative.	**4** The presentation flowed smoothly and stayed within the time limit.
3 The presenters revealed insight into some elements of mass communications and offered reasonable extensions.	**3** The presenters were helpful in illuminating some forms of mass media and their extensions.	**3** The presentation was attention-grabbing, interesting, and fun, but not very unique or imaginative.	**3** The presentation progressed fairly smoothly and stayed within the time limit.
2 The presenters did not seem to grasp some important elements of mass communications and the extensions were not completely logical.	**2** The presenters were minimally helpful in illuminating some forms of mass media and their extensions.	**2** The presentation was fairly interesting and fun, but not attention-grabbing, unique, or imaginative.	**2** The presentation had a few awkward moments and went a bit over or was noticeably under the time limit.
1 The presenters did not seem to understand very much about mass communications and failed to make plausible extensions.	**1** The presenters were not helpful in illuminating forms of mass media or their extensions.	**1** The presentation was not attention-grabbing or unique and only minimally fun and interesting.	**1** The presentation was not smoothly executed and went well over or was significantly under the time limit.

Communication *Past* and Present

Getting the News Out

From Town Criers . . .

In medieval England, the chief source of news transmission was a functionary known as a town crier. This person's responsibility was to travel from place to place within a specified region and walk through the streets of various villages, ringing a bell and loudly proclaiming whatever was deemed newsworthy or urgent—from royal proclamations about local laws to information about special sales and impending feast or market days.

A town crier shares the news of the day.

The task the town crier performed was absolutely essential: most people in rural areas and villages could neither read nor write. Town criers operated under the protection of the ruling monarch, since they often had to deliver bad news about such unpopular subjects as new taxes. Most town criers had a lot of miles to cover and consequently they did not have a great deal of time to spend in any one town or on any single news item. Often a proclamation was as simple as one brief sentence, such as "The king declared war today."

Even a one-sentence message from a town crier might have come in very handy for the opposing forces that fought the Battle of New Orleans, the final confrontation of the War of 1812. This war broke out in June of 1812 over the issue of trade restrictions imposed on the United States by Great Britain. Two and a half years later, on Christmas Eve of 1814, the British finally signed a peace treaty with the Americans. However, the signing took place thousands of miles from the fighting, in Ghent, in what is today Belgium. Communication from that distance moved so slowly in those days that the news of

Andrew Jackson

Reporters and pundits discuss the tabulations for a major election.

the Treaty of Ghent didn't hit American shores until many weeks later. Meanwhile, the American general Andrew Jackson led his forces into battle in New Orleans on January 8, 1815, scoring a decisive victory during what turned out to be a new era of peace between Great Britain and the United States.

. . . to Satellite Transmissions

Today's top news stories can be communicated within a matter of seconds to and from just about anywhere in the world. Through a variety of different media, the world has become smaller. For example, during the U.S. Democratic presidential primaries of 2008, interested viewers around the nation and around the world could track voting results in real time by means of satellite television. As presidential hopefuls Hillary Clinton and Barack Obama battled it out for primary wins, satellite affiliates were standing by for the breaking results. From cities, towns, and rural outposts in late-campaign primary states such as Indiana and North Carolina, county-by-county election tallies were released to the media as soon as they were tabulated. Within minutes these results were transmitted to people watching television, viewing news online, or listening to the radio anywhere from Kansas to Kuala Lumpur.

Chapter 24 Review

Using Vocabulary Words

Choose six of the following terms and answer these two questions:

- What is it?
- What is an example?

1. asynchronous media
2. cultivation analysis
3. disinformation
4. mass communications
5. media literacy
6. media piracy
7. mediated communication
8. misinformation
9. narrowcasting
10. plagiarism
11. propaganda
12. socialization
13. synchronous media

Reviewing Key Ideas

1. List some characteristics of mass communications.
2. What does mediated communication mean?
3. Identify and describe the four major purposes of mass communications.
4. Why is it important for people to develop media literacy?
5. Identify three examples of narrowcasting you have encountered in the mass media.

Reflecting on Your Project

Solicit feedback from your classmates about which parts of your project went especially well and which appeared to be the most difficult for you. Come up with two or three strategies for dealing with problem areas in future presentations.

Responding to the Essential Question

Create a brief summary that answers the question "What are mass communications?" When you finish, compare and contrast your summary with that of a partner.

Extending Your Understanding

Everyday Life

1. For generations millions of people around the world have counted on daily newspapers to keep up with current events. Today, however, there are so many alternative media sources that newspapers are in danger of becoming obsolete. Do you think newspapers will survive beyond the next twenty years? Write an essay telling why or why not.
2. Interview an older family member about the ways in which mass communications have changed since he or she was your age.

3. Today many people, including teenagers, post daily updates to their blogs. What do you think has fueled the interest in this form of self-expression? What are the advantages and disadvantages of posting private thoughts in a public forum?

In the Media

4. Compare front-page coverage of the same story across two or more newspapers or magazines and identify what is emphasized and what might constitute each publication's bias.
5. Write a review of a current television show or film. Use critical analysis to point out any instances of persuasive messages or stereotyping you notice.

Research

6. Write a report on the legal issues and changing trends involved in music downloading.
7. Research and report on the role of media watchdog organizations and the public's right to know.
8. Using a search engine such as Google, locate examples of U.S., British, and German military propaganda during World War II. Create a poster that illustrates and labels the propagandistic elements in terms of their purpose and intended effects.
9. Do historical research on various forms of media and prepare an informative speech to share your findings.

Interpreting Graphics

Copy the diagram below on a separate sheet of paper. Be sure the scale is large enough to allow you to write inside the circles. Then fill in the circles to identify at least three examples of each mass communications' purpose.

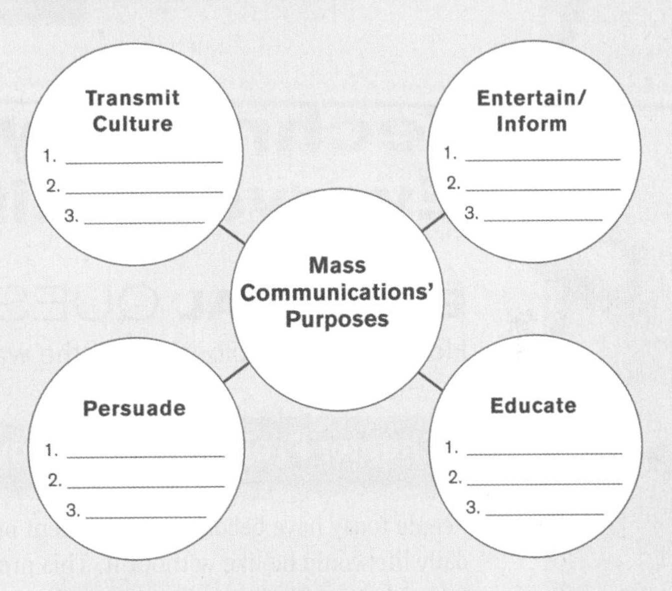

Additional Projects

1. **Group Project:** With a small group of classmates hold a panel discussion on why the Internet should or should not be federally regulated in the years to come. Each panelist should do some research and come into the discussion with a strong point of view.
2. **Individual Project:** Create a poster or graphic organizer depicting the role of the mass media in U.S. culture. Try to create an eye-catching design using illustration, stylish lettering, or images snipped from magazines. When you have finished, display your work for the class.

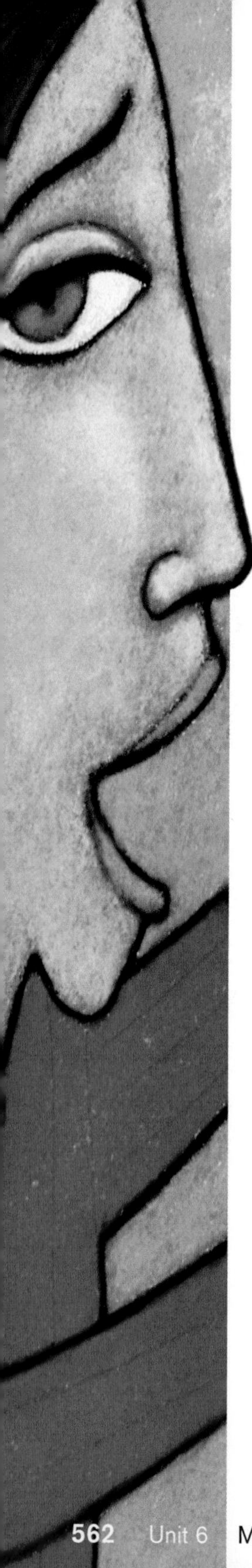

Technology in Everyday Life

ESSENTIAL QUESTION

How does technology affect the way people communicate?

Chapter Project: Technology Tales

People today have become so dependent on technology that it's hard to imagine what daily life would be like without it. This project will help you explore the impact of technology on the way you communicate.

With a partner, you will use storytelling—one of the oldest forms of communication—to describe the effects of technology on the way people communicate. First, one of you will tell a true story that shows a positive effect of technology on communication. Then, your partner will tell a true story that shows a negative effect of technology. Conclude by explaining what the two tales reveal about technology's impact. The entire presentation should take no more than five minutes. Refer to the CAPS guidelines below as you work.

The rubric on page 585 shows the traits on which your presentation will be evaluated.

CONCEPT	technology affects the way we communicate
AUDIENCE	classmates and teacher
PURPOSE	identify the positive and negative effects of technology on communication
SITUATION	narrative classroom presentation

KEY VOCABULARY

- e-learning
- videoconferencing
- teleconferencing
- convergence
- hybrid
- vlogs
- emoticons
- computer-mediated communication
- aesthetic
- Personal Digital Assistant (PDA)
- podcasts
- massively multiplayer online games
- telecommute
- cyberbullying
- cookies
- identity theft
- cyberstalking

Cell phones are one of many forms of technology that have reshaped communications in recent decades.

Speak Up!

With your classmates, create a two-column "technology" chart. In the first column, list the types of technology you use to communicate each day. In the second column, record the average number of times in a day you use each type of technology. Discuss your reactions to these numbers. Predict how the numbers might change in the future.

Pages 564–583 will provide the information you'll need to complete this project.

Technology's Impact on Communication

Modern technology has changed the way you live, learn, and work. It has created new channels for synchronous communication, in which messages are delivered immediately, and for asynchronous communication, in which messages are delayed. Technological advances have made the world smaller and made communication faster and easier. You can now exchange ideas with almost anyone, anywhere, at any time.

Technology has made all types of communication faster, easier, and more visual and has had an impact on all levels of communication, from intrapersonal to mass.

Impact on Intrapersonal Communication

Technology has provided new channels for intrapersonal communication, communication within yourself. It has also opened up creative channels for developing your self-concept, which is fundamental to all forms of communication. A blog can serve as an online diary for exploring your personal thoughts. You can use a profile on a social-networking site to convey your perception of yourself. Today, technology often helps people define who they are.

Impact on Interpersonal Communication

New communication technologies have also transformed interpersonal communication, the exchange of messages among two or more people. Cell phones, text messaging, instant messaging, and e-mail, for example, enabled American soldiers in Iraq to stay in close touch with their families. New technology has decreased the interference created by time and distance, putting people within reach of one another.

PROJECT PREP

With your **project partner**, discuss how your typical day would be different if you couldn't use technology for interpersonal communication.

The first laptop computers were developed in the early 1980s, although they did not become widely used until the mid-1990s.

Impact on Group Communication

New technology has broken down the walls of the classroom and the conference room. The growth of **e-learning**, in which instruction is delivered via technology, has expanded students' educational opportunities. **Videoconferencing**, or the holding of meetings using video links, enables high school students to attend a class given in a different school district. Across the globe, employees communicate in real time by **teleconferencing**, speaking to one another from different locations. Technology has transformed group communication by enabling people to learn and work together wherever they are.

A presentation can be shown in offices around the world just as easily as it can be shown in one office.

Impact on Public Communication

On March 18, 2008, presidential candidate Barack Obama delivered a landmark speech about race before an audience of about 200 people in Philadelphia, Pennsylvania. However, millions of other people were able to hear his speech. It was broadcast live on cable television and radio and viewed millions of times on YouTube. Technology can vastly expand a public speaker's audience and the influence of a message.

Impact on Mass Communication

The Internet and digitalization have made possible the merging of different communication technologies. This merging is called **convergence**. For example, newspapers and television stations now maintain extensive Web sites on which you can watch videos and comment on reporters' blogs. As a result of technological advances and convergence, mass communicators have new channels for reaching their audiences. In turn, audiences have new channels for providing feedback. Mass communications have become more interactive.

Hybrid Communication Types

Technology can blur the lines among intrapersonal, interpersonal, and mass communications. A blog, for example, can serve as a channel for all three types. Through e-mail and blogs, individuals can now provide more direct, immediate feedback to mass communicators. This feedback makes mass communications more like interpersonal communication. The relationship between the sender and the receiver has more dimensions in such mixed, or **hybrid**, types of communication.

Reliance on Visual Communication

With the increasing use of technology, communication has become more visual. People create **vlogs** (a word derived from videoblogs) to entertain or inform their readers and viewers. They also e-mail photographs back and forth with friends. **Emoticons**—pictures or images that represent emotions—increasingly pop up in personal and professional exchanges. They and other types of icons are a way to convey a message visually.

Some of the most powerful messages you receive each day are conveyed visually. Graphic artists use visual communication to promote both commercial and noncommercial products and ventures. Illustrators use visual communication to convey attitudes and insights into characters in books, and news photographers convey meaning through the visual representations they create. Knowing how to interpret, evaluate, and create visual messages will help you appreciate the power of visual communication.

Interpreting Visual Images

American writer William Saroyan said: "One picture is worth a thousand words. Yes, but only if you look at the picture and say or think the thousand words." In other words, visual messages, like all others, need to be decoded to be understood. And like other types of communication, visual messages use signs—elements that convey meaning—to get their point across. Learning how to interpret visual images and elements involves learning how to put their meaning into words. The questions in the chart below will help you interpret visual meaning.

Questions for Interpreting Visual Images

1. Who created the visual message?
2. What purpose is the message meant to serve?
3. How would I describe in words the images in the visual message?
4. What, if anything, is noteworthy about the creator's use of such visual elements as line, shape, color, texture, and perspective?

If you answered those questions about this poster, you would have a good interpretation of the message it conveys.

Questions for Interpreting Visual Images	Answers
Who created the visual message?	The logo in the bottom left indicates the creator is FACE, a non-profit organization devoted to fighting alcohol abuse.
What purpose is the message meant to serve, and who is the target audience?	The purpose of the message is to convey the idea that you can enjoy life to its fullest when sober. The poster seems to be targeting young, urban people.
How would I describe in words the images in the visual message?	The image shows a very active, very happy-looking, attractive young man enjoying music. His hairstyle, sunglasses, and clothing are visual signs that he is stylish and fun. The sweatband on the wrist and the athletic shirt give the impression he might be skateboarding or doing some other fun activity.
What, if anything, is noteworthy about the creator's use of such visual elements as line, shape, color, texture, and perspective?	The person's arm position suggests motion and/or balance; the shape of the sunglasses and the angle the face is photographed from reinforce the shape of the smile.

Like photographers, graphic artists create compositions to convey meaning, often by using culturally recognizable signs. In the poster, also created by FACE, what does the main graphic element communicate?

Evaluating Visual Images

After interpreting visual messages, you can evaluate their effectiveness. The following questions are especially helpful when evaluating visual communication.

Questions for Evaluating Visual Images

1. What attitude(s) come through the image?
2. How does the creator's choice of elements affect the attitude that is conveyed?
3. Do the image and the attitude accomplish the purpose of the visual for the intended audience?

If you answer those questions for the Road Kill poster, you might note that a strongly negative—even frightening—attitude comes through about accepting a ride from someone who has been drinking. What if, instead of the skull and crossbones, the creator had depicted two friends, one offering a ride, the other shaking his head "no"? While that might have conveyed the same literal message, the choice of the skull and crossbones creates a much stronger negative attitude. The target audience for this poster could be either young people or adults. For either audience, the image and the attitude seem to make a strong impression and get the point across.

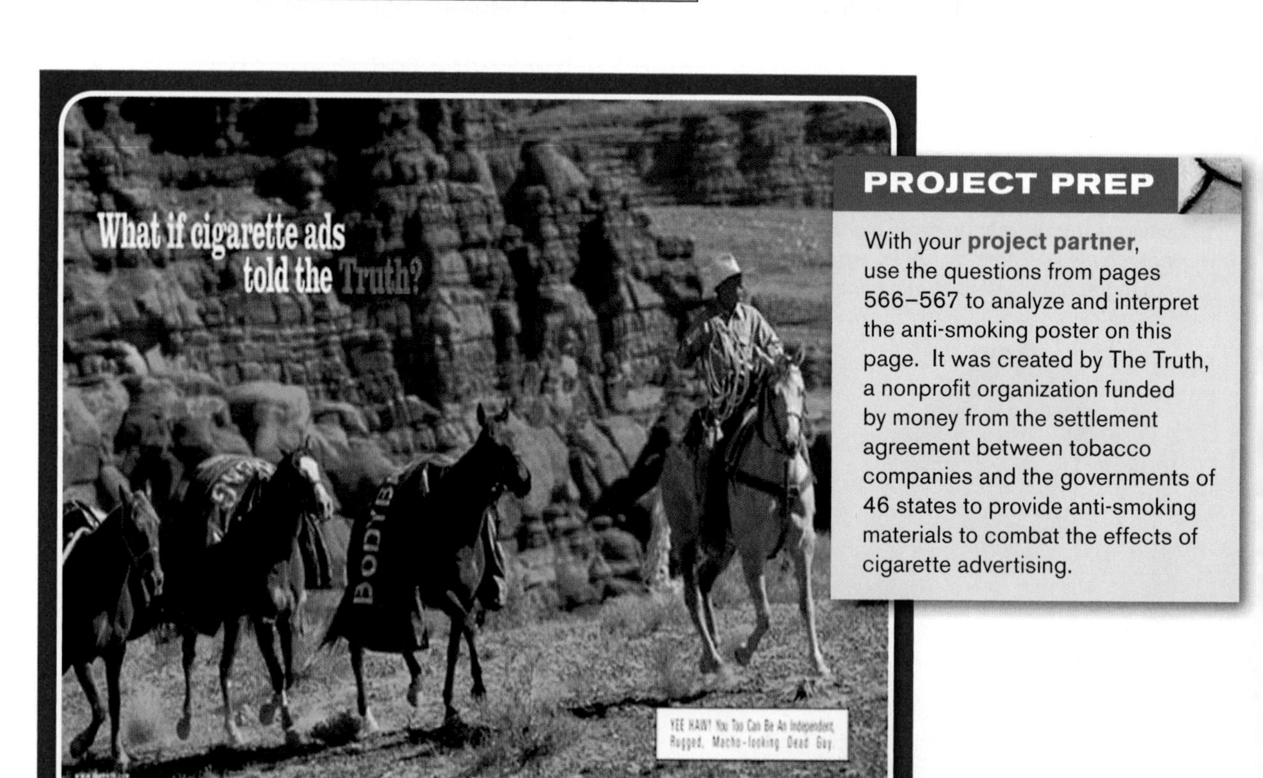

PROJECT PREP

With your **project partner**, use the questions from pages 566–567 to analyze and interpret the anti-smoking poster on this page. It was created by The Truth, a nonprofit organization funded by money from the settlement agreement between tobacco companies and the governments of 46 states to provide anti-smoking materials to combat the effects of cigarette advertising.

Creating Visual Images

Knowing how to create effective visual images will help you strengthen your presentations. It will also help make you a critical receiver of the thousands of visual messages you are bombarded with each day.

Creating a visual image is much like crafting a verbal message. The chart below shows similarities between the process of creating verbal presentations and the process of creating visual presentations.

While verbal communication in the mass media requires critical listening, visual communication requires critical viewing to interpret and evaluate the sender's message and to construct your own visual messages.

Strategies for Creating Verbal Presentations	Strategies for Creating Visual Presentations
identify purpose, audience, and occasion	identify purpose, audience, and occasion
use attention-getting quotes, incidents, or examples	use an attention-getting design
organize your words, sentences, and paragraphs to make them as clear as possible	organize the visual elements–line, shape, color, perspective, and texture–of your composition to get your ideas across
keep the focus on your main idea	make all the details support your message
choose words with evocative connotations when appropriate	choose visual signs that convey widely understood connotations
use visuals to enhance meaning	use words when appropriate to enhance meaning
evaluate the effectiveness of your message for your target audience	evaluate the effectiveness of your message for your target audience

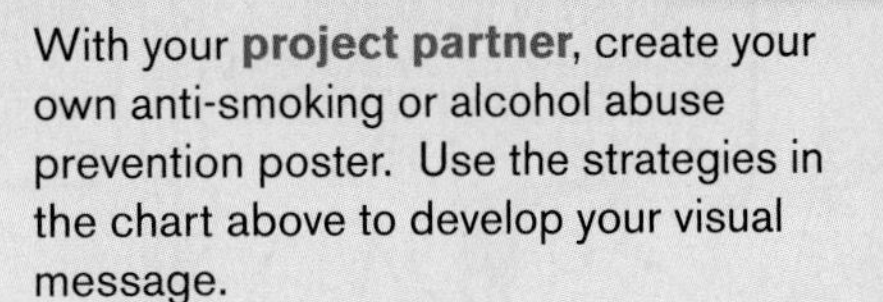

With your **project partner**, create your own anti-smoking or alcohol abuse prevention poster. Use the strategies in the chart above to develop your visual message.

How might you use this image in an anti-smoking campaign?

Technology's Impact on Democracy

With their ability to present instantaneous news and use compelling visual messages, television, the Internet, and other technological media are reshaping American political life. Craig Newmark, the founder of the Internet want-ad site called Craig's List, believes technology's influence "is as big a change as what we had in 1776." The impact of technology on democracy is especially noticeable in three key areas of political life: elections, leadership, and attitudes.

Technology and Elections

On election day 1980, exit polls—surveys of voters after they leave the voting booth—conducted by the broadcast media showed that Ronald Reagan was defeating Jimmy Carter in a landslide. The broadcast networks began to declare Reagan the winner—while the polls were still open in the western states. Before his supporters in the West even had a chance to vote for him, Carter conceded the election. Through television, the entire nation knew about his concession immediately. After a similar course of events in 1984, the networks agreed to refrain from projecting election results while polls are open anywhere in the nation. Everyone should have a chance to cast a ballot before the outcome is announced. Nonetheless, anyone watching television or checking Internet news on election day will learn plenty about the election. Other voter trends—voter turnout, for example—could still predict the outcome of the election.

The Internet especially has also changed the way politicians raise money and recruit volunteers for their campaigns. Political fundraising was once associated with expensive dinners for which contributors paid high prices, with the proceeds going to the candidates who made appearances at them. By 2008, though, candidates were using their Web sites to raise millions of dollars quickly and engage the support of volunteers. Now, instead of fundraising being limited to the wealthy at exclusive dinners, even the "average American" can easily become a donor online. Some argue, however, that the "average American" still represents only the comfortable middle class, since Internet usage is higher in that group than in lower socioeconomic classes.

The 2008 presidential campaign also included a technologically groundbreaking event: the YouTube debates. For this event, the public submitted questions for the presidential candidates in the form of videos. Young people took to this form of communication with enthusiasm, and traditional news sources began to scramble to come up with ways to lure young audiences away from the Internet.

What has remained constant about people since 1942?

Technology and Leadership

In 1960, presidential candidates Richard Nixon (Republican) and John F. Kennedy (Democrat) engaged in the first televised debate. Listeners of the radio broadcast felt the debate was a tie or favored Nixon. Viewers of the television broadcast gave the victory to Kennedy. Why the difference? One study suggested that Nixon, just getting over being ill, appeared tired. His "five o'clock shadow"—the beard stubble that grows between shavings—was very prominent on black and white TV. And he sweated very noticeably above his upper lip. Kennedy, in contrast, appeared relaxed and tanned. People found him attractive.

In the election, Kennedy edged out Nixon, but only by a very, very small margin of 100,000 votes among 68 million cast. Whether the one study was correct or not, media "image" has become a key factor in the public's perception of its leaders and their successful elections.

Technology and Attitudes

Technology can also shape political attitudes. Some studies have shown that Internet usage makes people feel more engaged in democracy. However, voter turnout has increased only slightly in national elections. Technology can also help shape the political agenda. For example, global warming had been an issue in the scientific community for more than 50 years. But after the widespread release of Al Gore's documentary film, *An Inconvenient Truth*, many people began to see the issue as an urgent one.

Technology has had an impact on democracy by affecting elections, citizen perceptions of leaders, and attitudes.

The race between John Kennedy (behind) and Richard Nixon (front) marked the true start of television as the most important form of communication in a political campaign.

Forms of Mass Technology

Over time, some forms of technology become obsolete. Through convergence, however, other forms arise that reach audiences through new channels. These forms have revolutionized the way people communicate on a daily basis.

The Internet

In the 1990s, the Internet began to transform communication. Now its reach is so extensive that many people forget how recently it developed. Every type of communication has been greatly altered, creating dynamic new channels for communicating. **Computer-mediated communication**, or communication that takes place between people via a computer connection, shapes both personal and professional lives. The Internet has also had a profound impact on public and political life. (See pages 564–565.)

Television

Television first became widely watched in the late 1940s, after the end of World War II. Studies show that the average American watches four hours of television a day. Many viewers are embracing new platforms for delivering content, such as digital video recorders, streaming video on the Internet, and cable video on demand, in place of traditional TV watching. These technologies enable viewers to watch what they want when they want to—often without commercials. With or without commercials, however, television conveys powerful messages. Critical viewers recognize the ingredients—and influence—of television's vast appeals.

Television's Aesthetic Effects and Appeal

Just as still visual images communicate with various signs and elements (see pages 566–569), so does television. Television uses the **aesthetic**, or artistic, techniques of its primary tool, the camera, to convey meaning. Camera shots convey a wide range of meanings. The close-up (focusing on a person's head or head and shoulders) helps create an intimate connection with the character, mimicking the way people move close to someone with whom they feel a connection. On a person, the extreme close-up (focusing on just part of the face) reveals subtleties of emotion. On an object, the extreme close-up calls attention to an important detail, like a clue in a mystery. Long shots (of the whole body) convey movement, as in dancing. Long shots of a set allow viewers to see characters in their environment. High-angle shots, with the camera up high, look down on characters and minimize their importance. In contrast, low-angle shots, looking up at characters, add to their intensity.

The Effects of Editing

All media presentations are affected by editing. Even "reality TV" is cast, edited, and manipulated. A fictional series is the most controlled, or filtered, because there is no objective reality to represent. The least controlled presentation might be a single live shot of something in the news—such as a picture of the Twin Towers in New York on 9/11/2001. But in some way, everything on television is subject to some degree of editing.

Radio

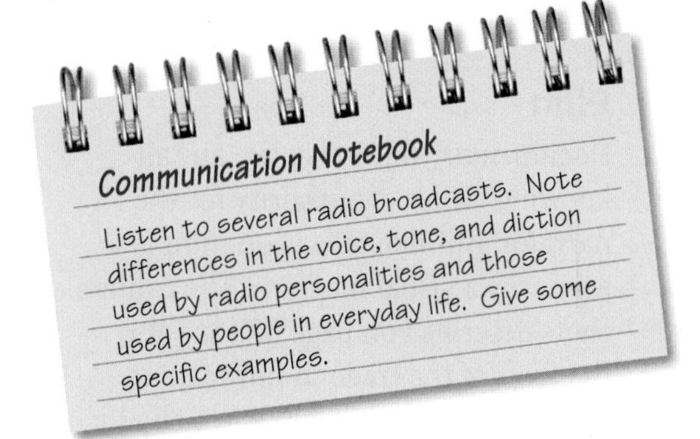

While the audience for traditional broadcast radio has remained strong, the audience for new listening platforms, such as Internet radio, MP3 players, and cell phone radio, is growing. The new platforms have given audiences greater choice and flexibility. No matter the platform, radio has its own tools for conveying meaning, many of them related to the human voice.

Voice, Tone, and Diction

Without visual cues to convey meaning, traditional radio conveys subtle meaning through the use of various voices. For example, radio anchorpersons or talk show hosts are considered voices of authority and are granted the power to address an audience directly as "you." The people they interview can address only the voice of authority, not the listening audience directly. Radio professionals are taught to imagine they are speaking to just one person, not the hundreds of thousands that may actually be tuned in. No matter what their role, radio professionals avoid sloppy speech habits and such filler expressions as "you know," "like," and "um."

Comparison with Television

Television also creates ranks of authority. In the case of television, these ranks are supported with visual messages. The anchorperson, at the top of the hierarchy, sits at a "throne" in an elaborate news set and orchestrates the rest of the newscast, introducing reporters and experts, who represent the level below the anchorperson. Reporters may address the audience directly in their "stand up" and speak with authority in the voiceover of their news stories. Experts typically discuss their expertise with the anchor but are rarely shown addressing the audience directly. Without the visual supports, rankings in radio are made clear by the use of authoritative tones of voice and careful use of language, reserving "you" as a reference to the audience for the anchorperson or main personality.

Listeners heard a voice of authority in the broadcast of the fictional War of the Worlds *in 1938 and were convinced Earth was under Martian attack.*

Film

Documentary films also use an "all-knowing" voice of authority for the narrator. But like television, film is primarily a visual medium. The camera shots described on page 572 are also the tools of the trade in filmmaking. Establishing shots in films—such as a long shot of a castle or a bustling city scene—let the viewer know where and when the action takes place.

In addition to camera shots, editing and the moving camera also create meaning. Fast cuts—several consecutive shots in a short amount of time, such as three seconds—indicate excitement and action. Other techniques that convey meaning include dissolves, gradual transitions from one scene to another, which convey a lyrical, flowing feel. A zooming lens takes the viewer from close up to faraway in an instant. The soft focus lens—through which the edges of a person or object are not sharply defined—is sometimes used to romanticize a character, especially a woman. Time lapse photography speeds up for the viewer a process that would take far longer in real time, such as the blossoming of a flower.

Lighting is instrumental in creating the mood of a scene, and the use of color—drab and gray or lively and vivid—also adds to the meaning of film.

KEY POINT

As a critical consumer of mass technology, understand the tools of the media and how they convey meaning.

And though primarily visual, film also makes use of music to add meaning, especially emotional meaning. Just think of how many times a movie's theme music has stirred you, maybe even bringing tears to your eyes.

Print Versus Film

Comparing print and film versions of a story reveals the strengths and communication tools of each medium. Consider, for example, *Harry Potter* or *The Lord of the Rings,* both of which involve characters and settings from an imagined world. The film version has a harder time conveying a character's thoughts and feelings than the book. Only in the book can the narrator dip into the character's mind. In addition, consider vivid scenes from the film. Even if they are based on the descriptions in the book, those scenes may be vastly different from the way you imagined them. Novels have time for dialogue and description. Movies are so short they usually focus on action. Keep these differences in mind as you create your own video (see page 576).

With a camera, a skillful photographer can capture reality—and shape how someone else views it.

Creating Messages in a Variety of Mass Media

Each media technology uses the symbols, signs, and conventions of its media to convey messages. The chart below summarizes the kinds of communication tools that work most effectively in each medium.

Print	
Books	Verbal explanations and descriptions; clear reasoning; expressive language; dialogue; narration
Newspapers	Factual reporting; clear and attention-grabbing headlines; occasional photos; persuasive writing in editorials; design elements in advertising
Magazines	Well-crafted articles for target audience; high quality photos and illustrations; design elements in advertising
Internet	
Web sites	Engaging graphics; succinct and often informal text; interactive features, such as blogs, message boards, social networking sites, and extensive searches; design elements in advertising
Audio and video applications	Streaming audio and video, podcasts, MP3s and video clips, live audio and video communication
Television	
Nightly News	Hierarchy of authority; video clips of events; serious tone; factual reporting
Newsmagazines	In-depth stories; usually multiple hosts; high degree of human interest details; carefully edited video clips; documentary feel
Documentaries	In-depth look at one topic; voice-of-authority narrator; edited film making the most of camera techniques to convey meaning; sound track
Entertainment	Wide variety of shows with wide range of camera techniques, scriptwriting, sound effects and sound track; audience involvement
Radio	
News	Voice of authority; factual reporting often with verbal descriptions; "ear-catching" targeted advertisements
Personality talk shows	Voice of authority; interviews; phone-in questions and comments; targeted advertisements
Sports and music shows	Strong on-air personalities; advertising targeted to an identified audience; music stations focused on one type of music; sports stations with play-by-play descriptions and commentary; news and talk stations
Film	
Documentaries	Voice of authority narrator; in-depth, well-researched coverage of topic; full use of camera techniques to convey meaning; careful editing; sound track
Fictional Movies	Full use of visual medium to convey meaning, time period, location, culture, characters; artful editing; crisp dialogue; plot development through the presentation of different scenes; often elaborate special visual effects and sound effects; sound track

Director's Cut: Creating Video Presentations

Creating a video presentation will help you develop skills you might use either in school or on the job. Further, it will help you become a critical consumer of media presentations. Try your hand at one or more of the following three-minute productions.

Working behind a camera is a great way to become a more educated viewer.

Purpose

To present well-researched factual information in a compelling visual way.

Elements

- *attention-getting opening, usually one that appeals to a viewer's emotions*
- *explanatory narration*
- *stills with narration*
- *interviews*
- *compelling video footage with well crafted shots and camera movements*
- *music*
- *memorable ending*

Purpose

To present factual and responsible reporting on the day's events.

Elements

- *spoken introduction by anchor*
- *compelling video with narration to provide background*
- *video interviews*
- *interview between reporter and anchor at end of video segment*
- *additional news stories, some with video, some just read by anchor*

Purpose

To present factual and in-depth reporting on a subject of high interest and/or controversy.

Elements

- *spoken introduction by reporter*
- *compelling video with background narration*
- *video interviews*
- *sometimes hidden cameras*
- *return of on-camera reporter at end of video segment for wrap-up*

Process of Creating Video Presentations

The process below will provide a good framework for creating your video presentation.

Pre-production

1. Determine the topic and your purpose and audience. Research as needed to feel you have accurate information.
2. Become familiar with the style and conventions of the genre you have chosen. Watch documentaries, nightly news shows, or newsmagazines, noting the order in which various elements appear and how the elements are unique in each genre.
3. Plan your video on paper. Create:
   - a *concept outline* describing the basic idea.
   - a *brief* detailing the purpose, the audience, and the effect on the audience you hope your video will have.
   - for documentaries, a *treatment* that describes the presentation in words scene by scene.
   - a *script*, which should include not only the words that will be spoken but also such details as the shots that will be used, the camera movements, and the background music.
   - a *storyboard* that contains a rough sketch of each scene, including shots and camera angles.
   - a *schedule* so you can keep the production on track.
4. Determine what recording equipment you need and make necessary arrangements to use it.

Production

5. Choose locations that will allow you to film without interference.
6. Use a tripod so the camera does not shake.
7. Set up your shots and moving cameras according to your script.
8. Be sure you film in enough light, and check the focus of your camera.

Post-production

9. If you have created digital video, transfer the video to a computer that has video editing tools on it, such as Final Cut Pro for the Macintosh. If you have recorded on analog film, first convert your film to a digital format.
10. Choose your best scenes and if necessary rethink the order in which they are presented.
11. Add music or other sound and/or insert still photos.
12. Add titles and credits.
13. Create a DVD as a finished product.

Leading an audience through a storyboard calls upon the same presentation skills as any other speech. If done in front of a movie producer, though, millions of dollars may be at stake.

Forms of Individual Technology

In addition to technology that allows publishers and broadcasters to reach millions of people at once, some new technology provides the means for personal or individualized communication.

Cell Phones and PDAs

When your parents were your age, the idea of a phone you could carry around was the stuff of science fiction. You've probably had a cell phone at your fingertips from a young age, and with the rapid advances in technology, your phone will be doing a lot more for you in the years ahead. You can now use it for text messaging, instant messaging, taking photos, and watching videos. You may already own a **Personal Digital Assistant** (PDA), the handheld computer that can also be used as a phone, but soon you will have 3G, the third generation of cell phone with broadband wireless data. With 3G, data can be transferred at around 64 to 384 kilobytes per second, a lightning speed compared to most phones. It will create a unified global phone standard and function like a multimedia center.

MP3 Players and Podcasts

MP3 players (portable digital players) and podcasts have helped to individualize how mass communications are received. Listening to music has become highly personalized—you can choose what you listen to on an MP3 player. Radio broadcasters, museums, and professors are all using **podcasts**, digital audio or video files that can be downloaded from the Internet, to deliver content to mass audiences. By playing these podcasts on MP3 players, you can determine not only which mass messages you want to receive, but also when and where to receive them.

Digital Cameras and Video Cameras

You've probably shared digital photographs or videos online with friends and family members. E-mail, blogs, Web sites, and social-networking sites all provide channels for the virtual community to view and respond to your photos and videos. Amateur journalists document significant national or global events by posting images online.

Video Games

In the early days of video games, people played games alone, and gaming was associated with isolation. With the creation of multiplayer games, gaming became a form of group communication. Today, **massively multiplayer online games** (also called MMOG or MMO) are played by vast numbers of people worldwide at the same time—and social interaction is the big draw. Through text and voice, players can communicate in real time and form global friendships in the process. Habbo Hotel is a Finland-based "social game" released in 2000. It boasts over seven million active users. World of Warcraft, released in 2004, claims over eight million subscribers, four million of whom are Chinese. Many MMOGs require payment of a subscription fee.

Is This Job for Me?

Search: Network Systems Analyst

It had been one of those days for Brooke. All morning long her phone was ringing off the hook because the company's e-mail system was down. After she found the source of that problem and fixed it, the server that hosts the company's website was disrupted by a virus and she and her team had to work for hours to get rid of it and get the server back online. Brooke is a *network systems analyst*. Her job is to design and evaluate the networks and data communications that enable employees to share information and access data from any location. She also researches and plans her company's networks, hardware, and software and manages the interfacing of computer and communications equipment. Without these tools, employees would be much less productive, and they would not be able to perform some tasks at all. Although her day was exhausting, Brooke enjoys her work and takes pride in the important role it serves in her company. She also enjoys the feeling that her skills will always be in demand. The U.S. Bureau of Labor Statistics projects that hers will be the fastest-growing occupation through the year 2016.

Does a job as a network systems and data communications analyst interest you? Measure yourself with this personality inventory to find out if you tend to have the traits of a network systems and data communications analyst. Are you:

- ✓ Good at using technology?
- ✓ Detail-oriented?
- ✓ Logical?
- ✓ Flexible?
- ✓ Analytical?
- ✓ Collaborative?
- ✓ Adept at problem-solving?
- ✓ Receptive to learning new skills?

If you became a network systems and data communications analyst, you might have job opportunities in the following organizations.

Clients	What You Would Do
Corporations	Create networks to increase productivity
Universities	Design networks to expand students' and professors' access to information
Hospitals	Devise communication and data networks to enhance patient care
Governmental agencies	Develop systems to improve intra- and interdepartmental communication and data-sharing
Cultural institutions	Design systems to help institutions achieve their educational mission

The Positive and Negative Impact of Technology

Technological advances have vastly improved your ability to communicate. However, there are drawbacks to communication technology as well.

On the Plus Side

The benefits of communication technologies fall primarily into two categories: 1) the ability to connect quickly with others, and 2) an increased access to information and knowledge.

Immediacy

In the past, when people could only rely on snail mail and landline phones, time and distance were great obstacles to communication. These days, friends or family members can live in another state or another country and contact one another with no delay via cell phone, text messaging, or instant messaging. New technologies have made communication much more immediate.

PROJECT PREP 

With your **partner**, discuss a time when technology helped you (either as a sender or a receiver) share the significance and meaning of an event.

Connectivity

Since technology has made communication quick and easy, it has helped people stay connected. Parents and children are in frequent touch during the day through cell phone calls and text messaging. Long-distance friends use e-mail to share news. Technology has helped people maintain and strengthen their bonds with others.

Distance and time are no barrier to people text messaging or instant messaging one another.

Shared Experiences

Advanced technology has made available multiple channels for sharing experiences. For example, you can post digital pictures of a vacation online. Or, using chat rooms and newsgroups, people with similar interests or concerns can trade information and offer advice. When technology is used for the exchange of ideas, it can strengthen the bonds between people. It can also create a virtual community of people who will probably never meet face-to-face.

By making communication so easy, computers have given people more flexibility about when and where they work than they have ever had. Here, astronaut Jeffrey Williams checks his computer on the International Space Station.

Social Networking

Social-networking sites have sprung up on the Internet almost overnight, creating online communities built around shared interests. These sites play a central role in many teenagers' lives, helping them to maintain bonds with old friends and to make new friends as well. Increasingly, these sites are also playing an important role in political life. (See page 570.)

Communication Support

Technology offers alternative channels for people who face obstacles in communicating verbally or face-to-face. Communicating online can put shy people at ease. People who stutter can participate in Internet discussion groups, share their experiences in blogs, and correspond with pen pals through e-mail. Online communication can help people feel less isolated—offering them a way to interact with a community.

Telecommuting

When people **telecommute**, they work in a location separate from their employer's office, usually their homes. They communicate with their colleagues and transmit materials online and by fax. Teleconferencing, videoconferencing, e-mailing, and other technological channels enable telecommuters and their colleagues to communicate swiftly and effectively. Where you live no longer inhibits where you work—so people have more freedom and flexibility.

More Communication Than Ever

How do astronauts on the International Space Station stay informed about current events? They play podcasts of *NBC Nightly News* transmitted by NASA. The convergence of technologies has created dynamic ways for transmitting and receiving information. Time and space now present few limits to communication, regardless of whether messages are in audio, written, or visual form. Convergence has enabled people to communicate more than ever before and to do so in more diverse ways.

Enhanced Learning

Today, an enormous quantity of information is just a mouse click away. On the Internet, you can use a search engine to locate information about almost any subject—movies, the Civil War, or presidential pets. You can explore a library's card catalog, access other online databases, and research information in e-books. Online courses have expanded educational opportunities for people of all ages. Never before have you had such quick and easy access to so much information.

Two benefits of using communication technologies are greater connectivity and increased access to information.

On the Minus Side

The benefits of communication technology have their flip side. The ease and speed of connecting to others and to vast amounts of information can have negative consequences.

Unrealistic Expectations

The more people rely on technology, the more they expect it to do for them. Since immediacy is a major benefit of communication technology, people often expect to receive feedback without delay. The receiver may be indisposed, however, or may need time to prepare feedback. This delay can annoy the sender. It can strain relationships.

Hasty Errors

The ability to communicate immediately can also lead to carelessness. Have you ever sent an instant message, a text message, or an e-mail only to immediately wish you had not? One minute you are uploading a personal video of your friend to YouTube that you anticipate will amuse everyone. The next minute you regret your decision as you anticipate her anger. Consider the consequences of your communication decisions—hasty communication can result in miscommunication or negative feedback.

Nonstandard Language

The cell phone has spawned a new language. Because of the immediacy, informality, and space limitations of text messaging, you may use abbreviations and omit proper punctuation and capitalization. Electronic communication style that is appropriate for a text message is not acceptable in formal writing.

Texting style does seem to be cropping up in students' schoolwork, however. Some educators are concerned that this is eroding language standards. Proofread your written schoolwork to be sure you haven't used unacceptable abbreviations or emoticons in your typed reports.

Abbreviation	Meaning
BCUZ	because
BFF	best friends forever
BTW	by the way
CUL8R	see you later
HAND	have a nice day
IMHO	in my humble opinion
IMO	in my opinion
MU	miss you
POV	point of view
THX	thanks

Single Channel

Single channel communication that conveys either visual or audio messages lacks the richness of multichannel, face-to-face communication. A single emoticon in an instant message, for example, can't express the complex emotions conveyed by a combination of facial expressions, posture, and the touch of a hand. Tone, such as irony or sarcasm, can easily be lost in single-channel e-mails. While communicating through single-channel forms can be highly efficient and productive, it can also be misinterpreted and ineffective.

Less Face Time and Civility

People sometimes forget how important face-to-face communication is. Talking to someone in person broadens your understanding of that person. It also builds trust and provides connection.

Relying too much on electronic communication can weaken bonds between people.

All too frequently, communication through technology lacks civility, or courtesy. The anonymous nature of electronic communication can lead to rude and hurtful comments that would never have been made in person. Always take responsibility for your words, written or spoken. Never write or say anything in secret that you wouldn't write or say in the open.

Rumors and Lies

The Internet has become a dangerously powerful channel for spreading falsehoods. The Internet's public nature enables anyone to begin circulating rumors or lies, and its anonymity protects circulators from being caught. Once a rumor or lie has been started, it can spread rapidly through e-mail, blogs, and social-networking sites. Spreading malicious rumors is one aspect of **cyberbullying**, or bullying that takes place online, which can be extremely harmful to its victims.

Privacy Issues

Your privacy can be sacrificed when you use technology to communicate. An e-mail sent to one person can be forwarded to others. Many Web sites collect information about you by placing **cookies**, or files used to track personal data, on your computer. Software installed on a computer without permission can seize personal information. Stealing personal data, such as credit card numbers, to make purchases is a crime called **identity theft**. Keep all your personal information secure.

Internet Safety Issues

Cyberstalking occurs when people use the Internet to stalk or harass their victims. Cyberstalkers can harass their victims through e-mail, chat rooms, and social-networking sites. They feed on the personal information spread on the Internet. The anonymity afforded by Internet communication also attracts them to online stalking. When you're online, guard your personal information.

- Don't give out any information about yourself, including your phone number and address.
- Recognize that people may not be who they say they are.
- If anyone harasses you or makes you uncomfortable, contact your Internet service provider.
- Follow your Internet service provider's rules.
- Avoid discussing personal problems with a stranger.

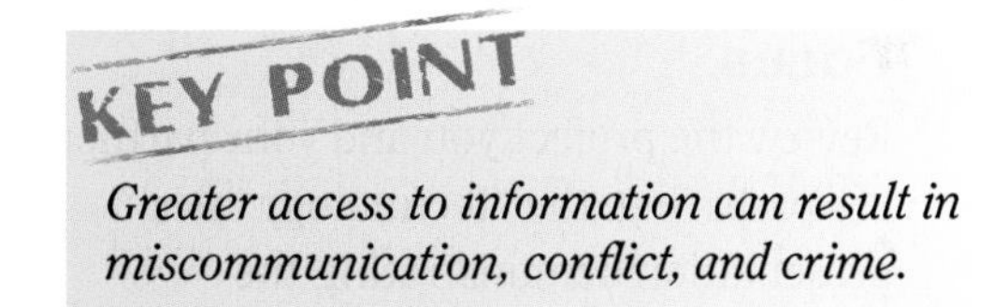

Greater access to information can result in miscommunication, conflict, and crime.

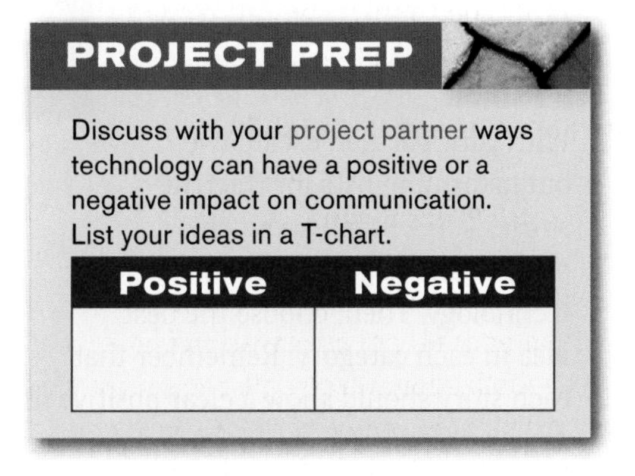

Discuss with your project partner ways technology can have a positive or a negative impact on communication. List your ideas in a T-chart.

Positive	Negative

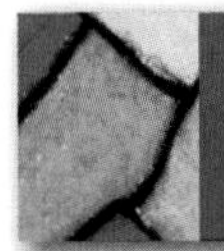

PREPARING THE PROJECT

Begin your project by looking back at the **Project Prep** activities in this chapter and using the directions below.

Make Connections

With your partner, discuss what you learned about the impact of technology on communication. What insights have you gained about technology's effects on communication in your own life? Discuss and summarize these important points:

- technology's impact on intrapersonal, interpersonal, group, public, mass, and visual communications and its role in creating hybrid communication types
- the growing presence of different forms of technology in our lives
- the benefits and drawbacks of using technology to communicate.

Focus

Review the project you and your partner are preparing: the "technology tales" presentation demonstrating the positive and negative effects of technology on communication.

Plan

With your partner, create two brainstorming lists for the true stories you will tell about the positive and negative effects of technology. Then, choose the best idea in each category. Remember that each story should show a clear positive or negative effect of technology and that the stories should work well together.

Develop

Decide who will tell each story. Prepare notes for the narrative. Then, review the notes together, giving each other feedback. For more on giving and receiving constructive criticism, see pages 159–160. Prepare a catchy opening and strong ending.

Surefire Planning

To plan effectively:

- stay focused on the assignment
- take all parts of the assignment into consideration
- be flexible if your original idea turns out not to be the best one
- be respectful of your partner's opinions and come to a consensus

Practice

Be sure that you and your partner are clear on who is saying what and when they are saying it. When you switch speakers, make the transition smoothly. Pay attention to volume, rate, and pitch when each of you speak. Pace yourselves to hold the audience's attention. Stay within the five-minute time limit.

PRESENTING THE PROJECT

Use the strategies that follow to help make your presentation as good as it can be.

You and your partner should now be ready to present your technology tales. Go over the CAPS guidelines on page 562 and the rubric on page 585 to meet the project requirements.

Interacting with the Audience

By maintaining eye contact with the audience, you'll give the impression that you're speaking directly to individual listeners. You'll convey your own investment in your message and hold your listeners' attention. As you speak, switch your focus so that you make eye contact with people in different parts of the audience.

EVALUATING THE PROJECT

Evaluate the presentations using the following rubric.

Score the demonstration on each point, with 4 being "outstanding" and 1 being "needs much improvement." Come up with an overall score, and write a brief paragraph that explains your score.

Understanding of Technology's Effect on Communication	Effectiveness of Narrative	Creativity and Originality	Preparation and Use of Time
4 Presenters demonstrated insight into technology's effects.	**4** Narratives were engaging and presented technology's effects convincingly.	**4** Narratives complemented one another; conclusions were supported by narratives.	**4** The presentation flowed smoothly and stayed within the time limit.
3 Presenters understood technology's effects.	**3** Narratives were generally engaging and presented technology's effects convincingly.	**3** Narratives complemented one another; conclusions were mainly supported by narratives.	**3** The presentation progressed fairly smoothly and stayed within the time limit.
2 Presenters demonstrated little insight into technology's effects.	**2** Narratives were not interesting and presented technology's effects in a limited way.	**2** Narratives complemented one another somewhat; conclusions were somewhat supported by narratives.	**2** The presentation had a few awkward moments and went a bit over or was noticeably under the time limit.
1 Presenters demonstrated little understanding of technology's effects.	**1** Narratives lacked clarity and did not demonstrate technology's effects.	**1** Narratives did not complement one another somewhat; conclusions were not supported by narratives.	**1** The presentation was not smoothly executed and went well over or was significantly under the time limit.

Communication *Past* and Present

Letter Writing

From Pen and Ink . . .

For more than two thousand years, people have been writing letters. The writers have expressed intimate thoughts about love or friendship. They've described significant events in history as they've experienced them. Sometimes letters have served as documents of both personal and national life, as in a famous letter written by Major Sullivan Ballou to his wife on July 14, 1861, during the Civil War. It is a hand-written letter in pen and ink, and he wrote it knowing that he might be killed in an impending battle. In the letter, Ballou expresses his feelings for his wife and his country:

> *Sarah my love for you is deathless. It seems to bind me with mighty cables that nothing but Omnipotence could break; and yet my love of Country comes over me like a strong wind and bears me unresistibly on with all these chains to the battlefield.*

A week after writing the letter, Major Ballou was killed at the Battle of Bull Run. His passionate feelings endure in his letter.

Letters convey a sense of immediacy—a flavor of life as it's lived in the moment. Letters from the past can make daily life in France or England during the Middle Ages feel vivid and real. Famous historical figures come alive through the hopes and fears they express in their letters. People who would otherwise remain anonymous in history pass along their names and stories in their letters.

The physical presence of letters also gives them a sense of the personal. The choice of paper, the writer's handwriting, the smell of the letter (a hint of perfume), even a wayward smudge (a teardrop, perhaps?) can reveal much about the writer. All of these details help shape the way the message is received. Letters, of course, are frequently thrown away or lost. Yet they are often saved—on purpose or by accident—tucked away in a drawer and forgotten until someone else stumbles upon them. The physical presence of letters is what gives them permanence.

. . . to E-mail

For decades, people have feared that communication mediated by technology might result in the death of the letter. As messages no longer had to be physically transported from place to place, whether by horse or rail or plane, distance posed less and less of an obstacle to communication. Consequently, communication became more rapid and more synchronous. First came the telegraph in the 1830s. Then came the telephone, patented in 1876, and in common use by the mid-1900s. In recent years, many have assumed that e-mail was the greatest threat to letters, as people have come to rely on it for personal and professional communication. Soldiers serving in Iraq can e-mail their loved ones, so few write letters on paper as Ballou did. People express concern that e-mail, because it makes communication so fast and easy, may lack the intimacy and reflection that characterize letters. They also note that it lacks permanence. Both of these are true to some degree, but there are those who think people are writing more deeply and more expansively now that communicating through the written word is so convenient and quick. By printing or archiving e-mail, thoughts and feelings delivered through the ether can be saved and "immortalized." Also e-mail messages can be stored on a computer for decade after decade and retrieved (with the permission and password of the owner) later.

Are letters themselves truly immortal? Perhaps the answer lies in how ***letter-writing*** will be defined in the future. It's a question that generations to come will have to answer.

How often do you mail letters? When letters were the most common form of long-distance communication, dropping a letter in a mailbox was an everyday activity.

The video game *World of Warcraft* mentioned on page 578 makes reference to Major Ballou and his famous letter. Players may find the body of a dwarf soldier under the Thandol Span bridge. The soldier's name is Sully Balloo, and in his hand he holds a sodden letter to his wife, Sara. The game player is charged with bringing the letter and sad news of Sully's death to his wife in Ironforge. This letter is very similar to the one written by Sullivan Ballou.

Chapter 25 Review

Using Vocabulary Words

How many different connections can you make among the following terms? List as many pairs as you can, and then explain the connection between the terms (you can use terms more than once).

1. computer-mediated communication
2. convergence
3. cyberbullying
4. cyberstalking
5. e-learning
6. emoticons
7. Personal Digital Assistant
8. podcasts
9. telecommute
10. teleconferencing

Reviewing Key Ideas

1. Briefly explain how technology affects intrapersonal, interpersonal, group, public, mass, and visual communication.
2. Provide an example of a hybrid type of communication.
3. Explain the impact of convergence on one form of technology discussed in this chapter.
4. Review the list of technology's benefits and drawbacks on pages 580–583. In your opinion, what are the two greatest benefits and the two worst drawbacks? Why?

Reflecting on Your Project

With your partner, discuss the most successful parts of your project. If you were doing your project over again, what would you do differently? What has the experience of completing this project taught you?

Responding to the Essential Question

Imagine that items were being collected for a time capsule, which would not be opened for one hundred years. You've been asked to contribute an answer to the question, "How does technology affect the way people communicate?" Write your response.

Extending Your Understanding

Everyday Life

1. Consider the benefits and drawbacks of cell phones, text messaging, instant messaging, and e-mail. Discuss which you would use to a) make a plan with a friend, b) discuss a conflict with a friend, and c) contact a friend with whom you've fallen out of touch.
2. Communication technologies have made it possible for parents and teenagers to be in touch throughout the course of the day. Discuss whether you think there are any drawbacks to this increased connectivity.
3. Should parents monitor or control their children's use of communication technologies? Debate the issue.

In the Media

4. Compare the way a current news story is covered in two of the following mass media: television, radio, the Internet, and your local newspaper. Discuss which media form communicates information about the story most effectively.
5. Compare the Web sites of two newspapers or two television stations to explore the impact of convergence. Discuss which Web site is the most informative and interesting.
6. With a partner, survey people of different ages to learn which form of mass media is their main source for news. What conclusions can you draw from the results of your survey? Present your findings to the class.

Research

7. Research the history of the telephone, radio, television, or the Internet. What has been its impact on communication? Present your findings to the class in a brief report.
8. Research the impact of technology on intercultural communication, or communication between members of different cultures. How has technology helped to make the world "flat"? Discuss your research with your classmates.
9. Conduct research to answer the question "How can playing video games be beneficial or harmful to you?" Present your findings in the form of a poster containing charts and diagrams.

Interpreting Graphics

What conclusions about online video viewers can you draw from the statistics in the chart below?

Online Video Viewers

Activities	Ages 18–29	Ages 30–49	Ages 50–64
Receive video links	76%	77%	71%
Send video links to others	67%	55%	45%
Watch video with others	73%	58%	34%
Post comments about video	25%	9%	5%
Post video links online	22%	7%	2%

Source: Pew Internet & American Life Project Tracking Survey, February 15–March 7, 2007

Additional Projects

1. **Group Project:** What are the advantages and disadvantages of using the Internet for research? How can you be sure that information is accurate and material is authentic? With a small group, write a guide for middle-school students about doing research on the Internet.
2. **Individual Project:** If you could create a new form of communication technology, what would its functions be? Create or draw a model of it, and write a press release explaining how it will enhance communication.

Unit Six

Culminating Activities

In this unit you have explored mass communications: the role of mass communications in society and the impact of technology on everyday life. The activities on these pages will help you apply your understandings to situations in everyday life.

Workplace Workout

Nick, a journalist, had to write a special article for high-school students to be posted on the website of the newspaper he works for. The topic was the long-standing controversy over the nuclear power plant. Nick found an article on the topic that had appeared in a magazine for elementary-school students three years earlier. He decided to use most of the article because the ideas were basic and the language was simple. Since the article seemed dry to him, he added some sarcasm and humorous bits. Nick knew he needed to update the information to include the new governor's role in the controversy, but he actually thought the governor's views were unsound. He devoted little space to discussing the governor's perspective, emphasizing a state senator's position instead.

When the article was posted, the newspaper was flooded with e-mails to the editor. Teachers from all over the state made their complaints known. The angriest e-mail was from the journalist who had written the earlier magazine article.

What Went Wrong?

Reflect on what you have learned about mass communications, including their characteristics, their purposes, and ethical issues. Then, write an e-mail to the newspaper's editor in which you point out the problems in Nick's article.

Make It Right

The newspaper plans to post other articles for high-school students. Create writer's guidelines to help prevent other journalists from making the same mistakes as Nick did. Present your guidelines to a small group. Then, discuss the similarities and differences in group members' guidelines.

Media Master

Use the Internet to research a former American president. Then, imagine that this person is currently running for president. Design the home page of his campaign website. As you develop the page and a menu of links, consider what you have learned about technology's impact on political life. You can design your home page on paper, or you can use a web-page creation tool. Present your home page to your classmates, and explain how designing it strengthened your understanding of this president and technology's impact on democracy.

Gender Journey

Over the years, researchers have documented gender-role stereotyping in the mass media. What kinds of stereotypes are still perpetuated on TV? With a partner, watch several popular TV shows in the course of a week. Take notes on any gender stereotypes you observe, and discuss these stereotypes. Together, develop an idea for a TV show that counters some of these stereotypes. Create a print ad to advertise your new show.

OWN IT!

Think about T. S. Eliot's statement at the beginning of Unit 6: "[Television] is a medium of entertainment which permits millions of people to listen to the same joke at the same time, and yet remain lonesome." (See page 541.) Reflect, too, on what you have learned in this unit and on your own experiences. How can television serve to unite us as well as isolate us? Can the Internet play the same two roles? With a small group, explore these questions in a panel discussion presented in front of your classmates.

Chapter 1

Abraham Lincoln: *The Gettysburg Address*

On November 18, 1863, President Abraham Lincoln gave a short speech at the dedication of the National Soldier's Cemetery in Gettysburg, Pennsylvania. In fewer than 300 words, he crystallized the historical significance of the Civil War—and of the United States. Notice how he repeats words and phrases to emphasize key points.

Fourscore and seven years ago our fathers brought forth on this continent a new nation, conceived in liberty and dedicated to the proposition that all men are created equal.

Now we are engaged in a great civil war, testing whether that nation or any nation so conceived and so dedicated can long endure. We are met on a great battlefield of that war. We have come to dedicate a portion of that field as a final resting-place for those who here gave their lives that that nation might live. It is altogether fitting and proper that we should do this.

But in a larger sense, we cannot dedicate, we cannot consecrate, we cannot hallow this ground. The brave men, living and dead who struggled here have consecrated it far above our poor power to add or detract. The world will little note nor long remember what we say here, but it can never forget what they did here. It is for us the living rather to be dedicated here to the unfinished work which they who fought here have thus far so nobly advanced.

It is rather for us to be here dedicated to the great task remaining before us—that from these honored dead we take increased devotion to that cause for which they gave the last full measure of devotion—that we here highly resolve that these dead shall not have died in vain, that this nation under God shall have a new birth of freedom, and that government of the people, by the people, for the people shall not perish from the earth.

For Discussion

1. Summarize Lincoln's message in one sentence.
2. Whom do you think Lincoln thought of as his audience for this speech?
3. Choose one phrase you think communicates well, and explain why you think it works.

Chapter 2

Mary Louise Gilman: *Courtroom Bloopers*

In a courtroom, lawyers ask people questions that they must answer on the spot. Sometimes, they don't interpret the questions as the lawyer intended. Or, they don't give the answer they might give with more time to reflect. Following are some examples of courtroom testimony compiled by Mary Louise Gilman. As you read them, think about how they would sound when spoken.

Q: What is your brother-in-law's name?

A: Borofkin.

Q: What's his first name?

A: I can't remember . . .

Q: He's been your brother-in-law for years and you can't remember his first name?

A: No. I tell you I'm too excited and nervous . . . (raising from witness chair and pointing to Mr. Borofkin). Nathan . . . tell them your first name!

Q: Doctor, did you say he was shot in the woods?

A: No, I said he was shot in the lumbar region [part of the back].

Q: Doctor, how many autopsies have you performed on dead people?

A: All my autopsies have been done on dead people.

Q: Mrs. Jones, is your appearance this morning pursuant to a deposition notice [a legal form] which I sent to your attorney?

A: No, this is how I dress when I go to work.

Q: Did he pick the dog up by the ears?

A: No.

Q: What was he doing with the dog's ears?

A: Picking them up in the air.

Q: Where was the dog at this time?

A: Attached to the ears.

....

Q: And lastly Gary, all your responses must be oral. O.K.? What school did you go to?

A: Oral.

Q: How old are you?

A: Oral.

....

Q: The truth of the matter is, that you are not an unbiased, objective witness, isn't it. You too were shot in the fracas [dispute]?

A: No, sir. I was shot midway between the fracas and the navel.

....

Q: (showing man picture) That's you?

A: Yes.

Q: And you were present when the picture was taken, right?

....

Q: Was that the same nose you broke as a child?

For Discussion

1. Analyze one of these exchanges, and explain why you think it is humorous.
2. Why are people more likely to make humorous comments by accident when they speak than when they write?
3. Give an example of when you have interpreted a question one way when the asker intended it in a different way.

Chapter 3

Helen Keller: *How to Help the Blind*

Helen Keller was born in 1880. When she was 19 months old, an illness left her blind, deaf, and unable to speak. She first learned how to communicate with gestures. Later, with the help of her teacher, Anne Sullivan Macy, she learned how to speak. Keller went on to be a successful author and public lecturer.

In this address given in 1925 in Cedar Point, Ohio, she is urging a service organization, the Lions Club, to support efforts to aid the blind. Keller's appeals to the imagination made this a powerful and effective speech.

Try to imagine how you would feel if you were suddenly stricken blind today. Picture yourself stumbling and groping at noonday as in the night; your work, your independence, gone. In that dark world wouldn't you be glad if a friend took you by the hand and said, "Come with me and I will teach you how to do some of the things you used to do when you could see"? That is just the kind of friend the American Foundation is going to be to all the blind in this country if seeing people will give it the support it must have.

You have heard how through a little word dropped from the fingers of another, a ray of light from another soul touched the darkness of my mind and I found myself, found the world, found God. It is because my teacher learned about me and broke through the dark, silent imprisonment which held me that I am able to work for myself and for others. It is the caring we want more than money. The gift without the sympathy and interest of the giver is empty. If you care, if we can make the people of this great country care, the blind will indeed triumph over blindness.

The opportunity I bring to you, Lions, is this: To foster and sponsor the work of the American Foundation for the Blind. Will you not help me hasten the day when there shall be no preventable blindness; no little deaf, blind child untaught; no blind man or woman unaided? I appeal to you Lions, you who have your sight, your hearing, you who are strong and brave and kind. Will you not constitute yourselves *Knights of the Blind* in this crusade against darkness?

I thank you.

For Discussion

1. What do you think Keller means when she says "a little word dropped from the fingers of another"?
2. What is Keller asking the Lions Club to do?
3. Research the Lions Club and its efforts on behalf of the blind.

Chapter 4

Plato: *When Is a Just Man Useful?*

Plato was born around 428 B.C. in Greece. His numerous writings featuring his teacher, Socrates, became the foundation for Western philosophy. Socrates was renowned for his willingness to listen closely to his students and to prompt them to clarify their ideas. In this passage, he is exploring the value of justice with Polemarchus. Socrates asks when a just man—a man who is fair and honest—might be useful. See if his answer surprises you.

Polemarchus: In a money partnership.

Socrates: Yes, Polemarchus, but surely not in the use of money; for you do not want a just man to be your counselor for the purchase or sale of a horse; a man who is knowing about horses would be better for that, would he not?

Polemarchus: Certainly.

Socrates: And when you want to buy a ship, the shipwright or the pilot would be better?

Polemarchus: True.

Socrates: Then what is that joint use of silver or gold in which the just man is to be preferred?

Polemarchus: When you want a deposit to be kept safely.

Socrates: You mean when money is not wanted, but allowed to lie?

Polemarchus: Precisely.

Socrates: That is to say, justice is useful when money is useless?

Polemarchus: That is the inference.

Socrates: And when you want to keep a pruning-hook safe, then justice is useful to the individual and to the state; but when you want to use it, then the art of the vine-dresser?

Polemarchus: Clearly.

Socrates: And when you want to keep a shield or a lyre, and not to use them, you would say that justice is useful; but when you want to use them, then the art of the soldier or of the musician?

Polemarchus: Certainly.

Socrates: And so of all the other things, justice is useful when they are useless, and useless when they are useful?

Polemarchus: That is the inference.

Socrates: Then justice is not good for much.

For Discussion

1. Why type of sentence does Socrates use primarily in this passage?
2. Select one point that Socrates makes, and explain why you agree or disagree with it.
3. What do you think Socrates believes about justice?

Chapter 5

Winston Churchill: *We Shall Fight on the Beaches*

World War II broke out in Europe in 1939. By the spring of 1940, the German Nazis were sweeping through France and were preparing to invade Great Britain. Many feared that the British, though they still controlled a world-wide colonial empire, could not stand up to the assault. On June 4, 1940, Britain's leader, Prime Minister Winston Churchill, spoke to the House of Commons to inspire the people of his country to defend their homeland. Churchill's several wartime addresses won him a reputation as one of the greatest English-language orators in history. As you read this, consider what ethical obligations Churchill had at the time.

I have, myself, full confidence that if all do their duty, if nothing is neglected, and if the best arrangements are made, as they are being made, we shall prove ourselves once again able to defend our Island home, to ride out the storm of war, and to outlive the menace of tyranny, if necessary for years, if necessary alone.

At any rate, that is what we are going to try to do. That is the resolve of His Majesty's Government—every man of them. That is the will of Parliament and the nation. The British Empire and the French Republic, linked together in their cause and in their need, will defend to the death their native soil, aiding each other like good comrades to the utmost of their strength. Even though large tracts of Europe and many old and famous States have fallen or may fall into the grip of the Gestapo [the German secret police] and all the odious apparatus of Nazi rule, we shall not flag or fail.

We shall go on to the end, we shall fight in France, we shall fight on the seas and oceans, we shall fight with growing confidence and growing strength in the air, we shall defend our Island, whatever the cost may be, we shall fight on the beaches, we shall fight on the landing grounds, we shall fight in the fields and in the streets, we shall fight in the hills; we shall never surrender, and even if, which I do not for a moment believe, this Island or a large part of it were subjugated and starving, then our Empire beyond the seas, armed and guarded by the British Fleet, would carry on the struggle, until, in God's good time, the New World [the United States and Canada], with all its power and might, steps forth to the rescue and the liberation of the old.

Winston Churchill

For Discussion

1. Describe the tone of Churchill's speech.
2. What techniques does Churchill use in the final paragraph to build up to his main idea, that Britain will never surrender?
3. What ethical responsibility as a speaker does a country's leader have in a time of war?

Chapter 6

Henrik Ibsen: *A Doll's House*

Norwegian writer Henrik Ibsen's play, A Doll's House, *caused controversy when it appeared in 1879. It portrayed a view of marriage that angered many. In this scene, Nora tries to explain her feelings about her marriage to her husband, Torvald Helmer. Analyze Nora's communication skills as you read.*

Nora: *(Shakes her head.)* You have never loved me. You just thought it was fun to be in love with me.

Helmer: Nora, what kind of way is this to talk?

Nora: It's the turth, Torvald. When I lived with Papa, he used to tell me what he thought about everything, so that I never had any opinions but his. And if I did have any of my own, I kept them quiet, because he wouldn't have liked them. He called me his little doll, and he played with me just the way I played with my dolls. Then I came here to live in your house—

Helmer: What kind of a way is that to describe our marriage?

Nora: *(Undisturbed.)* I mean, then I passed from Papa's hands into yours. You arranged everything the way you wanted it, so that I simply took over your taste in everything—or pretended I did—I don't really know—I think it was a little of both—first one and then the other. Now I look back on it as if I've been living here like a pauper, from hand to mouth. I performed tricks for you, and you gave me food and drink. But that was how you wanted it. You and Papa have done me a great wrong. It's your fault that I have done nothing with my life.

Helmer: Nora, how can you be so unreasonable and ungrateful? Haven't you been happy here?

Nora: No; never. I used to think I was, but I haven't ever been happy.

Helmer: Not—not happy?

Nora: No. I've had fun. You've always been very kind to me. But our home has never been anything but a playroom. I've been your doll-wife, just as I used to be Papa's doll-child. And the children have been my dolls. I used to think it was fun when you came in and played with me, just as they think it's fun when I go in and play games with them. That's all our marriage has been, Torvald.

For Discussion

1. List three words that describe how Nora presents her comments.
2. List three words you think describe Helmer's reactions.
3. Evaluate the effectiveness of Nora's interpersonal communication skills, and give examples from this excerpt to back up your evaluation.

Chapter 7

Deborah Tannen: *I Heard What You Didn't Say*

Deborah Tannen is a linguist and widely read author who writes frequently about how people can improve their communication. Here, she focuses on communication within families. Do you think she is accurate about the challenges of listening to the people closest to you?

Why does talk in the family so frequently leave us tied up in knots?

Through talk, we create and shape our relationships. Through talk, we are comforted; through talk we are hurt. We look to family members for come-as-you-are acceptance, but instead of an intimate ally, we sometimes find an intimate critic. A small remark can spark a big conflict because within the family, no utterance stands alone. Every remark draws meaning from innumerable conversations that came before. Consider this seemingly harmless comment, and the argument it triggered for one couple:

"This is recyclable," Helen says, brandishing a small cylinder that was once at the center of a roll of toilet paper.

"I know it's recyclable," says Samuel. "You don't have to tell me." He approves of recycling and generally practices it, but in a moment of haste, he had tossed the cardboard tube into the wastebasket. Helen has found it and wants to know why it is there. "You can't go through the garbage looking for things I threw away," Samuel exclaims. "Our relationship is more important than a toilet paper carcass."

"I'm not talking about our relationship," Helen protests. "I'm talking about recycling."

Helen is right: She was talking about recycling. But Samuel is right, too. If you feel like you're living with the recycling police—or the diet police, or the neatness police—it can take the joy out of living together. Sometimes you catch yourself wishing, for a fleeting moment, that you lived alone, in peace. In that sense, Helen's remark is also about the relationship.

Helen and Samuel could argue forever—and get nowhere—because they were focusing on different aspects of their conversation. Helen's concern, recycling, is the message: the literal subject at hand. Samuel's concern is the metamessage: the implication that Helen is always watching, always on the lookout for wrong moves.

Distinguishing the message from the metamessage (terms I have adopted from anthropologist

Gregory Bateson) is necessary to ensure that family members work things out rather than working each other over. It's frustrating to have the same arguments again and again. But some arguments can be constructive—if family members use them to articulate and understand the metamessages they are intending and hearing.

For Discussion

1. What advice would you give to Helen and Samuel to help them communicate better?
2. Give an example of the difference between a message and metamessage that you have seen or experienced.
3. How can listening for a metamessage improve communication?

Chapter 8

Margaret Chase Smith: *In Defense of Dissent*

Margaret Chase Smith represented Maine in the U.S. Senate from 1949 to 1973. She was still a newcomer to the Senate when, on June 1, 1950, she gave her most famous speech. She was responding to harsh, and often unfair, attacks made by Senator Joseph McCarthy against people he charged were communists or who associated with communists. While Smith is defending the right of political dissent, consider how her comments apply to dissent in other parts of life.

I speak as briefly as possible because too much harm has already been done with irresponsible words of bitterness and selfish political opportunism. I speak as simply as possible because the issue is too great to be obscured by eloquence. I speak simply and briefly in the hope that my words will be taken to heart.

I speak as a Republican, I speak as a woman. I speak as a United States Senator. I speak as an American.

The United States Senate has long enjoyed worldwide respect as the greatest deliberative body in the world. But recently that deliberative character has too often been debased to the level of a forum of hate and character assassination sheltered by the shield of congressional immunity. . . .

Those of us who shout the loudest about Americanism in making character assassinations are all too frequently those who, by our own words and acts, ignore some of the basic principles of Americanism—

The right to criticize;

The right to hold unpopular beliefs;

The right to protest;

The right of independent thought.

The exercise of these rights should not cost one single American citizen his reputation or his right to a livelihood nor should he be in danger of losing his reputation or livelihood merely because he happens to know someone who holds unpopular beliefs. Who of us doesn't? Otherwise none of us could call our souls our own. Otherwise thought control would have set in.

Margaret Chase Smith

For Discussion

1. What does Smith consider basic principles of Americanism?
2. How does Smith defend the importance of disagreements?
3. Do you agree with Smith's statements? Give reasons for your answer.

Chapter 9

Rachel N.: *My Grandmother, Shizue Kobayashi*

Shizue Kobayashi was born in 1934 in Japan. She lived there through World War II, and recalls the dropping of the first atomic bomb in 1945. After the war, she moved to the United States. This interview with her was conducted by her granddaughter, Rachel, who was a school student at the time. Rachel noted that "Although she [her grandmother] believes that the war [World War II] was terrible, she does not hold any harsh feelings against the United States." Note the style and length of questions that Rachel asks in the interview.

Where were you when the atomic bomb was dropped?
It was in the summertime, so I was in my yard. I was looking at the sky, and it was shiny, like a thunderstorm. My parents weren't home, and I don't even remember being scared.

Did you understand what was happening?
I did not know what was happening, but I knew something was wrong. Many people were dead or were dying. It was horrible, just horrible. The fire in Tokyo was burning so brightly it made the night look as bright as day. I was ten miles from Tokyo, and could feel the heat from the fire. After the second bomb, I heard the adults talking, and that is how I found out. There were no televisions, and the radio was hard to understand. . . .

How old were you when you came to the United States? How and when did you get here?
I came to the United States in 1956 when I was 22. I had met your grandfather at a war orphanage in Japan. I used to visit the orphans on Saturdays and Sundays, and he entertained the children with baseball. He was from the American air force, and they must have felt sorry

for the innocent victims of the atomic bomb because they sent them dried prunes. After his service at the war orphanage, we left Japan for America in a huge ship and arrived in San Francisco. Then we went to Texas where we got married. Then we moved to Michigan.

What was it like? How did you feel?
I thought America was so beautiful, especially San Francisco. I was so happy. It was exciting, but I was also a little scared.

For Discussion

1. Describe the style and tone of the questions that Rachel asks.
2. How does the second question follow up on the first question?
3. What might be a good question to ask Rachel's grandmother after her response to the final question?

Chapter 10

Cesar Chavez: *Recognizing the Power of a Group*

Cesar Chavez helped organize and lead the first successful union of migrant farm workers who toiled in the fruit and vegetable fields of California. Inspired by the nonviolent protests led by Mohandas Gandhi and Martin Luther King Jr., Chavez used marches, boycotts, and strikes effectively. In the following speech, given in 1984 to the Commonwealth Club of California, he describes how he became interested in organizing people. The Commonwealth Club is a nonprofit, nonpartisan group committed to public affairs. Its motto is "find the truth, and turn it loose in the world." What helps Chavez recognize the importance of groups in fighting for justice?

I'm not very different from anyone else who has ever tried to accomplish something with his life. My motivation comes from my personal life, from watching what my mother and father went through when I was growing up, from what we experienced as migrant workers in California. That dream, that vision grew from my own experience with racism, with hope, with a desire to be treated fairly, and to see my people treated as human beings and not as chattel. It grew from anger and rage, emotions I felt 40 years ago when people of my color were denied the right to see a movie or eat at a restaurant in many parts of California. It grew from the frustration and humiliation I felt as a boy who couldn't understand how the growers could abuse and exploit farm workers when there were so many of us and so few of them. Later in the 50s, I experienced a different kind of exploitation. In San Jose, in Los Angeles and in other urban communities, we, the Mexican-American people, were dominated by a majority that was Anglo. I began to realize what other minority people had discovered: that the only answer, the only hope was in organizing. More of us had to become citizens, we had to register to vote, and people like me had to develop the skills it would take to organize, to educate, to help empower the Chicano people.

For Discussion

1. What experiences shaped Chavez as he grew up?
2. What did Chavez learn from other groups about the power of groups in American society?
3. Review the motto of the Commonwealth Club. Do you think Chavez was effective in addressing the audience of this group? Explain.

Chapter 11

English College Students: *Organizing a Group*

The following dialogue is from a video made in England about group roles and processes. The five speakers are actors portraying college students who are meeting for the first time to work on a group project for a class. Their assignment is to prepare a presentation on the topic, "What are the barriers to effective learning and how can [they] be overcome?" Consider whether you think the group dynamics in this group are realistic.

Shireen: . . . There's gonna be quite a lot of stuff to cover, so do you wanna elect a group leader, and then we can be specific about the points? I don't mind doing that, because I've done group leading before.

Vikki: Maybe we could all have a go at running the sessions!

Shireen: Mmmmm.

Vikki: What does everyone else think?

Muzz: Yes.

Shireen: OK.

Shireen: What I'm saying is, I think we need to decide *now* what we're gonna do in the presentation, otherwise we're just gonna be discussing loads of things over the weeks and not have an idea of how we're *actually* gonna present it. So I've got a [prepared presentation] . . . .

Vikki: I think we should all *share* our ideas about what to include.

Shireen: Well yeah, but we need to have some idea *now* about what we're gonna do when we present, otherwise we're just gonna look stupid. . . .

Muzz: Excuse me.

Vikki: Yeah, but can we *all* share ideas?

Shireen: Well yeah, that's what I'm saying. I'm not saying "don't share our ideas."

Muzz: Excuse me. Excuse me. Excuse me! Sorry. I think we have to communicate our ideas onto the board.

Shireen: What for though?

Vikki: The way I see it, is that we'll start with the effective and ineffective approaches to learning.

Muzz: Yes.

Vikki: OK, so we've got good planning, relevant resources, sharing ideas, clear communication, and using feedback. Does that help?

Rob: Do you get it now, Muzz?

Muzz: What do you mean?

Rob: Well, it's taken you long enough!

Muzz: Well, it's clear for me, okay?!

Delia: Well, I didn't really understand before either, but it is a lot more clear right now.

Shireen: Yeah. Right, well, let's move on, because we've got ten minutes left, and we've only looked at effective. So do you wanna look at ineffective now?

Rob: I've gotta go.

Shireen: Brilliant.

Rob: Well, sorry. When are we meeting next week?

Shireen: Same time.

Rob: Fine. See you later.

Delia: See ya.

Shireen: Good commitment.

Muzz: He's very rude.

Vikki: Okay, how about we finish this list, and then we can update Rob next week.

Shireen: Right.

For Discussion

1. Who do you think is the leader of this group? Explain.
2. Describe the types of behavior that Rob exhibits.
3. How could this group work together more effectively?

Chapter 12

Daniel Goleman: *Humor and Problem-Solving*

In a group discussion, humor can be a welcome addition—or an annoying distraction. In this newspaper article, reporter Daniel Goleman explores the research of Alice M. Isen, a professor of psychology at Cornell University who studied how humor affects a group's ability to solve problems. Notice when Isen thinks humor is useful.

In the research, reported in a recent issue of *The Journal of Personality and Social Psychology,* Dr. Isen found that people who had just watched a short comedy film of television "bloopers" were better able to find a creative solution to a puzzling problem than were people who had watched a film about math or who had exercised.

The problem posed was one frequently used in such research: People were given a candle, matches and a box of tacks and asked to attach the candle to a corkboard wall so that the candle would burn without dripping wax on the floor.

Most people who try to solve this problem fall prey to "functional fixedness," the tendency to see the objects presented them only in terms of their conventional uses. Those who were in a good mood from watching the funny film, however, were generally able to solve the problem by seeing another use for the box holding the tacks: they tacked the box to the wall and used it as a candleholder.

In other studies, Dr. Isen found that the comedy film increased people's ability to think more broadly, seeing relationships that otherwise eluded them. This is a mental skill that is important in finding creative solutions to problems and in foreseeing the consequences of a given decision. The ability to recognize complex relationships and far-flung implications has also been found, in other research, to mark the most successful business executives.

"The mind associates more broadly when people are feeling good after hearing a joke," said Dr. Isen. "They think of things they ordinarily would not and have access to a broader range of mental material. And the more ideas present in your mind, the more ways you see to connect things; you're able to see more solutions."

For Discussion

1. What is "functional fixedness"? Why do you think Goleman defined that term in his article?
2. How does humor help people find solutions to problems?
3. Give examples of the influence of humor on how well groups you have been part of worked together.

Chapter 13

Rachel Donadio: *Revising Robert's Rules*

Robert's Rules of Order *are more than a century old. Despite their age, they remain the standard guidelines for running meetings using parliamentary procedure today. In this review of a new edition of the rules, Rachel Donadio considers their success. How have the rules survived so long?*

Although the name "Robert's Rules" passed into the public domain in the 1990s — prompting a wave of knockoffs like "Robert's Rules in Plain English" and "The Complete Idiot's Guide to Robert's Rules"—the original content remains under copyright and is a perennial strong seller. Since 2000, Da Capo Press has sold more than 450,000 copies of its eight different versions. The 10th and current edition has also been licensed for translation into Korean, Japanese, Chinese and Arabic. The book is "a machine," said Marnie Cochran, the executive editor of Da Capo. "It's a real institution."

It's also, as it happens, a family business. The original set of rules is still controlled by descendants of [Brigadier General] Henry Robert, an Army engineering officer who wrote the first several editions and died in 1923. . . .Today, Robert's descendants remain devoted stewards of their property, which brings in between $80,000 and $100,000 a year in royalties, according to the head of the 16-member family association. Robert's Rules may have attained near-governmental authority, but the last three editions were updated by four guys at occasional daylong meetings (with breaks for lunch) at the Johns Hopkins Club in Baltimore. . . .

Though mind-numbingly technical, with its recesses, adjournments, motions postponed definitely or indefinitely and its quasi-architectural jargon of tables and floors, Robert's Rules, like parliamentary procedure itself, has proven adaptable. In updating it, the committee's aim is to reflect changes in the culture while "maintaining certain standards of procedure," Balch said. "There's a tension there, a little bit like what's seen with dictionaries." The current incarnation — "Robert's Rules of Order: Newly Revised, 10th Edition" (2000) — was changed to acknowledge, for example, that "chair" and "chairwoman" are as valid as "chairman," and to accommodate video conferencing, deemed O.K. as long as participants can discuss a matter at the same time. (They frown on "asynchronous meetings" held via e-mail.)

For Discussion

1. How do Robert's Rules get updated?
2. Do you agree with the decisions about video conferencing and e-mail meetings?
3. What changes might you propose to Robert's Rules?

Chapter 14

Ray Suarez: *Writing Speeches for Presidents*

Clark Judge and Michael Waldman wrote speeches for presidents who were considered excellent speakers. Judge wrote for Ronald Reagan, and Waldman wrote for Bill Clinton. Journalist Ray Suarez interviewed the two about one of their most important assignments each year, writing the State of the Union Address. For more on the State of the Union Address, see Chapter 20. Pay attention to how the experiences of Judge and Waldman in preparing speeches differed.

Suarez: Clark Judge, let's go back to your White House, a couple of hours before the State of the Union address. Are you done? Are you finished?

Judge: Finished several days earlier. The president's been rehearsing. He may have tweaked things himself, may have made some minor modifications. But at this point, it's rehearsal, get it right, relax, and get ready to put on a good show.

Suarez: And as the speechwriter, you're not part of that part of it?

Judge: You may or may not be. It depends on the year; it depends on the president. But the important thing is for him to get in the zone and be ready to put on a good show for—to be as good as his text.

Suarez: Michael Waldman, here we are, oh, two-and-a-half hours before the sergeant-at-arms welcomes the president to the chamber. Are you done?

Waldman: Well, under President Clinton, it might be a somewhat different rhythm. He would be working on the speech, rehearsing and rewriting from the podium up until the day of, and, you know, asking questions, and as most presidents do, using these speeches to probe his own government and find out the political direction and try to set a stance. So he was working until the last minute.

Suarez: Still you're working pretty much until he gets up to that lectern?

Waldman: Pretty close.

For Discussion

1. According to Judge, why was finishing the speech several days early important to President Reagan?
2. According to Waldman, how does a speech influence policy?
3. Summarize the difference between Judge's and Waldman's experiences in writing speeches for presidents.

Chapter 15

Nicholas Carr: *Is Google Making Us Stupid?*

The Internet has revolutionized the way people do research. In particular, it has changed how people read. Writer Nicholas Carr reviewed the research on this topic and summarized it in a provocative article in The Atlantic *magazine. Some researchers think that using the Internet might be changing the way our brains work. Consider whether you agree.*

Thanks to the ubiquity of text on the Internet, not to mention the popularity of text-messaging on cell phones, we may well be reading more today than we did in the 1970s or 1980s, when television was our medium of choice. But it's a different kind of reading, and behind it lies a different kind of thinking—perhaps even a new sense of the self. "We are not only *what* we read," says Maryanne Wolf, a developmental psychologist at Tufts University and the author of *Proust and the Squid: The Story and Science of the Reading Brain*. "We are *how* we read." Wolf worries that the style of reading promoted by the Net, a style that puts "efficiency" and "immediacy" above all else, may be weakening our capacity for the kind of deep reading that emerged when an earlier technology, the printing press, made long and complex works of prose commonplace. When we read online, she says, we tend to become "mere decoders of information." Our ability to interpret text, to make the rich mental connections that form when we read deeply and without distraction, remains largely disengaged.

Reading, explains Wolf, is not an instinctive skill for human beings. It's not etched into our genes the way speech is. We have to teach our minds how to translate the symbolic characters we see into the language we understand. And the media or other technologies we use in learning and practicing the craft of reading play an important part in shaping the neural circuits inside our brains. Experiments demonstrate that readers of ideograms, such as the Chinese, develop a mental circuitry for reading that is very different from the circuitry found in those of us whose written language employs an alphabet. The variations extend across many regions of the brain, including those that govern such essential cognitive functions as memory and the interpretation of visual and auditory stimuli. We can expect as well that the circuits woven by our use of the Net will be different from those woven by our reading of books and other printed works.

For Discussion

1. Explain what Wolf means by "We are how we read."
2. According to Carr, what evidence suggests that using the Internet will change our brains?
3. Analyze how the way you do research might influence how you think.

Chapter 16

Sojourner Truth: *Ain't I a Woman?*

Sojourner Truth was born in slavery around 1797, but became a free woman when she was about 30 years old. She became widely known as a public speaker opposing slavery and supporting the right of women to vote. Her most famous speech is one attributed to her by Frances Gage, another woman suffrage advocate. According to Gage, Truth stood up in a meeting on the rights of women in Akron, Ohio, in 1851, and delivered the address below. Pay attention to how Truth organized her remarks.

Well, children, where there is so much racket there must be something out of kilter. I think that 'twixt the negroes of the South and the women at the North, all talking about rights, the white men will be in a fix pretty soon. But what's all this here talking about?

That man over there says that women need to be helped into carriages, and lifted over ditches, and to have the best place everywhere. Nobody ever helps me into carriages, or over mud-puddles, or gives me any best place! And ain't I a woman? Look at me! Look at my arm! I have ploughed and planted, and gathered into barns, and no man could head me! And ain't I a woman? I could work as much and eat as much as a man—when I could get it—and bear the lash as well! And ain't I a woman? I have borne thirteen children, and seen most all sold off to slavery, and when I cried out with my mother's grief, none but Jesus heard me! And ain't I a woman?

Then they talk about this thing in the head; what's this they call it? [member of audience whispers, "intellect"] That's it, honey. What's that got to do with women's rights or negroes' rights? If my cup won't hold but a pint, and yours holds a quart, wouldn't you be mean not to let me have my little half measure full?

Then that little man in black there, he says women can't have as much rights as men, 'cause Christ wasn't a woman! Where did your Christ come from? Where did your Christ come from? From God and a woman! Man had nothing to do with Him.

If the first woman God ever made was strong enough to turn the world upside down all alone, these women together ought to be able to turn it back, and get it right side up again! And now they is asking to do it, the men better let them.

Obliged to you for hearing me, and now old Sojourner ain't got nothing more to say.

Sojourner Truth

For Discussion

1. What does Truth say in her introduction?
2. How is the body of the speech organized?
3. How long is Truth's conclusion, and is it still an effective ending?

Chapter 17

Michael Hyatt: *What To Do When Technology Fails*

Using presentation software can greatly improve a speech. But just as speakers plan how to use supporting materials effectively, they should plan for what to do when their computer, projector, or other piece of technology won't work right. Michael Hyatt, president and CEO of Thomas Nelson Publishers, provides some tips. Note how he keeps the emphasis on what can be done, rather than on the problems.

I don't know when or how, but sometime, someplace, the stuff you are counting on to work is going to fail. What do you do then?

Apologize once, then stop apologizing. . . . [T]he audience will take their cues from you. If you are calm and at ease—even if you have to fake it—they will be calm and at ease. . . .

Make a decision to "fish or cut bait." You have to retain control. . . . Are you confident that they [the technical staff trying the fix the problem] know what they are doing? Or, are they clueless and just hoping they get lucky? Only you can make the call. If it is the latter, than you have to ditch the PowerPoint and get the techies off the stage. This is where you need to be direct but not rude. "Gentlemen, don't worry about it. I will make the presentation without my slides. Thank you very much." And then, to the audience, "Let's give these guys a big hand for a valiant attempt."

Remember, you are the presentation. You then have to take a big breath and make a powerful presentation. Now, before you panic, remember: the greatest speeches in the history of the world were made without presentation software. Lincoln's "Gettysburg Address," John Kennedy's "Ask Not What Your Country Can Do for You," and Martin Luther King's0 "I Have a Dream" speeches were all given—believe it or not!—without [it]. You can do it.

For Discussion

1. Do you agree that apologizing once is enough? Explain.
2. How does Hyatt provide a positive way to handle a problem that might make the technical staff feel embarrassed?
3. How important do you think technology is in any presentation by Hyatt?

Chapter 18

Richard Lederer: *Crazy English*

Richard Lederer has written more than 30 books, including several best-sellers about the quirks of English and the joys of discovering them. This excerpt is from one of these, Crazy English: The Ultimate Joy Ride Through Our Language. *His careful observations of the language have prompted many speakers to use language more carefully and more effectively. He focuses on everyday words and sayings that most people use without a second thought about their meaning.*

Sometimes you have to believe that all English speakers should be committed to an asylum for the verbally insane. In what other language do people drive in a parkway and park in a driveway? In what other language do people recite at a play and play at a recital? In what other language do privates eat in the general mess and generals eat in the private mess? In what other language do people ship by truck and send cargo by ship? In what other language can your nose run and your feet smell?

How can a slim chance and a fat chance be the same and a bad licking and a good licking be the same, while a wise man and a wise guy are opposites? How can sharp speech and blunt speech be the same and *quite a lot* and *quite a few* the same, while *overlook* and *oversee* are opposites? . . .

If appropriate and inappropriate remarks and passable and impassable mountain trails are opposites, why are flammable and inflammable materials, heritable and inheritable property, and passive and impassive people the same and valuable objects less treasured than invaluable ones? If *uplift* is the same as *lift up*, why are *upset* and *set up* opposite in meaning? Why are *pertinent* and *impertinent*, *canny* and *uncanny*, and *famous* and *infamous* neither opposites nor the same? How can *raise* and *raze* and *reckless* and *wreckless* be opposites when each pair contains the same sound?

Why is it that when the sun or the moon or the stars are out, they are visible, but when the lights are out, they are invisible; that when I clip a coupon from a newspaper I separate it, but when I clip a coupon to a newspaper, I fasten it; and that when I wind up my watch, I start it, but when I wind up this essay, I shall end it?

English is a crazy language.

For Discussion

1. Did you find this excerpt humorous? Why or why not?
2. Can you think of any other examples of words that sound like opposites but have similar meanings, or that sound similar but have opposite meanings?
3. What lesson does this excerpt suggest about choosing words for a speech?

Chapter 19

Taylor Branch: ***Presenting "I Have a Dream"***

When Martin Luther King Jr. presented his "I Have a Dream Speech" in Washington D.C. in 1963, he was already a skilled orator. (King's speech is reprinted in Chapter 18.) His years of preaching in churches and speaking at rallies made him a powerful, effective speaker. Like most public speakers, he often reused themes from previous speeches. For example, he had used the "dream" language in earlier speeches in Detroit and Chicago. But, as historian Taylor Branch notes in his book Parting the Waters: America in the King Years, 1954–63, *this langauge—the language that made the speech famous—was not in King's planned remarks. Why did King adjust his presentation as he went along?*

It was a formal speech, as demanded by the occasion and the nature of the audience. By then, ABC and NBC had cut away from the afternoon soap operas to join the continuous live coverage by CBS. . . . King delivered his address in his clearest diction and stateliest baritone. . . .

He recited his text verbatim [word for word] until a short run near the end: "We will not be satisfied until justice runs down like waters and righteousness like a mighty stream." The crowd responded to the pulsating emotions transmitted from the prophet Amos [a figure in the Bible], and King could not bring himself to deliver the next line of his prepared text. . . .

There was no alternative but to preach. Knowing that he had wandered completely off his text, some of those behind him on the platform urged him on, and Mahalia Jackson [a singer] piped up as though in church, "Tell 'em about the dream, Martin." Whether her words

Martin Luther King Jr.

reached him is not known. Later, King said only that he forgot the rest of the speech and took up the first run of oratory that "came to me." After the word "despair," he temporized for an instant. "I say to you today, my friends, and so even though we face the difficulties of today and tomorrow, I still have a dream. It is a dream deeply rooted in the American dream. . . ."

Mindful of his audience, he held himself to a far more deliberate pace than in Detroit, or in Chicago the week before. Here he did not shout or smile, and there was no chance to build upon cascading rhythms of response, as in a mass meeting. The slow determination of his cadence exposed all the more clearly the passion that overshadowed the content of the dream. It went beyond the limitations of language and culture to express something that was neither pure rage nor pure joy, but universal transport of the kind that makes the blues sweet. Seven times he threw the extremities of black and white against each other, and each time he came back with a riveting, ecstatic dignity.

For Discussion

1. How did the large size of King's audience influence how he presented his speech?
2. Why did King depart from his written speech?
3. What made King's departure from his text successful?

Chapter 20

Ralph Linton: *One Hundred Percent American*

For at least 200 years, people have debated the answer to the question, "What makes Americans American?" People usually answer this question with a combination of objective research and subjective beliefs. In the 1930s, anthropologist Ralph Linton made a classic contribution to the debate by looking at everyday objects. Note how he supports his viewpoint with extensive research.

There can be no question about the average American's Americanism or his desire to preserve this precious heritage at all costs. Nevertheless, some insidious foreign ideas have already wormed their way into his civilization without his realizing what was going on. Thus, dawn finds the unsuspecting patriot garbed in pajamas, a garment of East Indian origin; and lying in a bed built on a pattern which originated in either Persia or Asia Minor. He is muffled to the ears in un-American materials: cotton, first domesticated in India; linen, domesticated in the Middle East; wool from an animal native to Asia Minor; or silk whose uses were first discovered by the Chinese.

On awakening he glances at the clock, a medieval European invention, rises in haste, and goes to the bathroom. Here, if he stops to think about it, he must feel himself in the presence of a great American institution; he will have heard stories of both the quality and frequency of foreign plumbing and will know that in no other country does the average man or woman perform their ablutions [washing] in the midst of such splendor. But the insidious foreign influences pursue him even here. Glass was invented by the ancient Egyptians, the use of glazed tiles for floors and walls in the Middle East, porcelain in China, and the art of enameling on metal by Mediterranean artisans of the Bronze Age. Even his bathtub and toilet are but slightly modified copies of Roman originals. The only purely American contribution to the ensemble is the steam radiator, against which our patriot very briefly and unintentionally places his posterior.

Returning to the bedroom, the unconscious victim of un-American practices removes his clothes from a chair, invented in the Near East, and proceeds to dress. He puts on close-fitting tailored garments whose form derives from the skin clothing of the ancient nomads of the Asiatic steppes and fastens them with buttons whose prototypes appeared in Europe at the close of the Stone Age. He puts on his feet stiff coverings made from hide prepared by a process invented in ancient Egypt and cut to a pattern which can be traced back to ancient Greece and makes sure they are properly polished, also a Greek idea. Lastly, he ties about his neck a strip of bright-colored cloth, which is a vestigial [sign of something that no longer exists] survival of the shoulder shawls worn by seventeenth-century Croats [an ethnic group in southeastern Europe]. He gives himself a final appraisal in the mirror, an old Mediterranean invention and goes downstairs to breakfast. . . .

For Discussion

1. Did you find this speech informative? Why or why not?
2. What differences might there be between the way people reacted to these ideas in the 1930s and the way people today might react?
3. Do you think this article would have been as effective if Linton had provided his facts in a list? Explain why or why not.

Chapter 21

Carmen Hernandez: *In Favor of a Skate Park*

In a democracy, people use persuasive speeches to help shape public policy. This is true not only of national political leaders, but also of people active in their local communities. Carmen Hernandez helped persuade the New Jersey state legislature to provide funds for a skate park. Pay attention to how the tone and organization of the speech help make it persuasive.

Thank you for taking the time to meet with us today.

We'll begin with explaining our sport. There are some large annual events you may have heard of, such as X Games and Gravity Games. Our sport is about friendly competition with extreme athletic abilities. Like all sports, our kids have to practice to excel. Despite the fact that we are the minority in the world of "bikes, boards and blades," this is a rapidly growing sport and it's clearly more popular than other sports that already have public facilities.

You may not understand this sport or the way these kids dress, but make no mistake—they are athletes, and they are passionate about their sport. They will keep riding and skating. It benefits you to provide safe places for them to practice their sport.

This is an investment in their future. When children are looked after and cared for by adults, they grow up into responsible, caring adults. That's a known fact and that is why we have parks and recreation programs. As responsible adults, we cannot turn our backs on these kids.

According to a Rand Youth Poll, there are:

7–10 million skateboarders

4 million aggressive inline skaters

1 million freestyle bikers

There are over 300 skate parks in the USA now, and according to the International Association of Skateboard Companies, another 300 are currently under development and construction. Skate parks with smooth, well-built surfaces, and protective gear have a very low injury rate. . . .

We hope you can understand our passion and efforts to build this park. Our association, youths, parents, private citizens, small businesses, homeowners, and law enforcement have come together to try to resolve a community concern. With your continuous support and efforts, we believe this park can be built.

Thank you.

For Discussion

1. What do you think was the goal of the first part of Hernandez's speech?
2. What information did Hernandez provide to persuade the legislators?
3. Do you think Hernandez's conclusion was effective? Explain why.

Chapter 22

Sara Martinez Tucker: *A Commencement Address*

Sara Martinez Tucker was the president and CEO of the Hispanic Scholarship Fund when she spoke at the University of Texas at Austin graduation in 2005. She later went on to be an under secretary in the Department of Education of the federal government. She does an excellent job of connecting with her audience.

My message tonight starts with my father. It was December 1969 and my father got the family ready to watch what many were saying was the college football national championship game between number one Texas and number two Arkansas.

Never mind the excitement of the game—what I remember most was what my father said when we asked why this game was so important. He said, "Because this is the best school in Texas and it's your chance to see them win the national championship." The best school in Texas—that made such an impression on me.

Years later, when I was in high school, my father drove my classmates and me from Laredo to the campus for a UIL—University Interscholastic League—competition. We left Laredo at 3 a.m., arriving on campus just before 7. The campus was so quiet. As we walked away from him, I turned to thank him. I wish I could describe for you the look on his face. He said, "It's so beautiful here. Everything is so clean and fresh—I hope you get to come here one day." From that moment on, I knew I wanted to come to UT. And I immediately sensed that I would be part of an inspiring place!. . .

If I could have a conversation with my father tonight, I'd say, "Daddy, you were right. What I've learned is that first and foremost, I am Sara Martinez Tucker. I'm a woman of Hispanic heritage. But there's something else that defines me. I am also a graduate of the University of Texas."

Tonight, so is each and every one of you. Hook 'em! [a slogan used at University of Texas football games]

For Discussion

1. How does Tucker connect with the audience early in the speech?
2. What is the point of the story Tucker tells about her father?
3. How does Tucker connect with the audience at the end of the speech?

Chapter 23

Lindsay Morgan: *Pirate Myths and Realities*

While a student at Bob Jones Academy in Greenville, South Carolina, Lindsay Morgan competed in the Expository category of the National Forensic League's national tournament in 2007. Her well-researched, well-organized, and well-written speech landed her among the top finishers in the competition.

Ladies and gentlemen, we have been misinformed. We have been deceived, and what's more is, we know it. And they do too. We have been fed lies by writers and filmmakers alike. That's right, and I'm here to tell you the truth about . . . pirates.

We all know what a pirate is, don't we? The peglegs, and the eyepatches, and the swashbuckling, and "Aarrgh, matey." Right? Wrong. That, ladies and gentlemen, is part of the myth. So let's whip out the spyglass and take a good, long look at some of the popular ideas spread by fiction authors and filmmakers.

Now, there is one man responsible for 99.5 percent of all literary pirate mythology, and those responsible for the other 0.5 percent were copying him. For over 125 years now, fiction author Robert Louis Stevenson has deceived us all. In his book, *Under the Black Flag*, David Cordingly says that the effect of *Treasure Island* on our perceptions of pirates cannot be overestimated. Stevenson forever linked pirates with black schooners, tropical islands, and pegleg sailors with parrots on their shoulders.

But *Treasure Island* is more pirate fiction than pirate fact.

First, pirates did not mark buried treasure with an X. In fact, there are very few recorded instances of pirates burying their treasure at all. Most pirate treasure wasn't even kept in one place. Each sailor had his own share, and as one pirate authority noted, most preferred to blow whatever money they had on women, booze, and gambling upon returning to port.

Also, the black spot, dire warning to all pirates of their impending doom? It never existed. Stevenson's Billy Bones was the first pirate in all history to receive a black spot. But he was by no means the last. Fictional pirates have been dispatched in this way ever since. Just this past year, Disney's Captain Jack Sparrow received a similarly titled warning.

Now for that other 0.5 percent of literary pirate mythology. A contemporary and schoolmate of Stevenson, *Peter Pan* author James Barrie, shoulders a fair amount of myth responsibility as well. His Captain Hook would have been laughed out of the Caribbean, particularly with his choice of clothing. While the long coats and high boats, tailored breeches and those infamous poofy shirts do sit well in the imagination, and a few eccentric pirate captains may have looked similar, most pirates wore short coats, if any at all, went barefoot, and were among the earliest wearers of full-length trousers.

Another Barrie pirate myth is that of walking the plank. Now at best, there are two or three highly dubious records of anyone actually being forced to walk the plank. Most pirates preferred the time efficient method of heave-ho if someone must be put into the sea.

Then Hollywood gave us swashbucklers like Douglas Fairbanks and Errol Flynn. Unfortunately, real pirates weren't chivalrous. Probably not handsome. Neither were they swashbucklers. Oh, now we have all heard about pirates and pirate movies being swashbuckling epics and whatnot. But I have actually yet to see a swashbuckling pirate. The assumed meaning is usually something about being flamboyant or adventurous. But the actual definition is "one who makes noise by striking his own or his opponent's shield with his sword," a buckler being a small type of round shield.

Now when was the last time you saw a pirate with a shield? A Viking, maybe. But swashbuckling Vikings? It just doesn't have the same ring to it. I guess the flamboyant, adventurous definition will stick with movie-going audiences.

Another myth is that of Davey Jones. Now we've heard that one recently, haven't we? Unfortunately for Disney fans, Davey Jones was not an octopus man. Nor was he ever, even in legends, the captain of the *Flying Dutchman*. That title goes to a, surprise, Dutch captain by the name of Bernard Fokke. The Dutchman ran into a tempest rounding the Cape of Good Hope, and responding to the pleas of sailors, is said to have said that he would sail through the storm if it took until judgment day. Legend tells us he is still trying. But chances are, if this had happened on a pirate ship, sailors wouldn't have been pleading, they would have demanded. Now our imagination sees the captain as the overbearing dictator of the ship, but pirates actually had a strange form of democracy. A captain was actually an elected official. He only had complete authority only in times of battle.

But there is a reason that all of these myths have survived. The fact is that we want to believe pirates as they have been portrayed in the books, plays, and musicals throughout the years. We want the gallant captains with their parrots, the eyepatches, the swashbuckling, the buried treasure. Never mind the distasteful punishments, maroonings, and hangings. Just this past month, Disney's *Pirates of the Caribbean at World's End* had the best Memorial Day weekend debut in history, earning 142.1 million dollars in its opening weekend alone. People are more than happy to pay for more pirate mythology. And for most of us, pirates will always conjure up a romantic image of adventurous men and women sailing off into the horizon.

For Discussion

1. What makes Morgan's introduction effective?
2. What types of research does Morgan use?
3. Explain why Morgan's last paragraph is a good conclusion.

Chapter 24

Condoleezza Rice: *My Grandfather and Education*

At the Republican National Convention in 2000, the delegates nominated George W. Bush for president. Giving one of the major addresses in support of Bush was Condoleezza Rice. She was then on leave from her position at Stanford University to serve as an advisor to the Bush campaign. She went on to be Bush's first National Security Advisor and later his Secretary of State. Television, radio, and newspapers all covered the 2000 address, allowing her to reach a wide audience. How might her comments have helped introduce her to a nationwide audience?

In America, with education and hard work, it really does not matter where you came from; it matters only where you are going.

But that truth cannot be sustained if it is not renewed in each generation, as it was with my grandfather.

George W. Bush would have liked Granddaddy Rice. He was the son of a farmer in rural Alabama, but he recognized the importance of education. Around 1918, he decided he was going to get book-learning. And so, he asked, in the language of the day, where a colored man could go to college. He was told about little Stillman College, a school about 50 miles away. So granddaddy saved up his cotton for tuition and he went off to Tuscaloosa.

Condoleezza Rice

After the first year, he ran out of cotton and he needed a way to pay for college. Praise be, as he often does, God gave him an answer. My grandfather asked how those other boys were staying in school, and he was told that they had what was called a scholarship. And they said, if you wanted to be a Presbyterian minister, then you can have one, too. Granddaddy Rice said, that's just what I had in mind.

And my family has been Presbyterian and college-educated ever since.

But, you know, that's not just my grandfather's story, that's an American story—the search for hope, the search for opportunity, the skill of good, hard work.

For Discussion

1. What is the main point of Rice's story about her grandfather?
2. How does Rice connect her story with her support for Bush?
3. Explain whether you think Rice was speaking primarily to the convention delegates or to the public at large through the media.

Chapter 25

Sandra Tsing Loh: *Be Plus Like*

Writer Sandra Tsing Loh presents a regular broadcast called "Loh Down on Science" that is now heard on over 90 radio stations around the world. With humor, curiosity, and an energetic presentation, she gives listeners insight into the latest in scientific research. Note how she views the way technology is changing how young people communicate in everyday life.

Are you clueless about Valspeak? This is Sandra Tsing Loh with "The Loh Down on Science" . . . saying it now takes scientists to decipher what teens are saying. First the word "go" meant "said," like, "I go, Nuh-uh." The newest substitute: the verb "to be," plus "like." ("I'm like . . . She's like, what-EVERRR!")

Linguists call this fuzzy construction "be plus like," or the "quotative like." NYU anthropologist Bambi Schieffelin says it's on the rise in instant messaging. I-Ms normally read like super-concise shorthand. Nobody spells out "BE RIGHT BACK" or "JUST KIDDING"; everything's "B-R-B!" and "J-K!" Yet over a three-year period, college students' use of the "quotative like" in I-Ms increased EIGHT HUNDRED PERCENT.

Your kid would rather grind out "I WAS LIKE OH I'M SO SURE" than "I DISAGREED"... Why?! According to Schieffelin, I-Ms lack of nonverbal cues limits expressiveness. Young people TYPE the way they TALK, to enrich what would otherwise read as bland chatter.

And to avoid being mistaken for, like, adults.

This is STL for the LDOS saying L-O-L! Whatever that means.

For Discussion

1. Do you agree with Schieffelin that young people type the way they talk to enrich their messages? Explain.
2. How is "be plus like" an example of how technology affects communication?
3. Analyze how other changes in technology might influence how people speak to each other.

Glossary

A

abstain—not voting on a motion

abstract—referring to general concepts or ideas

active listening—the process of concentrating on what is heard, attaching meaning, and reacting to it

ad hominem—fallacy in which a person replies to a factual claim by attacking a belief or characteristic of the person who made the claim

adjourn—close a meeting

aesthetic—artistic

affirmative position—stance in favor of a resolution

agenda—outline of the issues and proposals for a meeting

alliteration—the repetition of an initial consonant sound

allusion—an indirect reference to something or someone

amend—alter or change

analogy—a comparison between two things, ideas, or situations

analytical—using logical reasoning

anecdote—brief story that demonstrates your main points

articulators—parts of the head, such as the tongue, teeth, lips, and palate, that help form words

assertive—expressing a confident and forceful personality

assonance—the repetition of stressed vowel sounds within words to create internal rhyming

asynchronous media—communication that does not occur in real time

attentive—listening with full concentration

attitude—opinion or general feeling

auspicious—significant; momentous

authoritarian leadership—leadership that involves a single leader who dominates and dictates processes to group members

B

bandwagon—a fallacy built on the idea that something is true because a lot of people think so

body language—gestures, eye contact, posture, facial expression, and proxemics as conveyors of feeling

C

call number—a number that indicates the subject of the book, with each number indicating a more specific subcategory

cause-effect order—an order that establishes a cause and explains effects.

chair—the presiding officer in a parliamentary group

challenging question—a question designed to prove a point

channel—the means used to transmit a message from sender to receiver

characterization—a description that brings a person's words and actions to life

chronological order—an order that presents things as they occur

circular reasoning—a fallacy in which an idea is just repeated in different terms rather than proved

civic groups—voluntary groups based on shared interests, concerns, and goals

claims—conclusions or ideas you want your audience to accept

clarity—clearness of style

classification order—an order that groups ideas before further organizing them

cliché—an overused phrase or expression

climactic order—an order that presents most important points last

closed question—a question that is limited to a specific piece of information or a simple "yes" or "no" answer

colloquialisms—words and phrases that are generally characteristic of spoken language and not of standard written language

committee—group of members within a group who meet to consider a subject

communication—a process for exchanging ideas and creating meaning

communication imperative—the idea that you are always communicating something, whether you do something or not

computer-mediated communication—communication that takes place between people via a computer connection

concrete—referring to specific items or processes you can see or instantly identify

connotation—a word's implied or suggested meaning

consensus—general agreement

consonance—the focused repetition of stressed consonant sounds

constructive criticism—helpful feedback

Glossary

context—time and place

controlling purpose—limited purpose or primary goal

conventions—traditions or a customs widely used to govern interactions

convergence—the merging of different communication technologies

cookies—files used to track personal data on your computer

courteous—being polite and respectful

credibility—worthiness of belief

criteria—standards

critical listening—analyzing and evaluating the information you take in

cultivation analysis—theory that proposes a link between habitual television watching and one's perception of the real world

cyberbullying—bullying that takes place online

cyberstalking—use of the Internet to stalk or harass people

D

database—a collection of related information

decoding—the process of translating communication into meaning

defensive climate—an atmosphere in which people feel the need to protect themselves from attack

delivery—a speaker's manner, or speaking style

democratic leadership—leadership in which the leader hears all ideas and lets the group develop its own identity

demonstration speech—a speech in which a speaker demonstrates a process

denotation—a word's explicit, literal meaning; dictionary definition

descriptive gestures—movements of the limbs, body, or head that help listeners visualize spoken words

Dewey Decimal System—an organizational system that categorizes books into ten general subject areas, each of which is assigned a range of numbers

dialect—a language pattern, often regional, that is different from the typical pattern

dialogue—conversation between two or more people as a feature of a book, play, or movie

diaphragm—an organ that separates the chest from the abdominal cavity

dignitary—famous or important person

digressions—ideas that depart from the main message

disinformation—intentionally misleading information

duration—the length of time you've known a person

E

economy—brevity and directness in expression

e-learning—instruction delivered via technology

emoticons—pictures or images that represent emotions

empathic listening—concentration, retention, judgment, and empathy while listening

emphatic gestures—movements of the limbs, body, or head that allow a speaker to emphasize spoken words

encoding—the process of turning ideas into messages

ethos—appeal to a person's sense of right and wrong

eulogy—a speech that honors a person who has recently died

euphemism—a word or phrase used as a substitute for an unpleasant or disturbing expression

excerpt—portion of a text

executive session—parliamentary meeting attended only by members

expectations—what an interviewer expects to see and hear from an applicant

exposition—the presentation of information

expository speech—a speech that provides information about an object, place, person, event, or idea

extemporaneous—a speech with very little preparation and rehearsal time

F

fallacy—a statement that sounds logical but is not true

false analogy—a comparison between two cases that are not enough alike to be compared meaningfully

false syllogism—fallacy in which two true statements are put together to reach a false conclusion

feedback—the receiver's response to the sender

follow-up question—a question that follows a closed question in order to gather more information

font—a typeface of a particular size

forensic—related to public speaking

formal group—a group with clearly expressed group norms

formal leadership—leadership that is designated as a norm of the group

framing—pauses on either side of a word or phrase for special emphasis

G

generators—larynx, or vocal chords

grace—the expression of ideas in an appealing and skillful manner

group discussion—an exchange of views on a topic

group dynamics—how groups work together in trying to solve problems and develop personal interactions

group leadership—leadership that helps a group meet its goals and develop positive communication

group maintenance roles—roles that help establish and maintain positive, cooperative relationships and group-centered interaction

group member roles—patterns of behavior exhibited by members in a group

group norms—standards of behavior expected from group members

H

hasty generalization—fallacy in which a conclusion about an entire population is drawn using too small a sample

hearing—the passive reception of sound waves

helping question—a question asked to gain information

hybrid—communications that blur the lines among intrapersonal, interpersonal, and mass communications

hyperbole—a deliberate and obvious exaggeration

hypothetical question—a question that calls on the person responding to take a guess or use the imagination

I

"I" comments—statements that begin with "I" and express how one feels

identity theft—crime of stealing personal data, such as credit card numbers, to make purchases

impromptu—done without planning

incidental motion—motions related to the main motion, which must be introduced right after a main motion

inflection—the pitch of the voice when speaking

informal group—a group without clearly expressed group norms

informal leadership—leadership that emerges from a group's interactions

informative speech—a speech that presents information or explains a process

interference—anything that blocks or distorts communication

interpersonal communication—communication in which people exchange messages

interpret—use your brain to assign meaning

interview—a structured conversation designed to gather information

intimacy—a feeling of closeness and trust for another

intrapersonal communication—communication within ourselves

irony—language that suggests the opposite of the literal meaning

J

jargon—the technical vocabulary of a hobby, occupation, or other specialized activity

L

laissez-faire leadership—leadership marked by a leader who allows the group to figure out its own processes

leading question—a question that directs or "leads" the listener to a desired answer

Library of Congress System—an organizational system that categorizes books by letters instead of numbers to indicate major subject areas

listening—an active process with four stages: sensing, interpreting, evaluating, and responding

listening barriers—physical, mental, and cultural forms of interference

logos—appeal to logical reasoning

M

main motion—motion that brings up business matters before the group

mannerism—a distinctive behavior

Glossary

mannerism—a distinctive behavior

manuscript—a delivery format making use of a prepared document

mass communications—messages sent by some form of technology to masses of people simultaneously

massively—multiplayer online games played by vast numbers of people worldwide at the same time

mass media—using technology to bring a message to many people

media literacy—set of skills in rationally interpreting the barrage of mass communications and sorting fact from fiction

media piracy—illegal copying of music, video, or computer software

mediated communication—communication that is media controlled

memorized—a delivery format

message—something you want to communicate

metacommunication—communication about communication

metaphor—a comparison that does not use the words *like* or *as*

minutes—records of a meeting

misinformation—wrong or inaccurate information spread in the guise of truth

misperception—flawed conclusion

mnemonic—a memory aid that uses associations or patterns

monotone—a flat, expressionless way of speaking

motion—proposal put to a group

motivated sequence—a five-step speaking process that uses a problem-solution method to organize information for effective persuasion

motivation—forces that cause people to act certain ways

multi-channeled—conducted through both verbal and nonverbal means

multimedia—using more than one medium of expression to communicate

N

narration—the recounting of the events in a story or incident

narrative—the spoken or written account of connected events; a story

negative position—stance opposed to a resolution

nonjudgmental listening—without expressing judgment

nonverbal communication—anything people communicate beyond the literal meaning of words

O

online—connected to the Internet

online catalog—a list of materials that can be accessed on the Internet

open question—a question that allows an interviewee to answer in any number of ways

oral interpretation—performance art that blends theatre and public speaking

P

panel discussion—a group that meets in front of an audience

paralanguage—the use of vocal effects to express meaning

paraphrase—restate

parliamentarian—person who makes sure proper rules are followed

parliamentary procedure—rules developed to facilitate business while maintaining group cooperation

pathos—appeal to feelings

perception—the process of using your senses to gather and interpret information

Personal Digital Assistant (PDA)—handheld computer that can also be used as a phone

personification—language that suggests human qualities for objects, animals, or ideas

person-to-group communication—communication in which a speaker addresses a group as one receiver

persuasion—a form of communication that tries to change attitudes, opinions, or behaviors

pitch—the relative highness or lowness of the voice

plagiarism—the act of passing off as one's own the written words of someone else.

podcasts—digital audio or video files than can be downloaded from the Internet

political groups—groups that form to create or maintain a power base

post hoc ergo propter hoc—fallacy of questionable causation

Glossary

post hoc ergo propter hoc—fallacy of questionable causation

posture—how you hold your body

precision listening—paying attention to details that offer clues to the speaker's emotion or state of mind

primary source—an original source of information

private group—a group that meets in private

privileged motion—motion to adjourn, recess, offer a question of privilege, and call for orders of the day

problem-solution order—an order that presents issues and then solutions

process speech—a speech that shows how something works or shows how to do something

projecting—making the voice heard

proof—evidence

propaganda—systematic output of information that reflects and promotes a certain cause or point of view

proposition—argument

protocol—specific conventions of behavior

proxemics—the use of space

public group—a group that meets in a public place and/or keeps written records

purpose statement—a written account of the specific outcomes you want your speech to achieve

Q

Q & A—question-and-answer period

question of fact—a question that can be answered by obtaining evidence or by direct observation

question of policy—a question attempting to discover what action should be taken

question of value—a question asking whether something is good or bad, needed or not needed, better or worse

quorum—the minimum number of members needed to hold a vote

R

rate—the pace at which one speaks—fast, medium, or slow

rebuttal—a statement countering the other's position

receiver—one for whom a message is intended

reconsider—take a second look at a motion that has passed

red herring—a fallacy that attempts to divert attention from the real issues by interjecting a related topic

reflective listening—active listening process during which you mirror a speaker's thoughts and feelings back for further processing

relevant—connected to the issue at hand

rescind—take back

resolution—proposition

resonators—areas in the head that pick up sound vibrations

résumé—brief account of your education, qualifications, and work experience

revise—to rework a written or spoken text

rhetoric—the art of using language effectively, especially in public speaking

rhetorical question—a question to which there is no answer or only one answer fits

roundtable—a discussion in which all participants have equal status

S

secondary source—information that comments on or develops information found in a primary source

secretary—a person who keeps a record of a meeting

selective listening—blocking out messages you don't want to hear

self-centered roles—roles that don't work well for a group as a whole

self-concept—how you would describe yourself

self-confidence—trusting in one's own abilities and judgment

sender—one who communicates a message

simile—a comparison that uses the words *like* or *as*

sincere—being honest, natural, and believable

slippery slope—fallacy in which a proposed course of action is presented as leading inevitably to a particular conclusion

snap judgment—an opinion based on one quick bit of information

social group—a group formed around the social needs of the members

socialization—the process by which people learn and adapt to the rules of society

spatial order—an order that presents ideas according to physical space

specific—detailed and particular

stage fright—a feeling of apprehension or dread when speaking to an audience

stance—how you distribute the weight of your body on your feet

statistics—numbers presented as facts

stereotype—an oversimplified image or idea about a person or a group

storyboard—a series of drawings showing a sequence of events

strategic questioning—a question asked with a purpose beyond getting information

style—the way a message is expressed

subcommittee—a small group within a committee that reports to the committee on their progress or findings

subsidiary motion—motion to put aside a previous question; limit or extend debate; or refer to committee, amend, or postpone a motion

substance—the content of a message communicated through words

summarize—use few words to communicate a main idea

supportive climate—a friendly and productive atmosphere

supportive providing—positive and helpful feedback

syllogism—a tool for reasoning by which a conclusion is inferred from premises

symposium—a group in which speakers address a topic

synchronous media—communication that occurs in real time

syntax—word order

T

table—to put a motion aside

tact—the quality that allows people to speak without giving offense

task group—a group formed around doing work or solving a problem

task roles—communication behaviors that help a group address an issue, solve problems, and perform a task

telecommute—work in a location separate from the employer's office, usually at home

teleconferencing—speaking to one another from different locations

terminology—of a certain profession or group

testimonial—a speech that honors a living person

testimony—the use of another person's words or ideas to support your claims

theme—controlling idea of your speech

thesis statement—a way of concisely and gracefully expressing the essential idea of your speech

tone—the spirit or manner in which something is said

topical order—an order that presents ideas in a logical flow from one to the next

town hall meeting—a discussion in which people in a community voice opinions and hear responses from public figures

transition—a word, phrase, or sentence that connects ideas in order to move from one point to the next

U

understatement—a way to express an idea in a less dramatic way than expected

usage—the relationship of language to a specific relationship, purpose, and audience

V

valedictory—a speech delivered by the student graduating with the highest grade-point average, or some other student leader

videoconferencing—the holding of meetings using video links

vlogs—videoblogs

volume—raising or lowering the voice or giving special emphasis to words

Acknowledgments

Text Credits

Excerpt from a speech by Winston Churchill. Reproduced with permission of Curtis Brown Ltd., London on behalf of The Estate of Winston Churchill.

Excerpt from *A Doll's House* by Henrik Ibsen, translated by Michael Meyer. Copyright © 1966 by Michael Meyer. Copyright renewed 1994 by Michael Meyer. Reprinted by permission of NY: Harold Ober Associated Incorporated.

Excerpt from "I Heard What You Didn't Say," *Washington Post,* May 13, 2001, copyright Deborah Tannen. Excerpt is based on her book *I Only Say This Because I Love You,* Ballantine, 2001. Reprinted by permission

Excerpt from a speech by Margaret Chase Smith, June 1, 1950. Found at http://www.mcslibrary.org/program/library/declaration.htm

Excerpt from an interview by Rachel N. of her grandmother, Shizue Kobayashi. Found at http://www.teenink.com/Interviews/article/17860/World-War-II-Survivor-Shizue-Kobayashi/

Excerpt from a speech by Cesar Chavez. Delivered to the Commonwealth Club of California, November 9, 1984. Found at http://www.commonwealthclub.org/archive/20thcentury/84-11chavez-speech.html

Excerpt from students organizing a group. This material is reproduced with the permission of the LearnHigher Centre for Excellence in Teaching and Learning, led by Liverpool Hope University, Liverpool, U.K. The full web-based resource is available at www.leanhighergroupwork.com and is free to use.

Excerpt from "Humor Found to Aid Problem-Solving" by Daniel Goleman from the *New York Times*, August 4, 1987. Copyright © 1987 by The New York Times Co. Reprinted by permission.

Excerpt from "Essay: Point of Order" by Rachel Donadio from the *New York Times,* May 20, 2007. Copyright © 1987 by The New York Times Co. Reprinted by permission.

Excerpt from interview on speechwriting by Ray Suarez. Found at http://www.pbs.org/newshour/bb/white_house/jan-june07/message_01-23.html

Excerpt from "Is Google Making Us Stupid?" by Nicholas Carr from the *Atlantic*, July/August 2008.

Excerpt from speech by Michael Hyatt. Copyright © 2008, Michael S. Hyatt. Used by permission. Originally published at www.michaelhyatt.com

Excerpt from *Crazy English: The Ultimate Joy Ride Through Our Language,* by Richard Lederer. NY: Pocket Books, 1989.

Excerpt from *Parting the Waters: America in the King Years, 1954-63,* by Taylor Branch. NY: Simon & Schuster, 1988.

Excerpt from "One Hundred Percent American" by Ralph Linton. Originally published from the *American Century,* Vol. 40, 1937.

Excerpt from speech by Carmen Hernandez. Found at http://flowskatepark.org/speech.htm

Excerpt from a speech by Sara Martinez Tucker delivered at the University of Texas at Austin Commencement. Found at http://www.utexas.edu/commencement/2005/address.html

Speech by Lindsay Morgan. Delivered at the National Forensic League's 2007 National Competition.

Excerpt from a speech by Condoleezza Rice delivered at the Republican National Convention, August 1, 2000. Reported in the *Washington Post*.

Radio commentary by Sandra Tsing Loh, "Be Plus Like. " Delivered KPCC on June 2, 2008. Found at http://lohdown.caltech.edu/script_archive?date_to_view=2008-06-02

The editors wish to thank the speakers, writers, and publishers who have allowed their copyrighted materials to be used in this book. Every reasonable effort has been made to contact all copyright holders. If we have omitted anyone, please let us know and we will include a suitable acknowledgment in subsequent editions.

Image Credits

Page 2: Jupiter Images, iStockphoto; Page 3: © Richard Hutchings/CORBIS; Page 5: iStockphoto; Page 6: iStockphoto; Page 7: Ariel Skelley / Blend Images / Getty Images; Page 8: Karen Moskowitz / Taxi / Getty Images; Page 9:iStockphoto; Page 10: iStockphoto; Page 11: Jupiter Images; Page 13: iStockphoto; Page 14: © Comstock / SuperStock; Page 15: © Stockbyte / SuperStock; Page 16: iStockphoto, Jupiter Images; Page 17: iStockphoto; Page 18: iStockphoto; Page 19: Illustration of Johannes Gutenberg Printing the First Sheet of the Bible, © Stefano Bianchetti/Corbis; Page 20: © Bettmann / Corbis; Page 21: Perfection Learning; Page 25: Jupiter Images; Page 26: Jupiter Images (left), © moodboard / Corbis (right); Page 27: Jupiter Images; Page 28: iStockphotos (left); Page 29: iStockphotos; Page 31: iStockphots (left), Punchstock (center), © C. Devan / zefa / Corbis; Page 32: © Reuters / Corbis; Page 34: iStockphotos; Page 36: Perfection Learning; Page 37: iStockphoto; Page 39: © Bettmann / Corbis; Page 40: iStockphoto; Page 42: © JP Laffont / Sygma / Corbis; Page 47: © Richard T. Nowitz/CORBIS; Page 48: Jupiter Images; Page 49: Jupiter Images; Page 50: Jupiter Images; Page 51: Jupiter Images, iStockphoto; Page 52: Jupiter Images, iStockphoto; Page 53: iStockphoto, Jupiter Images; Page 54: Jupiter Images, iStockphoto; Page 55: Jupiter Images; Page 56: Jupiter Images; Page 57: iStockphotos.com; Page 58: © ARND WIEGMANN/ Reuters/Corbis; Page 60: Jupiter Images; Page 61: Jupiter Images; Chapter 4; Page 65: iStockphoto; Page 66: iStockphoto; Page 67: iStockphoto; Page 68: iStockphoto; Page 69: iStockphoto; Page 70: © Tom & Dee Ann McCarthy/ CORBIS; Page 71: Perfection Learning; Page 72: © Gideon Mendel/Corbis; Page 73: Rubberball Productions / Getty Images; Page 74: iStockphoto; Page 75: Alloy Photography / Veer; Page 76: iStockphoto; Page 77: iStockphoto; Page 78: © image100/Corbis; Page 79: iStockphoto; Page 80: iStockphoto; Page 82: Becker Medical Library, Washington University School of Medicine; Page 83: Becker Medical Library, Washington University School of Medicine (top); © Bettmann/CORBIS (center); © George Steinmetz/Corbis (bottom); Page 87: iStockphoto; Page 88: © Louis K. Meisel Gallery, Inc./CORBIS; Page 89: iStockphoto; Page 90: PICASSO: MARIE-THERESE. Portrait of Marie-Therese by Pablo Picasso. Oil on canvas, 1937 / The Granger Collection, New york; Page 91: iStockphoto; Page 92: iStockphoto; Page 93: © Simon D. Warren/zefa/ Corbis; Page 94: iStockphoto; Page 95: iStockphoto; Page 96: Perfection Learning; Page 97: Perfection Learning; Page 98: Jupiter Images; Page 99: iStockphoto; Page 100: iStockphotos; Page 101: iStockphotos; Page 102: iStockphotos; Page 104: Library of Congress; Page 105: Universal Studios (left), Cartoonstock.com (right); Page 107: Stockbyte / Getty Images; Page 111: Paul Bradbury / OJO Images / Getty Images; Page 113: Yellow Dog Productions / Digital Vision / Getty Images; Page 115: Jupiter Images; Page 116: © Maria Taglienti-Molinari / Brand X / Corbis; Page 117: iStockphoto; Page 118: © amana/ amanaimages / Corbis; Page 119: © Sean Justice / Corbis; Page 121: Jupiter Images, iStockphoto; Page 122: © M. Thomsen / zefa / Corbis; Page 123: iStockphoto; Page 124: iStockphoto; Page 125: © Bettmann / CORBIS; Page 126: Jupiter Images, iStockphoto; Page 127: Jupiter Images, iStockphoto; Page 128: Piero Tonin / CartoonStock, iStockphoto.com; Page 129: © Tomas Rodriguez / Solus-Veer / Corbis; Page 130: © Jan Butchofsky-Houser / CORBIS, Photodisc / Getty Images; Page 132: © Leonard de Selva / CORBIS; Page 133: Jupiter Images, © Bettmann / CORBIS; Page 137: iStockphoto; Page 138: iStockphoto; Page 141: Paul Hawthorne / Getty Images; Page 142: iStockphoto; Page 144: © Punchstock; Page 145: iStockphoto; Page 148: © Bettmann/CORBIS, Jupiter Images; Page 149: Jupiter Images, © image100/Corbis; Page 153: © Darren Greenwood/Design Pics/Corbis; Page 154: iStockphoto; Page 157: © Heide Benser/zefa/Corbis; Page 158: iStockphoto; Page 159: Mike Baldwin / Cartoonstock.com; Page 160: iStockphoto; Page 161: Chabruken / Taxi / Getty Images; Page 162: Westend61 Photography / Veer; Page 165: iStockphoto; Page 166: © Image Source / SuperStock; Page 168: © Pascal Deloche / Godong / Corbis; Page 169: © Car Culture/Corbis; Page 173: iStockphoto; Page 174: iStockphoto; Page 176: iStockphoto; Page 177: iStockphoto; Page 179: iStockphoto; Page 180: © Najlah Feanny/CORBIS SABA; Page 182: iStockphoto, Blend Images Photography / Veer, iStockphoto, PhotoAlto Photography / Veer, © Artiga Photo/Corbis, Johannes Mann / Solus Photography / Veer; Page 183: iStockphoto; Page 184: © image100/Corbis; Page 185: Datacraft / imagenavi / Getty Images; Page 187: George Doyle / Stockbyte / Getty Images; Page 190: © Jack Moebes/CORBIS; Page 191: © Bettmann/CORBIS; Page 194: Stockbyte / Getty Images; Page 195: Zigy Kaluzny / Stone / Getty Images; Zigy Kaluzny / Stone / Getty Images; Chris Windsor / Stone / Getty Images; Page 196: Terry Doyle / Stone / Getty Images (top); Image Source Photography / Veer (2nd down); © Michael Prince / CORBIS (3rd down); Jupiter Images (bottom); Page 197: Yello Dog Productions / The Image Bank / Getty Images; Page 199: Ryan McVay / Photodisc / Getty Images; Page 200: © Steve Schapiro / Corbis; Page 201: © Jessica Rinaldi / Reuters / Corbis; Page 202: Don Smetzer / Stone / Getty Images; Page 203: Terry Doyle / Stone / Getty Images; Page 205: Eric Charbonneau / WireImage / Getty Images; Page 206: Yellow Dog Productions / Riser / Getty Images; Page 207: S. Harris / Cartoonstock; Page 210 & 211: Jupiter Images; Page 215: Image Source Photography / Veer; Page 217: George Doyle / Stockbyte / Getty Images; Page 218: Jupiter Images; Page 219: iStockphoto; Page 221: © Digital Vision Ltd. / SuperStock; Page 222: iStockphoto; Page 226: © Bettmann/CORBIS; Page 227: Ryan McVay / Stone / Getty Images; Page 231:

Acknowledgments

iStockphotos; Page 232: Bill Pugliano / Stringer / Getty Images; Page 234: © Ed Kashi / CORBIS; Page 235: Mike Kemp / Rubberball Productions / Getty Images; Page 236: iStockphoto; Page 237: Mike Shapiro / Cartoonstock; Page 238: © Liu Liqun / Corbis; Page 240: © Michael Prince / CORBIS; Page 241: iStockphoto; Page 242: © Reed Kaestner / CORBIS; Page243: iStockphoto; Page 244: Anderson Ross / Photodisc / Getty Images; Page 245: iStockphoto; Page 246: iStockphoto; Page 247: iStockphoto; Page 248: Ralph Notaro / Getty Images Entertainment / Getty Images; Page 249: iStockphoto; Page 250: iStockphoto; Page 255: Ryan McVay / Riser / Getty Images; Page 256: Jupiter Images; Page 257: OJO Images Photography / Veer; Page 258: iStockphoto; Page 259: S. Harris / Cartoonstock.com; Page 260: © Marilyn Angel Wynn / Nativestock Pictures / Corbis (left); iStockphoto (right); Page 263: iStockphoto; Jupiter Images (bottom); Page 265: © Bettmann / CORBIS; Page 268: © Gianni Dagli Orti / CORBIS; Page 269: © Somos Images / Corbis; Page 272: iStockphoto; Page 273: © Brooks Kraft/Corbis (top); Sparky / The Image Bank / Getty Images (bottom); Page 274: iStockphoto (top); Jupiter Images (2nd down); iStockphoto (3rd down); Photodisc Photography / Veer (4th down); iStockphoto (5th down); Digital Vision / Getty Images (bottom); Page 275: Paul Burns / Photodisc / Getty Images; Page 277: © Tom Stewart/CORBIS; Page 278: Jupiter Images; Page 279: F64 / Digital Vision / Getty Images; Page 280: iStockphoto; Page 281: iStockphoto; Page 282: © Randy Faris / Corbis; Page 284: iStockphoto; Page 285: iStockphoto; Page 286: iStockphoto; Page 287: iStockphoto; Page 288: iStockphoto; Page 289: © Bettmann / CORBIS; Page 292: Library of Congress; Page 293: © NADER / CORBIS SYGMA; Page 297: iStockphoto; Page 298 & 299: © Tim Tadder / Corbis; Page 300: © Franck Robichon / epa / Corbis; Page 301: © Peter M. Fisher / Corbis; Page 302: Standard RMI © CORBIS; Page 303: Tetra Images / Getty Images; iStockphoto; Page 304: iStockphoto; Page 305: Albrecht Frans Lieven Vrlendt / Fine Art Photographic / Hulton Archive / Getty Images; Page 306: © CORBIS (top); iStockphoto (bottom); Page 307: Andersen Ross / Photodisc / Getty Images; Page 308: Jupiter Images (top); iStockphoto (bottom); Page 309: iStockphoto (top); Andersen Ross / Blend Images / Getty Images (bottom); Page 310: iStockphoto; Page 311: © Blue Lantern Studio / CORBIS (both bottom images); Page 312: © Bettmann / CORBIS; Page 313: Jupiter Images; Page 314: iStockphoto; Page 316 & 317: © Bettmann / CORBIS; iStockphoto.com (bottom); Page 317: © Underwood & Underwood / CORBIS; Page 321: mana productions inc / amana images / Getty Images; Page 322: Digital Vision / Getty Images; Page 323: Jupiter Images; Page 324: iStockphoto; Page 325: © Keystone/Corbis (top); iStockphoto (bottom); Page 326: © Bettmann/CORBIS; Page 327: iStockphoto; Page 328: AFP / Roslan Rahman / Getty Images; Page 329: iStockphoto; Pages 330 & 331: © Randy Faris / Corbis; iStockphoto.com; Page 332: © Somos Images/Corbis; Page 333: © C. Devan/zefa/Corbis; Page 334: Blend Images Photography / Veer; Page 336: iStockphoto; Page 337: Jupiter Images; Page 338: Jupiter Images; Page 339: iStockphoto; Page 340: iStockphoto; Page 341: iStockphoto; Page 342: iStockphoto; Page 343: iStockphoto; Page 344: iStockphoto; Page 346: The Granger Collection, New York; Page 347: Getty Images / Getty Images News / Jason Connel; Page 349: iStockphoto; Page 351: Image Source Photography / Veer; Page 352: Alloy Photography / Veer; Page 353: Somos Photography / Veer; Page 354: iStockphoto; Page 356: iStockphoto; Page 357: iStockphoto; Page 358: © Richard T. Nowitz / CORBIS; Page 359: PhotoAlto Photography / Veer; Page 361: Getty Images Entertainment / Jeff Daly / Getty Images (top); Don Farrall / Digital Vision / Getty Images (bottom); Page 363: iStockphoto; Page 364: iStockphoto; Page 365: STOCK4B / Getty Images; Page 366: Photodisc Photography / Veer; Page 367: iStockphoto; Page 368: © Frans Lemmens / zefa / Corbis (top, left); © Bettmann / CORBIS (top, center); Ron Chapple / Taxi / Getty Images (top, right); © CORBIS (bottom, left); © Christie's Images/CORBIS (bottom, center); C Squared Studios / Photodisc / Getty Images (bottom, right); Page 369: iStockphoto (top, right corner); © Estelle Klawitter / zefa / Corbis (center, left); Getty Images / Hulton Archive (center, 2nd from left); Triangle Images / Digital Vision / Getty Images (center, 2nd to right); iStockphoto.com (center, far right); Stockbyte / Getty Images (bottom, left); © Beathan / Corbis (bottom, center); © Krista Kennell / ZUMA / Corbis (bottom, right); Page 373: NBAE / Randy Belice / Getty Images; Page 374: iStockphoto; Page 375: © Bettmann / CORBIS; Page 376: Greg Glume / Getty Images Sport / Getty Images; Page 378: Mike Baldwin / Cartoonstock.com; Page 380: Jupiter Images; Page 381: iStockphoto; Page 385: © Hulton-Deutsch Collection/CORBIS; Page 387: iStockphoto; Page 390: Library of Congress; Page 392: Jupiter Images; Page 393: Jupiter Images; Page 395: iStockphoto; Page 396: © Joseph Sohm/ Visions of America/Corbis; Page 397: Perfection Learning Corporation; Page 398: iStockphoto; Page 400: © Brad Edelman / Corbis; Page 402: Mark Segal / Stone / Getty Images; Page 403: Digital Vision / Getty Images; Page 404: Dave & Les Jacobs / Blend Images / Getty Images (far left); Matthew Antrobus / The Image Bank / Getty Images (2nd to left); Martin Poole / Riser / Getty Images (center); Norma Zuniga / Riser / Getty Images (2nd to right); Ellen Stagg / Riser / Getty Images (right); Page 405: Digital Vision / Getty Images; Page 406: iStockphoto; Page 407: Jon Feingersh / Blend Images / Getty Images; Page 408: Artiga Photo / Corbis / Veer; Page 410: Rubberball / Punchstock; Page 411: Photodisc / Punchstock; Page 412: Digital Vision / Punchstock; Page 414: Jupiter Images (left), © CORBIS (right); Page 415: © Bettmann / CORBIS (left); © Brooks Kraft / Corbis (right); Page 417:

iStockphoto; Page 418: Andreas Pollok / Taxi / Getty Images; Page 419: © Blend Images / SuperStock; Page 420: Jupiter images (top); Tim Graham / Tim Graham Photo Library / Getty Images (top, center); iStockphotos (bottom, center); Jupiter Images (bottom); Page 421: Hamish Blair / Getty Image News / Getty Images; Page 423: Jose Luis Pelaez Inc / Getty Images; Page 425: iStockphoto; Page 426: Jupiter Images; Page 427: Jupiter Images; Page 428: iStockphoto; Page 431: iStockphoto; Page 432: iStockphoto; Page 433: iStockphoto; Page 434: Jupiter Images (right); iStockphoto (center); Jupiter Images (left); Page 435: iStockphoto; Page 436: Dave & Les Jacobs / Blend Images / Getty Images; Page 438: iStockphoto, Jupiter Images, iStockphoto; Page 439: iStockphoto; Page 440: Jupiter Images; Page 441: © moodboard / Corbis; Page 446: Jupiter Images; Page 447: FPG / Taxi / Getty Images (left); AFP / Larry Downing / Getty Images (right); Page 451: Todd Wright / Blend Images / Getty Images; Page 452: John Morris / CartoonStock; Page 453: iStockphoto; Page 454: iStockphoto (right), Comstock / Punchstock (left); Page 455: iStockphoto; Page 456: Dirk Anschutz / Stone / Getty Images; Page 457: Valueline / Punchstock; Page 458: iStockphoto; Page 459: Jupiter Images; Page 460: Paul Maguire / Dreamstime; Page 461: Hulton Archives / Getty Images; Page 462: © Joe Skipper / Reuters / Corbis; Page 464: Tim Graham / Tim Graham Photo Library / Getty Images; Page 465: Tim Graham / Tim Graham Photo Library / Getty Images; Page 466: Tim Graham / Tim Graham Photo Library / Getty Images; Page 467: Fancy Photography / Veer; Page 470: iStockphoto; Page 474: Jupiter Images; Page 475: Erik Dreyer / Stone / Getty Images; Page 479: © Gary Hershorn / Reuters / Corbis; Page 480: iStockphoto; Page 481: iStockphoto; Page 482: Kevin Winter / Getty Images; Page 483: Jupiter Images; Page 484: Jupiter Images; Page 486: Daniel Sannum / AFP / Getty Images; Page 487: AFP / Getty Images; Page 488: © Frank Trapper / Corbis; Page 489: WireImage / Getty Images; Page 490: Robert Spencer / Getty Images; Page 491: © Los Angeles Daily News / Corbis Sygma; Page 492: AFP / Getty Images; Page 493: © Tony Frank / Sygma / Corbis, © William Coupon / Corbis; Page 494: Scott Olson / Getty Images News / Getty Images; Page 495: © Jason Szenes / Corbis; Page 496: iStockphoto; Page 498: George Doyle / Stockbyte / Getty Images; Page 500: Per-Anders Pettersson / Reportage / Getty Images; Page 501: iStockphoto; Page 502: iStockphoto; Page 504: © PoodlesRock / Corbis; Page 505: © Richard Olivier / Corbis; Page 509: Keith Brofsky / UpperCut Images / Getty Images; Page 510: iStockphoto; Page 511: iStockphoto, Dreamstime; Page 512: © Cultura / Corbis; Page 513: iStockphoto; Page 514: iStockphoto; Page 515: iStockphoto; Page 516: iStockphoto; Page 517: AFP / Getty Images; Page 518: iStockphoto; Page 519: iStockphoto; Page 520: © Thinkstock / Corbis; Page 521: © Comstock / Corbis; Page 522: Amy Sussman / Getty Images Entertainment / Getty Images; Page 523: iStockphoto; Page 524: Jupiter Images; Page 525: Jupiter Images; Page 526: © Whitney Curtis / epa / Corbis; Page 527: Time & Life Pictures / Getty Images; Page 528: Jupiter Images; Page 529: Jupiter Images; Page 530: Time & Life Pictures / Getty Images; Page 531: Timothy A. Clary / AFP / Getty Images; Page 533: Dreamstime; Page 534: Dreamstime; Page 535: iStockphoto; Page 537: iStockphoto; Page 538: iStockphoto; Page 539: iStockphoto (top), Time & Life Pictures / Getty Images (bottom); Page 540: Dreamstime (top), Jupiter Images (bottom); Page 541: Asia Images Group / AsiaPix / Getty Images; Page 543: Dreamstime; Page 544: iStockphoto; Page 545: Weeping Lincoln by Bill Mauldin, Bill Mauldin estate; Page 546: Corbis Photography / Veer; Page 547: iStockphoto; Page 548: Bru Garcia / AFP / Getty Images; Page 549: iStockphoto; Page 550: Dreamstime; Page 551: © Olivier Polet / Corbis; Page 552: © Matthew Cavanaugh / epa / Corbis (top), Photodisc / Veer (bottom); Page 553: © Steve Hamblin / Corbis (top), Blank Archives / Hulton Archive / Getty Images; FPG / Hulton Archive / Getty Images; Page 555: Dreamstime; Page 556: Jayme Thornton / Stone / Getty Images; Page 558: © Bettman / Corbis; Page 558 - 559 © Bettman / Corbis; Page 559: Emmanuel Dunand / AFP / Getty Images; Page 563: Jupiter Images; Page 564: iStockphoto; Page 565: iStockphoto; Page 566: Face.org; Page 567: Face.org (right); Jupiter Images (left); Page 568: frankwbaker.com/counteradexamples; Page 569: Dreamstime; Page 570: The Other Coast © 2008 Hairy Dog Productions, Inc. Used with the permission of Hairy Dog Productions, Inc. and Creators Syndicate. All rights reserved.; Page 571: © Bettman / Corbis; © Bettman / Corbis; Page 573: © Bettman / Corbis; Page 574: iStockphoto; Page 576: iStockphoto, Jupiter Images; Page 577: Brad Barket / Getty Images; Page 578: iStockphoto; Page 580: iStockphoto; Page 581: NASA Human Spaceflight Collection; Page 586: iStockphoto; Page 587: Dreamstime; Page 590: iStockphoto; Page 591: Jim Spellman / Wire Image / Getty Images (top), iStockphoto (bottom); Page 593: iStockphoto; Page 597: Dreamstime; Page 601: © Bettman / Corbis; Page 605: iStockphoto; Page 609: Hulton Archives / Getty Images; Page 613: Popperfoto / Getty Images; Page 617: iStockphoto; Page 619: © epa / Corbis

Index

C

Index

D

E

F

G

H

I

Index

M

Index

P

Index

Index

T